Sustainability Principles and Practice

This new and expanded edition builds upon the first edition's accessible and comprehensive overview of the interdisciplinary field of sustainability. The focus is on furnishing solutions and equipping the student with both conceptual understanding and technical skills for the workplace.

Each chapter explores one aspect of the field, first introducing concepts and presenting issues, then supplying tools for working toward solutions. Techniques for management and measurement as well as case studies from around the world are provided. The second edition includes a complete update of the text, with increased coverage of major topics including the Anthropocene; complexity; resilience; environmental ethics; governance; the IPCC's latest findings on climate change; Sustainable Development Goals; and new thinking on native species and novel ecosystems.

Chapters include further reading and discussion questions. The book is supported by a companion website with links, detailed reading lists, glossary, and additional case studies, together with projects, research problems, and group activities, all of which focus on real-world problem solving of sustainability issues.

The textbook is designed to be used by undergraduate college and university students in sustainability degree programs and other programs in which sustainability is taught.

Margaret Robertson is a member of the American Society of Landscape Architects (ASLA) and teaches at Lane Community College in Eugene, Oregon, USA, where she coordinates the Sustainability degree program.

Sustainability Principles and Practice

Second Edition

Margaret Robertson

Routledge
Taylor & Francis Group

LONDON AND NEW YORK

from Routledge

Second edition published 2017
by Routledge
2 Park Square, Milton Park, Abingdon, Oxon, OX14 4RN

and by Routledge
711 Third Avenue, New York, NY 10017

Routledge is an imprint of the Taylor & Francis Group, an informa business

© 2017 Margaret Robertson

First edition published by Routledge 2014

British Library Cataloguing in Publication Data
A catalogue record for this book is available from the British Library

Library of Congress Cataloging-in-Publication Data
Names: Robertson, Margaret, author.
Title: Sustainability principles and practice / Margaret Robertson.
Description: Abingdon, Oxon ; New York, NY : Routledge, 2017. | Earlier
    edition: 2014. | Includes bibliographical references and index.
Identifiers: LCCN 2016036622| ISBN 9781138650213 (hbk) | ISBN
    9781138650244 (pbk) | ISBN 9781315625478 (ebk)
Subjects: LCSH: Sustainability. | Sustainable development. | Environmental
    economics.
Classification: LCC HC79.E5 R6243 2017 | DDC 338.9/27—dc23
LC record available at https://lccn.loc.gov/2016036622

ISBN: 978-1-138-65021-3 (hbk)
ISBN: 978-1-138-65024-4 (pbk)
ISBN: 978-1-315-62547-8 (ebk)

Typeset in Times New Roman
by Swales & Willis Ltd, Exeter, Devon

Visit the companion website: www.routledgesustainabilityhub.com

"The great strength of Robertson's book is its breadth of coverage. From marketing to life cycle costing to the latest science on climate change, *Sustainability Principles and Practice* serves as a welcoming guide into the often jargon-laden field of sustainability."

—Jay Antle, Johnson County Community College, USA

"This book is a solid and well-crafted introduction to the field, conveying both the substance and the heart of sustainability work with style and grace. It will help students and other new entrants to the field get oriented to the special interdisciplinary challenges of sustainability, and to its core mission: helping us learn to be better caretakers of our planetary future."

—Alan AtKisson, President & CEO AtKisson Inc., USA & AtKisson Europe AB, Sweden. President, ISIS Academy GmbH, Germany. Member, President's Science and Technology Advisory Council (PSTAC), European Commission

"This is an important book. Robertson has a keen sense of the situation and an even keener sense of alternatives and means to achieve them. The author gives it to you the way it is and then provides some important pointers to resilient futures. This book contains both a diagnosis and a treatment. Read it."

—Simon Bell, Open University, UK

"An organized, engaging, and even inspiring collection of ideas that—if internalized and used to inform policies—would enable societies to thrive within a healthy environment. I wish this book had been available when I was first learning about social and environmental systems."

—Robert Dietz, Editor, The Daly News, *Center for the Advancement of the Steady State Economy*

"A comprehensive and practical map of the evolving field of sustainability. This well-organized and thoroughly researched textbook provides both students and educators with a useful guide to the essential sustainability topics. Robertson delivers an important work that will help to define the knowledge base in the sustainability field."

—Andrés R. Edwards, Founder, EduTracks, USA. Author of The Sustainability Revolution *and* Thriving Beyond Sustainability

"Robertson places sustainability in the connectedness between human culture and the living world. She links technical knowledge with tools for developing positive solutions and putting them into effect, including working collaboratively in organizations with other people."

—Bruce K. Ferguson, University of Georgia, USA

"Robertson has distilled the essential background information that students, our rising decision-makers, need so that they can follow her clearly defined roadmap to a sustainable future for the planet."

—Lee Kump, Pennsylvania State University, USA

"*Sustainability Principles and Practice* covers a broad range of topics, principles and concepts—at several scales from energy, water, pollution, ecosystems, food, and cities—to a charge to future 'agents for change' at policy, institutional, and personal, experiential levels. A must-have book to refresh your knowledge and to make a better world."

—Alison Kwok, University of Oregon, USA

"From now on when someone asks me what is sustainability, I will tell them to read Margaret Robertson's book, *Sustainability Principles and Practice*, which presents clearly and thoroughly the multi-faceted concept of sustainability in a very readable form."

—Norbert Lechner, Auburn University, USA

"Everyone thinks they know what sustainability is, but few people truly understand it—and fewer still can explain it well. Robertson cuts through the greenwash and the clichés with a top-notch exploration of the topic in all its complexities. It's an enjoyable read that's both thoroughly grounded in science and steeped in wonder at our fascinating, fragile planet."

—Daniel Lerch, Post Carbon Institute, USA

"Robertson's incisive analysis is both global and specific, comprehensive and inclusive. There is careful blending of facts and values, what is and what ought to be. You will find yourself engaged. I guarantee it."

—Holmes Rolston, III, Colorado State University, USA

"This book grabbed my attention and kept me engaged. The focus on creating solutions is refreshing. This publication will enhance and deepen the work of any general reader, student or faculty member working to bring sustainability into the curricula."

—Debra Rowe, Oakland Community College, USA

"This book masterfully integrates human and natural systems and the relationships between them into a grand and detailed picture of the world we live in. It provides a highly accessible introduction to sustainability suitable for anyone who cares about where we are going as a species, translating this knowledge into practical action."

—Arran Stibbe, University of Gloucestershire, UK

"This is a comprehensive, useful account of what sustainability is all about and what is needed for building it. It describes the many facets that collectively determine the degree to which a system, at any scale, is sustainable, and explains how they interact. It is a valuable guide and reference for anyone wishing to get involved in the practice of sustainability."

—Brian Walker, CSIRO Ecosystem Sciences, Australia.
Author of Resilience Thinking

"Sustainability champions practice systems thinking, connecting the dots between green buildings, sustainable cities, corporate CSR, and all the global sustainability meg-aforces besieging us. This book is their indispensable primer and wonderfully practical handbook to ensure they are effective change agents. It is a coherent encyclopedia of sustainability issues, with answers."

—Bob Willard, Sustainability Advantage, Canada

Contents

Illustrations

Figures

Boxes

Supplementary Material

Additional resources are available on the Companion Website for this book: http://routledge textbooks.com/textbooks/_author/robertson-9780415840187/.

- Throughout the book, defined words are printed in bold the first time they appear. The bold font signals that a definition of this term can be found in the online glossary on the website.
- A limited number of suggested books for Further Reading are listed at the end of each chapter in the printed book. A more extensive Further Reading list is available on the Companion Website as an annotated bibliography with additional books, articles, and links to websites, listed by chapter.
- The printed book provides questions for review and discussion at the end of each chapter. Additional exercises with end-of-chapter questions, activities, and projects are available on the Companion Website.
- Case studies and white papers on the Companion Website examine additional topics and specific skills.
- Educators can find presentation slides to accompany lectures for each chapter on the Companion Website.

Abbreviations

A	ampere (amp)
AASHE	Association for the Advancement of Sustainability in Higher Education
AC	alternating current
APC	American Plastics Council
ASHRAE	American Society of Heating, Refrigerating and Air-Conditioning Engineers
B-2	2 percent biodiesel
B-100	100 percent biodiesel
BAN	Basel Action Network
BART	Bay Area Rapid Transit
BAT	best available technique
bbl	blue barrel
BCE	before common era
Bcf	billion cubic feet
BEV	battery electric vehicle
BHAG	big, hairy, audacious goal
BMP	best management practice
BOD	biochemical oxygen demand
BP	before present
BPA	bisphenol A
BREEAM	Building Research Establishment Environmental Assessment Method
BRT	bus rapid transit
Bt	*Bacillus thuringiensis*
Btu	British thermal units
C2C	Cradle to Cradle (certification)^{CM}
C&D	construction and demolition
CAFO	concentrated animal feeding operation
CCOF	California Certified Organic Farmers
CCS	carbon capture and sequestration
CE	common era
CERCLA	Comprehensive Environmental Response, Compensation, and Liability Act
CFC	chlorofluorocarbon
CFL	compact fluorescent light
cfm	cubic feet per minute
CH_4	methane
CHP	combined heat and power
CII	commercial, institutional, industrial

CO	carbon monoxide
CO_2	carbon dioxide
CO_2e	carbon dioxide equivalent
COP	Conference of the Parties
COPR	Canada Organic Product Regulation
CPTED	crime prevention through environmental design
CRZ	critical root zone
CSA	community-supported agriculture; Canadian Standards Association
CSD	Commission on Sustainable Development
CVP	Central Valley Project
DC	direct current
DDT	dichloro-diphenyl-trichloroethane
DFD	design for disassembly
DFE	Design for the Environment
DMS	dimethyl sulphide
DNA	deoxyribonucleic acid
DO	dissolved oxygen
DoD	Department of Defense
E10	10 percent ethanol
E85	85 percent ethanol
EC	European Commission
EIA	Energy Information Administration
EMAS	Eco-Management and Audit Scheme
EMS	environmental management system
ENSO	El Niño-Southern Oscillation
EPA	Environmental Protection Agency
EPAct	Energy Policy Act of 1992
EROEI	energy returned on energy invested
ESA	Endangered Species Act
ESCO	energy services company
ESY	Edible Schoolyard
EU	European Union
EUI	energy utilization index
FAO	Food and Agriculture Organization
FDA	Food and Drug Administration
FERC	Federal Energy Regulatory Commission
FFTH	Food From the 'Hood
FLO	Fairtrade International
FSC	Forest Stewardship Council
FWS	Fish and Wildlife Service
GATT	General Agreement on Tariffs and Trade
GBI	Green Building Initiative
GDP	gross domestic product
GM	genetically modified
GMO	genetically modified organism
gpf	gallons per flush
GPI	Genuine Progress Indicator
gpl	gallons per load

gpm	gallons per minute
GPRC	Great Plains Restoration Council
GRAS	Generally Recognized As Safe
GRI	Global Reporting Initiative
GW	gigawatt
GWP	global warming potential
H_2O	water
HAP	hazardous air pollutant
HBN	Healthy Building Network
HCP	habitat conservation plan
HDPE	high-density polyethylene
HFC	hydrofluorocarbon
HID	high-intensity discharge
HRS	Hazard Ranking System
HVAC	heating, ventilating and air conditioning
ICI	institutional, commercial, industrial
ICPD	International Conference on Population and Development
IEA	International Energy Agency
IMF	International Monetary Fund
IPBES	Intergovernmental Platform on Biodiversity and Ecosystem Services
IPCC	Intergovernmental Panel on Climate Change
IPM	integrated pest management
IPMVP	International Performance Measurement and Verification Protocol
IPPC	Integrated Pollution Prevention and Control
IPPUC	Urban Planning Institute of Curitiba
ISEW	Index of Sustainable Economic Welfare
ISO	International Organization for Standardization
IUCN	International Union for Conservation of Nature and Natural Resources
KAB	Keep America Beautiful
kW	kilowatt
kWh	kilowatt-hour
LCA	life cycle assessment (or analysis)
LED	light-emitting diode
LEED	Leadership in Energy and Environmental Design
LEED AP LEED	Accredited Professional
LEED GA LEED	Green Associate
LEED-ND LEED	for Neighborhood Development
LID	low-impact development
LTL	less than a load
M&V	measurement and verification
Mcf	thousand cubic feet
MDG	Millennium Development Goal
MHCHS	Mole Hill Community Housing Society
MRF	material recovery facility
MRL	maximum residue limit
MSC	Marine Stewardship Council
MSW	municipal solid waste
MW	megawatt

N_2	nitrogen
N_2O	nitrous oxide
NAPL	nonaqueous phase liquid
NASA	National Aeronautics and Space Administration
NEPA	National Environmental Policy Act
NGO	nongovernmental organization
NMFS	National Marine Fisheries Service
NO	nitric oxide
NO_2	nitrogen dioxide
NO_x	nitrogen oxides
NOAA	National Oceanic and Atmospheric Administration
NPL	National Priorities List
NPO	non-product output
NRC	National Recycling Coalition
NREL	National Renewable Energy Laboratory
NSF	National Sanitation Foundation
O_2	oxygen
O_3	ozone
O&M	operations and maintenance
OECD	Organization for Economic Cooperation and Development
OTEC	ocean thermal energy conversion
OWC	oscillating water column
P2	Pollution prevention
PBT	persistent, bioaccumulative, and toxic
PCB	polychlorinated biphenyl
PBDE	polybrominated diphenyl ether
PEFC	Programme for the Endorsement of Forestry Certification
PHEV	plug-in hybrid electric vehicle
$PM_{2.5}$	particulate matter less than or equal to 2.5 micrometers in diameter
PM_{10}	particulate matter less than or equal to 10 micrometers in diameter
POP	persistent organic pollutant
ppb	parts per billion
ppm	parts per million
psi	pounds per square inch
PURPA	Public Utility Regulatory Policies Act of 1978
PV	photovoltaic
PVC	polyvinyl chloride
RCRA	Resource Conservation and Recovery Act
REC	renewable energy certificate (or credit)
RNA	ribonucleic acid
ROI	return on investment
R-value	resistance to heat flow
SCS	Scientific Certification Systems; Soil Conservation Service
SER	Society for Ecological Restoration
SES	Soil Erosion Service
SETAC	Society for Environmental Chemistry and Toxicology
SFI	Sustainable Forestry Initiative
SHGC	solar heat gain coefficient

SO_2	sulfur dioxide
SOx	sulfur oxides
SPI	Society of Plastics Industries
STARS	Sustainability Tracking, Assessment & Rating System
STRAW	Students and Teachers Restoring a Watershed
SUV	sport-utility vehicle
TBL	triple bottom line
Tcf	trillion cubic feet
TDM	transportation demand management
TDML	total daily maximum load
TDS	total dissolved solids
TFR	total fertility rate
TOD	transit-oriented development
TSCA	Toxic Substances Control Act
TSDF	treatment, storage, and disposal facility
TSE	Truck Stop Electrification
TSS	total suspended solids
UGB	urban growth boundary
UN	United Nations
UNEP	United Nations Environment Programme
UNFCCC	United Nations Framework Convention on Climate Change
US	United States
USDA	US Department of Agriculture
USGBC	US Green Building Council
USGS	US Geological Society
U-value	heat transfer coefficient
V	volt
V2G	vehicle-to-grid
VICS	Voluntary Interindustry Commerce Solutions Association
VMT	vehicle miles traveled
VOC	volatile organic compound
VT	visible transmittance
WASCO	water service company
WBCSD	World Business Council for Sustainable Development
WCED	World Commission on Environment and Development
WHO	World Health Organization
WRI	World Resources Institute
WTE	waste-to-energy
WTO	World Trade Organization
WWF	World Wildlife Fund

Part I
Context

1   What Is Sustainability?

We live in a vast, three-dimensional, interconnected web of energy flows and life forms. Years ago our world appeared to be the size of whatever culture we lived within and felt as if it were stable and unchangeable. Our world is now understood to be planetary in scale, to be changing very fast, and to be situated either at the threshold of a planetary disaster of unprecedented magnitude or at the beginning of a sustainable new era. Whatever the outcome, the new state of the world will not be like it is today.

In this world of planet-scale crises and opportunities, sustainability is a topic of increasing focus. Many people are familiar with some of the strategies employed in sustainability efforts: solar panels, recycling, or harvesting rainwater, for example. These are important positive steps. They and many others are discussed in more detail later in the book, but by themselves they cannot make the current conditions sustainable. So, what does it mean to be sustainable?

What Is Sustainability?

Sustainability means enduring into the long-term future; it refers to systems and processes that are able to operate and persist on their own over long periods of time. The adjective "sustainable" means "able to continue without interruption" or "able to endure without failing."[1] The word "sustainability" comes from the Latin verb *sustinēre*, "to maintain, sustain, support, endure," made from the roots *sub*, "up from below," and *tenēre*, "to hold." The German equivalent, *Nachhaltigkeit*, first appeared in the 1713 forestry book *Sylvicultura Oeconomica* written by Hans Carl von Carlowitz, a mining administrator in a region whose mining and metallurgy industry depended upon timber and who realized that deforestation could cause the local economy to collapse. Carlowitz described how through sustainable management of this renewable resource, forests could supply timber indefinitely.

We are part of linked systems of humans and nature, so the study of sustainability goes beyond environmentalism. A key attribute of the field is a recognition of three interrelated dimensions: ecological, economic, and social. The planet faces many problems that are connected, including poverty, impaired health, overpopulation, resource depletion, food and water scarcity, political instability, and the destruction of the life support systems we all depend on. Scholars debate about whether environmental destruction causes poverty, or whether poverty causes environmental destruction out of sheer desperation, but it is agreed that they go together (Caradonna 2014, 224). We cannot fix one problem in isolation because they are all connected.

The three dimensions of ecological sustainability, economic opportunity, and social inclusion are captured in the phrase sustainable development. The term was introduced in *World Conservation Strategy*, a 1980 report by the International Union for Conservation of

Nature (IUCN) and the first international document to use the term (ibid. 141). It was made popular in the 1987 report *Our Common Future*, produced by the World Commission on Environment and Development (WCED) and commonly known as the Brundtland report, which explicitly points at the connection between environment, economics, and equity. In the Brundtland report, "sustainable development" is defined as "development that meets the needs of the present without compromising the ability of future generations to meet their own needs" (WCED 1987, 43). Sustainable development recognizes the rights of all people, including future generations, to grow and flourish.

These three dimensions—environment, economics, and equity—are sometimes called the "triple bottom line" (TBL), a term introduced in 1997 by corporate responsibility expert John Elkington (Elkington 1998, 70). They are also known as the "three E's" and sometimes referred to as the three pillars of sustainability or, in the business world, as planet, people, and profit (Elkington 2012, 55).

Sustainability and Resilience

Much sustainability work focuses on the concept of resilience. Resilience science originated in the field of ecology and is based on the understanding that life is not static, that change is inevitable. Resilience is the capacity of a system to accommodate disturbance and still retain its basic function and structure (Walker and Salt 2006, xiii); it is the capacity to cope with change. A resilient system adapts to changes without losing its essential qualities. All systems which are resilient share common traits: they are self-organizing and feature diversity, redundancy, and connectivity. We understand that humans and nature are not separate, and so in sustainability work the systems are known as social-ecological systems: linked systems of humans and nature (Walker and Salt 2012, 1).

Sustainability and resilience are not synonymous but are interrelated concepts. They provide complementary frameworks that are employed toward the same goal: to enable social-ecological systems to continue into the long-term future. A sustainability approach identifies long-term goals, examines strategies for achieving those goals, and systematically evaluates using indicators. A resilience approach emphasizes change as a normal condition, recognizes that a system may exist in multiple stable states, and focuses on building adaptive capacity to respond to unexpected shocks and disturbance. Sustainability scholar Charles Redman explains it this way: "sustainability prioritizes outcomes; resilience prioritizes process" (Redman 2014, 37).

Systems Thinking

The study of sustainability is the study of systems. A system is a coherently organized set of interconnected elements that constitute a whole (Meadows 2008, 188), where the identity of the whole is always more than the sum of its parts. The properties of the whole cannot be predicted by examining the parts; they are emergent properties, arising from the relationships and interactions of the parts. Systems are nested within other systems. A cell, an organ, and a human body are all systems, as are an ecosystem, an ocean, and an economy. The Earth itself is a system, made of myriad other nested and interconnected systems; it is the focus of a field of study known as Earth system science.

The field known as systems science became part of the public conversation in 1972 with the publication of the groundbreaking *Limits to Growth*, the result of a study by MIT systems scientists Donella and Dennis Meadows and Jorgen Randers commissioned by a think tank called The Club of Rome. The report included the first modern use of the word "sustainable" (Caradonna 2014, 138). Using cutting edge computer models, the researchers analyzed in detail how economic growth, consumption, and population growth would cause humans to exceed the limits of Earth's **carrying capacity** and lead to a condition of **overshoot.**

Carrying capacity is the maximum number of individuals a given environment can support indefinitely. Its inverse is the **Ecological Footprint**, the demand placed on nature for resources consumed and wastes absorbed, expressed as land area. Earth is currently operating at 140 percent of its capacity (Ewing et al. 2010, 18) and on track to be operating at 200 percent by the 2030s (Gilding 2011, 52). That is, we are already in overshoot: the condition in which human demands exceed the regenerative capacities of the biosphere. Ecological economist Herman Daly identified four conditions for avoiding overshoot: In order to live sustainably within Earth's carrying capacity, humans would need to maintain the health of ecosystems (our life-support systems); use renewable resources at a rate no faster than they can be regenerated; use nonrenewable resources at a rate no faster than they can be replaced by the discovery of renewable substitutes; and emit wastes and pollutants at a rate no faster than the rate at which they can be safely assimilated (Daly 1990).

Humans have already overshot Earth's carrying capacity and are living by depleting its **natural capital** and overfilling its waste sinks (Rees 2014, 192). Natural capital consists of the resources and services provided by ecosystems (Folke 2013, 19). Renewable resources can support human activities indefinitely as long as we do not use them more rapidly than they can regenerate. This is analogous to living off the interest in a savings account and not spending the capital. We have the planetary equivalent of a savings account, but it is made of plants, animals, soil, water, and air (Hawken et al. 2008). This natural capital provides **ecosystem services**, the biological functions that support life, including provision of materials and food, assimilation of wastes, seed dispersal, pollination, nutrient recycling, purification of air and water, and climate regulation.

The problems facing the planet, such as climate change, mass extinction, water scarcity, and poverty, are challenging because they are intrinsically systems problems (Meadows 2008, 4). Systems are complex.[2] Complexity refers to systems that have outcomes which are indeterminate and cannot be predicted (Ehrenfeld 2008, 100); their behavior is nonlinear (Heinberg and Lerch 2010, 31; Wessels 2006, 120). The many systems which make up the larger Earth system are known as **complex adaptive systems** (CAS). Their elements are interconnected, and it is not possible to change one component of a complex adaptive system without affecting other parts of the system, often in unpredictable ways.

Complex adaptive systems feature emergent behavior which means not only are they inherently unpredictable, but they can have more than one stable state (Walker and Salt 2006, 36). Natural systems have "tipping points" or critical thresholds at which seemingly small changes cause a system to shift abruptly and irreversibly into a new state (OECD 2012, 26). These state shifts can be planetary in scale and can be difficult to predict; changes accumulate incrementally and the actual threshold is usually not known in advance (Barnosky et al. 2012, 52). One potential tipping point is global temperature, where a small increase in average temperature may trigger abrupt, large-scale, and irreversible changes in the global climate system (AAAS Climate Science Panel 2014, 15; Blaustein 2015, 34).

Living in the Anthropocene

Geologists divide time on Earth into segments based on physical characteristics of geology, climate, and life.[3] The Holocene was the 10,000-year epoch spanning all of written human history until now, a time between ice ages with a warm and unusually stable climate which allowed civilization to develop. These extraordinarily stable conditions made it possible for population to expand, agriculture to appear, and human cultures to arise and flourish (Wijkman and Rockström 2012, 38). We live at the beginning of a new geological epoch known as the **Anthropocene**, a time in which human activity has become such a powerful force that it has major, planet-scale impact on climate and on every living system. Geologists are working to formalize the geological unit as an official designation and to determine what physical evidence should be used as its marker (Anthropocene Working Group 2016).[4]

In 2009, a group of scientists undertook a collaborative research effort to define the crucial processes and global boundary conditions which could ensure that the planet remains in a stable, Holocene-like state, a "safe operating space" within which human society could continue to develop (Wijkman and Rockström 2012, 44). Researchers defined planetary boundaries for nine interdependent areas of the global commons: climate change, biodiversity loss, excess nitrogen and phosphorus production, stratospheric ozone depletion, ocean acidification, freshwater consumption, land-use change, air pollution, and chemical pollution; they mapped these onto a radial graph with one wedge for each area of concern and with boundaries denoted by concentric rings. The concept of planetary boundaries and their graphic illustration was a powerful way to communicate complex scientific issues to a broad lay audience (Folke 2013, 29). The researchers found that humanity has already exceeded the safe boundaries for the first three: climate change, biodiversity loss, and nitrogen production (Rockström et al 2009a; 2009b). As is typical of complex systems, the planetary boundaries are interconnected, so that crossing one boundary may shift the positions or critical thresholds of other boundaries (Folke 2013, 26).

We face multiple, global-scale issues including food scarcity, aquifer depletion, pollution, habitat destruction, extinction, depletion of renewable and nonrenewable resources, climate destabilization, social inequity, failing states, growing control by powerful corporate interests, and widening gaps between rich and poor. A mass extinction is underway, with species disappearing at 1000 times the normal rate (Primack 2008, 126). Storms and wildfires are growing, mountain glaciers are melting, sea level is rising, and indications are that we may be approaching a climate-system tipping point. Many of these issues are what are known as **wicked problems**, problems that are difficult to solve because they are complex, interconnected, and continually evolving (Steffen 2014, 1). Behind them all lie two fundamental drivers: consumption, built on the economic growth model, and human population growth.

Humans have gone through several major transitions in their history: the discovery of fire, the development of language, the development of agriculture and civilization, and the Industrial Revolution. Today we live on the threshold of what has been called the "fifth great turning" (Heinberg 2011, 284), a turn away from a fossil fuel-powered, climate-destabilizing, growth-based industrial economy and toward a sustainable, regenerative society.

We live in a new geological epoch, the Anthropocene. The Holocene has apparently come to an end, and humanity faces novel conditions it has not encountered before. The question is not whether we will change, but how, and what form the transition will take. Navigating the shifting conditions, fostering the fifth great turning in the sociocultural realm while we strive to avoid crossing planetary-scale thresholds into an undesirable state shift in the biospheric realm, will require that we find ways to live better and to work together like never before. We will need to shift rapidly away from fossil fuels, power our lives with renewable energy sources, use energy more efficiently whatever the source, reduce per-capita resource consumption, provision ourselves from zero-waste circular economies, reduce population growth, provide food to increasing numbers of people without converting new areas of land or destroying habitat, protect biodiversity, protect ecosystem services, and generally live within the planet's capacity to support us and our fellow creatures into the long-term future. We will need to define what is meant by "sustainability," use those definitions to measure and monitor trends so that we can assess where we are moving toward or away from sustainability, and develop evidence-based strategies with the potential for real, measurable progress (Engelman 2013, 13). We will need not just technological adaptations, but social and political ones as well. Sustainability will depend on having informed, ecologically literate citizens working toward healthy ecosystems, genuine social inclusion, and equitable distribution of resources. We will need strong communities, networks of all kinds, and participatory governance at multiple scales, as we build the foundations for a thriving, sustainable human civilization and biosphere (ibid., 17).

Notes

1 American Sign Language (ASL) has a sign for extinction: the two signs "death" and "forever." However, ASL does not have a sign for "sustainability," so environmental educator Susan E. Fowler combines the two signs for "life" and "forever." Thus extinction is "death forever" and sustainability is "life forever" (Sitarz 2008, 13).
2 In systems science, "complex" does not simply mean "more complicated." The word "complicated" (from the Latin verb *complicare*, to fold together) refers to a system with many parts where there are knowable causes and effects and one can predict the outcomes given enough information. For example, a jet engine is a complicated system. "Complex" (from the Latin verb *complectere*, to braid or to entwine around) refers to a nonlinear system in which interactions are emergent and outcomes cannot be predicted. For example, the Amazon rainforest is a complex system.
3 Geological time is subdivided into hierarchical segments. From the largest to the smallest division, the terms are eon, era, period, epoch, and age.
4 The Anthropocene is discussed further in the next chapter.

Further Reading

Brown, Lester R. *Plan B 4.0: Mobilizing to Save Civilization*. New York: W. W. Norton & Company, 2009.
Caradonna, Jeremy L. *Sustainability: A History*. New York: Oxford University Press, 2014.
Heinberg, Richard and Daniel Lerch, eds. *The Post Carbon Reader: Managing the 21st Century's Sustainability Crises*. Berkeley, CA: University of California Press, 2010.
Meadows, Donella, Jorgen Randers, and Dennis Meadows. *Limits to Growth: The 30-Year Update*. White River Junction, VT: Chelsea Green, 2004.
Thiele, Leslie Paul. *Sustainability*. Cambridge: Polity, 2013.
Worldwide Institute. *State of the World 2013: Is Sustainability Still Possible?* Washington, DC: Island Press, 2013.

Critical Thinking and Discussion

1 An elevator speech is a concise summary that can be conveyed within the span of a 30-second elevator trip. If a neighbor learned you were studying sustainability and asked, "So, what is sustainability?" what would you say? Write an "elevator speech" to explain the basic concepts of sustainability.
2 An elevator speech gives you a period of time, albeit short, to describe a concept. But what about situations where you are called upon to give an even shorter, concentrated summary? If you were in a checkout line at a market, you mentioned to the clerk that you were studying sustainability, and the clerk said to you, "Sustainability? What is that?,"

what would you say? Write one to two concise sentences that give a quick, comprehensible overview, understandable by someone for whom the subject is unfamiliar.

3   Think about a sustainability issue the planet faces, one with which you are familiar. Does the knowledge needed for finding solutions come from one academic discipline, or more than one? List the disciplines you think might be involved in addressing this issue.

4   Our species has had an extraordinary impact on the biosphere. Why do you think that is?

5   Modern society is experiencing rapid innovation and change. Do you think the rate of change is a sign of unsustainability or progress? Is there a simple answer?

6   Do you think that laws and regulations are necessary in order to move society toward a sustainable future?

7   Two common diagrams for representing sustainability use simple circles. The triple bottom line of sustainability is traditionally illustrated by three intersecting circles representing environment, economics, and social equity. Some scholars prefer to illustrate the triple bottom line of sustainability with concentric circles by placing the economic and social spheres within the circle representing environment. What messages does each version convey? What do they say about the relationships between ecology, economics, and equity? Once you have answered, can you think of a different possible message each version could represent?

8   People sometimes feel overwhelmed by the magnitude of the problems our planet faces. If you were working on a sustainability project and someone told you, "There is no point in trying to be sustainable, since it is hopeless anyway," how would you respond?

9   Are the terms "sustainability" and "sustainable development" interchangeable? If not, how do they differ?

10   Imagine a community of bacteria living on a Petri dish. A single bacterium was placed on the dish at midnight. Their population doubled once an hour. At 1:00 a.m. there were 2 bacteria, by 2:00 a.m. there were 4 bacteria, and so forth. At noon, 12 hours later, their food supply ran out. At what time of day was half their food used up?

2   A Brief History of Sustainability

Sustainability is a multidisciplinary field that encompasses the entire planet, its constituents and inhabitants as a whole. Earth's planetary system has until recently maintained a balance of dynamic equilibrium—it has been sustainable—since its beginnings approximately 4.5 billion years ago. So the history of sustainability as a concept, the state of being sustainable, could in one view encompass the entire long and interwoven story of our planet. Telling the life story of our planet involves most of the science disciplines including atmospheric science, geology, chemistry, and biology.

Sustainability as a concept is also about the human role within the biophysical world, and the history of sustainability includes examination of how humans have related to the rest of nature through time. The study of human relationships to the natural world through time is a field of study called **environmental history**.

Understanding the past helps us plan for the future. The global social-ecological system that has evolved during the Holocene exhibits complex webs of interconnections and emergent properties that are characteristic of complex adaptive systems. Thus the future cannot be predicted. But understanding how humans and the rest of nature have interacted over time can help us to clarify the options for creating a more sustainable future (Costanza et al. 2007, 522).

Recent History: The Last 200 Years

In general, Western culture has maintained a belief that economic growth and ever-improving standards of living can continue forever. However, a few influential books which suggested that some human activities might not be sustainable began to appear in the last 200 years or so.

Beginning in 1798 Thomas Malthus, a British scholar in the fields of political science and economics, wrote six editions of his influential treatise, *An Essay on the Principle of Population*. He wrote: "The power of population is so superior to the power of the earth to produce subsistence for man, that premature death must in some shape or other visit the human race" (Malthus [1798] 2008: 61). This work predicted that population growth was inevitable and that it would continue until it outstripped the resources available. Malthus said that population was expanding at geometrical rates while food supplies were increasing at only arithmetical rates. He argued that in any society, population would continue to increase until it reached the carrying capacity of its resources, when various natural controls—disease, famine, or war—would cause ecological and social collapse, reducing the numbers again. This process is known as the Malthusian cycle (Christian 2011, 312).

Henry David Thoreau was one of the first Americans to question the belief that nature and its resources were inexhaustible (Nash 1988, 36). He was a careful observer, and he noticed that wild species were beginning to disappear from his region in Massachusetts. In an effort to understand nature better, he built a cabin in the woods on Walden Pond where he lived alone for two years, observing and writing. Foreshadowing the science of ecology, Thoreau saw nature as an interconnected community. In *Life in the Woods*, he wrote: "What we call wildness is a civilization other than our own" (ibid.).

In 1864 George Perkins Marsh, a US diplomat and historian, published *Man and Nature; Or, Physical Geography as Modified by Human Action*, a description of the destructive impacts of human civilization on the environment. Marsh used scientific reasoning to show how the rise and fall of past civilizations were connected to overuse of resources. He suggested that stewardship of the planet was more than an economic issue, that it was an ethical issue (ibid.).

John Muir was a naturalist who spent several years exploring the North American wilderness from Alaska to California. His journal entries were published in several books which became popular. Muir championed the idea of national parks as a way to save vanishing wilderness and was largely responsible for establishing Yosemite National Park in 1890. Two years later, in 1892, he founded the Sierra Club. He was a proponent of the idea that nature has intrinsic value independent of its usefulness to humans (Thiele 2013, 17).

The first warnings about climate change probably came in 1908, from Swedish chemist Svante Arrhenius. Arrhenius argued that industrial activity, specifically increasing emissions from burning fossil fuels, was making the planet warmer and would lead to global climate change (Arrhenius 1896; IPCC 2007a, 105). The warnings would surface again in the mid-1970s, this time from the international scientific community.

Early Conservation

In the late nineteenth century nonhuman animals were being killed in great numbers for sport and for fashion, and women's hats adorned with plumage were popular. US congressman John Lacey, alarmed at the slaughter of birds for the purpose of decorating hats, sponsored the Lacey Act of 1900 which made the interstate transport of illegally killed wildlife a federal offense. This early thinking about the rights of other species to life and habitat later developed into endangered species legislation (Nash 1988, 49). The Lacey Act helped some birds, but not all, and in 1914, following years of decimation from hunters, the last passenger pigeon died in captivity at the Cincinnati Zoo.

Theodore Roosevelt, US Republican president from 1901 to 1909, was a passionate conservationist. In 1903, shortly after passage of the Lacey Act, he established the first National Wildlife Refuge at Pelican Island in Florida for the protection of endangered brown pelicans. A few years later he used a new law, the Antiquities Act, to protect the Grand Canyon and other areas that became national parks, set aside federal lands as national monuments, and added vast tracts of land to the system of federal forest reserves (Miller et al. 2009, S34).

In the first half of the twentieth century, many scientists and policymakers saw nature as a resource to be managed for the benefit of humans. Gifford Pinchot, a name often associated with this view, was appointed the first chief of the newly formed US Forest Service in 1905. In contrast to people such as John Muir, who argued for preserving wilderness in its untouched state, Pinchot believed that forests were in essence a kind of crop and that public forest lands should be managed scientifically (Merchant 2007, 143).

Transformation from Conservation to Ecology

Scientific understanding of the living world underwent a transformation in the twentieth century. **Conservation** and the view of nature as a resource to be efficiently managed had tended to look at each crop or element in isolation. The science of **ecology**, which first appeared in the nineteenth century and flowered in the twentieth century, studied not objects but relationships and connections in the larger environment (Edwards 2005, 12). The word ecology comes from the Greek word *oikos*, meaning "household." German biologist Ernst Haeckel began using the term "ecology" in his books and articles in the 1860s (Merchant 2007, 180). He wrote that biologists had overlooked "the relations of the organism to the environment, the place each organism takes in the household of nature, in the economy of all nature" (ibid.).

The concept of the food web and food pyramid, outlined by zoologist Charles Elton in 1927, helped to put the human position in the natural world into a different perspective. Elton presented the feeding relationships in nature as a pyramid, with a few predators at the top and very large numbers of plants and bacteria at the bottom. If the predator at the top of the food pyramid—the human—is removed, the system is hardly affected. But take away plants or bacteria at the base, and the pyramid collapses. The food pyramid revealed that humans are far from indispensable and in fact are vulnerable. Elton also developed the concept of ecological niches, finely tuned functional roles within the structure of an ecosystem (Nash 1988, 57).

Frederic Clements was a central figure in the emerging field of ecology known for his theories about ecological **succession** in plant communities, a process that he believed led to the stable equilibrium of **climax** vegetation (Merchant 2007, 182). The view he laid out in his 1916 book *Plant Succession* is called the organismic approach to ecology because for him a plant community was like a complex living organism. Other scientists in the organismic school of ecology developed the idea that cooperation among individuals in a community was at least as important as competition and the old Darwinian idea of "survival of the fittest."

An economic approach to ecology developed as a kind of alternative to organismic ecology. British ecologist Arthur Tansley first introduced the term **ecosystem** in a 1935 paper. Tansley had studied thermodynamics and applied terms from that field, including "energy" and "systems," to the field of ecology. A few years later, in 1942, ecologist Raymond Lindeman re-introduced the concept of the "food chain" or **trophic levels** (ibid., 186–87). "Trophic" refers to nutrition. In the food chain, food is metabolized at each trophic level, and in metabolizing, each plant or animal converts energy from the trophic level below it.

The chemist Ellen Swallow developed the concept of human ecology, an approach in which humans are not separate from nature or managers of nature; they are part of nature and work within it. This branch of ecology was expanded during the 1960s by ecologist Eugene Odum, who argued that the economic approach that works for maximizing productivity of ecosystems can lead to degraded ecosystems. He proposed applying science and ethical principles to repair damaged ecosystems. Odum's perception of the Earth as a network of interconnected ecosystems was one of the guiding principles in the environmental movement that emerged in the 1960s (ibid., 186–89).

Chaos theory and complexity theory, a branch of mathematics that developed in the 1970s and 1980s, influenced the study of ecology. In their 1985 book *The Ecology of Natural Disturbance and Patch Dynamics*, ecologists S. T. A. Pickett and P. S. White described ecosystems as dynamic rather than the homogeneous stable systems of successional climax communities. The idea of a stable balance of nature had implied that humans were capable of repairing degraded ecosystems, that it was in effect just a matter of getting the mechanics right. Complexity and chaos theory meant acknowledging that while nature does have patterns that can be recognized, nature is unpredictable; it is not only more complex than we know, it is more than we *can* know. We can work in partnership with nature but can never master it.

The Beginnings of the Environmental Movement

What we think of as sustainability as a field of study got its start with the environmental movement in the 1960s and 1970s. Books, conferences, and college classes on environmental topics first began to appear in the early 1970s. The movement was heralded by the publication of Rachel Carson's book *Silent Spring* in 1962. The book, which documented the destructive effects of pesticides on the environment, was widely read and became a best seller.

Rachel Carson was a biologist with the US Fish and Wildlife Service (FWS) at a time in American history when the old DuPont advertising slogan, "Better Things for Better Living . . . through Chemistry," expressed the spirit of the age. World War II had propelled the growth of the petrochemical industry, resulting in an explosive proliferation of varieties of plastics, chemical compounds, and synthetic pesticides. One of the most popular chemical pesticides was dichloro-diphenyl-trichloroethane (DDT), widely used on crops, forest lands, roadsides, and residential lawns across the country. Technology was seen as a positive tool for progress, although the appearance of dead birds on front lawns began to raise questions for some people.

The title of Carson's book, *Silent Spring*, was a reference to a world without birds that could be the ultimate outcome of indiscriminate pesticide use. As a scientist, Carson researched her book meticulously and grounded it in rigorous science. She made a forceful case for the severe damage that reckless spraying of pesticides had inflicted on wildlife and exposed the potential threat to humans as well. She did it with an eloquent, poetic writing style that made the subject accessible to ordinary people. Up to that time, technology had been seen as the realm of scientists and government regulators, and Americans generally entrusted it to the experts who appeared to understand the complicated details of biology and chemistry. Carson pulled back the curtains and allowed ordinary citizens to see into the world of the experts. *Silent Spring* encouraged citizens to become informed and to become actively engaged, and in so doing helped usher in the spirit of participatory democracy that characterized the 1960s (Magoc 2006, 227).

The Population Bomb, published by biologist Paul Ehrlich in 1968, was another influential best seller in the 1960s that raised awareness of environmental issues. This book, too, raised the level of understanding about technical topics for ordinary citizens. *The Population Bomb* illustrated exponential growth for lay readers, presented existing data about population, and let people see what would happen if these patterns continued (Merchant 2007, 195). *The Population Bomb* had been presaged in 1948 by the influential best seller *Road to Survival* by ecologist William Vogt, who showed that declining resources and overpopulation were trends that were connected.

The environmental awareness raised by Rachel Carson and others, underscored by telling events such as a 1952 fire on the Cuyahoga River in Ohio, culminated in the first Earth Day on April 22, 1970. First suggested by US Senator Gaylord Nelson of Wisconsin and organized by Harvard graduate student Denis Hayes, Earth Day was billed as an "Environmental Teach-In." New York City shut down Fifth Avenue for the event, thousands of colleges and universities organized rallies, and 20 million people participated in cities across the country. Some historians see Earth Day as the beginning of the modern environmental movement in the US (ibid., 199).

Topics of alternative energy and appropriate technology entered the public awareness in the 1970s. In 1973 conflict in the Middle East led to an Arab oil embargo and a fuel shortage known as the "oil crisis." While the energy crisis lasted only a few months, it spurred public interest in both energy conservation and the search for alternatives to fossil fuels.

At the same time as the energy crisis, in 1973, British economist E. F. Schumacher published *Small Is Beautiful: Economics as if People Mattered.* The book was an early introduction to the idea that perpetual economic growth is not sustainable. It suggested that human well-being was a more appropriate measure of progress than was gross national product and it encouraged people to think about the connections between environmental, social, and economic health. It also introduced the concept that nonrenewable natural resources such as fossil fuels should be treated as capital, not as expendable income. It encouraged people to consider appropriate use of technology and the value of small, local economics. The book became another best seller.

The 1970s began with Earth Day and continued to be years of activism and participation. New environmental organizations including Worldwatch Institute, Greenpeace, and the Natural Resources Defense Council were founded. The battle over a community named Love Canal put environmental threats from hazardous waste in the public spotlight and made them personal: toxins were not just things that affected other species and distant places; they could affect you in your own home. It also showed how ordinary citizens could be effective agents for change.

Love Canal was a pleasant community near the iconic Niagara Falls whose homes and school were built on the former waste site of a chemical company. As mothers of school children talked to each other they discovered an unexpected and alarming pattern of miscarriages, birth defects, and childhood cancer. One of the mothers, Lois Gibbs, organized a community group whose members educated themselves about hazardous waste and put pressure on the state and on the federal government. In 1978 President Carter declared a State of Emergency. The Love Canal disaster led to the passage of legislation in 1980 that became known as Superfund, establishing a system for identifying and cleaning up hazardous waste sites. Gibbs, whose two children had both experienced serious health problems as a result of living at Love Canal, devoted her life to the antitoxics movement. She organized the Citizens' Clearinghouse for Hazardous Wastes, a coalition of community groups headquartered in Washington, DC. She also founded a magazine called *Everyone's Backyard* aimed at helping local groups move beyond the "NIMBY" (Not in My Backyard) phenomenon to what she called Not in Anyone's Backyard (Magoc 2006, 250–52).

US Legislation in the 1970s

The public awareness that was awakened by Rachel Carson's *Silent Spring* and that bloomed on the first Earth Day was part of a process that led to a series of legislative moves for the protection of the environment. The 1970s was an extraordinary decade for environmental law (Lazarus 2004, 67–75).

The year 1970 began with the National Environmental Policy Act (NEPA) being signed into law by President Nixon on January 1 with great fanfare. Called the "Magna Carta of environmental law" by many commentators (ibid., 68), NEPA was established "to create and maintain conditions under which man and nature can exist in productive harmony, and fulfill the social, economic and other requirements of present and future generations of Americans." The year ended with an executive order from President Nixon that reorganized the Executive Branch to create the Environmental Protection Agency (EPA), a federal agency charged with administering environmental laws enacted by Congress.

A string of sweeping legislation followed NEPA, beginning with the Clean Air Act in 1970. The Clean Air Act required the EPA to publish a list of hazardous air pollutants, set emissions standards, and achieve reductions at specified levels. It also required the EPA to review the scientific bases for air quality standards every five years and to include an adequate margin of safety to protect the public health.

The Water Pollution Control Act of 1972 was an amendment to an earlier act. It required that all navigable waters in the US be "fishable and swimmable" by 1983 and prohibited all discharge of pollutants into navigable waters without permit by 1985. The Act also regulated the potential filling of wetlands. The 1974 Safe Drinking Water Act established standards for contaminants in public water supplies. Like the other environmental laws of the 1970s, the Act passed overwhelmingly in the House and the Senate with bipartisan consensus. One legislator, Senator Cotton, later commented: "After all, if one votes against safe drinking water, it is like voting against home and mother" (Lazarus 2004, 69). Protection of water expanded in 1977 with the Clean Water Act.

Energy conservation was promoted by the Energy Policy and Conservation Act of 1975. Two years later the US Department of Energy was created. The National Energy Act of 1978 was a response to the 1973 energy crisis and included tax credit incentives for the development of renewable clean energy sources, although they were eliminated a few years later.

In 1972 the use of DDT was banned and the Federal Pesticide Control Act, an amendment of the earlier Insecticide, Fungicide, and Rodenticide Act, was passed. The Toxic Substances Control Act (TSCA) was passed in 1976; it regulated manufacture, sale, use, and disposal to prevent "unreasonable risk of injury to health or the environment." The Resource Conservation and Recovery Act (RCRA), also passed in 1976, regulated the generation, transportation, treatment, storage, and disposal of hazardous wastes "as necessary to protect human health and the environment."

A number of other acts were revisions of older natural resource laws. Earlier laws, with their roots in the nineteenth century, had focused on using and exploiting natural resources. The new laws focused on conservation and preservation.

Perhaps the most far-reaching legislation was the Endangered Species Act (ESA) of 1973. This landmark law was groundbreaking in at least two ways: it gave legal protection to the rights of at least some nonhumans and it adopted an ecosystem approach to environmental protection. Its primary goal was to prevent the extinction of species imperiled as a "consequence of economic growth and development untempered by adequate concern and conservation" (*Endangered Species Act of 1973*, 16 US Code 1531 et seq.). It protected species and "the ecosystems upon which they depend." The ESA is administered by the US FWS and the National Oceanic and Atmospheric Administration (NOAA), which includes the National Marine Fisheries Service (NMFS). In addition to preventing extinction, the ESA is also intended to help **threatened** or **endangered** species recover. Once a species has gone through a **listing** process and has been listed as threatened or endangered, FWS and NMFS are required to create a detailed recovery plan. A 1978 amendment to the ESA noted that the goal of the law is to make itself unnecessary, and recovery plans are a means toward that goal. Existence of this law has not prevented species from going extinct at an accelerating rate, both in the US and worldwide.

The transformation of the legal landscape during the 1970s was not limited to the federal government. New federal laws gave substantial roles for implementation to states. For example, under the Clean Water Act states were to develop their own permitting programs, which meant that they were responsible for overseeing compliance with the federal water pollution control law. The other federal environmental laws gave the states similar roles.

Environmental Justice

Growing awareness of the dangers of pesticides and other hazardous chemicals beginning in the 1960s led to one of the key attributes of the field of study we now call sustainability: the triple bottom line of environment, economics, and equity (Edwards 2005, 21).

One arena for concerns about equity was the labor union movement. Efforts to organize farm workers laboring in the fields of California began in 1962, the year *Silent Spring* was published. Cesar Chavez and Dolores Huerta, co-founders of the drive to organize the United Farm Workers of America, made protection from pesticide exposure for farm workers a top priority (Magoc 2006, 232). They and other union organizers insisted that only a union contract could guarantee protection for workers. Through their work, as well as the work of Rachel Carson, increasing numbers of people began to realize that the goals of a safe and healthy workplace and the goals of a healthy environment were intertwined. People also began to realize that the old dependence on trusting the experts was not enough and that citizen participation was essential.

Another arena was the civil rights movement. In 1982 a disposal site for polychlorinated biphenyls (PCBs), a toxic chemical used as a coolant in electrical transformers and as an additive in many industrial compounds, was proposed for a Warren County, North Carolina neighborhood that was primarily African American. Protests began immediately. Residents and civil rights organizers joined together to block roads and stage rallies that raised awareness about the dumping of toxic chemicals in minority neighborhoods.

One of the protest leaders in Warren County was the civil rights activist Ben Chavis. He coined the phrase "environmental racism" to describe the proposed Warren County dump site. In 1987 Chavis authored a report for the United Church of Christ's Commission on Racial Justice, "Toxic Wastes and Race in the United States." His report, which located hazardous waste sites by zip code, showed that almost every major city in the country located its hazardous waste sites in areas whose residents were members of minority communities. The report helped to spark a nationwide **environmental justice** movement (Merchant 2007, 202).

Environmental Ethics

Growing awareness of social and environmental concepts, including the interconnectedness of life, led to increased interest in the moral relationship between humans and the rest of the natural world (Brennan and Lo 2015). Philosophers, scholars, activists, and citizens began to ask questions about the rights of nature. The result was the development in the early 1970s of a modern branch of philosophy known as environmental ethics, a field which considers whether only humans are morally considerable, or whether **moral standing** should extend to other species or even to ecosystems; whether non-human species and larger systems have **intrinsic value** or only **instrumental value;** and whether humans are part of nature or separate (McShane 2009, 407; Rolston 2012, 517).

Intrinsic value is the assumption that a thing has value in itself, regardless of its usefulness for humans. Instrumental value is the assumption that a thing is valuable insofar as it benefits humans (Kopnina and Shoreman-Ouimet 2015). Some early conservationists, such as Gifford Pinchot, believed that the human species had intrinsic value, while non-human species and systems had only instrumental value. Others, including Henry David Thoreau, John Muir, and Aldo Leopold, saw the interconnectedness of all life and believed that all elements of the biosphere had intrinsic value (Brennan and Lo 2015). Most environmental ethics thinkers ascribe intrinsic value not only to human beings but to entities other than humans.

Discussions of animal rights formed an early element in an emerging environmental ethic. In the seventeenth century French philosopher René Descartes had asserted that animals had no moral standing because, he thought, they were not sentient and had no ability to feel pleasure or pain, but by the late eighteenth century this view was changing. British philosopher Jeremy Bentham had argued that skin color should not be a basis for treating some humans differently than others. In 1789 he extended the logic, arguing that number of legs or whether one has fur or a tail should not be a basis for mistreatment, writing about animals in an often-quoted statement, "The question is not, Can they *reason* nor, Can they *talk*? but, Can they *suffer*?" (Nash 1988, 23). Nineteenth-century philosophers including John Stuart Mill and Henry S. Salt continued to advance the thinking on animal rights. In 1975 philosopher Peter Singer published *Animal Liberation*, a book which vividly brought issues of animal rights into the awareness of the general public and which became popular with readers outside the academic world. Referring to the dismissal of animals' rights as speciesism, Singer and philosopher Tom Regan became influential voices for the rights of non-human animals. In the academic world the ethics of animal rights, or what Singer called animal liberation, was sometimes criticized by other scholars because it was utilitarian, an approach that typically ascribes intrinsic value only to sentient beings but not plants or landscapes, and because it was individualistic, that is, ascribing intrinsic value to individuals only but not to ecological wholes such as ecosystems (Brennan and Lo 2015).

Valuing ecological wholes was at the core of an idea known as the land ethic. Aldo Leopold was an ecologist, conservationist, philosopher and author whose lyrical essays had a powerful influence on how people thought about nature. His most famous work, *A Sand County Almanac*, originally published in 1949, became a best seller during the flowering of environmental awareness in the 1970s. Its culminating chapter, "The Land Ethic," expanded the moral sphere from humans to animals to the land itself (Leopold 1987). Beginning his essay with a dramatic story about Odysseus' hanging of his slave girls, Leopold laid out parallels between human slavery and human approaches to land as merely a commodity.

Leopold described an ethical sequence in which the "extension of ethics" from individual to society to land itself "is actually a process in ecological evolution" (Leopold 1987, 202). He saw the possibility that ethics was a social instinct which was evolving in human society (Callicott 1989, 15). Some scholars agree, noting that superorganisms, including humans and some insects, have developed various social restraints for regulating behavior. Ethics is one method; social insects such as ants and termites use other methods (Callicott 1989, 65). Membership in a community confers evolutionary advantages for survival.

Leopold said that "[e]thics are possibly a kind of community instinct in-the-making" (Leopold 1987, 203). With the land ethic, he expanded what constitutes a community beyond individuals to other animals, plants, soil, and water as a collective whole. He stressed the importance of the integrity of the biotic community and saw humans as members of that larger community. In one of his most well-known statements in the closing section of "The Land Ethic" he wrote, "A thing is right when it tends to preserve the integrity, stability, and beauty of the biotic community. It is wrong when it tends otherwise" (ibid., 224).

This underscores a theme running throughout both environmental ethics and sustainability generally: the nature of the distinctions between parts versus wholes or individuals versus communities, a notion considered in more detail in the next chapter. Philosopher J. Baird Callicott wrote of them all as "nested communities" (Light and Rolston 2003, 26). Philosopher Holmes Rolston III noted that what we perceive as individual competition, such as the relationship between cougar and deer, may be cooperation when viewed from another scale (Rolston 1989, 250). He described individuals as close-coupled systems and communities as weak- or loose-coupled systems, "though not less valued," pointing out that "[a]dmiring concentrated unity and stumbling over environmental looseness is like valuing mountains and despising valleys" (ibid., 253). Rolston said thinking that ecosystems do not count morally because they lack sentience or a sense of self "makes another category mistake. To look at one level for what is appropriate at another faults *communities* as though they ought to be organismic *individuals*" (ibid., 255).

Legal scholars look for ways to codify environmental ethics into law. One arena is animal rights law. For example, a team of animal law attorneys at the Animal Legal Defense Fund works to protect animals from abuse by filing civil lawsuits on their behalf. Legal scholar Steven M. Wise teaches animal rights law at several US law schools; he and other attorneys from the Nonhuman Rights Project argue in the courts for the rights of animals including, as a starting point, legal personhood for certain nonhuman primates (Wise 2000).

In 1972, law professor Christopher Stone argued for the legal rights of trees and other natural objects in a groundbreaking essay, "Should Trees Have Standing?" Stone constructed the legal argument for a case being heard before the US Supreme Court, *Sierra Club v. Morton*. The Sierra Club was fighting a massive development in Mineral King Valley in the Sierra Nevada Mountains; a US Court of Appeals had ruled that the Sierra Club did not have legal standing, and the case was being reviewed by the Supreme Court. Stone took up the question in his famous essay, published in the *Southern California Law Review*, which he sent to Justice William O. Douglas. Although the Court majority ruled against the Sierra Club, three justices ruled in its favor. Justice Douglas wrote an impassioned dissenting opinion, citing Stone's argument on the first page of his opinion and concluding with a reference to Leopold's "Land Ethic" (Stone 1972, 73–84). Although the Sierra Club did lose its appeal to speak for the valley, the cost of years of delays convinced Walt Disney Enterprises to abandon the development, and a few years later the US Congress added the valley to Sequoia National Park.

Some governments "are expanding fundamental rights to the planet itself" (Assadourian 2013, 120). In 2008, Ecuador declared that nature has the "right to exist, persist, maintain and regenerate its vital cycles, structure, functions and its processes in evolution." Intrinsic value was codified in Bolivian law in 2011, which defined 11 "Rights of Mother Earth" including "the right to life and to exist; the right to continue vital cycles and processes free from human alteration; the right to pure water and clean air; the right to balance; the right not to be polluted; and the right to not have cellular structure modified or genetically altered" (Moore and Nelson 2013, 230).

The concept of ethics within the work of sustainability also concerns, of course, the rights of all humans to survive and thrive. Environmental justice works to address environmental inequalities, particularly among low-income people and people of color impacted by toxic pollution and unfair land use patterns. Intergenerational equity concerns the rights of people not yet born and our obligations to them. Social equity, generally, involves equal access to resources for all people, equal opportunity to participate, and efforts on behalf of the rights of humans who are less able to speak in their own defense: people who live in poverty, in conditions of power imbalance, and at the bleeding edge of climate change impacts.

Expanding to a Global Scale

Our perspectives on issues of sustainability have expanded. *Silent Spring*, Love Canal, and environmental racism focused on issues that were, in some ways, local. Meanwhile our view has opened up also to encompass a global dimension. The expanding perspective may have started with "Earthrise."

In 1968, Paul Ehrlich published *The Population Bomb*, protests over the Vietnam War raged in the streets, and the Apollo 8 mission sent astronauts around the moon. On December 24 the astronauts entered the lunar orbit planning to take photos of the moon's surface. They looked up to see the Earth rising over the moon's horizon; amazed, they grabbed a camera and took an unplanned picture (Poole 2010, 1). When the photograph of "Earthrise" reached Earth in a live broadcast, people saw a tiny blue and white planet floating in the black void of space. The impact of that image was significant. People began to use the term "spaceship Earth" as a reminder that this world on which we live is finite and the only home we have. Galen Rowell, a photographer for *Life* and *National Geographic* magazines, called Earthrise "the most influential environmental photograph ever taken" (Hosein 2012).

An even more dramatic photograph was sent back to Earth by the crew of Apollo 17 on their way to the moon in 1972. The sun was behind them, the Earth was fully illuminated, and this time the camera captured the entire planet floating in blackness. The crew dubbed the photograph the "Blue Marble." The picture captured people's imaginations during a surge in environmental awareness (Miller 2009, S35). DDT had just been banned, a series of environmental laws had just been passed, and memories of the first Earth Day were still fresh. The "Blue Marble" vividly reinforced, in an immediate and inescapable way, the vulnerability and isolation of the planet in the vast expanse of space. These two photographs, "Earthrise" and "Blue Marble," enabled ordinary people to conceive of their world on an unprecedentedly global scale.

The same year as the Apollo 17 flight the United Nations (UN), a union of countries worldwide that by definition is global in scope, organized the first-ever global environment summit, the 1972 UN Conference on the Human Environment, in Stockholm, Sweden. The UN commissioned economist Barbara Ward and microbiologist René Dubos to prepare a report, *Only One Earth*, to guide the conference discussions (Ward and Dubos 1972). Dubos is credited with coining the phrase "think globally, act locally" which became popular a few years later (Mackenbach 2006, 575; Evans 2012, 84).

In advance of the summit, 30 leading scientists signed a work titled *Blueprint for Survival*. Released as the January 1972 issue of the journal *The Ecologist*, and soon after published as a widely read book, the text presented technical details about ecosystems and their disruption, social systems and their disruption, population and food supply, and nonrenewable resources. It emphasized not just environmental problems but the overwhelming need for "change towards a stable and sustainable society," setting out steps that would be needed to build a "stable and sustainable society" (Goldsmith 1974, 25). The UN Conference on the Human Environment that followed attempted to connect environmental concerns and economic issues (Smil 2002, 22). One of the results was the establishment of the United Nations Environment Programme (UNEP), whose mission was to "provide leadership and encourage partnerships in caring for the environment by inspiring, informing and enabling nations and people to improve their quality of life without compromising that of future generations" (Edwards 2005, 15). Global leaders were beginning to recognize the importance of including all three pillars of sustainability.

More global-scale efforts followed. The Worldwatch Institute was founded by Lester Brown in 1973 to measure worldwide progress toward sustainability; in his 1980 sustainability roadmap *Building a Sustainable Society*, Brown defined a sustainable society as "one that is able to satisfy its needs without diminishing the chance of future generations" (Brown 1981). The term "sustainable development" was first used in the 1980 report, *World Conservation Strategy: Living Resource Conservation for Sustainable Development*, by the International Union for Conservation of Nature (IUCN), commissioned by UNEP. In 1983, the UN created the World Commission on Environment and Development (WCED), headed by Gro Harlem Brundtland, former prime minister of Norway. The Commission was asked to set out shared definitions and goals, propose long-term strategies for sustainable development, and recommend ways to address environmental and economic concerns through international cooperation. The Commission's 1987 report *Our Common Future*, often called "the Brundtland report," adopted Brown's phrase in what has become the most often quoted definition of sustainability: it said that sustainable development is "development that meets the needs of the present without compromising the ability of future generations to meet their own needs" (WCED 1987, 43).

The Worldwatch Institute released its first annual *State of the World* report in 1984. The report made a clear connection between economic development and the environment. An overview chapter observed, "We are living beyond our means, largely by borrowing against the future" (Edwards 2005, 17).

Attention to climate changes on a global scale began to coalesce. In the 1970s the international scientific community had begun issuing the first modern warnings of global climate change caused by the buildup of greenhouse gases from human activity. In 1983 the EPA and the National Academy of Sciences published reports connecting the buildup of greenhouse gases and rising temperatures (Miller 2009, S37). By 1988 the UNEP acknowledged the magnitude of the issue and, together with the World Meteorological Organization, established the Intergovernmental Panel on Climate Change (IPCC). The IPCC assesses and synthesizes published peer-reviewed scientific research, producing reports considered by most governments and international organizations to be authoritative (Blockstein and Wiegman 2010, 9).

In 1992 the UN organized the United Nations Conference on Environment and Development, known as the Earth Summit, in Rio de Janeiro, Brazil. Delegates from 180 countries agreed to a set of 27 principles in the Rio Declaration on Environment and Development, often called simply the Rio Declaration. They adopted Agenda 21, a "comprehensive blueprint for a global partnership [that] strives to reconcile the twin requirements of a high quality environment and a healthy economy for all people of the world" (UN Sustainable Development 1992; Sitarz 1994). They generated the UN Convention on Biological Diversity, a legally binding international treaty. They also generated the UN Framework Convention on Climate Change, a nonbinding treaty that later led to creation of the **Kyoto Protocol**.

Many of the agreements made at the Rio Earth Summit have not been realized. In 1997, the UN General Assembly held a special session called Earth Summit+5 to evaluate progress on implementing Agenda 21. Their report found progress was uneven and identified trends including widening economic inequalities and continued deterioration of the global environment. In 2002, the UN organized the World Summit on Sustainable Development in Johannesburg, South Africa, known as the Earth Summit 2002, boycotted by the US, at which delegates reaffirmed their commitment to Agenda 21 and a new set of goals known as the Millennium Development Goals (Evans 2012, 89).

In 2000, members of the United Nations ushered in the new millennium at a special Millennium Conference, where they adopted a set of goals aimed at halving extreme poverty in all its forms, including hunger, illiteracy, and disease, by 2015 (Sachs 2015, 144). The agreement was called the Millennium Declaration and it established a set of 8 Millennium Development Goals (MDGs), coordinated by the United Nations Development Programme: (1) Eradicate extreme poverty and hunger; (2) Achieve universal primary education; (3) Promote gender equality and empower women; (4) Reduce child mortality; (5) Improve maternal health; (6) Combat HIV/AIDs, malaria and other diseases; (7) Ensure environmental sustainability; and (8) Develop a Global partnership for Development. The goals were not met by 2015. However, they did draw the world's attention to the challenges of extreme poverty, generate new partnerships, and mobilize global efforts. As a result, the number of people living in extreme poverty declined by more than half, the percentage of undernourished people in developing countries fell by almost half, the number of 5- to 11-year-old children not in school fell by almost half, and the death rate for children under 5 fell by more than half (UN 2015, 4).

In 2001 the UN initiated the first of a series of reports called the Millennium Ecosystem Assessment. This report synthesized the work of over 1,360 scientists and other experts from around the world to present measurable indicators of the condition of "Earth's natural capital" (Millennium Ecosystem Assessment 2005). Its prognosis was not encouraging. The report concluded that it was still possible to reverse much of the degradation of the planet's ecosystems over the next 50 years, but "the changes in policy and practice required are substantial and not currently underway."

Still, joining together to face and resolve an environmental crisis that is global in scope is possible. Evidence for that can be seen in the story of the thinning ozone layer that became a global problem in the 1980s. **Chlorofluorocarbon** (CFC) had originally been introduced in the 1930s as an improvement, a more benign substance to replace the use of toxic ammonia, methyl chloride, and sulfur dioxide as refrigerants. In 1976, however, a report from the US National Academy of Sciences reported that CFCs were causing the thinning of the protective ozone layer that shields the earth from excessive ultraviolet rays. In 1985, 20 nations signed the Vienna Convention for the Protection of the Ozone Layer. That same year, dramatic seasonal thinning was discovered in the ozone layer above Antarctica. It became known in the popular press as the "ozone hole" and increased public attention to the issue. In a 1987 multinational agreement called the Montreal Protocol, signed by 43 countries including the US, the industrial world agreed to phase out CFCs and to stop producing them altogether by 1996 (Evans 2012, 83). Some 196 nations have signed subsequent revisions of the Protocol; scientists predict that at the current rate the ozone layer will recover by 2050.

Progress in addressing the threat of global climate change has not been so encouraging. Although awareness of climate change is broad, the causes and potential solutions are more complex. CFCs were produced by only a small number of corporations, primarily DuPont, and their production was concentrated in the industrialized nations (ibid.). Greenhouse gases that lead to climate change, particularly carbon dioxide and methane, are produced by humans in every nation and are connected and augmented through feedback loops and other global-scale, complex mechanisms.

The UN Conference on Sustainable Development, often referred to as Rio+20, was held in Rio de Janeiro, Brazil, in 2012. Its outcome document, *The Future We Want*, laid out a common vision including a concise description of principles of sustainable development (UN 2012, 2). The agreement surveyed the results of UN declarations and conventions from the previous 40 years and laid the plan for a new set of sustainable development goals to carry forward the work of the MDGs (ibid., 46).

Over the next two years, working groups and stakeholders developed a system of 17 goals with 169 measurable targets and indicators. There are many goals and targets because, rather than being written by a few specialists, they were developed by stakeholders from both developed and developing countries and agreed upon by consensus. In 2015, world leaders at the United Nations Sustainable Development Summit adopted the Sustainable Development Goals (SDGs), which aim to end poverty and hunger, fight inequality and injustice, support economic progress for all people, sustainably manage freshwater resources, restore terrestrial and marine ecosystems, address climate change, and make cities and human settlements inclusive, safe, resilient, and sustainable by 2030, to be accomplished through partnerships, participation, and good governance.

Modern Trends

By the mid-1980s, sustainability activists were seeing a need for alternatives to large-scale projects. An anti-environmental backlash in the US in the 1980s had weakened some of the legal controls for environmental protection (Merchant 2007, 199). The early promises of the Rio Earth Summit had not materialized. Wars continued to threaten stability worldwide. The threats of pollution, declining biodiversity, and increasing global temperature seemed daunting. One possible response could have been to feel helpless in the face of the immensity of these challenges and to give up. But many activists decided that the thing to do was to focus on what they could do within their individual spheres of influence. Bumper stickers with the slogan "think globally, act locally" began to appear. **Bioregionalism** and **place-based learning** programs were introduced in schools and universities (Orr 1992, 73; Plant et al. 2008, 8). Local food programs developed. Since the 1980s the numbers of sustainability organizations, programs, and initiatives have increased dramatically, with an explosion in the numbers of community organizations both in physical locales and in Internet communities.

The 1990s and 2000s were lively years in the field of sustainability as the number of sustainability-related organizations increased dramatically and sustainability became firmly established within schools, colleges, and universities. Professionals moved beyond simply recognizing that problems existed to developing ways of measuring both problems and progress. New closed-loop approaches to product design and manufacturing appeared. Architects and builders took up the challenge of sustainability and increasingly sought to get their projects certified by organizations such as the US Green Building Council.

Scholars within higher education have taken an active role in shaping the sustainability movement. The first US college to offer a major in Environmental Studies was Middlebury College, in 1965. The US green-campus movement got its start in 1987 when David Orr of Oberlin College set up quantified studies of the use of energy, water, and materials on several college campuses. Today, hundreds of colleges and universities offer degrees in environmental studies, environmental science, and sustainability. Sustainability has taken an increasingly important position in primary and secondary education as well. Beginning in Europe, sustainability science became a recognized academic discipline.

As sustainability began to mature into an established subject, measurable data became important. In the early 1990s, two scholars at the University of British Columbia developed the idea of measuring human impact and comparing it with the biophysical world's carrying capacity, calling this approach the Ecological Footprint. Another set of data-driven tools, sustainability indicator reports, have become standard components of sustainability programs for many companies and institutions.

A related approach called life cycle analysis or **life cycle assessment** (LCA) was developed around the same time as Ecological Footprint tools (Giudice et al. 2006, 87). This accounting process, now used by some manufacturing companies and many architects, measures the environmental impacts of a material or thing from cradle to grave. In the 1990s American architect William McDonough and German chemist Michael Braungart recognized that something was still missing, and in 2002 published their seminal book *Cradle to Cradle: Remaking the Way We Make Things*. Their approach suggested that we imitate nature's systems, where the concept of waste does not exist and where byproducts from one cycle become nutrients for another.

Data are only useful when they are reliable, and so the practice of formal certification, with verification by independent third parties, became an accepted element of sustainability practice. Beginning in the 1990s and 2000s, certification processes were developed for a range of areas that included greenhouse gas reporting, organic food, green buildings, products and materials, and fair labor practices.

Socio-economic trends

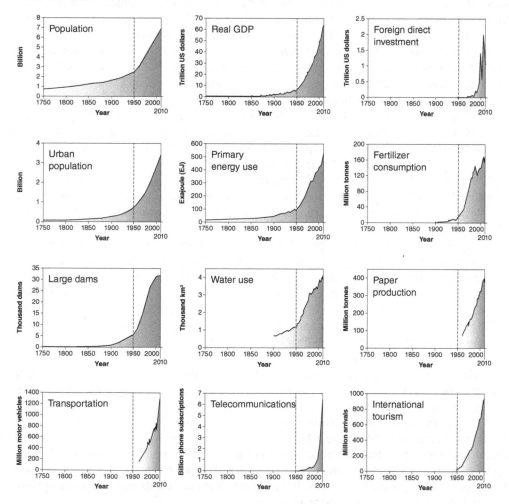

Earth system trends

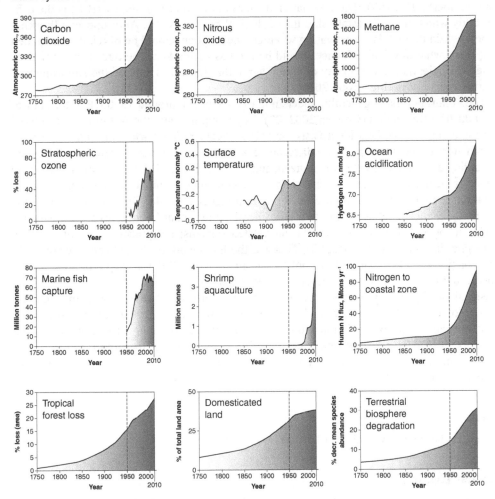

Figure 2.1 Socio-economic and Earth system trends of the Great Acceleration from 1750 to 2010

Source: Will Steffen et al., "The Trajectory of the Anthropocene: The Great Acceleration." *Anthropocene Review.* January 16, 2015.

Into the Anthropocene

We live at the dawning of a new geological epoch, the Anthropocene, an unprecedented period in which human activity has become the primary driver of physical planetary change. The recent geological epoch has been formally known as the Holocene, a period of warm and extraordinarily stable climate conditions between ice ages that was ideal for the development of human civilization. Research indicates that without negative human impacts, the ideal conditions of the Holocene would probably continue for several thousand years more (Wijkman and Rockström 2012, 40).

The term 'Anthropocene,' from the Greek words *anthropo*, 'human,' and *–cene*, 'new' or 'recent,' was proposed in 2000 by atmospheric chemist Paul Crutzen and biologist

Eugene Stoermer. Each time period, such as an epoch, leaves behind a physical, "stratigraphic signature" that will still be visible in the geological record millions of years from now (Kolbert 2014, 109). The International Commission on Stratigraphy (ICS) is the official body which formally establishes the geological time scale; the Anthropocene Working Group within the ICS is investigating whether a new epoch should be officially designated and, if so, what physical evidence should be used as its marker. The term is already used widely by scientists, the majority of whom agree that Earth has entered the Anthropocene (Anthropocene Working Group 2016).

The Anthropocene is generally understood to have begun around 1800 CE at the start of the Industrial Revolution (Crutzen 2002, 23). Beginning in 1945, the Anthropocene entered a second stage researchers identify as the "Great Acceleration," when multiple aspects of human impact including population, resource use and environmental deterioration began expanding exponentially (Steffen, Crutzen, and McNeill 2007, 617). Graphs of each of these impacts reveal a similar curve, with a shape often compared to the blade of a hockey stick.

Humans have become a geological force on a planetary scale. One way to address the enormous challenges that confront us is to identify the global boundaries within which it is safe to operate for each of several interrelated systems: the preconditions of a stable, Holocene-like state (Folke 2013, 22). This was the framework of the collaborative research effort on planetary boundaries, first published in an influential 2009 article in *Nature*, "A Safe Operating Space for Humanity" (Rockström et al 2009a).[1]

Sustainability as a movement began as many small, quiet revolutions. In countless corners of the world, it has gradually coalesced—from small pockets of awareness and grassroots action, from legislation and global cooperation, from innovative designers, from the work of leaders, scholars, and educators. The future shape of the field is still forming, but it seems clear that sustainability will prove to be the most consequential discipline of the twenty-first century.

Note

1 Planetary boundaries were discussed in the previous chapter.

Further Reading

Burke, Edmund III and Pomeranz, Kenneth, eds. *The Environment and World History*. Berkeley, CA: University of California Press, 2009.
Caradonna, Jeremy L. *Sustainability: A History*. New York: Oxford University Press, 2014.
Magoc, Chris J. *Environmental Issues in American History: A Reference Guide with Primary Documents*. Westport, CT: Greenwood Press, 2006.
Merchant, Carolyn. *American Environmental History: An Introduction*. New York: Columbia University Press, 2007.
Nash, Roderick Frazier. *The Rights of Nature*. Madison, WI: University of Wisconsin Press, 1988.

Chapter Review

1 In what ways are the environmental movement and the sustainability movement different?
2 What are some of the benefits of environmental regulations?
3 Why was DDT seen as beneficial?

4   What approaches did Rachel Carson use in *Silent Spring* to argue against indiscriminate pesticide use?
5   During the 1950s and 1960s it was reported that rivers caught fire. How is this possible?
6   If your 10-year-old neighbor asked you "What was Love Canal?" what would you say?
7   What was the significance of the National Environmental Policy Act?
8   What was the origin of the Environmental Protection Agency?
9   Do you think environmental racism exists? What kind of evidence would make you believe that it did or did not exist in a particular situation?
10   What did the Water Pollution Control Act regulate?
11   What is the Anthropocene epoch?

Critical Thinking and Discussion

1   Working for sustainability takes many forms, from personal lifestyle choices to activism to policies and laws. How likely do you think it is that sustainability can be achieved solely by individuals taking responsibility without the addition of systemic changes?
2   Why are people of color and low-income people more likely to suffer from environmental hazards?
3   List some ways that life in the US might be different today if the legislation of the 1970s such as the Clean Air Act and Water Pollution Control Act had not been enacted.
4   Environmental laws enacted in the 1970s had beneficial effects on human and environmental health. Why do you think there was a backlash in the 1980s?
5   What are some arguments in support of a market approach to controlling pollution? What are some arguments in support of a regulatory approach?
6   Why was the Montreal Protocol so successful at addressing damage to the ozone layer, while attempts to address the larger issue of climate change have been so unsuccessful?

3 The Biosphere

This book is not a science textbook. Most students of sustainability will take courses in the sciences such as ecology, biology, chemistry, and physics, where the workings of the world can be studied in detail. This chapter simply introduces how the sustainable world works and picks out some key themes that appear in more specialized science books and courses.

Why Study Living Systems?

Sustainability practitioners often try to pattern their solutions on sustainable living systems that operate and endure over long periods of time. Life has been pursuing its way on the planet for about 3.8 billion years (Hazen 2012, 149); it has done so successfully, and for all but the last 150,000 years it has done it without the presence of us, *Homo sapiens*. As Galileo wrote in 1623: "The great book of Nature lies ever open before our eyes" (Margulis and Sagan 1997, 39). Right outside our doors is a vast, living "instruction manual." Our task is to understand as much as we can about how systems function, that is, to read the instruction manual carefully, so that we can propose positive solutions that work.

One key to understanding the living planet is to recognize that nothing about the physical world is static. The transfers of energy and the movement of matter in the physical world may be hard to see, as the cycles happen over scales that may be microscopic or vast.[1] Mountains, continents, stars, and galaxies may appear permanent and unchanging to us but the entire universe, with us in it, is in fact constantly moving and changing, reusing and recycling, dying and regenerating, in all places and at all scales. On our unusually lively planet much of the flux among biological systems is accelerated and concentrated, so changes here are easier for us humans to perceive than the longer, slower cycles. However, there really are no static elements anywhere in the universe. Changes happen through flows of energy and flows of materials, and these flows take place in regenerative patterns that are cyclical.

Energy and Matter

A system is an integrated whole, made up of parts (Meadows 2008, 11). A living cell, a turtle, a forest, and the planet are all systems. In any system, energy is constantly being transferred and matter is constantly being moved around. Energy drives the movement of matter, allowing systems to change constantly and to interact with other systems. The ways in which energy is transferred and matter is moved often make systems seem static and unchanging, but this is mostly appearance. Look a little deeper, and many networks of dynamic flows can be seen.

Energy is the ability to do work. It can change form and can appear as mechanical, chemical, nuclear, electrical, light, or heat energy. Energy flows into a system, is transformed, and flows out; it only flows one way through a system and cannot be reused. That means that all living things require a flow of energy. The only constant source of energy on our planet is the sun (Wijkman and Rockström 2012, 12).

Thermodynamics is the study of the transformation of energy; the name comes from Greek words for "heat" and "power." One of the most famous laws of science is the first law of thermodynamics, sometimes referred to as the conservation of energy, which says that energy cannot be created or destroyed.[2] Energy cannot be destroyed, only converted from a higher to a lower level of quality, and the energy coming into a system must equal the energy flowing out of the system.

The second law of thermodynamics says that entropy or disorder will increase in any system until the system finally comes to a state of thermal equilibrium. Heat energy is often the byproduct of other, more useful kinds of energy. The second law means that when energy is used it tends to convert to heat, and systems tend to lose heat to their surroundings. For example, when an animal eats a plant about 10 percent of the stored chemical energy in the plant is converted to chemical energy in the animal and the rest is given off as waste heat (AGI 2011, 39).

Matter is the name we give to all physical substances. It can be stored, transferred, and moved around in systems. The same atoms are reused and recycled again and again (Hazen 2012, 6), which means that no feature on the planet is permanent (Trefil and Hazen 2010, viii). The atoms that make up matter can recombine but matter cannot be created or destroyed.[3] For example, if a carbon atom enters a system, a carbon atom must eventually leave the system. A carbon atom you just exhaled in your breath was flung into interstellar space billions of years ago by an exploding star, re-forged in the furnace of our own star, and among many other stops in its journey might have helped build the structure of a bacterial cell three billion years ago, been exhaled by a dinosaur 100 million years ago, been pulled beneath Earth's crust and later expelled by a volcano 30 million years ago, circulated around and around through water and atmosphere, and been breathed in by an oak tree 100 years ago.

Matter is composed of atoms which are made of three kinds of particles: negatively charged electrons, positively charged protons, and electrically neutral neutrons.[4] Protons and neutrons have similar mass and are clustered in equal number in the nucleus, the center of the atom. Electrons are much lighter and orbit the nucleus at the speed of light. Protons and electrons are held together by electromagnetic force, 10^{40} times stronger than gravity (Giancoli 2005, 895). The reason we do not feel these electrical forces, although we are composed of an enormous number of them, is that atoms almost always have the same number of positive protons and negative electrons in balance, so that we are electrically neutral. Chemistry, the combining and separating of atoms, is essentially electrical in nature. All of chemistry and biology and much of physics are based on the remarkable existence of "positive" and "negative" particles within atoms and on the fact that like charges repel and opposite charges attract.

Matter consists of elements. An element is made of atoms that cannot be broken down any further by ordinary chemical means. It is the number of protons and electrons that determines the characteristics of the element: for example, oxygen, with 8 protons and 8 electrons, behaves differently than iron, which has 26 protons and 26 electrons. Just four elements—carbon, hydrogen, nitrogen, and oxygen—make up all but 4 percent of the mass of all life forms on Earth, including us (Cunningham and Cunningham 2010, 53). These four, together with phosphorus and sulfur, are the most important elements for life; they can combine and interact in an almost-infinite number of ways.[5] Atoms are sometimes referred to as the building blocks of life, but they are never isolated objects. Atoms are always interacting and interconnecting.

The Earth is a closed system for matter. Except for tiny bits of debris from space, no matter comes in and no matter goes out. All of the elements used in the processes and structures of life come from elements that were part of the Earth when it formed over 4.5 billion years ago (Harding 2006, 99).

Cycles

Matter and energy move through every kind of system in regenerative patterns that are cyclical. Cycles happen at all scales of systems, from the metabolism of a bacterium to the pumping of carbon around the planet to the recycling of fundamental matter in the great star factories of interstellar space.

A typical star, about the size of our sun, lives for about 10 billion years. Our own star is about halfway through its lifespan. The most massive stars are much brighter but have shorter lives, living only about 10 million years (Smolin 1997, 119). Stars are constantly dying and being born; galaxies are the systems where they are made. Galaxies themselves, of which there are billions, are arranged within clusters and superclusters. The largest structures known so far are enormous walls of galaxies, each containing many galaxy clusters, each of which contains dozens to thousands of galaxies (ibid., 34). Current estimates are that our particular galaxy contains about 400 billion stars (Kump et al. 2010, 388). Not all types of galaxies contain star factories. The arms of spiral galaxies are the places where conditions are just right to generate new stars. The cosmic-scale process of the recycling of dying stars and the enormous waves that generate new star formation recur perpetually in the great star factories of spiral galaxies.

We know from the second law of thermodynamics or the law of entropy that everything, including the universe itself, should be moving toward thermal equilibrium. The reason the universe remains dynamic, nowhere near thermal equilibrium, is because there are stars. Stars are concentrations of energy and matter within vast and highly complex, finely tuned, and self-organizing systems. When they are born, stars forge atoms of hydrogen and helium into carbon, oxygen, nitrogen, and other elements, and in the process convert nuclear energy into radiation and light energy (Smolin 1997, 34). They fling their transformed matter and energy out into the universe. We are made of star material, and every atom of matter on Earth originated in the core of a star.

Here on our local planet, material is constantly moving. Energy flows through systems in one direction while matter cycles around and around. We can think of these cycles as flows and storage compartments. A storage compartment where matter is stored is known as a **reservoir** or **sink**. For example, carbon from dead organisms accumulates on seabeds; the oceans are considered a "carbon sink." A storage compartment that releases matter to another location is known as a **source**. A forest fire releases into the air the carbon that had been stored in trees; it is one kind of "carbon source."

Carbon, nitrogen, and other elements are rearranged, transported, and stored in places where they can be used. They move through ecosystems, organisms, earth, water, and air in cycles known as **biogeochemical cycles**. These cycles of elements flow through sets of nested loops that include biological processes, geological processes, and chemical processes, which is why we call them biogeochemical. They take many different pathways and use a variety of reservoirs where materials may be stored for short or long periods of time. Some carbon atoms, for example, make a complete circuit within a few days, while others remain locked in ocean sediments for millions of years.

Carbon is one of the fundamental building blocks of life and is transferred among systems in the carbon cycle. Plants take carbon dioxide out of the air during photosynthesis.

Photosynthesis means "to put together with light." Using energy from the sun, plants take water from the soil and carbon dioxide from the air and from them "put together" sugars and oxygen. Plants that are eaten by other organisms become part of eating sequences known as food chains. When terrestrial plants die or when the animals who ate them die, the carbon originally captured from the air is broken down by microbes and becomes part of the soil. In warm weather, some of it rises back into the air as carbon dioxide. Oceans absorb carbon dioxide from the air by folding it into the water through wave action and by the work of tiny algae who pull it into the first stage of the ocean's food chain. Rocks are the planet's largest carbon reservoir (Smil 2002, 135). Earth's atmosphere and plants on land are also carbon reservoirs.

Nitrogen is also essential to life. Every living cell on Earth contains nitrogen in the form of amino acids and nucleic acids made available through the nitrogen cycle. Nitrogen gas makes up 78 percent of the air we breathe and is made of two atoms of nitrogen held together with one of the strongest bonds in chemistry. This bond makes the molecule very unreactive, requiring a great deal of energy to break apart so that it can be used by living organisms. Some nitrogen is fixed, or made available, by lightning that provides enough energy to break the atomic bonds. But most of the work of fixing nitrogen is done by the few types of bacteria who have the unique ability to break the strong molecular bonds and capture nitrogen out of thin air (AGI 2011, 40). When these nitrogen-fixers are eaten, or die and decompose, their nitrogen enters the food chain where it is used by all the other organisms; without these bacteria, most life on Earth would cease to exist (Margulis and Sagan 2000, 107). When living things die, other bacteria who use nitrogen as their energy source convert the nitrogen compounds back to the nonreactive form of nitrogen where it passes back to the atmosphere again.

Many other organisms play specialized roles in the nitrogen cycle. Lichens growing in old-growth forest canopies capture nitrogen hundreds of feet in the air, releasing it to the soil when they fall to the forest floor (Denison 1973, 77). Spawning salmon carry nitrogen from the ocean many miles up rivers and are caught by bears who carry them into the forest to eat and then leave the partially eaten carcasses where they release their captured nitrogen into the soil (Klingle 2007, 18; Cunningham and Cunningham 2010, 52).

Phosphorus is made available through the phosphorus cycle. Phosphorus, sometimes called the "energy element," is a component of compounds involved with transferring and using energy within cells. Phosphorus cycles through food webs in the ocean and is recycled between land and ocean by salmon and migratory birds.

Sulfur is another element that is necessary for the function of living cells. Rivers carry it from weathered rocks to the ocean before it can be used by plants on land and it is very scarce in soil. However, coral reefs and certain kinds of algal seaweed around the continental shelves are able to extract sulfur from the sea. They incorporate it into a compound called dimethyl sulphide, which is what gives ocean air its tangy aroma. This gas is carried inland by ocean winds, where it falls back to earth as rain, making sulfur available to plant roots. Sulfur in the form of dimethyl sulphide also plays an important role in seeding clouds. Dust particles cause some of the condensation that results in clouds, but most of the cloud-forming work is done by this sulfur compound (Harding 2006, 131). Thus sulfur captured by tiny algae performs two big jobs as it cycles from ocean to land: it generates the abundant clouds that cool the surface of the planet and circulate water in the form of rain, and it becomes part of the building of proteins in cells.

Some 24 elements are needed by living things. Several, including silicon, calcium, and sulfur, play important roles in regulating the temperature of the planet. For every element used by life there is an intricate and dynamically balanced cycle, ensuring that quantities are always just right and keeping the element circulating through the crust, the atmosphere, the water cycle, and living organisms.

The Four Spheres

Systems can be defined at many scales. At the scale of the entire planet there are four major systems, or spheres: rock, air, water, and organism. Ecologists call these the lithosphere, the atmosphere, the hydrosphere, and the **biosphere**.

Lithosphere

The lithosphere is made of rock; it is the outer part of the solid earth, about 60 miles thick (Keller and Botkin 2008, 42), composed of the crust and the upper layer of the mantle. *Lithos* is the Greek word for "stone." The larger system of which the lithosphere is a part is the geosphere, the entire solid matter of the Earth.

At the center of the geosphere is Earth's core, made mostly of iron and nickel. It is very hot because of residual primordial heat plus ongoing radioactive decay left over from the supernova explosion that forged the elements of our planet. Tremendous pressures at the depth of the inner core keep it solid. The outer core is liquid (AGI 2011, 8), and fluid motion in this liquid iron core generates a magnetic field that is amplified by Earth's rotation. Earth is a giant two-pole magnet; compass needles point toward the north pole, one pole of the planetary magnet. The outer core's fluid motion is the reason the north pole is constantly moving around (Hazen 2012, 118). Most good-quality maps list a declination, which is the number of degrees the magnetic pole was located away from the geographic or "true north" pole in the particular year in which that map was made. Earth's magnetic field helps to protect living things from cosmic radiation.

Above the core is the mantle, the layer of rock that makes up most of the geosphere. Not all of it is solid. The upper part of the mantle is plastic, which is a state between solid and liquid. It appears solid on short time scales but exhibits fluid motion over time scales of millions of years (ibid., 123). Large convection currents caused by temperature variations keep the mantle material in constant motion. Where two convection cells come together flowing downward, deep ocean troughs form. Where two convection cells come together flowing upward, marine mountain ridges form as material from the mantle emerges and flows down both sides of the ridge.

The crust is the thinnest layer of the geosphere. The crust and the rigid uppermost mantle form the layer known as the lithosphere. The rocks of the lithosphere are constantly changing, and all rocks on the surface are present only temporarily. Weathering breaks big rocks into little rocks and smaller grains. Erosion moves these pieces of rock, gravel, sand, and silt from higher to lower elevations with the help of gravity and running water. Eventually sediment reaches a place where it can settle out and accumulate, and over time it changes into sedimentary rock. Larger-grained sand changes into sandstone, finer sediment made of clay changes into shale, and ocean sediments containing minerals from seawater and the remains of tiny creatures become limestone. When enough sediment has built up, the pressures and temperatures at very deep levels are so great that the rocks change, or metamorphose, into a new type of mineral. In some places below the crust, the heat is so great that rock melts. When it encounters a weak place in the crust the magma, or melted rock, breaks through and rises to the surface to form new igneous rock, and this cycle, known as the rock cycle, starts over again (AGI 2011, 10).

As the mantle material sinks, rises, and moves from place to place it breaks the crust above it into pieces, moving them around like floating islands. These moving pieces of broken crust are called plates. Plates move at about the same rate that human fingernails grow. The movement of the plates continually reshapes continents, bringing them together and splitting them apart, opening and closing oceans. When two plates come together the older of the two plates, which is colder and denser, sinks below the younger plate. The sinking older plate carries water with it that causes the rock beneath partly to melt, forming magma that can eventually makes its way back to the surface again (ibid., 213).

Life is a partner in the lithosphere. On land, as it extracts nutrients it needs from rock it plays a role in physical and chemical weathering and breaking apart of rock. In the oceans, the calcium- and silica-rich bodies of dead organisms settle onto the moving plates of the sea floor and are eventually carried deep into the lithosphere when an oceanic plate meets and slides beneath a continental plate. High temperatures and pressures deep in the earth split and reform atomic bonds, recombining the carbon from the calcium carbonate in the bodies of dead organisms and the oxygen from the silica in their bodies to form fresh carbon dioxide that is released during volcanic eruptions. The calcium, silicon, oxygen, and other elements recombine to create new granite, which can then resurface and erode again (Harding 2006, 113).

Since the Industrial Revolution, the lithosphere has become the source for 70 percent of the materials used in human civilization (Thorpe 2006, 28), including fossil fuels, minerals, and various kinds of metal ore. Once material is taken out of the lithosphere, it cannot be put back. Extraction, manufacturing, and eventual disposal break the extracted materials of the lithosphere into little dilute bits that are then spread across the atmosphere, hydrosphere, and biosphere. Once these lithosphere materials are distributed, they cannot easily be removed from the other spheres (ibid., 31).

Atmosphere

The atmosphere consists of the layers of air above the solid crust. It is full of turbulent motion as winds with complex flow patterns at varying elevations constantly swirl through the realm of the clouds. Air is a mixture of unstable and nearly combustible gases. For the last 700 million years the atmosphere has remained about 78 percent nitrogen and 21 percent oxygen. All free oxygen in the air is the result of life, the product of plants. If life disappeared from Earth, oxygen would quickly recombine with elements in rocks and oceans and vanish from the atmosphere (Flannery 2010, 44). If the oxygen level were to rise even 1 percent, the likelihood of forest fires would increase by 70 percent, and if the oxygen level rose to 25 percent even wet vegetation in a rain forest would ignite (Lovelock 2000, 65). In spite of all this volatility and turbulence the atmosphere somehow manages to maintain a constant chemical composition and constant temperature. The atmosphere is the system responsible for carefully regulating conditions to make them just right for life on Earth. No other planet in the solar system has an atmosphere like ours.

The atmosphere is divided into layers. The lowest and liveliest layer is the troposphere, 6 to 10 miles high. Air here is kept constantly swirling and churning by differences in temperature and moisture. This is where birds, bats, and insects fly, where weather happens, and where most of the clouds are. About midway up in the troposphere are several so-called jet streams, bands of wind 200 to 300 miles wide circling the globe at speeds up to 200 miles per hour; these rivers of air sometimes branch and rejoin like braided streams (Henson 2002, 29). Temperatures in the troposphere get colder and colder as altitude increases. At the top of this layer at a boundary called the tropopause, temperatures reverse and begin to get warmer again.

The layer above the troposphere is called the stratosphere, so named because, in spite of its fierce winds, the air remains in layers or strata at constant levels and does not easily mix above or below those levels. Temperatures increase with altitude in the stratosphere as it absorbs ultraviolet radiation from the sun. Air in the stratosphere is too thin and cold for most clouds to form. In the middle of the stratosphere is a layer called the ozone layer, formed from oxygen released by organisms. Oxygen molecules are usually made of two oxygen atoms bonded together as O_2. In the ozone layer ultraviolet radiation from the sun breaks and joins oxygen's chemical bonds to form oxygen molecules with three atoms, O_3 or ozone (AGI 2011, 17). The ozone layer absorbs ultraviolet light and protects living things below from damage.

Above the stratosphere is the very thin air of the mesosphere, where temperatures get very cold. What we call shooting stars are meteors falling through this layer and heating because of friction with the remaining air molecules. Above that is the thermosphere, where gas molecules are fewer and fewer in number as the layer gradually merges into outer space. The sparse molecules in the thermosphere get electrically charged by streams of high-energy particles from the sun, making this layer home to the northern lights, or aurora borealis, and southern lights, or aurora australis.

We are creatures of the bottom of the sky. Some animals, the so-called benthic organisms, live at the bottoms of lakes or oceans, where they are adapted to the pressures on their bodies and to extracting the oxygen they need from the water around them. We and most other land creatures are benthic creatures of the sky, our bodies adapted to lighter atmospheric pressures and designed to extract oxygen from the air (Roth 1981, 293). Plants have their roots in soil, but they are literally made from air, making their roots, stems, and leaves using oxygen and carbon they get directly from the air (Capra 1996, 178).

Hydrosphere

The hydrosphere consists of water. Earth is the water planet, and we often use water as the reference to which we compare. We measure elevations relative to mean sea level. We measure acidity and alkalinity in terms of the concentration of hydrogen ions compared to water; pure water, with a pH of 7, is considered neutral. We measure the specific gravity or density of a substance by comparing its weight to the weight of an equal volume of water. The Celsius temperature scale is based on changes in the physical state of water; $0°$ is set at water's freezing point and $100°$ is set at water's boiling point. Earth is the only planet in the solar system where water on its surface can exist in all three states of matter: solid, liquid, or gas (AGI 2011, 13).

Water plays multiple roles in all the spheres on the water planet. It stores heat from the sun and distributes it around the world; its largest reservoirs, the oceans, regulate the composition of the air, play central roles in planetary water and chemical cycles, and underlie global food webs (Lovelock 2000, 78). Water condenses to form clouds that help keep Earth's temperature cool enough for life. It wears down mountains, redistributes materials, and helps form magma deep underground. Water is essential to all living beings; it moves nutrients through ecosystems, is essential to metabolism, and makes up most of the volume of every living cell.

Water circulates around the planet in a cycle known as the hydrologic cycle. Through all the physical changes and upheavals the planet has undergone since life first appeared around 3.8 billion years ago, the total volume of water on the planet has remained unchanged (Lovelock 2000, 79; Trefil and Hazen 2010, 379). The hydrologic cycle influences all the other biogeochemical cycles.

In the hydrologic cycle, water rises into the atmosphere, condenses into clouds, falls back to earth, runs off the surface and into rivers, lakes, and oceans, and infiltrates into soil and groundwater. The sun drives the hydrologic cycle, causing water to evaporate from land and surface waters. Combining evaporation and transport in the process called transpiration, plants pump water from underground through their stems and out through pores in their leaves. Each large tree pumps many gallons each day. About 90 percent of the water that evaporates over the land comes from transpiration (Miller and Spoolman 2009, 65). Molecules of water vapor in the air come together in clouds, rejoin, and condense into liquid water droplets or ice.

Water molecules cycle through the oceans every 30,000 to 40,000 years (Flannery 2010, 51). Ninety percent of the water that evaporates from the ocean falls back to the ocean as rain; the other 10 percent is carried by winds and falls over land (Cunningham and Cunningham 2010, 66). Some soaks into the ground; some runs off the surface, where it flows into streams, then rivers, then back to the ocean. The salinity of oceans has remained constant over billions of years through an interplay of the hydrologic cycle, with streams adding salt eroded from land, and the rock cycle, with water recirculating through hydrothermal vents on the ocean floor every 10 to 100 million years where salt is removed (Flannery 2010, 53).

Some water that falls on land changes to ice and is stored in glaciers. A small amount of the water that falls on land is taken up by plants and temporarily enters a food chain. Although the atmosphere has an important place in the water cycle, it contains only 0.001 percent of all water (AGI 2011, 14).

Water is found nearly everywhere on Earth, above and below the surface. Even in places that look like dry and lifeless deserts, clay particles and porous rocks are home to thriving communities of microscopic organisms, swimming happily in the thin layers of water that adhere to underground surfaces (Wolfe 2001, 22).

Biosphere

The biosphere is the part of the Earth system inhabited by living organisms and includes the other three spheres: the lithosphere, atmosphere, and hydrosphere. The biosphere is explored in more detail in the following section.

The Biosphere

The biosphere is the thin layer at the surface of the planet where life exists. It extends five to six miles down into the ocean and crust and several miles up into the atmosphere (Capra 1996, 214). The biosphere includes all the living and nonliving parts, the organisms and the rocks, water, and air with which they interact as materials are interchanged in the biogeochemical cycles.

Biologists currently recognize five kingdoms of living beings: plants, animals, fungi, protists, and bacteria. These life forms can be grouped into two super-kingdoms: prokaryotes, whose cells lack a nucleus, and eukaryotes, whose cells have a nucleus. Prokaryotes, or bacteria, represent most of the history of life on the planet until very recently. They are still by far the most numerous, can survive in the most diverse range of living conditions, and are the most necessary (Wolfe 2001, 62). Eukaryotes include the other four kingdoms:

protists (including amoebas and paramecia), fungi, plants, and animals. A diagram of life forms, first developed in 1977 by Carl Woese using ribonucleic acid (RNA) and deoxyribonucleic acid (DNA) analysis, showed that the history of life, its "family tree," is more like a bush than a simple tree. It also revealed that plants and animals make up only a small portion of all life.

All living things circulate energy and chemicals through the biosphere. Energy moves through in one direction; chemical materials cycle around and are reused. Every organism must obtain energy to live either directly from its environment or by eating other organisms.

A diagram of who eats whom in a particular ecosystem is called a **food web**. We sometimes use the term "food chain" in casual conversation, but the flows and exchanges are so complex that a simple, linear chain does not describe them accurately. Food webs are divided into levels called trophic levels. Each trophic level includes all the organisms in that ecosystem who get their energy from the same source. Plants, producers who get their energy from the sun, are the first trophic level in many ecosystems. The second trophic level includes herbivores, animals who eat plants. Carnivores who eat herbivores are on a third trophic level. In food webs, plants are called producers; carnivores and herbivores are called consumers. Scavengers and decomposers are the recyclers of the food web, disposing of remains and returning carbon dioxide and water to the biogeochemical cycles. Everything gets used; waste from one organism is always food for another. At each trophic level only about 10 percent of the energy an organism gets from its food becomes tissue that organisms at the next trophic level can eat. The organism uses the other 90 percent just to stay alive, eventually releasing that energy as heat. That means that each trophic level contains 10 percent of the energy and 10 percent of the biomass, the mass of living material, of the level below it (Hazen 2001, 58). This is why large carnivores are relatively rare, and why it takes around 16 pounds of grain to produce just one pound of meat (Sachs 2009, 36).

When we think of wildlife we often picture the visible creatures we all like such as birds, butterflies, or beavers. But the big creatures we like must live off the small things we cannot see. In many environments bacteria are the primary producers or first trophic level. Within rock layers far below the surface lithotrophs, or rock eaters, get their energy not from the sun but from the minerals around them, or from hydrogen gas in pore spaces of the rock (Wolfe 2001, 48). In the deep ocean, microbes use chemical energy they get from rocks and from hot gases emitted by hydrothermal vents.

In fact, it turns out that bacteria are not only the oldest, most numerous, and most diverse organisms on Earth; they run the planet. Every living system on Earth depends on these tiny complex beings (Margulis and Sagan 1997, 21). Without them, carbon, nitrogen, and other materials would be unavailable to plants and animals. Bacteria regulate the temperature and chemical composition of the atmosphere and without them the planet would grow too hot to support life.

These amazing creatures invented photosynthesis and the ability to metabolize a vast array of chemicals. Various strains can detect light, break down decaying matter, fix nitrogen gas, make food from hydrogen sulfide in place of sunlight, and live at temperatures above boiling or below freezing. Bacteria are not genetically programmed to grow old and die; unless affected by starvation, heat, or desiccation, a bacterium can live indefinitely.

Ecosystems

Ecologists study the biosphere at various scales: individuals, populations, communities, ecosystems, biomes, and the entire biosphere itself. A **population** is a group of individuals of the same species living in an area. A **community** is all the populations that live in an area. An ecosystem is a community plus its rocks, soil, water, and air.

An ecosystem is a combination of living and nonliving parts, with each part playing an important role. A functioning ecosystem depends on webs of interactions among all the species of plants, animals, fungi, and microbes together with rocks, soil, water, and climate. Every organism in an ecosystem occupies a niche. Its **niche** is how it earns its living, its role in the system. Every organism must compete for resources in its niche, so generally more than one species will not occupy identical niches. In a forest, for example, two species of birds might live in the same tree, but one will live in the canopy and eat one kind of insect and the other will live in the lower branches and eat a different kind of insect.

Every organism is part of a **habitat**. Its habitat is its physical address. An organism's habitat is where it lives and finds food, water, cover, and space to grow and reproduce. Habitats can be found two miles below the ice of Antarctica or inside fiery deep-sea vents belching scalding-hot hydrogen sulfide gases, with residents perfectly adapted to living there. Depending on whose living space you are talking about, a habitat might be microscopic in size or it might cover several square miles.

Every place is unique, each finely tuned to the special conditions at its particular location. However, to help develop broad understanding about how habitats function, scientists identify major regional habitat types known as biomes. A **biome** is a particular type of community that covers a large geographical area. Each biome has particular soil, moisture, and climatic patterns and a distinctive community of microbes, fungi, plants, and animals that have developed in response to those conditions. Biomes are terrestrial systems and include deserts, grasslands, tropical forests, temperate forests, boreal forests, and tundra.

In marine and freshwater environments, major categories of ecosystems have developed in response to salinity, depth, permanence, and movement of water. Saltwater aquatic ecosystems include the intertidal zone or coastal zone where ocean meets land; the pelagic zone or open ocean, with coral reefs found in some places; the benthic zone or seafloor; and the abyssal zone, the deepest, darkest zone, often including hydrothermal vents. Freshwater aquatic ecosystems include rivers and streams, lakes, and wetlands. Estuaries are a mix of saltwater and fresh.

Ecosystems are not permanent; nature is constantly changing. Two essential and related processes of change are **disturbance** and **succession**. A terrestrial ecosystem is never static and lives in a state of dynamic equilibrium, periodically undergoing some kind of disturbance, a destructive event such as flood, wind, or fire. Many ecosystems need periodic disturbance to remain healthy.

Succession follows disturbance. Succession is an important process in most ecosystems and it follows some general patterns. Plants known as pioneers are the first to establish because they can tolerate harsh conditions such as full sun and poor soil. They tend to be small plants, they grow fast and have relatively short lives, and they make seeds that spread quickly. As they die and decay, their vegetation returns nutrients to the soil where the next generation can use them. After the pioneers, larger plants including trees begin to take hold. Several stages of succession move through over time, each with plants adapted to different conditions. Most ecosystems are not uniform and homogeneous, but are mosaics of patches of different ages and different stages of succession, and this complexity increases biodiversity by increasing the kinds of habitats available.

Disturbance is a basic process of life that happens at all scales including planetary. The history of life on Earth includes repeated patterns of catastrophes, followed by mass extinctions, followed by periods of intense flowering of new life forms as life and diversity surge forward (Primack 2008, 126).

What Is Life?

So, what is life, anyway? This is a question we cannot answer precisely, but we can describe some general patterns. We know that on our planet all life consists of cells. Some cells have nuclei; some do not. Some organisms have only one cell; some consist of complex interconnections of multiple cells. The cells all have certain features in common.

All cells have membranes that define their boundaries, dividing what is inside a cell from what is separate from the cell. However, membranes are open to exchanges with the outside world. A membrane is a thin film that is the cell's interface with the outside world, allowing certain substances in and keeping certain other substances out. Metabolism cannot take place without membranes.

Within each cell, metabolism of some kind takes place. The word "metabolism" comes from a Greek word meaning "change." Metabolism is a process of exchange and chemical reactions, with energy and food coming in and waste going out. A constant flow of energy and matter is a feature of all life.

All life, at all scales, is made of networks. Within a cell, metabolism is essentially a chemical network. Within each multicelled organism are networks of cells and circulation systems. Within an ecosystem, organisms are connected in networks of food webs. Within the biosphere, ecosystems are connected by complex networks of energy flows and biogeochemical cycles. You could say that life is more about the relationships between things than about the things themselves. A living system is a network made of components that interact with each other so that the entire system, whether a cell or the biosphere, organizes and regulates itself.

All life is made of networks, but not all networks are living systems. The difference is that living systems are constantly regenerating. All life constantly replaces itself. The scientific name for this is autopoiesis, or "self-making." Living systems not only regenerate themselves, they also are able to reproduce themselves, to make new copies of themselves.

Life constantly develops and evolves. One reason it does is that living systems always operate at a state of non-equilibrium (Capra 2002, 13). When a system is in equilibrium, the flow of energy coming in equals the flow of energy going out, such as when temperature outside equals temperature inside, or chemical composition outside equals chemical composition inside. The only time an organism is in equilibrium is when it is dead (ibid.).

The constant flows of energy and matter within the complex network structures of life mean that new forms and structures can emerge spontaneously, a feature of life known as **emergence**. Life is not just a constantly repeating cycle; life consists of systems whose processes continually generate novelty.

This constant, dynamic change allows systems to be resilient (Walker and Salt 2006, 78). Resilience is the ability of a system to accommodate disturbance and still retain its basic function and structure. Ecosystems are resilient because they are made of a diversity of component parts at a range of scales. When a disturbance happens, small parts react and recover quickly while larger, slower parts maintain the continuity of the system. For example, when floods scour a riverbank, the small and fast parts are affected: individual trees are uprooted, birds must find other places to nest, and new trees subsequently sprout and grow. The large and slow parts—the role of birds, the role of trees, and the function of the riverbank ecosystem—absorb the shock and continue on.

Emergence and resilience happened in a big way early in the history of life. Photosynthesis, the ability to manufacture food from sunlight, was invented by ancient bacteria who used not sunlight and water but sunlight and hydrogen sulfide, a gas that was being discharged in large quantities by volcanoes. About two billion years ago the greatest pollution disaster in Earth's history threatened to wipe out all life on the planet: photosynthetic blue-green bacteria had begun emitting oxygen for the first time, and it began to accumulate. This reactive gas happened to be highly toxic to the life forms then living on the planet, the **anaerobic** bacteria. Many species were completely wiped out. Others were driven underground, to live in muds at the bottoms of lakes and oceans. Today we find these same anaerobic bacteria living in the guts of all animals, where we provide the anaerobic environment they need while they digest our food for us. But in this early oxygenated atmosphere, in a dramatic example of emergence some life forms actually developed the ability to breathe this formerly toxic chemical (Hazen 2012, 228–29).

When we talk about the evolution of life, we may think of what we learned in school about competition and survival of the fittest. But while it is true that competition plays a role in determining which organisms survive long enough to reproduce, it turns out that cooperation is even more fundamental to life. A form of cooperation called **symbiosis** occurs when two different organisms live with and interact with each other, benefiting both of them. Symbiosis led to the development of the cells that now make up all plants and animals (Margulis and Sagan 2000, 103–06).

Every cell contains tiny power factories called mitochondria which use oxygen to generate energy for the cell. Biologists have learned from studying the DNA of cells and the DNA of their mitochondria that in ancient times they were actually different species of bacteria. In the newly oxygenated world, these smaller oxygen-breathing, energy-producing bacteria invaded larger bacteria but instead of killing their targets, the invaders took up residence. The larger hosts provided food and shelter, and in return the smaller bacteria provided energy and aerobic viability. Both invader and host thrived, and mitochondria inside cells still provide energy today (Smil 2002, 220).

Symbiosis is the reason plants can produce food and oxygen through photosynthesis, a process invented not by plants but by cyanobacteria. Cyanobacteria are closely related to chloroplasts, the component of plant cells responsible for photosynthesis. Around 2 billion years ago a single-celled organism first ingested a cyanobacterium without killing it. The host provided nutrients, and the cyanobacterium provided energy in the form of oxygen. Today plant cells and their chloroplasts still contain distinct and separate DNA, reflecting their early history as separate beings (ibid., 224).

Examples of symbiosis can be found in every ecosystem. The organisms we call lichens are not really plants but communities, a symbiosis of algae and fungi. Coral reefs are made of calcium deposits from small sea anemones; algae living inside the cells of each coral animal provide food from photosynthesis to the anemone in exchange for shelter and nutrients.

Symbiosis is critical to the survival of most modern plants. Specialized symbiotic fungi live in the soil around the roots of about 90 percent of all higher plants in every region but the Arctic in a fungus–root partnership called mycorrhizae (Wolfe 2001, 94). The fungi act as surrogate roots, completely encasing the plant rootlets and sending out very fine threads that give the plants access to nooks and crannies in the soil they could not otherwise penetrate. The fungi help supply plants with nutrients and water, and in return the plants produce food that feed the fungi.

Mycorrhizae do more than feed individual plants. They also connect nearby plants in mycorrhizal networks. Some plants, including legumes, alder trees, and various tropical trees and vines, are home to bacteria who can fix nitrogen out of the air. Mycorrhizae transfer some of this nitrogen to neighboring plants who are not nitrogen-fixers (ibid., 102). Some botanists who study these mycorrhizal networks have discovered that in many forests, the trees in the ecosystem, including those of different species, communicate with each other; they share resources, adjust the transfer of nutrients and water based on the needs of individuals in the network, and signal neighbors to activate defenses to prepare for approaching threats from pathogens (Marshall 2010, 14). In some systems the connections between members of some plant communities are so interconnected that it becomes difficult to distinguish exactly where the boundary between individuals is (Wolfe 2001, 102).

The lack of a sharp distinction between individuals and communities is another feature of life on Earth (Rolston 1989, 255). Some distinctions are clear. You can see that an alder tree is not a raccoon, for example. But in other places dividing lines are less certain. In the US, a mass of quaking aspen clones living in Utah shares one 106-acre root system and all the stems in this colony are identical genetically (Beattie and Ehrlich 2004, 17). Is this one tree? It depends on your definition of an individual tree. A single armillaria fungus in Michigan covers 37 acres (ibid., 18); another in Oregon covers over 2,300 acres and is several thousand years old (Casselman 2007). Are these single individuals? Or are they communities?

In societies of social insects such as ants, bees, and termites, individuals have tiny brains and do not make voluntary decisions in the same way mammals do. Yet they use highly organized division of labor to farm, tend flocks, wage war, share child-rearing, build air-conditioned structures, manage production centers, haul off garbage, and tend to the dead. They are members of cooperative communities known as superorganisms, whose actions initially look like random patterns but which turn into organized wholes that emerge out of their interactions as a community (Hölldobler and Wilson 2009, 58). In social insects, complex behaviors are orchestrated by exchanges of chemicals called pheromones. In humans, another superorganism, behaviors are coordinated through exchanges of ideas using language (Flannery 2010, 136).

Distinctions between individual bacteria are even less clear. Similar to social insects, they coordinate their collective behavior by releasing chemical signals in a process known as quorum sensing (Harding 2006, 157). Bacteria do not sexually reproduce; they simply divide to form two identical offspring. They exchange genetic material freely, even among different "species." As such, they are part of a huge planetary gene pool that changes and adapts to shifting environmental conditions.

Various scientists over time have suggested that distinctions between individuals and communities are somewhat arbitrary. In the 1890s, for example, biologist Frederic Clements, an early proponent of the succession model, described climax vegetation as a "complex organism," saying that many living things functioning together resembled a single being, with individuals mutually dependent in a way quite analogous to organs in the body (Rolston 1989, 246). Eighty years later, Lynn Margulis' and James Lovelock's Gaia hypothesis held that individual beings were parts of indivisible wholes, analogous to cells and organs in the body. We know that organisms not only live within ecosystems; they are each ecosystem themselves, containing myriad smaller organisms. In general, it is the degree of connectedness that differentiates individuals and communities (Flannery 2010, 55). For example, organs within an individual are tightly coupled, individuals within an ecosystem are more loosely coupled, and both levels of connection are essential (Rolston 1989, 249).

Scientists, including mathematician Alfred North Whitehead (Nash 1988, 59) and physicists Fritjof Capra (1996, 36) and Paul Davies (Davies and Gribbin 2007, 14), have pointed at the physics discovery that all matter is essentially energy to support the idea that everything is, in fact, connected and that we cannot completely distinguish between the identity of an individual and the identity of the whole.

All life is made of connections. Whether a human body, a termite mound, an ecosystem, or a planet, ecological systems cannot be understood by studying individual parts. The processes that make a living system only take place when the individual parts interact together. It is a feature of all emergent systems, that is, of all life, that the whole is always greater than the sum of its parts.

Earth System Science

In the 1960s the National Aeronautics and Space Administration (NASA) was looking for life on Mars. To help them design their instruments for detecting signs of life they hired a consultant named James Lovelock. Lovelock was an atmospheric chemist and the inventor of an electron capture device that could precisely measure the presence of DDT in the environment, the same device that allowed scientists a few years later to understand how chloroflurocarbons (CFCs) were eroding the ozone layer (Harding 2006, 52). Lovelock is best known, however, not for a machine but for developing the concept of the planet as a self-regulating system, which became the foundation of the field known as Earth system science.

From Idea to Hypothesis to Theory

In the early days of NASA's planetary exploration program at the Jet Propulsion Laboratory, Lovelock studied telescope data showing the composition of the atmospheres of Mars and Venus and noticed something interesting. Their atmospheres were chemically in equilibrium, with no chemical reactions going on at all (Barlow 1997, 162). The difference between the state of Earth's atmosphere and that of Mars was striking.

Lovelock knew that every organism has a metabolism. Each of us eats or otherwise takes in matter, processes it, and gives off wastes in some form. We can't all be doing the same thing; if every organism on Earth took in oxygen and breathed out carbon dioxide, after a while the air would be saturated with carbon dioxide and there would be no more oxygen available. Instead, some of us breathe in one kind of gas and others another kind, and as all of us are eating and breathing and excreting, our gaseous waste products spend a little time in the air until they are taken in by another being in the food web. Life alters our atmosphere and keeps it churning with chemical activity.

Lovelock reasoned that if there were living organisms on Mars they would need a fluid medium for acquiring raw materials and disposing of wastes, and the only medium available there was the atmosphere. So if there were life on Mars, life would change the composition of its atmosphere. Instead, information from telescopes showed that the thin atmosphere of Mars was almost entirely carbon dioxide, with no chemical reactions going on at all. Lovelock told NASA that their Viking mission would not find life on Mars (Harding 2006, 54).

Lovelock continued to study the atmosphere of Earth. He observed that, against all logic and rules of chemistry, the oxygen level in Earth's chemically unstable atmosphere has stayed within a close range that is just right for aerobic life for hundreds of millions of years. He also observed that despite the fact that the sun is burning 30 percent hotter than it did when life first appeared, the temperature at the surface of the Earth has remained constant and just right for life as well.

When scientists collect evidence that needs an explanation they formulate a hypothesis, a proposal to explain the known facts that can then be tested by experiment and either proven or disproven. Lovelock formulated a hypothesis that he first presented in a 1968 scientific paper that the planet was a self-regulating system and that life was responsible for regulating the temperature and composition of the atmosphere in order to keep conditions suitable for life. One day in 1969 Lovelock was discussing the concept with his neighbor William Golding, author of the novel *Lord of the Flies*, and Golding suggested that he call it the "Gaia hypothesis," after the Greek goddess of the earth (Lovelock 2006, 22).

When microbiologist Lynn Margulis heard about Lovelock's hypothesis she recognized its potential. Margulis was known for her work with bacteria and for proving that mergers among strains of ancient bacteria gave rise to the complex cells that make up life today. She and Lovelock began to collaborate, and in 1974 began publishing joint papers on the Gaia hypothesis proposing that the biosphere regulates the climate and chemistry of the atmosphere in its own interest. Lovelock and Margulis later realized that it was not life alone that regulated the atmosphere, but the whole system—life plus air, oceans, and rocks—that worked together as a tightly coupled, self-regulating, evolving system to keep conditions within the range that is right for life (Harding 2006, 65).

Lovelock needed a way to test this hypothesis experimentally and so he and oceanographer Andrew Watson developed a computer model of a planet they called Daisyworld. The virtual planet orbited a star similar to our sun that, like ours, got hotter as it aged. Growing on the planet was just one form of life: daisies. The daisies came in two varieties, black and white. When Daisyworld's sun was young the planet's surface was too cold for seeds to germinate. At some point when the sun had warmed enough for daisies to begin sprouting, black daisies had the advantage because they could absorb sunlight and warm the atmosphere. They survived and reproduced, and eventually the planet was covered with black daisies. But as the sun aged and got hotter the surface grew warmer and the white daisies, which reflected sunlight, began to compete for space. As the sun's output increased, the white daisies came to dominate the surface. In the face of a changing sun, the system of daisies kept the surface temperature within the range needed for plant growth (Kump et al. 2010, 26), and they did it without making decisions or planning ahead. Each individual daisy acted in its own self-interest, but collectively the white and black flowers acted in a way that kept the temperature acceptable for both of them. Self-regulation turns out to be a property that emerges in a world where each form of organism simply grows and reproduces whenever it gets the chance.

Mechanisms: How the System Regulates Climate

Planet Earth is composed of more than just daisies. Earth is a complex adaptive system made up of life coupled to its abiotic environment. How does the system self-regulate to keep conditions right for life? Earth system services operate on a global scale, with multiple interconnected characteristics of the planet controlled over short and long periods of time, including temperature and the chemical composition of the atmosphere (Folke 2013, 21).

Climate scientists have worked to understand something known as the "faint young sun paradox" (Kump et al. 2010, 18). Our sun is one of a class of stars that get hotter as they age. Ours is currently about halfway through its life and about 30 percent hotter than it was when life began. Yet despite changes in the composition of the atmosphere since that time, the average surface temperature on Earth has never varied by more than a few degrees. The planet has regulated its temperature primarily by adding greenhouse gases such as carbon dioxide and methane to its atmosphere when it was too cold and by removing them when it grew too hot. The planet also regulates its temperature by changing its **albedo**, the lightness or darkness of its surface, and by changing the proportion of its cloud cover through the action of chemicals emitted by trees and marine algae (Flannery 2006, 15).

Carbon dioxide is pulled from the atmosphere by the chemical weathering of rocks, transported to the sea by rivers, deposited on the floor of the oceans, and sequestered in sedimentary rock. Plants on land and bacteria in soil pump CO_2 out of the air. In the oceans, wave action mixes CO_2 from the air. Algae metabolize CO_2 and shell-forming plankton and coral reefs use it to build their structures. When these beings die they settle to the seafloor, part of a mechanism known as the biological pump (Wolfson 2008, 396).

Oxygen (O_2) is an explosive, reactive chemical that makes up about 21 percent of the atmosphere, a level just right for aerobic life. With even a small increase, the danger of fires would rise sharply (Lovelock 2000, 69). This volatile gas is so reactive that without life's processes to keep it constantly cycling it would vanish from the air altogether in a relatively short time. Photosynthesis is the principal source of oxygen in the atmosphere (Kump et al. 2010, 210). Almost all the oxygen cycles continuously through the atmosphere and biosphere, but a little extra accumulates. Meanwhile, a little extra oxygen is withdrawn from the atmosphere as it reacts with other chemicals in the weathering of rocks. Methane, produced by anaerobic bacteria in marshes, lakes, and seabeds, and complex feedback loops between carbon and phosphorus also help to regulate oxygen levels (Harding 2006, 127).

Clouds forming over the ocean keep the Earth cool by reflecting sunlight back into space. They form not only through physical evaporation, but because algae floating near continental shelves emit the sulfur gas dimethyl sulphide (DMS) as a waste product. DMS molecules form nuclei around which water droplets condense. When nutrients get depleted in an area of ocean, algae respond by blooming in vast numbers. Their DMS emissions cause dense clouds to form, algae get sucked up into them, and they can be carried for many miles before they are washed out into a new area that may be richer in nutrients (ibid., 136).

Systems

The realization that Earth is a self-regulating system has had benefits and disadvantages. On one hand, understanding how systems work with as much accuracy as possible is critical to making good decisions. On the other hand, a cursory knowledge of the Earth system can make people feel complacent, believing that "the planet" has everything under control and will work it out, which may be true over time scales of tens of millions of years (Flannery 2010, 276). Unfortunately, the system's correction may involve removing us and it is likely that before we went we would cause massive damage to Earth's biodiversity and climate that would take millions of years to repair.

The study of sustainability is the study of systems. Earth system science studies the interactions of systems within the atmosphere, hydrosphere, lithosphere, and biosphere (Kump et al. 2010, ix). Beginning early in the twenty-first century the field of sustainability science, too, focuses on interactions among systems, striving to understand the dynamics of ecological systems, social systems, and their interconnections as a framework for sustainability (Kates 2011).

Notes

1 Everything gets recycled. For example, the water cycle occurs over timescales of days to months; the carbon cycle and other geochemical cycles occur over timescales of years; the rock cycle occurs over timescales of millions of years; and star and galaxy cycles occur over timescales of millions or billions of years.

2 Barry Commoner paraphrased the first law: "There is no such thing as a free lunch" (Commoner 1971).

3 Commoner restated this concept as: "Everything must go somewhere" (ibid.).
4 We use the words "negative" and "positive" to indicate charges that are opposite, but there is otherwise nothing inherently negative or positive about these charges, and we could have called them by other names.
5 Some organic chemistry students remember these elements with the acronym CHNOPS.

Further Reading

Flannery, Tim. *Here on Earth: A Natural History of the Planet.* New York: Atlantic Monthly Press, 2010.

Harding, Stephan. *Animate Earth: Science, Intuition and Gaia.* White River Junction, VT: Chelsea Green Publishing, 2006.

Kump, Lee R., James F. Kasting, and Robert G. Crane. *The Earth System.* 3rd ed. Upper Saddle River, NJ: Prentice Hall, 2010.

Lovelock, James. *Gaia: A New Look at Life on Earth.* Oxford: Oxford University Press, 2000.

Margulis, Lynn and Dorion Sagan. *What Is Life?* Berkeley, CA: University of California Press, 2000.

Wilson, Edward O. *The Diversity of Life.* Boston, MA: Belknap Press of Harvard University Press, 2010.

Withgott, Jay and Matthew Laposata. *Environment: The Science behind the Stories*, 5th ed. San Francisco, CA: Pearson Benjamin Cummings, 2013.

Chapter Review

1   State the two energy laws in your own words. These laws are usually called the first and second laws of thermodynamics.
2   What does entropy measure?
3   Why is carbon such an important element on our planet?
4   Name some processes that remove carbon from the atmosphere.
5   Name some processes that return carbon to the atmosphere.
6   What role does the moving of continental and oceanic plates play in the carbon cycle?
7   List the layers of the atmosphere beginning at sea level, and describe them briefly.
8   What are the three most abundant gases in the atmosphere?
9   How has life altered the chemistry of Earth's atmosphere?
10   What is life? What characteristics distinguish life from inanimate matter?
11   What organisms first produced oxygen?
12   What kind of organism first used photosynthesis?
13   Why was photosynthesis such a fundamental development in the history of life on Earth?
14   In what ways are bacteria important to life on Earth?
15   List the five kingdoms of organisms.
16   What is the difference between prokaryotes and eukaryotes?
17   What is the difference between a food chain and a food web? How are they similar?
18   How do periodic fires and floods affect ecosystems?
19   What are some characteristics of pioneer species that first recolonize disturbed areas?
20   What is resilience?
21   What is albedo?
22   What effect does albedo have on temperature?
23   What is Daisyworld?
24   What maintains the oxygen in the atmosphere at its current level?
25   Has the sun's temperature changed over its lifetime? If so, in what way has it changed?
26   Describe the relationship between clouds and algae in the oceans.

Critical Thinking and Discussion

1 Compare and contrast the history of bacteria and the history of the human species.
2 Give two examples of symbiotic types of relationships.
3 Predators are generally less numerous than their prey. How does this relate to the second law of thermodynamics?
4 Matter cycles around the biosphere while energy flows through. What is the primary source of this energy?
5 What are some factors that might cause microclimates to develop within a larger ecosystem?
6 How can nonscientists decide whether or not to trust the claims made by modern science?
7 Why is peer review important for scientific research?
8 Do you think that "Gaia theory" or "Earth system theory" is a better name for communicating with nonscientific members of the public? Why? What are the advantages of each approach?
9 What is feedback? Give an example of negative feedback and an example of positive feedback.
10 A magazine runs an article claiming that patterns in Martian rock prove that there is life on Mars. What would you say?
11 List as many mechanisms as you can that the Earth system uses to regulate its temperature.
12 A colleague has recently taken a course in Earth System science and tells you we should not be concerned about human-caused damage to natural systems because natural processes always restore the balance of nature. What would you say?

4 The Human Sphere

Sustainability is built on three interdependent pillars: environment, economics, and equity, guided by good governance. The multidimensional issues of poverty, health, overpopulation, resource depletion, food and water scarcity, political instability, and the destruction of the biosphere are all connected.

During discussions of the challenges that are facing Earth systems someone often asks, "Isn't human population growth really the only problem?" It is true that challenges including damaged ecosystems, resource depletion, pollution, and water shortages have increased exponentially, driven by human population numbers. However, the primary driver of the sustainability crisis now gripping the planet is economic growth (Heinberg 2011, 7).

Human Impact

Carrying capacity is a scientific term that defines the number of individuals an environment can support without degrading a population's ecosystem. For humans, some environments have a larger carrying capacity than others depending on the patterns of consumption of the human culture that lives there. Ultimately, the planet as a whole is our support system and it has a carrying capacity. The planetary system is currently operating at 140 percent of its capacity (Gilding 2011, 50). If all humans on the planet lived with the same standard of living enjoyed by people in the United States and Canada, we would need 4.5 more planet Earths even if the population did not grow at all. Given that the quantities of resources are more or less fixed, the fewer people there are the more resources are available to divide equitably; as population rises, the same resources must be divided among more people and so the per capita quantity that can be consumed sustainably shrinks (Engelman 2013, 9).

Environmental scientists summarize the drivers of environmental degradation with a formula called "IPAT," first developed by biologist Paul Ehrlich and physicist John Holdren and written $I = P \times A \times T$ (Ehrlich 1971). This is a shorthand way of saying that environmental *Impact* is a product of the size of human *Populations*, their *Affluence* or consumption per capita, and the *Technology* that determines the environmental impact of each dollar spent. Developing countries have the most room for improvement in reducing *Population* growth. Industrial countries have the most room for improvement in reducing their *Affluent* consumption patterns. Making *Technology* choices to minimize environmental impact is a focus of work in renewable energy, building and site design, product design, and industrial ecology. As growing numbers of people around the world strive for higher living standards, it is consumption per capita, the *Affluence* in the IPAT formula, that poses the gravest threat (OECD 2012, 20).

Stages in Human Population

The fossil record tells us that our species, *Homo sapiens*, first appeared on the planet around 150,000 years ago (Wessels 2006, 50). Like earlier hominid species several million years before us, through all but the last 10,000 years modern *Homo sapiens* survived by gathering plant materials and hunting animals, living what is called a hunter-gatherer way of life. Life expectancy was short, infant deaths were common and population numbers were small, limited by the amount of available food. During most of the last several million years Earth has been in the midst of an ice age, marked by abruptly fluctuating temperatures (Henson 2011, 194; IPCC 2007a, 449). Every 100,000 years, approximately, conditions warmed dramatically and an interglacial climate settled in (Stanley 2004, 488). The most recent ice age ended around 12,000 years ago and a warm and stable interglacial period known as the Holocene epoch began. Rainfall over continents increased. Growing seasons got longer.

These benign and unusually stable conditions set the stage for a new form of human culture: agriculture, as people learned to grow crops and raise domestic animals (Wijkman and Rockström 2012, 38). Humans no longer had to spend all their time looking for food to stay alive. They settled down in permanent villages. Agriculture meant that people could store extra food during good years that could help get them through lean years. Settlements and storage of food led to more complex societies, with specialization of labor, social hierarchies, and trade with other groups (Ponting 2007, 37). People began living longer, birth rates rose, and death rates fell. The world's population grew steadily. At the beginning of the agricultural revolution around 10,000 years ago the human population was probably 4 million people. By 5,000 years later it had grown to 5 million. From then on the world's population nearly doubled every 1,000 years until it reached 50 million by 1000 BCE, then 100 million by 500 BCE, and 200 million (ibid.) by 200 CE.[1]

Another revolution and accompanying population surge, the Industrial Revolution, was launched in the mid-1700s with the harnessing of fossil fuels beginning with coal (Sachs 2015, 74). Petroleum products that could power farm equipment boosted agricultural productivity. By 1804 the world's population had reached the 1 billion mark. A few decades later Louis Pasteur and others demonstrated that bacteria spread disease. Sanitation improved, vaccines were developed, and antibiotics were subsequently developed. Infant mortality dropped. By 1930 the population had doubled again, reaching 2 billion (Wessels 2006, 50).

Population Growth

Human population is growing approximately exponentially (Figure 4.1). Unlike arithmetic or linear growth that occurs when a quantity increases by adding the same number repeatedly, exponential growth means that the quantity increases by a fixed percentage over a given time. It works like compound interest in a savings account: the percentage may stay the same, but every year the amount added is that same percentage of a larger number. The more time that goes by the larger the amount that gets added, and before long the original amount will have doubled. Even if the rate remains steady, the size of a population will increase by larger numbers with each generation.

The "rule of 70" is a handy, if rough, formula for calculating how many years it will take for an original amount to double. 70 divided by the annual growth rate equals approximately the number of years to double. For example, if a quantity such as a savings account or a population is growing at 2 percent, it will double in 70/2, or 35 years. If it is growing at 7 percent, it will double in 70/7, or 10 years. The rate of global human population growth peaked at

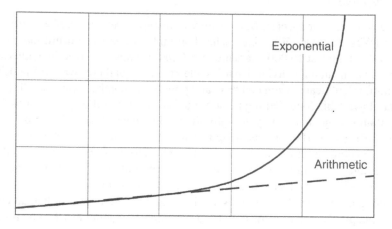

Figure 4.1 Arithmetic versus exponential growth

2.1 percent in the 1960s. At that rate, using the rule of 70 the population would double about every 33 years (Withgott and Brennan 2009, 118). The world's population growth rate has fallen and today is slightly over 1 percent (US Census Bureau 2015). At that rate the population will still double, but it will take longer—about 70 years—to do so.

The growth rate has not remained constant, however; it has changed over time. In 1650, the numbers in Europe were recovering from the Black Plague, the world's population was around half a billion people, and it was growing at a rate of 0.3 percent per year, with a doubling time of almost 240 years. It took all of human history until just after 1800 for the global population to reach the first 1 billion mark (Speth 2008, 13). By 1900, with changes in technology and healthcare, the population had reached 1.6 billion and the growth rate was around 0.8 percent per year, with a doubling time below 100 years. The population, which had first reached 1 billion in 1804, had doubled to 2 billion by 1927. Sometime around 1965 the world's population numbered 3.3 billion and the growth rate reached a peak of 2.1 percent per year with a doubling time of only 36 years. Growth rates began to fall as birth rates fell but the numbers kept rising, and by 2000 the population was just over 6 billion, with a growth rate of 1.2 percent per year and a doubling time of 60 years. The rate had dropped, but because of exponential growth more people, 75 million, were added to the planet in 2000 than the 68 million that had been added in 1965 (Meadows et al. 2004, 29).

Over the past century the planet's population quadrupled from 1.5 billion to 6 billion, with a billion people added to the planet every 33 years on average. It took all of human history through about 1927 to put 2 billion humans on the planet. It took 47 years to add another 2 billion, and 25 years to add the next 2 billion (Worldwatch Institute 2010, 14). By 1999, the world's population had reached 6 billion, and in 2011 it reached 7 billion (Figure 4.2).

The study of the growth, decline, and changes in populations is called population ecology. When the statistical principles of population ecology are applied to human populations, the result is a field of social science known as **demography** (Withgott and Brennan 2009, 121).

The formula for measuring the growth or decline of a population begins with an existing population size. If the birth and immigration rate is higher than the death rate, the population will grow. If the death and emigration rate is higher than the birth rate, the population will decline.

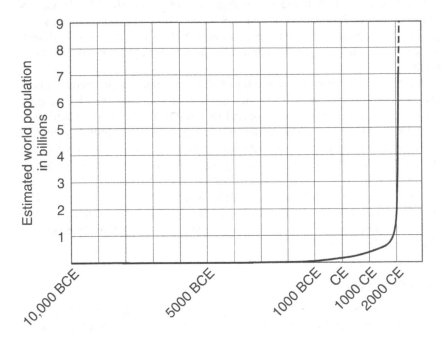

Figure 4.2 World population since 10,000 BCE

In addition to measuring the **birth rate**, which is the total number of people born in a given year, demographers also measure the **total fertility rate** (TFR). The fertility rate is the number of children born per woman during her lifetime. The **replacement fertility rate** is the number of births per woman that will keep the population size constant at zero population growth. For humans, the replacement fertility rate is 2.1 (ibid.), slightly above 2.0 to compensate for infant and child mortality. If the fertility rate drops below 2.1, human population will start to decline. If the fertility rate is above 2.1 even slightly, the population will experience exponential growth. It will double more slowly the lower the fertility rate, but it will double nonetheless.

The worldwide fertility rate in 1960 when the human population growth rate reached its peak was an average of 4.3 children per woman. By 2000, the fertility rate had dropped to 2.6 worldwide and 2.1 in the US (Wilson 2002b, 29). In all of the industrialized nations of the developed world, fertility rates are now at or below the replacement level. The population continues to grow, with almost all of the increase taking place in developing nations.

Future Population Trends

Demographers expect four trends in the world's human population over the next 50 years: the population will be older than it was in the previous century and bigger than it is now; it will continue to grow, but at a slower rate; migrations will continue; and populations will be increasingly urban.

The international organization that monitors and evaluates population trends is the United Nations Population Division. Every two years the organization issues a revised population projection called *World Population Prospects*. Using demographic data from each country and statistical methods, the 2015 UN report predicted that the world's population will reach approximately 9.7 billion around 2050 and 11.2 billion in 2100 (Wilmoth 2015, 3); the US Census Bureau projection for 2050 is 9.4 billion (US Census Bureau 2015). Previous UN analyses had projected that population would peak around 2050 and then decline; although growth rates continue to decline, population stabilization in this century is now thought to be unlikely (Wilmoth 2015, 18).

Virtually all the population growth in the future will be in urban areas. Between now and 2050 the world's rural population will remain approximately constant at 3 billion people while the world's urban population is expected to roughly double from 3 billion to 6 billion people (OECD 2012, 20). Economic, social, and environmental conditions will be affected. If cities double in size by spreading out over agricultural land, the impact on food production will be significant. If cities limit their physical size but grow in density, drastic changes to infrastructure for power, water, transportation, and housing will be required. This presents an opportunity for positive change: if half the urban infrastructure that will be needed by 2050 must be built in the next decades then we have the opportunity to design and construct places that are healthy, safe, delightful, regenerative, and that provide economic opportunities for everyone.

Stabilizing Human Population

One of the recurring themes in sustainability work is that several elements of the transition to a sustainable world are inextricably connected. They include reducing population growth, social inclusion, and a new economic model.

The Demographic Transition

Countries in the industrial world have passed through a period of population growth demographers call the **demographic transition** that occurs as countries move from one stage of development to the next. Preindustrial societies are characterized by both high birth rates and high death rates. As a society moves toward industrialization, death rates fall as food production and medical care improve while birth rates temporarily remain high. As education, social and economic conditions improve, birth rates fall and population growth stabilizes. The demographic transition is the shift from high birth rates and death rates to low birth rates and death rates. Japan, China, most of Europe, and the US appear to have passed through their demographic transitions. Their populations will continue to grow for several more years because large numbers of young people are still moving into their reproductive years. Once these population bulges pass out of the reproductive years these countries' populations will stabilize.

Demographers worry about demographic transitions in developing countries. Death rates in some of these regions dropped sharply with the introduction of modern medicine. However, decades later their societies remain trapped in conditions of poverty that keep birth rates high; they are in a poverty/population trap. Social and economic progress holds the key to escaping from the demographic trap (Meadows et al. 2004, 28).

Countries that successfully pass through the demographic transition benefit from what economists call "the demographic bonus" (Brown 2009, 185). As their birth rates fall the proportion of both dependent children and older people relative to the number of working adults decreases. Society can spend less of its resources caring for and educating its children and providing medical care for its older citizens. Instead, these resources can be invested in economic activity, with the result that productivity surges. This demographic window remains open for several decades, but it is only open once. Countries that have recognized this opportunity have been able to take advantage of the window (Wright and Boorse 2011, 224). For example, during its transition Brazil has put policies in place to help reduce poverty and promote more equitable social and economic development.

Social Progress and Population

Poverty and lack of education lead to high birth rates. In turn, high birth rates lead to perpetual poverty and lack of opportunity. People living in poverty in developing countries have no social power and no way to get ahead except to hope that their children can help with family labor or help bring in income. For women in particular, childbearing is one of the few forms of investment available to them. Living off the land is labor-intensive, and having more children means more hands cultivating or gathering wood and water. At the same time, in poor countries childbearing often prevents women from being able to bring in income. And without education or adequate healthcare, family planning is out of reach, even for women who want to limit the number of children.

Three dimensions of social progress are essential to stabilizing population: education, employment, and reproductive health (Cohen 2005, 53). The empowerment of young women, many of whom still lack both the knowledge and the freedom to choose how many children to have, is especially important in breaking the cycle of poverty and population growth. Young women in developing countries who are educated are able to enter the labor market and experience an improved standard of living. They have social status that is no longer tied only to how many children they bear. Educated young women postpone marriage, so that births in a population are spaced more years apart. With education and with careers outside the home, women choose to have fewer children and have access to family planning techniques that make fewer children possible. The most important predictors of falling birth rate are education and employment, particularly for women. In a clear and direct way, social equity for women results in fewer children.

As a country's birth rate begins to decline, more resources can be devoted to providing clean water, medical care including reproductive health, and support for the elderly. Improved medical care results in lowered disease rates and means that more children survive to adulthood. When parents have the expectation that their children will survive they choose to have fewer children. When they have access to family planning and can afford family planning services, they have the ability to choose their own family size. When some form of social security exists, parents no longer need so many children to support them when they are old and unable to work.

Family planning services fall under the rubric of reproductive health. Reproductive health is a term used by United Nations agencies to include maternal health, child health, and family planning; it also covers prevention of sexually transmitted diseases such as HIV/AIDS and prevention of gender-based violence including rape, abuse, and genital mutilation. Many women in developing countries do not have access to contraceptives, either because they are costly or because they are simply not available. The UN estimates that over 200 million women lack access to contraception (Brown 2009, 184). According to the Population Reference Bureau, access to contraception is the single factor that most determines birth rate. Family planning, supported by government funding, international aid, and private donations, is the most direct way to lower population growth rates.

Policy: National and International Efforts

Education, career opportunities, lower childhood mortality, access to family planning, and security in old age are all outcomes of national laws and policies. National governments play a central role stabilizing population. Countries or regions with public policies that have made these outcomes a priority, such as Thailand, Iran, and Brazil, have successfully moved through the demographic transition (Wright and Boorse 2011, 228). The countries that have put effective family planning programs in place have experienced the most rapid decline in birth rate. Approaches include providing family-planning information, providing contraception, imposing taxes or other penalties, and offering rewards.

Singapore, for example, limits the amount of tax allowances for children, puts restrictions on maternity benefits, gives school admissions preference to children from smaller families, and allocates the same size government-funded housing regardless of family size, so that smaller families live more comfortably (Keller and Botkin 2008, 31). Thailand offers government-sponsored family planning education and access to contraceptives.

China had perhaps the world's most talked-about population policy. In the late 1970s its policymakers recognized that because of population momentum already built into its demographics, even a birth rate of 2.0 would soon overshoot the available resources. The Chinese government established a range of rewards and penalties aimed at achieving a goal of one child per family. Families with only one child receive extra food rations, housing preferences, and hiring preferences, plus extra medical care if the family's only child is a girl. Families with a second child paid higher prices for food, paid taxes for the second child, and were required to return bonuses received from the first child. China's total fertility rate dropped from 5.5 in 1970 to 1.5 in 2010 (Wright and Boorse 2011, 240). However, the policy was unpopular and sometimes led to brutal results including infanticide and forced late-term abortions, and it left the Chinese population with a disproportionate number of old people and males (Fong 2016, 1). The policy was ended in 2015.

In 1994 the United Nations hosted a conference in Cairo, Egypt, known as the International Conference on Population and Development (ICPD). Participants turned away from older approaches of using strict laws to set birth-rate limits and punish violations in favor of a more holistic approach. In the Program of Action signed by 179 nations, the Cairo conference linked poverty, education, and population growth and urged all governments to provide access to reproductive healthcare, provide better education, promote gender equality, and address the causes of poverty. Member nations have reaffirmed the terms of the Cairo agreement every five years since 1994 (Withgott and Brennan 2009, 128).

Economics

We live on a rapidly changing planet that is fundamentally different than it was when any of us were children. In the last 50 years population has more than doubled, global consumption of water has more than tripled, and the use of fossil fuels has quadrupled (Foley 2010, 54). Synthetic pesticides and heavy metals are found in the tissues of every animal on earth. The end of cheap fossil fuels is looming. The planet's sixth mass extinction is underway, with 50 percent of species alive today predicted to be gone by the year 2100 (Wilson 2002b, 102). Ninety percent of large fish have disappeared from many ocean fisheries, victims of overfishing. Where rivers empty into oceans, runoff laden with synthetic fertilizers has pulled oxygen out of coastal waters and left dead zones devoid of animal life. Coral reefs are dying and mollusk populations shrinking as carbon dioxide concentrations make ocean waters increasingly acidic. Mountain glaciers are melting, deserts are growing, sea level is rising, and waves of climate refugees are likely in the near future.

The driver of all this change is economic. In particular, the driver is the economic growth model that has been at the core of human commercial activity since World War II. Ecological economists and other researchers say that continuation of the growth model is not just a bad idea, it is a physical impossibility (Daly and Farley 2003, 63). The current economic system releases wastes into the environment faster than natural systems can process them and consumes renewable resources faster than they can be replenished. It consumes nonrenewable resources; once those are gone they cannot be replenished.

Economics: A Brief History

Around 10,000 years ago human societies made the transition from the hunter-gatherer mode of earning a living to the agricultural mode. This transition marked a change in human economies. With the advent of agriculture the idea of ownership appeared—ownership of surplus food and ownership of the land on which to grow it—along with the specialization of labor, forms of government including class division, and some form of money as a medium of exchange (ibid., 9).

The Industrial Revolution began to dawn in 1712 when British inventor Thomas Newcomen developed a steam engine that could burn coal to generate steam pressure. The new invention could replace a team of 500 horses to drain water from coal mines, making it easier and cheaper to extract the coal (McKibben 2007, 5). With coal, and the subsequent discovery of oil and then natural gas, humans had access to vast amounts of underground, concentrated energy. Advances in medicine and hygiene allowed populations to grow dramatically and advances in technology led to an explosive increase in the production of consumer goods of all kinds, available for the first time not just to the wealthy but to the middle class as well.

The idea of economic growth was born. In 1776 Adam Smith wrote *An Inquiry into the Nature and Causes of the Wealth of Nations*, usually called simply *The Wealth of Nations*, which asked the question: why had some nations become so much wealthier than others? Smith wrote that "it is not the actual greatness of national wealth, but its continued increase" that causes incomes to rise (Smith [1776] 1976, 78). Smith put forward the idea that individuals acting purely out of self-interest are benevolently guided by the invisible hand of markets. One of his best-known contributions is the division of labor, the idea that dividing work into pieces with each performed repetitively by a separate worker will increase productivity. Many of Smith's ideas were developed and expanded by others and became the basis of the discipline we now call economics.

Through the nineteenth century the subject of economic growth was the focus of classical economists such as Thomas Malthus and Karl Marx, who wrestled with the question of whether growth could continue indefinitely, or whether there were limits. Malthus in particular concluded that populations would increase until they bumped up against the carrying capacity of their resources, at which point they would collapse, a theme repeated 170 years later by biologist Paul Ehrlich in *The Population Bomb*.

However, it has only been since the Great Depression of the 1930s that policymakers and economists have become fixated on the concept of economic growth (Daly and Farley 2003, 13). Through the end of the Depression, economists believed that the economy had essentially matured. With the launching of World War II, however, industry mobilized for war with surprising speed, demonstrating that an economy could still grow and could grow quickly. By the end of the war industrial production was vigorous and scientists and engineers were launching one discovery or invention after another. People enthusiastically adopted synthetic pesticides, plastic, television sets, refrigerators, and air conditioning. Supported by the inexpensive, concentrated energy in fossil fuels, the production of consumer goods expanded at an astonishing rate. With automobiles, inexpensive fuel, and air conditioning, suburban development was now possible in whole new regions, and people embraced the trappings of this new lifestyle with optimism. Economists scrambled to adapt economic theory to fit the new reality.

Hints of a different view of reality began appearing in the 1970s. Oil shortages followed by rising gasoline prices led to a widespread concern about the potential scarcity of non-renewable resources. Recent best-selling books such as Rachel Carson's *Silent Spring* and Paul Ehrlich's *Population Bomb* had planted doubts. These, together with televised images such as Los Angeles blanketed by dense smog and the Cuyahoga River in Ohio so polluted it caught fire led some people to begin questioning whether limitless growth was an altogether positive phenomenon. A group of industrialists who called themselves The Club of Rome commissioned a study by a team of systems analysts at MIT to examine facets of growth. Their scientifically rigorous work was published in 1972 in an influential and widely read book, *The Limits to Growth*. The authors concluded that if current trends continued, the planet would reach its limits to growth within 100 years. In 1973 British economist E. F. Schumacher wrote *Small Is Beautiful*, which caught people's imaginations. The same year a World Bank economist, Herman Daly, examined the idea of limits to economic growth in his book, *Toward a Steady State Economy*. Daly soon went on to become a central figure in the new field known as ecological economics.

By 1980 the political climate had shifted. Politicians talked about the benefits of unregulated growth. The concept of globalization of trade took hold, with a vision of an ever-expanding global economy (McKibben 2007, 9).

Some Drivers of the Growth Model

The economic engine of modern society is driven primarily by the combustion of fossil fuels. At an earlier time, fossil fuels were abundant and easy to extract. For 150 years this cheap, accessible energy source drove economic expansion at an average rate of about 3 percent per year (Heinberg 2011, 10), a rate that came to be accepted as the natural state of things.

No other energy source contains as much energy concentrated into such a small volume for such a relatively low cost. Almost all of our buildings and the activities within them depend on electricity, most of it generated by the burning of coal. We produce massive quantities of food using petroleum-derived fertilizer and petroleum-powered machinery, then use more petroleum to ship almost all of it to somewhere else. The majority of people now live in cities and suburbs, much of them in the developed world organized around automobiles and roads laid out when oil was cheap and plentiful. Our settlement patterns maximize the volume of goods that must be transported in and the volumes of wastes that must be transported out. Almost all of the goods we consume are shipped by boat, airplane, or railroad from somewhere and distributed by trucks, millions of them, powered by diesel fuel. We live in a high-energy civilization driven by a finite, one-time supply of fossil fuels.

Meanwhile, humans' innate tendency to acquire things has assumed a central position in contemporary culture. Acquisitiveness had survival value at an earlier stage in human evolution. It would have helped to drive the search for food and according to some anthropological research it also likely improved individuals' ability to find mates and to reproduce. Even 200 years ago survival was not a sure thing, and the drive to meet basic needs for food, clothing, and shelter meshed rationally with new economic tools provided by the emerging Industrial Revolution. In modern society, however, acquisitiveness is an evolutionary adaptation out of control. While there exist physical controls to counterbalance this drive such as limits on the carrying capacity of the Earth, they are still invisible to most people. And much of what is consumed consists of once-through, disposable, or short-lived products, increasing the rate of production and the flows of materials and wastes.

Globalization, also known as economic openness, is a controversial driver of economic growth. Up to a certain level, it has a positive effect on well-being and economic health. Beyond a certain threshold, globalization can contribute to social inequity and environmental damage.

Three international entities organize and structure global economic activity. The World Bank, established by treaty in 1944, provides loans to developing countries with the stated goal of reducing poverty. A related institution, the International Monetary Fund (IMF), monitors currency exchange rates, oversees loans, and restructures debts between nations. Almost all the United Nations member countries participate in the IMF. The World Trade Organization (WTO) was set up in 1995 as a replacement for the 1948 General Agreement on Tariffs and Trade (GATT). The WTO is a trade organization intended to eliminate barriers and improve the free flow of goods and capital between countries. Critics charge that the WTO is influenced by the largest transnational corporations whose representatives fill some of the seats in national delegations. Critics note that in their roles in the WTO these corporations promote policies of trade, finance, and intellectual property based on their own financial interests, while weakening the autonomy of national and local economies (Korten 2001, 173–80) and allowing regions to exceed their local carrying capacities (Rees 2014, 196).

Neoclassical and Ecological Economics

Economics is the study of how to allocate limited resources among alternative or competing interests (Daly and Farley 2003, 3). The words "ecology" and "economy" both come from the same Greek word *oikos*, meaning "house." Ecology is literally the study of the household, and economy the management of the household. Modern economists typically fall within one of three schools of thought: neoclassical economics, environmental economics, or ecological economics.

The majority of economists today are neoclassical economists. Classical economics, following Adam Smith, looked at the economy as a whole. This large-scale view is known as macroeconomics. Around the end of the nineteenth century economists began to shift their focus to individual markets within an economy, a view known as microeconomics. The new approach to classical economics, or neoclassical economics, has been the standard approach since the end of World War II. In this approach, it is assumed that markets have an inherent, efficient logic subject to supply and demand and that markets always choose the optimal alternative. Conventional neoclassical economics holds that economic growth can continue forever (Daly 2005, 102). If an economy runs short of a resource—fossil fuel or clean air, for example—neoclassical economics says that shortage will provide incentives to the market to innovate and that as a result technology will be developed that can address any environmental challenges.

Environmental economics, a subset of neoclassical economics that developed within the last 100 years, takes a step further to consider environmental values. This branch of economics recognizes that human welfare depends upon ecosystem services, the biological functions that support life, including purification of air and water, mitigation of floods and droughts, provision of materials and food, decomposition and processing of wastes, seed dispersal, pollination, and climate stabilization. The term "ecosystem services" was first used by Paul and Anne Ehrlich (1981); in 1997 ecological economists including Robert Costanza and Gretchen Daily published detailed assessments of the monetary value of these services (Costanza et al. 1997; Daily 1997). The Economics of Ecosystems and Biodiversity, known by its acronym TEEB, is an international initiative organized by the European Commission and hosted by UNEP to analyze and report the economic value of ecosystem services (TEEB 2010).

Environmental economics assigns values to ecosystem services and pollution so that they can be incorporated into markets (Daly and Farley 2003, 5). Environmental economics shares many assumptions in common with conventional economics: it assumes that people behave rationally and will do the best that they can; it assumes that people will always prefer more to less; and it is anthropocentric, seeking positive outcomes primarily for humans.

Ecological economics is a branch of economics that developed within recent decades through the work of economists including E. F. Schumacher and Herman Daly and systems ecologist Robert Costanza. Conventional neoclassical economics sees nature as a supply depot and waste disposal service nested within the macroeconomy; Herman Daly referred to it as "empty world" economics because it developed during a time when humans were less numerous and it appeared that more forest, more prairie, and more ocean would always be available. In contrast, ecological economics sees the macroeconomy as a subsystem nested within the biosphere upon which it depends (ibid., 15). The field recognizes that on a planet now filled with billions of humans, economics and ecosystems are interconnected in important ways, and that it would be unrealistic to focus on either one to the exclusion of the other. Ecological economics can be thought of as "full world" economics.

Bringing together multiple disciplines can sometimes yield insights that were not previously known to either discipline by itself. Ecological economics is an example. Ecological economics joins together the fields of ecology and economics, applying natural laws, in particular the laws of thermodynamics, to the study of economics. A key idea is the recognition that growth cannot in fact go on forever, that nature has fundamental thresholds, and that there is no assurance that technological innovation can overcome problems caused by overshooting these limits. Instead of perpetual growth, ecological economics works toward optimization: a steady-state economy in dynamic equilibrium at an optimal scale. In this approach to economics without perpetual growth, equitable distribution will become important (ibid., 12).

Basic Concepts in Economics

The most commonly used definition of sustainability is actually a definition of sustainable development: "development that meets the needs of the present without compromising the ability of future generations to meet their own needs" (WCED 1987, 8). To an ecological economist, **growth** is different from **development**. Growth is quantitative; it means an increase in size or an increase in production. Development is qualitative; it means an improvement in the quality of goods and services, with or without growth. **Sustainable development** involves an increase in quality without a quantitative growth in consumption or production. Sustainable growth is physically impossible because the biosphere is finite. For example, on one hand, the production of petroleum cannot grow forever because only a finite quantity exists; once it is used up, it is not replenished. On the other hand sustainable development, a qualitative change in which well-being does not decline and may improve, is possible.

Well-being includes both human quality of life and the health of all other parts of the biosphere. Sustainable development would keep natural capital intact, living off nature's income rather than consuming its capital.

Capital is the supply of resources; it is wealth used for the production of more wealth. Human-produced or manmade capital includes things such as machinery, fishing boats, or money. Natural capital includes ecosystem services and physical natural resources. Neoclassical economists generally believe that manmade capital can be substituted for natural capital as long as the total amount remains unchanged (Costanza and Kubiszewski 2014, 180). The idea is that scarcity of natural resources will raise market prices, reducing their demand, and that technological innovation will then find substitutes (Sustainable Scale Project 2003b), an example of the notion that technology can solve any problem. This concept was introduced in the 1970s, and by the 1990s had become known as **weak sustainability**. Weak sustainability is an approach to economics which says that human-made capital can be substituted for natural capital (Daly 2005, 103).

Ecological economists believe that human and natural capital are not interchangeable and that natural capital is the limiting factor, an approach known as **strong sustainability**. The climate system and biodiversity are examples of critical natural stocks that cannot be replaced by human-made capital (IPCC 2014c, 11). Herman Daly offers an example from marine fisheries: the number of fish in the oceans constitutes natural capital. Originally the total wealth, measured in quantity of catches, was limited by the number of fishing boats. When the number of fish declines, however, substituting more manmade capital in the form of more fishing boats and more nets will not restore the quantity of catches or maintain the original quantity of total wealth (Daly 2005, 103). Strong sustainability has implications not only for economics but also for environmental ethics, the rights of nature, and **intergenerational equity** or the rights of future generations. Economist David Pearce, author of the 1989 best seller *Blueprint for a Green Economy*, illustrated the anthropocentric and ecocentric attributes of weak and strong sustainability along a 'sustainability spectrum' (Pearce 1993, 18–19).

A country's annual market value of all the physical objects purchased plus all the services purchased plus the net amount exported is quantified with a measure known as **gross domestic product** (GDP). GDP was developed during World War II as a way to measure wartime production capacity and is now the most commonly used indicator of economic progress. All financial transactions are counted as part of the GDP whether they benefit or degrade our well-being.

Costs of what are known as defensive expenditures, such as the costs of cleaning up pollution, contribute to GDP. Alaska's GDP went up as a result of the 1989 Exxon Valdez oil spill. McDonough and Braungart (2002, 37) note that based on their contributions to GDP, car accidents, hospital visits, and toxic spills are all signs of prosperity, and McKibben (2007, 28) notes that, using GDP as a measure, "the most economically productive citizen is a cancer patient who totals his car on his way to meet his divorce lawyer."

GDP is a measure of economic activity. It does not measure well-being and does not differentiate between activities that pollute or damage and activities that regenerate our planetary life support systems. Ecological economists have proposed various alternative metrics. One system is the Index of Sustainable Economic Welfare (ISEW); another is the Genuine Progress Indicator (GPI). These systems measure economic and social welfare, and they include the costs of environmental damage, pollution, crime, international debt, and income disparity, and the benefits of volunteer work and uncounted household services such as childcare. Analysis shows that although global GDP has continued to climb, real progress as measured by the ISEW and the GPI has actually declined since 1978 (Kubiszewski et al. 2013, 57).

Flaws in the Growth Model

The market is a remarkable institution that functions surprisingly well. It balances supply and demand and efficiently allocates resources in a highly complex modern world. It is not perfect, however. In its current unsustainable form, the market requires continuous economic growth. Ecological economists point to several problems with the economic growth model.

The growth model results in inequities. Growth generally occurs in already affluent countries, and its mechanisms result in a small number of people accumulating most of the wealth while the incomes of those at the bottom decline (Meadows 2004, 42).

Continued growth is not making us happier. According to research, well-being increases with income only up to a point and beyond that point stops increasing (Easterlin 1974, 89; Daly 2005, 105). In addition, research indicates that the connection between income and feelings of happiness is relative. If everyone's income rose equally, no one's relative income would rise and so relative happiness would remain constant. The good news this implies is that if a society gives up the economic growth model and reaches a sustainable economic balance, its citizens may not have to sacrifice greatly in terms of happiness. Two systems sometimes used as measures of social well-being and happiness are Gross Domestic Happiness (GDH) and the Happy Planet Index (HPI) (Caradonna 2014, 212).

The growth model does not account for real costs (Brown 2009, 16). It does not recognize that natural systems have limits, as indicated by its failure to count the costs of depleting or damaging natural systems. For example, the future costs of climate change are not part of the price of petroleum. The real cost of burning gasoline is high, but its price in the marketplace tells us it is cheap. Economists express this by saying that externalities are not valued. An **externality** is a cost that is external to the entity creating the damage. Long-term growth is impossible if there are no natural resources to underpin that growth. As Daly notes, under the economic growth model "we count consumption of natural capital . . . as if it were income rather than capital drawdown—a colossal accounting error" (Randers 2012, 75).

The growth model does not set a value on ecosystem services. When a timber company estimates the value of the trees in a forest, it counts the number of board feet of timber but not the habitat value or the flood control services that will be lost if the forest is clear-cut. In 1998 massive flooding of the Yangtze River in China left 3,700 people dead, 15 million people homeless, and $26 billion in economic loss. The Chinese government did an analysis and determined that the flood control services provided by forests were worth three times as much as the timber would be worth if the trees were cut. The government banned tree-cutting in the Yangtze River basin as a result of their analysis (Brown 2009, 16). However, not all environmental assets can be assigned monetary values. A dollar cost is not relevant for species that go extinct, for example.

Not only do markets fail to include the costs of externalities, but prices are artificially kept even lower through subsidies. Some subsidies are helpful in correcting inequities among disadvantaged people. Others are what are known as perverse subsidies, those that are harmful to both the economy and the environment, including subsidies for mining, over-logging, over-fishing, driving, and industrial farming.

The most fundamental flaw in the economic growth model is that it does not correspond to natural laws that govern the physical world. Ecological economists point to the laws of thermodynamics in particular. Earth, like a planetary island, is a closed system for matter.

The atoms that make up matter can recombine, but matter cannot be created or destroyed. Everything must go somewhere. Solar energy flows into the system, is transformed, and flows out. Energy flows through the system, while matter cycles within the system. As matter flows through an economic system—extracting fossil fuels from the lithosphere and burning them, for example—the matter is taken from one location, the source, and moved to another, the sink. In the process matter always increases in entropy or disorder. Matter always changes quality, moving from a low-entropy or more-ordered state to a high-entropy or less-ordered state. No matter how efficient the process, some resources are depleted from their source and some waste is produced that flows into a sink.

The mathematics of exponential growth of any kind mean that economic growth cannot continue into the long-term future. At some point, any exponentially increasing quantity will become infinite in size.

The upshot of all this is that constant growth is physically impossible. At some point any system, whether a tree or a bear or an economy, must stop growing and make the transition to a steady state of dynamic balance (Daly and Farley 2003, 64).

Reconfiguring the Growth Model

Continued economic growth is as unsustainable as continued population growth. Either one will result in an Ecological Footprint that exceeds the planet's carrying capacity. What is needed is an equitable distribution of goods and food in the developing world and an adjustment to consumption patterns in the developed world, from a condition of excess consumption to a condition of adequate consumption.

A **paradigm** is a fundamental framework for understanding the world, a coherent set of assumptions and concepts that defines a way of viewing reality. Growth as the core economic paradigm has been developing for several hundred years and has become solidly entrenched since the last century. Although an end to growth seems inevitable, moving to a different economic model will involve dramatic change. The question is whether the transition will be wrenching and chaotic or orderly and reinvigorating.

One aspect of an economic transformation will involve reconfiguring the current consumer–product manufacturing system that now extracts resources from the earth, creates small products and big wastes, then sells the products to consumers who use them briefly before sending them to landfills. The new economy will need to find ways to reuse and recycle every material, a pattern known as a **circular economy**. Reuse and recycling are particularly important for nonrenewable resources; in addition, the new economy will need to consume renewable resources at a rate lower than their natural rate of renewal (Heinberg 2011, 247). The condition in which development occurs without increases in environmental impact is referred to as **decoupling** (Jackson 2009, 67).

The energy base of world economies will change as fossil fuel supplies diminish and as policymakers recognize the implications of climate change. Renewable sources of energy will need to replace fossil fuels. Energy efficiency strategies will provide de facto more energy from the same amount of fuel, essential during the transition period as well as afterward. Transportation systems will become increasingly diverse as transport gives up its dependence on fossil fuel technology.

Reconfiguring national and global economic structure involves policy change. Several approaches are commonly recommended. Policy can ensure that prices reflect the true value of natural capital and ecosystem services through devices such as tradable water rights, payment for ecosystem services from forests or watersheds, natural park entrance charges, or eco-labelling certification schemes (OECD 2012, 28). Policy can make pollution and environmental damage more costly than greener alternatives through environmental taxes and trading schemes so that the right to deplete resources or to pollute sinks would no longer be a free good but a scarce asset that could be bought and sold. Cap and trade systems for controlling pollution and transferrable quotas on fish catches are the beginnings of such a system. The tax structure could shift so that instead of taxing things we want, such as labor, we tax things we don't want, such as carbon emissions, pollution, resource depletion, or groundwater consumption (Daly 2005, 107; Rees 2014, 196). Perverse, or environmentally harmful, subsidies of such activities as fossil fuel production, water withdrawal, and unsustainable agricultural and aquacultural practices must be removed (OECD 2012, 29).

The change to a non-growth model will require addressing inequities in distribution, the way resources are allocated among individuals (Daly and Farley 2003, 12). While command-and-control approaches to regulation are still necessary in some situations—to protect endangered species or vulnerable resources, for example—sustainable development will need to involve shared, democratic governance with additional emphasis on local ecosystems, local economies, and local culture. Sustainable development will mean that most production is smaller in scale and finely tuned to place. Whatever the shape of the new economy, it will in all probability place far more emphasis on local production and consumption, for a variety of reasons.

Failing States

The whole world is interconnected, and certain sustainability issues by their nature can only be considered by looking at connections on a global scale. The problem of failing states is one such issue.

In many periods throughout history, the durability of groups or nations and their leaders has been threatened by states that accumulate too much power. Many wars have been fought over the perceived accumulation of too much power. World War II dealt with this threat. The Cold War was based on perception of a similar threat. Too much power is dangerous. Yet in a different way the absence of power is just as dangerous. In an absence of power social order disintegrates; governments are unable to provide basic services including food security, water, sanitation, and healthcare; violence and starvation stalk the land; and ecosystems and their inhabitants are destroyed.

A **failed state** is a state—that is, a self-governing political body—in which the ability to govern has broken down. The political structure that originally provided order may have been a monarchy, a democracy, or some other system. Whatever that system was, when it ceases to function and no stable system replaces it, the state begins to fail. The rule of law breaks down, social and economic systems stop functioning, and the state becomes unable to provide basic public services (Brown 2009, 18). A **failing state** is one that is in the process of such disintegration.

The natural world is one of the first casualties of a failing state. Starving people cannot make ecosystem preservation their top priority when they are struggling just to stay alive, and armed conflicts almost always result in severe degradation or destruction of habitat. For example, when governing descended into chaos in Rwanda and the Democratic Republic of the Congo in the 1990s, the populations of endangered mountain gorillas plummeted. The poorest people in the world are the most likely to depend on natural resources for their survival, and thus alleviating poverty is integral to alleviating pressure on environmental resources (Flannery 2010, 232).

The Index of Failed States

Several national and international organizations monitor conditions worldwide and maintain lists of states that appear to be failed or failing. The most systematic and well-respected effort to track and analyze failed states is the Failed States Index, a project of the American non-profit organization Fund for Peace. Like other thorough, global-scale analyses such as that by the Intergovernmental Panel on Climate Change or the International Union for Conservation of Nature and Natural Resources (IUCN) Red List of Threatened Species, this research compiles and evaluates peer-reviewed data from thousands of sources. The Failed States Index is published annually on the Fund for Peace website and in the July/August issue of *Foreign Policy* magazine.

The Index identifies 177 sovereign countries and examines 12 social, economic, and political indicators within each country that measure "their vulnerability to violent internal conflict and societal deterioration" (Brown 2009, 20). Each indicator for each country is given a score ranging from 1 to 10, so that the maximum possible score is 120. The total score is that country's Failed States Index. A country with a score of 120 would be totally failed in every category. Countries with scores from 1 to 30 are categorized as "Sustainable," those with scores over 30 to 60 as "Moderate," and those with scores over 60 to 90 are listed in a "Warning" category. Countries with scores over 90 are placed in the "Alert" category.

Many of the same countries have appeared at the top of the list since the index began in 2005. Some have or are developing nuclear capability; several are petroleum-exporting countries. Many countries experiencing water shortages and desertification appear at the top of the "Warning" category. Numerous countries are on a watch list, the so-called "Alert" category, including familiar names from the Middle East, Africa, and Central America.

It is possible for countries to recover. As with other topics of sustainability, it is because there is hope of recovery that people expend effort toward repair and restoration. Effort has paid off in Sri Lanka, Sierra Leone, Liberia, Colombia, and the Dominican Republic, once among the top 20 failed states (Fund for Peace 2013).

Characteristics of Failed States

According to research compiled by the Fund for Peace, 12 social, economic, and political characteristics are most likely to indicate a country is at risk of becoming a failed state.

The social indicators are demographic pressure, floods of refugees, human flight, and entrenched patterns of group grievances. Demographic pressure may be manifest as too many people and too little food, or it may be an age structure with a high proportion of desperate young people unable to find work. Human flight includes intellectuals and professionals and, as conditions deteriorate, a mass exodus of a country's former middle class.

Among the economic indicators are inequality between a few elites and a desperately poor majority, and sharp or severe economic decline. Many failing states are facing what are essentially natural resource crises: water shortages, desertification, and food shortages. James Gasana, the minister of agriculture and environment in Rwanda when 800,000 people were murdered there in 1994, observed that "the genocide may have been driven by hatred, but it was set into motion by hunger" (Steffen 2006, 20).

The political indicators of a failing state are an illegitimate government, deteriorating public services, widespread human rights violations, an elite security apparatus, warring factions, and often outside intervention.

Whose Land?

In a practice that has become known as "land grabbing," affluent countries with insufficient land or water, plus corporations and speculators looking for profits, lease or buy up huge blocks of land in poorer countries (Pearce 2012). No official registry for these transactions exists and the negotiations are confidential, so no one knows for sure how many there are or how much land is involved. These deals are typically made by governments, private agribusiness and financial corporations in affluent, food-importing countries which make large acquisitions of farmland in at-risk countries.

These land deals involve few stakeholders other than investors and government officials. A **stakeholder** is a person or group with a stake in the outcome, someone who can be affected by the decision. Many of the stakeholders who are farmers do not learn deals are being made until after agreements have been signed. Their land is often either confiscated or bought at a low price.

The larger land-acquisition issue is a subject of controversy. The World Bank and the UN Food and Agriculture Organization (FAO) believe that such land deals can benefit people living in poverty. Opponents argue that the practice results in greater inequality and food insecurity; they point out that because land grabs result in industrial monoculture production by absentee owners, and in some cases deforestation, they accelerate ecosystem destruction and contribute increased quantities of greenhouse gas emissions (Brown 2009, 12).

Governance

Governance refers to the processes by which humans make and implement collective decisions. Governance at a national level serves functions that allow states to operate. National or regional governments build and maintain infrastructure such as roads, power, and water. They underpin the legal system, provide laws, provide functional courts to ensure that those laws are enforced fairly, ensure that contracts are enforced, and regulate banking and financial systems (Sachs 2015, 130).

Governance is fundamental to sustainable development. Progress toward sustainability involves four dimensions: social inclusion, economic opportunity, healthy ecological function, and good governance. These make up complex systems at multiple scales, and so governance needs attributes of complex systems. In a rapidly changing world of pressing issues, resilience is a central goal, and so institutions should strive to include diversity and redundancy (Walker and Salt 2006, 148). Polycentric and overlapping governance structures at multiple levels can appear messy, but are better able to cope with complex issues and adapt to change (Ehrlich and Ehrlich 2013). The problems facing us are of great magnitude and interconnected; we will need polycentric structures: governance systems at multiple scales, global, national, and local; public and private. Some issues are appropriate for one scale; others are appropriate at another.

Governance adapts to particular situations, but some general principles are universal. Governments must have accountability, transparency, and participation in decisionmaking by stakeholders (Sachs 2015, 503). Any robust system needs a feedback loop with monitoring and assessment, and the concept of accountability means that governments will report these publicly. Transparency makes this possible; in order to hold a government accountable, we need to know what they are doing. Transparency makes it less likely that information critical for decisionmaking will be overlooked.

Governments develop guiding policies which are then implemented through regulations. Several forms of policy tools are available (OECD 2012, 28–30). Tax restructuring can make environmentally damaging actions more costly than greener actions: raising taxes on pollution and emissions and implementing emissions trading, for example (taxing the "bad") while lowering income taxes for individuals (not taxing the "good"). Values and pricing can be placed on natural assets and ecosystem services, for example through tradeable water rights, payments for watersheds and forests, or eco-label certifications, while eliminating subsidies on environmentally harmful activities such as fossil-fuel production that keep prices artificially low. Policies can set standards for such things as air and water quality, pollution levels, emissions, energy efficiency, and land use. Meanwhile, policies can be used to encourage technological innovation and then to diffuse innovations, thereby moving the "T" in the "IPAT" formula in a positive direction.

The Commons

"The Tragedy of the Commons" was an influential article by biologist Garrett Hardin. The scenario laid out by Hardin (1968) described herdsmen sharing a common pasture, in which each individual reaps a benefit from adding an animal to his herd and so is motivated to keep adding animals, while the disadvantage of degradation from additional overgrazing is shared by all the herdsmen. "The Tragedy of the Commons" has been used as a metaphor for the problems of overuse and degradation of natural resources (Ostrom 1998, 1). Hardin later clarified that what he described was actually a "tragedy of an unmanaged commons" (Bollier 2014, 27).

Common pool resources (CPRs) are resources from which it is difficult to exclude or limit users and in which use of the resources by one person decreases the benefits for other users (Ostrom 1990, 31). Examples include forests, fisheries, aquifers, and the atmosphere. A **commons** is a CPR plus a community plus a set of protocols: the rules and social practices for managing the resources (Bollier 2014, 141).

Understanding of commons governance was advanced by Elinor Ostrom, who was awarded the Nobel Prize in Economics for her analysis of how local groups of users devise arrangements for managing common-pool resources. Ostrom's field studies of a diverse range of hundreds of enduring, self-governing CPRs found they all exhibit similar design principles: in each commons there are clearly defined boundaries with respect to who has rights to appropriate the resource and the extent of the resource itself; users create rules based on local conditions; users participate in creating or influencing roles; there are methods of monitoring resource use; there is a system of graduated sanctions for free riders and users who violate the rules; there are mechanisms in place for resolving disputes; external governmental authorities do not prevent users from creating their own rules of use; and the commons are nested in multiple layers within larger systems of governance, a pattern she called polycentric governance (Ostrom 1990, 88–101). These polycentric, overlapping systems featuring multiple governing authorities at differing scales illustrate that there is no one ideal approach. In some situations self-organized community rules work best; in others, laws of larger government jurisdictions work best; and often it is a combination of scales that works best (Ostrom 2012, 70).

Commons are evolving social contracts for using shared resources, with rules finely tuned to local place that constantly adapt to changes. They are, according to Ostrom, complex adaptive systems, a theme that recurs again and again in many arenas of sustainability work. Commons are not the result of centralized direction or a single authority; they are self-organized groups of elements "whose rich patterns of interactions produce emergent properties that are not easy to predict by analyzing the separate parts of a system"

(Ostrom 1998, 21). Such systems adapt by incrementally changing their rules, modifying the details but retaining coherence under changing conditions and thereby exhibiting the attributes of resilience. As with all resilient systems, diversity and the "emergence of complex larger-scale behavior" (ibid.) from interactions of smaller elements are key features. Such systems often look messy but are in fact robust.

Note

1 CE stands for "common era," year 1. BCE stands for "before common era."

Further Reading

Daly, Herman E. and Joshua Farley. *Ecological Economics: Principles and Applications*. Washington, DC: Island Press, 2003.

Evans, J. P. *Environmental Governance*. London: Routledge, 2012.

Heinberg, Richard. *The End of Growth: Adapting to Our New Economic Reality*. Gabriola Island, BC: New Society Publishers, 2011.

McKibben, Bill. *Deep Economy: The Wealth of Communities and the Durable Future*. New York: Henry Holt and Company, 2007.

Ostrom, Elinor. *Governing the Commons: The Evolution of Institutions for Collective Action*. Cambridge: Cambridge University Press, 1990.

Speth, James Gustave. *The Bridge at the Edge of the World*. New Haven, CT: Yale University Press, 2008.

Chapter Review

1 How does carrying capacity affect population size?
2 Describe the difference between arithmetic growth and exponential growth.
3 In what ways did the agricultural revolution have an effect on human population size?
4 Why did the Industrial Revolution have such an impact on human population size compared to other periods in human history?
5 Describe the difference between a decreasing population and a decreasing rate of population growth.
6 Can a country's population increase when its birth rate is declining?
7 Why is the replacement fertility rate for humans 2.1, and not 2?
8 How does a population's age structure affect its economic health?
9 Why do people living in poverty tend to have larger families?
10 What factors influence people to limit the number of children they have?
11 What are the connections between empowering women and slowing population growth?
12 How are environmental economics and ecological economics different?
13 Give some examples of ecosystem services.
14 What is the difference between growth and development?
15 What is a failed state?
16 Who decides which countries get listed as failed states?
17 Once a country becomes a failed state, what kinds of changes could help it recover?
18 Give some examples of the phenomenon Hardin called "The Tragedy of the Commons."
19 Why is the pasture described in "The Tragedy of the Commons" technically not a commons?

Critical Thinking and Discussion

1 Some people assert that human population growth is the sole environmental problem affecting the planet. Do you agree? Why or why not?

2 In the eighteenth century Thomas Malthus wrote that every population will increase until it overshoots its carrying capacity, which will cause it to collapse. Why has a Malthusian collapse not occurred in developed countries?

3 In what ways could human activities enhance Earth's carrying capacity?

4 Should increasing Earth's carrying capacity be an ongoing goal of human effort?

5 What can you say about a society by looking at its age structure?

6 What do you think is the ideal world population size?

7 Population experts advocate improved public health as part of a population stabilization strategy. Yet improved health means that in the short term population will rise as more infants and children survive childhood. How do you explain this apparent contradiction?

8 What are the impacts of the economic growth model on the triple bottom line of environment, economics, and equity? In what ways might a transition to an ecological economics paradigm affect the triple bottom line?

9 Do you think that buying greener products has a net positive effect on limiting climate change, reducing pollution, preserving biodiversity, and so forth? Or do you think that buying biodegradable, nontoxic, and recyclable products simply spurs more consumption?

10 Do you think that environmental sustainability in developed nations has improved over the last 20 to 30 years?

11 How do you think globalization might impact the health of the environment?

12 Do you think that countries which have trade agreements with each other should use international environmental standards? Why or why not?

13 Do you think that laws and regulations could be effective tools for limiting consumption? Why or why not?

14 Would it be possible to lower our consumption rates and still maintain an adequate quality of life? If so, how might we do that?

15 Is economic growth inevitable? Do you think that a steady state economy is possible?

16 Other than simple financial assistance, how might industrialized countries help developing countries to reduce pollution?

17 Think about how climate change might affect the distribution of agricultural crops. What impacts might this have on regional economies in developing countries?

18 Could massive loans from the World Bank prevent states from failing?

Part II
Issues and Solutions

5   Climate

Many scientists believe that climate change is the most serious crisis facing our planet. People intending to work in fields related to sustainability need a clear understanding of what climate change means and the basic science behind it. As climate-related risk management becomes a common topic of concern, sustainability practitioners will be called upon to advise their organizations about climate impact, to provide **greenhouse gas** inventories and indicator reports, and to develop climate action plans.

Climate is not weather. Weather is the short-term variation in temperature, precipitation, and wind that occurs day to day (IPCC 2007a, 104). When we say, "It's hot today," we are talking about weather. Climate is the long-term trends in these atmospheric conditions measured over decades, centuries, or longer. When we say, "The cherry trees are blooming three weeks earlier than they did when I was a child," we are talking about climate.

Scientific thinking is always based on evidence. Scientists collect evidence by making precise observations or by conducting controlled experiments; evidence is considered valid only if the same results can be reproduced repeatedly using the same methods. Scientists submit their work to public scrutiny in peer-reviewed publications. Data and explanations are debated, tested, and re-tested. Only when an overwhelming body of data accumulates to support a particular explanation and the majority of experts within the scientific community reach a general consensus that the explanation is reliable does it become scientific theory.

All of the accepted scientific data and explanations we have about climate change have been reviewed by an international group called the Intergovernmental Panel on Climate Change, or IPCC, who was awarded the Nobel Peace Prize in 2007. The IPCC is an example of scientific consensus at work, at one of the largest scales in history. The IPCC was formed in 1988 by the United Nations Environment Programme and the World Meteorological Organization and consists of a jury of several hundred top scientists from around the world, on loan from their employers, who volunteer their time. Panel members are all respected researchers at their home governments or universities, but when they are on loan to the Panel they do not conduct original research; instead, they work as peer reviewers of existing research (Blockstein and Wiegman 2010, 10). After collecting, reviewing, and synthesizing thousands of studies from thousands of researchers, the Panel issues periodic assessment reports. The first IPCC report on climate change was issued in 1990, followed by reports in 1995, 2001, 2007, and 2014.

Is Earth Warming?

The IPCC has collected temperature measurements from 1850 to the present from locations all over the globe. They analyzed deviations in temperature at different kinds of

world, using the average temperature from 1961 to 1990

temperature moved up and down but overall stayed rela-
of the twentieth century the average temperature rose. In
y the average temperature dropped slightly, then remained
years. In the last 30 years of the twentieth century the tem-
...d continues to rise (Figure 5.1). The rate at which the average
accelerated.

...a few degrees in the global average temperature has a significant impact
...s a whole. Temperatures are rising more than twice as fast over land as over
...they are rising faster in the Northern Hemisphere, where most of Earth's land
area is, ...nan in the Southern Hemisphere. Temperatures in the Arctic have risen fastest of all,
four times as fast as for the rest of the world at large, a ratio that was typical of climate oscil-
lations in the geologic past (Wijkman and Rockström 2012, 40). A small increase in average
temperature means a bigger warming in temperatures over continents and an even bigger
warming in the Arctic (Wolfson 2008, 406). And even a small change in average temperature
can mean a big change in the frequency of extreme hot weather events such as heat waves and
high-energy storms (IPCC 2007a, 53).

Analyses from IPCC reports indicate that, depending on carbon dioxide concentration levels, by 2100 the global average temperature will be 1.5°F to 8.5°F warmer than it was in 1900
(IPCC 2013, 1055). What is striking to note is that the global average temperature during the
coldest part of the last ice age, when ice a mile or two deep covered parts of Europe and North
America, was only 9°F colder than it is now (AAAS Climate Science Panel 2014, 8). A few
degrees difference in average temperature can mean a major change in climate.

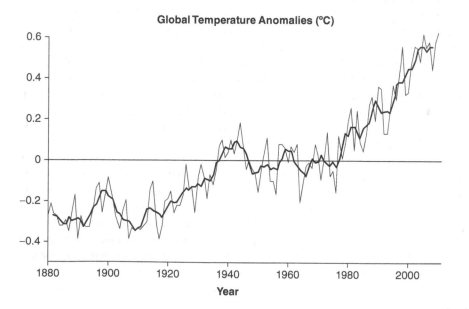

Figure 5.1 Global average temperature anomalies, 1880–2010, relative to 1961–1990 average temperature.
The thin line represents annual data, while the thick line is a five-year running mean.

Source: NASA Earth Observatory/Robert Simmon

Other changes around us are fingerprints of a warming climate. The upper layers of the oceans are warming, salinity is changing, and seawater is becoming more acidic. Sea level is rising. In the mid-latitudes growing seasons have gotten longer, the numbers of frost days per year have decreased, and springtime events such as flowering are occurring earlier. Species of plants and animals in the Northern Hemisphere are moving northward and higher in altitude. Differences between daytime and nighttime temperatures are decreasing. Heat waves are longer and more frequent. The amount of water vapor in the atmosphere has increased as evaporation rates have grown. The intensity of hurricanes is increasing. The number of storms with intense rainfall has increased in some regions, while the number and intensity of droughts has increased in drier regions. The amount of snow cover has decreased everywhere, permafrost has begun melting across Canada, Alaska, Siberia, and the Tibetan Plateau, Arctic sea ice is shrinking, and the world's glaciers are shrinking.

Is Earth warming? On one hand, the answer from data in thousands of studies over 150 years is clear: Yes, Earth is warming. On the other hand, continual change is a characteristic of climate and of all complex systems. So a climate that is changing is nothing new. In order to understand whether the recent temperature changes are unusual, it is necessary to look at Earth's climate history over a longer time period than 150 years. A review of ancient climates shows that Earth has been warmer in the past than it is now. During the age of the dinosaurs, for example, the average global temperature was around 9°F warmer than it is now (Henson 2011, 211). What is unprecedented, however, is the speed of the change. Never in the history of the planet has the temperature increased so rapidly.

How Temperature Records Are Compiled

Earth's temperature can be determined in multiple ways. The most straightforward is by actual measurement. Weather stations around the world have been measuring the surface temperature on land and at the surface of the oceans with thermometers since about 1850. Stations are chosen where consistent measurements have been made over most of the period under consistent conditions. Researchers correct for variations in sampling methods and for changes in the surroundings that might skew the data, such as increased urban development.

For measurements before 150 years ago, scientists use proxies: indicators that stand in for temperature. One example of a **proxy** is the use of tree rings examined in small cores cut from living trees without harming them. In temperate regions, trees tend to grow more in spring and summer and to slow down in fall and winter. Annual rings of wood are laid down in their trunks, with thicknesses that respond to temperature variations. Some living trees, such as bristlecone pines, are thousands of years old. From other places such as bogs where dead tree trunks are preserved, the record can be pushed back in time thousands more years.

Coral reefs also form annual layers that give researchers information about ocean temperature at the time they were formed. Coral reefs work best for warm tropical water temperatures, while tree rings work best for temperate-region land temperatures. The two complement each other to give a more complete picture.

Tree rings and coral reefs are biological proxies. Temperature records can also be constructed using geological proxies. One version is lake sediments, which form thick or thin annual layers depending upon the rate of snowmelt feeding sediment-bearing streams, which changes with temperature. Pollen within lake sediments also shows what kind of plants were growing nearby, another indication of temperature. Fossils of all kinds give clues to what the climate was like at the time they were formed. Ocean sediments contain the remains of tiny creatures, including plankton and foraminifera, which help form a picture of how deep the water was and what proportions of various elements it contained. Stalagmites in caves formed by layers of limestone laid down by dripping water are another kind of geological proxy.

Ice cores are proxies that can go back in time nearly a million years, collected by drilling into an ice sheet in Greenland, the Arctic, or Antarctic. These ice sheets are formed by snowfall that gets compacted, trapping bubbles of air inside; the layers within the ice cores give a record of the temperatures at the time precipitation fell. Those temperatures are determined using ratios of oxygen or hydrogen isotopes. An isotope is a version of an element with a different number of neutrons in its nucleus. Because neutrons are electrically neutral they do not change the chemical properties of the element, but because they do have mass their presence or absence makes an element heavier or lighter.

Oxygen is the most abundant material in Earth's crust. It usually has 8 protons and 8 neutrons in its nucleus, so it is called ^{16}O, pronounced "oxygen 16." About 1 in 500 oxygen atoms is ^{18}O, which has two extra neutrons in its nucleus and thus is heavier. When water evaporates and becomes water vapor, the lighter ^{16}O tends to evaporate first and the heavier ^{18}O tends to stay behind. The proportions of each depend somewhat on temperature. Measuring the quantities of the two isotopes within layers of ice gives a piece of data that can be used to reconstruct temperature. The same technique can be used with hydrogen isotopes (Wolfson 2008, 411).

The Long View: Climates through Time

From a range of geological, fossil, and ice core evidence we can reconstruct a climate history for much of Earth's life. A combination of natural forces, including plate tectonics and variations in Earth's orbit patterns, has resulted in dramatic climate changes in the past.

Three deviations in Earth's orbit combine to influence climate. These changes in Earth's orbit are known collectively as the **Milankovitch cycles** (Houghton 2009, 86). The Earth's axis tilts, relative to its orbit around the sun, with the tilt swinging back and forth from 21.8° to 24.4° over a period of 41,000 years; the tilt now is about 23.4° and decreasing. When the angle of tilt is the greatest, differences between summer and winter are more pronounced. In addition to tilting, Earth's axis changes position like the wobble in a spinning top. This cycle, known as the precession of the equinoxes, takes about 26,000 years. It, too, affects how intense seasonal differences are. The shape of Earth's orbit is eccentric and slightly elliptical. Currently we are closer to the sun in January and farther from the sun in July, which moderates the climate somewhat. The shape of the orbit results in one cycle that is about 100,000 years long and another that is about 400,000 years long, which make the contrast between seasons either more or less intense.

Earth's surface is constantly on the move, with continental plates rafting about on top of heavier oceanic plates. Locations of continents affect where ocean currents can flow. In addition, when land masses are near the poles, large ice sheets can develop. About a billion years ago a supercontinent known as Rodinia broke up into several pieces. The pieces rejoined and formed a supercontinent known as Gondwana, which drifted around the South Pole 300 to 400 million years ago, allowing ice sheets to form. Gondwana broke apart and became part of a supercontinent known as Pangaea, which eventually broke into the continents we see today.

As the continental plates float around, heavier oceanic plates dive under them and begin melting. Melting magma comes to the surface, forming volcanoes. Volcanoes can cause short-term cooling, as their particles block sunlight, but can cause long-term warming because of the carbon dioxide they add to the atmosphere.

Scientists think that a combination of extra tilt of Earth's axis and locations of land masses led to a period called Snowball Earth that covered the planet with ice from 750 to 580 million years ago (Henson 2011, 210). A **positive feedback** effect—in which white surfaces reflected incoming sunlight back into space, making the planet colder, resulting in yet more reflective snow—could have kept the planet locked in ice (Wolfson 2008, 9).

Other periods have been warmer than today. A dramatic warming happened around 250 million years ago. An explanation has not been settled; theories about the cause include increased volcanic activity and the greenhouse gas methane pouring out of the ocean floor (Henson 2011, 211). This warming period marked the greatest mass extinction in history. After this event, known as the Permian/Triassic extinction, life came surging back, although it took millions of years. The Mesozoic era, the age of the dinosaurs, saw global averages 9°F warmer than present temperatures. Another dramatic warming happened around 56 million years ago, known as the PETM, or Paleocene-Eocene Thermal Maximum, in which high carbon dioxide levels and methane from the seafloor and melting permafrost caused the global average temperature to rise by 9°F. The ocean acidified and many marine species went extinct, but because the changes happened over several thousand years, most terrestrial species were able to adapt or migrate (Kump 2011, 61).

Regular ice ages began to occur 2.5 to 3 million years ago with warm periods in between about every 41,000 years, corresponding to the cycle in the tilt of Earth's axis (IPCC 2007a, 449). Around a million years ago the cycle of ice ages lengthened and began occurring about every 100,000 years (Stanley 2004, 481). The last ice age peaked around 20,000 years ago, ending around 12,000 years ago.

The past 10,000 years, known as the Holocene epoch, featured mild climate with stable temperatures. This brief interglacial period, with its ideal and unusually stable climate conditions, was an exception to the extreme temperature variations of the past, a window which made it possible for humans to invent agriculture and for civilization to develop (Wijkman and Rockström 2012, 39). Research indicates that, without human impact on the climate system, these conditions would likely continue for several millennia more (ibid., 40).

Modern Climate Change and Greenhouse Gases

Earth's climate is warming and it is doing so at a rate that is unprecedented. The primary driver is something called the greenhouse effect.

Electromagnetic energy from the Sun hits Earth's surface in a range of wavelengths. Some of the solar radiation is in the visible spectrum, light in wavelengths we can see; some of it we cannot see because its wavelength is in the infrared spectrum. Most of the radiation hits the surface as visible light. Where it strikes white ice or snow, much of it is reflected back into space. Where it strikes darker land or open water, much of it is absorbed. Solar radiation absorbed by the Earth is re-radiated at a longer wavelength in the infrared part of the spectrum (Kump et al. 2010, 2).

Earth's average surface temperature is about 59°F. If Earth had no atmosphere, light would quickly be reflected out as infrared radiation and the average surface temperature would be around 0°F (Wolfson 2008, 362). Earth does have an atmosphere, and gases in the atmosphere absorb some of the infrared radiation coming from the surface. Less radiation can escape to space, and as a result the planet is warmer than it would otherwise be. These gases are called greenhouse gases. The more greenhouse gas there is, the warmer the surface.

The term "greenhouse effect" is one of those historic terms that does not match physical reality. The term was first used in the 1820s by a French physicist, who observed that the atmosphere was like a hothouse, or greenhouse (Henson 2011, 21). Actually, a greenhouse traps hot air and keeps it from escaping. The atmosphere does not do that; it keeps infrared radiation from escaping (Wijkman and Rockström 2012, 99).

A closer analogy is that greenhouse gases act like a blanket, insulating the surface and making it harder for energy to escape. As infrared radiation goes out, some of it is absorbed by greenhouse gases. The surface is warmed by this radiation coming back to it and so radiates more infrared in order to maintain an energy balance (IPCC 2007a, 97).

The most abundant gases in our atmosphere are nitrogen in the form of N_2, which is about 78 percent of the atmosphere, and oxygen in the form of O_2, which is around 21 percent of the atmosphere. They are simple **diatomic**, or two-atom, molecules and because of their simple shapes do not block much outgoing radiation. A few other gases have larger and more complicated molecules, and these are the so-called greenhouse gases. The most common are water (H_2O) and carbon dioxide (CO_2). These **triatomic**, or three-atom, molecules are larger, have more ways to rotate and vibrate, and in many cases vibrate at the frequencies of infrared radiation (Wolfson 2007, 62). The other common greenhouse gases are ozone (O_3) and nitrous oxide (N_2O), both of which are triatomic, and methane (CH_4), which is larger.

Water vapor is not as powerful a greenhouse gas as carbon dioxide, but it is abundant. Unlike carbon dioxide, it adjusts quickly to changing conditions and cycles through the system rapidly. A typical water molecule only remains in the atmosphere for about a week. Carbon dioxide, the gas released by burning fossil fuels, plays a more significant role in modern climate change.

A typical carbon dioxide molecule remains in the atmosphere about five years (ibid., 93). However, the carbon cycle is complicated. Different flows of the carbon cycle act over different time scales and the effect of added atmospheric carbon dioxide can last for a century or more. About 55 percent of the carbon humans put into the atmosphere as carbon dioxide is absorbed by the oceans and taken up by plants and soils. The other 45 percent stays in the atmosphere, where it is added to the carbon already cycling (Henson 2011, 34). As human activities release it into the air, the total amount of added CO_2 accumulates over time.

The climate record reveals a correlation between past climates and greenhouse gas concentrations (IPCC 2007a, 511). Data from the Vostok ice core in Antarctica show that global temperature and global carbon dioxide levels over the last 400,000 years follow similar patterns. When temperature is up, carbon dioxide is up. When temperature is lower, carbon dioxide levels are lower. That does not mean there is a simple mechanical connection, but it is clear that temperature and carbon dioxide levels do move together.

The amount of carbon dioxide in the atmosphere is usually reported in parts per million by volume, abbreviated **ppm**. Ice core records show that during ice ages the atmospheric carbon dioxide concentration is an average of around 170 ppm. During warm interglacial periods, such as the one we live in now, atmospheric carbon dioxide concentration rises to 280 to 300 ppm (Flannery 2010, 96). Before the Industrial Revolution, that is, before 1750, the carbon dioxide concentration was about 280 ppm (Blockstein and Wiegman 2010, 34). With the discovery of coal and oil, it began to climb. It is now over 400 ppm—a concentration last seen 3 million years ago when temperatures and sea levels were much higher than today (Sachs 2015, 40)—and rising by about 2 ppm per year.

Once carbon dioxide is added to the air, the constant churning of the atmosphere mixes it and spreads it evenly around the globe, where its effect remains for at least a century.

That means that carbon dioxide released in one region becomes everyone's problem. It also means that measurements in one place can accurately reflect the carbon dioxide concentration worldwide. A monitoring station high up on the Mauna Loa volcano in Hawaii has been sampling clean Pacific air and recording carbon dioxide levels since 1958 (Figure 5.2). A graph from the monitoring station known as the Keeling curve shows that carbon dioxide concentrations oscillate seasonally as growing plants take carbon dioxide out of the air in summer and release more carbon dioxide in winter, but the saw-tooth pattern of the graph shows a steady rise since measurements began (Kump et al. 2010, 4).

Methane is another significant greenhouse gas. It is produced when anaerobic bacteria digest organic matter, emerging from decaying plant matter in marshes, the belching of cows, rice paddies, landfills, sewage treatment plants, mining, and leaks from natural gas systems. It occurs at much lower concentrations than carbon dioxide, but it has a greenhouse effect 28 times as powerful as CO_2. Methane is measured in parts per billion by volume, or **ppb**. Ice core measurements from the last 800,000 years show that methane levels have ranged from 350 to 850 ppb. Like carbon dioxide, methane levels in ice core data rise and fall with the rise and fall of temperatures. Preindustrial levels of methane were 750 ppb; the current concentration is nearly 1,800 ppb (ibid., 310).

Greenhouse gases can be compared using a unit called the **global warming potential** (GWP), also known as carbon dioxide equivalent (**CO_2e**), which gives their impact relative to the same mass of carbon dioxide for a particular time horizon. GWPs differ depending upon what time horizon is used in the calculations. For example, 1 ton of methane is equivalent to 28 tons of CO_2 over a 100-year period but 84 tons of CO_2 over a 20-year period (IPCC 2014d, 87). One ton of leaking hydrofluorocarbon (HFC) refrigerant is the equivalent of anywhere from 124 to 14,800 tons of CO_2 over a 100-year period or 437 to 12,000 tons of CO_2 over a 20-year period, depending upon the type of HFC (IPCC 2007a, 33). The UN

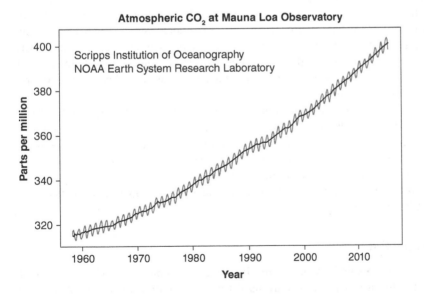

Figure 5.2 Record of carbon dioxide concentrations measured at the Mauna Loa station, 1958–2010. CO_2 levels rise and fall with the seasons, but the average concentration shows a steady rise.

Source: NOAA, Earth System Research Laboratory

Framework Convention on Climate Change adopted the 100-year GWP, which is commonly used as the default metric (IPCC 2014d, 87).

The Human Factor

Scientists studying climate change look at two kinds of studies: detection and attribution. Detection studies try to detect whether or not unusual changes in climate have happened, but they don't say anything about causes. Attribution studies look at the causes. If unusual changes are detected, we want to know to what to attribute them. We want to know if the changes are **anthropogenic**, or human-caused. One approach is to determine what kind of climate behavior would be expected without anthropogenic greenhouse gases, then compare that to the actual observed changes.

One way scientists can do controlled experiments with global climate is to run computer models. Basic physical laws plus variables including the chemical composition of the atmosphere, locations of oceans and landforms, energy from the sun, dust from volcanoes, and variations in Earth's orbit are entered into computer programs that simulate climates changing over time. Anthropogenic factors include the warming effects of various greenhouse gases and the cooling effects of pollutants in the air. The IPCC has analyzed the collective results of hundreds of climate models, each one an ensemble of multiple simulations.

Predictions of computer models without human inputs match actual temperature measurements from the nineteenth through the first half of the twentieth century fairly well. However, after the second half of the twentieth century the predictions diverge from actual measurements. Only when all the factors are fed into the computer models, natural and anthropogenic factors together, do they accurately reproduce the observed temperature rise (Henson 2011, 243). We cannot explain the changes in climate unless we take into account humans and the greenhouse gases they produce.

The combination of exploding population numbers, economic growth, and 150 years of industry based on fossil fuels has brought about our rapidly warming climate. A massive amount of ancient carbon has been **sequestered** or stored underground, which we are now burning in our cars and power plants. Millions of years ago decaying organic matter was buried by sediments and in the heat and pressure underground became coal, oil, and natural gas. When we burn these materials we release the sequestered carbon all at once, throwing Earth's carbon cycle far out of balance.

Since the start of the industrial era the concentration of CO_2 in the atmosphere has risen almost 40 percent (Houghton 2009, 29). The burning of fossil fuels is the primary culprit; wood-burning, farming, deforestation, and cement production also contribute significant amounts (Blockstein and Wiegman 2010, 38). CO_2 concentration is rising by 2 ppm each year (Wolfson 2008, 112); if the pattern continues at the same rate, we will see CO_2 concentrations of 550 to 600 ppm by the end of this century, a level high enough to be catastrophic (Blockstein and Wiegman 2010, 43).

Projecting into the Future

Climate scientists make predictions of future climate using computer models. Computer models combined with past observations are used to predict future impacts of increasing greenhouse gases. When the IPCC calculated their projections about climate change, they had to make assumptions about many variables, including how much greenhouse gas concentrations would change, whether population growth would stabilize, and whether people's

choices about fossil fuels and energy consumption would change. They orga
variables into four plausible pathways with a large number of scenarios, base
ing assumptions about energy sources, technology, land use, population growth
activity, and climate policy (IPCC 2014d, 57).

Changes predicted by computer models reviewed by the IPCC include he.. waves;
extremes of weather conditions including floods, droughts, and hurricanes; melting of glaciers and polar ice; sea level rise; changing ocean currents; changes to terrestrial and marine
ecosystems including extinctions; and changes to human lifestyles including agriculture and
economic issues. Actual measurements such as sea level rise, melting of ice, and changing
ecosystems show systems changing faster than IPCC predictions (Blockstein and Wiegman
2010, 43).

Extreme weather events such as prolonged heat waves are predicted to continue increasing in intensity and frequency, with more crop failures, forest fires, and ecosystem damage.
Warming will affect the distribution of water; some regions of the world will experience
more severe droughts while other regions will see increased intensity of rainfall and large-
scale flooding (Black and King 2009, 32). The frequency of hurricanes may not increase, but
the frequency of intense hurricanes is increasing (Wolfson 2008, 443).[1]

One area of great concern in the cryosphere, Earth's ice and snow cover, is the melting of both polar ice and glacial ice. It is believed that sometime this century the Arctic
Ocean will be entirely free of ice during the summer for the first time in about a million
years. While this will have short-term economic benefits as new shipping lanes open up,
it will have disastrous effects for some ecosystems and species such as polar bears. Much
of the disappearance of Arctic sea ice is due to a positive feedback loop: White polar ice
reflects some of the incoming sunlight back to space, but as the ice disappears darker water,
which absorbs more sunlight, is exposed, warming the air and causing more sea ice to melt
(Henson 2011, 78).

On land, Greenland and Antarctica are covered by massive ice sheets. An increase in
global average temperature causes an increase in precipitation in the form of snow in the dry
Antarctic interior, where the ice may actually be growing. The concern is that as glaciers
slowly advance, increased calving of chunks of ice at the continents' perimeter removes a
plug holding back the seaward flow of inland glaciers (IPCC 2014a, 355). An additional concern is that if meltwater works its way to the bottom surface of a glacier, the water can act as
a lubricant allowing the glacier to flow faster (ibid., 354).

Mountain glaciers all over the world, from the Himalayas to the Alps to the Andes, are
disappearing at a rapid rate. In the short term increased flow of meltwater will fill rivers and
increase irrigation to crops. But once the glaciers are gone, the cities that depend upon them
as their primary water source will face a water crisis with no immediate solution (Hambrey
and Alean 2004, 346).

Permafrost in Alaska and Siberia appears to be melting. Permafrost, as its name implies,
is ground that remains below freezing year-round. A great concern is the massive reservoir of
densely concentrated methane in the form of ice-like methane hydrates, 150 times as concentrated as methane gas, trapped within the permafrost ice (Henson 2011, 86). If this methane
is released, its added greenhouse effect could dwarf that of carbon dioxide.

Rising sea level is perhaps the most familiar potential outcome of climate change
reported in the popular press. The 2013 IPCC report projected a mean sea level rise of 17 to
29 inches by the year 2100 (IPCC 2013, 1180). These are conservative numbers; the IPCC
is a conservative body whose scientists and diplomats from every member nation must reach
consensus on each finding before it can be reported. Some climate scientists believe sea-level

rise from 3 feet to tens of feet in the next century is likely if humans continue with business as usual (Hansen 2010, 258).

Melting sea ice does not cause sea levels to rise. Like ice cubes in a glass of water, sea ice is less dense than the water it floats in, and when it melts the water level does not change. Like all materials, water expands when it is heated and sea-level rise is caused primarily by the thermal expansion of water as the oceans warm (Blockstein and Wiegman 2010, 51). Melting of floating ice at the edges of Greenland and Antarctica do not contribute to sea-level rise; however, if the Greenland ice sheet melts, that new water will eventually result in a sea level rise of up to 23 feet (IPCC 2014d, 74).

As ice melts more freshwater is added to the ocean, changing its salinity. A possibility exists that the increase in freshwater could shut down part of the global conveyor belt or thermohaline circulation, a deep-ocean circulation system driven by temperature and salinity (Kump et al. 2010, 318) (Figure 5.3). The concern is that changes in water density could slow the conveyor belt (IPCC 2013, 282; Randers 2012, 123), leading to climate changes in Europe. While there is no evidence that Europe could become covered by ice, ecosystems would probably be significantly affected by changes in the conveyor system (Henson 2011, 120).

Marine ecosystems are vulnerable to changing climate for several reasons. Plankton, the tiny plants and animals on which the ocean's food chains depend, are sensitive to even small rises in water temperature; changes in the mix of plankton can result in mass die-offs of fish and birds (Heinberg 2011, 150). Coral reefs also face threats from warmer water temperatures, which lead to massive die-offs called coral bleaching. Ocean water is becoming more acidic as the increasing amount of carbon dioxide in the atmosphere is mixed into the churning water and changing its pH, a measure of acidity. The sea is still slightly alkaline, but less so than it was. In the increasingly acidic waters, corals and shell-building mollusks find it more difficult to build their structures (Houghton 2009, 211).

An ecosystem change that is already occurring in both marine and terrestrial environments is that some kinds of organisms begin their annual growth and reproduction cycles earlier in

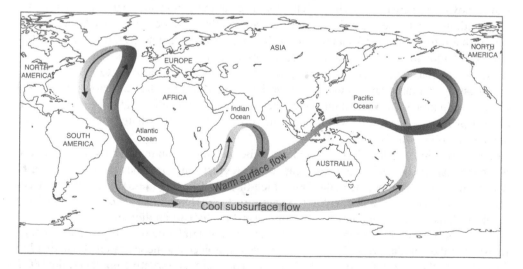

Figure 5.3 The global conveyor belt or thermohaline circulation

Source: Adapted from NASA

the year while timing for some other organisms has not changed. The result is a mismatch in growth and feeding times on a large scale.

On land, warming temperatures are transforming ecosystems and species ranges. As the Earth warms species who can are moving to places with living conditions that suit them. The ranges of many plants and animals are moving poleward at an average rate of 3.7 miles per decade (Blockstein and Wiegman 2010, 45). For those who live in mountain ecosystems, the only direction they can move easily is upward and these species are moving upwards in elevation at a rate of about 20 feet per decade (Henson 2011, 151). Many species are unable to adapt by moving, however. Conservative projections are that if the Earth warms only 3° to 4°F, 20 to 30 percent of all species will be at risk of extinction by the end of the century (ibid., 148). Other projections put the extinction rate much higher.

One focus of concern is the boreal forest or taiga, which circles the globe north of the 50th parallel and is warming twice as fast as the rest of the world. As the planet's largest terrestrial biome, it is a major carbon-sequestration sink. This vast forest region is in steep decline, with widespread insect outbreaks, tree die-offs, wildfires, and permafrost thawing and even burning. Scientists worry about the potential for the forest to reach tipping points this century, in which thawing permafrost could lead to runaway methane emissions and the forests could switch from being carbon sinks to major greenhouse gas emission sources (Gauthier et al. 2015, 819; Robbins 2015).

Climate change will make it harder to grow food in some places, undermining food security (IPCC 2014d, 13). Agriculture evolved within the constant and benign climate of the Holocene; adapting to unpredictable, rapidly shifting conditions will present unfamiliar challenges. Some parts of the world will face threats from heat, drought, and water shortages; in other parts of the world crop yields may actually rise in the short term due to the increased amount of carbon dioxide in the air or the warming of regions formerly too cold to grow crops (IPCC 2014b, 494). Ocean acidification, warming, and increases in extreme storm events will affect fisheries and aquaculture (ibid.)

Planet Earth has what is called **climate commitment**. We are committed to a warmer climate based on the increased amount of carbon dioxide already released into the atmosphere (IPCC 2013, 1104). Even if the burning of fossil fuels stopped completely tomorrow, the planet would continue to warm for several hundred years because of the greenhouse gases already in the system (ibid., 1107). We know that the planet will get warmer. The question will be how much warmer it will get, and how we and our fellow living beings will adapt.

It is not just gradual warming of the planet that is of concern. The Earth system is a complex system, with the potential to experience a critical transition, or tipping point. A tipping point occurs when the climate system crosses a critical threshold beyond which positive feedbacks drive the system from one stable state to a new, irreversible state (Glikson and Groves 2016, 147). As a system approaches a critical transition, conditions may appear to be changing gradually, or even not at all, until a critical threshold is reached and a tiny perturbation causes the system to shift from the old state to a new one. Climate researchers have identified multiple potential climate tipping points or "self-accelerating transformations set off when natural thresholds are crossed" (Blaustein 2015, 36), including the melting and collapse of Greenland and west Antarctic ice sheets, melting of permafrost, boreal forest dieback, Amazon forest dieback, changes in Indian and west African monsoons, ozone hole growth, changes to the El Niño-Southern Oscillation (ENSO) ocean circulation, and changes to the Atlantic thermohaline circulation (Lenton et al. 2008, 1786). The IPCC explicitly discusses tipping points, concluding that with increased warming, some systems "may be at risk of abrupt and irreversible change;" they note that "the precise levels of climate change sufficient to trigger abrupt and irreversible change remain uncertain, but the risk associated with crossing such thresholds increases with rising temperature" (IPCC 2014a, 13). One area of climate-change research is working to identify warning signals of an approaching threshold, with a focus on a phenomenon known as critical slowing down which occurs as a system takes longer than usual to stabilize itself after a disturbance, a symptom of loss of resilience (Blaustein 2015, 35, 38).

United Nations Convention on Climate Change

United Nations members are parties to an international treaty known as the United Nations Framework Convention on Climate Change (UNFCCC), first adopted at the Earth Summit in Rio in 1992. The parties meet every year in what is known as the Conferences of the Parties (COP). The Kyoto Protocol was an agreement to reduce emissions signed in 1997. After years of preparation and a series of failed climate talks it was replaced by the Paris Agreement, which emerged from the 21st Conference of the Parties (COP21) following intense negotiations and signed in 2015. In the Paris Agreement, countries agree to limit global average temperature to "well below 2°C above pre-industrial levels" and to strive for a more ambitious target of 1.5°C above pre-industrial levels (UNCOP 2015, 21).[2] They agree to reduce deforestation and to conserve and enhance existing forests, given their role in carbon sequestration (ibid., 22). They commit to a long-term goal of net zero emissions by the second half of the century through a balance between emissions by sources and removal by carbon sinks (ibid., 21). They agree to review emissions reductions and to establish new and deeper emissions targets every 5 years beginning in 2023, and to do so "on the basis of equity, and in the context of sustainable development and efforts to eradicate poverty" (ibid.). Developed countries agree to share financial burdens to help developing countries transition to renewable energy and adapt to climate impacts, although the finance elements are not specific and not legally binding.

COP21 acknowledged the scale of the threat and began to respond politically in a way that previous conferences did not. However, climate scientists, and the text of the Paris Agreement itself, state that emissions-reduction pledges submitted by participating countries still fall far short of what is needed in order to avoid dangerous and potentially runaway climate change (Gillis 2015). The agreement by itself is not enough to avoid catastrophic warming, but it does begin a process, laying a foundation and committing the parties to improve on emissions targets substantially in the years ahead.

Climate Stabilization

A significant component of sustainability work is aimed at reducing the impact of climate change. Many organizations take the formal step of setting up a climate action plan with a goal of becoming **climate neutral**. Climate neutral is a term to describe living or doing business in a way that results in an overall net climate impact of zero. Many people use the term **carbon neutral** to refer to the same condition of no net greenhouse gas emissions. People focus on carbon neutrality because carbon dioxide is the most significant greenhouse gas. However, methane, nitrous oxide, and the fluorocarbons are climate-heating gases, too, and some people choose to use the term "climate neutral" in order to include all the greenhouse gases.

The task of averting climate disaster is large in scope. Acting on multiple fronts is essential; no strategy by itself will be enough. Just as multiple approaches are needed, contributions of many people in multiple organizations are needed. The work begins with each of us as individuals and the choices we make—what we eat, how we consume energy, how we move ourselves around, what we buy, and how we vote.

Many cities have climate plans. Students at many colleges and universities have developed their own climate action plans. Hundreds of college and university presidents have signed the American College & University Presidents' Climate Commitment, agreeing that their institutions will measure and report their greenhouse gas emissions, develop and implement action plans for becoming climate neutral, and make climate neutrality part of their curriculum.

Many businesses view climate destabilization as not only an ethical mandate but also as a business threat and business opportunity. Companies assess potential financial risks that may arise from increased fire, severe storms, water shortages, or disruption of supply chains; risks from costs they may incur if regulations to curb emissions are enacted; and risks from loss of market share if they are perceived negatively by customers. As an opportunity, climate mitigation programs improve brand recognition, take advantage of growing market demand, motivate employees, and can attract new investors. Actions to reduce emissions by reducing energy use or managing transportation also lower costs.

Climate Action Plans

The steps for setting up a program to reduce greenhouse gas emissions arc similar whether they are for an individual, school, business, organization, or government. Those steps are: (1) make a plan; (2) measure; that is, prepare a greenhouse gas inventory; (3) reduce emissions; (4) offset the emissions that remain.

Best results come from following these steps. However, there may be reasons why planning is difficult, and establishing an accurate inventory can be complicated. The important goal is reducing emissions. Any enterprise can still reduce its emissions without having a complete greenhouse gas inventory.

Make a Plan

Planning is an important first step in any activity, laying out a roadmap for the tasks ahead. Depending upon the size of the organization planning may be done by a team or by an individual. The first planning task is to define the goal or goals. As business managers sometimes quip, "do good things" is not a real goal; likewise, "become climate-friendly" is not a real goal. Goals should be measurable so that it is possible to verify whether or not they have been met. A goal could say something such as, "Reduce net greenhouse gas emissions by 5 percent per year, compared to 2010 emissions" or "Become climate neutral by 2020."

Part of defining the goal is defining the boundaries. If the goal is a certain percent reduction, will that apply to the entire organization or just parts? Some organizations decide a program has the greatest chance of success if it is applied to the entire enterprise from the beginning. In other organizations a project can be made more manageable if it starts with a goal of reducing emissions in one product line, one department, or one business unit. Or, a goal might be limited to one type of source the first year: emissions only from transportation, for example, or emissions only from energy use. Finally, when setting up the greenhouse gas inventory you need to define the scope: will you track simply the direct emissions for which you are responsible, such as exhaust from your heating plant or fuel burned during employee commutes? Or will you expand the inventory's boundaries to include indirect emissions embedded in the products you buy, such as emissions from the trucking company that delivers your office supplies, or carbon released in the logging of trees that were used in the paper you buy, or methane released from food waste you send to the landfill?

Determine who will be involved. Select a leader for the climate action plan and assemble a representative steering committee or leadership team, if the organization is large enough to have one. Be sure that the individual or team has adequate authority to get the job done. In an organization with limited time or limited expertise it may be efficient to hire an outside consultant. Ensure that top leadership in the organization endorses the plan's goals. Find ways for the organization's leaders to communicate their support to others whose cooperation will be important. A kickoff event and regular updates through newsletters or announcements are two useful tools.

An organization's climate action plan, including the goals, should always be in writing. If the organization is a commercial business, it may be wise to analyze risks and opportunities or costs and benefits. There may be financial risks if emissions are not reduced, or there may be competitive advantages if they are. These provide the business case to which people can refer, helping ensure that the goals are achieved.

Measure

In a climate action plan, the measurement step refers to conducting a greenhouse gas inventory, sometimes known as measuring your carbon footprint. The greenhouse gas inventory gives you information about sources of emissions and clarifies which ones are the most significant sources. This allows the organization to set priorities so that it can tackle the biggest sources first and reduce its planet-heating emissions as much as possible, as soon as possible. In addition, knowing where you started allows you to track future performance so that you can evaluate your progress.

Protocols are used in situations where consistency across organizations is important. A protocol is a written method that can be followed in the same way by everyone who uses it. The Greenhouse Gas Protocol is an internationally recognized, standardized method for measuring and reporting climate impact developed through a partnership between the World Resources Institute (WRI) and the WBCSD. The standard ISO 14064 was subsequently developed based on the Greenhouse Gas Protocol. ISO 14064 is an internationally recognized standard for reporting and verifying greenhouse gas inventory data, reporting and monitoring greenhouse gas emission reductions, and validating and verifying inventory and reduction data.

Establish an Emissions Boundary

In the Greenhouse Gas Protocol, after the boundaries of the organization have been defined the first step is to decide which emissions sources are to be included. The Protocol has three categories known as Scope 1, Scope 2, and Scope 3. Scope 1 includes the direct emissions from sources owned by or controlled by the organization; it can include direct emissions from generating heat or electricity, emissions from company vehicles, emissions from manufacturing processes, and "fugitive" emissions such as leaks from pipelines and equipment. Scope 2 includes indirect emissions from purchased electricity or purchased heat. Scope 3 includes indirect emissions from other sources such as vehicles owned by others and used to transport people or goods, the extraction and production of materials purchased by the organization, and emissions generated in the end use and disposal of items produced by the organization.

According to the Greenhouse Gas Protocol all Scope 1 and Scope 2 emissions should be included in every inventory; Scope 3 emissions are considered optional.

Collect Data

After the sources have been identified, the next step is to collect activity data. This is the most time-consuming step in the greenhouse gas inventory. Data come from numerous sources. You will need to think carefully to identify all the sources in your own organization. Data on quantities of purchased electricity and heat can be found in utility bills. For electricity and heat generated on-site, data can include fuel volumes from purchase orders or fuel tank logs. Data on vehicle emissions begin with either mileage taken from expense reports or odometer readings, or fuel volumes taken from purchase records or expense reports. Air travel mileage may be available from an organization's travel agent records or using online calculators to find distances between cities. Data on vehicle emissions from freight transport begin with mileage from shipping and delivery invoices. Data on materials used in production begin with purchase orders; online calculators can help find information about associated emissions. If your organization does printing, a printing company or printing department can provide data on pounds of paper used and its recycled content percentage.

Calculate

The next step is to calculate greenhouse gas emissions using the data collected in the previous step. Tools are available from many sources to help with this step. The website for the Greenhouse Gas Protocol provides a selection of emission calculation tools.

If you collect data on more than one type of greenhouse gas you will convert each one to an equivalent amount of carbon dioxide, written as CO_2e. Be sure that your data are converted to carbon dioxide equivalent, CO_2e, as opposed to carbon equivalent.[3]

Quality Control

It is important that the greenhouse gas inventory be credible the first time it is released. You will be managing a lot of data and will have done many calculations; since each piece of data is an opportunity for error, the work needs to be checked. If possible, have someone else do the checking, reviewing data entry sheets and calculations. How much time is spent on checking depends upon the magnitude of risks and opportunities. If shareholders have demanded an inventory that will be reported in an annual report, or if the organization is preparing to meet regulations or to enter an emissions trading market, legal requirements are involved and the risk of error is greater than if the purpose is simply to look for opportunities for improvement. For large-scale projects with risk of financial penalties or legal exposure, consider having a consultant or an accounting firm review the data. Consult the *Greenhouse Gas Protocol Corporate Standard* for details about setting up a quality management system in an inventory program. For small projects with no public exposure, self-checking may be adequate.

Monitor

Evaluate your organization's progress regularly as part of the measurement activities. Most organizations review their inventories on an annual basis (Lingl et al. 2010, 27). An annual assessment shows whether the climate action plan's goals are being met. If they are not, evaluate the reasons and take action. If they are, evaluate whether more ambitious goals could be set. Measuring and reducing emissions is an iterative process.

Reduce

Reducing emissions is the exciting part of the climate action plan. Here you determine how you can meet the reduction goals you set during the planning phase. The greenhouse gas inventory can help identify projects with the best opportunity to reduce emissions.

There are several approaches to selecting projects. One approach is to find projects that can be done easily and quickly with low cost. Energy efficiency measures fall into this category. Another approach is to begin with a pilot project, an initial small-scale test version of a larger project, which is useful when it is not certain whether a strategy will be effective. A pilot gives an opportunity to collect data, analyze performance, and make adjustments. Not every project will be successful, and doing a pilot is a way to minimize cost and protect the reputation of the project until a strategy can be proven.

Some projects have a lot of visibility and appeal. Putting a wind microturbine on top of a building or covering a roof with solar panels are examples of projects that attract positive publicity and raise awareness. Grants from utilities, government programs, or donors may be available to help with funding. High-visibility projects are easiest to accomplish as part of new construction or major renovation, more costly and harder to accomplish when they are retrofits. When considering a visible, glamorous project, evaluate not only the potential for emissions reductions but also financial costs and payback period. Particularly in the early stages of implementing a climate action plan, it is important to be able to make the business case and to avoid negative reactions that can threaten the program. Above all else, you need greenhouse gas reductions to continue into the future.

Offset

Few organizations can achieve climate neutrality through on-site changes alone. When your organization has made all the changes possible, use offsetting to bring the total net emissions to zero. With offsetting, an organization pays someone else in another location to reduce emissions or sequester carbon. Offsetting is a net benefit to the planet but will not directly reduce an organization's own emissions. A later section in this chapter discusses details of offsetting and emissions trading.

Strategies for Reducing Emissions

Energy Use

It is surprising how many people do not understand that energy use and greenhouse gases are connected. The connection is simple: if an organization uses energy made from fossil fuels, it emits greenhouse gases. The most effective method of reducing emissions is to cut energy use.

Energy efficiency means using less energy to do the same amount of work, whether lighting a light bulb, heating or cooling a room, or turning an electric motor. For most organizations the largest and most cost-effective emissions reductions come from energy efficiency.

Fuel switching means changing the source of energy to do the same work, such as converting a furnace from oil to natural gas. Natural gas is still a fossil fuel, but its emissions per unit of heat are lower than oil.

Reducing global emissions will require replacing fossil fuels with clean, renewable energy sources. Ending dependence on coal-fired power plants is the most urgent need on the climate-stabilization agenda. If energy from renewable sources is not available, an organization may choose to purchase **renewable energy certificates** (RECs), also known as renewable energy credits, green certificates, or green tags.

Transportation

Transportation accounts for a significant share of carbon dioxide emissions from the burning of fossil fuels, so many organizations develop a transportation plan. Reducing single-occupancy vehicle travel is a primary goal of such a plan.

Air travel is a large source of greenhouse gas emissions. It is a difficult emission source to change because current jet-engine technology requires fossil fuel in enormous quantities with no nonfossil fuel substitutes available. Strategies for reducing emissions focus on reducing the number of air miles traveled. Travel by train or bus produces significantly lower greenhouse emissions per passenger-mile than flying (GRID-Arendal 2008, 122), and teleconferencing avoids travel emissions. Air travelers can purchase carbon offsets, but offset programs can distract people from making more significant behavioral changes such as flying less, and in some cases actually encourage people to travel more. Meanwhile, air-travel offsets cover only a fraction of a trip's emissions (Rosenthal 2009).

On occasions when air travel seems necessary, avoiding nighttime flights reduces impact somewhat. Night flights constitute only a quarter of total air travel but contribute 60 to 80 percent of total jet greenhouse gas emissions (Reed 2006, 28). During the day, while jet contrails do trap heat and prevent it from radiating into space they also reflect sunlight and block incoming radiation. At night, however, there is no blocking of solar radiation to offset the trapping of heat, and only the greenhouse effect remains.

Buildings

Buildings have enormous impact on energy use. In existing buildings, opportunities include improving energy efficiency, fuel switching, and converting to renewable energy sources. In the construction of new buildings designers, planners, and citizens can choose high-performance, zero-emission buildings, carefully sited to reduce energy use and take advantage of local climate characteristics such as sun and wind.

Operations and Purchasing

Because HFC refrigerants used in heat pumps, air conditioning, and refrigeration are extremely potent greenhouse gases, even small leaks result in major global warming potential. An important strategy is a scheduled maintenance program with a regular leak-detection routine, along with switching to less-polluting refrigerant technologies.

Every organization purchases supplies and materials, including paper. Paper is made from trees, which store carbon. When they are cut they release carbon, as does the equipment used to cut, haul, and process the paper. Changing the way paper is used gives an opportunity for reducing emissions. Using doubled-sided printing and copying, printing only when necessary, and switching to 100 percent post-consumer recycled paper can reduce emissions by up to 40 percent (Lingl et al. 2010, 36).

Companies involved in manufacturing or construction purchase large quantities of a range of materials. Using recycled materials still requires energy, but it requires fewer raw materials; thus less fossil fuel is expended to acquire the materials and less carbon dioxide is emitted. Recycling also keeps at least some material out of the waste stream, so greenhouse gas emissions from incinerators or methane from landfills is reduced.

Organizations can set up purchasing policies that promote energy efficiency, recycled content, and local sourcing. Some purchasing policies also include criteria for selecting vendors and rewards for suppliers who reduce their emissions.

Forests, Farms, and Soil

Automobiles and power plants are carbon sources. Forests are carbon sinks: they sequester or store carbon.[4] About a quarter of the living biomass in a forest is carbon, snags and fallen logs store other carbon captured long ago, and the soil beneath a forest stores even more carbon than the trees (Vogt et al. 2007, 199). Clear-cuts are carbon sources that often continue to emit carbon for years, despite the rapid growth of young trees. Decomposer microbes in forest soil work more quickly after a stand has been logged, releasing carbon dioxide as they break down dead branches and roots (Levy 2008, 38). Reducing deforestation is an important mitigation strategy (IPCC 2014c, 24); it is estimated that 15 percent of global carbon emissions each year result from deforestation (Flannery 2010, 260; Sachs 2015, 472). The more frequently a forest is harvested, the more carbon is emitted. Conversely, each acre of new tropical forest takes up a quantity of carbon in its first 12 years of life equivalent to the carbon emitted by an average automobile driven 500,000 miles (Batterman et al. 2013, 224). Fast-growing trees sequester more carbon in their first 10 years of life. Slow-growing trees have denser wood, which sequesters more carbon later in life (Nair et al. 2010, 281).

Managing croplands and restoring organic soil is another important mitigation strategy (IPCC 2014c, 24). In photosynthesis, plants use sunlight and water to take carbon dioxide out of the air and store it. When they die, a third of their carbon becomes organic matter in the soil (Nair et al. 2010, 253), where complex biochemical processes create a stable, long-lived form of carbon. About 58 percent of soil organic matter is carbon (Toensmeier 2016, 22). Carbon farming is a suite of agricultural practices in which farmers and other land managers sequester carbon in the soil (ibid., 3). Carbon farming practices include minimal tilling, mulching, composting, and long-lived perennial crops.

Another strategy for sequestering carbon in the soil is biochar, a type of charcoal made by burning organic material in the absence of oxygen at relatively low temperatures in a process known as pyrolysis (Lehmann and Joseph 2009, 1). Biochar was used thousands of years ago by pre-Columbian civilizations to improve soil fertility (Bruges 2010, 26). Evidence of its use in extensive farms and orchards by these large, complex societies in what is now the Amazon rainforest is found in pockets of black soil known as *terra preta*[5] (Mann 2011, 354–59). Biochar added to soil increases soil fertility: its structure provides myriad microscopic surfaces where microbes can colonize and hyphae from mycorrhizal fungi can form networks; microbes and mycorrhizae are fundamental elements of healthy soil ecosystems. Biochar also increases soil's ability to hold water.

The biggest benefit of using biochar is its role in stabilizing climate. Plants pull carbon dioxide out of the atmosphere and become temporary carbon sinks, but when they decompose or burn, they return that carbon to the air. Converting their biomass to charcoal instead renders that carbon inert, keeping it out of the atmosphere. When this biochar is added to soil, it magnifies fertility while sequestering carbon. Climate scientists are studying biochar's potential as a long-term carbon sink because of its ability to lock up carbon in stable form for long periods of time, for at least centuries and in most cases millennia (IPCC 2014c, 832).

There is a multiplier effect, too: not only is organic waste used to produce biochar, which locks up the carbon long-term, but if that organic waste had been allowed to decompose, it would have resulted in emissions of the potent greenhouse gas methane, emissions which are avoided by processing waste into charcoal.

Carbon Capture and Sequestration

Carbon capture and sequestration (CCS) refers to technology that captures, or removes, carbon dioxide from industrial processes, particularly those powered by coal, and sequesters, or stores, it deep underground in geological formations (GRID-Arendal 2008, 88). The captured carbon dioxide is pumped into porous locations, primarily either depleted oil and gas fields or porous saline rock formations. Captured carbon dioxide is also sold to oil companies who inject it under pressure into producing oil fields in order to increase their yield. Researchers are studying carbon storage in basalt formations under the oceans, where assuming the formations will store the carbon dioxide permanently, the volcanic rock is converted to limestone, locking in the carbon. CCS comes with tradeoffs and risks. It would primarily be used to extend the period of transition to post-carbon energy, but is not a permanent fix (Wolfson 2008, 463).

CCS is an example of geoengineering, using technology to change the dynamics of the Earth system in order to mitigate climate destabilization. Other examples of geoengineering include releasing sulfur aerosols into the stratosphere to absorb sunlight, seeding clouds to increase reflectivity, and spreading iron particles over the ocean to speed the growth of algae, which can then absorb carbon dioxide. These approaches have in common an assumption that the planet behaves like a machine, treating problems as if they were parts of linear systems. Earth's systems, however, are complex and nonlinear, which means that predicting the outcome will always be impossible no matter how much data one has.

Offsets

Once all the possible reductions have been found and implemented, if some emissions still remain the last step is offsetting. **Offsets** are voluntary payments made to initiatives that reduce the level of greenhouse gases in the atmosphere. An offset is a way of quantifying an emission reduction created by one enterprise, which is then purchased by another enterprise. An offset can be generated by one of many different greenhouse gas reduction activities including wind farms, solar installations, methane-capture facilities, cogeneration plants, and some forests. The offset can then be purchased by anyone, anywhere.

Offsetting is based on the fact that climate change is a global problem. Carbon dioxide emitted in one part of the world spreads throughout the atmosphere, affecting the climate in other parts of the world. Depending upon the industry or activity involved, reducing emissions may cost a great deal more in one sector than in another. Offsets are a way of distributing the impacts and sharing the solutions. For example, an organization that has not become climate neutral might purchase offsets through a wind farm, thus investing in wind power and resulting in more greenhouse gas reduction than would have been possible if it were acting solely on its own.

Offsets are sold on the market in tons of CO_2e. They can be purchased from carbon exchanges, from brokers, or directly. In the US, carbon offset brokers include The Climate Trust. There are as yet no US laws governing the carbon market so it is what is known as a voluntary carbon market. This means that the buyer must be especially careful since there is no regulation. Quality varies, prices vary, and whether or not an offset actually creates an emissions reduction depends upon the extent to which it meets quality criteria.

High-quality carbon offsets are registered with a standard. One of the most reliable international standards is known as the Gold Standard. Offsets registered with the Gold Standard must be verified by third-party auditors accredited by the UN using recognized methodologies. The Climate Registry is a nonprofit organization that establishes standards in North America.

Emissions Trading

Emissions trading is, in a way, the inverse of offsetting. An offset is a reduction in emissions created by one entity and purchased by another entity. Emissions trading, also known as a **cap and trade** system, refers to the buying and selling of permits to pollute. Regulations impose a maximum limit, or cap, on the amount of pollution that may be released. A company that reduces its emissions below the cap can sell its excess emissions allowances. A company whose emissions remain above the cap can buy emissions allowances to make up the difference. Emissions can be verified using a standard such as ISO 14064. The emissions allowances are traded like a commodity.

In Europe, emissions are traded through the European Union (EU) Emissions Trading Scheme, the world's largest system for trading emissions allowances. In the US and Canada, emissions are traded through three voluntary regional markets: the Western Climate Initiative, the Regional Greenhouse Gas Initiative, and the Midwestern Greenhouse Gas Reduction Accord.

Adaptation

Two kinds of responses to Earth's changing climate are required: mitigation, or lowering greenhouse gas emissions to stabilize the climate insofar as possible, and adaptation, adapting to new circumstances that will inevitably come from changes that are already in the pipeline (Henson 2011, 118). Even if the most aggressive climate stabilization efforts are successful and greenhouse gas concentrations are brought lower, the fact remains that we now inhabit a different planet than the one on which human civilization developed and on which it has lived throughout its history. It is hot and getting hotter. Polar ice and mountain glaciers are disappearing. Tropical climates and deserts are advancing. Species are disappearing. Sea level is rising, seawater is acidifying, and coral reefs and fish are vanishing. Hurricanes, floods, and wildfires are increasing in strength and frequency. Climate refugees are growing in numbers. Even greater changes appear to be inevitable in the foreseeable future. We will need to figure out strategies for adapting to changing conditions. This, too, is part of the work of sustainability professionals.

Final Thoughts

After two centuries of fossil fuel consumption, scientists tell us that the Earth system has become destabilized and its condition is guarded. Nevertheless, there are grounds for hope. If we are very committed, soon enough to avoid tipping points, the climate will eventually stabilize and the atmospheric carbon dioxide concentration will begin to fall below 350 ppm. At that point, assuming geochemical cycles, remaining ecosystems, and other planetary components have stabilized, the parts of the Earth system that survive will be able, slowly, to soak up the excess carbon dioxide and restore balance. However, much will have changed. Earth, when it settles into a new state of dynamic equilibrium, will not be the same as it was before (Orr 2009, 157).

Between now and then lies the transition; that is where we live now. The transition back to stability is likely to take centuries. Scientists, from physicists to biologists to climatologists, tell us that the climate impacts of fossil fuels are expected to last at least hundreds and probably thousands of years (Henson 2011, 224). The work we do now is for a future we will never see. This work, contributing to the stabilization of Earth's climate to maintain livability of the biosphere for us and so many fellow creatures, may be the most consequential work any of us will ever do.

Notes

1 These storms are called "hurricanes" when they form in the Atlantic or Pacific oceans off North America, "typhoons" when they form in the north Pacific off Asia, and "cyclones" when they form in the Indian Ocean or in the Southern Hemisphere. There is currently no evidence of changes in either the frequency or intensity of the funnel-shaped columns known as tornados.
2 The average global surface temperature has already increased 0.85°C above pre-industrial levels (IPCC 2014d, 40). An increase of 2°C equals an increase of 3.6°F.
3 A carbon molecule has an atomic weight of 12; it contains 12 protons in its nucleus. A carbon dioxide molecule has an atomic weight of 44; it contains 12 protons from the carbon plus two oxygen atoms with 16 protons in each. So a carbon dioxide molecule is 44/12 heavier than a carbon molecule.
4 Burning firewood releases a tree's lifetime store of carbon back into the atmosphere.
5 *Terra preta* are Portuguese words meaning "black earth."

Further Reading

Blockstein, David E. and Leo Wiegman. *The Climate Solutions Consensus: What We Know and What to Do about It*. Washington, DC: Island Press, 2010.
Henson, Robert. *The Rough Guide to Climate Change*. 3rd ed. New York: Rough Guides Ltd., 2011.
Houghton, John. *Global Warming: The Complete Briefing*. 4th ed. Cambridge: Cambridge University Press, 2009.
Lingl, Paul, Deborah Carlson, and the David Suzuki Foundation. *Doing Business in a New Climate: A Guide to Measuring, Reducing and Offsetting Greenhouse Gas Emissions*. London: Earthscan, 2010.
Orr, David W. *Down to the Wire: Confronting Climate Collapse*. New York: Oxford University Press, 2009.
Stern, Nicholas. *The Economics of Climate Change: The Stern Review*. Cambridge: Cambridge University Press, 2007.
Wolfson, Richard. *Energy, Environment, and Climate*. New York: W. W. Norton, 2008.

Chapter Review

1 What is the difference between weather and climate?
2 If someone said to you that a few degrees warmer would actually be nice, especially for gardeners, how would you respond?
3 Describe the greenhouse effect and how it works for someone who is unfamiliar with the concept.
4 What benefit does the greenhouse effect provide for life on Earth?
5 Without the greenhouse effect, Earth would be too cold for life as we know it to exist. So why is the "greenhouse effect" considered a problem?

6   Why are some gases considered greenhouse gases?
7   Water is a greenhouse gas. Why are scientists usually not concerned about increases in water vapor?
8   What is global warming potential?
9   Give an example of a positive feedback loop.
10 Some observers believe the IPCC understates the risks of climate change. If true, what might cause the understatement?
11 How do scientists use the Vostok ice core to determine temperatures in the past?
12 What is a proxy? Give five examples of proxies used in climate records.
13 Does the melting of Arctic ice cause a rise in sea level?
14 Does ice that slides across Antarctica and drops into the ocean cause a rise in sea level?
15 It is possible that Antarctica's ice sheet may actually grow as the climate warms. How can that be?
16 What do scientists mean when they refer to the "conveyor belt" in the oceans?
17 How could melting permafrost affect climate change?
18 How do oxygen isotopes tell us about climates in the past?
19 What is currently the primary cause of sea-level rise?
20 What is the approximate difference between the average global temperature today and that of the last ice age? Give your answer in both Fahrenheit and Celsius.

Critical Thinking and Discussion

1   While the surface of the Earth has grown warmer in recent years, temperatures in the upper atmosphere have actually gotten cooler. Some people say this means that global warming is a myth. What would you say?
2   People concerned about the possibility of a future ice age say that we must continue adding carbon dioxide to the atmosphere to prevent an ice age from happening. What would you say?
3   Is the hole in the ozone layer related to global warming?
4   In what ways is global climate change a social equity problem, as well as an environmental problem?
5   What examples can you identify in your own experience that indicate a changing climate?
6   A typical carbon dioxide molecule stays in the atmosphere for about 5 years, yet the increase in atmospheric carbon dioxide caused by burning fossil fuels lasts for many years. How do you explain this difference?
7   Human history is full of examples of adaptability and innovation. Some observers believe that predictions of climate impact do not take human adaptability into account, and so climate impacts tend to be overestimated. Do you agree?
8   What do you think conditions might be like in the area where you live if the average temperature increases 6° to 7°F? How will crops, precipitation, water supply, and building design change? You may be able to find a region at a lower latitude than yours where those conditions exist now to use as a guide.
9   Why is the climate changing faster in the Arctic than in other parts of the world?
10 Do you think your carbon footprint has increased or decreased since coming to the college or university where you are studying now?
11 Which do you think is a more effective strategy for lowering carbon dioxide emissions: a carbon tax on emissions, a tax on gasoline, or an incentive such as a tax credit for renewable energy alternatives, or some combination? Why?

12   How can a vegetarian diet have a lower climate change impact than a beef-based diet?

13   Do you think laws should require clothing companies or appliance manufacturers to provide carbon footprint information on their labels? Why or why not?

14   The burning of landfill gas can in some cases qualify as a method for creating carbon offsets. Why is this burning considered a reduction in greenhouse gas emissions? Doesn't combustion create more greenhouse gases?

15   Many of us are aware that burning gasoline contributes to greenhouse gases, yet we continue to drive our cars. If knowledge alone is not enough, what else is needed to get us to change our behavior?

16   The Montreal Protocol was successful at reducing ozone-depleting pollutants. Why have treaties aimed at reducing greenhouse gas emissions not been successful?

17   A coworker argues that with technological innovation and economic growth, the world a few decades from now will have better resources at its disposal for mitigating or adapting to climate change. How would you respond?

18   Most climate-change action plans set a planning horizon at the year 2100 or before. Do you think planners now should be looking beyond 2100, or is that too far in the future to be practical?

19   As other countries rush to compete in the global market, their greenhouse gas emissions rise rapidly as well. Leaders in developing countries argue that they should have the same opportunities to grow and compete that the developed world enjoyed. What strategies and approaches could induce developing nations to reduce their emissions?

20   One carbon sequestration strategy that has been proposed is to capture carbon dioxide from the atmosphere and sequester it in the oceans, which already store large amounts of carbon. What problems might result from this approach?

6   Water

Earth is often called the water planet. Water makes up most of the volume of every living cell, maintains the temperature of the climate, and reshapes mountains and land. Although it covers more than 70 percent of the surface of the blue planet (Stanley 2004, 19), only a tiny percentage is available for human use. The freshwater that is not frozen and is available for use makes up only about 0.76 percent of the total. About 97.5 percent of Earth's water is salt water. The remaining 2.5 percent is freshwater, most of which is frozen in ice and snow. About 30.1 percent of the freshwater is available as groundwater. The water we can see—rivers, lakes, wetlands, clouds, soil moisture, plants and animals—makes up the remaining 0.4 percent of the freshwater (Black and King 2009, 21). Some water, including water in rivers, soil, and living things, recirculates within a time scale of days. Other water, including saltwater in the oceans and freshwater held in glaciers and underground aquifers, has a **residence time** measured in thousands of years (Cunningham and Cunningham 2010, 374). Freshwater in rivers, lakes, and aquifers is known as blue water; water which falls as rain or infiltrates the soil is known as green water.

Freshwater is generally a renewable resource. A constant volume of water moves through the hydrologic cycle where it is continually filtered and recycled, and the total volume of water never changes (Black and King 2009, 12). The problem is not that Earth is running out of water; the problem is that humans pull it from the hydrologic cycle faster than it can be purified and replaced, and that human activities pollute some of the remaining water so that it is not safe to use. The imbalance is further complicated by global climate change.

The combination of overpopulation, overconsumption, and uneven distribution of available water has led to a number of problems involving water. The most visible problem is water scarcity. Less visible, but more long-term, are the resulting symptoms of water scarcity: water pollution, underground aquifer depletion, and damage to ecosystems.

Water scarcity is defined as the point at which all the demands on the supply of water or quality of water cannot be met (FAO 2013, 5). Demands on the world's water include domestic use, manufacturing, irrigation for agriculture and landscapes, and the needs of natural ecosystems. Given growing populations, growing consumption patterns, and changing dietary expectations, there is not enough water to feed people, meet urban needs, and protect the health of the life-support systems of the biosphere. Water scarcity escalates competition between people; particularly in developing countries, water scarcity is an issue of poverty that leads to political conflict (Black and King 2009, 44).

Uneven Distribution

Most of the freshwater on the planet is frozen and not accessible for us to use. In addition, there is a mismatch between where water is located and where people live, a problem that is especially serious in developing countries. Many countries have areas both of water scarcity and of water abundance.

In the US, most of the fastest growing cities are in regions with the least water: Texas, Arizona, California, and Nevada, and a large percentage of the nation's irrigated agriculture is concentrated in areas with limited water supplies, including the Great Plains and southern California. In California, 80 percent of the demand for water lies in the southern two-thirds of the state, most of which receives only a few inches of rainfall a year, while about 70 percent of California's available water falls as precipitation in the less-populated northern third of the state (Bourne 2010, 141). A massive system of pipes, tunnels, and canals called the Central Valley Project (CVP) moves water from northern California to the cities and farmlands to the south, where more than half the nation's vegetables, fruits, and nuts are produced. Continued water extraction from the Sacramento–San Joaquin Delta in northern California has taken a growing environmental toll on endangered salmon, smelt, and larger ecosystems. Cutbacks in water shipments in an effort to protect these endangered species have taken a financial toll on farmers. Moving all that water requires a large amount of energy and releases carbon emissions.

The other major source of water for southern California is the Colorado River. Beginning in the Rocky Mountains, the river flows through the Grand Canyon, crosses into Mexico and empties into the Gulf of California. Along the way it is impounded by massive dams including Glen Canyon and Hoover Dam. Its water is used for agriculture and cities in seven western states, where it also irrigates desert golf courses, keeps lawns bright green, fills desert swimming pools, and gushes through fountains in Las Vegas casinos. On many days the river's flow is so depleted that it does not reach the Gulf of California at all (Withgott and Brennan 2009, 262). The plant communities, fish populations, and other members of the river's once-rich ecosystems have been devastated by these severe reductions in flow.

Water rights to the Colorado River were established for 7 western states in 1922. The Prior Appropriation Doctrine gives priority to those who claim it first, but water rights must be used or they are forfeited, encouraging farmers to take more than they need. Federal subsidies give farmers incentives to grow cotton and other water-hungry crops. Alternatives could include phasing out subsidies, redistributing water rights more equitably, or creating a water market where farmers could trade water rights (Lustgarten et al., 2015).

Box 6.1   The Aral Sea Disaster

The Aral Sea in Central Asia was once the fourth largest lake in the world, covering an area of 26,000 square miles. In the 1960s, the Soviet Union began diverting water from the two major rivers that fed the Aral Sea to supply irrigation for the production of cotton and other export crops across millions of acres of desert land in Uzbekistan, Kazakhstan, and other Central Asian states (NASA Earth Observatory 2000). While desert cotton crops blossomed, the Aral Sea was devastated. The surface area of the lake has since shrunk by about 74 percent (Aral Sea Foundation n.d.). A drought in 2009 stopped the flow of one of the rivers, and in 2014 the eastern basin disappeared completely (NASA Earth Observatory 2014). According to a UN estimate, if present trends continue the Aral Sea will be gone by 2020 (Aral Sea Foundation n.d.).

(continued)

(continued)

The lake was once so large that it influenced local climate, but as it dried up, its moderating influence on climate disappeared. Local summers became hotter and drier. Local winters became colder and longer, with shorter growing seasons.

The salt concentration in the Aral Sea rose from 10 percent to over 23 percent, killing most of the creatures who once lived there (Campbell 2001). A once-thriving fishing industry employing 60,000 people was destroyed, and the communities that depended on it collapsed. Towns such as Muynak, Uzbekistan, which once flourished on the shore of a sea now over 90 miles away, feature ghostly piers stretching out over expanses of desert littered with the rusting hulks of stranded ships (Heintz 2010).

The salty water is polluted by fertilizers and pesticides used on cotton crops. Dust storms stir up the dry, salty soil from the former lakebed, spreading toxic dust, salt particles, and chemical residues through the air. Widespread respiratory and nutritional illnesses have resulted, along with high rates of some forms of cancer including throat cancer (Aral Sea Foundation n.d.). The salty, polluted dust from the dried lakebed settles onto farm fields. Crop yields have fallen, even in the fields that the irrigation diversion was intended to help.

The cotton that is destroying the Aral Sea is picked by forced labor (Hoskins 2014). Although a number of apparel brands worldwide have signed pledges through the Responsible Sourcing Network and Anti-Slavery International never to use Uzbek cotton, complicated supply chains and a lack of traceability make such pledges difficult to enforce.

Depletion of Nonrenewable Aquifers

About a fifth of the water we use comes from aquifers (Black and King 2009, 26). Some of this water is considered a nonrenewable resource. When rain falls in the hydrologic cycle, some evaporates, some runs off the surface, and some infiltrates through the soil and into sand, gravel, and pore spaces in the rock layers below. When all the spaces in the lower soil layers are filled with water, the soil is saturated; this zone of saturation is called **groundwater**, and the top of this zone is called the **water table**. Almost half the water used in the United States comes from groundwater. A large deposit of groundwater is called an **aquifer**. Places where water can infiltrate the ground and eventually reach the aquifer are called recharge zones.

The world's largest known aquifer, the Ogallala Aquifer, has helped to turn the US Great Plains into one of the world's most productive agricultural regions. The Ogallala is what is known as a fossil aquifer; its water was deposited millions of years ago and it will take thousands of years to recharge (Kostigen 2010, 125). The Ogallala is for all practical purposes a nonrenewable resource, and it is disappearing. About 11 percent of the aquifer's volume has been lost since pumping began in the 1950s (Sandford 2009, 190). In some parts of Texas, Oklahoma, and Kansas, the water table has dropped more than 100 feet (Brown 2009, 40) and wells have gone dry on thousands of farms. As water tables fall, the energy required to pump the remaining water increases. The gap between rich and poor increases as farmers must drill deeper wells, buy larger pumps, and consume more electricity to run the pumps. Farmers who cannot afford the additional expense may lose their farms.

No one knows how much water is actually being withdrawn. Water managers on the High Plains have made conscious decisions to mine this resource for one-time use and not to maintain accurate drilling records (Sandford 2009, 195). Someday it will no longer be economical to draw water from the Ogallala and at that point, current forms of agriculture on the High Plains will either need to change or disappear.

Water rights to the Ogallala Aquifer in Texas are governed by an agreement called the Rule of Capture or Prior Appropriation (ibid., 191). Under this rule, the first person to lay claim to a piece of land can use as much water as they want and then owns that right in perpetuity. The next person to lay claim can take as much as they want of what is left. The rule also says that residents of Texas can legally withdraw all the water they want to from under neighboring states.

Aquifer depletion sometimes leads to subsidence, or sinking, of land. The San Joaquin Valley in California has sunk more than 33 feet in the last 50 years because of excessive pumping of groundwater (Cunningham and Cunningham 2010, 382). The cities of Baton Rouge, Phoenix, Houston, and Mexico City are all dealing with subsidence caused by excess groundwater pumping (Withgott 2009, 263).

If groundwater near coastal areas is overpumped, saltwater can be pulled into freshwater aquifers, contaminating them so that they are no longer usable. This **saltwater intrusion** is occurring in parts of southeastern US and California. Many of the world's largest cities, which are heavy users of groundwater, are located in coastal areas and can expect increasing problems with saltwater contamination (Miller and Spoolman 2009, 323). Rising sea levels from global climate change will further increase the incidence of saltwater intrusion and decrease the amount of usable groundwater in coastal areas.

As populations increase and people move out of poverty demand for freshwater rises, and much of the increased demand is met by pumping water out of the ground. Satellites which measure the gravitational pull of water masses show that 13 of the world's 37 largest aquifers are being depleted, with the greatest water stress occurring in four aquifers in Saudi Arabia, India and Pakistan, northern Africa, and California's Central Valley (Richey et al. 2015, 5217).

Threats to Human and Ecosystem Health

Salt is not the only contaminant of water supplies. In the developing world, 90 percent of human waste is discarded, untreated, into rivers (Black and King 2009, 14). In many parts of the world, lack of access to clean water is the largest cause of disease transmission and, as a result, poverty.

Chemical pollution is damaging to ecosystems and to human health as rivers and lakes are increasingly polluted by fertilizer, pesticide residues, chemical wastes, and industrial spills. Pesticide and fertilizer contamination has been found in aquifers including many areas of the Ogallala, and it is not known how much more is still percolating through the soil on its way to the aquifer (Sandford 2009, 193). For years, people used water as a convenient place to dump wastes, with the idea that water would dilute any harmful substances. An old saying was, "dilution is the solution to pollution." We now know that saying is generally not correct. Many chemical toxins are cumulative, which means that when they enter the food chain they build up in the tissues of larger animals who have eaten smaller animals. Many humans eat fish or other animals and so, similar to large predators, are at the top of a food chain where toxins can accumulate and cause long-term health problems.

Depletion of aquifers is another threat to biodiversity. Plants, animals, and other organisms in lakes, rivers, and underground water systems have evolved to suit the particular ecosystems where they live. When water is drawn down, those ecosystems change and the organisms in them face local extinction. Aquifers such as the Ogallala move underground, but they also flow onto the surface of the land in some places, creating wetlands that cleanse water, absorb floodwaters, and are important habitats for wildlife (Cunningham and Cunningham 2010, 376). Wetlands work as natural sponges, holding back surface runoff, producing an even stream flow year round, and allowing time for water to infiltrate back into aquifers. When water tables that are the top surfaces of aquifers fall, many of these wetlands disappear.

While water is distributed unevenly in space, it is also distributed unevenly in time. Many regions have rainy seasons and dry seasons. People build dams to create temporary water storage, and while the dams help to even out the variation in water availability, they create other problems in the environment.

Dams present a major threat to biodiversity. Not only do they kill outright the living things that are inundated when reservoirs first fill, they also alter the original flows of rivers and streams, interrupting natural processes and damaging ecosystems both above and below the dams. Migrating fish are blocked from swimming upstream to spawn and juvenile fish are blocked from moving downstream. Fish ladders of various designs have been added along-side many dams, some more successful than others. Even in dams where fish ladders allow migrating salmon to pass, sedimentation behind the dams makes it hard for salmon to thrive and can shift the fish community toward more silt-tolerant species.

Dams alter the natural flows of rivers. Undammed rivers are like living things. Year to year they meander back and forth across the land, leaving behind complex channels, rich soil deposits and mosaics of habitats as they go. Along their margins and in the **hyporheic zones** below, plants, animals, and other organisms adapted to shifting river patterns thrive. This changes when dams are built. As mechanical flood control devices, dams turn water flows on and off like giant faucets. Seasonal flow variations are dampened, more or less steady streams of released water scour the bottoms of channels, side channels disappear, and river meanders become fixed in place.

With steady year-round flows and water held back behind dams, rivers no longer do their primary work of moving rock and building soil. Sediment starvation below dams results in scouring, loss of habitat, loss of native fish species, and degradation of native streamside eco-systems (Riley 1998, 355). Meanwhile the sediment that would have been carried by the rivers builds up in the reservoirs behind the dams where even along the banks it blocks the amount of light that can penetrate. Aquatic plant communities change, and with them the inverte-brate and fish communities. Decaying organic matter trapped in sediments releases methane, a powerful greenhouse gas (Black and King 2009, 36).

Consumption

Humans in the industrialized world use huge quantities of water to support our lifestyle of a meat-rich diet and plentiful consumer goods. Direct water use is only a small part of the total picture of water consumption. Everything we eat not only contains water but also used addi-tional water when it was grown. The concept of **virtual water** describes the quantity of water embedded in food and products, measured at the places where they were actually produced (Hoekstra and Chapagain 2008, 8). The virtual water content of a thing is also sometimes referred to as its **water footprint** (ibid., 3).

The higher we go up the food chain, the greater the virtual water content. The virtual water content of a pound of wheat is 172 gallons, while the virtual water content of a pound of beef is 1,500 gallons (ibid., 13). Switching from a hamburger to a vegeburger for one meal can save about 750 gallons of water (Kostigen 2010, 44).

Every object we use required water for its manufacture. For example, the virtual water content of a new pair of jeans is about 3,000 gallons (ibid., 67) and the virtual water content of a new car is about 39,000 gallons (ibid., 92). Paper, metal, and electronics industries are big water users. The manufacture of computer chips uses large volumes of several toxic chemicals and then requires enormous quantities of high-quality treated water. The mining industry uses chemicals including mercury and cyanide to extract ores and must then wash the ores, producing large volumes of polluted water. Chemical plants, petroleum plants, and machinery manufacturers are other major industrial users of water. These industries tend to be heavy polluters as well.

More than half the water used by industry goes into producing energy. Some electricity is generated by hydropower, using water behind dams to turn turbines. In fossil fuel and nuclear power stations, water is used for cooling. A growing consumer of water is irrigation water used to grow alternative biofuels including corn.

Worldwide, agriculture makes up 70 percent of the embedded water use, 20 percent of water use comes from industry, and 10 percent comes from domestic use (Sachs 2015, 189). In the US about 41 percent of water use is for agriculture, 46 percent comes from industry, and 13 percent is for domestic use (Black and King 2009, 116). We use a lot of water for drinking, bathing, and cleaning, but the proportion appears modest compared to our consumption of virtual water embedded in the food we eat and the things we buy.

Box 6.2 Bottled Water

Bottled water is a curious industry in which companies make billions of dollars a year selling drinking water in bottles. Consumers drink bottled water because they believe it is more benign than tap water. Is bottled water healthier? According to government and industry estimates, about 25 percent of bottled water is actually just tap water, often with no further treatment (Gleick 2004, 29). And in many jurisdictions, water quality and testing standards for bottled water are surprisingly less stringent than those for tap water (Gleick 2011, 41). In the US, tap water is regulated by the EPA which requires testing in certified laboratories; bottled water is regulated as a food by the Food and Drug Administration (FDA), which makes bottlers responsible for their own testing and does not require them to disclose the water's source, treatment, or contaminant content (Leonard 2010b).

Not only is the purity of bottled water questionable, the consumption of bottled water comes with heavy environmental costs including groundwater depletion, fossil fuel consumption, and pollution. Some companies simply bottle tap water, but others pump it from springs and aquifers. Additional water is required to produce the bottled version; 3 gallons of virtual water are embedded in every 1 gallon of bottled water.

Plastic is made of petroleum; millions of barrels of oil a year are consumed to produce plastic bottles for water, and millions more consumed to transport them, sometimes thousands of miles from their source (Gleick 2011, 95). Manufacturing the plastic generates toxins and greenhouse gases. Once bought by consumers, plastic bottles are usually thrown away after a single use. Most of them end up in landfills and incinerators, where incineration releases more toxic gases and more greenhouse

(continued)

(continued)

gases. It is estimated that 25 percent of our discarded plastic bottles end up in the ocean (Grossman 2008). Over time they break apart into tiny pieces of plastic that get eaten by marine animals who mistake them for food and then either suffocate or starve because the plastic bits in their digestive systems prevent them from eating real food. Meanwhile the bits of plastic and the toxins they carry move up the food chain (Cole et al. 2011, 2588).

Regardless what kind of water is in that bottle, consider the meaning it represents: we are so uncertain about the condition of modern water that we pay more for bottled water than we do for gasoline. On the water planet, where all of life depends utterly upon this liquid resource, which cycles continuously around the planet and through every living cell, that bottle of water says, in effect, we give up; our fundamental resource is so ruined that we cannot use it, and rather than fix it we have turned to artificial life support systems.

In any organized water system, water has to be delivered and it has to be paid for. In current water systems worldwide, water is heavily subsidized. Users pay much less than the actual cost of providing water, and they do not pay at all for the ecosystem services lost through the environmental damage caused by dams, pollution, and groundwater depletion. Subsidized water means that users have little incentive to reduce their usage. On one hand, low water prices create the impression that water is abundant when it is not, and often result in low water productivity (Brown 2009, 174). On the other hand, higher water prices create hardships for people who already live in poverty.

Effects of Climate Change

A final, big piece of the water puzzle is global climate change. Currently, population and economic growth are the most significant factors affecting water issues; after 2050, climate change is expected to be the major driver (OECD 2012, 213). Much of the danger from climate change will arise from water, either too much or too little. In some regions flooding will increase; in others droughts will become more frequent and more severe. Countries already suffering from water scarcity will be the hardest hit. Globally, crop irrigation requirements may rise 5 to 20 percent by 2080 (FAO 2011b, 123). Glaciers that now feed rivers during the dry season will retreat.

Meltwater from glaciers in the Himalayas, the Andes, and other mountain ranges is currently the primary source of freshwater for one billion people (Black and King 2009, 32). These glaciers are shrinking as the temperature warms. As glaciers melt, the rivers they feed will temporarily see increased water flow, but once they are gone, the people who depended on them will face serious and permanent water shortages.

Water Conservation

Water is a renewable resource, constantly replenished by the hydrologic cycle. Renewal takes time, however, and the quantity available for use is declining. Humans must find ways to increase the amount of water to which we have access. Two options are possible: the traditional approach to solving water problems is to locate new supplies; an alternative approach is to use less water. Using less water or using it more efficiently is known as water conservation or water efficiency. Water conservation can take place on the supply side or the demand side.

Supply-side activities include harvesting rainwater, desalinizing seawater, or protecting an aquifer or a watershed that supplies drinking water. New York City faced a supply-side problem in the 1990s. The City's water originates in the Catskill Mountains, and for years was exceptionally clean. However, increased development in the watershed brought run-off and pollution loads, and New York's water quality dropped below EPA water quality standards. A new water filtration plant would handle the problem, but would cost $6 to $8 billion to construct and $300 million a year to operate. The city chose instead to restore the watershed. They purchased forest land and signed agreements with 30 watershed communities. The agreements provided money to protect the working landscapes of family farms and woodlots, upgrade septic systems, and foster partnership projects for innovative agriculture and forestry programs (Wilson 2002b, 107). The conservation program was so successful that in 2007 the EPA, which requires filtration in almost all the water systems in the US and generally requires re-evaluations every 5 years, ruled that New York's water supply was so clean and their conservation plans so effective that the city's water did not need to be filtered for at least another 10 years (DePalma 2007).

On the demand side, more efficient use results from initiatives such as installing low-flow plumbing fixtures, repairing leaks, recycling water from cooling systems, or implementing more efficient landscape irrigation practices. Reduced water consumption can also come from individual consumer choices. Eating lower on the food chain reduces virtual water use, and reusing or recycling products reduces consumption of the virtual water embedded in new consumer goods.

In many cities, reducing water consumption has decreased or eliminated the need to construct expensive new public water infrastructure, including pipes, equipment, and buildings, which would have been needed to supply additional water and treat additional wastewater (Kats 2010, 33). Using water consumes energy for pumping, heating, conveying, and treating water and wastewater, so reducing water consumption results in reduced energy use as well.

Residential Water Conservation

Programs to reduce residential water consumption are offered by most local utilities, who hire water conservation technicians or other water specialists. Landscape irrigation is often the biggest residential use of water (US EPA 2013b). However, utility programs typically focus on indoor water use first because indoor efficiency measures are relatively inexpensive and easy to accomplish.

A water efficiency program includes two types of measures, technical and behavioral. Technical measures include installing water-saving fixtures such as low-flow showerheads or converting landscapes to efficient irrigation systems. These measures tend to be long-lasting. Practices or process measures include changing water-use behavior, such as taking shorter showers or reducing the amount of water applied to a lawn. These changes can be encouraged through periodic informational brochures and mailings, in-school educational programs, and personal contact through activities such as home water audits. Behavioral changes require investments of time spent on education, ongoing reminders, and follow-up. Studies show that the most effective water efficiency programs involve both kinds of measures, technical and behavioral (Vickers 2001, 6).

One of the first steps in a water efficiency program is to analyze existing conditions using a water audit. A water technician uses utility bills to determine how much water a household uses, looks for leaks in toilets and faucets and recommends repairs. They may also evaluate landscape irrigation methods and make recommendations. The water audit provides the homeowner with written materials including a checklist of findings, a list of recommended efficiency measures, and a sheet with calculations of costs, potential savings, and payback period (Green 2010, 20). Education is a component of an audit; the customer learns about efficiency ratings on fixtures and appliances, how to read their water meter, how to detect leaks, and how to apply for any rebates that are available.

Commercial Water Conservation

Sites in the commercial sector use large quantities of water and thus some of the greatest improvement opportunities in water efficiency are possible in these types of sites. This sector includes three categories of users: (1) commercial sites include all types of businesses that provide or distribute retail services or products;[1] (2) institutional sites include all types of public facilities such as government buildings, schools, prisons, and hospitals; (3) industrial sites are facilities that are involved in the manufacturing and processing of products. These three categories of commercial, institutional, and industrial sites are collectively referred to as CII or ICI (ibid., 71).

Water utilities often hire engineers or experienced water technicians to conduct or assist with audits at ICI sites, which are typically complex. Audits and efficiency upgrades can also be managed by water service companies or WASCOs (ibid.). The site and the WASCO sign a performance contract, and the WASCO's fee is paid from a portion of the savings realized by water-use upgrades they implement.

Cooling systems use water and are often the largest water consumers in an ICI facility (Vickers 2001, 288). Several types of cooling systems are used. Water may be used in some medical facilities, machine tools, and older cooling equipment in a configuration known as once-through or single-pass cooling, where the water flows through, absorbs heat, and is disposed of. Water conservation specialists try to replace single-pass equipment or find ways to reuse the cooling water.

A common type of cooling system is called a cooling tower, used in most large buildings. Water flows through a building space or piece of equipment, picks up heat, and flows through the cooling tower, where evaporation lowers the temperature of the water. The water is then recirculated. Total dissolved solids (TDS) in the water must be kept below a maximum range; when TDS are above a certain level, some water must be bled off and replaced with make-up water. Thus maintaining water quality is an important step in water conservation. One efficiency measure is to use condensate water from large air conditioning systems, which contains almost no minerals and can be reused as makeup water in cooling towers (ibid., 307).

Domestic Water Use

Domestic water use refers to water used by fixtures such as toilets, showerheads, and faucets together with appliances such as clothes washers and dishwashers. These fixtures and appliances are used in all types of buildings in residential, commercial, industrial, and institutional settings.

Toilet flushing is the largest single domestic use of water in the US, with an average of 5.1 flushes per person per day in homes and 3 flushes per person per day in the workplace (ibid., 26). The US Energy Policy Act of 1992, known as EPAct, requires that all toilets sold and installed in the US must be low-volume fixtures using no more than 1.6 gallons per flush (gpf); urinals are required to use 1.0 gpf or less. Prior to EPAct, toilets typically used 3.5 gpf. (Those sold before the late 1970s used from 4.0 to 7.0 gpf.) Toilet replacement is often the first action in a water-efficiency program.

High-efficiency toilets feature a dual-flush design. Selecting a full flush for solid waste, usually by pushing a button, uses 1.6 gpf; selecting a half flush for liquid waste uses half the volume, or 0.8 gpf (Green 2010, 38). Automatic electronic flushing controls found in some commercial and public restrooms are used to reduce the spread of bacteria; they are not water-saving devices (Vickers 2001, 30).

The second largest use of water in residential settings is clothes washers. Americans wash an average of 0.37 loads per person per day (ibid., 117). Older washing machines use 35 gallons per load (gpl) or more; high-efficiency residential washers use an average of 27 gpl. Commercial washers are larger. Dishwashers make up a small portion of residential use, using an average of 1 gallon per person per day (ibid., 127). In commercial restaurants and hotels they are large consumers of water; in other settings they may be absent.

In residential settings, the third largest use of water is showerheads. Showerhead use in commercial and institutional settings varies by location. EPAct rules require that all showerheads sold and installed in the US must be low-volume fixtures using no more than 2.5 gallons per minute (gpm) at a water pressure of 80 pounds per square inch (psi) or 2.2 gpm at a water pressure of 60 psi. Showerheads sold prior to 1992 used 3.0 to 8.0 gpm.

Faucets have the same EPAct flow requirements as showerheads: 2.5 gpm at 80 psi or 2.2 gpm at 60 psi. Low-flow showerheads and faucets achieve their efficiency by injecting air into the water stream. They can be inexpensively retrofitted by inserting aerators. Hospitals have special faucet requirements and restrict the use of aerators to prevent the spread of water droplets and bacteria (Green 2010, 74).

Irrigation

Landscape irrigation can be a major consumer of water in both residential and commercial sites. In parts of the arid US West, 70 percent of residential water may be used for keeping lawns green (Kostigen 2010, 13). In existing landscapes, professional irrigation system design can be used to reduce the amount of water wasted. Drip irrigation uses 30 to 70 percent less water than conventional sprinklers (Ayres and Ayres 2010, 156). Mulching, letting leaves stay where they fall, and building healthy soil allow landscapes to retain water longer. The most effective strategy for reducing outdoor water use is to use native or regionally adapted plants and to replace lawns with plantings that need less water.

Globally, agriculture is the largest consumer of water. Seventy percent of the water used worldwide and 41 percent of the water used in the US is for agriculture (Black and King 2009, 13), but most of the water applied to fields runs off and is never used by plants. Organic farming strategies that improve soils and retain soil moisture increase water efficiency.

Desalination

Earth has a fixed volume of water that continuously circulates through the hydrologic cycle. When we take water supplies from rivers or from groundwater we are borrowing water from that cycle. Another and very large storage compartment from which we might borrow water lies in the world's oceans. This water is salty, so it must be desalted before humans can use it. Desalination, sometimes called desalination, takes water from the sea, removes the salt, and distributes it to users. The water eventually flows back to the sea as some part of the hydrologic cycle.

Two technologies are used to remove salt from seawater: reverse osmosis and distillation. Reverse osmosis is a form of microfiltration or nanofiltration. In this process, water under pressure is pushed through a membrane; water molecules pass through, but salt molecules do not. A reverse osmosis desalination plant in Tampa Bay, Florida supplies about 10 percent of the region's drinking water (Lohan 2008, 127), and a plant in San Diego, California supplies about 8 percent of that region's needs (SDCWA 2015). The largest installations are in the Middle East, whose countries produce 70 percent of the world's desalinated water (US Geological Survey 2013). Distillation is the process of boiling water to produce steam, which is then captured by condensing the water vapor. The method is ancient. It was used on early sailing ships to produce drinking water from seawater and is still used on ships today. Distillation removes more contaminants than any other water treatment method.

Both methods of desalination are expensive. Drinking water produced through either reverse osmosis or distillation costs 3 to 5 times as much as water from conventional treatment methods, sometimes more. The processes require large amounts of energy, leading to concerns about greenhouse gas emissions (Pearce 2006, 233). Engineers are researching strategies for using combined heat and power (CHP) for desalination plants that use distillation. Biologists are concerned that marine environments and sea life can be threatened by concentrated brine effluent, and high numbers of fish and other organisms can be killed in desalination plant intake structures (Lohan 2008, 127).

Rainwater Harvesting

During a single rainstorm, millions of gallons of rainwater can run off into storm sewers. Meanwhile owners of buildings, some of which consume millions of gallons of freshwater per day, pay to treat and import other water. The entire water supply is treated to highest-quality drinking water standards whether it is used for drinking, washing cars, or flushing toilets, while clean water from the sky is sent down drains.

Rainwater harvesting is the practice of collecting rainwater, storing it, and using it later. Water that falls as rain is known as **stormwater**. Strategies for collecting, cleansing, and infiltrating stormwater runoff include rain gardens, bioswales, porous paving, and green roofs.

When stormwater is collected and then stored for later use, the process is known as **rainwater harvesting**. Collecting and storing rainwater is not a new idea. As designer Michael McClary observed: "Irrigation of the land with seawater desalinated by fusion power is ancient. It is called Rain" (Kinkade-Levario 2007, 1). Rainwater cisterns are found in archaeological and historical sites from around the world (ibid., 6).

A rainwater harvesting system contains six basic components: a catchment area such as a roof; conveyance devices such as pipes or gutters; filters and roof washing to remove debris; storage in a tank, also known as a cistern; a distribution system using either gravity or pumps; and purification systems for filtering and disinfecting the water if it is to be used as **potable** water. Potable water is water that is suitable for drinking. Less than half the domestic water use in buildings requires potable water (Mendler et al. 2006, 88). Nonpotable uses include toilet flushing, cooling, fire sprinklers, and irrigation.

A building roof is usually used as the catchment area. In arid climates such as Texas and Arizona, additional open sheds known as rain barns are built for collecting rainwater from as large an area as possible. Galvanized roofs, which contain zinc, and copper roofs should not be used for collecting rainwater. The best water quality comes from smooth surfaces such as metal or tile roofing. Several brands of elastomeric or rubber-like paint have been approved by the National Sanitation Foundation (NSF) for coating roofs that will collect water for potable uses.

Once rain falls on a roof it must be conveyed to the storage location. This is done through some form of gutters or channels together with downspouts or other pipes. Gutters and down-spouts are used on both residential and commercial buildings. They must have screens to prevent debris from entering, and need to be large enough to handle the volume of water that will flow from the particular roof being drained. Rain chains hung from gutters are some-times used in place of downspouts to guide the flow of water.

Debris and pollutants build up on a roof between rains. When rain first falls on the roof it carries the majority of the debris and pollutants with it. This is called the **first flush**. First flush devices collect and discard this first quantity of rainfall. One simple form of first flush device is a standpipe that fills with contaminated first-rainfall water, then diverts subsequent water to the main conveyance pipe. These devices typically collect about 10 gallons of rainwater for every 1,000 square feet of roof area (Kinkade-Levario 2007, 23) and must be emptied after each rainstorm. Larger rainwater systems add roof washers that include holding chambers and filters.

Storage makes it possible to use harvested rainwater during times when no rain is falling. The container for storing water is known as a cistern, whether it is above or below ground. It can also be called a tank. Water storage is usually the most visible and highest-cost compo-nent of a rainwater collection system. Some designers avoid strictly utilitarian tanks, which convey the message that sustainable choices are unattractive. Although utilitarian tanks made of fiberglass or polyethylene are available, most commercial designs feature either aestheti-cally appealing aboveground tanks that celebrate the use of rainwater, integral cisterns that are built into a building's structure, or large underground cisterns. The tank lining must be rated as food grade if water is to be for potable uses. Small tanks may be 500- or 1,000-gallon capacity, while large cisterns may hold over 100,000 gallons.

The distribution system moves water from where it is stored to where it will be used. If the tank is higher than the place where water is used, water will flow. However, domestic fixtures require water pressure in order to operate properly. Municipal water systems provide water at 40 to 80 psi, which they do by storing water in elevated tanks or reservoirs. It is the weight of the water that creates the pressure. Because a water tank would need to be about 92 feet above a fixture in order to supply 40 psi through gravity alone, most distribution sys-tems use pumps (Banks and Heinichen 2004, 32). Filters screen out particulate matter before water reaches a pump.

If water is used for nonpotable uses such as irrigation and toilet flushing, no additional purification is needed. For potable water systems, additional microfiltration and disinfection are required, and the water must be tested regularly. Ultraviolet light is often used to kill bacteria and viruses. A backflow preventer is required to prevent non-treated water from contaminating the potable supply.

Large rainwater harvesting systems are designed by architects, landscape architects, or engineers. Smaller residential systems can be designed by homeowners. Knowing how much rainwater can be captured, referred to as the **rainwater endowment**, requires knowing the area of the roof, the annual rainfall amount, and the monthly rainfall distribution, available from the local weather service. About 75 percent of the average rainfall can actually be stored; the rest will be lost from evaporation, roof washing, and catchment inefficiencies (Kwok and Grondzik 2007, 246).

Calculating the sizes of rainwater system components requires developing a water budget, a process somewhat like balancing a checkbook. Calculation begins with a monthly water balance. For each month the amount of demand—for irrigation or toilet flushing, for example—is subtracted from the cumulative balance and the average amount of rainfall expected in that month is added to the balance. Months in which demand exceeds rainfall are months where supplemental storage will be required. The maximum volume of storage needed determines tank size. The system can only collect as much rainfall as the tank will hold.

Graywater Reuse

Water treatment facilities consume a lot of energy treating water to bring it up to potable standards. Much of this highest quality drinking water is then used to wash cars, flush toilets, and water shrubbery. An alternative to rainwater is to use **graywater** for those secondary uses. Graywater, also spelled greywater, is wastewater collected from bathroom sinks, showers, bathtubs, and clothes washers.

In some US states and European countries, plumbing codes allow this water to be collected in a separate plumbing system, filtered, and stored, then used for toilets or outdoor irrigation. Graywater must be separated from potable water supply and requires clearly labeled dual plumbing systems. Graywater is traditionally conveyed through purple pipe. Some designers of new buildings in regions where graywater reuse is not yet legal provide separate plumbing so that if building codes change in the future, a graywater system can be installed with minimal disturbance and cost.

To make a graywater reuse system effective, the building must have enough potable water demands to produce sufficient graywater and must have enough nonpotable uses, such as toilet flushing and irrigation, to accommodate the graywater generated. In commercial buildings graywater can come from showers, sinks, and laundries as well as air conditioning condensate water and foundation drain water, and can be used for toilets and irrigation as well as cooling-tower makeup water and fire suppression systems.

Blackwater, which is wastewater from toilets, kitchen sinks, and dishwashers, must be drained away from a building in separate blackwater pipes, and by law cannot be mixed with graywater.

Blackwater is often treated on-site in green building projects. Modern treatment technology may be slightly modified and repackaged, but it is not new. For years, municipal wastewater treatment plants have been using biological methods to purify water before it is used in irrigation or released to rivers.

Wastewater Treatment

Wastewater is all of the water that runs into building drains. In most buildings the blackwater and graywater flows into the same wastewater drain lines. All of this wastewater is required by law to be treated before being released. Regardless of technology, all wastewater treatment relies on living organisms to break down organic and chemical wastes.

In non-urban areas wastewater flows into individual underground septic tanks where bacteria break down wastes. Water then flows from the tanks into underground drain fields and finally infiltrates the soil.

In urban areas wastewater is transported to sewage treatment plants where bacteria do the work of breaking down wastes. A sewage treatment process includes three levels: primary treatment is a mechanical process in which solids are removed. Debris is removed by screening, then grit is removed by allowing the wastewater to rest in settling basins. These basins are usually the largest structures in a conventional wastewater treatment plant. Secondary treatment is a biological process in which aerobic bacteria break down organic wastes and some metals and chemicals. Tertiary treatment, also known as polishing or finishing, is the final filtering and disinfection process. Although bacteria do most of the work, wastewater treatment still uses energy. Almost 4 percent of the electricity produced in the US is used to pump and treat wastewater (Kats 2010, 37).

Sewage treatment lagoons have been used for decades by colleges and small towns as an alternative method. Like treatment plants, lagoons use primary, secondary, and tertiary stages. Wastewater passes through a grinder which pulverizes or removes debris, then flows to a primary lagoon, where particulates settle out and bacteria begin breaking down wastes. From there the water flows to a secondary lagoon and then to a final tertiary lagoon.

Some communities use **constructed wetlands**. These wetlands may be combined with existing wastewater lagoons or they may provide the sole treatment system. A constructed wetland is engineered to use the natural processes from the communities of plants, soils, and bacteria living in association with plant roots which are found in wetlands. Most constructed wetlands used for wastewater treatment are a form known as subsurface-flow wetlands, in which wastewater flows through gravel below the surface (Campbell and Ogden 1999, 101). Aerobic and anaerobic bacteria break down wastes and the water then flows to a drain field. Microclimates around plant roots provide habitats for both anaerobic bacteria surrounding the root zones and for aerobic bacteria around the root hairs, where roots fix oxygen transported from plant stems (ibid., 22).

Membrane biological reactors or bioreactors are essentially compact constructed wetland processes contained within a series of large tanks, where bacteria living on membranes break down nutrients. They are used in commercial buildings, where they are often installed in basements.

Living Machines are patented wastewater treatment systems. Primary treatment takes place in a series of large open tanks where solids are settled and aerobic bacteria warmed by sunlight begin to break down organic matter. From the primary tanks wastewater flows into tanks filled with water hyacinths, cattails, bulrushes and other aquatic plants that take up nutrients and provide habitat for bacteria in their root zones. The water then flows through subsurface gravels where plants filter remaining organic wastes, take up metals, and secrete compounds that kill pathogens. Bacteria-laden water flows into other tanks, where zooplankton and snails consume the microorganisms and are themselves eaten by fish who can then be eaten or sold. Finally, the water flows into polishing wetlands for final filtering. If potable water is needed, it is disinfected using ultraviolet light or ozone generators. Living Machines are typically seen in greenhouses, but systems can also be designed to work outside.

A design known as a natural swimming pool or natural swimming pond cleanses water using constructed wetlands. The design uses two basins: one pool for swimming and one regeneration pool where water is cleansed by aerobic bacteria and wetland plants including iris, cattails, and water lilies growing in gravel. Community or public pools using this technology are permitted in Europe. Building codes do not allow them to be built as public pools in the US but they can be installed at private residences.

Stormwater

Where land is left undisturbed the natural processes connecting water, soil, and living things work together in self-sustaining systems. Root hairs of plants, surrounded by thriving communities of fungus and other microorganisms, separate particles of soil. Tiny animals burrow among the grains and loosen the soil. As roots die and decompose they leave more spaces between soil particles where more animals burrow. Leaves and stems from above ground fall and form a protective layer of mulch. Earthworms pull them below the surface where bacteria break them down. What might have begun as powdered rock becomes a spongy, permeable ecosystem perfectly designed to receive and infiltrate rainwater.

Rainwater in such a system stays where it falls or moves slowly. Soil does not usually become completely saturated during a rainstorm, so only a small portion of the water runs off the surface. What little water does run off usually flows at a slow, meandering pace, during which suspended sediments have time to settle out. This water has been cleansed of particulates before it finally reaches stream channels. Deep below the surface, water slowly accumulates into pools of groundwater. Between rainstorms and during dry seasons, this groundwater gradually seeps into streams and wetlands, maintaining a steady baseflow and providing water to invertebrates, fish, and other aquatic creatures.

Wherever forests and grasslands are replaced by rooftops and roads, the water-retaining function of the soil is cut off and the flow of water is radically altered. The vast underground reservoir of water becomes disconnected from its source of recharge in the stormwater runoff system. Water that before might have been held below ground in this reservoir to be released slowly over days or weeks now flows rapidly across the surface and arrives in streams in short, concentrated bursts, a condition known as "flashy" flow. Floods downstream are bigger. Streambanks erode. Water quality declines. When summer arrives, soils dry out. Streams and wetlands are cut off from their supplies of water. Fish struggle to breathe in warm, sluggish, low-oxygen water. Local extinctions follow.

Water that falls as rain is known as stormwater. The conventional approach to stormwater is to use "gray infrastructure," that is, concrete and steel. This approach manages water through conveyance and detention, using gutters and pipes to get rid of the water and send it either to detention ponds or straight to streams. Surface streets and buried pipes take the place of streambeds.

A more-sustainable approach to stormwater uses infiltration. This approach mimics the kinds of conditions that would have existed on the land before development by giving water access to the soil. Strategies for treating and infiltrating stormwater all use permeable surfaces and include rain garden depressions and vegetated swales that replace concrete channels or pipes, porous paving that lets water infiltrate the soil instead of running off, and green roofs that soak up water instead of shunting it away.

All sustainable stormwater strategies are based on the same fundamental principles: (1) think small; (2) start at the source; (3) minimize impervious surface areas and maximize permeability (BASMAA 1999).

Think small: sustainable stormwater management focuses on small storms. Larger storms have less effect on groundwater replenishment overall because they happen infrequently. Most of the rain that falls and thus most of the water that infiltrates the soil and recharges groundwater does so in small, frequent 1- and 2-year storms.[2] Allowing water from these small, frequent rainfalls to infiltrate will restore most of a watershed's function. Small, frequent rainfall amounts can be infiltrated on every site.

Start at the source: sustainable stormwater management retains the water where it falls instead of transporting it. Treating and infiltrating a small amount of water at a time, when repeated in multiple locations across the land and when repeated for every small storm and the beginning of every large storm, will restore water quality, most of a stream's baseflow, and most of the groundwater level.

Minimize impervious surfaces: water that runs off impervious surfaces, especially paving, picks up pollutants including oil, antifreeze, and pesticides. Without access to plants and soils that could remove suspended particles, break down petroleum, and sequester metals and pesticides, the pollutants become concentrated. This contaminated water then moves into pipes with its pollutant load and empties into streams. Sustainable stormwater management, in addition to restoring stream baseflows and replenishing groundwater, is essential for removing pollutants from water.

Natural stormwater systems achieve multiple goals. They reduce the velocity and peak volume of runoff, restoring stream baseflows, limiting erosion, and reducing flooding. They recharge aquifers. They remove or neutralize pollutants. They can lower costs by replacing much of the expensive stormwater infrastructure that would otherwise have been constructed. At the same time, they provide habitat for native plants and animals and aesthetically pleasant places for people. Many places designed to infiltrate and treat stormwater also function as landscape elements or as public open space for recreation during dry weather.

Under the US Clean Water Act, urban stormwater runoff must be managed using best management practices (BMPs) to reduce or prevent pollution from entering lakes and streams. Low-impact development (LID) is a term that is sometimes used to describe the approaches to stormwater management that work with natural systems to manage stormwater close to its source. The best-known stormwater BMPs are LID strategies and include rain gardens, vegetated swales, porous paving, green roofs, and constructed wetlands.

Rain Gardens and Swales

Rain gardens are planted depressions in the landscape, small basins where stormwater runoff is allowed to collect temporarily as it infiltrates into the soils below. Water collects in these depressions after a storm and is gone in 72 hours or less. The soils and plants in a rain garden are an easy way to keep pollutants from residential yards and driveways out of streams. A typical rain garden is 2 to 10 feet wide at the bottom and 6 to 12 inches deep, with sloping sides and permeable soil underneath so that water can percolate through it. Plants in a rain garden can include native or locally adapted grasses, groundcovers, shrubs, and trees.

A rain garden is one way of contouring the ground to retain water. Working with existing depressions and then shaping the ground with additional depressions, swales, and sloping sidewalks is in effect creating multiple small watersheds. On all but residential scales regrading of the ground should be minimal and contouring of the land should be done in consultation with a landscape architect. Unless a site is highly disturbed, the goal is to preserve the naturally occurring topography and its natural drainage patterns where possible. Additional swales and rain gardens that mimic the naturally occurring topography of the site can be created to compensate for development impacts. Natural forces have established a balance of landform and water flow over thousands of years; this equilibrium should be considered a resource (Balmori and Benoit 2007, 14).

A **swale** is a drainage channel with a vegetated surface. Swales have greater water-holding capacity than rain gardens. Because swales are linear, they can transport water from one place in the landscape to another. They are useful for catching and treating runoff from parking lots and for disconnecting impervious sections of parking lots from each other. Swales reduce stormwater velocity, infiltrate and recharge groundwater, and cleanse stormwater by removing, breaking down, or storing pollutants.

A stormwater treatment swale is planted with native or locally adapted plants and often referred to as a **bioswale**. That is because the dense vegetation in a swale does a lot of the work of slowing, retaining, and treating stormwater runoff. Dense vegetation increases the length of path as water flows through the swale, increasing the time water is in contact with plants and increasing their ability to capture particles. Plants in a swale work as sponges, storing a lot of water; wetland plants, which are designed to take up water in wet sites, do this best. Both the aboveground parts and the roots of plants provide many surfaces for removing and holding sediments and other particulate pollutants. The plants also take up heavy metals and hydrocarbons; woody plants keep these materials locked up through the seasons and keep these pollutants out of streams. Bacteria and other microorganisms in the soil break down petroleum-based pollutants and other organic compounds including nitrates and phosphorus. Since they do this work slowly, the water needs to stay in the soils beneath a swale long enough to let the bacteria do their work.

The amount of time that water resides in a swale is called its **residence time**. The typical residence time for a bioswale is 1 to 4 days, long enough for the sediment and debris to settle but not so long that mosquitoes breed there. Swales designed to treat stormwater have gentle slopes so the water has enough residence time for pollutant removal. Check dams are often added in swales with steeper slopes to slow the velocity of the water and allow sediment to settle out. Check dams are very low walls; they can be made of concrete but are often simply large stones or even wood placed across the channel to promote ponding of water. Most swales include a drain inlet at their low end that can handle overflow during heavy storms if necessary.

Porous Paving

Building roofs, sidewalks, parking lots, and roads are all impermeable surfaces, also called impervious surfaces, that prevent rainwater from reaching the soil. Of the impervious surfaces, paving for automobiles constitutes by far the major barrier. Porous paving is a way to provide surfaces where people can walk and vehicles can drive or park, while removing stormwater pollutants and allowing rainwater to infiltrate and recharge groundwater.

Like any specialty field, paving has its own language. **Aggregate** is the word used to refer to coarse particles of rock, such as sand or gravel. Aggregate is graded by sorting it through vibrating screens. **Open-graded** is a term that means aggregate that is all the same size.

The component of a porous paving system that is visible is the surface paving layer, which is porous to let water flow through. The surface can be made of unit pavers such as cobbles, bricks, or interlocking concrete pavers; crushed stone or gravel; or what is known as turf paving or grass paving, consisting of plastic or concrete grid cells through which grass can grow. It can be porous concrete, which is a concrete mix made with cement and open-graded aggregate without sand, or porous asphalt, which is mixed like standard asphalt but with open-graded aggregate. The cement or asphalt clings to the aggregate, allowing stormwater to drain through. A layer of finer gravel is sometimes used just under the surface layer of paving to provide a smooth, stable surface for the upper paving.

Below the paving surface is a reservoir, a prepared area excavated and filled with open-graded rocks 1 to 2 inches in size and 18 to 36 inches deep. This is the heart of the porous paving system. The aggregate reservoir serves two primary purposes: (1) it stores rainwater in what is essentially a rock-filled tank, holding the water while it slowly infiltrates through the soil below; (2) the reservoir is a bioremediation site where communities of bacteria that develop on the many rock surfaces break down petroleum-based pollutants.

Below the layer of aggregate is a layer of filter fabric on top of the soil to prevent soil particles from migrating up into the rock layer. The subgrade soil itself has been leveled so that the water will be retained rather than running off but has not been compacted so that it remains permeable.

Bioswales are components of many parking areas. They are particularly important elements where parking surfaces remain impervious. When impervious areas are connected, stormwater running across paved expanses can rapidly form concentrated flows of contaminated runoff, cut off from groundwater. One stormwater management goal is to break up these impervious areas into isolated, disconnected patches. Swales, rain gardens, and other infiltration areas are used to disconnect these areas and direct their flows back into plants and soil. The soil and groundwater underneath remains connected; the impervious patches above are disconnected. Draining impervious surfaces into infiltration areas reduces the effective impervious area.

Green Roofs

A green roof is a kind of roof covering consisting of a waterproof layer, growing medium, and plants. It is like a rain garden up in the air, absorbing stormwater runoff, removing pollutants, and providing habitat. Green roofs store carbon, reduce urban heat buildup, and lower energy consumption in buildings. We will talk about these roofs again in Chapter 10, Green Buildings and Sites.

Water circulates in a continuous global cycle and its volume is unchanging. Threats to water are not due to diminishing supply but to the dual impacts of excessive demand and pollution loads, coupled with fluctuations in the hydrologic cycle caused by climate changes. Thus strategies for sustainable water use involve reducing demand and preserving water quality. Some of the freshwater supply comes from surface waters and some lies in aquifers that are not renewable over time scales meaningful to humans; protecting those aquifers is essential to avoid wrenching water supply problems in the future.

We reduce pressure on the water supply through water conservation: using less water. Water conservation practices occur at the residential scale and the commercial scale. Every object we use requires water; we can reduce our demand for the virtual water embedded in elements of our civilization by lowering our consumption and by eating lower down the food chain as well as by improving the processes by which we manufacture our goods and grow our food. We can augment water supply at a local scale by harvesting rainwater from the sky and reusing graywater.

Also essential, for both aquifers and surface waters, is reducing pollution loads from human wastes, industrial and agricultural chemicals to levels that the natural water system is able to absorb. We can minimize loads through pollution prevention, then use living systems to treat wastewater and cleanse stormwater.

The same water has been circulating through the planetary hydrologic system for millions of years. Our goal for sustainability is to borrow water for our use and return it to the cycle in healthy condition, ready to circulate again.

Notes

1 The word "commercial" is used in two different ways, as a sector and as a user category.
2 A 2-year storm has a 1-in-2 probability of occurring each year; a storm of this size occurs on average once every 2 years. A 50-year storm has a 1-in-50 probability of occurring in a given year; a storm of this size is much larger and occurs on average only once in every 50 years.

Further Reading

Black, Maggie and Jannet King. *The Atlas of Water: Mapping the World's Most Critical Resource.* 2nd ed. Berkeley, CA: University of California Press, 2009.

Ferguson, Bruce K. *Introduction to Stormwater: Concept, Purpose, Design.* New York: John Wiley & Sons, 1998.

Hoekstra, Arjen Y. *The Water Footprint of Modern Consumer Society.* London: Routledge, 2013.

Kwok, Alison G. and Walter T. Grondzik. *The Green Studio Handbook: Environmental Strategies for Schematic Design,* 2nd ed. Oxford: Architectural Press, 2011.

Lohan, Tara, ed. *Water Consciousness.* San Francisco, CA: AlterNet Books, 2008.

Pearce, Fred. *When the Rivers Run Dry.* Boston, MA: Beacon Press, 2006.

Sandford, Robert William. *Restoring the Flow: Confronting the World's Water Woes.* Surrey, ND: Rocky Mountain Books, 2009.

Vickers, Amy. *Handbook of Water Use and Conservation.* Amherst, MA: WaterPlow Press, 2001.

Chapter Review

1 What is potable water?
2 For what purposes may nonpotable water be used?
3 What is the difference between graywater and blackwater?
4 What kind of water use typically consumes the largest amount of water in suburban neighborhoods?
5 Describe some strategies that can be used to reduce water use in commercial buildings.
6 Why do residential water conservation programs from public utilities tend start with a focus on indoor water fixtures, although landscape irrigation typically consumes a larger proportion of total water usage?
7 What water conservation opportunities are available for commercial cooling systems?
8 Do electronic flushing controls reduce water consumption?
9 What is the purpose of placing water tanks on top of city buildings, in addition to just storing water?
10 What is the purpose of a first flush device in a rainwater harvesting system?
11 What is a water table?
12 What is groundwater?
13 How is the water in an aquifer replaced?
14 What is the difference between a fossil aquifer and other kinds of aquifers?
15 Describe some of the negative impacts of dams.
16 What causes saltwater intrusion? What effects might a warming climate have?
17 What is stormwater runoff?
18 List impermeable surfaces in the built environment that can result in rainwater runoff.
19 Why is secondary sewage treatment sometimes referred to as biological treatment?

Critical Thinking and Discussion

1 An early newsletter of the American Water Resources Association proposed that deforestation of mountain slopes could direct more snowmelt into reservoirs rather than being transpired away by trees, thereby providing more runoff water for irrigation in the western US. Was this a sensible idea?
2 In what ways do you think global climate change might affect the hydrologic cycle? In what ways might it affect aquifers?

3 Why do experts predict that wars will be fought over water in this century?

4 How do subsidies for meat production affect water consumption?

5 Do you think that water should be considered a shared commons, or is it more appropriate to be priced and traded in the marketplace?

6 A town that gets its water from an aquifer has found that the rate of water entering the aquifer is about 0.5 percent less than the town's residents and businesses are withdrawing. What, if anything, should they do?

7 Waterless urinals are the ultimate low-flow fixtures. Why are they not used in every commercial building?

8 Maintenance staff in the organization where you work park their vehicles in a small gravel parking lot. People in your organization have become interested in sustainability, and someone suggests scraping off the gravel and putting down porous paving in this parking lot. They ask you what kind of paving you recommend. What would you say?

9 Porous concrete is sometimes specified as a paving material because it allows stormwater runoff to infiltrate. However, some users avoid concrete because of the energy needed to produce it and the pollution and greenhouse gases emitted during its production. If someone at your company asked for your recommendation for a parking lot surface, what would you say?

10 Material continually cycles in the natural world, where waste from one organism or process becomes food for another. If that is so, what prevents humans from taking advantage of the potential value in human biological waste?

11 What do you think might be some of the components of a wastewater treatment plant's carbon footprint?

7 Ecosystems and Habitat

The state of the world's ecosystems has changed more rapidly in the last 50 years than at any time in human history (Millennium Ecosystem Assessment 2005, 1). Ocean fisheries are collapsing, forests and wetlands are disappearing, and deserts are advancing. A process known as the "sixth mass extinction" is underway, with species going extinct at a rate not seen in 65 million years. Human habitation is increasingly urbanized, and nature is moving to the cities in many places and at many scales. The global climate is changing, the ranges of many plants and animals are shifting, and novel ecosystems are appearing. This is life in the Anthropocene, in which we see vividly illustrated the emergent properties of complex adaptive systems.

Populations and Extinction

Understanding populations and how they interact with their environments is a field of study called **population ecology**. A population is a group of individuals of one species living in the same area. A population may be as small as a patch of bacteria growing under a stone, or as large as all the pileated woodpeckers living in a 1,000-acre forest, or even larger, such as the millions of bison living on the North American Great Plains in 1850 or all the humans covering the planet today.

The size of any population fluctuates naturally. The larger a population, the greater its ability to recover from negative impacts such as storms, floods, drought, or fire. A small population can be impacted by such a natural disaster and can move to the brink of extinction by the naturally occurring fluctuations in population size.

If a population is too small, close relatives are more likely to mate with each other and an impact called inbreeding depression can occur in which genetic defects multiply. The higher the level of inbreeding, the greater the chance that some of the offspring will receive defective genes from both parents, be unable to reproduce, or be weakened and die prematurely. Inbreeding depression is common in rare and endangered plants and animals.

Individual characteristics in a population change slightly over time with genetic variation. Genetic diversity is critical to a population's survival because it increases the chance that its members will be able to adapt to adverse conditions that arise, such as new diseases, habitat changes, or changing climate.

Species diversity in an ecosystem is also important for survival. If one species disappears, another species may be able to fill its niche if there is a large-enough pool of candidates. **Biodiversity** is the term used to describe the biological diversity of genes, species, and ecosystems. The greater the biodiversity in an ecosystem, the more stable and resilient it will be.

Populations usually begin decreasing in size before they go extinct. As a population gets smaller it becomes increasingly vulnerable to all of the challenges to survival: variations in population size, **genetic drift**, environmental changes, and natural disasters. A change in one factor makes a small population more vulnerable to the other factors, and the population can be trapped in what population ecologists call an extinction vortex, with the population moving faster toward extinction the closer it gets to the "center" of the vortex (Primack 2008, 153).

If a population living in an area disappears, we say it has gone locally extinct. If other local populations within a **metapopulation** survive, the species may be able to recover if enough intact habitat is available. A metapopulation is a collection of local populations, a "population of populations." For example, in the 1960s DDT caused populations of brown pelicans to go extinct in California, Louisiana, and several other regions of the US. After DDT was banned in the 1970s, individuals from surviving populations within the metapopulation began to recolonize the affected regions. Today the brown pelican is no longer listed as endangered.

Once all the subpopulations of a species disappear, the species is extinct. Extinction is irreversible. Extinction is a natural part of the cycles of life and death in the biosphere. We know from the fossil record that, on average, about one species in every million goes extinct each year (Wilson 2002b, 99). New species develop simultaneously, although very slowly. The rate of new species development typically equals or exceeds the **background rate of extinction**, and biodiversity increases over time.

Five times in the history of the planet, however, massive worldwide extinctions have sent large numbers of species into oblivion.[1] The first mass extinction happened about 500 million years ago, with another about 345 million years ago. The most massive die-off happened about 250 million years ago at the end of the Permian period, when over 75 percent of land animals and up to 96 percent of marine animals went extinct (Primack 2008, 125). This was followed by another mass extinction about 180 million years ago. Perhaps the most famous mass extinction occurred 65 million years ago at the end of the Cretaceous period, when the dinosaurs along with about 80 percent of all animal species went extinct. Commonly referred to as the K-T Extinction, this disaster may have been caused by a very large meteor that struck the Earth near the Yucatán Peninsula.

The causes of these mass extinctions are not known with complete certainty. Current theories based on the geological record are that they were caused by climate changes, perhaps triggered by volcanism, asteroid collisions, or massive releases of methane from the seafloor.

A sixth mass extinction is now underway and is progressing rapidly. Extinction rates have reached 1,000 times the background extinction rate (ibid., 126), with species going extinct at a rate not seen in 65 million years. Conservation biologists estimate that if current trends continue, about 20 percent of species will be gone by 2030 and about 50 percent of all known species will have vanished by 2100 (Wilson 2002b, 102). This time we know the cause: human activities. The primary weapon of extinction is habitat destruction, followed by pollution and overexploitation; some ecologists include invasive species. Climate change and increasing human population numbers exacerbate all these causes.

The International Union for Conservation of Nature and Natural Resources (IUCN) is the most comprehensive global inventory of the status of species. Current data on conservation status and risk of extinction are maintained in the IUCN Red List of Threatened Species. Like the IPCC approach to compiling research on climate change, the IUCN Red List compiles peer-reviewed research data from recognized conservation experts worldwide.

Mass extinctions create conditions where new kinds of life can emerge. After each major extinction biodiversity has surged. Extinction on a slow, global scale might be compared to the way disturbances on a fast, local scale can open up patches of forest to succession. This is part of the cyclical nature of life on our planet. However, the surging back of life happens slowly in human terms. Over 50 million years passed before Earth regained the biodiversity that had been lost in the Permian extinction. The fossil record shows that it takes 10 to 100 million years for the biosphere to recover from a mass extinction (Perlman and Milder 2004, 59).

Drivers of Ecosystem Change

Traditional conservation biology over the past several decades has held that the primary threats to species and ecosystems—the primary drivers of extinction—are habitat destruction, invasive species, pollution, population, and overexploitation. Conservation biologists summarize these threats using the acronym HIPPO. These forces are listed in their order of importance, with the exception of population: a higher population of humans means a greater intensity of all the other HIPPO forces.

During the Paleolithic period the sequence was reversed, or OPPIH, with overexploitation the most damaging factor. The fossil record shows that each time humans have entered a region, large mammals and flightless birds have been driven to extinction within a few hundred years (Primack 2008, 127). Prominent examples include Australia about 40,000 years ago, North America about 12,000 years ago, and Hawaii about 1,600 years ago (Flannery 2001, 191). With the development of agriculture and the resulting spread of civilizations in the Neolithic period the sequence reversed, and habitat destruction became the predominant force.

Most threatened species and ecosystems face more than one of the HIPPO forces, which can interact and reinforce each other. Species stressed by HIPPO forces are more vulnerable to death from natural causes as well.

Habitat Destruction

Habitat is the place where an organism lives and finds food, water, cover, and space to grow and reproduce. Each organism has evolved over time to be adapted to a particular kind of habitat. Habitat destruction is the most significant driver of ecosystem damage, biodiversity loss, and species extinction and comes about because of a variety of human activities.

In the oceans, habitat destruction occurs out of sight as bottom trawlers drag 5-ton weights and 200-foot chains and nets across the floor of the ocean. In the process creatures who live on the seafloor such as anemones and sponges are destroyed, along with thousands to millions of fish, sharks, and occasional dolphins and whales who are trapped in each of the massive nets with no way to escape. Vast areas of ocean floor habitat are destroyed each year by trawlers. Deep-sea mining is an additional threat.

Clearcutting of forests does on land what bottom trawling does on the ocean floor. Clearcutting is a method of logging in which every tree in a given area is cut regardless of size. Ecosystems in the soil and all the plants on the forest floor are destroyed along with the cutting of trees, and with them the habitat on which the forest's species depend. With the trees and undergrowth removed, sediment washes into streams, destroying stream habitat as well.

Land clearing for crops destroys the largest percentage of terrestrial habitat. In the US, approximately 97 percent of the Midwestern tallgrass prairie habitat has been destroyed to make way for farmland, with some states losing more than 99 percent of their prairie habitat in the last 150 years (ibid., 83). In dry regions of the US, grazing of livestock has converted many grassland habitats to sagebrush-and-tumbleweed deserts.

The planet is being deforested at a rate of about 1.3 percent of the total forest area per year (Brown 2011, 137). Tropical rainforests are of particular concern. They are considered **biodiversity hotspots**, habitats that constitute the richest and most threatened reservoirs of species in the world; they are also important sinks for sequestering carbon, important for slowing global warming. Deforestation in Asia is driven primarily by demand for timber and expansion of palm-oil plantations; in South America it is driven by demand for beef and soybeans for cattle feed (Brown 2011, 137). Much of the destruction results from cultivation of small-scale crops by poor subsistence farmers in response to demand for cheap food products including palm oil, sugar, beef, and soybeans; large-scale deforestation also occurs at the hands of industrial pulpwood and palm-oil conglomerates (Boucher et al. 2011, 1–3).

Urban development is responsible for another large percentage of habitat destruction. A development pattern known as suburban sprawl has chewed up large expanses of land and fragmented much of those that remain, while creating an automobile-dependent culture with its voracious consumption of fossil fuels.

Wetlands, land areas where soil is saturated with water at least part of the year, are important habitats that provide many ecosystem services. They function as sponges that absorb floodwaters, even out stream flow, purify water, recharge aquifers, and provide critical habitat for a diverse number of birds, fish, frogs, and smaller animals. Once referred to as swamps and considered simply wasteland, more than half the wetlands in the US and Australia and over 60 percent in Canada, Europe, and China have been filled or drained to create farmlands and build cities (Mitsch and Gosselink 2007, 48), and many disappeared with the eradication of beaver populations.

Lakes and river systems may be the most threatened terrestrial ecosystems of all. The plants, animals, and other creatures who live in them have evolved particular characteristics adapted to their local sites. Organisms in lakes are isolated as much as organisms who live on islands; organisms in rivers can move only upstream or downstream. The natural flows of rivers have been altered by dams that also create barriers to fish migration. Development that removes streamside vegetation also removes necessary habitat, causes pollution of the water by silt from erosion and toxins from pavement and, by removing shade, results in water too warm for many creatures to survive.

A great deal of habitat can be lost not through outright destruction but through a process known as **habitat fragmentation**. Fragmentation happens when a road or other human activity divides a large habitat patch into two or more smaller patches. Fragmentation does not just make patches smaller, it changes their makeup.

Habitat consists of three kinds of elements: patches,[2] corridors connecting the patches, and the surrounding matrix. It does not matter what type of habitat is involved, the patch-corridor-matrix elements are universal for any terrestrial habitat (Dramstad et al. 1996, 14). It is the spatial pattern that affects how habitat functions and how it is impacted by fragmentation. This is the specialty of a field of study known as landscape ecology.

The conditions at the edge of each patch are different from conditions in the interior. This perimeter zone is subject to **edge effects** including increased heat, faster wind speeds, and dry soil. Fragments are vulnerable to invasion by exotic species. Some species are specialists and require interior habitat. Forest-interior bird and frog species and shade-tolerant forest plants, for example, disappear when patches become too small and are mostly edge.

Even though roads themselves take up little space they split habitat areas into fragments, reducing interior habitat and multiplying edge effects. Dividing a large patch into two smaller patches increases the amount of edge habitat and greatly decreases the amount of interior habitat. Creatures in the interior are closer to edges and if the new patches are too small may not have enough core habitat to survive. Smaller populations in remnant fragments are more vulnerable to genetic drift and inbreeding depression, may not be large enough to survive normal fluctuations in population size, and may go locally extinct. Fragmentation can bring wild populations into contact with domestic plants and animals where they are vulnerable to new diseases; small wild animals are particularly vulnerable to domestic cats, which are efficient predators.

Roads are barriers to movement and are particularly potent forces of fragmentation and destruction. Animals have not evolved to understand objects moving at the kinds of speeds automobiles travel. Many animals are killed as they try to cross in search of food or water, or when they are lured to warm surfaces for basking. Some animals are not able to cross roads at all, with the result that their populations become divided; the subpopulations created may be too small to persist over time, and may go locally extinct.

Corridors connect patches. Many animals need to move freely across the landscape in search of water and food, which may be scattered or which may change with the seasons. They may use corridors to move seasonally from one food source or nesting area to another, to find new territory, or to find mates. Many plants depend on animals to spread their seeds as the animals move around. When corridors are destroyed, patches become islands, species may be unable to find scarce resources or mates, and local populations may go extinct. Corridors can be destroyed by land development.

Invasive Species

Plants, animals, other organisms, and the ecosystems where they live historically evolved together in a closely tuned balance. These are what are traditionally called **native species**, species that developed in the place where they live and are adapted to conditions there. Species that move in after having developed someplace else are traditionally called exotic species. These newcomers may not have evolved to be susceptible to the same predators, parasites, and diseases that keep the populations of native species in balance with their surroundings. Some exotic species are not adapted to their new surroundings and cannot become established, but some can.

A small number of so-called nonnative or exotic species become what are known as **invasive** species. Invasives are more efficient than the natives at exploiting nutrients and other resources, and without natural controls they can take over a habitat, driving some of the natives to extinction. The ultimate invasive species is *Homo sapiens.*

Invasive species can be introduced accidentally. Smallpox was an invasive species of virus that killed the majority of American Indians when it arrived with Europeans (Mann 2011, 70). Insects, rats, and snakes may arrive as stowaways on ships and airplanes. Oceangoing ships carry large quantities of water in their holds as ballast and if they release this water when they arrive at their destinations they can discharge thousands of larvae and adults of many exotic aquatic species. The zebra mussel, for example, was originally native to Russia and was discharged into Lake Erie from the ballast of a European ship in 1988 (Primack 2008, 112; Davis et al. 2011, 153). It spread quickly through the Mississippi River drainage and threatens other Great Lakes. Lake Erie was heavily polluted by the Cuyahoga, the river known for catching fire in the 1960s, and humans had hunted the lake's top predator, the sturgeon, almost to extinction. Some ecologists think that zebra mussels would not have taken hold had the lake's ecosystem been intact (Pearce 2015, 62). Shipments of plants or food can arrive with insects and pathogens attached. A fungus from the Himalayas, brought to the US on wooden crates made of infected elm wood, has destroyed most of the elm trees that once lined parks and streets.

Some invasive plants are introduced intentionally when they are grown as ornamentals because of their attractive flowers or foliage, thrive in their new homes, and then escape. In some cases the results can be relatively benign; in other cases the plants become invasive and result in local extinctions. An example is Purple Loosestrife, an ornamental flower that escaped and now dominates wetlands in the eastern US where it has crowded out cattails and other natives. Perhaps the most famous example is the Kudzu vine, imported to the US as an ornamental vine and later promoted by the Soil Conservation Service (SCS) for its ability to prevent soil erosion; today it is referred to by some people as "the plant that ate the South." Genetically modified organisms, or GMOs, are another category of invasive organisms with an unpredictable future; scientists do not yet know how GMO escapees may affect ecosystems and biodiversity.

Some invasive animals are introduced intentionally. One of the most serious predators of wild birds and other small land animals everywhere is the domestic cat. In Everglades National Park in Florida Burmese Python snakes, who escaped when a hurricane destroyed a pet-snake breeding facility, are spreading rapidly and appear poised to move to the top of the Everglades food chain. The European starling, a widespread nest parasite, was brought to the US in 1890 as part of one person's plan to introduce all of the birds mentioned in the works of Shakespeare. Some exotic species, often insects, were originally brought in as solutions to some other pest problem, only to become worse pests than the originals.

Most so-called nonnative species are not invasive. In fact what constitutes native or nonnative is not clear-cut. Species and ecosystems constantly change, adapt, and form new relationships. Camels, for example, were originally native to North America but around 4 million years ago began migrating elsewhere (Flannery 2001, 127). The mammoth, a kind of elephant, was native to Asia but during one of the ice ages walked across a land bridge to North America and settled in (ibid., 155). Later, the invasive species *Homo sapiens* hunted the mammoth to extinction. Humans themselves were native to Africa but later spread to other continents. Meanwhile, ranges of plant species have shifted repeatedly over time as temperatures grew warmer or cooler, glaciers advanced and retreated, landforms rose and eroded, and rivers changed course, with combinations of species constantly shifting and remixing, too (Jackson 2006, 553).

Box 7.1 Reconsidering Invasive Species

Traditional conservation theory has held that invasive species are the second leading cause of extinction. The field of invasion biology was built on the work of zoologist Charles Elton, described in his 1958 book *The Ecology of Invasions by Animals and Plants* (Elton 2000). In 1992 ecologist Edward O. Wilson wrote about preserving biodiversity and identified four "mindless horsemen of the environmental apocalypse." In order of importance, he said they were habitat destruction, invasive species, overexploitation, and diseases spread by exotic species (Wilson 2010, 253).

(continued)

(continued)

In an influential paper six years later, a team of ecologists reported on their study quantifying the causes of extinction, which they concluded were, in order, habitat destruction, invasive species, overexploitation, pollution, and disease. The authors emphasized that the data they tabulated were usually based on the opinions of agents such as US Fish and Wildlife Service employees or state Fish and Game employees and that "their evaluation of the threats facing that species may not be based on experimental evidence or even on quantitative data. Indeed, such data often do not exist" (Wilcove et al. 1998, 608). Further, the high ranking of non-native species as extinction threats was skewed by the paper's focus on species in Hawaii (Davis 2011, 269). Nevertheless, the idea took hold.

Modern ecologists are reexamining that idea. Conservation biology is full of examples in which a nonnative species has apparently moved into an area and a native species has become threatened, yet a careful examination reveals that the original driver was damage to the ecosystem by human impacts such as pollution, which degraded the system and wiped out the native species, which then opened up a niche for a new species (Pearce 2015, 35, 62). Even the whole notion of native versus alien is based on an earlier view of nature as unchanging and what it means to be native as absolute and enduring; it is a notion which does not reflect reality. Throughout the history of life on Earth, species have constantly moved about and ecosystems have constantly reorganized, always in novel ways. What is now the rolling open countryside of Britain, for example, was covered in forests 5000 years ago; 15,000 years ago it was covered in ice; and in the interglacial period before the last ice age it was home to hippopotamus, lions, and Barbary apes (ibid., 188).

Research confirms that when new species are introduced to a system, biodiversity almost always increases (Davis et al. 2011, 153). Many ecologists now recognize that what matters in conservation and restoration work, particularly in the changing climate of the Anthropocene, is not so much where a species originated but whether it contributes to biodiversity and system health.

Pollution

Habitat destruction, fragmentation, and exotic species invasions are mechanisms of extinction that are visible. Although some forms of pollution such as large oil spills or chemical plant explosions are visible and dramatic, most pollution is more subtle. Pollution introduces toxic substances into environments that are not adapted to absorb them. Pollution can come from single sources such as industrial waste pipes or from diffuse sources such as automobile exhaust, fertilizer washed from farm fields by irrigation, or contaminated rainwater as it runs off paved city streets and parking lots. Pollution in the atmosphere can spread out and damage entire ecosystems with toxic metals, ground-level ozone, acid rain, and other substances.

Most of this pollution is invisible. Quantities that constitute only a few parts per million are often enough to cause damage. Animals cannot recognize it as a threat; safe and contaminated food or water look and smell the same. Humans, too, may be unaware that damage is occurring until much time has gone by. Many toxins are cumulative, becoming increasingly concentrated as they rise through successive layers of a food chain.

Population

The most adaptable and destructive invasive species is *Homo sapiens*. Our species evolved on the African savanna but later spread and adapted to every continent except Antarctica. Everywhere the species went, extinctions followed as human hunters encountered prey who had not evolved with them (Flannery 2001, 191; Ponting 2007, 34). Supremely adaptable and with few natural controls, *Homo sapiens* populations have expanded exponentially.

Some observers argue that human population growth is the primary cause of the current mass extinction. They argue that if the human population lived within Earth's carrying capacity there would be little to no habitat destruction, spread of invasive species, pollution, or overexploitation.

Overexploitation

When humans use up a resource faster than it can be replenished, the situation is unsustainable. That resource has been overexploited. Overexploitation is a sign that humans are spending Earth's natural capital rather than living off its interest.

The overharvesting of marine fisheries is a prominent example. The word **fishery** can mean either a particular species of fish or a particular marine area being fished commercially. Fish stocks are said to be in collapse when they have been 90 percent depleted, which is now the case for a third of large marine fish species. Biologists calculate that if current trends continue, all the major fish stocks could be in collapse by 2050 (Cunningham and Cunningham 2010, 235).

Overharvesting of old-growth trees is another example. Old-growth forests are those that have developed over time without human intervention. They are hundreds to over 1,000 years old and consist of a mix of tree ages, a range of vertical layers, and a rich diversity of microhabitats. Once these habitats are destroyed, they cannot be replaced by simple replanting. Old-growth forests are home to many interior species that cannot survive in monoculture tree farms. Over 90 percent of the old-growth forests in the US have been destroyed, and most of those that remain are scheduled for logging in the near future (ibid., 260).

Conservation and Restoration

Ecosystem conservation and restoration is an important focus of sustainability work. Conserving or restoring ecosystem health involves three broad fields of endeavor: Conservation refers to protecting biodiversity; it is about minimizing damage. Restoration is about repairing damage, returning the condition of an ecosystem to a state of health. Reconciliation involves acknowledging that humans are part of the natural world and finding ways to live together, weaving into the fabric of the biosphere the activities of its most visible and ubiquitous species, *Homo sapiens*. There is no single solution. We live on a complex, constantly changing planet which faces a broad range of threats and restoring biospheric health calls for a diversity of approaches. Several themes from ecology that underlie this work are discussed next.

DISTURBANCE

Natural processes including wind, flood, fire, grazing, insects, and disease play major roles in structuring ecosystems. Disturbance processes produce constantly shifting mosaics of micro-habitats at different successional stages, resulting in a great diversity of living conditions, which can support more species than could a uniform habitat. Some ecosystems cannot survive without disturbance. A prairie without fire may be taken over by trees; a forest without landslides or wind has no open patches where pioneer species can begin the regeneration process; a river floodplain without floods loses its infusions of nutrient-rich silt and its mix of young and old fast-growing riparian trees.

STRUCTURAL COMPLEXITY

Disturbance regimes produce varied three-dimensional structures. Diverse vertical structure, with vegetation at various layers from ground covers to low and tall shrubs to trees, creates multiple niches for a wide range of plants and animals. The diverse horizontal structure of mosaics produces a range of microhabitats with multiple niches. **Microtopography**, or small-scale variations in the shape of the surface, is critical to many ecosystems. It results from a variety of processes including animal burrows, wallows, and mounds and pits from the root wads of fallen trees. Diverse age structure is also important for accommodating a range of organisms with different habitat needs. Biodiversity depends on structural complexity. The more species that can live in an ecosystem, the more stable it will be.

CONNECTEDNESS

We cannot save parts and pieces of nature. The organisms within an ecosystem are connected to each other through flows of energy, food, and waste, and the ecosystem is connected to the world outside it and influenced by the context in which it is embedded. Ecologists always consider what is at a smaller scale and what is at a larger scale, thinking not just about a particular patch, but about the microhabitats it contains and the larger framework of ecosystems within which it is nested.

RESILIENCE

Resilience, the capacity of an ecosystem to accommodate change while retaining its essential function, structure, and identity, is an emergent property of complex systems. Maintaining diversity is the key to maintaining resilience. Ecosystems constantly change through processes of disturbance occurring at multiple scales. Resilience allows systems to rebuild themselves, to adapt, and to absorb disturbance while maintaining their basic function.

Conservation

Conservation is one of the three approaches to maintaining the health of the natural world, together with restoration and reconciliation. Conservation is the first line of defense for preserving biodiversity. Its goal is to preserve existing populations, species, and habitats and prevent their disappearance. It does this by establishing protected places, which may be reserves, refuges, parks, or private lands with special legal protection. The scientific discipline is known as conservation biology.

The sixth mass extinction is well underway, and conservation biologists say that it is no longer preventable. With tens of thousands of species now listed by the IUCN as threatened with extinction, there are too few resources to save them all, so conservation planners are forced to make choices about how to spend the limited resources available. They must choose what to protect, where to protect it, and how best to do it.

Conservation science suggests three criteria for selecting species or ecosystems on which to focus resources: distinctiveness, endangerment, and utility (Primack 2008, 206). Distinctiveness means that an ecosystem that contains mostly rare species has a higher priority than an ecosystem that contains mostly common species. Endangerment means that species in danger of extinction have a higher priority than species that are not threatened. Utility means that species or ecosystems that have potential value to humans have a higher priority than those that do not.

Conservation planners must be realistic, since resources are limited. To spend most of the resources on a plan with little hope for success would not be the best way to protect the natural world. So conservationists consider the "four Rs": representation, resiliency, redundancy, and reality (ibid., 214). To be considered for conservation, an ecosystem should be representative, that is, it should contain the species and habitat features of a functioning ecosystem of its type. For example, an area of degraded prairie on which overgrazing had caused the grassland to be replaced by sagebrush and tumbleweed would not be a good candidate for conservation, although planners may consider it for restoration work. An ecosystem should be resilient, that is, it must be large enough and intact enough to be able to maintain ecosystem function in the face of natural disturbances for the foreseeable future. An ecosystem should contain redundancy, that is, it should include enough species that if one population became extinct, the niche it filled could still function. Finally, the conservation planner must be realistic about the funding and political support that are available. In the modern human-filled world, simply acquiring a reserve is not enough to guarantee its survival. Every reserve, large or small, requires monitoring and management.

Conservationists take one of three different approaches to selecting areas for protection: a species approach, an ecosystem approach, or a hotspot approach.

Species Approach

The species approach is one way to set priorities and to protect multiple organisms as a consequence. It is often true that efforts to protect one species protect an entire ecosystem at the same time, since that species cannot survive without its habitat.

The presence of an endangered species is an obvious impetus to conservation effort. In the US, the Endangered Species Act (ESA) mandates protection for any species officially listed as endangered, together with the ecosystems on which it depends. It does this by prohibiting any activities that harm either the species or its habitat. Occasionally protection is so successful that a formerly endangered species can be removed from the list, or **de-listed**. Well-known examples of species which have been de-listed include the Rocky Mountain wolf, American alligator, brown pelican, peregrine falcon, and bald eagle.

The federal ESA offers greater protection to animals than to plants. Harming endangered animals or their habitat is illegal on all land, both public and private. Endangered plants are protected by the ESA if federal lands, funding, or permits are involved; if the plants are on private land, however, they may not be protected. In addition to the federal ESA, each state determines standards for listing species that live within their borders independent of how rare or common they are outside state borders. All 50 states have some form of legal protection for threatened and endangered animals. Not all states have legal protection for threatened and endangered plants.

Conservationists may focus on a particular type of species for protection and in doing so protect an entire habitat. An indicator species is one that indicates the presence of a particular type of endangered ecosystem. For example, the northern spotted owl is an indicator species in old-growth forests of the Pacific Northwest. Efforts to protect the spotted owl have the effect of also protecting old-growth forests (ibid., 208).

A keystone species is one that plays a disproportionately large role in determining the structure in an ecosystem. For example, the Rocky Mountain wolf, reintroduced to Yellowstone Park, is a keystone species. Populations of trees in Yellowstone Park including aspen and cottonwood had crashed due to overgrazing by elk whose populations had boomed in the absence of wolves. With the reintroduction of wolves in 1995, elk stopped grazing along rivers where they were vulnerable to ambush. Riparian vegetation regrew, riverbank erosion decreased, rivers meandered less, and deeper channels and pools formed (Monbiot 2014). Trees throughout the park are recovering as are other affected species including the red fox (Perlman and Milder 2004, 90).

A flagship species is a large, charismatic animal species that can generate public support, in effect acting as an ambassador for a habitat. A focus on saving the individual species also helps protect many other species who share its habitat. Examples of flagship species include elephants and mountain gorillas in Africa, giant pandas in Asia, polar bears in the Arctic, and whales in marine environments. A flagship species may or may not be an indicator or keystone species.

Many indicator species and flagship species are also what are known as umbrella species: protecting them also protects populations of many other species who share their habitat. The grizzly bear and northern spotted owl are examples of umbrella species. Umbrella species typically require large home ranges and often more than one type of habitat. Selecting an umbrella species for conservation can make gathering data for prioritizing faster and less expensive and can make conservation decisions easier.

Ecosystem Approach

Most of the living organisms and processes in an ecosystem are not visible to us. Thus the most effective way to preserve existing biodiversity is to protect not just species but entire ecosystems that are healthy and intact. Several tools are available to the conservationist.

One tool is part of the ESA and is known as habitat conservation plans (HCPs). HCPs are compromises worked out by multiple conservation and business stakeholders in situations where preservation and development are in conflict. They protect parts of ecosystems containing endangered species while allowing private landowners to develop in designated adjacent areas. While HCPs do typically result in net loss of habitat, they involve multiple stakeholders in conservation planning and protect species that might not otherwise be protected (Primack 2008, 195).

Ecosystems come in all sizes. Large reserves are critical for protecting large carnivores and some bird species and are important for minimizing edge effects. However, many small animals, plants, and microorganisms can survive in patches of a few acres (Perlman and Milder 2004, 152).

Hotspot Approach

The concept of hotspots developed as a way to identify areas that are most critical to preserving biodiversity so that limited funding and research can then be targeted toward areas where protection is likely to have the greatest positive impact. Ecologists have identified 35 of "the richest and most threatened reservoirs of plant and animal life on Earth" (Conservation International n.d.). These are regions which contain the greatest diversity of species facing the highest risks of extinction (Myers et al. 2000). To qualify as a bio-diversity hotspot, a region must support at least 1,500 plant species found nowhere else in the world and it must have lost at least 70 percent of its original habitat. The 35 biodiversity hotspots identified cover just 2.3 percent of the Earth's land surface yet are home to 42 percent of all terrestrial vertebrate species and over 50 percent of all plant species (Pimm and Jenkins 2005, 70).

Tools for Establishing Protected Areas

The largest protected areas in the US are owned by the federal government and include wilderness areas, national parks, national monuments, and wildlife refuges. While national forests and grasslands managed by the US Forest Service are often conserved, the forests can be logged. Other large tracts of land are owned and managed by Native American tribes, research universities, conservation organizations such as the Audubon Society, land trusts such as The Nature Conservancy, and individuals.

A **land trust** is a nonprofit organization that works to acquire land, to help others acquire land or conservation easements, and to provide stewardship. One of the most well-known is an international land trust, The Nature Conservancy. There are over 1,600 other land trusts in the US (Primack 2008, 272). In addition to accepting donations of land and making outright purchases of land, land trusts can be facilitators and negotiators, working with landowners and community members to craft conservation agreements.

One of the tools a land trust may help facilitate is called a **conservation easement**. A conservation easement is a legal agreement in which landowners retain ownership of their property but permanently relinquish the right to build on or develop the property. Conservation easements are usually donated, but in some cases landowners get a benefit in exchange such as a cash payment or lower taxes.

In places threatened by development, a form of compromise is sometimes used known as conservation banking or mitigation banking. **Mitigation** is used in conflicts between wetlands and development pressures. Developers are given permission to destroy wetlands if they mitigate, that is, create or restore the same number of acres of wetlands at another site. In mitigation banking, wetland areas can be set aside in advance of anticipated losses. Wetlands in a mitigation bank then provide credits that can be bought and sold, a concept somewhat similar to emissions trading. Conservation banking is similar and can be used for any type of habitat.

A criticism of mitigation is that it is impossible to reproduce the hydrology, soils, and species composition of wetlands that have developed over centuries or millennia; new constructed wetlands cannot really replace the function and complexity of the wetlands that were lost. However, "no net loss" is an improvement over earlier practices that failed to address ecosystem loss (Perlman and Milder 2004, 207). Mitigation does create a financial incentive to developers for restoring or enhancing wetlands, and the practice of mitigation banking does consolidate many small projects into larger, potentially more ecologically valuable sites.

The National Environmental Policy Act (NEPA) provides a mitigation process in regulations which all federal agencies must follow. Under these regulations, land use planning strategies use a priority sequence of "avoid, minimize, mitigate, and compensate." Agencies must: avoid impact altogether by not taking an action if possible, then minimize impacts by limiting the magnitude of any action that is taken, then mitigate any losses in ecological function by repairing or restoring the affected environment, and finally, compensate for the impact by replacing or providing substitute resources.

Restoration Ecology

Restoration is a second approach to maintaining the health of the natural world, following conservation. According to the Society for Ecological Restoration (SER): "Ecological restoration is the process of assisting the recovery of an ecosystem that has been degraded, damaged, or destroyed." Restoration involves assessing existing conditions, identifying the processes that led to degradation, making a plan for addressing the causes of damage and for restoring health, implementing, monitoring progress, and using adaptive management to adjust the plan as conditions require. Restoration is a long-term commitment. Once a restoration project is implemented much monitoring, watching, and waiting lie ahead. Ecological restoration is a process; degradation took decades or centuries, and decades more of managing the site may be required before it can be considered fully restored.

One question planners must address is how actively they want to manage a site since systems are never static. The question "restore to when?" is not an easy question to answer. If a decision is made to keep a landscape looking as it does today, the situation is in fact more like a managed park than a functioning ecosystem. Ecosystems at all scales change constantly over time and the process of succession does not follow the same path forever. Many plant communities that are common today did not exist a few thousand years ago. Conditions changed, ranges covered by species shifted, and species from those earlier communities were reassembled in new combinations. In the future, global changes in climate are guaranteed to result in whole new habitat ranges and whole new combinations that have not existed before. To insist on putting something back the way it was, to restore historical fidelity, may not only be unwise, it may also be impossible because conditions today are radically different than before. What matters is the restoration of ecosystem functioning. Resilience, the property that allows the fundamental functions of an ecosystem to persist in the face of disturbance, may be the single most important characteristic for modern ecosystem recovery.

Degraded ecosystems are often fragmented patches surrounded by dissimilar matrix. A fundamental goal for restoration is to reconnect fragmented habitats. The science of landscape ecology has recognized several essential patterns that apply at any scale. The indispensable patterns include large natural patches, connectivity between patches with corridors and stepping stones, vegetated stream corridors, structural diversity, and natural remnants distributed across the matrix of human-dominated areas.

Large habitat patches with circular or square shapes are best for maximizing core habitat and reducing edge effects. Convoluted edges with coves and lobes offer greater habitat diversity than straight edges, although they increase the proportion of edge habitat. The optimum shape is thus generally circular, with some curvilinear boundaries and a few fingers extending outward for species dispersal (Dramstad et al. 1996, 32). Whatever the shape, it is important to avoid fragmenting habitat patches with human activities.

Restoring Terrestrial Sites

Forests

The process of forest restoration begins by removing barriers that prevent natural forest processes from working. This includes closing roads, removing invasive species, and controlling livestock grazing. Forest diversity depends on disturbance regimes including fire and wind; in some locations controlled fires known as prescribed burns are used to mimic natural lightning-caused fires. Ecologists may excavate soil to mimic the pit-and-mound microtopography caused by windthrown trees. The goal is a diverse stand of mixed ages, full of living and dead wood and a complex range of microhabitats.

Prairies

Prairie restoration involves removing pressure from livestock grazing, clearing the soil, and planting native prairie species. Techniques of prairie restoration are similar to gardening and farming, so these can be popular projects for volunteer groups. Prairies were historically adapted to fire disturbance regimes; in some places on the US Great Plains, ecologists use prescribed burns as part of the restoration.

Wetlands

Restoring a wetland means restoring hydrology. It begins with removing pollution sources. If the wetland has been filled, which was once common practice, the fill is removed and the site is then regraded to simulate natural topography and hydrology. Native species appropriate to that particular type of wetland are replanted using genetic stock from the same geographical area. Wetlands are complex, self-regenerating ecosystems, and in some cases ecologists choose to let native species recolonize an area on their own.

Stream Restoration

When streams are not in pipes and are allowed to flow, they are active systems that inherently seek their own dynamic equilibrium. The goal of restoration is essentially to remove the obstacles so that the system can do the natural work of a stream. Every stream restoration project has two fundamental goals: (1) a self-sustaining stream system in dynamic equilibrium, with a structure of meanders, pools, and riffles modeled on the stream as it might have been without development, if possible; and (2) healthy, diverse, and self-sustaining ecosystems within the stream and along its banks (Riley 1998, 32).

Geometry and vegetation are the two basic components of any stream restoration project. Once the streambed geometry is in place, the streambank is planted with native vegetation. Because of the active, constantly shifting environment of meandering streams, native riparian plants are usually pioneer species which like disturbance and which grow fast, such as willows.

Many urban streams have been diverted to pipes underground. **Daylighting** is the act of bringing a stream to the surface and allowing it to flow above ground again. Daylighting projects have multiple community benefits, acting as catalysts for redevelopment and investment. In some situations a stream is visible but has been relegated to a narrow flood control channel. In rural areas these channels are trapezoidal; in urban areas they are rectangular and lined with reinforced concrete. A challenge in restoring a buried or channelized stream is the urban development that often sits close to the channel in what was formerly its floodplain. However, even in close urban situations the goal is always to foster a more self-sustaining stream. Restorationists look for ways to provide appropriate width and depth, meander shape, and slope, as well as floodplain where possible, in order to help the stream find a new equilibrium.

The floodplain is part of an active stream channel and plays an important role in minimizing damage from floods. Where possible, the 100-year floodplain[3] is preserved or restored along with the main channel, and can be a multiuse greenway zone with paths and open space. An ideal system includes three zones: the streambank zone with riparian forest; a middle zone covering the 100-year floodplain which can include vegetation, stormwater management, and recreational uses; and an outer zone often consisting of residential back-yards that functions as the buffer's "buffer," providing a space between the floodplain and the nearest structure (ibid., 10).

Dam removal is stream-and-habitat restoration on a big scale. Dams, built for flood control and power generation, cause large-scale damage in spite of their role as renewable energy sources. They destroy habitat, block fish migration, raise water temperatures, interfere with the work of rivers in transporting sediment, displace human cultures, and sometimes destroy archaeological sites. The silt and decaying plant matter that builds up behind them emits methane, a powerful greenhouse gas (Brown 2015, 121). Across Europe and the US, hydro-electric dams have been removed to allow rivers to assume their natural function again. It is multidisciplinary, collaborative work with big payback. Old channels and meanders are recreated, riverbanks are replanted, and rivers are allowed to reconnect with their floodplains (Pearce 2013). Once a dam has been removed, wildlife returns, sometimes with astonishing speed and diversity (Mapes 2016).

Living Together: Reconciliation Ecology

Conserving wildlife reserves and restoring habitats are important work, but by themselves they are not enough. These places are too small, too few, and too isolated. As the global climate changes, these reserved ecosystems will change, too, and in some cases collapse. In the modern era of growing human population, urban development, habitat destruction, and changing climate, we need to find ways to integrate ourselves with the rest of the biosphere, to fuse the bits and pieces together into a larger, coherent living whole.

Ecologist Michael Rosenzweig uses the term **reconciliation ecology** to describe the deliberate sharing of the places where we live with other species (Rosenzweig 2003, 7). To do this, we must first try to understand what other species need in order to be able to get along with us, then adapt our surroundings to accommodate them. Habitats in the midst of humans are not ideal for most species, but can allow at least some of them to survive. As Rosenzweig points out, those species evolved in a different world whose conditions no longer exist (ibid.). Over time, natural selection and resilience may allow us and many of our nonhuman neighbors to adapt to living together in the new world as it is.

Conceptually, we can imagine a green fabric or green net linking parts of the planet including our cities. Our task is to repair "breaks in the net" and reweave the fabric. Imagine, for example, a city where green roofs, small backyards, town squares, larger parks, school grounds, and tree-filled cemeteries are all functioning ecosystems dotting the city with patches of habitat, all connected together into a green network by greenways, vegetated swales, and healthy stream corridors.

Yards and Parks

Two potential habitats that may come immediately to mind are backyards and parks. The more structural diversity and diversity of plant communities we can provide in these sites, the more kinds of organisms are able to live there. A healthy site with structural diversity has multiple layers of vegetation and varied ground surfaces to provide multiple habitat niches. It should provide water where possible, natural elements for cover and shelter, and escape cover such as shrubs and low trees. It allows dead trees to remain standing where it is safe to do so, allows fallen leaves and debris to remain on the site to provide microhabitat and recycling of nutrients, and uses native or regionally adapted plants to provide resources for animals who live there. All of these strategies can be done in ways that are still attractive to human sensibilities. The goal is not for a place that "looks natural" but for a place that functions as a healthy ecosystem.

Birds

Many communities provide places for birds to nest. In European cities one of the most loved birds, the white stork, builds massive nests on utility poles, roofs, and tall chimneys, with some rooftop nests in use for hundreds of years; many humans build platforms on their roof-tops to encourage storks to take up residence. Ospreys, too, are attracted to poles and towers, and workers in many cities erect nesting platforms to give them alternative places to build. Peregrine falcons, once listed as endangered, have made a comeback and are known to nest on high-rise buildings and bridges across the US and Europe, with human inhabitants check-ing on them from webcams. At millions of homes, schools, and parks, humans erect nest boxes to help compensate for lost nesting space. Some city parks and college campuses leave dead tree snags standing, with interpretive signs to help educate people about their benefits for wildlife.

Bats

Bats are not only fascinating animals, but they can also consume up to half their weight in insects every night. In areas where large trees and other bat habitats have disappeared, some communities install bat boxes, and some towns in Europe have built larger bat roosts. All bats and their roosts are legally protected in Britain. In Austin, Texas the underside of the Congress Avenue Bridge features expansion joints that are just the right size for Mexican free-tail bats to roost; protected by the city, over a million bats live under the downtown bridge, where tourists and residents gather every night to watch them emerge.

Green Roofs

Green roofs offer wildlife habitat for butterflies, other insects, and birds. Many city parking structures are constructed underground with parks above them in place of traditional concrete roofs. The parks are in effect a type of green roof.

Cemeteries

Urban cemeteries are among the largest and most stable of all open space systems. They are relatively large and because they are used for burial, they are protected from development and remain undisturbed for centuries. In the nineteenth century cemeteries were intention-ally designed to function as public parks; cemeteries from that period often contain large tree canopies which provide habitat for many kinds of animals. In a new twenty-first-century version, places known as eco-cemeteries prohibit the use of embalming fluids and heavy metals, and are designed to serve as habitat restoration projects at the same time as they are working cemeteries.

Golf Courses

Golf courses are regarded as environmentally devastating, typically using large quantities of water, fertilizers, and pesticides to maintain uniform, monoculture surfaces. In an emerging trend known as natural golf courses, multi-use courses serve dual roles of recreation and wildlife habitat. Such courses use less irrigation, avoid spraying and mowing around water, use native plants, leave dead trees standing as nesting sites, and develop unmanaged wildlife habitat areas between holes and along streams. Golf course managers post signs explaining habitat and management practices to promote acceptance by users.

Public Lands

Street and highway rights-of-way, highway medians, utility and power transmission line easements constitute significant areas of land that cannot be built upon. Public agencies in many countries plant and maintain these linear spaces as habitat corridors, including plantings for butterflies, honeybees, and other pollinators. When used as part of a stormwater management system, these open spaces are known as green infrastructure.

Military Sites

Many kinds of military exercises are devastating to wildlife. However, wide security zones around military bases and other government installations offer protected natural areas. LIFE, the EU's funding instrument for the environment, works with the LIFE-Nature project to restore and protect habitat on military sites across Europe. In the US, The Nature Conservancy has a cooperative agreement with the Department of Defense to create or conserve protected buffer zones amounting to hundreds of thousands of acres (Rosenzweig 2003, 34). According to The Nature Conservancy, "more threatened and endangered species live on military bases across the United States than on land managed by the Forest Service, Bureau of Land Management, Fish and Wildlife Service or the Park Service" (The Nature Conservancy n.d.).

The Korean Demilitarized Zone (DMZ) forms the border between North and South Korea. Two and a half miles wide and 155 miles long, filled with land mines and guarded by 2 million soldiers on both sides, no human has walked there since its creation in 1953. It is surrounded by countries that are among the most densely populated in the world. In spite of the land mines, because of the lack of human intervention this zone is home to 67 endangered species including migratory birds, the rare Amur leopard, and an occasional Siberian tiger (Kim 1997, 242).

Agricultural Lands

Most traditional farmland is not perfectly flat; it is rolling countryside, where fields are interspersed with small streams, hedgerows, and woodlands. Hedgerows are narrow strips of plants, shrubs, and trees that grow along fence lines. In addition to serving as windbreaks and reducing water loss they provide rich habitat for large numbers of insects, reptiles, birds, and mammals. Hedgerows, stream corridors, and woodlands provide movement corridors for wildlife. Many federal programs in the US are available to help farmers conserve habitat by providing detailed technical assistance, rental payments, and cost-sharing to farmers who agree to conserve wetlands, buffers, and woodlands on their farms.

Roads and Wildlife Crossings

Roads and highways are significant problems for wildlife. In addition to fragmenting habitat patches, they are barriers that make it difficult to forage for food, find mates, and colonize new areas. Vehicles on roads kill millions of animals every year (Gaskill 2013). Short of eliminating roads, the next best way to help wildlife survive these threats is to give them safe ways to move across the roads, either by passing under them or by passing over them. Many departments of transportation have wildlife crossing programs. The most common style is the wildlife underpass, which can be as simple as a large culvert; others are vegetated overpasses. Fencing is added in some places to protect animals from traffic and to guide them to safe crossings. One of the most-photographed wildlife overpasses crosses a highway through Banff National Park in Canada, where instituting a program of fences, underpasses, and overpasses reduced the death rate for large mammals by 96 percent (Primack 2008, 222).

Rewilding and Large-Scale Corridors

The reestablishment of resilient, healthy ecosystems which are able to function and evolve over time is the goal of ecological restoration. Research data from multiple disciplinary fronts paints the same picture: large habitats and connectivity are critical to resilience and long-term species survival. The foundational concept was put forth by E. O. Wilson in a theory known as island biogeography, which showed that in isolated habitats as area decreased, the number of species decreased (MacArthur and Wilson 1967, 3–4). In the early 1990s a group of biologists began to develop an approach known as rewilding, built on the importance of large-scale habitat cores, corridors to connect them, and large predators to regulate prey and smaller predators, together with other keystone species, summarizing the essential elements with the phrase "cores, corridors, and carnivores" (Soulé and Noss 1998, 22). As was shown in Yellowstone National Park when communities of aspen trees, willows, beavers, trout, birds, and frogs surged back to health following the reintroduction of wolves, carnivores perform regulating functions that are essential to keeping ecosystems healthy (Ray et al. 2005, 105–107). But keystone species at the tops of food chains need areas bigger than Yellowstone Park in which to do their work, with connections between them where the animals can disperse, find mates, and maintain genetic diversity.

In North America the Wildlands Network proposes to link isolated protected areas into one large network to restore large-scale habitats and migration corridors for animals who need large ranges (Primack 2008, 222). It envisions restoring four Continental Wildways or large-scale corridors. The goals are to reintroduce keystone species and to reduce fragmentation, assembling corridors from existing wildlands that have minimal fragmentation, such as national parkland, together with linkages connecting many smaller cores. Strategies include wildlife overpasses and underpasses, wolf-friendly ranching practices, and collaboration with private landowners (Wildlands Network 2015).

A US-Canadian organization known as the Yellowstone to Yukon Conservation Initiative (Y2Y) is working to assemble an interconnected system along the entire Rocky Mountain corridor, with enough space for large animals to travel safely. It makes restoration decisions using the habitat requirements of the grizzly bear as an umbrella species. Y2Y lobbied for wildlife crossings, which led to wildlife-friendly fencing and crossings throughout the area including the famous wildlife overpasses in Banff National Park (Fraser 2009, 35), modeled on examples found throughout Europe.

Europe has long been a center for major conservation efforts and is now the site of a major large-scale corridor. During the Soviet era, Europe was split by a heavily guarded barrier known as the Iron Curtain. Although socially devastating, the border turned out to offer protection for wildlife. Today it is an ecological network covering over 7700 miles known as the European Green Belt (Fraser 2009, 81). Launched in Germany, with support from the last leader of the Soviet Union Michail Gorbachev, the European Green Belt initiative has been adopted by the IUCN, national governments, and other partners.

Another approach to large-scale restoration is known as Pleistocene rewilding, based on the concept that large animals are critical to the health of ecosystems and that their disappearance sparks chains of reactions that throw ecosystems out of balance. Pleistocene rewilding in North America proposes the reintroduction of proxies for megafauna who were once native to North America and were driven to extinction by the arrival of humans around 13,000 years ago (Donlan 2007, 70). In some cases, megafauna species went extinct worldwide but have close relatives who survived elsewhere. For example, mammoths are extinct, but their relatives the elephants survive in small numbers on other continents and might be used as proxies for the niche that mammoths filled. The incremental plan began by reintroducing endangered Bolson tortoises from Mexico to a private New Mexico ranch. The next step would introduce Asian asses, an endangered species of wild horse, and Bactrian camels to fenced reserves (Donlan et al. 2005, 914). In the second and more controversial phase, ecologists propose establishing populations of cheetahs, elephants, and lions in a vast, securely fenced park similar to arrangements found in Africa. As an additional conservation benefit, settling at-risk and endangered species into new habitats beyond their current narrow ranges may help protect their populations from extinction, while ecotourism and new jobs can provide economic benefits (ibid.).

In Russia, the goal of Pleistocene Park in the overgrown woodlands of northern Siberia is to restore a former grassland known as the mammoth steppe through rewilding (Flannery 2010, 277). During the Pleistocene epoch, ecosystem processes on the steppe were driven by large herds of herbivores including woolly mammoths, woolly rhinoceroses, bison, yaks, and musk oxen. Scientists at Pleistocene Park hope to reproduce the self-maintaining processes and functions that kept the steppes open and the permafrost frozen by reintroducing proxies for now-extinct megafauna, and in the process to prevent runaway melting of permafrost and resulting methane release (Zimov 2007, 111).

Wilderness or Managed Landscape?

There are commonly understood to be two general types of landscapes on the planet: places which have been impacted by humans, and pristine wilderness, which has not been impacted by humans. But one must go far back in time to find ecosystems not impacted by humans. It is now understood that indigenous humans likely were keystone species in many ecosystems, exerting widespread influence (Cole and Yung 2010, 43). Most megafauna, the largest mammals ever to roam the earth, were driven to extinction by humans over the last 80,000 years, with all of them gone worldwide by 10,000 years ago (Sandom et al. 2014; Bartlett et al. 2015). Humans and ecosystems have lived in interconnected relationships for thousands of years.

North America, for example, was heavily managed by Native American people who lived there, using fire regimes and other techniques. European explorers arrived in 1492 on the shores of a managed landscape where for centuries humans had modified vegetation and built earthworks, roads, settlements and cities throughout the Americas. However, those European explorers brought with them diseases to which the Indian people had no resistance, and native populations were reduced by 90 percent as a result (Mann 2011, 106). Without human land managers to burn, clear, and plant, trees filled in the cleared places and dense forests formed. This was the landscape EuroAmerican travelers saw in the years from 1750 to 1850, a re-grown forest they thought was wilderness (Vale 2002, 195).

In what is now the Amazon rainforest of South America, archaeological evidence reveals that complex agrarian societies once managed large farms and orchards and built cities, roads, and extensive earthworks (Mann 2011, 354–59). Sixteenth-century Spanish explorers described the urban centers and highways they encountered there (Pearce 2015, 121). The pathogens they carried with them launched a pandemic that wiped out 90 percent of the local population; the forest took over and the few survivors fled into the jungle to become the remnants of isolated tribes we find today (Bruges 2010, 25). So, too, in the Amazon basin, what we now think of as pristine rainforest was until 500 years ago the managed landscape of a sophisticated civilization (Heckenberger 2003, 1710).

Ecology in the Anthropocene

The traditional view of ecology was that ecosystems were stable, static, and balanced. However, we now know that ecosystems are dynamic and somewhat unpredictable because life on Earth is made of complex adaptive systems which feature emergence and resilience. Life continuously innovates and generates novelty as it explores new niches and adapts to shifting conditions. Emergence and resilience mean that change is inevitable. Ecosystems and species distributions have always changed over time throughout the planet's history (Cole and Yung 2010, 198).

Restoration efforts often work to return an ecosystem to some state in the past, a target known as a historical baseline (Hobbs 2012, 26). For example, at a site in North America, the goal might be to restore plant and animal communities that were present before European colonists arrived. Managers may remove nonnative species or reintroduce species which have vanished locally in order to restore a system to a historical baseline, in the belief that ecosystems that look like the past are more natural or more wild (Cole and Yung 2010, 43).

However, life moves on, and many of the changes in state are irreversible (ibid., 38). The global climate is changing; temperatures will continue to warm for centuries or longer because of greenhouse gases already in the atmosphere. Plants and animals are adapting by steadily shifting their ranges toward the poles and higher in elevation. As they do, the combinations of who lives with whom are shifting, too, in a major turnover of species within habitats (Dornelas et al. 2014, 296). As climate and composition change, historical assemblages of species become less well adapted to current conditions.

The details may be novel, but the movement of species is not new: many species shift hundreds of miles every time ice ages come and go or climate warms or cools (Marris 2011, 33). Meanwhile, human activities have moved all kinds of species to new locations, where they have adapted and settled in. The new communities being created which are not managed by humans are known as **novel ecosystems** (Hobbs et al. 2009, 599). Of course, since species and habitats have changed continually throughout the history of life, every ecosystem has been a novel ecosystem at some time in the past.

A decision restorationists must make is whether to emphasize historical fidelity, or whether to emphasize ecological function and resilience, particularly given that future climate conditions will be different than today. To conserve assemblages of species and ecosystems inherited from the past would demand active intervention and management into the indefinite future. To support nature's dynamic processes of regeneration and evolution would mean allowing and promoting change, rather than trying to hold it back (Pearce 2015, 187). Ecosystems which are allowed to operate on their own can be expected to drift into new and unprecedented conditions (Cole and Yung 2010, 24) as species move and remix in new ways (Hobbs 2012, 27). This is the new face of restoration ecology, as scientists incorporate concepts of change and resilience as fundamental features of ecosystems (ibid., 25).

Notes

1 The massive destruction of bacterial life that happened about 2 billion years ago when oxygen began filling the air is not included in this count.
2 What constitutes a patch depends on scale. A piece of landscape that functions as a patch for an elephant can be a diverse region of multiple patches for a butterfly (Andel and Aronson 2012, 47).
3 A 100-year storm has a 1-in-100 probability of occurring in a given year; flooding from such a storm occurs on average once in every 100 years.

Further Reading

Apfelbaum, Steven I. and Alan W. Haney. *Restoring Ecological Health to Your Land.* Washington, DC: Island Press, 2010.
Flannery, Tim. *The Eternal Frontier: An Ecological History of North America and Its Peoples.* New York: Grove Press, 2001.
Marris, Emma. *Rambunctious Garden: Saving Nature in a Post-Wild World.* New York: Bloomsbury, 2011.
Pearce, Fred. *The New Wild: Why Invasive Species Will Be Nature's Salvation.* Boston, MA: Beacon Press, 2015.
Primack, Richard B. *A Primer of Conservation Biology.* 4th ed. Sunderland, MA: Sinauer Associates, 2008.
Riley, Ann L. *Restoring Streams in Cities.* Washington, DC: Island Press, 1998.
Rosenzweig, Michael L. *Win–Win Ecology.* New York: Oxford University Press, 2003.
Wilson, Edward O. *The Future of Life.* London: Abacus, 2002.

Chapter Review

1   Extinction is a naturally occurring process. What is unusual about that process today?
2   Why should we be concerned about a species going locally extinct if populations still exist elsewhere?
3   What kinds of species are most vulnerable to extinction?
4   What does HIPPO stand for?
5   What is biodiversity and why is it important?
6   What factors promote biodiversity?
7   Why does a large population preserve genetic diversity more than a small population?
8   How is a tree plantation different from an old-growth forest?
9   List some examples of edge effects.
10   What is the difference between conservation and restoration?
11   How can you tell whether a restoration project is successful?
12   What is resilience and why is it important to ecosystems?
13   What is a biodiversity hotspot?
14   What roles do land trusts play in conserving ecosystems?
15   How is an umbrella species different from a keystone species?

16 How would you describe the core goal of stream restoration?
17 What is daylighting?
18 What is a novel ecosystem?

Critical Thinking and Discussion

1 How are invasive species different from nonnative species?
2 The 2007 film *The Story of Stuff* stated that the US had less than 4 percent of its original forests left. A critic of the film countered that between 1920 and 2000, the number of forests in the US actually increased. Are these statements mutually exclusive? What is the difference between so-called "original forests" and new forests? Explain how both these statements can be true.
3 What is the value of setting aside roadless areas? What harm do roads do?
4 Do you think that overconsumption of resources could have greater impacts on future generations than on the current generation? If so, why?
5 Ecologists and environmental ethicists debate the relationship of humans and the rest of the biosphere. An anthropocentric view places humans at the center and gives human needs higher priority. A biocentric view considers humans as one among many species and holds that all life has intrinsic value independent of its usefulness to humans. Which approach would you say more closely aligns with your own?
6 Do you think that universally accepted values about the human relationship to the rest of nature should be a goal? Do you think it is acceptable for different communities to hold different values?
7 List several human impacts on the health of the oceans. Describe how elements of your life connect to each impact.
8 Imagine that a coworker tells you that extinction is a natural process that has been going on for millions of years, and so a species going extinct a little earlier than it would have as a result of human activity is not a cause for concern. How would you respond?
9 Can you name any species that have gone extinct within your lifetime?
10 What is "nature"? Are humans outside nature, or are we part of nature?
11 What is wilderness? Does wilderness still exist, or has the concept become only symbolic?
12 When we are restoring an ecosystem, should we try to restore it to a set of conditions from a particular time in the past? How do we pick which time? Is there another approach?
13 Fire is sometimes used as an ecosystem management tool, but it causes suffering and death for many smaller creatures. What alternative tactics might there be that could accomplish similar goals?
14 How does reintroducing beaver into an area from which they were once extirpated affect ecosystems there now?
15 Do you think it would be possible to hold city council or planning commission meetings in which not just diverse human interests but also the interests of ecosystems were represented? How would it be decided who would speak for these ecosystems?
16 A developer in your town wants to build on a wetland. They have offered to buy and conserve a similar-sized natural area in a different place to mitigate for the wetland they are destroying. Is that a reasonable trade?
17 Should we try to assign a monetary value to ecosystem services? Why or why not?
18 Some people think the word "stewardship" implies caring and protection; others think it implies an anthropocentric view of the human relationship to nature. What does the word "stewardship" mean to you?

19   Some people think the ESA is too strict; others think it is not strict enough. What do you think? Can you think of examples?

20   What are some advantages and disadvantages of living in a river's floodplain?

21   What are some benefits of floods?

22   If you were the manager of a park, how would you establish conservation and restoration goals to accommodate changing climate over the next 100 years?

8   Pollution

Every system from a cell to a planet uses energy and cycles material, taking in matter as nutrient, using it, and releasing it as waste. In the biosphere, waste from one organism becomes food for another. For a system to be sustainable, the rate at which waste is released can be no greater than the rate at which it can be processed, recycled, or absorbed.

Pollution is an unwanted substance that is harmful. The word comes from the Latin verb *polluere*, meaning to soil, defile, or contaminate. Pollution comes from a variety of sources. It can be from a natural source such as a volcanic eruption, or it can be from an organic source such as sewage, a naturally occurring byproduct of life, which becomes pollution when it accumulates at rates greater than natural processes can accommodate.

Toxicity depends upon dose. Many substances are toxic at certain quantities but have negligible effects below certain concentrations. Nitrogen, for example, is necessary to plant growth, but added in excess amounts as fertilizer can result in nitrate contamination of drinking water and causes dead zones along coastlines. Carbon dioxide is essentially for keeping Earth's temperature warm enough for life, but when it builds up faster than the earth system can accommodate, climate regulation is disrupted.

In addition to natural or organic sources, pollution can come from synthetic chemicals produced by human activity. Some can be metabolized and eventually rendered harmless by bacteria. But for many other such chemicals, which have never before existed on the planet, no organisms and no natural processes have evolved which can break them down. These compounds are called **xenobiotic**: they are foreign to living systems. Some xenobiotic pollutants are toxic at even minute quantities.

Pollution can be categorized by where it occurs: it can be air pollution, soil pollution, or water pollution. It can be categorized by content: it can be composed of particulate matter, organic compounds, inorganic salts, and metals. When the behavior of certain pollutants is of particular concern, they may be listed by a regulatory agency such as the Environmental Protection Agency (EPA). In the US, air pollutants of concern are listed as **criteria pollutants** and water pollutants of concern are listed as priority pollutants. Especially problematic pollutants are found on lists of **persistent organic pollutants** (POPs); persistent, bioaccumulative, and toxic (PBT) pollutants; or both.

Types of Toxins

Some toxins are **allergens**: they cause a response when a response is not necessary by activating the body's immune system. Formaldehyde is a strong allergen that can also sensitize the immune system and trigger reactions to other substances. It is used in plywood, particle board, foam insulation, and other building materials.

Immune system depressants are substances that work the opposite way. Instead of activating the immune system they suppress it, making the organism susceptible to infections. Examples include some pesticides and the now-banned polychlorinated biphenyls (PCBs), formerly used in electrical transformers and as fire retardants.

Mutagens are substances that damage genetic material, or DNA, in cells. There appears to be no safe threshold level for mutagens. Some mutagens are **carcinogens**, substances known to increase the risk of developing cancer. Toxins that also cause abnormalities in developing embryos, such as mercury, lead, and alcohol, are known as **teratogens**.

Neurotoxins attack nerve cells, causing permanent neurological damage. Neurotoxins include heavy metals such as lead, arsenic, cadmium, mercury, and many pesticides, including the now-banned DDT and Aldrin and the still-used Malathion and Parathion. Mercury is a persistent and powerful neurotoxin. Most of the mercury accumulating in the environment comes from coal-fired power plants.

Endocrine disruptors interfere with normal hormone functions. Hormones are substances produced in the endocrine system that regulate processes such as growth, metabolism, behavior, and organ function. Endocrine disruptors are also known as environmental estrogen because they can mimic the hormone estrogen. Atrazine, a common herbicide, is an endocrine disruptor linked to increased rates of birth defects among infants born in farm regions. Endocrine systems are designed to function with minute quantities of hormones, and so are vulnerable at even very low concentrations of substances that can mimic hormones.

Some toxins affect living systems in multiple ways. For example, PCBs work as immune system depressants, mutagens, and endocrine disruptors. PCBs have been banned in the US but a closely related chemical, polybrominated diphenyl ether (PBDE), has been banned in Europe but is still widely used in the US as a flame retardant, in upholstery foam, and various plastic products. Phthalates are carcinogens and endocrine disruptors, widely used as plastic softeners in toys and food packaging and as fragrance-enhancers in cosmetics. Bisphenol A (BPA) is another mutagen and endocrine disrupter used in manufacturing polycarbonate plastics for products including water bottles, food can linings, and tooth sealants; BPA leaches into water and food (Hill 2010, 84).

Box 8.1 Cancer Clusters

When biologist Sandra Steingraber developed cancer in her early twenties, she began researching the evidence linking high rates of cancer to high concentrations of toxins in the environment. Her 1998 book *Living Downstream* reported what she found. Steingraber's approach was similar to that in Rachel Carson's *Silent Spring*, and like Carson's book *Living Downstream* was eloquent, passionate, scientifically rigorous yet easy to read, and a best seller. It introduced many readers to the concept of **cancer clusters.**

A cancer cluster is a greater-than-expected number of cancer cases, usually associated with exposures to toxins in the workplace (Steingraber 2010, 64). The US Centers for Disease Control and the World Health Organization (WHO) make some of the connections visible through cancer mortality data tables and maps. Areas of high cancer concentrations are obvious in industrial regions.

Epidemiologists conduct studies to identify possible cancer clusters that might link cancers and exposure to potential carcinogens. They suspect a cancer cluster when statistics in one geographical area show an above-average number of cancer cases, a large number of one type of cancer, rather than a mix of several types, or an above-average number of cases of a rare type of cancer.

Pollution Transport and Fate

Pollution comes from a source and moves into a sink. Natural and human activities, or sources, produce byproducts and wastes that are then emitted back into the various planetary systems, or sinks. These products move through the environment at different speeds and in various ways: through air, through water, and through the food chain. **Transport** refers to how pollutants move through the environment. **Fate** refers to how they change over time.

Pollutants can be transported by flows of air or through water. The atmosphere is constantly in motion, so pollutants that get into the air in one region are easily carried to another. Wind currents carry contaminants around the globe and emissions from one continent become pollutants on other continents. For example, PCBs are a class of persistent organic pollutants (POPs) that have been banned since the 1970s, yet the highest levels of PCBs in human blood are found not near former manufacturing sites but in Inuit people living above the Arctic Circle (Cunningham and Cunningham 2010, 357).

Toxins that are water-soluble move through the environment easily because water is everywhere on this water planet. Water, the universal solvent, readily dissolves other substances. Water-soluble pollutants are readily absorbed by organisms since all cells are made primarily of water.

Some compounds are fat soluble and do not dissolve in water. However, when these substances get inside the body they easily penetrate cell membranes. Once inside cells, the toxins tend not to break down and instead tend to accumulate.

Bioaccumulation is the cell's process for absorbing and storing materials it needs. The same mechanism that allows the cell to accumulate useful substances also lets it accumulate harmful ones. Toxins may be diluted in the environment, perhaps a few parts per million, but inside the cell can build up to dangerous levels.

Bioaccumulation is multiplied by the effects of **biomagnification**, in which compounds can also move up through food chains and become more concentrated. On each level of a food web, one predator eats many prey animals from the level below. The toxins that bioaccumulated in the tissues of the prey animals get concentrated in the tissues of the predators who eat them. One of the earliest examples of biomagnification was the accumulation of DDT in bald eagles, top predators in their particular food webs. Long-lived predators such as bears and humans can accumulate dangerous concentrations of toxins. In the Pacific Northwest, toxicological studies found that not only do salmon remain contaminated with PCBs, but the Puget Sound orcas who eat them contain PCB levels that are 400 to 500 times those found in humans (Cullon et al. 2009, 148).

Pollutants can spread by dispersion as a plume, or volume of contamination, moves away from the center of an area of contamination, growing in size and decreasing in concentration as it moves. This is what happens when pollution from a smokestack disperses downwind or when fuel from a leaking underground fuel tank moves through the soil.

Contaminants can move by changing state, as when a solid becomes dissolved in water or a liquid evaporates and becomes a gas. The movement of a contaminant can also be retarded, or slowed, if it becomes associated with solid particles such as in soil, a process known as sorption. A long-lived pesticide easily sorbed to soil particles is more likely to remain near the surface and be carried by runoff into a stream or lake. A long-lived pesticide that is more mobile is more likely to be leached through soil and to contaminate groundwater.

Chemical compounds undergo reactions in air, water, and soil as they move and are slowly converted to other chemicals. Some transformations take millennia and are too slow to be perceived during human lifetimes; others are faster. Some herbicides degrade into simpler, less harmful substances known as breakdown products. Other toxins, such as DDT, break down into substances that are just as toxic as the original chemicals.

The fate of a contaminant—what happens to it—is determined by the combination of transport and transformation processes. A pollutant's resistance to change is described as its **persistence**. Toxins that last a long time without changing are known as **persistent**. Heavy metals, polyvinyl chloride (PVC), some pesticides, and the family of carcinogenic and endocrine-disrupting chemicals used to make nonstick cookware and waterproof fabrics are highly persistent (ibid., 169). The more readily a contaminant is transported and the more resistant it is to being transformed, the greater its pollution potential. The greatest health risks come from contaminants that are highly mobile, highly persistent, and highly toxic.

The next sections looks at pollution categorized by where it occurs: air, soil and land, water, and global-scale issues.

Air Pollution

Airborne pollutants cause more health problems than any other transport mechanism because the entire biosphere is surrounded by air (ibid., 166). Humans and other animals breathe several times a minute, taking in far greater volumes of air per day than they do food or water. Our lungs are designed to absorb gases out of the air efficiently; that means they also absorb pollutants efficiently.

In the US, the Clean Air Act requires the EPA to publish a list of hazardous air pollutants and to set maximum standards for them. It identifies six major air pollutants, known as criteria pollutants. The EPA develops criteria for setting permissible levels based on human health and/or ecosystem health. The six criteria pollutants are particulates, carbon monoxide, sulfur oxides, nitrogen oxides, lead, and ground-level ozone. These pollutants are considered to pose the most serious threats to human health and constitute the largest volume of pollutants in the atmosphere. All six are produced by the burning of fossil fuels.

Five of the criteria pollutants are called primary pollutants: they are released directly into the air from their sources, already formed. The sixth criteria pollutant, ground-level ozone, is a secondary pollutant: it forms as a result of chemical reactions between primary pollutants and other constituents in the air.

Particulates

Particulate matter is matter in the form of minute particles small enough to be suspended in air or water. When suspended in air, particles are called **aerosols**. Fine particulate matter constitutes one of the biggest health threats in industrialized countries. Particles can be solid or liquid and can be made of a wide range of substances, including soot, smoke, dust, pollen, metals, organic chemicals, and acids such as sulfates and nitrates. This is the only category of pollutant that is described by its size of particle, not by its chemical composition.

The EPA divides airborne particulate matter into two categories: PM_{10} or "inhalable coarse particles," refers to particles with diameter less than or equal to 10 μm (10 micrometers or 10,000 nanometers) in diameter. $PM_{2.5}$, or "fine particles," refers to particles less than or equal to 2.5 μm (2.5 micrometers or 2,500 nanometers) in diameter. For comparison, an average human hair is 50 to 70 μm in diameter. Particles larger than 10 μm (sand and large dust) are not regulated by the EPA.

$PM_{2.5}$ particles are the most dangerous aerosols (Pepper et al. 2006, 125). Because they are so small, they can be drawn deep into the lungs where they damage lung tissue, clog tiny airways, and put stress on the heart. Bacteria, fungi, synthetic chemicals, and heavy metals that adhere to particles get carried deep into lungs as well. While PM_{10} particles typically settle out of the air in less than a day, $PM_{2.5}$ particles remain suspended for days and travel greater distances, so the risk of exposure is increased.

Most $PM_{2.5}$ aerosols are anthropogenic. Primary particles such as soot enter the air already formed from sources such as construction sites, incomplete combustion, and metal smelting. The major component of soot is black carbon, which in addition to health impacts, contributes to climate change by accelerating the melting of snow and ice (IPCC 2013, 685; OECD 2012, 135). Secondary particles form in the air from other components including sulfur dioxide and nitrogen oxides; they come from vehicle exhaust, power plants, industrial processes, incinerators, and wood burning. In some regions coal-fired power plants produce the largest percentage of $PM_{2.5}$ aerosols; in other regions the largest percentage comes from roads, industrial processes, or residential wood burning.

Some materials occur in nature, but become problems because of the great quantities in which humans use them. For example, asbestos is a naturally-occurring mineral. It occurs in a fibrous structure and forms tiny, sharp particles that can embed in lungs, causing scar tissue or cancer. Asbestos removal from buildings is closely regulated to prevent exposure. Silica is another naturally occurred mineral used in jack-hammering and in sand-blasting to clean building surfaces. Silica crystals can embed in lungs, resulting in scar tissue and fibrous growths.

Carbon Monoxide

Carbon monoxide (CO) is the major pollutant in urban air, most of it released by incomplete combustion of fossil fuels. CO concentrations are highest along heavily traveled roads (ibid., 381). Long-term exposure can lead to heart damage and poses an increased health risk to people with congestive heart failure and people who are pregnant. Carbon monoxide also reduces the ability of the Earth system to regulate levels of the greenhouse gas methane. At sufficient concentrations carbon monoxide also weakens or kills forest trees, thus diminishing a carbon sink and potentially increasing the quantity of the greenhouse gas carbon dioxide (Meadows et al. 2004, 166).

Sulfur Oxides

Most atmospheric sulfur pollution is sulfur dioxide, SO_2, sometimes called "sox" for short when speaking. It is a colorless gas with a strong, distinctive smell, the same odor given off when a kitchen match or fireworks are lit.

Ninety percent of the sulfur dioxide in the air comes from the burning of fossil fuels, particularly coal (Pepper et al. 2006, 382). Oil refineries, ore smelters, and cement manufacturing also emit significant quantities of SO_2 (Hill 2010, 127). Sulfur dioxide is corrosive and is damaging to both plants and animals. It causes respiratory problems and is believed to be second only to tobacco smoke as a cause of air pollution-related health problems (ibid., 125).

Sulfur dioxide can be further oxidized in the air to form sulfur trioxide, SO_3, which then reacts with water vapor or rainwater to form sulfuric acid. Some of the health impacts from sulfur dioxide on humans and other animals are due to its ability to form the highly irritating sulfuric acid in reaction with moisture in mucous membranes and lungs. We experience the same process when chopping a raw onion and the sulfur compound emitted by the onion combines with moisture in the eyes to produce sulfuric acid. The eyes then produce tears to wash out the irritant.

Sulfuric acid, together with nitric acid, is a major component of **acid rain**. Acid rain refers to precipitation that contains higher than normal amounts of these two acids. The acids form through chemical reactions in the air when sulfur dioxide and nitrogen oxides released by power plants and vehicle exhaust mix with oxygen, water, and other atmospheric components. Acid rain damages historic buildings and sculptures, damages forest trees, and upsets ecosystems of lakes and streams through acidification.

Nitrogen Oxides

Nitrogen oxides include nitric oxide, NO, nitrogen dioxide, NO_2, and nitrous oxide, N_2O, one of the common greenhouse gases. They are referred to using the general abbreviation NOx, sometimes pronounced "nox" when speaking. NO_2 is the NOx on which the EPA focuses, using NO_2 as an indicator of the presence of the other nitrogen oxides as well.

Nitric oxide (NO) is produced during the burning of fossil fuels. It oxidizes further in the atmosphere to produce NO_2, recognized by its distinctive reddish-brown color. The brown color in the smog that settles over urban areas is caused by the presence of NO_2. Similar to sulfur dioxide, nitrogen oxides can be further oxidized in the air to form NO_3, which then reacts with water vapor or rainwater to form nitric acid, a component of acid rain.

Like sulfur dioxide, the nitrogen oxides are damaging to both plants and animals. They irritate lungs and mucous membranes, inflaming the lungs of healthy people, aggravating symptoms in people with respiratory diseases and putting people with congestive heart failure at greater risk of premature death (Pepper et al. 2006, 383).

Nitrogen oxide pollution is an environmental justice issue. According to the EPA, NO_2 concentrations near major roads are 30 to 100 percent higher than away from roads. Housing within 300 feet of a major highway, railroad, or airport and thus vulnerable to increased impact from nitrogen oxides is more likely to include non-white and low-income people (US EPA n.d., Nitrogen Dioxide).

Lead

Lead is a highly toxic heavy metal, a neurotoxin that can cause behavioral problems and learning disabilities. As an air pollutant, it comes from lead smelters, waste incinerators, coal-fired power plants, and lead-acid battery manufacturing. Before it was banned in the 1980s, the largest source of lead in the atmosphere was from the burning of leaded gasoline.

Ground-Level Ozone

Secondary air pollutants are formed by chemical reactions that occur after substances enter the air. One of the most important secondary pollutants is ground-level ozone, one of the EPA's six criteria pollutants.

Ordinary atmospheric oxygen (O_2) consists of two atoms of oxygen joined together. Ozone (O_3) contains three oxygen atoms instead of two. Ozone can often be recognized by its smell, a sharp odor said to resemble chlorine bleach or the smell of clean bed sheets. Ozone gives urban smog its characteristic odor, the same odor detected outdoors after lightning storms or indoors near some electrical equipment. The word "ozone" comes from the Greek verb meaning "to smell."

Ozone can be protective or damaging depending upon in which level of the atmosphere it is found. It forms when solar radiation strikes oxygen molecules in the stratosphere or upper atmosphere, where the ozone shields organisms on Earth from incoming ultraviolet radiation. Ozone in the stratosphere is necessary for life. In the troposphere or lower atmosphere, however, and particularly near the ground, excess ozone is considered a pollutant.

Ground-level ozone forms in a chemical reaction between nitrogen oxides and **volatile organic compounds** (VOCs) in the presence of sunlight. Because these secondary chemical reactions are driven by energy from the sun, the results are called photochemical oxidants or simply photochemical smog. The word **smog** was first coined in London 100 years ago by combining the words "smoke" and "fog." Photochemical smog formed from hydrocarbons in car exhaust is most common in urban areas with strong sunlight. It is often called "brown cloud" because of the color of its nitrogen oxide component. Industrial cities without strong sunlight also have photochemical smog, but there it tends to be higher in particulate pollution including tiny particles of soot and sulfur dioxide from burning fossil fuels. These particulates give the smog a gray color and it is often called "gray air."

Breathing ozone can reduce lung function and irritate mucous membranes; lungs can be permanently scarred with repeated exposure. Being made of oxygen, ground-level ozone causes oxidation, damaging building materials and plastics; making plants more susceptible to disease, insect attacks, and other pollutants; and reducing growth in forests and crops (Pepper et al. 2006, 384). Ozone, a three-atom molecule, is one of the greenhouse gases.

Other Air Pollution Concerns

In addition to the six criteria pollutants, the EPA has identified a list of chemicals that they consider particularly dangerous. Known as the **hazardous air pollutants** (HAPs), the list includes 187 carcinogens, mutagens, neurotoxins, endocrine disruptors, and other highly toxic compounds. Most are heavy metals, chlorinated hydrocarbons (pesticides), or VOCs. The hazardous air pollutants are not as pervasive nor do they occur in as large quantities as the criteria pollutants, but they are dangerous, can accumulate, and often persist in the environment for long periods of time.

Soil and Land Pollution

Pollution sources that can contaminate soil include mining, oil drilling, and agriculture. Mining, including strip mining and pit mining, involves removing mass quantities of soil and rock from the earth, processing it using chemicals, and depositing the remains in large piles. Rock that contains a metal of interest is leached with acid solutions until most of the metal ore has been dissolved and removed. The processed crushed rock, known as mine tailings, is then pumped together with liquid into pits. Gold-mine tailings contain cyanide; copper-, silver-, and lead-mine tailings contain sulfuric acid and heavy metals including cadmium and lead. Wastewater from these tailings washes into streams and lakes.

Drilling for oil uses large quantities of drilling fluids to force crude oil to the surface and as cutting fluid for the drill bits. On land, the fluids are disposed of in storage pits or evaporation ponds; if drilling off-shore, they are released into the ocean. Some oil and gas also leaks from every drilling operation. Wastes generated by oil and gas drilling are known as exploration and production waste, or E&P waste, and in the US are exempt from hazardous waste regulations.

Water Pollution

Hydrogen oxide, commonly known as water, is the universal solvent. One of its most significant chemical properties is its ability to dissolve other substances, which makes it easily contaminated, allowing it to dissolve and carry pollutants for long distances. Once water is polluted it is difficult, and thus expensive, to restore.

Several laws protecting water quality were enacted in the US during the 1970s. The most current version, the US Clean Water Act, requires each state to establish and monitor Total Daily Maximum Loads (TDMLs) for pollutants. The federal Clean Water Act lists water pollutants under several categories: conventional pollutants, priority pollutants, and nonconventional pollutants.

Conventional Pollutants

Just as the Clean Air Act requires the EPA to regulate criteria pollutants in air, the Clean Water Act requires the EPA to regulate **conventional pollutants** in water. The conventional pollutants are biochemical oxygen demand, total suspended solids, fecal coliform bacteria, pH, and oil and grease. What is noteworthy about these pollutants is that none of them is an individual chemical.

Biochemical oxygen demand (BOD) is a measure of oxygen depletion. Most of the bacteria in water who decompose organic matter require dissolved oxygen (DO) to do so. The greater the proportion of decomposing organic matter in the water, the greater the oxygen demand. High organic content, or high BOD, thus depletes the dissolved oxygen in the water. Oxygen depletion, called hypoxia, can suffocate animals living in the water who depend on dissolved oxygen.

Total suspended solids (TSS) describes the concentration of fine particles suspended in water. TSS are quantified by **turbidity**, a measure of water clarity. With greater turbidity less light can penetrate the water, which reduces photosynthesis and the production of dissolved oxygen. Greater turbidity also increases water temperature, which lowers the concentration of dissolved oxygen; warmer water holds less dissolved oxygen than colder water.

Coliforms constitute a group of bacteria who live in the digestive tracts of humans and other animals and are consequently found in feces. Strains include the well-known *Escherichia coli*, abbreviated *E. coli*. Many kinds of microorganisms live in digestive tracts and it would be time-consuming to test for all of them, so **fecal coliform bacteria** are used as indicators for a range of pathogenic organisms including other bacteria, viruses, and protozoans. If fecal coliforms are found, it is assumed that other fecal organisms are likely to be in the water as well.

The **pH** scale is a measure of the concentration of hydrogen ions in water or water-based fluids, measured on a scale from 1 to 14. A pH of 7 is neutral, less than 7 is acid, and more than 7 is alkaline or basic. Distilled water has a pH of 7. Most aquatic animals prefer a range of 6.5 to 8.0. Acidic water, that is, water with a lower pH, not only harms organisms but also makes toxic pollutants more mobile and more easily taken up by plants and animals. Changes in pH can be caused by acid rain and by discharging of pollutants in wastewater.

Oil and grease is one category of conventional pollutant. Although the EPA does not regulate wastes from oil and gas exploration and production, it does regulate wastes from aboveground and underground oil and gas storage tank leaks and spills.

Priority Pollutants

The category called "priority pollutants" is a set of pollutants listed by their individual chemical names and for which the EPA has published analytical test methods. The current EPA list contains 126 priority pollutants, many of which are found on other EPA lists as well. Pollutants on this list include heavy metals, volatile hydrocarbons, and many pesticides.

Nonconventional Pollutants

The third group of water pollutants regulated by the EPA is called "nonconventional pollutants," covering any pollutant not already identified as a conventional or priority pollutant. The category includes such components as color, salt, and heat. Color comes from dye discharged by textile mills; its concentration is regulated. Salt is used to dissolve ice and snow from roads in colder climates.

An unhealthy change in water temperature is known as **thermal pollution**. Biological processes in any ecosystem, including photosynthesis and metabolism, are tuned to operate at particular temperatures. For example, tropical fish do best in warmer water; trout do best in colder water and can die if water temperatures get too warm. Thermal pollution can result from releases of cooling water from power plants or manufacturing facilities or from runoff from pavement.

Eutrophication

Eutrophication is the gradual build-up of organic matter and nutrients in a waterway. Excess nitrogen and phosphorus from fertilizer runoff and livestock manure washes into rivers or oceans where it acts as a nutrient for algae. The result is algal blooms, large masses of dense algae growth. As individual algae die and begin to decompose, they increase biochemical oxygen demand, depleting the water of oxygen so that aquatic life dies from lack of oxygen. The dead zone in the Gulf of Mexico near the mouth of the Mississippi River is an example of eutrophication.

Groundwater Pollution

Once water in an underground aquifer is polluted it is very difficult to decontaminate. When surface water is contaminated, photochemical reactions from sunlight, evaporation in contact with air, and the mixing of oxygen with water through wind and wave action begin the process of transforming and breaking down the pollutants. Groundwater, by contrast, is sealed away from light and air.

Preventing pollution from entering groundwater in the first place is critically important. An aquifer with the highest risk of being contaminated is one near the surface, topped by porous soil, and located in an area of high rainfall (Pepper et al. 2006, 265). Pollutants with the highest risk of contaminating groundwater are those that are water soluble and that are persistent.

Previous sections looked at pollution categorized by location. Pollutants can also be categorized by content. The following sections examine two categories of pollutant content: organic pollutants, that is, synthetic chemicals containing carbon; and inorganic pollutants, including salts and heavy metals.

Organic Pollutants

Organic compounds are chemicals that contain carbon atoms. They usually contain hydrogen atoms as well as carbon. Hydrocarbons are compounds made only of carbon and hydrogen. All of the fossil fuels are hydrocarbons, as are their derivatives including benzene, toluene, and xylene. Pesticides and synthetic plastics contain hydrocarbons.

Synthetic organic compounds are carbon-containing chemicals made by humans. They include chlorinated solvents such as trichloroethene and carbon tetrachloride; pesticides such as DDT, 2,4-D, and atrazine; PCBs; CFCs; and a number of pharmaceuticals and food additives. Volatile organic compounds (VOCs) are organic compounds that vaporize at room temperature. Many VOCs occur in nature. Methane is a VOC emitted by decomposing organic matter. Terpenes and isoprenes are VOCs emitted by trees and other plants. Terpenes give pine trees their distinctive aroma.

It is the synthetic VOCs that are of concern as pollutants. Many hydrocarbons from fossil fuel combustion, such as benzene, are carcinogens. Other sources include solvents, many household cleaning products, cosmetics, air fresheners, and dry-cleaned fabrics. **Off-gassing** refers to the vaporization of VOCs. The smell inside new cars is caused by the off-gassing of several toxic VOCs.

Formaldehyde is a VOC that is found almost everywhere in modern life, particularly indoors. It is an irritant to the respiratory system and is considered a probable carcinogen by the EPA (ibid., 198). It is common in the woodworking and textile industries and is a component of paint, adhesive, plywood, particleboard, new furniture, and carpeting.

Inorganic Pollutants

Another category of pollutants classified by content is the inorganic contaminants. These include the inorganic salts, including halogens, sodium, calcium, nitrate, and sulphate; and the heavy metals, including lead, mercury, arsenic, cadmium, and chromium.

Salts

Salts are extremely mobile in water, which makes them a pollution concern. One kind of salt is ordinary table salt, sodium chloride, used to de-ice roads and in oil-drilling fluids. Runoff changes the salinity in waterways, harming plants and animals. Groundwater near military bases is vulnerable to perchlorate, a salt used in explosives and rocket fuel. Perchlorate is water soluble, highly mobile in groundwater, resists chemical and bacterial degradation, and is extremely persistent (Pepper et al. 2006, 277).

A halogen is one of a group of elements that forms a salt in union with a metal. The halogens, fluorine, chlorine, bromine, iodine, and astatine, are highly reactive and toxic. Chlorine, toxic at higher concentrations, is used in low concentrations to disinfect drinking water. Chlorine and fluorine are components of the ozone-destroying CFCs. Although banned for most uses, they are still used in spray propellants, foam blowing agents, and in the chemical process to create non-stick cookware (Cunningham and Cunningham 2010, 351).

Heavy Metals

Heavy metals are metals that have high atomic weights. They include mercury, chromium, cadmium, arsenic, and lead. The oceans once contained high concentrations of heavy metals. Ancient bacteria used these metals as catalysts to hasten the chemical reactions that were essential to life. As these microorganisms died they drifted to the seafloor, carrying dissolved metals with them, where they accumulated. The metal-rich sediments were carried deeper into the crust, forming what are now ore deposits. As humans mine the lithosphere, they rapidly release and redistribute the metals once accumulated over eons by the work of microorganisms (Flannery 2010, 48–50).

Over 50 heavy metals are known to be toxic; 17 of these are considered very toxic and are also readily available. The heavy metals are toxic at relatively low concentrations, persistent, and bioaccumulate in the food chain. They are given off by metal smelting and the burning of fossil fuels and used in manufacturing processes including batteries and circuit boards. As with many pollutants, the dose makes the poison. Chromium, copper, and zinc are toxic metals, but in minute concentrations are trace elements needed by the body.

Two particularly widespread and highly toxic heavy metals are lead and mercury, both potent neurotoxins that can cause neurological problems and developmental disabilities in children. The phrase "mad as a hatter" stems from mercury poisoning, common among nineteenth-century hat-makers who used mercury to cure felt for hats (Pepper et al. 2006, 284). Lewis Carroll's *Alice in Wonderland* featured a character named the Mad Hatter. Hat-making was the main trade in Stockport, England near where Carroll grew up.

Mercury, once common in thermometers, is still used in thermostats, switches, batteries, pesticides, and fluorescent lights including compact fluorescents. Most mercury contamination comes from coal-fired power plants, incinerators, and cement plants. It is carried in the atmosphere, deposited on land, and carried by streams into lakes and oceans. Because it is persistent and cumulative, it biomagnifies in the food chain; most human exposure comes from eating contaminated fish (ibid., 286).

Previous sections looked at pollution categorized by location and by content. The following sections examine two particularly hazardous classes of pollutants categorized by behavior: endocrine disruptors and persistent organic pollutants.

Endocrine Disruptors

Every animal with a nervous system possesses an endocrine system composed of glands that secrete hormones in tiny amounts. Hormones are chemical messengers, each carried in the bloodstream to its own particular target sites in the body where it delivers its message by attaching to hormone receptors. Examples include estrogen, testosterone, adrenalin, and insulin.

A number of modern synthetic pollutants interfere with the endocrine system. They are called endocrine disruptors, sometimes also known as hormone mimics, estrogen disruptors, pseudoestrogens, or environmental hormones. Many of them mimic hormones in the body. Some have chemical properties similar to hormones and plug into hormone receptors before the real hormones do. Others affect the production and release of hormones by the endocrine glands, and still others block the actions of hormones at the target sites.

Box 8.2 *Our Stolen Future*

In 1996 Theodora Colborn, a senior scientist with the World Wildlife Fund, published a book that alerted the world to the threat of endocrine disruptors. Titled *Our Stolen Future*, the book told the story of how endocrine disruption was discovered, how it works, and what it means. Like Rachel Carson's *Silent Spring* over 30 years before, *Our Stolen Future* used a vivid narrative style that made the discovery immediate and real, backed up by ample scientific evidence, along with simple, clear language that made the scientific concepts understandable to a broad, nonscientific audience. Dr. Colborn called it "a scientific detective story" (Colborn et al. 1996). Discussing how hormones work in minute quantities, Colborn described how typical dose-response curves do not work with endocrine disruptors, showing that low doses of these chemicals have biological effects often missed in high-dose studies. She explained that the way modern society uses chemicals is like performing a vast experiment whose variables and outcome we cannot control.

One example of an endocrine disruptor is the hormone estrogen itself, taken by millions of women for birth control or for hormone replacement during menopause. These pharmaceuticals must be able to resist being broken down in the body so that they can reach their target sites intact, which means that quantities of hormone are excreted and carried into sewage treatment facilities. Sewage treatment does not remove estrogen nor myriad other prescription drugs, which pass out of wastewater treatment plants into streams (Pepper et al. 2006, 507).

Other endocrine disruptors are not designed as pharmaceuticals but bind to hormone receptors in humans and other animals because of their chemical structure. Two are common in plastic products: BPA and the family of phthalates. The EU and the State of California have banned toys containing phthalates (Hill 2010, 85).

Among the most dangerous and widespread endocrine disruptors are those found in **pesticides**, such as the herbicide atrazine. Atrazine, an effective weed killer, is one of the most widely used pesticides in the US and is the herbicide most often found in groundwater (Pepper et al. 2006, 250).

Persistent Organic Pollutants

The trait of persistence is used to name a class of toxins, the persistent organic pollutants (POPs), widely produced in the industrial boom following World War II. Most are produced intentionally, but some including PCBs can also be byproducts of other processes, and dioxins are only produced as byproducts. Dioxins are created by the burning of plastics, the manufacturing of vinyl or PVC, and the burning of medical waste containing chlorine.

Production of POPs is outlawed or restricted by an international treaty, the 2001 Stockholm Convention. Some including DDT are still sold to developing countries where they are valued for their role in controlling mosquitoes. POPs no longer produced remain environmental health hazards because they are transported worldwide by wind and water, they persist for very long periods of time, and they accumulate in the tissues of predators as they are passed from one level of the food chain to another. Nearly every human on earth carries detectable levels of POPs within their body (Cunningham and Cunningham 2010, 169).

Many of the POPs are pesticides, most of them used in agriculture. A pesticide is designed to kill some kind of living organism; it is released into the environment precisely because it is toxic. Under the definition in US law, pesticides may be insecticides, rodenticides, herbicides, fungicides, growth regulators, defoliants, or desiccants (Pepper et al. 2006, 250).

Point Source and Nonpoint Source Pollution

In addition to being categorized by location, content, or behavior, pollutants can also be categorized by source. Three types of sources are point source pollution, nonpoint source pollution, and radioactive pollution.

Point source pollution comes from a single, well-defined source of emission. Point sources are facilities that concentrate pollutants, then pass them through a pipe, ditch, or canal for disposal. Common examples include a pipe discharging effluent into a river, a leaking storage tank, a ship, or a smokestack.

Nonpoint source pollution comes from diffuse sources that are more difficult to identify. As opposed to point source pollution, which comes from a specific location, nonpoint source pollution occurs over a wide area. The term is often used to describe stormwater runoff. Examples of nonpoint sources include streets, parking lots, agricultural areas, and logging sites. Automobile exhaust can also be considered nonpoint source pollution.

Radioactive Pollutants

Pollution from **radioactivity** can come from naturally occurring sources including radon gas and background radiation, or it can be a byproduct of human activities, including medical diagnosis and treatment. Radiation at high enough levels can damage tissue and cause cancer to develop.

Radioactive elements such as uranium are naturally occurring, their radioactivity left over from the supernova explosion that gave rise to the elements of our planet (Harding 2006, 112). Uranium occurs in a number of different isotopes, forms that have the same number of protons but different numbers of neutrons. The one that is important in nuclear power, uranium-235, is rare so naturally occurring uranium does not fission readily. In order to create enough critical mass to start a chain reaction, for example to fuel a nuclear power plant, the uranium must be enriched or concentrated. That is, it must be changed so that a larger percentage of it becomes uranium-235.

Some electrical power is generated in nuclear power plants. Safety is one of the major concerns with nuclear power. While the risk of accidents is low, any accidents that might occur would be significant. Disposal of radioactive waste is the larger environmental concern. Half-life is the time it takes for half of all the nuclei of an element to decay. Because the half-life of radioactive materials used in nuclear power is long, it may be hundreds of thousands of years before their radioactive levels are safe (AGI 2011, 386). Uranium mines produce large piles of radioactive tailings; fuel production, reactor operation, and spent fuel rods produce more waste. When power plants reach the end of their useful lives, the plants themselves must be decommissioned, disassembled and their massive pieces handled as waste. The challenge environmentally is the need for a storage method that could safely store all this radioactive waste for many thousands of years.

Pollution Remediation

Pollution **remediation** means stopping and reversing damage to environmental systems caused by pollution. Remediation is, essentially, applying a remedy to the problem of pollution.

In many cases the remedy comes from living organisms including bacteria, fungi, and plants. A pollutant for one organism may not be a pollutant for another organism. For example, petroleum spilled on a beach is a pollutant that can be fatal to birds, clams, otters, and many other organisms. However, it is considered food by the trillions of bacteria living along the same beach.

In the European Union (EU), pollution is regulated by the European Commission (EC) Integrated Pollution Prevention and Control (IPPC) Directive. Activities that have a high pollution potential, such as energy production, metal processing, mining, chemical manufacturing, waste management, and livestock farming, are required to have a permit. Applicants must prove that they practice pollution prevention using the best available techniques (BATs). The Directive is administered by Member States.

In the United States, pollution is regulated by several federal laws. Pollution in groundwater and surface water is regulated by the Water Pollution Control Act, usually known as the Clean Water Act. Air pollution is regulated by the Clean Air Act. Hazardous wastes on land and in navigable waters are regulated by the Comprehensive Environmental Response, Compensation, and Liability Act (CERCLA), also known as the Superfund program, and by several other laws. According to the EPA, hazardous waste is harmful or potentially harmful to humans or the environment and is either flammable, corrosive, reactive, or toxic.[1]

The Clean Water Act, the Clean Air Act, and Superfund laws are all administered by the EPA. Hundreds of thousands of polluted sites are found across the US but not all are designated as Superfund sites. Because cleanup is expensive and there are many more sites than there are funds, the EPA has developed a system known as the Hazard Ranking System (HRS) for prioritizing polluted sites. The sites are ranked so that limited resources are spent on the most critical sites first. When a hazardous waste site is being considered as a potential Superfund site it is placed on a list called the Superfund Site Inventory. The site is then assessed. If preliminary EPA assessment results indicate a problem of a particular magnitude, the site is placed on a list called the National Priorities List (NPL) and can then be called a Superfund site. Many site remediation projects are coordinated by state or local agencies and are not supervised by the EPA.

Every pollution remediation project, regardless of scale, begins by gathering and analyzing information about the site and the problem. This step is known as site characterization. Analysis is typically performed by environmental engineers or other specialized contractors.

Once site conditions have been characterized, a remediation plan is drawn up and implementation can begin. Contamination is dealt with through containment, removal, or treatment. Containment uses barriers to prevent the pollutant from spreading further. Removal physically moves contaminated soil or water to a different location. Treatment transforms the pollutant into a form that is considered no longer harmful and can be done on-site or off-site. Some treatment involves physical processes, but much of the cleanup work is done by the workhorses of pollution remediation, the bacteria. There are no simple solutions, and most sites require multiple remediation approaches. Following remediation, continued monitoring is necessary. Some sites require monitoring for 10 years or longer.

Characterization

Site characterization involves understanding the pollution and where it is. This step consists of identifying the types of contaminants, locating their source, measuring or estimating their concentration, and determining the extent of contamination. A map is drawn that shows the extent of the contamination. In the case of soil or groundwater, the map is three-dimensional, showing the extent both horizontally and vertically.

First, the types of contaminants must be identified. Knowing what kind of business or industry was involved provides basic orientation. For example, dry cleaning businesses, metal plating businesses, and gasoline stations with storage tanks each use particular types of chemical compounds. Company records including purchase orders, bills of lading, inventory records, and waste disposal records, together with interviews of present or former employees, provide more detailed information.

Mapping the contamination involves sampling, or taking measurements at a number of points. Then points of equal concentration can be connected by contour lines to produce an image of the contaminant plume, similar to the way points of equal elevation are connected by contour lines in a topographic map. Sampling points can be randomly selected to give a broad picture of an entire study area. If the contamination source and probable dispersion paths are known, sampling points can be selected systematically. Points might be evenly spaced along a path or located in a grid pattern covering an area.

Samples are often taken not only at different points in space, but at different points in time. Contaminant maps drawn at different times help engineers understand whether the contamination is staying in place or moving. If it is moving, samples over time give information about how fast and in what directions it is spreading.

Air samples are taken from air monitoring stations, with source location and topography helping to determine where pollution concentrations are likely to be highest. Air samples are also taken upwind of the source to establish baseline conditions. Soil samples are collected using augers and sampling tubes. Groundwater samples are collected from monitoring wells. Surface water samples are collected and taken to a laboratory for testing. Portable water quality kits can give rough indications of surface water quality in the field, but the results are not as accurate as laboratory testing.

Laboratory testing does not automatically reveal every pollutant that exists on a site. Different tests must be used to test for different chemical compounds. If the composition of the contaminants is not known, testing is done in several stages beginning with priority pollutants.

It is also important to know whether the contaminant is a liquid, gas, or solid; how dense it is; and if liquid, whether the contaminant is an immiscible liquid, that is, a liquid that does not mix with water. Immiscible liquid is known as a nonaqueous phase liquid (NAPL). For example, gasoline is an immiscible liquid that is less dense than water, so it may collect in a layer above the water table. It is easy to detect from wells or boreholes but difficult to remove. Chlorinated solvents may have been used in dry cleaning, metal cleaning, paint removal, or urethane foam manufacturing. They are denser than water and so do not collect and float above water. They form small, local pockets that are hard to find and so require a large number of samples to be taken. When groundwater is polluted with VOCs, the contaminants can change into gas and migrate upward through the soil. Soil gas sampling can reveal areas of VOC concentration in the subsurface to help identify optimal boring and well locations.

If pollution occurs in soil or groundwater, site characterization also involves developing an understanding of conditions underground in three dimensions. Information is collected about the makeup of the soil, its layers or horizons, how porous it is, where the groundwater is located, where permeable or impermeable layers lie above and below it, and the direction and speed with which it is flowing. Data collection methods range from standard monitoring wells combined with existing well drillers' logs to state-of-the-art instruments and advanced mathematical modeling. Once the site has been characterized, treatment can begin.

Containment

Containment involves using a barrier to prevent, or try to prevent, a contaminant from moving. It is used in some cases when removing contaminated material is too costly, as happened at Love Canal, a Superfund site introduced in Chapter 2. In some cases it is determined that given time, bacteria will be able to metabolize the contaminant into harmless products, so containment is used to allow the bacteria time to work. In other cases, containment is used to isolate a site when analysis shows that even if treatment continued for centuries the pollutant would remain toxic.

The most commonly used containment barrier is a physical barrier known as a slurry wall, built by digging deep trenches and filling them with a nonpermeable material such as bentonite clay or a mixture of clay and soil. The slurry wall is cut into an impermeable layer below the site to prevent contaminated water from flowing under the barrier. Containment sometimes involves completely encapsulating a contaminated site with thick layers of clay.

More costly physical barrier methods include grout curtains and sheet piling. Grout curtains, used when the subsurface is rock, are formed by injecting a cement-like chemical into the ground that then hardens. Sheet piles, used when the subsurface is soil or sand, are large sheets of steel driven into the ground; they can develop leaks at seams where two sheets come together.

In addition to physical barriers, hydraulic barriers can be formed by creating zones of different water pressures. A contaminant plume will not flow from a low-pressure to a high-pressure zone. High pressure is created by injecting water into a well, forming a high-pressure mound of water. Multiple wells are used to create barriers for large areas.

Low-pressure zones are created in shallow areas by installing perforated drain pipe in trenches and in deeper zones by pumping water out of a well. The pumping brings large quantities of contaminated water to the surface, which must then be dealt with. Low hydraulic pressure zones are sometimes created not with electric pumps but by planting species of poplar trees. These trees work by doing what poplars do best: pumping large quantities of water up from deep in the ground.

Removal

A critical early step in remediation is the removal of the source generating the pollution. For example, if an underground fuel tank is leaking, before any treatment of surrounding soil or water begins the tank must first be emptied or removed so that no more fuel can be released. If a solvent or other NAPL has accumulated near an aquifer, the substance must be pumped out before treating the groundwater can begin.

Removal generally involves pumping contaminated water to the surface or excavating and disposing of contaminated soil. However, moving a pollutant from one location to another does not change its chemical makeup. Thus removal of contaminated soil or water is often combined with treatment.

Physical Treatment

Treatment means changing a contaminant into a form that is no longer hazardous. This can involve leaving a compound in its current chemical state but rendering it unavailable to living things who might be harmed by it, typically done with inorganic pollutants such as heavy metals. Treatment can also involve transforming a compound into a different chemical that is not toxic, the approach taken with hydrocarbons and other organic chemicals.

It is impossible to clean up many sites completely. When a contaminated site is to be treated a decision must be made about the level of cleanup. The question to be answered is how clean is "clean"? The higher the level of decontamination, the higher the cost. One factor is intended use. If an industrial site is being remediated and will be returned to industrial uses, it may be decided that removing 95 percent of the contaminants is adequate.

Methods such as hazardous waste incineration can remove 99.99 percent of pollutants; this condition is referred to in the trade as "four nines." Some situations with high risk and high toxicity require more sophisticated and costly processes that result in "five nines" or "six nines," that is, removal of 99.9999 percent of contaminants.

Contaminated soil or water can be treated in place if the right conditions exist. This is known as *in situ* remediation. *In situ* is a Latin phrase that means "in position." *In situ* remediation is less costly and usually reduces the potential that contaminants will affect workers or be released into the environment, and is a good approach for treating large volumes.

Contaminated soil or water can also be removed for treatment. This is known as *ex situ* remediation. *Ex situ* means "out of position." *Ex situ* remediation is more costly, but it is faster and conditions are more predictable and easier to control.

Cleanup can involve physical methods or biological methods. Biological methods using microorganisms or plants are the lowest cost and least disruptive approaches and are used whenever possible. However, biological actions are gradual. More costly and energy-intensive physical methods are used when it is necessary to clean up toxic hot spots quickly.

Physical soil pollution treatment methods include venting, distillation, incineration, and chemical reactions. One form of venting uses vacuum and is known as soil vapor extraction. In this method, wells are dug near the pollution source and a vacuum is introduced that extracts volatile components of petroleum products. The air is then filtered through activated carbon to remove the volatile compounds.

Another form of venting uses pressure. Also known as bioventing, it is a way of helping bacteria do the work of breaking down pollutants by forcing oxygen into the soil. Sparging involves forcing oxygen into groundwater to drive volatile compounds out of the saturated zone and into the unsaturated zones above, where aerobic bacteria who live there can break down the pollutants. In addition, groundwater does contain some populations of aerobic bacteria who become active in breaking down pollutants when oxygen is added.

Contaminated soil can be treated using distillation. In this process, steam is driven through contaminated soil where it picks up contaminants. The steam is fed through a distillation column; substances with higher boiling points remain behind while volatile substances with lower boiling points vaporize and are captured.

Incineration or burning is done *ex situ*. It involves excavating, then heating contaminated soil to a high temperature. This is the method used for PCB contamination. Treated soil is either returned to the site or moved to a landfill. Incineration is also used as a final stage after trees have been used to extract heavy metals from contaminated soil. The trees are burned and the metals are concentrated in the ash that remains. While incineration removes the majority of contaminants, metals remain and organic compounds do not break down completely. Even a sophisticated process that removes 99.9999 percent cannot destroy the last 0.0001 percent of the pollutant. In addition, some of the compounds transform into others which, although less toxic, are still pollutants. Some chemicals are formed which are given off in emissions and which can then be filtered separately. Other chemicals become concentrated in the ash that is left over, which is then moved to a landfill.

Chemical methods used *in situ* usually involve injecting a reagent of some kind into the soil or water. A reagent is a substance that causes a chemical reaction resulting in a different substance being produced. For example, cyanide is destroyed by introducing oxygen in the form of ozone or O_3, which causes the cyanide to oxidize. If the contaminant is a heavy metal, it may not be broken down, but is stabilized so that it cannot leach into groundwater. Stabilizing metal is usually done by adding a highly alkaline substance that renders the metal insoluble and causes particles of it to precipitate where they can be collected.

In another chemical approach, permeable underground treatment walls break down substances while allowing water to flow through. For example, iron filings may be embedded in a treatment wall near a plume of chlorinated solvent such as trichloroethene, a metal degreaser. The iron filings partially break down the compounds in the solvent into relatively benign substances as the water passes through.

Physical treatment of contaminated groundwater can be done *ex situ* in a process known as pump-and-treat. The groundwater is pumped to the surface, treated, and returned underground. If the water has been contaminated with solvents or other hydrocarbons, biological treatment using bacteria can be used. The water can also be filtered through activated carbon, which concentrates the contaminant by moving it from one location, the water, to another location, the filter, where it is easier to dispose of later in a landfill. If the water has been contaminated with metals, a chemical process is used that precipitates the metal out. This does not change the composition of the metal, but concentrates it for disposal.

Bioremediation

Bioremediation means using microorganisms to break down and convert synthetic chemicals to inorganic products, such as water and carbon dioxide. It is the primary method of treating pollution. Microbes are already responsible for most of the global recycling of matter.

Microbes are remarkably versatile. Every naturally occurring substance on Earth is broken down by at least one species of organism in some environment (Alexander 1999, 5). If it were not so, some compounds would have accumulated over time in enormous amounts. The microbial world is filled with specialists. Some like to live in boiling-hot temperatures. Some like to live without oxygen. Some prefer an atmosphere rich in sulfur. Some prefer acid, some prefer alkali. At least one known strain is resistant to radiation. The challenge for treating pollution is that most modern contaminants are new to nature. They were created recently by humans, and may not have any bacteria evolved to use them as food sources. In some cases, one bacterium breaks down a toxic chemical into a different toxic chemical, which is then eaten by a different species. This is what happens with persistent organic pollutants including the pesticide DDT, a toxin that breaks down very slowly (Vesilind et al. 2004, 532).

Many kinds of bacteria break down—that is, eat—petroleum products. Petroleum consists of the remains of microorganisms that would have been eaten by ancient bacteria had they not become buried. It contains the same organic compounds, and is still considered edible by modern bacteria. So many bacteria like to eat petroleum that some are actually considered pests in refineries and oil fields (Dyer 2003, 119).

Sometimes the easiest and lowest cost approach to bioremediation is to take no action and to wait for the natural processes of indigenous microorganisms, using the supply of nutrients on site, to break down the pollutants. This is known as bioattenuation, also called intrinsic bioremediation, natural bioremediation, or passive bioremediation. Some kind of risk assessment must be done before making this choice to ensure that living systems will not be placed as risk. Long-term monitoring must be done as well. In most cases bioattenuation is not enough and another, more direct intervention will be needed.

Bioremediation has been used to treat wastewater in a process known as landfarming for at least 300 years (McCutcheon and Schnoor 2003, 5). In this process, waste or contaminated soil is spread in a thin layer on the land so that it is easily accessible by aerobic soil microorganisms. The soil is mixed by tilling to provide oxygen to more bacteria. Where soil is prone to drying out, supplemental irrigation is provided as well. Landfarming is effective at breaking down petroleum and is widely used to treat soil at oil refineries and contaminated soil excavated from around underground storage tanks (Vesilind et al. 2004, 533).

A more controlled form of bioremediation can be done in a prepared bed bioreactor, used at many Superfund sites. An impermeable liner such as plastic or clay is placed in the bottom of the bed. Sand and a system of perforated pipes are placed above the liner to collect **leachate**, the water that picks up contaminates as it flows through the soil. The bed is kept moist by overhead irrigation, and nutrients are added to stimulate bacterial action. Leachate is removed for additional treatment, sometimes at an adjacent bioreactor. If the contaminants being treated are volatile, as with many organic solvents and petroleum products, the bed is covered by a plastic greenhouse to prevent fumes from polluting the air.

Bioaugmentation means inoculating a site with additional microorganisms if not enough or not the right kinds are present already. In most cases bioaugmentation is not necessary, as every environment on earth contains populations of indigenous microorganisms adapted to that particular site (Alexander 1999, 348). In addition, introducing new microbes is often unsuccessful since they are not as closely adapted to conditions at the site, so may not be able to establish a niche and may not survive (Pepper et al. 2006, 327).

However, indigenous microorganisms can be helped along by the addition of oxygen and nutrients. The bacteria and other organisms that eat hydrocarbons and other organic pollutants are aerobic: they need oxygen to live. Soil can be exposed to additional oxygen by turning or by bioventing. In groundwater, oxygen is slow to replenish once it is used up, so extra oxygen is provided through sparging, injecting air directly into the water.

The bacteria that eat hydrocarbons and organic pollutants also need other nutrients, especially nitrogen and phosphorus. Sites contaminated with petroleum and other hydrocarbons are generally rich in carbon and poor in nitrogen and phosphorus. As bacteria break down the hydrocarbons they use up the existing nitrogen, so more needs to be added. After testing, technicians calculate the amount of nitrogen and phosphorus to be added based on the amount of carbon to be degraded. If there is not enough, bacteria work slowly; if there is too much, they may not be able to survive. This addition of nutrients is sometimes called biostimulation.

Biostimulation is sometimes used to help clean up oil spills (Dyer 2003, 119). In 1989 the Exxon Valdez tanker ran aground, dumping millions of gallons of crude oil into Alaska's Prince William Sound. Hydrocarbon-eating bacteria living along the shores began eating the oil, receiving ample oxygen as wave action mixed air with seawater. Environmental engineers added calculated amounts of nitrogen fertilizer to some stretches of shoreline and found that oil along stretches that had been fertilized was broken down 3 to 5 times faster than oil on untreated beaches (Hill 2010, 362).

Almost all bioremediation uses aerobic microorganisms. However, some anaerobic bacteria can metabolize some kinds of contaminants that cannot be broken down by aerobic bacteria (Alexander 1999, 369). It is anaerobes who digest food in animal digestive tracts, sewage in wastewater treatment tanks, and buried matter in landfills. Research is being conducted on other applications.

Phytoremediation

Phytoremediation is the use of plants to treat pollutants. Depending on the type of pollution and the type of plant, plants can be used for each of the three approaches to dealing with contaminants: containment, removal, and treatment.

Poplar trees are used to contain a groundwater contaminant plume by providing a hydraulic barrier. Their roots reach 20 feet deep or more; poplars can withdraw large amounts of water and nutrients, with a mature tree pumping 50 to 250 gallons a day through its roots for transpiration out through its leaves (Mackova et al. 2006, 24). Poplars are sometimes planted close together around landfills to absorb landfill leachate and prevent it from moving away from the landfill area; a planting of mature poplars pumps half a million to a million gallons of water per acre each year (McCutcheon and Schnoor 2003, 32). Poplar trees are sometimes planted as wide riparian buffer strips along the edges of streams next to farm fields in order to take up excess nutrients and chemicals moving across farmlands or spilled into soil, where they efficiently absorb and partially metabolize organic agricultural chemicals such as atrazine (Mackova et al. 2006, 168).

Plants can be used to remove pollutants from soil. Contaminants, extracted as plants pull moisture and nutrients up from the soil, accumulate in stems and leaves. This is the primary approach used for remediating heavy metals, which cannot be broken down by any physical or biological method (Pepper et al. 2006, 495). The plants are then harvested and incinerated or placed in a hazardous waste landfill. Animals must be protected from eating leaves from these plants.

Plants have evolved to extract nutrients from the soil along with micronutrients they also need in tiny amounts, including metals. Most plants do not accumulate more micronutrients than they need for metabolism. A few plants, however, known as **hyperaccumulators** can accumulate and store metals in their tissues at 100 times greater concentrations than most plants (Lasat 2000, 10), possibly a strategy for deterring insect attacks. Each such plant hyperaccumulates one specific metal. No plant species has yet been found that hyperaccumulates multiple types of metal, nor has a species been found that can hyperaccumulate lead, one of the most widespread metal contaminants (Mackova et al. 2006, 115). The idea has been proposed that metals might be reclaimed from plants and recycled. However, the hyperaccumulators, including hybrid corn, alpine pennycress, duckweed, and water hyacinth, are nonwoody plants that do not produce the quantity of biomass of larger trees and thus are not suitable for reclamation and recycling processes.

Plants can be used to stabilize a contaminant such as a metal so that it is no longer mobile. This happens in the root zone (Pepper et al. 2006, 495). Unlike plants used as accumulators, plants chosen for use as stabilizers are those that do not take up or mobilize contaminants (McCutcheon and Schnoor 2003, 28).

Plants transform some contaminants into less toxic substances. Inorganic elements such as metals cannot be transformed, but organic pollutants such as hydrocarbons can be (Pepper et al. 2006, 496). Some transformation happens within plant tissues (ibid., 37), but the majority happens within the root zone (Mackova et al. 2006, 23).

Plants provide an environment that helps soil microorganisms metabolize contaminants such as petroleum and chlorinated pesticides more efficiently, known as plant-assisted bioremediation. The area of soil immediately around plant roots, the rhizosphere, is intensively colonized by bacteria and the fine root hairs are covered by fungi. Plants exude compounds from their roots that provide oxygen and food for these communities of microbes. In return, the bacteria and fungi help the roots absorb nutrients and secrete compounds that protect the plants against pollutants (McCutcheon and Schnoor 2003, 35). Symbiotic interactions between roots and soil microorganisms may offer the best potential for eventually breaking down persistent organic chemicals (Mackova et al. 2006, 194).

Plant-assisted bioremediation also helps promote the work of anaerobic bacteria. During dry years tree roots follow water tables downward. In wet years water tables rise and numbers of small roots die. These dead roots add significant amounts of carbon to the soil, creating new places for microorganisms to attach. Decomposition of dead roots consumes dissolved oxygen, creating low-oxygen zones where anaerobes can thrive. Some of these anaerobes are able to break down explosives and chlorinated solvents that are resistant to degradation (McCutcheon and Schnoor 2003, 35).

Some plants break down organic compounds such as hydrocarbons into inorganic products such as water and carbon dioxide, a process known as mineralization. Although mineralization occurs when plants are used, the process is actually carried out by microorganisms. Pollution specialists using phytoremediation must determine whether their goal is actually mineralization, the breakdown of contaminants into harmless components, or whether their goal is accumulation, the concentration of contaminants such as metals, which will then be collected and incinerated or disposed of in other locations.

Brownfields

A great deal of sustainable urban planning and development involves **brownfields**. A brown-field is an abandoned industrial site where the presence of pollutants complicates redevelopment or reuse. A brownfield may be a former factory site, gas station, airfield, utility substation, railroad yard, firing range, or industrial waterfront. Remediating and reusing a brownfield is considered more sustainable than building on a **greenfield**, open space that has never been built upon. Rehabilitating a brownfield can involve some or all of the processes discussed in this chapter.

Pollution Prevention

The goal of remediation is either to break down pollutants to concentrations that are undetectable or to break them down to concentrations that are below the limits established as safe by regulatory agencies. However, even the best remediation is not optimal. Even 99.9999 percent clean is not the same as 100 percent. And substances or concentrations once thought to be safe may later be found to be hazardous; the insecticide DDT is an example. Simply stopping production does not necessarily stop contamination. For example, PCBs have been banned for many years, yet these highly persistent compounds continue to leak into the environment from landfills and old storage sites. Thus, preventing pollution in the first place is the more sustainable option.

A philosophy of prevention is embedded in a principle known as the Precautionary Principle. It was one of 27 principles set forth in the 1992 Rio Declaration, subsequently underpinning multilateral environmental agreements such as the Montreal Protocol and some environmental law in the EU (Evans 2012, 190). The Precautionary Principle says that if the health of the environment and humans is at stake, precautionary measures should be taken even if cause-and-effect relationships have not been scientifically established with certainty. The principle says, in effect, if you are not completely sure, always err on the side of caution.

Pollution prevention is a framework embedded in the US Pollution Prevention Act of 1990. This framework, also used in waste management and known as P2, provides a hierarchy of methods for dealing with waste streams (US EPA 2013, Pollution Prevention). The highest priority is prevention, reducing or eliminating pollution at its source. The next strategy is to reuse or recycle what cannot be reduced, then to treat pollution, and finally to dispose of pollution as a last resort.

Pollution does not have to be inevitable. It is in fact a symptom of poor design (Van der Ryn and Cowan 2007, 135) and inefficiency (Meadows et al. 2004, 125). When dealing with pollution, sustainability professionals need some knowledge of the concepts covered in this chapter, both in order to understand conditions as they are and to provide a framework for mitigating existing problems. More importantly, practitioners need to go beyond current conditions to help envision how we might structure our ways of provisioning ourselves differently. Other chapters throughout this book offer ideas for wrestling with this fundamental issue.

Note

1 A hazardous material, sometimes referred to as "hazmat" for short, is a substance which poses a risk to humans or the environment when transported. It does not become a hazardous waste until it is accidentally or intentionally discarded (Russell 2012, 2).

Further Reading

Cunningham, William P. and Mary Ann Cunningham. *Environmental Science: A Global Concern.* 13th ed. New York: McGraw-Hill, 2014.

Pepper, Ian L., Charles P. Gerba, and Mark L. Brusseau, eds. *Environmental and Pollution Science.* 2nd ed. Boston, MA: Academic Press, 2006.

Vesilind, P. Aarne, Susan M. Morgan, and Lauren G. Heine. *Introduction to Environmental Engineering,* 3rd ed. Stamford, CT: Cengage Learning, 2009.

Withgott, Jay and Matthew Laposata. *Essential Environment: The Science behind the Stories.* 5th ed. San Francisco, CA: Pearson, 2014.

Chapter Review

1   How would you define pollution?
2   Why is the word "photochemical" often used in connection with smog?
3   Vehicles powered by fossil fuels do not emit ozone. Why are they singled out as the major cause of ozone pollution?
4   What pollutants are responsible for acid rain?
5   How do contaminants get into groundwater?
6   What is an endocrine disruptor?
7   What is a pesticide? List the four categories of pesticide, that is, words that all end in the suffix "-icide."
8   Describe BOD and turbidity.
9   What causes eutrophication?
10   Why is $PM_{2.5}$ more dangerous than other particulates?
11   Why are persistent organic pollutants (POP) levels higher in meats than in vegetables?
12   What is the Montreal Protocol?
13   Why is ground-level ozone considered a problem, when ozone in the upper atmosphere is considered beneficial?
14   What is the difference between remediation and prevention?

15 What is the Superfund program?
16 What is a brownfield development?
17 How is phytoremediation different from bioremediation?
18 Why do you sometimes see bands of poplar trees planted at the edges of farm fields?
19 How would you summarize the Precautionary Principle?

Critical Thinking and Discussion

1 Agricultural runoff is a major source of pesticide and excess nutrient pollution. Why do you think more has not been done to control these contaminants?
2 A few decades ago, people dealing with industrial pollution would say, "Dilution is the solution to pollution." Why is dilution no longer considered a good strategy?
3 How probable do you think it is that laws will be enacted requiring automakers to pay for environmental damage due to cars, and that automobiles will be more costly in the future as a result?
4 Why are urban residents advised to do outdoor exercising early in the morning on warm summer days?
5 Should we be concerned about low levels of a pesticide?
6 Do you think a business should be held liable for damages from hazardous waste on its site, even if the pollution came from a previous owner?
7 Why are young children exposed to greater quantities of contaminants in house dust than adults?
8 Some people believe that nuclear power is necessary in order to deal with the climate crisis. How do you think the dangers from nuclear waste compare to the dangers from a destabilized climate?
9 Why is prevention considered the only practical approach to maintaining groundwater quality?
10 List some benefits of living in an advanced industrial society. Do you think that some risks are a reasonable tradeoff for being able to enjoy these benefits?
11 Do you think that corporate funding of research influences the results? What research strategies maintain neutrality and credibility?
12 Can bioremediation be used in every kind of pollution situation?
13 Does bioremediation have any disadvantages or risks? If so, what are they?
14 What financial incentives are there for corporations to prevent or reduce pollution?
15 Do you think that shooting hazardous wastes into space aboard rockets is a practical solution?
16 If the herbicide atrazine were found in your town's drinking water, what actions would you suggest?
17 Are there ways to control the release of hormones into sewage systems and waterways?
18 A community has a persistent air pollution problem caused largely by particulates from the burning of wood. Do you think the city council should prohibit the use of wood stoves and fireplaces?
19 Pollution control policies can be of two general types: they can be command-and-control policies, that is, laws which forbid certain things; and they can be policies that provide economic incentives. Give at least one example of each type.

9 Energy

Fossil Fuels

Every living thing depends on flows of energy. Plants use flows of energy from the sun to make food. Humans use food to power their bodies and a variety of other energy sources to carry on the complex activities of modern life. Most energy used by humans today comes from fossil fuels.

Fossil fuels are a nonrenewable resource. Some renewable resources, such as the energy from sunlight and wind, are constantly replenished; others, such as wood or grain, are renewable over relatively short periods of time, from months to centuries. Fossil fuels may eventually be replenished, but regeneration takes place over a time scale of hundreds of millions of years, a duration that is not relevant for human civilization. That means that, unlike sunlight, there is a finite supply. Once it is gone, it is no longer available.

A fossil is literally a rock or mineral dug out of the earth. The word "fossil" comes from a Latin word meaning "to dig." Thus **fossil fuels** are fuels—that is, substances that provide energy—dug out of the earth. They are found in three forms: oil, natural gas, and coal. Oil and natural gas are hydrocarbons, which means they are made of hydrogen and carbon. Natural gas is made of simple hydrocarbon molecules, mostly methane. Oil is a mixture of hundreds of different complex hydrocarbon molecules. Oil is also referred to as **petroleum**, a word that puts together *petra*, the Latin word meaning "rock," and *oleum*, the Latin word meaning "oil." Coal is a solid material, and like the other fossil fuels it contains carbon and hydrogen, in addition to minor quantities of other minerals. Coal is mostly carbon, and when burned it releases the most carbon dioxide per unit of energy of the fossil fuels (Smil 2006, 107).

Petroleum consumption is measured in **barrels**, a unit left from the early days of the oil industry. One barrel contains 42 US gallons. Barrel is abbreviated "bbl," which stands for "blue barrel," the original standard container for oil. Natural gas is measured in cubic feet. It may be also be listed as thousand cubic feet (written Mcf), billion cubic feet (written Bcf), or trillion cubic feet (written Tcf). While oil and gas are measured by volume, coal is measured by the ton.

Oil and natural gas are fossilized marine plankton; coal is fossilized terrestrial plant material. In the early part of the twentieth century, as automobiles assumed a central role in American life, oil company advertisements featuring pictures of brontosaurs and stegosaurs promoted the idea that oil came from dinosaurs. In fact, however, 95 percent of the world's petroleum came not from giant land animals but from microscopic marine organisms (AGI 2011, 369). In warm Mesozoic-era seas nutrients, washed down by continental rivers and brought up from the sea bottom by upwelling currents, promoted a rich seawater environment teeming with plankton; floating microscopic life forms that included diatoms, a class of algae; and foraminifera, an order of animals. As these beings died, their remains drifted to the sea bottom and built up in black muddy sediments. The seawater at that time was so rich in life that the organic debris built up on the bottom faster than bacteria could break it down. As the sediments grew thicker and thicker, their weight pressed the lower layers deeper into the crust, where heat from below and pressure from above cooked the material at ideal temperatures of 120° to 210°F, and a series of chemical reactions transformed the organic debris into crude oil (Broad 2010).

Most of the current petroleum deposits formed 90 to 150 million years ago during the Cretaceous period, when continents and seas were in different locations than today. Seas that were somewhat isolated were less diluted by currents in the world's oceans, allowing nutrients to accumulate and concentrate in the mud. One such sea was the Tethys Sea, which ran approximately east to west near the equator; some of its coastal sediments formed the rich deposits that are now buried beneath the Gulf of Mexico. As the Tethys Sea later closed up, leaving the Mediterranean Sea as one of its remnants, its fertile southern coastal waters became the lands that are now the oil-rich Middle East. Land masses that are now Africa and South America began pulling apart, a small sea that is now the South Atlantic began forming, and nutrients from the continents poured in to develop what are now oil fields off the coast of Brazil.

Petroleum is less dense than water or rock. Over time the petroleum that was dispersed within sedimentary rock migrated through cracks and pores in the rock and accumulated. Rock above these accumulations, known as traps, prevented the petroleum from migrating further. Accumulations within traps are oil and gas fields. Some petroleum was not able to accumulate and remained more dispersed. It is found in what are called the nonconventional oil resources: oil shales, heavy oil, and tar sands.

Natural gas formed when some sediments were buried even more deeply and heated to higher temperatures. The organic matter and carbon-rich molecules broke down further and formed the simpler molecules of natural gas. In some oil fields, natural gas escaped from parent rocks and accumulated in reservoirs above the oil. Natural gas is the cleanest-burning of the fossil fuels. Although it, too, emits greenhouse gases, it emits less carbon dioxide and less pollution than oil or coal, and may play a role as a bridge in the transition to renewable energy.

Coal formed on land as plant material condensed. Most of the present coal deposits were formed during the Carboniferous period, 286 to 360 million years ago, when the climate was warm and humid and vast forests of ferns and trees flourished along river deltas and floodplains. In swamps and bogs decaying dead plant material, known as **peat**, accumulated. Sediment carried by rivers eventually buried the peat. As with oil, pressure from above and heat from below caused chemical reactions. The resulting coal contains less moisture and more concentrated carbon than the original peat.

As pressures and temperatures increase, coal is transformed through several stages. Peat is first converted into lignite, a brownish, high-moisture coal material with about 50 percent carbon and low energy output. As the process continues, the lignite converts to black bituminous coal, the most abundant coal in the US and the coal typically used for power generation and heating. The final stage formed under considerable heat and pressure is anthracite, a hard, lustrous black coal that is over 90 percent carbon (Smil 2006, 107).

Extraction

Petroleum is extracted by drilling wells. Typically 10 or more exploration wells must be drilled before an actual oil or gas field is discovered. The drilling process uses a high-pressure fluid called drilling mud, which can be oil, water, or synthetic fluid (Smil 2006, 120); waste drilling mud must be stored somewhere. Petroleum wells also produce about 6 barrels of water for every barrel of oil; produced water contains salt and traces of petroleum, so it too must be stored somewhere where it will not contaminate surface water or groundwater (AGI 2011, 388).

As land-based oil fields have become depleted, petroleum producers have turned to marine deposits, where extraction is known as offshore drilling, and to nonconventional sources of oil: oil shales and tar sands. Extraction processes for these sources are more expensive and difficult and carry even higher environmental risks than conventional drilling, with a lower net energy yield. The difference between the energy used to produce a fuel and the energy contained in the final product is the energy returned on energy invested (EROEI). The EROEI for crude oil is an average of 15:1; the EROEI for tar sands is from 5:1 to 3:1 (Wijkman and Rockström 2012, 70).

Producers have also turned to new technology for extracting non-conventional natural gas in shale deposits, particularly horizontal well drilling combined with hydraulic fracturing or "fracking." In the fracking process, water is pumped deep underground where it fractures the surrounding rock, releasing the natural gas. Some of the gas escapes into the atmosphere before the rest of it is captured. This is a concern in many rural areas of the US, where oil companies have purchased minerals rights on working agricultural farms and use fracking to produce natural gas. The additional release of methane is a climate-change concern.

Once oil or gas is produced it must be processed in a refinery that boils the crude oil. Vapors from the boiling oil are distilled as they rise and condense in tanks known as distillation columns. Long, complex hydrocarbon molecules are heavier and condense at high temperatures near the bottom of the column. Short, simpler hydrocarbon molecules are lighter and condense at lower temperatures near the top of the column. Each type of hydrocarbon is called a fraction, and the distilling process is called fractionation. The heaviest residues, settling at the bottom of the column, are asphalt and tar. Slightly higher in the column, oil and grease settle out. Above that are fuel oil, kerosene, and diesel oil. Above the oils, gasoline condenses in the upper part of the column. At the top of the column, polymer chains are extracted, which are later used to manufacture plastics. Refineries produce about half a ton of waste sludge for every 1,000 barrels of oil produced; some waste can be recycled or reprocessed, and about 20 percent is placed in landfills (ibid.).

Oil deposits are not evenly distributed around the globe and they are not generally found near where the petroleum is used, so extensive transportation systems are required. Currently about 2.2 million miles of pipelines collect the petroleum, carry it to refineries, then transport it to various distribution centers (ibid., 379). It is stored above ground in collections of large tanks sometimes called "tank farms" and below ground in millions of small individual tanks. Petroleum is carried across oceans in massive ocean-going tankers and over land in railroad tanks and freight trucks.

Uses for Fossil Fuels

Petroleum forms the basis of contemporary society. It is difficult to find any non-metal object in everyday life that does not have a petroleum component. Some are obvious: oil, grease, solvents, paint, credit cards, computer keyboards, and almost anything else made of plastic begins with petroleum. Others may be less obvious. Among the millions of examples are artificial vanilla flavoring, red food coloring, vitamin capsules, shampoo, lip balm, shoes, shoe polish, fertilizer, and glue. The majority of synthetic chemicals used in agriculture and manufacturing come from petroleum products. Fossil fuels are used for transportation, electricity generation, industry, and buildings. The machinery used to grow almost all the food in the developed world is powered by petroleum.

Problems Associated with Fossil Fuels

Many pollution problems are associated with the burning of fossil fuels. Coal combustion emits mercury, generates the SOx and NOx that result in photochemical smog and acid rain, and leaves behind coal ash contaminated with heavy metals that piles up in landfills and holding ponds. Coal mining results in the destruction of entire mountains, the burial of streams and valleys, and massive quantities of contaminated waste.

A major issue associated with exploration is the release of petroleum into the natural world during an accidental spill. The massive 2010 oil spill at the Deepwater Horizon drilling platform in the Gulf of Mexico resulted in the deaths of thousands of creatures and the suffering of countless more. The impact on marine ecosystems is not yet known. The Deepwater Horizon spill was just one of a large number of such accidents over several decades. Other spills have occurred when ocean-going tankers have broken up or run aground, as happened during the 1989 Exxon Valdez oil spill in Prince William Sound, Alaska. Some land-based spills have caused massive pollution and ecosystem destruction.

Spills and emissions also come from pipeline accidents. With 2.2 million miles of pipeline, inspections and maintenance get overlooked in some places. Pipes and valves corrode and leaks occur. Spills also occur when people not connected with the petroleum industry dig in areas where pipelines are buried. While some pipelines carry petroleum, others carry natural gas which is mostly methane, a powerful greenhouse gas. Even well-maintained pipelines lose 1 to 2 percent of the gas they carry (Smil 2003, 215).

The most dangerous byproduct of fossil fuel combustion is the buildup of carbon dioxide and other heat-trapping greenhouse gases. Increase in carbon dioxide is the primary cause of rising global temperatures and climate disruption. It is emitted from the tailpipes of trucks and automobiles and the smokestacks of coal-burning power plants. More is emitted during flaring, the pressure-relief process of venting and burning natural gas through smokestacks at oil and gas wells and refineries.

Energy and Automobiles

We live in a high-energy society based on fossil fuels. One of the hallmarks of modern society is the private automobile, powered by the very portable, very high-energy fuel, gasoline. Diesel has nearly as much energy per volume, and its use in farm equipment has led to a revolution in agricultural output. We will eventually run out of this nonrenewable resource, and before that happens we will be forced to make changes to our lifestyles to prevent runaway climate change. But in terms of energy and cost, nothing else can match petroleum.

Physicists define energy as the ability to do work. Power is a measure of that work, done at a certain rate. A farmer plowing a field 100 years ago with a team of 6 large horses would have had about 6.7 horsepower or 5 kW of power available. One hundred years later, a farmer plowing the same field with a diesel tractor would have over 400 horsepower or 300 kW of power available—60 times as much as a team of big horses—and would be able to do it from within an air-conditioned cab equipped with stereo and computer (ibid., 8). It is not hard to see why the farmer would prefer diesel power to horse power.

We like fossil fuel because of its energy. We like it, too, because of its relatively low cost. Gasoline used to be a lot cheaper than it is now, in the days following World War II when oil was plentiful, no one yet knew about pollution, and technology seemed to hold all the answers. Planners designed towns and road systems for a culture where every person had their own automobile instead of using public transportation. Developers built homes in the suburbs, far from town. It was a luxury that was affordable when gasoline was cheap, although development brought with it other problems.

Energy Data

Two organizations with similar names, one global and one national, provide standard sources of data on energy production and consumption. The International Energy Agency (IEA) is an intergovernmental organization of representatives from 28 countries including Japan, Korea, Australia, New Zealand, Turkey, the United States, and most of the European countries. The IEA program was implemented in 1974 as part of a group of 30 democratic governments known as the Organization for Economic Cooperation and Development (OECD). The IEA acts as an energy policy advisor to the member OECD countries and publishes data, projections, and analysis in an annual document titled the *World Energy Outlook*.

The IEA uses scenario planning in its work. Most of its work focuses on the New Policies Scenario; its Current Policies Scenario predicts global energy markets if governments make no changes to their existing policies, what could be called a business-as-usual scenario. Its 450 Scenario, an alternative scenario, lays out an energy pathway if governments take collective action to limit the atmospheric concentration of greenhouse gases to 450 parts per million (ppm) (in CO_2 equivalent units).

The US Energy Information Administration (EIA) is the agency within the US Department of Energy charged by Congress with providing energy data, analysis, and projections. Like the IEA, the EIA was established in 1974 following the oil shortages of 1973. The EIA publishes an annual document titled the *International Energy Outlook*. Among other useful data that can be downloaded from the EIA website, the *International Energy Outlook* reports energy consumption by country, by fuel type, and by sector.

Peak Oil

Fossil fuel is a nonrenewable resource. We are not sure exactly how much fossil fuel remains, but we are sure that it consists of a finite and limited amount. Thus at some time, perhaps still in the future, fossil fuel production will reach a peak quantity and then begin to decline. That midway point, when half the reserves have been used up and after which there will be less in reserve each year than there was the year before, is sometimes referred to as **peak oil**. Geologists, economists, and policymakers debate about when that peak might happen.

The reason some analysts are concerned about peak oil is that two trends are on diverging trajectories. One trend includes the rising human population, expected to continue rising until at least 2100. Coupled with the increase in population are growing global economies with rising affluence; people everywhere aspire to live easier, more pleasant lives, and that translates into increased consumption. The other trend is declining oil reserves. As oil supply declines while population and consumption rise, a gap between supply and demand will appear and grow larger. As fossil fuel becomes more scarce, it will become increasingly expensive. It is not the exact timing of the peak that is important, but the years following the peak when the gap opens wider as demand outpaces supply. The diminishing oil supply will not turn off suddenly like a faucet. Rather, oil depletion will show up first as decreasing returns on investment for exploration and production companies and then as a gradual decline in total production. Our task between now and then is to figure out how we will make the transition between the current fossil fuel-dependent economy and a new, more sustainable economy based on renewable sources of energy.

Oil production follows an observable pattern. After new oil or gas fields are discovered in a region, more deposits continue to be found. At some time the rate of discovery reaches a peak and then begins to decline. Meanwhile the deposits are tapped and begin producing, with producers exploiting the largest and easiest reserves first, an approach known as "best first" (Heinberg 2011, 109). At some time the rate of production in an area reaches a peak and then begins to decline.[1] The repeated pattern, known as the Hubbert curve, is that a region's peak in production tends to occur 30 to 40 years following its peak in discovery (Hopkins 2008, 22).

The pattern was first observed by a geologist named M. King Hubbert. In the 1930s and 1940s the United States had been one of the largest oil producers in the world. Its rate of new oil field discoveries peaked in the 1930s. In 1956, Hubbert predicted that US oil production would peak in 1970, which proved to be correct. Worldwide, discoveries peaked in 1965 and have been falling since that time. New oil fields are still being found but they are dramatically smaller than those found in past years. In 1940, the average size of fields found was 1.5 billion barrels of oil. Since then the sizes of discoveries have steadily declined until by 2004, the average size had dropped to 45 million, just 3 percent the size of the earlier average (ibid.). The world currently consumes about 4 barrels of oil for every 1 barrel discovered.

A **resource** is the total quantity of material that exists in the Earth's crust. We have depleted some of the petroleum resource, and some of that resource remains. **Reserve** is the quantity of material that has been discovered and that can still be used in the future. Resources get used, and can only go down. Reserves can go up as additional discoveries are made or production technology changes.

Some analysts believe peak oil occurred in 2005, other estimates place the peak between 2010 and 2015, and others place it in 2020 or 2025. Meanwhile the world's population will continue to grow, setting up a widening gap between supply and demand.

This section has focused on peak oil, but of course coal and natural gas are nonrenewable resources as well. That means that they, too, will have peaks and subsequent declines. Although oil's peak is predicted to occur somewhere between 2005 and 2025, oil resources could last another 50 years if consumption does not increase. Meanwhile, natural gas is predicted to last decades to centuries more. Coal is the most plentiful of the fossil fuels, although if consumption continues to increase at its current rate it, too, could be depleted within the next decade (Lovins 2011, 8; MacKay 2009, 265). It is not coal supply, but coal's damaging effects on the environment and climate, that will prove to be its limiting factor.[2]

Renewable Energy

"Alternative energy" is a term used to describe a range of alternatives to fossil fuel-based energy. The most immediate and effective strategy is simply to use less energy by increasing efficiency. Other ways to reduce demand include changing the way our buildings are designed and built, including how they are heated, cooled, and lighted; changing land-use patterns to reduce the need to drive everywhere; and providing other modes of transportation as alternatives to single-passenger vehicles.

One alternative strategy, known as combined heat and power, treats "waste" heat as a resource rather than as a waste. Another approach uses alternative energy sources in place of petroleum to power vehicles; options include electricity, biofuels, and hydrogen fuel cell technology. Most alternative energy strategies use energy from renewable resources to generate electricity. These sources include sunlight, wind, waves, geothermal heat, and biomass. Using renewable energy offers multiple benefits: improved energy security with independence from fossil fuels, few or no greenhouse gas emissions, reduced air pollution, better worker safety during production, and local employment opportunities (IPCC 2014c, 7).

Energy Basics

Energy is the ability to do work. Power is the rate at which work is done and is measured in watts. One kilowatt, abbreviated "kW," is 1,000 watts. A typical small house uses power for lights and appliances at the rate of around 1 kW, not including any additional amount used for heat. Utility companies measure the amount of energy used in kilowatt-hours, abbreviated "kWh." If you use power at a rate of 1,000 watts and do that for an hour, you have used 1 kWh. Power is a rate, not a quantity. We cannot say a power plant produces so many kilowatts per day, because the word "watt" has rate already built into it.

The output rate of power plants is measured in megawatts (MW), a million watts, or gigawatts (GW), a billion watts. Small power plants typically produce 40 to 100 MW. One MW is enough power for about 1,000 homes (without air conditioning), so a 100 MW plant can provide power for about 100,000 homes. A typical large coal-fired or nuclear power plant produces power at the rate of about 1 GW. Power plants are sized so that they have the capacity to meet not only the base load, the electricity that must be delivered all day, every day to power things like lighting and electric motors; but also peak load, the intermittent, extra demand from conditions such as a hot afternoon when many people come home from work and turn on air conditioners at once.

Power plants use mechanical energy to turn generators. A **generator** is a device that converts mechanical energy into electrical energy. Mechanical input for generating electricity can come from a wind turbine, a turbine in a hydroelectric dam, ocean wave action, diesel engines, or a steam turbine. Steam turbines are common in power plants and are driven by heat; that heat can come from a nuclear reactor, geothermal heat, a solar concentrator, or from burning biomass, coal, oil, or natural gas.

When a coil of wire in a generator rotates inside a strong magnetic field, the motion induces electrical current to flow in the coil. This is the principle of induction. Because generators turn in a circular direction, the voltage and current they produce continually changes in magnitude. This regularly-varying voltage and current produced by a spinning generator is known as alternating current (AC). Electricity delivered to buildings and city streets is always AC.

All the mechanical energy sources listed above are used to turn generators. One source of electricity uses a different principle: **photovoltaic** (PV) panels, often called solar panels, instead rely on the photoelectric effect in which energy from sunlight causes electrical current to flow. While generators deliver alternating current, PV panels and batteries produce direct current (DC).

In the eighteenth century people though that electricity was a fluid. We now know it is not, but many people still use the water analogy as a way of remembering electrical vocabulary.

If you were to compare electricity to flowing water, current would be like water flowing. You could imagine current flowing in a river. Current is the rate of flow of electrons and is measured in amperes (A), usually called amps for short. If you were to compare electricity to flowing water, voltage would be analogous to pressure. Voltage, measured in volts (V), is potential energy difference, a measure of energy pushing electrons through a conductor. Just as a difference in pressure makes a current of water flow through a pipe or through the turbines in a dam, it is a difference in voltage that makes current flow through a wire.

Centralized Power and Distributed Power

Almost all of the electricity generated in Europe and the US is distributed over large, centralized power systems. Electricity from thousands of power plants is delivered through the power **grid**, a vast network of interconnected transmission and distribution lines. The grid makes it possible to send power from regions that have excess electricity to regions that do not have enough, and it enables power to be delivered to cities from power sources that cannot be moved, such as wind farms or hydroelectric dams.

If power companies were privately owned, each company would need to make huge investments in its own transmission lines, its own substations, and its own networks of wires. Instead, power is generated and distributed in each area by a single utility company. To prevent the problems that could accompany their being run as monopolies, utilities are federally regulated. Regulations explicitly allow power generation by independent power producers.[3]

Power that comes from a utility enters the user's site at a meter, which measures the usage. Thus centralized power generated at power plants and distributed over the grid is sometimes referred to as power on the utility's side of the meter. That power is usually generated by conventional sources such as coal, natural gas, and nuclear reactors. However, such centralized power can also be generated by alternative sources including wind turbines. Wind power is an example of power generation by independent power producers, who usually sell the power they produce back to the grid, that is, back to the utility.

Other alternative power sources are located on the customer's side of the meter. Small, independent power sources are referred to as distributed generation. Distributed power comes from small, on-site generating equipment and is used close to where it is produced. This local power might be produced in an industrial plant using combined heat and power, or by a homeowner with rooftop solar panels, or by an apartment building with small-scale wind turbines. Federal regulations allow independent power producers to connect to the grid and to sell any surplus power back to the utility at the standard retail price. Most power meters record accurately in both directions. The practice of giving credit to a customer for the electricity they generate is known as **net metering**.

An approach known as community energy offers local ownership, with the energy consumed in a community owned and controlled by that community (Pahl 2012, 71). Investment may come from partnerships, cooperatives, or community-owned public utility districts. In regions where group net metering is permitted communities can offer community solar, in which solar panels are owned by a utility, a nonprofit organization, or a collaboration of community members (Brown 2015, 75). A solar garden is a solar array with multiple subscribers connected to the utility grid; subscribers buy or lease some of the panels in the array and get credit on their utility bills as if the panels were on their own roofs, but at lower cost than if they had bought panels individually. Other renewable energy sources including wind, micro-hydropower, biomass, and biogas are also used in community energy projects. Setting up community energy requires collaboration and hard work, but can result in greater community self-sufficiency and resilience.

Distributed Generation and Microgrids

As users generate their own power close to where it is used and share it across interconnected networks, this distributed generation changes the structure and scale of distribution from large centralized grids to networked microgrids. Microgrids are local, small-scale versions of the centralized power grid featuring many small units rather than one large, central unit. Networks of microgrids operate like virtual utilities in scale-free networks analogous to the structure of the Internet.

Smart grids are distributed generation networks that are integrated by sensors and information technology to allow more active control of distribution networks (IPCC 2014c, 32). They use two-way meters, intelligent controls, telecommunications, and distributed storage, and include digital sensors and processors at every power-generating device, appliance, electric car, switch, and distribution line. Each microgrid can generate and store power independent of the larger grid if needed, making it easier to withstand and recover from regional grid failures (Lovins 2011, 203). When connected, it can exchange information with the larger grid, using power at off-peak times when the price is lower and allowing consumers to manage their own energy consumption. Electric vehicles become part of a distributed storage network, both using power for charging, and storing and selling power to the larger grid. Critics raise concerns about privacy, cyber security, and potential health impacts of radio frequency emissions (Pahl 2012, 30).

The US government and the EC have both implemented standards for interconnecting distributed resources that allow microgrids to operate both on their own and as part of larger networks. The Danish government is developing a smart energy network as part of its national Smart Grid strategy. The US Department of Defense (DoD), already the world's largest buyer of renewable energy (Lovins 2011, 210), is implementing microgrids in its military bases. The DoD has made energy resilience a priority because it considers both climate change and fossil fuel decline to be security risks.

The following sections look at distributed power sources, or power from renewable energy produced on the customer side of the meter. They include solar PV, geothermal energy, combined heat and power, and biomass.

Solar Photovoltaic Panels

Whenever alternative energy is mentioned, the version that comes to most people's minds is solar panels made of photovoltaic (PV) cells. These solar cells are **semiconductors** which convert sunlight to DC electricity. They are based on the same semiconductor principles as those on which computer processor chips are based and are manufactured using similar materials and a similar method. They have no moving parts and silent operation. Photovoltaic cells were first used in the space program in the 1950s to generate power for satellites.

Individual solar cells produce about half a volt each, so they must be connected together in series to increase the voltage. Single cells are connected to form modules and several modules are connected in a supporting frame to form a panel. A solar array is a group of panels, electrically connected and fastened to a supporting structure. Solar cells produce DC. In order to be able to use their output to power lights and appliances, the current must be converted to AC using an inverter.

Solar cells cannot store energy. In a standalone system, batteries are used to store DC electricity. When power is called for, electricity travels from the battery through the inverter and then to the load. In a system connected to a utility grid, the grid functions as the storage device, and power from the solar cells goes through a utility-interactive inverter and then to the load. A standalone system is more complicated and more difficult to design.

Energy from sunlight is free. Generating electricity from sunlight is not free. Although costs are coming down, the initial costs of installing a PV system remain high. Government subsidies will be essential until the solar industry comes up to scale. In Germany, government policy which guaranteed a long-term premium price and access to the grid led to rapid growth of solar power in that country (Brown 2015, 68).

The major advantage of PV systems is that, while they do use chemicals and embodied energy during their manufacture, they emit no pollution and no greenhouse gases during operation. The monetary cost is still high, but the environmental cost of burning fossil fuels may be higher. Some people choose PVs because of the environmental philosophy they communicate. In addition, PVs can be used in applications without easy access to the grid such as emergency call boxes, on-street parking meters, and remote rural sites.

Light from the sun can be harnessed in two different ways. One way is to use the photoelectric effect to generate electricity in PV cells. The other way is to use the heat from the sun, known as solar thermal energy. Solar thermal energy can be used to preheat water, using panels that contain tubes that heat in the sun. Solar thermal energy can also be used passively to heat building spaces. In addition, heat from the sun can be collected and concentrated, then used to provide heat for steam boilers. This approach is known as concentrating solar.

Geothermal Power

The temperature inside the Earth is hot. This heat comes from three sources: residual heat left from the violent collisions that formed the planet, radioactive decay, and the tremendous pressure deep in the Earth caused by gravity. Geothermal heat can be used to generate electricity.

In some places, including Iceland, Hawaii, Alaska, and some regions in the western US, volcanism and hydrothermal activity (steam or hot water) are active near the surface. This heat can be used in the same way coal and nuclear reactors are used to turn steam turbines and drive power generation. Power plants drill wells to make it easier to capture this naturally-occurring steam.

Generating power from geothermal resources is only possible in regions with high tectonic activity; it is different from using the thermal mass of the earth for heating and cooling buildings. Research is underway to make use of the geothermal heat that is available everywhere on the planet at depths of several miles below the crust, not just at volcanically active sites. In these enhanced geothermal systems, deep wells are dug and water is pumped through the hot rocks below and then returned to the surface as steam. These systems are not yet producing power commercially.

Combined Heat and Power (Cogeneration)

In many manufacturing facilities, industrial processes use large amounts of power and release large amounts of waste heat. In addition, about two-thirds of the energy produced by power plants is discarded as waste heat. Combined heat and power (CHP), formerly known as cogeneration, produces both heat and power as usable resources in the same facility.

For example, the US Steel Company and the ArcelorMittal Steel Company in Indiana are steel producers that each generate about 90 MW of free power from waste heat left over from steelmaking which would otherwise be blown into the air (Smil 2003, 33). The free power is then used for rolling steel. This electricity is produced without any additional carbon dioxide or pollution emissions beyond what would have been produced in the steelmaking process itself. The cost of producing this power with waste heat from blast furnace gas is about half the cost of power from the local utility.

Waste heat is similarly available from a number of other industrial processes that burn fossil fuels including smelting, oil refining, and chemical processing. This heat can be recycled to produce electricity without any additional fossil fuel input. Blast furnace gas from iron smelting, flammable gas from oil refineries, and gases from chemical plants all must be flared to remove toxic or flammable components; plants that capture this gas instead get low-cost power and reduce their greenhouse gas emissions.

Nonindustrial facilities that generate heat are also candidates for CHP. Examples include hospitals, college campuses, hotels, apartment buildings, and airports. These facilities can use microturbines, small combustion engines that generate electricity and give off waste heat, which can then be used to heat water or building spaces. Microturbines can be powered by natural gas, diesel, or even methane from landfills.

Biomass

Biomass consists of plants or plant waste that can be converted into energy through burning or through conversion into a gas or liquid fuel, which is then burned. Many renewable energy sources—solar, wind, wave, even hydroelectric—all trace back to the sun. Biomass, too, uses energy from the sun, converted into plant matter and chemical energy through the process of photosynthesis. Biomass material can be wood waste from sawmills, agricultural byproducts, or municipal solid waste.

As with any choice, there are tradeoffs. When biomass is burned, if the material contains heavy metals or synthetic chemicals these can become toxic emissions. Even without those pollutants, wood smoke contains particulate matter and carcinogens. Refining biomass into another fuel requires energy, often from fossil fuels, and emits some carbon dioxide. Nevertheless, the burning of biomass is considered by some to be carbon neutral because it uses only carbon in the form of plant matter, which is part of the recent carbon cycle and thus does not increase the net amount of carbon in the cycle. Burning of biomass releases only the carbon dioxide the plants recently removed from the atmosphere, together with emissions released during processing (Randolph 2008, 543).

So-called "traditional biomass" is wood, charcoal, agricultural residues, and animal dung burned for cooking and heating in developing countries. This material often comes from unsustainable harvesting and results in unhealthy air pollution, greenhouse gas emissions (IPCC 2014c, 48), and climate impacts from black carbon (OECD 2012, 135). Facilitating universal access to modern energy is one of the targets of the UN's Sustainable Development Goals (IEA 2015, 23).

The following sections review large-scale sources of centralized power, that is, power from renewable energy produced on the utility side of the meter. They include hydroelectric, concentrating solar, wind, and wave power, plus biogas or methane from landfills. Some scholars argue that because the crisis of climate change is so urgent, nuclear power should be included as an alternative energy source. Others argue that the levels of uncertainty are too high and the risks from very long-term storage of lethal waste too great.

Hydroelectric Power

The use of potential energy released by water as it falls from a higher to a lower elevation is the oldest method of generating electricity. Hydroelectric power changed the impact of the Industrial Revolution in the late nineteenth century by providing large-scale, centralized power distributed over interconnected grids. Using flowing water to drive machinery was not new; waterwheels had driven grain mills and manufacturing shops for centuries. But to use waterwheels, those machines had to be located near falling water. What was new was the ability to use that power far away. With the invention of generators that could produce AC using water stored behind dams, electricity could be transmitted and used miles from where it was produced.

Hydroelectric power is classified as renewable energy and makes up a large percentage of the total power produced by renewable energy sources. A coal-fired plant burns coal to produce steam, which turns a turbine; in a hydroelectric plant, falling water spins the turbine. While a coal-fired power plant is about 33 percent efficient, a hydroelectric plant is about 90 percent efficient as it converts the kinetic energy of the water into electrical energy (Wengenmayr and Buhrke 2008, 22).

A primary advantage of hydroelectric power is that it produces no greenhouse gas emissions. However, construction of dams destroys ecosystems, blocks fish migration, raises the temperature of river water, and changes hydrological function (Brown 2015, 121). It also displaces people and obliterates cultural and archaeological sites.

The World Commission on Dams estimates that 40 to 80 million people worldwide have been displaced and forced to move because of dam construction. The Nile River in Egypt created rich farming soil for millennia as it did its work of conveying and depositing millions of tons of silt each year. However, since construction of the Aswan Dam in 1960, the silt has been deposited behind the dam instead of fertilizing the Nile Valley and delta. To compensate for this loss, Egypt is now one of the largest users of synthetic fertilizers in the world (Smith 2005, 28).

Although hydroelectric power generation itself does not emit greenhouse gases, water backed up behind dams does. Plants flooded and killed by reservoir waters emit methane as they decompose. Silt accumulating behind dams is rich in organic matter and bacteria that emit methane as well. Since methane is a greenhouse gas with 28 times the greenhouse effect of carbon dioxide, some researchers believe that dams cause more climate change damage than conventional power plants (Brown 2015, 121).

Concerns about declining fish populations and impaired stream flows have modified some of the thinking about the costs and benefits of dams. Dam removal projects, which are in fact wildlife restoration projects, have been completed on the Loire River in France, the Douro River in Spain, and the Elwha River in the US state of Washington, with numerous others under consideration.

A small-scale alternative known as microhydropower is suitable for streamside homes, farms, and small businesses on sites with adequate flow rate and adequate head or vertical water drop (US DOE n.d.). In a standard run-of-the-river microhydro system, a portion of the river's flow is temporarily diverted to a turbine and can generate up to 100 kW without needing a storage reservoir. Portland, Oregon and Riverside, California, installed in-pipe turbines that generate power within city gravity-fed water supply pipes.

One of the advantages of hydroelectric power is that it is constant, while one of the challenges for renewable energy sources such as wind and solar is their intermittent nature, absent a storage method such as batteries. One approach in places with significant elevation change is pumped hydroelectric storage using two reservoirs (Smil 2006, 205). During off-peak hours when electricity costs are lower, electric pumps send water to the upper reservoir. During peak demand times, water flows from the upper reservoir, through turbines, to the lower reservoir, from which it can be pumped again later (MacKay 2009, 190). Pumped storage is difficult to site and expensive to construct (Randolph and Masters 2008, 397).

Concentrating Solar Power

Solar thermal technology provides another way to generate electricity from the sun, in addition to solar PV panels. Solar thermal plants use the same technology as coal-fired plants: heat turns a steam turbine, which turns a generator, which produces electricity. Reflectors are used to focus the sun's rays on a small area, similar to sunlight focused through a magnifying glass, concentrating the rays to obtain a high temperature. This technology is a closed system that uses little water and lots of sun, so it is appropriate for desert climates. Unlike solar PV systems, which can generate power effectively even in diffuse sunlight, solar thermal systems are economical to use only in latitudes below the 35th parallel where the sun angle is closest to overhead year round (Wengenmayr and Buhrke 2008, 26).

Concentrators come in several shapes. Dish concentrators focus the sun's rays on a single point. Parabolic trough concentrators focus the sun's rays on a linear heat collection tube. Larger parabolic trough systems are used with conventional steam turbines. Dish systems are used with a technology known as a Stirling engine, a heat engine that uses temperature difference to drive pistons.

A third style of solar thermal plant uses heliostats or concentrator mirrors that move so that they always reflect sunlight in a constant direction. The heliostats are adjusted to concentrate sunlight on a central receiver system at the top of a tall tower several hundred feet high, often referred to as a power tower. A 390 MW concentrating solar installation in Ivanpah, California, is a power tower system; Ivanpah uses molten salts to store heat energy so that the plant can generate electricity after sundown. The world's largest concentrating solar installation is the 580 MW Noor plant, under construction in Morocco.

There are always tradeoffs between benefits and costs that must be evaluated when making decisions about energy sources. Concentrating solar plants have visual impact on the landscape and are responsible for some incineration deaths of birds. German solar energy researcher Robert Pitz-Paal used life cycle analysis to calculate the total carbon emissions due to manufacture, construction, operation, and disposal of various renewable energy sources. His analysis showed that for every MWh of electrical energy generated, solar thermal plants emit 26.5 pounds of carbon dioxide, compared to 37.5 pounds for wind energy plants, 39 pounds for hydroelectric plants, 243 pounds for solar PV plants, 960 pounds for gas and steam turbine plants, and 1,980 pounds for coal-fired power plants (ibid., 33).

Wind Power

Wind is a byproduct of sunlight, a free, continually renewable resource. Generating power with wind emits no greenhouse gases once the equipment has been manufactured. Wind has been used as a source of energy for around 4,000 years to propel sailing ships, pump water, and operate mills, and windmills became an iconic source of power in the Netherlands during the Renaissance. In the nineteenth and early twentieth centuries windmills were widely used across the US Great Plains, mostly for pumping water, but also for generating electricity in rural areas.

Modern wind turbine design is based on different principles and is capable of generating far more electrical power than the old models. A typical wind turbine has 3 blades, each 50 to 100 feet long, on a horizontal axis mounted on a steel tower 200 to 300 feet in the air. The generator sits behind the hub of the blades in an enclosure the size of a large truck known as a nacelle. Inside the nacelle are the generator, a gearbox for stepping up the speed of the generator, and a hydraulic system that optimizes the adjustment of the blades to match wind speed and direction.

Vertical-axis turbines are less efficient and far less common. However, they are relatively quiet and can harvest wind energy from any direction. Hence, a vertical-axis turbine provides the power needed by the first-floor visitor pavilions at the Eiffel Tower in Paris.

The higher the elevation, the faster the wind speed. Elevation is important because the power of wind increases with the cube of wind speed. For example, if the wind speed doubles, the power increases by 2^3, or 8 times the power. Power also increases with the area swept by the blades, so longer blades generate greater power. However, increased size does not necessarily increase the amount of power produced per acre. Because each turbine casts a wind shadow, larger turbines must be spaced farther apart (MacKay 2009, 265).

Most wind energy plants are large scale, owned by independent power producers who sell power to the grid on the utility side of the meter. However, smaller-scale turbines can be used to provide power for individual buildings.

The best locations for wind turbines are, of course, places with strong and reliable winds. The National Renewable Energy Laboratory (NREL), a division of the US Department of Energy, produces wind resource maps for each state, for the US as a whole, and for a number of other countries, showing the quality of the wind resource at 30, 50, 80, and 100 meters, or about 100 to 328 feet, above the ground, ranked by a 7-category wind power classification scheme. Like solar thermal plants, wind power plants do not use water, so they can be located in arid areas. In the US, land in a large swath across the Great Plains is considered an ideal location. It is generally flat and relatively easy to access. Turbines have relatively small footprints and are often located on farmland or grazing land where the land can serve dual purposes, generating power while providing lease income for farmers who may be struggling to stay in business.

Appropriate siting is critical for protecting wildlife. Wind turbines placed in the path of bird migration routes result in high numbers of bird fatalities. This has been a particular problem in the Altamont wind farm in California constructed in 1981. Sensitive siting of modern wind installations has been able to avert this problem.

Wind turbines are a bigger problem for migratory tree-roosting bats, who are killed in greater numbers than birds by turbines all over the world, mostly in late summer and fall (Cryan 2015). Tree bats appear to confuse airflow paths around turbines with those that flow around tall trees where they feed and roost (Cryan 2014, 15126). Bats fly in low winds, so operators mitigate accidents during migration season by increasing the speed at which turbines cut in (Nyári et al. 2015, 4).

Aesthetic landscape impact is another concern that must be addressed. Many sites with good wind resources are also places of natural beauty, and proposed installations of wind turbines near coastlines have prompted protests from residents. Installations located miles offshore may be able to address that problem, although costs are incurred for undersea transmission lines.

Wind turbine noise is an additional concern. With improved aerodynamic design of modern blades, measured decibel levels at a distance of around 300 yards are typically 40 to 50 decibels, similar to those of a refrigerator, dishwasher, or air conditioner (GE Global

Research 2010). Some observers have raised concerns over infrasound, low-frequency sound below the level of human hearing; the issue is considered controversial.

Visual Impacts of Centralized Power

Utility-scale wind and solar facilities cover huge areas, are visible for very long distances of 35 miles and more, (Sullivan and Meyer 2014, 46), and have major impacts on scenic resources. During the day the surfaces of solar devices and the white color of wind turbines mandated for aviation safety are highly reflective; at night, facilities are brightly lit, with impacts on both scenic resources and wildlife. The combination of large size, long-distance visibility, and siting in open landscapes makes these facilities significant sources of cumulative impacts. Researchers evaluate two attributes: visual impact and visual contrast or a change in what is seen. A combination of careful siting and mitigation strategies can reduce visual impacts (US DOI 2013); nevertheless, the transition to renewable energy is likely to change landscape character and sense of place.

Wave and Tidal Energy

Truly massive amounts of energy flow through the world's oceans, driven by gravity and the sun. Researchers have studied four options for using these energy sources: wave energy, tidal energy, energy from ocean currents, and thermal energy conversion.

Several approaches to making use of the energy of waves have been explored. The standard technology is the oscillating water column (OWC), which uses an enclosed chamber in which rising and falling water caused by wave action compresses air in the chamber, driving a turbine. This technology has been used for several decades to power ocean buoys. Larger scale prototypes are being tested.

Tidal energy technology takes advantage of differences in water level between low tide and high tide. The potential energy from this difference is captured by barrages, or low walls, similar to how a dam captures water in a reservoir. Tidal heights vary from location to location and tidal energy technology requires a substantial height difference to be effective. The location with the greatest such difference is in the Bay of Fundy between the Canadian provinces of New Brunswick and Nova Scotia, famous for its 52-foot tidal variation; a 20 MW facility is located on the shore of the bay. In France a 240 MW tidal power station is located on the estuary of La Rance River; the world's largest tidal power station is a 254 MW plant in South Korea. Tidal stations have the potential to inflict environmental damage; changing the tidal heights can kill plants and animals in estuaries where they are installed, can increase suspended sediments in the water, and can kill fish who are trapped by turbines.

Another form of moving water occurs in ocean currents. A global system of oceanic loop currents called the thermohaline circulation is driven by differences in temperature and salinity. Also known as the global conveyor belt, these currents take about 1,000 years to complete one cycle (MacKay 2009, 242). The potential for tapping this resource using submerged water turbines similar to wind turbines is being researched. Several prototypes have been tested, but no commercial installations exist.

Differences in temperature between the surface and depths help drive these global ocean currents. The fact that the layers of ocean have different temperatures makes possible the use of some kind of heat engine such as a Stirling engine. The technology is known as ocean thermal energy conversion (OTEC). The US Department of Energy has conducted experiments with several test installations near Hawaii, but commercial installations do not yet exist.

Biogas from Landfills

People in developed countries generate massive quantities of solid waste each year. With that waste comes planet-heating methane, produced by anaerobic bacteria as they break down organic matter in waste materials and emitted even from capped landfills, which are vented for safety reasons. Landfills are a major source of methane emissions. Many landfills now capture that landfill gas (LFG) and use it to generate electricity or as fuel in heaters and other equipment. Natural gas is methane, so methane biogas from landfills can be used in the same ways natural gas is used for energy production. Anaerobic digesters are also used to produce biogas, or methane, at sewage treatment plants and at livestock farms. Methane-rich biogas is used extensively in Europe to fuel combined heat and power systems.

Alternative Energy for Transportation

Transportation, most of it cars and light trucks, is the world's biggest user of petroleum and accounts for a significant share of global carbon dioxide emissions. A range of approaches will be needed to redirect this trajectory. One strategy is to improve vehicle efficiency and thus burn less fuel in the trips we do take, for example by redesigning drive trains and by using ultralight materials. Another approach is to reduce vehicle miles traveled by providing public transportation options and by rethinking our urban planning and land use decisions so that travel is less necessary. A third approach is to find other energy sources as alternatives to fossil fuels. Alternatives include electricity, biofuels, hydrogen and fuel cells.

Natural Gas

Natural gas is a fossil fuel and so its use contributes to climate change. However, burning it releases about 25 percent less carbon dioxide than gasoline combustion (Randolph and Masters 2008, 580), so it can be considered as a transition fuel. Vehicles must be modified to use natural gas or be equipped with dual fuel systems. Many college campuses and manufacturing facilities use natural gas-powered utility vehicles. Natural gas is also used to produce hydrogen gas, which can be used in hydrogen fuel cells.

Electricity

One way to power vehicles is to skip fuel combustion and go directly to electricity. Electric-powered vehicles use batteries. They are typically driven during the day and recharged during off-peak hours at night. Because of this they can take advantage of idle capacity in the grid, using additional power for battery chargers without increasing demand for power generation capacity. The cost per mile for a car run on electricity is several times less than that of a gasoline-powered car (Brown 2015, 33).

Electric vehicles face two challenges: one is emissions released by electricity production. Even if every gasoline-powered car were replaced by an electric car, greenhouse gas concentrations could remain at the same level or even rise if all the electricity were generated by coal, oil, and natural gas (Blockstein and Wiegman 2010, 42).

Another challenge is energy storage. Electric vehicles depend on batteries. Until recently batteries were so heavy and bulky that electric cars were not practical. Research for the kind of small, lightweight batteries used in cell phones and laptop computers has resulted in improved battery technology that can be applied to vehicles as well. In addition to reduced battery weight, the development of ultralight composite body materials has made it possible to cut the size of engine and drive train needed and has therefore reduced the weight that must be moved around. Electric vehicles as currently designed use nonrenewable resources: rare-earth metals for motors and lithium for batteries (Jacobson and Delucchi 2009, 62), in addition to the materials used in bodies and drive trains.

Automobiles can be driven completely by electricity or they can be hybrids of electric and gasoline drives. An all-electric car is driven by electric motors and uses batteries to store and supply charge. This battery-powered car is known as a battery electric vehicle (BEV).

A vehicle that can use electricity from its batteries but which has the option to get power from a gasoline engine is known as a plug-in hybrid electric vehicle (PHEV). A conventional hybrid vehicle uses a gasoline engine together with an electric propulsion system. Its engine and braking system both recharge the batteries. When power demands are low enough, the gasoline engine shuts down and only the electric motor moves the vehicle. In contrast to a PHEV, a conventional hybrid cannot be recharged by connecting to the grid. A PHEV is a hybrid vehicle with extra batteries that can be driven longer distances before needing the gasoline engine. Its batteries are charged not only by the engine and braking, but can also be charged by plugging into the grid.

A PHEV with excess charge could also sell power back to the grid. This kind of application is known as V2G, or vehicle-to-grid. As with PV panels, while V2G is not an economical choice for base load power generation for utilities, it can be useful for balancing and regulating fluctuating loads.

Biofuels

Biofuel is fuel made from plant material. The substance referred to as biofuel is usually ethanol, which is ethyl alcohol, generally used as a partial substitute for gasoline. The fuel known as E10 or gasohol is a mix of 10 percent ethanol and 90 percent gasoline. Ethanol contains less energy per gallon than gasoline, but in a 10 percent mix the difference in mileage is barely noticeable. The fuel known as E85 is a mix of 85 percent ethanol and 15 percent gasoline. Vehicles driven using E85 get from 5 to 12 percent fewer miles per gallon than when using pure gasoline (Randolph and Masters 2008, 540).

The production of ethanol involves converting some kind of plant matter to sugars. Four types of plant matter are used: sugar cane; grain, usually corn or wheat; cellulosic crops, either trees or grasses; and biomass, such as crop residues or wood waste. The majority of ethanol in the US is made from corn, and this is what makes biofuel controversial. Using corn as the feedstock results in greater synthetic fertilizer use, greater eutrophication in waters such as the Gulf of Mexico, increased water use, fossil fuel-burning cultivators, large subsidies granted to agribusiness corporations, consumption of agricultural land, clearing of forests, and rising world food prices. Corn ethanol has a low net energy return, with an EROEI ranging from 0.87:1 to 1.73:1 (Hughes 2013, 138), compared to petroleum's current EROEI of 15:1. That is, corn ethanol is not really an energy source; it simply transforms one fuel, petroleum, into a different fuel, ethanol (Heinberg 2011, 158). Analysts note that if the goal were to reduce greenhouse gas emissions, converting cropland to forest would reduce emissions more effectively than converting forests to cropland for growing corn (Smil 2003, 107).

Cellulosic materials avoid some of the negative side effects. Woody crops such as fast-growing poplar trees are one option. Perennial grasses such as switchgrass and miscanthus are another. These grasses can be harvested and regrown without cultivation, which also means they provide some habitat and contribute to soil health and erosion control. Grasses and woody crops contain residual biomass that can be used instead of the fossil fuels usually required to produce heat for the conversion process for producing ethanol. Because of their low energy density compared to petroleum, very large land requirements are still an issue for cultivated biomass crops (Smil 2006, 197).

Biodiesel is a different kind of biofuel. It is made from oils and is used to replace diesel as a fuel. Biodiesel can be blended with petroleum diesel at a range of mixes. B-2 is 2 percent biodiesel and 98 percent petroleum diesel; B-100 is 100 percent biodiesel. The oils can be vegetable oils such as soybean or rapeseed oil. Oil can also be obtained on a small scale from recycling used cooking oil in a process that is relatively simple. Another source being actively tested is the use of algae to produce biodiesel. Algae have a higher yield per acre than soil crops, producing 10 to 300 times more fuel per acre than other biodiesel crops. They can be intensively grown in lagoons, in enclosed plastic tubes, or on thin-film membranes suspended in racks, although after years of research, commercialization has remained elusive (Hughes 2013, 138).

Hydrogen

Hydrogen is the element of which stars are made. It is the most plentiful element in the universe and one of two elements that make up the abundant water on this planet. A lot of excitement is generated around the possibility of what is sometimes called a "hydrogen economy." The idea of an energy source that is around us everywhere, releases no greenhouse gases, and produces only water as a waste is appealing. But a number of technical issues must be worked out first.

Hydrogen is not a fuel like gasoline; it is not a source of energy. Hydrogen is a storage medium, a way to transport energy. It can be used in a device such as a fuel cell where chemical energy is converted into electricity. Extracting hydrogen from water or methane requires energy. The energy source can be fossil fuels or it can be electricity from solar, wind, hydroelectric, or geothermal power. Hydrogen is only carbon neutral if the energy source used to produce it is carbon neutral. If electricity used in the conversion process comes from coal-fired power plants, hydrogen production results in greenhouse gas emissions.

Water is a ready source of hydrogen. The process of using electrical current to separate water into its separate chemical elements is called electrolysis, a mature and well-understood technology. Methane is currently the most common source of hydrogen. The majority of methane used as feedstock is natural gas, although methane from biomass has large potential. The most widely used process for extracting hydrogen from methane, steam methane reforming, uses fossil fuels and releases carbon dioxide as a byproduct so it is not an ideal process, but so far is the lowest-cost way to produce hydrogen.

Hydrogen has other issues. It is difficult to store and transport. At room temperature, hydrogen is a low-density gas. Storing it involves compressing it to pressures of 10,000 psi, which requires heavy, thick-walled tanks. Even when compressed, the gas is only half as dense as liquid, so it takes up a lot of space. Hydrogen in liquid form takes up less space, but to change hydrogen to a liquid state it must be supercooled to minus 423°F, which requires special, costly insulated bottles called dewars (Muller 2010, 11). While hydrogen is less flammable than gasoline and disperses quickly, it is still flammable, so safe storage and handling are critical. Finding a better storage method is a major thrust of current hydrogen research.

Another complex challenge is infrastructure for producing, delivering, and distributing hydrogen economically. Developing this infrastructure and bringing it up to scale, that is, developing a large-enough distribution system, is predicted to take several decades. As a transition, it may be possible to transport hydrogen in some existing natural gas pipelines. Because hydrogen's properties make it costly to store and transport, it is likely that in its mature configuration hydrogen will be produced in multiple regional plants, and even at local stations and individual homes, where natural gas is likely to be the feedstock. Electricity could be used at off-peak hours, when power costs are lower.

Once these issues can be resolved, hydrogen has advantages. The primary advantage is reduced greenhouse gas emissions. If renewable energy sources are used to split off the hydrogen, then no greenhouse gases are released when it is produced. Even if fossil fuel energy sources are used, cars powered by hydrogen fuel cells release less carbon dioxide than gasoline-powered cars. And unlike oil refineries that release carbon dioxide and other pollutants, hydrogen plants release only water.

Many of the mechanical and hydraulic subsystems in conventional gasoline-powered cars can be eliminated in hydrogen-powered cars, which operate using fuel cells and electricity that they generate. Vehicles could themselves function as mobile sources of electricity that could be used for other purposes.

Hydrogen storage takes up a lot of space. However, the gas itself is several times lighter than fossil fuels. Thus it may be put into place first for large vehicles such as buses and heavy trucks. It is conceivable that hydrogen could be used to address the problem of greenhouse gas emissions in airplanes. Because weight is a significant factor for airplanes, more important than volume, space-consuming but lightweight compressed hydrogen gas may be feasible for aircraft.

And while costs of hydrogen-powered vehicles are many times that of fossil fuel vehicles using current technology, according to an assessment by the National Research Council and the National Academy of Engineering, the cost per mile in a fuel cell car will be lower than in a conventional gasoline-powered car once large-scale production and distribution are developed (Ogden 2006, 99).

Fuel Cells

Hydrogen stores and transports energy. This energy can be converted into electricity in a fuel cell, a device that converts hydrogen and oxygen into water and in the process produces electricity. Fuel cells are currently used in space shuttles, where they provide electricity, heat, and drinking water and produce no carbon dioxide waste requiring disposal.

A fuel cell looks a lot like a battery and is similar to a battery in that it contains cells where chemical reactions produce electricity. In a battery the chemicals are stored together permanently in the same cell. Once all the chemical has been used up, the battery must either be discarded or recharged using electricity produced elsewhere. In a fuel cell the chemicals are hydrogen and oxygen, they are housed in separated cells, and they continually flow through and are replenished. Hydrogen flows through one side of the cell; oxygen is removed from air as it flows through the other side. Hydrogen and oxygen combine to form water. In the process chemical bonds are broken and formed and electrons begin to flow, producing electrical current. A fuel cell can use other types of fuels instead of hydrogen, but hydrogen is the most benign and thus is the focus of current research and development. Platinum, a nonrenewable resource, is a component of fuel cells; long-term use of platinum will depend upon developing effective recycling processes (Jacobson and Delucchi 2009, 62).

Fuel cells are often discussed as power sources for vehicles, but they can also be used to provide power for buildings. Quiet and vibration-free, they can be located indoors. At larger scales, their waste heat can be used in combined heat and power systems. Some commercial facilities with large-scale outdoor fuel cells, including several Google and Verizon data centers, use natural gas as their hydrogen source; facilities at eBay and Adobe headquarters use biogas from landfill waste.

Energy Efficiency

When organizations look for alternatives to fossil fuels, the first place they typically look is to efficiency improvements. Energy efficiency is the lowest-cost alternative to fossil fuels and the easiest to accomplish; saving fuel is a lot cheaper than buying it. It is, in effect, a free supply of energy. In addition, it reduces greenhouse gas emissions: the greenest energy source of all is the one not used.

Buildings make up a sizable sector of all energy consumption. While principles of green building design can greatly decrease the energy required by buildings, new construction makes up only a small portion of the total building stock. Existing buildings outnumber new by more than 50 to 1 (Landsberg and Lord 2009, 3). Thus finding more efficient ways to use energy in existing buildings is one of the most effective ways to reduce fossil fuel use and emissions, with potential for large cost savings.

The steps in improving energy performance of buildings are similar to the steps in many problem-solving processes. Typical problem-solving steps are, after defining the problem, to gather information, propose and select solutions, implement, and evaluate. In an energy improvement process, the first step is to measure the energy performance of the building. A formal process usually includes energy audits. Once energy performance has been evaluated, the next step is to set goals. Implementation begins with no-cost or low-cost adjustments, and may continue with equipment replacements and other capital improvements over time. Evaluation can be as informal as reviewing utility bills, but often it includes more formal commissioning and financial analysis. Incorporating energy management into an organization's policies and procedures, including purchasing policies and operations and maintenance policies and manuals, helps to ensure ongoing performance tracking.

A sustainability coordinator is typically employed by a corporation, educational institution, government agency, or NGO. They are likely to be involved with commercial buildings, where they may work with an energy analyst, engineer, or other energy professional.[4] Commercial buildings consist of all buildings, including schools, in which at least half of the floor space is used for a purpose that is not residential, manufacturing, or agricultural.

Measuring Energy Efficiency

The energy efficiency of a building is measured and characterized in terms of an **energy utilization index** (EUI). Using this index to measure building efficiency is similar to using miles per gallon to measure the fuel efficiency of a vehicle. Miles per gallon allows a buyer to compare cars; EUIs allow energy managers to compare buildings with other similar buildings.[5] The EUI is a ratio, usually expressed as a ratio of Btu (British thermal units) per square foot of gross floor area per year.

To find the total energy used in a building over the course of a year, energy managers determine the total amount of each kind of fuel or energy source used per year. They can collect data from utility bills, purchase orders, and equipment such as data loggers, which record the amount of energy used. Utility meters record overall consumption. Many buildings also use submetering, in which owners provide their own meters to record energy use in selected portions of the facility.

Setting Goals

Once a building's energy performance has been characterized, the next step is to set goals for improvement. Goals should be (1) measurable and (2) attainable. Measurable goals could include statements such as the following examples: improve energy utilization index by 10 percent over the previous 5-year average. Earn an ENERGY STAR score of 70 or higher. Earn an ENERGY STAR label (which requires a score of 75 or higher) each year.[6]

Once the goals have been defined, the energy manager or team writes an energy efficiency plan. The plan describes existing conditions, goals, measures to be implemented, evaluation steps, a timeline, and a budget.

Effective plans take an integrated approach, considering a building as a whole system whose components influence each other. For example, a plan may call for upgrading lighting, adding window shades, and replacing air conditioning systems. The new lighting probably produces less waste heat and the window shades reduce heat from summer sun, so a new cooling system could be sized smaller than the old one it replaces.

Improving Energy Efficiency Performance

Energy efficiency measures take several forms. They can address the end uses of energy, such as plug loads, or devices that are plugged into wall outlets; lighting; water heating; refrigeration; and heating, ventilating and air conditioning (HVAC; pronounced with the letter "H" followed by "vac") equipment and distribution. Energy efficiency measures can include changing behavior, such as turning off lights in unoccupied rooms. They can involve elements that influence energy use such as operations and maintenance procedures and upgrades to the building envelope.

Energy managers look first for what is often referred to as low-hanging fruit, targets that are easy to achieve and carry no or low cost. Examples include locating and repairing air, steam, and water leaks; checking and calibrating thermostats to ensure they are set correctly; identifying hours when buildings are unoccupied and programming thermostats to reduce heating and cooling demands during those hours; and coordinating with cleaning staff so that custodians clean each floor as a team, turning lights on and off again as they go.

Changing occupant behavior, another example of low-hanging fruit, involves an education and energy awareness program. The program may include newsletters, reminders or updates via the organization's email system, and posters. These communication tools can remind employees to turn off equipment, including computers, when not in use; to turn off lights when leaving a room; to use company-provided task lighting instead of area lighting, when appropriate; or to close south-facing blinds in the summer. Many users have incorrect ideas about turning lights or computers off and on, based on what they learned years ago, so education efforts can help users learn that life expectancies of modern lighting ballasts and modern computer screens are not affected by turning them off and on.

Heating and cooling are the largest energy consumers in a typical building, followed closely by lighting. Lighting upgrades are lower cost than replacing heating and cooling plants. Thus lighting upgrades are a frequent element of energy efficiency measures, replacing incandescent lights with either fluorescent lights or light-emitting diodes (LEDs). Incandescent lights use 4 times as much energy as fluorescent lights to provide the same amount of illumination.

Standard fluorescent lighting is used to light large areas; compact fluorescent lights (CFLs) are used for task lighting. LEDs are as efficient as CFLs; they cost far more but last 3 times longer and unlike CFLs do not contain mercury.

Lighting controls can be used to address inefficiencies. A common control is a switch that includes a timer and a motion detector. When a room is occupied, the lights are on. When a room is unoccupied for a period of time with no motion detected, lights automatically turn off. Other controls detect the amount of daylight entering a space and adjust lighting in response. Manual dimmer controls allow users to adjust lighting levels individually; they improve user satisfaction and typically result in energy savings of 10 to 20 percent per light (ibid., 37).

Some US organizations have purchasing policies mandating ENERGY STAR-labeled electrical products whenever they are available. These appliances and devices can reduce energy use by up to 60 percent over conventional equipment (ibid., 38).

Equipment lacking sleep mode features can be connected to power strips with timers or occupancy sensors that shut off when a room is unoccupied. These reduce consumption of what is known as **phantom power** load, the energy that is consumed by electronic devices when they are turned off or in standby mode.

HVAC equipment is usually the biggest user of a building's energy. Replacing an HVAC system may require capital outlay and is usually done at the time of major renovation. However, an engineer or HVAC technician can optimize a system for improved efficiency. Pump and fan motors can be replaced with high-efficiency motors or can be fitted with variable-frequency drives. Air handling systems can include fan controls that bring in cooler outside air to supplement cooling requirements, when conditions permit, known as an economizer cycle. Ventilation controls can limit fan use and air conditioning during times of low occupancy.

The building envelope consists of floors, walls, roofs, windows, and doors. All of these have an impact on amount of energy used. Envelope components are typically upgraded as part of major renovations. Lower-cost upgrades to building envelopes can be performed by addressing air leaks around windows, door thresholds, or where pipes come through walls as part of regular building maintenance.

Higher-cost projects, known as **capital projects**, are usually the final step in an energy efficiency plan. A capital project is a long-term investment in the improvement of a fixed asset, such as a building or infrastructure, requiring a comparatively high financial outlay. Such projects may include major lighting upgrades, HVAC upgrades or system replacements, or building envelope upgrades. For example, in 2008 the owners of the 1931 Empire State Building in New York City invested $13 million in energy efficiency upgrades including windows, lighting, and HVAC systems as part of a massive renovation project. Their investment is expected to reduce energy costs and greenhouse gas emissions by up to 38 percent with a payback period of three years (Empire State Building 2013).

Energy Audits

Most commercial energy efficiency programs identify efficiency measures through **energy audits** and **commissioning**. An energy audit is a systematic, detailed analysis of how and where a building uses energy. It is a complex process requiring the services of an experienced energy analyst or auditing firm. Prior experience conducting energy audits in a variety of buildings and contexts is an important advantage. The end product of an energy audit is a written report.

Commissioning

Commissioning is the process of verifying that building systems are functioning as intended and taking corrective action if they are not. Commissioning of new buildings is often required by contracts and is required for buildings certified under Leadership in Energy and Environmental Design (LEED). It is such an important part of building construction that commissioning has become a specialty, with many building-commissioning companies and building-commissioning departments in larger engineering firms. Commissioning of new buildings can reduce operating costs significantly.

Commissioning of existing buildings is known as retrocommissioning. Retrocommissioning compares a building's actual operation to its intended design potential. Once retrocommissioning has been completed, ongoing measurement and verification ensures that the building continues to operate as commissioned.

A **measurement and verification** (M&V) plan is a value-added service often provided by energy auditors or commissioning specialists. An M&V plan verifies that investments in energy efficiency measures provide the benefits expected; this is especially useful for validating energy efficiency measures to upper management in large organizations. Buildings applying for LEED certification can earn a point for M&V. To qualify for the point the written M&V plan must follow a protocol known as the International Performance Measurement and Verification Protocol (IPMVP), sponsored by the US Department of Energy.

Audits, commissioning, and M&V are often performed by an **energy services company** (ESCO) under contract to the building owner. Under the contract, a part of the energy savings is paid to the ESCO in its monthly fee. The ESCO can perform audits, identify and install energy efficiency measures, guarantee their performance, and verify that performance using M&V. The ESCO's fee is less than the energy savings, so the owner saves money with no up-front costs for energy upgrades. The owner repays the ESCO for the upgrade costs as part of its monthly payment.

Operation and Maintenance

Successfully implementing an energy efficiency plan requires support from upper management to provide operations and maintenance (O&M) staff with the tools and skills they need. Managing energy O&M is a fulltime job. Many organizations, especially those without ESCOs, hire an energy manager and pay for the position with the energy savings produced by the energy manager.

Box 9.1 Jevons' Paradox

In 1865, British economist William Stanley Jevons published a treatise called *The Coal Question*. Jevons analyzed exponential growth in consumption, pointing out that consuming nonrenewable resources such as coal uses up the supply and means that coal will eventually run out, an early recognition of the limits to growth (Alcott 2005, 11) and the concept of peak oil (MacKay 2009, 19). His calculations of British peak coal production were surprisingly accurate (ibid., 158). He offered a formula for society's impact that was an early version of the I = PAT formula, stating that consumption consists of "the number of people, and the average quantity consumed by each" (Jevons 1866, 196).

Jevons is best known for his analysis of the history of steam engine technology. Early engines were inefficient and thus impractical to use. As steam engines were improved to consume coal more efficiently their use became more attractive, they were used more often, and thus more coal was consumed. Jevons had discovered a paradox: "It is the very economy of its use which leads to its extensive consumption" (ibid., 141). Increased efficiency does not by itself lower consumption; instead, efficiency makes energy less expensive so that people can afford to use more of it (Heinberg 2011, 171; Smil 2006, 193). This paradoxical situation is known as the rebound effect or Jevons' Paradox. Scholars are in agreement that the rebound effect exists, but are not in agreement on the magnitude (IPCC 2014c, 28).

Making the Transition

We live at the beginning of an energy transition, from a world powered by fossil fuels to one powered by sun and wind. Modern society has massive amounts of infrastructure and technology all built around fossil fuels. Trucks, cars, airlines, ships, power plants, paved highways, steel production, plastic production, heating and cooling of buildings, even the manufacturing of alternative-energy equipment and its infrastructure, all depend upon fossil fuels. It is not possible just to switch the massive momentum of the entire world economy abruptly to a new mode of energy without causing economic collapse. Even if renewable energy sources grow rapidly and cultural and political forces are motivated, analysts project that it will require decades to make the transition to a carbon-free economy (Ayres and Ayres 2010, 1), while greenhouse gases continue to accumulate in the atmosphere.

Developing and implementing renewable technologies as fast as we can go is critical. But even if these sources grow exceptionally quickly, doubling in size every year, it will take a number of years before they are reliably online at the necessary scale. Meanwhile, recognizing that it will take many years before fossil fuels have moved out of the system, the other obvious solution is to find ways to use less fuel. The technical term for this approach is increasing the **energy service**, the amount of useful work done by each unit of fuel. Energy efficiency and combined heat and power are two effective ways to increase energy service. Technologies that double the amount of energy put out by a given amount of fossil fuel can in effect double the quantity of fuel reserves available during the next few years while renewable energy sources are developed and scaled up. Combined heat and power is attractive to businesses because the energy produced using process waste heat is currently far cheaper than energy from solar photovoltaics or wind turbines.

Some analysts believe that natural gas should be used as a transition fuel because burning it releases less greenhouse gas than petroleum or coal. Fuel switching in a central heating plant by changing from oil or coal to natural gas is one approach. Natural gas can be used as a feedstock for producing hydrogen used in fuel cells. It can also be used to power internal combustion engines, although since petroleum has about 1,000 times as much energy density as natural gas, use of natural gas as a transportation fuel is limited. Methanol, a liquid fuel derived from methane gas and used in some fleet cars and buses, is a possibility, although it has only half the energy density of gasoline (Muller 2010, 69). Because methanol is less flammable and volatile than gasoline, it is used in Indianapolis-type race cars. Finding an alternative for petroleum jet fuel remains the most challenging fuel issue.

Of all the fossil fuels, burning natural gas emits the least pollution. It contains fewer carbon atoms per volume than oil or coal, so its combustion produces about half as much carbon dioxide as the other fossil fuels. However, it is a far more powerful greenhouse gas than carbon dioxide; methane releases are a serious concern. Natural gas flaring at refineries and leaks during transportation currently account for about 10 percent of global methane emissions (Smil 2009, 215), although some critics say that leakage is significantly under-reported, and analyses have shown that natural gas actually worsens the climate outlook in many cases because of extensive leakages (Brown 2015, 9). Some researchers propose tapping deposits of methane hydrates, or clathrates, ice-like structures of methane molecules frozen under permafrost and in deep ocean sediments. However, large releases of methane on land or depressurizing it in ocean deposits carry grave risks.

Energy efficiency means using less energy to do the same amount of work. Energy efficiency offers the biggest opportunity for cutting carbon emissions and provides, in effect, free energy. Conservation, or reducing demand, is a related but different strategy.

The fact remains that no energy source can match the energy density of fossil fuels. Alternative energy sources are critical for making the transition away from planet-cooking fossil fuels, but because of their lower energy density, they cannot substitute for fossil fuels at a one-to-one rate. Today's system is based on what turns out to be a special case, a one-time windfall of cheap energy, available from a continuous, uninterrupted supply and able to meet whatever demand we place upon it. The energy system in a low-carbon future will not be a facsimile of that system (Butler et al. 2012, 73). It is probable that in future decades, global society will have less energy available than today (Heinberg 2011, 117). Thus a fundamental task of the energy transition will be to adjust our expectations as we learn to limit demand; a low-carbon future necessarily means lower consumption (Hagens 2015, 34).

Diversity is essential. So is a focus on local conditions. Renewable energy resources vary by location. Each energy strategy is well suited to some places, less so to others, and each has a list of pros and cons. Each community figures out what works in its particular place.

The Water-Energy-Food Nexus

Sustainability is a systems problem. Water, energy, and food are interconnected. Large amounts of water and energy are used to grow food. Large quantities of water are used to extract and process fossil fuels, to generate power with fossil fuels or nuclear energy, and to grow feedstock for biofuels, while large amounts of energy are used to pump, treat, and transport water. An abundance of one allows an abundance of the others, and a shortage of one can lead to a shortage of the others (Webber 2015, 63). As global population rises and becomes increasingly urbanized, demand for all three will rise. Added to this, climate change will have major impacts on the availability of water and food and on the range of appropriate energy choices.

Although they are elements of a complex system, water, energy, and food sectors typically operate within silos, with separate regulators, agencies, infrastructure, and funding streams. Water planners often assume they will have all the energy they need, and energy planners often assume they will have all the water they need (Webber 2008, 40). By missing the fact that these are inherently interconnected and interdependent processes, a focus on optimizing separate pieces one subject at a time exacerbates unintended negative consequences and overlooks important opportunities (Dodds and Bartram 2016, xix).

All three are critical to sustainable development. A nexus approach is fundamental to improving water, energy and food security and effectively implementing global Sustainable Development Goals (ibid., xxiii). This approach integrates governance and management across the three sectors and promotes their interconnectedness (Hoff 2011, 7). In addition, explicitly considering the interactions of water, energy, and food plays an important role in making decisions about climate change mitigation (IPCC 2014d, 112). The water-energy-food nexus is the subject of conferences, research, and global initiatives.

Conclusion

Making the transition to a post-carbon world is a multi-faceted undertaking. Fossil fuels are a one-time, nonrenewable resource; they do not regenerate and can only be depleted. We are far from running out any time soon, but we have run out of sources that are cheap and easy to access. As reserves continue to deplete, extraction will eventually become so expensive that it will be economically untenable. Before that happens, a destabilizing climate will make curtailing greenhouse gas emissions imperative. One major strategy is to switch to renewable sources of energy derived from sun, wind, water, and earth. Government-supplied subsidies will be needed to allow renewable technologies to be economically competitive until they come up to scale. Another major strategy is to increase the amount of useful work from the same amount of energy through energy efficiency and combined heat and power. A final strategy is to reduce the amount of energy we need. Potential strategies are available through building design, material selection, product and manufacturing process design, recycling, changing our consumption rate, reducing the amount of water we pump over long distances, and urban land use planning. All these strategies together are elements of a larger whole.

Notes

1 EROEI declines, too. In 1930 the EROEI for oil produced in the US was about 100:1 (Heinberg 2011, 112); today it is at most 15:1, and falling.
2 "The stone age didn't end because we ran out of stones." Statement made by Sheik Ahmed Zaki Yamani in 1973, at the height of the first oil crisis (quoted in Evans 2012, 148).
3 In the US, the regulations are the Public Utility Regulatory Policies Act of 1978 (PURPA), Energy Policy Act of 1992 (EPAct), and Order 888, 1996 from the Federal Energy Regulatory Commission (FERC).
4 Energy efficiency work can be done by professional facilities managers, energy analysts, technicians, or engineers. For simplicity, any person involved in managing energy will be referred to in this chapter as an energy manager.
5 US building codes typically base their energy requirements on an energy standard from the American Society of Heating, Refrigerating and Air-Conditioning Engineers (ASHRAE, pronounced "ASH-ray"). The standard is ASHRAE Standard 90.1, and is available for free download from ASHRAE. This standard is updated about every 3 years. Energy efficiency requirements in Standard 90.1 have become more stringent with each revision. High-performance buildings, sometimes called green buildings, are typically 15 to 40 percent more energy efficient than the minimum standards set forth in ASHRAE Standard 90.1.
6 ENERGY STAR Portfolio Manager from the US EPA is a tool for tracking building energy performance. The rating tool assigns a score from 1 to 100. A score of 50 means that 50 percent of similar buildings use more energy and 50 percent use less energy. Top-performing buildings, those with a score of 75 or higher, can earn an ENERGY STAR label, which is good for one year.

Further Reading

Heinberg, Richard and David Fridley. *Our Renewable Future: Laying the Path for One Hundred Percent Clean Energy.* Washington, DC: Island Press, 2016.

IEA. *Key World Energy Statistics 2015*. Paris: International Energy Agency, 2015.

Landsberg, Dennis R. and Mychele R. Lord. *Energy Efficiency Guide for Existing Commercial Buildings: The Business Case for Building Owners and Managers.* Atlanta, GA: ASHRAE, 2009.

Lovins, Amory B. *Reinventing Fire*. White River Junction, VT: Chelsea Green Publishing, 2011.

MacKay, David J. C. *Sustainable Energy—Without the Hot Air*. Cambridge: UIT Cambridge Ltd., 2009.

Muller, Richard A. *Physics and Technology for Future Presidents*. Princeton, NJ: Princeton University Press, 2010.

Randolph, John and Gilbert M. Masters. *Energy for Sustainability: Technology, Planning, Policy*. Washington, DC: Island Press, 2008.

Smil, Vaclav. *Energy Transitions: Global and National Perspectives*, 2nd ed. Santa Barbara, CA: Praeger, 2017.

Chapter Review

1   Why are coal, oil, and natural gas called "fossil fuels"?
2   Describe the origins of petroleum, natural gas, and coal. Does one of them come from dinosaurs?
3   Why are we predicted to run out of petroleum in the next several decades if there are still substantial oil supplies remaining?
4   What is the difference between reserves and resources?
5   Plankton are still dying and falling to the bottoms of oceans. Why do we not classify fossil fuels as renewable energy sources?
6   Why can we not just decide to stop using fossil fuels and immediately convert everything to renewable energy sources?
7   When people talk about "Hubbert's peak," what are they referring to?
8   What is "the grid"?
9   Describe how a smart grid differs from the grid system currently in use.
10   If your neighbor had never heard of combined heat and power, or cogeneration, and asked you what it was, how would you explain the basic idea to them in just a few words?
11   Would switching to hydroelectric power from another method of power generation be an effective strategy for reducing greenhouse gases?
12   Why is generating electricity using geothermal power not practical as a major source of power?
13   Why have hydrogen automobiles not replaced gasoline models?
14   List some energy conservation steps an organization can take at no cost.
15   List some energy conservation steps that have initial costs but that will pay for themselves.
16   What is the purpose of the commissioning process? Could the same commissioning plan be used for two different projects?

Critical Thinking and Discussion

1   Some advertisements declare that natural gas is a "clean" fuel. Is this an accurate label?
2   If the US has much larger reserves of coal than of petroleum or natural gas, why did industry shift in the twentieth century from coal to the other two fuels?
3   Do you think policy efforts should focus on increasing miles per gallon in vehicles or on reducing the total miles driven? Why?
4   Markets tend to respond to supply and demand, with price reflecting the scarcity of a commodity. Do you think the price of oil reflects how much oil is left in the ground? Why or why not?

5   How could governments use tax policies, subsidies, or payments to certain businesses to discourage the use of fossil fuels?

6   If Jevons' Paradox is correct, does this mean that government policies for efficiency are counter-productive? What other policy approaches could be considered?

7   What social and economic issues might follow the decline of fossil fuel production?

8   What kinds of facility or site conditions would make cogeneration a good choice for power generation? For wind power? Solar photovoltaic cells? Hydropower?

9   List three forms of renewable energy and discuss the social costs that might be connected to these sources.

10 Do you think wind turbines should be installed in wilderness? Should they be installed in scenic areas? What criteria should be used for making such decisions?

11 How probable is it that 50 percent of the world's energy needs will be supplied by renewable resources within the next 20 years? Explain your reasoning.

12 Except for hydroelectric and geothermal power, renewable energy sources do not deliver steady power 24 hours a day. Is this a problem?

13 Hydroelectric dams provide clean power compared to coal-fired power plants. Do you think the advantage is worth the related environmental and social costs? Why or why not?

14 Your city owns 4 square miles of land outside of town that it intends to use for generating power. How would you decide whether it would be best to use this land to grow biomass, to install solar photovoltaic panels, to install solar thermal panels, or to mount wind turbines? If this were the city in which you are living now, what would you recommend?

15 How can governments advance renewable energy if it means sacrifices by individuals? Would a transition to renewable energy be possible if it required additional revenue such as from increased taxes?

16 If a significant portion of vehicles become electric vehicles, how might this alter goals for energy efficiency or onsite renewable energy for buildings?

17 When architects and engineers design buildings, they often compare building performance to code requirements and then describe the design as a certain percentage "better than code." However, owners and maintenance and operations staff see invoices that measure energy use in kilowatts, therms, and gallons. Is there a gap between building performance measurement during design and during operation? If so, what kinds of approaches might close that gap?

18 Research indicates that people are willing to tolerate wider temperature ranges if they have control over their environment. How does designing buildings that give users personal control affect energy efficiency? What are some of the tradeoffs to consider?

10 Green Buildings and Sites

Buildings are large consumers of resources with big impacts on sustainability. They sit at the intersection of three converging crises: climate change, natural resource depletion, and the impending end of the era of cheap fossil fuels. Buildings in the US consume 74.9 percent of all electricity and 47.6 percent of all energy produced (Architecture 2030, 2013). Globally they consume even more. In the US they generated 44.6 percent of all greenhouse gas emissions in 2012, far more than transportation's 34.3 percent or industry's 21.1 percent (ibid.).

Yet buildings offer significant opportunity to reduce greenhouse gas emissions and avert a climate change tipping point. Buildings are constantly being torn down, renovated, or built. Existing buildings and infrastructure developed in the building booms of the last century are aging, populations are still growing, and urban development patterns continue to change. It is predicted that between now and the year 2035 approximately 75 percent of the built environment will be either new or renovated (ibid.).

Approaches to architectural design develop along historic trends, just as music or art develops in particular periods. In much of the twentieth century buildings were seen as "machines for living." This era was heralded as the machine age, and prominent architects designed buildings to celebrate and to meet the demands of the new age. By the middle of the century electrically powered air conditioning was increasingly common. Windows no longer needed to be opened, the direction of sunlight and shade became less important, and modern buildings became separated from the outdoors. Tall and wide modern buildings, thin-skinned, covered by expanses of glass, sealed and sporting windows that couldn't be opened, fueled by cheap fossil-fuel energy and cooled mechanically, could be built in any climate using exactly the same forms and technologies. Dependent on energy-hungry mechanical systems, they could only be occupied as long as the power was on and the air conditioning was operating.

In the twenty-first century, a dramatic change in the way buildings are designed and built is gaining momentum. One visible manifestation is known as LEED. Leadership in Energy and Environmental Design (LEED) is a rating system for buildings developed by the US Green Building Council (USGBC). LEED certification provides third-party verification that a building's design, construction, and operation will reduce greenhouse gas emissions, use water and energy efficiently, minimize environmental impact, promote social equity, and promote economic viability.

Sustainability practitioners need a basic understanding of how buildings and sustainability strategies in buildings work so that they can talk with designers and participate in collaborative planning teams. Green buildings are often designed using collaborative processes involving multiple stakeholders, with planning teams sometimes including sustainability professionals.

What Is a Green Building?

While traditional twentieth-century buildings used the machine as a metaphor, green buildings use ecology as a metaphor. The term "green building" is used to describe a healthy building that minimizes negative impacts on the environment. The USGBC defines green buildings as "buildings that are environmentally responsible, profitable and healthy places to live and work" (Whitson 2003, iii). According to the EPA: "Green building is the practice of creating structures and using processes that are environmentally responsible and resource-efficient throughout a building's life-cycle from siting to design, construction, operation, maintenance, renovation and deconstruction" (US EPA n.d., Green Building). Green buildings are also known as high-performance buildings.

A green building follows examples of living things in nature. It uses the free sources of energy and water that are available around it, particularly sunlight, wind, and rain. Like a living organism, it is adapted to the specific conditions in the particular place where it is. Green buildings are conceived of not as isolated objects but as interacting elements connected to their site and neighborhood. Many get their water supply primarily from water that falls on site and their energy supply primarily from electricity generated on site. They use locally sourced, nontoxic materials wherever possible. They are highly insulated, use high-quality window systems, and are topped by roofs that reflect rather than absorb heat. They take advantage of free sunlight and wind so that they can use natural daylighting, passive solar heating, and natural ventilation to reduce energy requirements.

The term "sustainable building" is sometimes used, but no buildings are actually sustainable. As architect William McDonough (McDonough and Braungart 2002, 51) points out, being "less bad" is not the same as being sustainable. A sustainable building would use only materials and energy resources that are available in the place where it is located, would provide nutrients but produce no net waste, would foster the health of systems that sustain life, and would be able to continue functioning on its own into the future. It would support not only environmental but also social and economic well-being. Some designers aspire someday to go beyond sustainable buildings to regenerative buildings, which would give back more than they use and would contribute to restoring the health of land, air, water, and biosphere. Current green buildings are not themselves sustainable or regenerative, but they are incremental steps in that direction.

Green design results in buildings that have different appearances in different regions. A building suited to hot desert climates, where the primary strategies are ventilation, night cooling, and **thermal mass**, will have one look. It will be quite different from a building designed for snowy winters, where ample windows on the southern face are needed to let in warming sun. Thermal mass makes sense in a hot, dry place with wide daily temperature swings from day to night, such as Egypt or Phoenix, Arizona, but would not be a good choice in a hot, humid place with only small daily temperature differences such as Singapore or Miami, Florida.

One of the features of green design is that its solutions address many goals simultaneously. Designs strive to reduce or eliminate greenhouse gas emissions, reduce energy use, minimize or eliminate dependence on fossil fuels, reduce water use, reduce waste, avoid pollution, protect natural resources, preserve or restore local ecosystems, provide places that are comfortable and healthy for people, and build community. Designers integrate multiple strategies for meeting these goals.

Reusing an existing building is often a more sustainable choice than demolishing and replacing it with a new building (Preservation Green Lab 2011, vi). As historic preservationists say: "The greenest building is the one that already exists" (Moe 2007). When new buildings must be built, they can be designed for long life using materials that are durable. Choosing a design that is aesthetically attractive to many people will help the building to realize a longer life. Designing a building whose interior is flexible and adaptable to changing uses helps ensure the building will be reused. Architects call this "long life, loose fit."

Designers of green buildings plan for recycling of building materials in the event that, despite their best intentions, the building is taken down. The building is viewed as a storehouse of materials for another project, with building components designed for disassembly and reuse. Components of permanently attached mixed materials prevent disassembly and recycling, and are avoided where possible.

A popular slogan says, "reduce, reuse, recycle." This familiar set of approaches for minimizing waste and resource consumption in consumer goods is relevant to buildings as well. When new construction is planned, owners and occupants can begin by evaluating how much space is really needed. Smaller is better. The smaller a building space, the fewer the building materials needed to construct it and the fewer the resources needed to operate it.

By far the greatest costs of a building come from its operation over its lifetime. Green buildings cost on average 2 percent more to design and build. However, the average payback time for this additional cost is about 6 years from energy savings alone; after 6 years, the reduced operating cost continues to add to the bottom line. Analyzed over a 20-year period, the financial payback from energy savings is 2 to 3 times greater than the original additional cost of greening (Kats 2010, xvii). Water costs, too, are significantly lower, and occupant health and productivity are higher than in conventional buildings.

The Process of Green Building Design

Green buildings are more than simply conventional designs with a set of individual products stuck on once the designs are complete. These buildings are integrated systems that require a different, whole-building way of thinking. Bringing green goals and approaches into the process from the beginning is critical to a successful and cost-effective green building. While residential designs are usually developed by a single designer, for commercial buildings, not only is a green building different from a traditional building, the green building design process is different. No one person has all the knowledge needed to allow the parts of the system to work together. The old image of the solitary genius designing behind closed doors, with individual specialists who each develop isolated subcomponents on their own, has been replaced by a motivated, interdisciplinary team, working together, where each member has important knowledge to contribute and where synergy means that the final result is something no one person could have developed on their own.

This whole-system, collaborative method of building design is known as integrated design, and it provides simultaneous solutions to multiple problems. The shape of a building; where it sits on its site; whether it is lit by natural daylight, warmed by just the right amount of solar radiation, and kept cool by passive ventilation; whether it gets some or most of its water through what falls on the site; whether it generates its own power; and whether it provides spaces that support the well-being of people; each of these elements affects the form and size and cost of the others.

An integrated design process brings together a range of specialties and diverse viewpoints. This process is often more difficult than conventional design because of the expanded range of issues being considered and the interconnections between them. But the collaboration between disciplines also offers greater potential.

The process of collaboration in the design of a green building often begins with a **charrette**. A charrette is a fast-paced, highly collaborative, carefully orchestrated method for exchanging and building upon ideas, common in community planning as well as building design. The word *charrette* is the French word for cart, and comes from nineteenth-century design competitions in Paris where designers would jump onto the slow-moving carts carrying their drawings to the judges, working as fast as they could to finish their work while sharing materials and information with other competitors (Lennertz and Lutzenhiser 2006, v).

An important feature of a charrette is the inclusion of a broad range of stakeholders, people who have a stake in the building. While it is important to include professionals with expertise in green building, it is also important to include anyone who might have information about the building and anyone who might be affected by the building. The process helps to ensure that a diverse range of potentially relevant information is considered.

Together the teams work to develop a shared vision. Brainstorming is used to help generate the most innovative sustainable strategies possible. It is common for the facilitated design charrette process to begin by referring to the LEED checklist. LEED provides a way to organize the thinking about goals and strategies. In addition, LEED itself was developed through a consensus process and vetted by experts, so most participants feel comfortable using its tools.

Once building systems have been designed and constructed or installed, it is important to verify that they are functioning as intended. This is done through the process called building commissioning. Originally limited to mechanical systems such as heating and cooling equipment, it has since expanded to include all the systems in a building. LEED standards emphasize building commissioning, and often a commissioning agent is hired at the beginning of the design process and included in charrette work. Savings in operations costs due to building commissioning may be greater than the savings due to energy conservation measures.

Lighting with Daylight

About one-third of the electricity in most buildings is used for lighting. Many green buildings use daylight instead of electric lighting. **Daylighting** is the use of natural sunlight or daylight for illumination in order to reduce or eliminate electric lighting. Not only does it lower a building's energy consumption, it can be part of a passive solar heating design so that less heating is required in winter; and because daylight is cooler than electric lighting, it means less mechanical cooling is required in summer. A daylit building supports the human need for connection with the natural world and thus lowers stress, improves productivity, and improves students' ability to learn; this is why building codes in Europe require that workers have access to views and natural daylight (Lechner 2008, 386).

In a building lit by natural daylight, the building itself is the system. The amount of daylight that can enter depends on the building's form, its orientation, and its window size and location. The amount of daylight that can enter a window depends on how much clear sky is visible from that window; if sky cannot be seen from windows in a room, those windows will not be able to provide significant daylight to the room. Direct sunlight is visually uncomfortable for performing most tasks, and so daylit rooms are designed to bring in comfortable indirect light, evenly distributed and brought deeper into the space as it is reflected off light-colored room surfaces. Daylight can be brought into a room with sidelighting, toplighting, clerestory windows, and light shelves.

Sidelighting is daylight that comes in through windows in a vertical wall. Sunlight enters at an angle determined by the sun's location in the sky. In the summer it is high in the sky;

in the winter it is lower in the sky. On average, daylight can be used to illuminate space in a room within about 15 feet of a window and an additional 15 feet beyond the primary space can be illuminated with daylight if supplemental electric lighting is used. Beyond 30 feet from a window, electric lighting will be needed (Kwok and Grondzik 2007, 65). This implies that not only does a building need windows, its width needs to be relatively narrow from one wall to another.

Toplighting is daylight that comes into a room from above. Skylights, essentially windows in a roof, are one method. Since skylights are located in roofs, they allow direct sun to enter from overhead in the summer when the sun angle is high in the sky and can result in heat gain. Light can also be brought in through solar tubes, or light pipes. In the nineteenth century, multistory buildings brought in daylight through small enclosed spaces called light wells; modern buildings also use large enclosed spaces called atria (or atriums).

Toplighting does not have the depth limitation that sidelighting has. A building can be wide and still receive daylight throughout a room. However, toplighting is limited either to single-story buildings or to the top floor of a multistory building. In addition, while toplighting provides daylight, it does not provide a connection to the outdoors that has been shown to be important to human well-being.

Clerestory windows are vertical openings near the roof. They provide a way to bring indirect light from above and let it reach deeper into a room. While sidelighting is limited to narrower widths, clerestories allow a building of any width to be daylit. Like other toplighting, their use is limited to top stories. Depending upon building orientation, shading may be required to prevent heat gain.

Light shelves are used on the south walls of many buildings to bounce light rays deeper into rooms, and are usually white in color for reflectivity. Light from outside strikes the top of the light shelf, bounces up to the ceiling, then bounces from the ceiling into the room. A light shelf needs to have a window directly above it. The shelf itself may be either inside or outside the building wall. If it is outside the building, it can also function as a shading device to reduce solar heat gain.

Basics of Heating and Cooling

In every culture before the industrial age, people built structures that were tuned to place and local climate conditions. Buildings in cold places were oriented to take advantage of the sun. Buildings in hot places were designed to take advantage of breezes and provide ventilation paths for passive cooling. Modern green building designers study these vernacular examples for sources of inspiration for energy-efficient design. Four general climate types call for four different kinds of responses.

Hot, arid climate zones, such as in the Middle East and the US Southwest, have hot, dry summers, mild to cool winters, low rainfall, and extreme diurnal or day-to-night temperature fluctuations. Designs in these desert places minimize windows and feature light-colored, thick walls for thermal mass; they avoid daytime ventilation, when it's hot, and promote nighttime flushing with cool evening air. Sometimes they add surrounded courtyards and water features for cooling.

Hot, humid climate zones, such as in parts of Southeast Asia and the US Southeast, have hot summers, mild to cool winters, high rainfall, high humidity, and minor diurnal temperature fluctuations. Designs in these humid places strive to promote evaporation and breezes and to increase shade. Instead of thermal mass they use lightweight materials that do not hold heat, roofs with large overhangs for shade, windows that can be open at all times to promote air flow, and often a building form that provides a stack effect.

Temperate climate zones in the middle latitudes have hot, often humid, summers, cold winters, fairly high rainfall, and seasonal temperature fluctuations. Designs in these varied places use passive solar heating in winter, passive ventilation and shading devices in summer, and insulation. Understanding solar angles is particularly important for these locations where the same buildings must provide both heating and cooling.

Cold climate zones, such as the northern US and northern Scandinavia, have mild summers and very cold winters. The primary goals for designs in these places are to block winter winds and promote solar gain and heat storage. Window orientation, thermal mass, and insulation are important.

Each site has microclimates that can be different from regional climate. These small, local climates are the micro-effects of topography, moisture, sun, and shade. Designers must evaluate site conditions because they affect the heating and cooling of a building. Sunlight warms south-facing slopes but will have less access to slopes facing north.[1] In hills and valleys, warm air rises during the daytime, while at night cool air flows downhill, driven by gravity, and collects in cool pockets at the bottom (Brown and DeKay 2000, 17). Topography and vegetation block wind or channel it; they create spots that are shady and cool or sunny and warm.

Because Earth's axis is tipped, the sun never shines directly overhead. Its angle in the sky varies with latitude, and at each location its angle in the sky changes over the course of a year. Designers use sun angle charts or software to determine how sunlight will fall on their particular building's site. Windows and shading devices are then designed with sizes, heights, and locations to match the sun angles at that site. The sun is higher in the sky during summer, so a roof overhang over a window may block some of the sun's rays then. The sun is lower in the sky during winter, so the sun's rays may come in through that same window.

Designers also determine prevailing wind directions at a given time of year for their site. Knowing a few details about sun and wind allows them to determine placement and sizes of windows, trees, and shade devices so that the building will let sunlight come in when heat is needed, block the sun when heat is not wanted, promote airflow in summer to carry away heat and block cold winds in winter. Cool breezes in summer help with cooling; cold winds in winter make heating more difficult.

Trees cool the air around them not only by shading but also by evapotranspiration, the process by which trees transport water from the soil through stems and leaves and evaporate it into the air. They can reduce local air temperatures up to 15°F (Brown 2010, 52). Trees should be located where they can provide shade in summer, let in sunlight during the winter, and block wind flow during winter. As a starting point, the way to do this is to plant deciduous trees to the south of a building and evergreen trees to the north. Deciduous trees have leaves in summer, when shade is needed, and are bare in winter, allowing sunlight through.

Passive design uses the natural movement of heat and air to condition a space and provide comfort. Sun provides heating. Wind or air movement carries away heat and provides cooling. In a passively heated space, sunlight is allowed to enter the building when heat is needed and is blocked by shading devices when heat is not wanted. Inside the building thermal mass made of heavy materials such as stone or concrete is used to store heat energy and even out temperatures. Passive design uses the building's location and the site around it to take advantage of sun, wind, and shade. It depends upon the design of the building itself, including its orientation, shape, and windows.

Heating

Passive Solar Heating

In passive solar heating, the sun is the only energy source and the building itself is the system. There is no energy use, resource consumption, or greenhouse gas emission beyond what was used in constructing the building. The system lasts as long as the building and provides spaces that are pleasant.

The system has two fundamental elements: south-facing windows and thermal mass. Similar to a greenhouse, the windows act like one-way heat valves, letting in short-wave energy from the sun and trapping long-wave infrared radiation, or heat. Thermal mass in the walls or floors stores the heat energy, reradiating it slowly back into the space.

Designers balance the proportion of window size to room size. With too little glass, not enough radiation can enter. With too much glass, spaces can overheat. The windows are located to face approximately south. The building is oriented with its long axis running east to west to maximize southern exposure and to minimize overheating on summer afternoons, when sun from the west is low in the sky and difficult to block. A building heated by passive solar energy will look different on each of its four sides, with largest windows on the south, smallest windows on the north, and some kind of shading on any west-facing windows.

The thermal mass is a heavy, dense material that absorbs heat. It can be concrete, stone, adobe, brick, or even tanks of water. It is located where it will receive direct sunlight, commonly the floor or a wall, and is given a medium to dark surface color (low albedo) to absorb more heat. The thermal mass is a heat sink; it heats slowly, radiates slowly, and reduces the magnitude of temperature swings.

Shading is provided to keep spaces from heating in the summer. The best shades are overhangs and deciduous trees. Overhangs are sized to match sun angles so that low winter sun can enter while high summer sun is blocked. Overhangs are not as effective on west windows, so vertical shades and deciduous trees are often used there.

Depending upon situation and climate, passive solar heat may or may not be able to provide all of the heat needed during a year. The approach is to use solar energy to provide as much heat as possible, then to use a supplemental heating system when additional heat is required, for example, on especially cold and cloudy winter days.

Active Solar Heating

Active solar heating uses the sun's energy to heat water in a solar collector. It is most often used to heat water for domestic uses such as bathing, cooking, dishwashing, or laundry. Heated water is stored in a tank, which can be a conventional water heater tank or a separate preheat tank. A conventional water-heating backup system provides supplemental heat if necessary. Hot water from a solar collector can also be used as a medium to distribute heat in a radiant heating system, where hot water is run through a network of tubing in a radiant floor system or through radiators.

Collectors can be flat plate or evacuated tube collectors. A heat-transfer fluid, either water or glycol solution, flows through tubes where the liquid picks up heat. The most common type of collector is a flat plate collector. It features a thin, insulated, rectangular box, a dark-colored absorber plate, and small fluid-filled tubes running through the box. The cover is high solar gain, low-iron glass to let in as much solar energy as possible. A flat plate collector system can produce water 50 to 120°F warmer than the outside air temperature (Walker 2010).

Evacuated tube collectors use glass tubes with a vacuum inside. The tubes contain a heat-transfer fluid such as glycol, which can become hotter than the boiling point of water. They can be mounted on roofs or hung on the south side of a building where they look a little like window blinds made of vertical glass tubes.

Larger systems are mounted on the ground next to a building. They often include curved mirrors to focus and concentrate the sunlight, together with tracking mechanisms to keep the collectors oriented toward the sun. These systems can be used for commercial and institutional water heating or to turn a steam turbine for generating electricity.

Heat Pumps

When a mechanical heating system must be added to a building, a heat pump is an energy-efficient choice, providing 4 times more heat energy than the electrical energy consumed (Mumovic and Santamouris 2009, 91). Heat pumps use a refrigeration cycle. A refrigerator works by absorbing heat from the food inside and moving it to the air outside; that is why the back of a refrigerator feels warm. A heat pump works like a refrigerator with a reversing valve, and is used for both heating and cooling. In winter it takes heat energy from outside, which is available even at cool temperatures, and releases it inside the building. In summer it removes heat from inside the building and releases it outside. Conventional air-source heat pumps are most efficient when the temperature differences between inside and outside are not extreme and work best in moderate climates.

A ground-source heat pump takes advantage of the thermal mass of the earth, which maintains a stable temperature year round, and can be used for heating and cooling in any climate. At depths below about 6 feet, soil temperature is typically 50 to 60°F. Air or glycol, used as the heat-transfer medium, is piped from the building through tubes buried underground. In summer, the fluid removes heat from the building and releases it into the ground. In winter, the fluid removes heat from the ground and releases it into the heating system of the building. These systems have very low operating costs and very low maintenance requirements. In commercial buildings, a ground-source heat pump can operate at 50 percent of the cost of a conventional air-source heat pump (Kats 2010, 29).

The initial cost of installing a ground-source heat pump is high because of excavation costs, although the payback period is generally only 2 to 5 years (ibid.). In a horizontal system, pipe is laid in horizontal trenches. Excavation costs are lower, but a large area of land is required. In a vertical system, pipes are placed in vertical boreholes 150 to 650 feet deep. Installation costs are higher but land area requirements are low. Vertical systems are the most common arrangement in commercial and urban settings.

Passive Cooling

Cooling systems in green buildings rely on natural ventilation to replace some or all of the demand for mechanical air conditioning. In the process they generally result in better indoor air quality and productivity. Note that using daylighting in place of some or all artificial light reduces the cooling load in a building.

Modern air conditioning began appearing around 1950. Air conditioning made it possible to design buildings of almost any size and shape, with any amount of windows facing any direction. It made possible buildings that look the same regardless of climatic region, contributing to a phenomenon known as placelessness.

Air conditioning is a large consumer of energy, and as global climate warms the demand for air conditioning rises. It has become common for engineers to size air conditioning systems in modern buildings 30 to 50 percent above their actual cooling requirement in anticipation of future climate warming (Roaf et al. 2005, 224). It is likely that the warming climate of the future will require smaller heating systems and make it possible to heat many buildings using passive solar heat alone, while increasing the demand for cooling and making it more difficult for passive natural ventilation to cool buildings adequately for comfort.

Natural ventilation depends upon building shape and orientation. As with passive solar heating, the building is the system. Green buildings are designed to allow natural ventilation to move air through the spaces. A passively cooled building is opened when outside temperatures will improve comfort, and closed when outside temperatures are too hot or too cold. Operable windows, windows that can be opened, are important elements of natural ventilation.

Natural ventilation for cooling is based on fundamental physical principles: warm air rises; cool air is more dense than warm air; air moves from higher pressure to lower pressure and from warm to cool; wind blowing against a building or other object creates high pressure on the windward side and low pressure on the leeward side; and air moving at speeds of 1.5 to 10 feet per second aids heat loss, cooling people through evaporation and convection.

Three approaches are possible. Stack ventilation uses buoyancy, or the fact that warm air rises. Cross ventilation uses wind pressure. Night ventilation uses day-to-night temperature swings and thermal mass.

Box 10.1 Natural Cooling Inspired by Termites

In a high-rise dwelling in Africa, residents cultivate crops in the lower levels of their structure. They use precisely tuned stack ventilation to maintain their gardens and their living spaces at just the right temperature, humidity, and carbon dioxide level for themselves and their food crops. An underground cellar, the coolest area in the structure, is kept cool without refrigeration using evaporative cooling. As heat flows upward through the tops of the chimneys, cool air from the cellar is pulled through the living quarters and passageways. Thermal mass, stack ventilation, solar chimneys, and night flushing keep conditions constant inside while temperatures in this desert climate fluctuate from 107°F during the day to 37°F at night. The inhabitants of this structure are mound-building termites.

Inspired by the effectiveness of these building systems, the design team for the Eastgate Center, a shopping center and office building in Zimbabwe, used the principles of termite mounds to design the passive cooling and ventilation system of the building. The project cost $35 million in 1995 and saved 10 percent of the cost, or $3.5 million, by not purchasing an air conditioning system. Today the building uses 35 percent less energy for heating and cooling than similar conventional office buildings. The architect and engineer studied the details of termite mound technology and used similar strategies in the Eastgate building. Like local termite mounds, the building uses thermal mass in the building and below ground to absorb heat, together with an interior atrium, chimneys, and a system of vents to draw in cool air at night and flush hot air in the daytime. Local people refer to the building as "the anthill" (Kellert et al. 2008, 35; Biomimicry Institute n.d., Ventilating Nests).

Stack Ventilation

Stack ventilation uses rising heat in the building itself to create a stack effect. Warm air rises and then exits through high-level vents. As it does so, cooler, denser outdoor air is drawn in through low-level vents. The taller the building space, the greater the potential for the stack effect to pull air through the building. Some buildings use an indoor atrium, open stairwell, or raised roof section such as a cupola or monitor roof to increase air flow. Some buildings feature solar chimneys, tall ducts that heat up when exposed to sunlight to enhance the stack effect. Buildings that rely on stack ventilation can be more flexible in orientation and do not depend on a narrow building footprint.

Cross Ventilation

Cross ventilation allows air to flow from one side of a space to another. The moving air picks up heat from the building and its occupants. Air flows because of pressure differences generated by wind; the faster the wind speed, the greater the cooling potential. Building orientation, narrow building footprint, and operable windows are important for this method of cooling. Some buildings feature roof-mounted ventilators, with wind creating pressure on one side to drive air into the space and suction on the other side to draw air out of the space. Some buildings use devices to funnel the wind; vegetation can be used to direct wind toward lower floors of a building, and wing walls, small vertical projections on the outside of a building, can channel wind into any floor of a building.

Night Ventilation

Night ventilation is used to flush heat accumulated during the day and to draw in cool night air from outside. Thermal mass absorbs heat gain in the daytime. Air flowing over the thermal mass at night picks up that heat and removes it. The following day the thermal mass provides cooling again by absorbing heat from the indoor air. A building can use natural ventilation for night flushing. Night ventilation requires a day-to-night temperature difference of 20°F to be effective (Kwok and Grondzik 2007, 157). Some buildings in hot climates augment night ventilation by slab cooling, which passes cool night air through tubes in a concrete floor slab.

Other Strategies for Cooling

Earth Tubes

The thermal mass of the ground can be used as part of a natural ventilation system. Earth tubes are large diameter, long tubes buried underground. Air is pre-cooled inside these tunnels before it is introduced into the indoor building space. Mechanical fans or pumps may be added to help move the air. This is a simple technology, different from ground source heat pumps. Installation is costly because a large quantity of very long tubes is required.

Evaporative Cooling Towers

Evaporation is the principle behind refrigeration. When water evaporates, air temperature drops. This principle is used in so-called swamp coolers, small-scale evaporative coolers seen on top of houses in hot, dry climates in which a fan blows air across a wetted pad.

The same strategy is at work in evaporative cooling towers, common on large commercial and institutional buildings. As in the smaller swamp coolers, air is blown across wetted pads at the top of the cooling tower, where evaporation cools the air. The cool, dense air falls in the resulting downdraft and enters the building spaces. Large buildings have multiple cooling towers.

Some green buildings use rainwater from roofs or graywater from the building as cooling-tower water. Large buildings also use recycled condensate water, water that has condensed from large air conditioning systems, as makeup water to replace water that is dumped to remove mineral buildup.

A cooling tower is also used in conjunction with another type of equipment, the water-cooled chiller, a commercial-scale mechanical system that uses refrigeration to chill water. The chilled water is circulated from the chiller through coils or heat exchangers, and air is blown across the coils where heat is removed from the air.

Chilled Beams

Radiant cooling is a strategy in which cold water circulates through tubes, usually in the ceiling. A common version is known as a chilled beam, used in commercial and institutional buildings. The chilled beam is not used by itself, but in conjunction with other chilled water and ventilation systems. It reduces energy consumption and qualifies for LEED points.

Absorption Chillers

Standard chillers use compressors as part of a refrigeration cycle. Chillers are the largest single users of energy in commercial buildings, consuming 23 percent of a building's energy (Kibert 2005, 201). In addition, because they are used primarily during the daytime when power demands are already at a peak, they contribute to peak loads, which lead to the construction of additional power plants. Chillers are usually oversized to allow an operating margin for the future. Even when sized appropriately, chillers are only efficient when operating at peak load, a condition that occurs only a fraction of the total time.

Absorption chillers are an alternative to refrigeration chillers. Rather than using a mechanical compressor, they use a heat source to drive the refrigeration cycle. In commercial buildings, this heat source is usually waste heat from a gas turbine or water heater. It is their ability to use waste heat that makes absorption chillers energy efficient. For example, the same gas-fired source can produce electricity, hot water, and air conditioning, adding one more output to a combined heat and power system.

Ventilation

Heating and cooling systems are referred to as HVAC. Ventilation is an essential element in all heating and cooling and is the key to providing healthy indoor air quality. One of the 7 sections in the LEED green building standard for new construction is devoted to indoor air quality.

Adequate air exchange and fresh air intake prevents the buildup of carbon monoxide, carbon dioxide, moisture, and mold. The air exchange rate can be measured in two ways: number of air changes per hour or cubic feet per minute (cfm). Building codes and ASHRAE standards specify minimum cfm and minimum air changes per hour. One air change is the exchange of a volume of air equal to the interior volume of a building.

Buildings can be ventilated using only natural ventilation, using mechanical ventilation, or using mixed-mode ventilation. Mixed mode uses mechanical ventilation to assist natural ventilation systems. A mixed-mode building ventilates using natural methods when possible; at times when the stack effect or pressure differences from wind are not available, then fans are used to supply air to and exhaust air from rooms.

Building Envelope

An efficient, thermally resistant building envelope is the basis of an energy-saving building. The envelope is the outer skin of the building and includes the walls, windows, roof, floor, and foundation.

Walls

Inside a wall is insulation. Insulation prevents heat energy from leaking in or out, keeping a warm space warm and a cool space cool. A material's ability to insulate is quantified by its **R-value**, which measures resistance to heat flow. The higher a material's R-value, the greater its insulating properties and the lower the rate of heat flow through it. Purchased insulation is labeled with its rated R-value. Building codes specify a minimum R-value for insulation that is seldom adequate for an energy-efficient structure; green buildings typically use a greater amount of insulation.

Some alternative wall-construction methods are available for residential buildings including straw-bale construction, cob, and rammed earth. While they provide excellent insulation properties, they are labor-intensive to construct and are not appropriate for commercial or industrial buildings.

In straw-bale construction, bales of straw are stacked like bricks, then pinned together by steel reinforcing bar (rebar) or bamboo. The stacks are then covered with metal lathe (wire mesh) and plaster or stucco. Once enclosed, they have good fire resistance. The bales provide insulation between structural posts and do not carry any load themselves. Protecting the straw from moisture is essential.

Cob, from an Old English word meaning a round loaf, is a composite mixture of clay, sand, straw, and water similar to adobe. It is mixed by hand and built up slowly in large clumps, or cobs, without formwork. Cob examples are found in Africa and the Middle East. Cob was a house-building material for several centuries in parts of England, where it was made of clay-based subsoil and straw. Sculptural, fire resistant, and insulative, cob construction is a slow and labor-intensive method best done with groups of people. The mixture is so variable that standardization and reliable calculations of structural strength are nearly impossible.

Rammed-earth construction uses soil laid in layers within formwork, then rammed or compacted by manual or pneumatic tampers. Early examples can be seen along parts of the Great Wall of China and in parts of North Africa, where rammed-earth structures may be several stories high. It is also seen in Mediterranean climates of Portugal, Spain, and southern France, where the soil is mixed with cement and known as *pisé*. Rammed earth provides good thermal mass to help reduce the need for cooling and is best suited to warm, dry climates. This method, too, is slow and labor-intensive.

Another method of construction that uses the whole earth as part or all of a wall is known as earth-sheltered design. Earth-sheltered buildings can take advantage of contoured topography. Buildings can be either underground construction, dug into an existing slope, or bermed construction, with earth banked around the perimeter and partially covering the structure. Below several feet in depth, earth maintains a relatively constant temperature, cooler than surrounding air in summer and warmer than surrounding air in winter. Although construction costs are typically higher than for conventional buildings, earth-sheltered structures can substantially reduce the need for heating and cooling. Because of its ability to resist fire and high winds, this method can result in lower insurance premiums as well. Strategies to avoid moisture are essential.

Windows

Windows are a part of the building envelope that have significant impact on lighting, heating, and cooling. In building design, windows are referred to as glazing. Designers select different types of glazing depending upon which side of the building they are on and whether they are part of a system with daylighting and passive solar heating. Windows are an important link between life inside buildings and the world outside. On one hand, too few windows results in not only a need for artificial light but also in lowered productivity and even increased health problems. Too much glazing, on the other hand, results in overheating, a need for artificial air conditioning, and bird deaths.

The thermal resistance of windows and wall assemblies is rated by their **U-value**, or heat transfer coefficient. The U-value is the reciprocal of the R-value. For example, if a wall's R-value were 20, its U-value would be 1/20, or 0.05.

Window glass is described by other ratings as well. The solar heat gain coefficient (SHGC) is a measure of what percentage of sunlight enters the window and becomes heat. Daylight potential or visible transmittance (VT) is a measure of what percentage of the visible spectrum of sunlight is transmitted through the window. Both SHGC and VT are expressed as values from 0 to 1. South-facing windows used in passive solar heating have high SHGC. West-facing windows, which could overheat in the afternoon, have low SHGC. In a room to be lit by natural daylight, windows have high VT. A window with high VT and low SHGC is able to let in sun for daylighting without overheating.

Low-emissivity glass, or low-e glass, admits the full spectrum of sunlight but blocks the escape of infrared radiation. If the low-e coating faces outward, it will reflect heat from the sun and prevent it from building up inside. If the low-e coating faces inward, it will retain heat energy. A type of low-e coating known as spectrally selective coating is transparent to visible sunlight but reflects infrared heat. Windows with spectrally selective coatings can reduce cooling requirements.

Building windows can be deadly to birds, who mistake reflections for continuation of the sky and fly into them. Windows are deadlier to birds than their other major threat, domestic cats, and far deadlier than wind turbines. Bird fatality statistics indicate that while wind turbines in the US kill around 30,000 birds per year, domestic cats kill around 100 million and collisions with buildings kill over 500 million birds per year (Randolph and Masters 2008, 481; Erickson et al., 2002; US Government Accounting Office 2005). Some cities, including Toronto, New York, and Chicago, have developed bird-friendly design guidelines for designers and developers. It is particularly important to avoid monolithic expanses of glass. Strategies that make glazing look less like sky and more like solid objects include shading devices, screens, and differences in material and texture that help fragment glass reflections.

Roofs

Roofs covering tops of buildings are continually heated by the sun. On large buildings, roof surfaces in summer can easily reach 150°F (Kibert 2005, 198). This leads to two problems: increased energy use for air conditioning and a multiplying of the **urban heat island effect**. The urban heat island effect is the phenomenon in which air temperature in cities is several degrees warmer than in surrounding areas. It increases energy use, air pollution, greenhouse gas emissions, and health problems. The primary contributors are paving and rooftops. Buildings help mitigate the urban heat island by using either cool reflective roofs or vegetated green roofs.

A roof that reflects rather than absorbs sunlight is called a **cool roof**. Light-colored or white roofing or roof coatings increase a roof's albedo, or reflectivity. Buildings with light-colored roofs use less energy than similar buildings with dark-colored roofs. However, a cool roof does not have to be white. Highly reflective coating pigments are available that reflect infrared radiation even when they are darker in color.

A **green roof** is a kind of roof covering made of layers that include a waterproof layer, a lightweight, soil-like growing medium, and plants. Other layers include a root barrier, drainage, and filter cloth. Green roofs have multiple benefits, including extended roof life, improved air quality because of particulate removal, habitat creation, and urban amenity. However, the primary reasons for installing a green roof are typically to capture and slow stormwater runoff, to cut energy demand by minimizing heat gain in summer and heat loss in winter, and to help reduce the urban heat island effect.

The types of roof plants that can be grown depend on the depth of growing medium. An extensive green roof is a roof planted at a depth of 6 inches or less. Because of its low weight, many existing building structures can be retrofitted with an extensive green roof without requiring structural changes. These thin roofs do not use irrigation, and only certain plants will grow in the harsh sunbaked, windy, and dry environment of the roof. The most commonly used plants are species of sedums.

An intensive green roof, or roof garden, is planted in growing medium over 6 inches deep. If the medium is deep enough, even trees can be grown. In dense urban environments, many urban plazas and gardens are in fact green roofs. This kind of roof features the greatest plant diversity. It is also the most expensive to install and maintain. An intensive green roof needs provisions for irrigation, either through a conventional irrigation system or through collected rainwater and recycled graywater. The building's structural capacity must be calculated by a structural engineer.

Green walls are sometimes mentioned together with discussions of green roofs. A green roof covers the roof with plants while a green wall covers a wall with plants. Green walls provide cooling through shade and evapotranspiration while also capturing particulates, providing habitat, and providing the amenity of living plants. Two different technologies can be used for greening a wall surface.

The most common green wall approach is a green façade. Climbing plants or vines are rooted in soil at the base of the wall and climb upward from there. Walls covered by self-clinging vines such as Boston Ivy are a traditional form, and are the feature from which the "Ivy League" universities get their name. Aerial plant roots can damage mortar and building materials, however, so modern green façades instead use metal cables or panels as trellises to support the vines.

A more technically challenging, costly, and less common approach to green walls is vertical planting on what is known as a living wall, modeled on growing conditions found on cliff faces or tree trunks. Plants are hydroponically grown without soil in vertical modules that receive a steady flow of water and nutrients (Blanc 2012, 98).

Foundations

A foundation transfers and distributes the load of a building to the earth below. Most building foundations involve concrete. Concrete is a mixture of cement, sand, coarse aggregates, and water. Humans use a lot of concrete, which generates a lot of greenhouse gas: cement production is the second largest industrial source of carbon dioxide emissions, after power generation. About 5 percent of all CO_2 emissions worldwide are generated by the cement industry, more than the entire aviation industry (Calkins 2009, 105). Of those emissions, about half are from the chemical process of converting limestone and other carbonates to Portland cement and about 40 percent from the burning of fossil fuels used in the process.

Green building designers often specify a concrete mix with fly ash used as a substitute for part of the cement. Fly ash is a byproduct of burning ground coal to produce electricity. Like Portland cement, it will react and harden when mixed with water. Using fly ash as a cement substitute reduces demand for planet-warming cement and recycles what would otherwise be a waste product. Ground granulated blast furnace slag, a byproduct of steelmaking, is another waste product that can be substituted for cement. As with fly ash, it produces concrete with improved strength and durability.

Construction

Contractors are a critical part of green building: they are how green designs become translated into actual green buildings. Their essential role means collaboration from the beginning is important. In building projects larger than residential scale, construction usually begins with a bidding process. Designers schedule a pre-bid conference for contractors interested in bidding, where the green design goals and requirements are discussed. Once contractors and subcontractors have been selected, a meeting is held before construction begins. This meeting educates all the participants about what is expected, and why, but it can do more. Effective green building projects respect the knowledge and experience of contractors and include them as genuine participants. Contractors can make valuable contributions in identifying alternative materials and technologies for meeting a project's green-building goals. Regular on-site meetings are usually held throughout the phases of the project.

Forty percent of landfill waste in the US each year comes from construction and demolition debris (*LEED Visual GA* 2009, 68). Managing and minimizing construction waste is an important part of green building and is part of the LEED rating system.

Rating Systems

LEED

The most well-known certification standard for building design and construction is LEED developed in 1993 by the USGBC. Some level of LEED certification is now required in publicly funded new construction and major renovation in most US states and federal agencies and in many cities, schools, and universities. Like other certification systems, LEED was developed through a consensus-based process involving multiple stakeholders and requires assessment and evaluation by neutral third parties.

Designers choose the LEED rating system that best fits their building or project type. LEED, version 4 offers five rating systems:

- LEED BD+C: Building Design and Construction
- LEED ID+C: Interior Design and Construction
- LEED O+M: Building Operations and Maintenance
- LEED for Homes
- LEED ND: Neighborhood Development.

Each rating system has a checklist designers use to evaluate their project. The checklists for Building Design and Construction, Building Operations and Maintenance, and Homes are divided into 8 categories:

- Location and Transportation
- Sustainable Sites
- Water Efficiency
- Energy and Atmosphere
- Materials and Resources
- Indoor Environmental Quality
- Innovation
- Regional Priority.

The checklist for Interior Design and Construction includes all of the above except Location and Transportation, so it has 7 categories. Each of the categories contains prerequisites, characteristics that are required. For example, the Water Efficiency category contains a prerequisite of at least a 20 percent reduction in water use over conventional construction. The project will receive additional points if it achieves greater water use reduction, but it must achieve 20 percent at the minimum or the rest of the project will not be considered for certification.

In addition to prerequisites, each category offers a menu of optional strategies. Each additional strategy has a particular number of points assigned to it, based on its environmental impact and human benefit. Prerequisites do not have points assigned because they are compulsory. One hundred base points are possible from the first 6 categories, including 1 point if an Integrative Process was used. In addition, 10 bonus points are available, including up to 6 points for Innovation and up to 4 points for Regional Priority. The basic level of certification, LEED Certified, requires 40 to 49 points. Silver requires 50 to 59 points, Gold requires 60 to 79 points, and Platinum, the highest level, requires 80 points or more.

LEED ND is different from the other rating systems. It integrates the principles of smart growth, New Urbanism, and green building and is organized into entirely different categories than the other rating systems. This standard focuses not just on buildings but on where they are located and how they relate to each other. Developments must achieve a minimum degree of density and disconnected greenfield developments are not eligible. LEED ND addresses social issues including affordability, diversity, community participation, and visitability for people of all abilities. Its five categories are:

- Smart Location and Linkage
- Neighborhood Pattern and Design
- Green Infrastructure and Buildings
- Innovation in Design
- Regional Priority.

Specialists who meet one of the eligibility requirements—employment in a sustainable field of work, experience working on a LEED-registered project, or education in a related field—are eligible to take an examination to be certified as an LEED Green Associate (LEED GA). Professionals who pass the LEED Green Associate exam and who have additional work experience are eligible to take an examination to be certified as an LEED Accredited Professional (LEED AP).

Green Globes

Green Globes is a green building rating system used primarily in Canada and occasionally in the US and administered by the Green Building Initiative (GBI). Currently its primary users are large developers and property management companies. LEED and Green Globes have common origins and similar goals. About 80 percent of the point categories of the two systems overlap, although points are weighted and allocated differently.

BREEAM

The Building Research Establishment Environmental Assessment Method (BREEAM, pronounced "BREE-am") was the first green building rating system, developed in the United Kingdom in 1990 and still used in Europe. Both LEED and Green Globes were substantially based on BREEAM.

Living Building Challenge

The Living Building Challenge is a rating system that intends to move beyond LEED Platinum toward buildings and sites that are truly regenerative and sustainable. The LEED rating system can be a constructive tool to aid in planning for a green building project, whether or not LEED certification will be sought. One of the risks, however, is that designers may use the LEED checklist like a shopping list, selecting a collection of the easiest and lowest-cost strategies in order to get as many LEED points as possible for as few dollars as possible, without thinking deeply and holistically about sustainability. And as noted earlier, even a building with the highest rating of LEED Platinum is not truly a sustainable building.

Green buildings are steps along a healthy path. They are, as William McDonough says, "less bad" (McDonough and Braungart 2002, 51). However, according to green building expert Jason McLennan, "A world full of typical green buildings doesn't get us where we need to be to avoid environmental catastrophe" (Wendt 2009). McLennan, together with other members of the USGBC, developed a building rating system more stringent than LEED known as the Living Building Challenge. To be certified as a Living Building, a building must generate its own energy using renewable resources, must capture and treat its own water through ecologically sound techniques, must use only nontoxic, regionally sourced materials, must be healthy and not be harmful to its occupants or its environment, and must be beautiful.

In contrast to the historic metaphor of a building as a machine, the Living Building Challenge uses the metaphor of a building as a flower, a living organism rooted in its place that receives all of its energy from the sun, its water from the sky, and its nutrients from the soil. At the same time, a flower is itself an ecosystem sheltering myriad microorganisms, and it is a thing of beauty.

A Living Building must meet 20 prerequisites known as "imperatives" grouped into 7 categories consisting of Place, Water, Energy, Health and Happiness, Materials, Equity, and Beauty. The 7 categories of imperatives are called petals, in reference to the flower metaphor. The system provides a Red List, a list of materials including lead, mercury, pesticides, and PVC that are not permitted. Unlike LEED, there is no menu of credits and points. All imperatives are required in order to receive Living Building Certification. Incremental pathways to certification are an option: A building that achieves 3 of the 7 petals can apply for Petal Certification, and a building that supplies 100 percent of its energy needs from on-site renewable energy can apply for Net Zero Energy Certification. A building must prove itself by being in operation for at least one year before it can be certified. Several projects have earned Living Building Certification since its launch in 2006, and scores of project design teams report that they are using the Living Building Challenge in their design process.

Aesthetics

Some people wonder what style a green building is. The answer is that there is not a green-building style. A green building can be designed and built in any architectural style and generally looks like any other building. We measure how green a building is not by its appearance but by its performance. It uses energy and water efficiently. It protects the health of its occupants and its environment. It conserves natural resources and uses materials that are not harmful or polluting.

If there is a style at all, it lies in regional differences growing from the fact that each green building is adapted to its local place. Buildings use different climate strategies if they are located in hot, dry Phoenix, Arizona; in hot, humid New Orleans, Louisiana; in wet, temperate Seattle, Washington; or in Minnesota with its hot summers and cold winters. Green buildings minimize their carbon footprints by using regional materials that do not need to be shipped over long distances, so building materials differ from region to region as well.

There is an unfortunate perception among some people that green buildings are ugly. This perception probably arose from early attempts at environmentally responsible building design (McLennan 2004, 227). Many of the early projects were built by people who were passionate do-it-yourselfers or enthusiastic technophiles but not necessarily the most accomplished designers. People who have learned about sustainability and are able to "read" one of these earlier green buildings may appreciate its character. They may recognize, for example, that a particular floor material was sustainably sourced, or that a particular pipe system is for catching rainwater. However, these fine points are lost on most people, who expect good buildings to be attractive.

In fact, green buildings must be attractive if they are to be sustainable. Buildings that endure can be reused. In these durable buildings, new resources are not being consumed in construction, and demolition waste is not being sent to a landfill. Buildings will endure if we care for them, and we tend to care for buildings we think are beautiful. Consider historic stone buildings built with care in Europe, some of them nearly 1,000 years old, still loved and still standing. Even functional brick warehouses and factories designed and built with care in the nineteenth century have become popular for renovation into urban offices and high-end residential lofts. It is not likely that modern low-cost warehouses will live as long. The old brick warehouses are examples of how a building constructed for long life and durability can be sustainable.

Beauty is one of the required imperatives for certification as a Living Building. As the Living Building Challenge observes, requiring beauty is an impossible task because defining or assessing beauty is an impossible task. What the Living Building Challenge requires is simply that designers demonstrate an intention to create something of beauty, that they demonstrate an effort to "enrich people's lives" with every square foot of a building. If we surround ourselves with places that are unattractive, as happens in strip malls and warehouse compounds, we develop a habit of not seeing (Smith and Williams 1999, 229). The danger is that we are unaware that we are not seeing; we become perceptually numb. When strip malls and seas of parking become acceptable, we may tend not to notice forest clearcuts and strip mines. The Living Building Challenge says that the intent of requiring beauty in a building "is to recognize the need for beauty as a precursor to caring enough to preserve, conserve and serve the greater good."

When green buildings are beautiful, we pay attention to them and they then become a source of learning. We more easily understand things that are tangible. A green building is oriented toward the path of the sun. It lets in daylight. Fresh air flows through it. Rain falling on it becomes a resource. Its occupants can begin to sense changing seasons, the local climate, and the natural processes of the living world.

Sustainable Sites

Buildings and landscapes are more than single, detached objects. Together they are connected elements whose flows of energy and materials contribute to a larger environmental context. Habitat conservation areas are important, but 80 to 90 percent of the land that humans use and inhabit is not addressed by these conservation areas (Perlman and Milder 2004, 1). In order to have a healthy biosphere we need to retain healthy ecosystem functions—on every site. Any landscape whether it is a single residential yard, a city park, a college campus, or a shopping mall has the potential to purify air, cleanse water, provide habitat, support pollinators, and restore ecosystem function.

A healthy, resilient landscape is self-sustaining, able to persist through time with minimal outside input from people. A sustainable site includes a diversity of plant and animal life, with species that are either native or adapted to the local region; site disturbance is minimized, native topsoil is conserved, stormwater is managed on the site, and irrigation is minimized.

A healthy site is fitted to the local conditions in its **ecoregion** and built around the concept of plant communities. An ecoregion is an area with a particular combination of environmental conditions including climate, topography, geology, and vegetation. In each ecoregion, plant communities there have adapted to that set of conditions of temperature, rainfall, and soil. It is these ecoregions that make each place different from every other place. Plants that only thrive under particular conditions are the plants that tell us where we are.

By studying a site and the ecoregion within which it sits, designers learn what processes and plant communities would operate there in the absence of human intervention. They can then replicate the functions of healthy, local ecological systems. The goal is not to produce a "natural look;" the goal is actual, functioning ecosystems.

Landscapes are always place-specific. A designer cannot just create a landscape design in an office, then go out and find a site on which to install it. To achieve a healthy site, the landscape must be carefully fit to the existing site, and in order to fit a landscape to a site, the designer must thoroughly understand the details of the site. The process of learning about, documenting, and evaluating a site's characteristics is known as site inventory and analysis. Site inventory is the process of collecting data about the physical, biological, and social or cultural characteristics of the site and mapping their locations. Site analysis then evaluates the site's suitability for specific uses, based on those attributes.

Vegetation

Plants are central to a functioning planetary system. They oxygenate the air, capture particulate matter from the air, take up pollutants in soil, sequester carbon, and provide habitat for communities of organisms that depend on them. For plants to be able to fulfill their potential as providers of ecosystem services, they must be part of healthy, self-sustaining systems.

The use of native plants has traditionally been a fundamental element of ecologically sensitive design. They are part of an interconnected web of plants, animals, microorganisms, soil, and water that have evolved together. They are adapted to their region's amount of rainfall, so that once they are established they require little or no irrigation. They are adapted to their region's soil type and nutrient level, so they do not need fertilizer. They have evolved natural controls and defenses against their region's pests and diseases, so they do not need applications of pesticides. Native plants attract local insects, which in turn attract local birds and other animals who feed on them. These native plants help to restore local habitat networks, beginning to knit the so-called green fabric back together.

Most sites include a variety of microclimates, the result of small variations in sunlight, moisture, and soil composition. Choosing plants involves understanding not just the ecoregion and its conditions at a macro scale, but also the characteristics at each location around the site, the conditions at a micro scale. The goal is to determine which plants might have naturally occurred on the site without human presence, and work with them.

A palette is a selection of materials chosen for a design. An interior designer chooses a particular color palette for a room. A landscape designer chooses a particular plant palette for a site. Native plants can be used as design materials just as any other kind of plant material can. There is a common, and unfortunate, misperception that native plantings are messy. There is no reason that landscapes composed of native plants should appear any less attractive than any other planting. A designer can follow good design principles, regardless what palette they use. After all, every plant is native to somewhere. Highly designed Italian Renaissance gardens used plants native to Italy. Highly designed Chinese scholars' gardens used plants native to China. A garden in New England can use plants native to New England and arrange them in ways that both humans and wildlife can appreciate. In order for places to be sustainable, to last into the future without needing high inputs of resources to maintain them, they must be attractive to the people who use them on a daily basis.

One common landscape where appearance always trumps ecological function is the American lawn, a cultural remnant of a style popularized in the late 1800s. This monocultural planting style consumes resources, generates pollution, and offers little habitat value. Fertilizers, pesticides, and large quantities of water are required in order to keep turf grass bright green and uniform. Lawn mowers used to keep grass at an unnaturally uniform low height consume hundreds of millions of gallons of gasoline per year while releasing greenhouse gases into the air.

In select places where turf is valued, such as recreation areas, some managers allow mixed low-growing meadow plants to be part of the turf and allow lawns to go naturally dormant in the summer. Organic soil amendments and compost tea are used in place of fertilizer, and **integrated pest management** (IPM) is used to control insects and disease without chemicals in most cases.

In an era of changing climate, shifting species ranges, remixing of communities, and the rise of novel ecosystems, defining which species should count as "native" plants in a particular place is not clear-cut. Designers and ecologists of the Anthropocene are beginning to rethink the entire concept of "native" and what it might mean in the years of transition ahead.

Issues of Light and Sound

Excess noise from human activity is damaging to both humans and wildlife. In ecosystems, just as each animal has its own niche, each also has its own acoustic territory. Many animals have evolved to vocalize in particular ranges of sound so that they can hear and be heard by potential mates and members of their group. One bioacoustics researcher who has collected 3,500 hours of ecosystem sounds since the 1960s found that at least 40 percent of these natural soundscapes have been so radically altered that many of their former members appear to be locally extinct (Tennesen 2008, 24). In addition to using sound to find mates and to maintain group contact, predators use sound cues including footfalls and breathing to help locate prey, and prey animals use those same cues to escape predators. Human sounds can cause problems for wildlife by masking these quieter cues.

For humans, noise from traffic, mechanical systems, and other unnatural levels of noise have been shown to interfere with sleep quality, increase stress, and contribute to anxiety; noise-induced stress can contribute to a sense of helplessness in children (Sustainable Sites Initiative 2009, 161). Where noise sources exist nearby, one strategy is to provide barriers to noise, but prevention through planning and policy measures is always more effective than barriers.

Light from human activity is another impact that affects both wildlife and human health. Light pollution can be of three types: astronomical, ecological, or light trespass. Light trespass is unwanted light that violates property boundaries. Astronomical light pollution interferes with the ability to use telescopes and makes people unable to see most features of the night sky. In most of the developed world the sky is so brightly lit that our own Milky Way galaxy, once a dominant feature of the night sky, is no longer visible. Many modern people never use the structures that make up over half of the retina in the human eye, the rods, which are structures adapted for seeing in darkness.

Ecological light pollution interferes with the normal functioning of animals, plants, and entire ecosystems by disrupting organisms' daily rhythmic cycles of activity known as circadian rhythms. Most above-ground animals rely on seasonal and daily differences in light and dark to feed, reproduce, and migrate. Plants rely on periods of light and dark to provide signals for growth and reproduction. Birds, insects, amphibians, sea turtles, fish, and zooplankton are known to be impacted, often disastrously, by artificial light. A bird-safety program in Canada estimates that 100 million birds a year are killed because of artificial lighting on urban structures (Fatal Light Awareness Program n.d.). Research has implicated artificial night lighting in increased rates of a range of health problems in humans as well (Thompson and Sorvig 2008, 296). Many cities have regulations requiring light fixtures to control the direction and spread of light, such as shielded or cut-off light fixtures to prevent light from being emitted upward. However, while these fixtures mitigate astronomical light pollution, they may not improve ecological light pollution and nature's need for regular darkness.

Biophilic Design

A growing body of research has demonstrated that humans are healthier, both psychologically and physically, when they have access to nature. One of the most intriguing early pieces of research was a study by behavioral scientist Roger Ulrich (1984, 420) on the recovery times of gall-bladder surgery patients, in which some of the patients had a view of trees and shrubs and others had a view of a brick wall. Patients with the view to nature had a shorter average recovery period, took fewer painkillers, had lower heart rates, and made fewer nursing request calls. This research, and other subsequent studies on healing times and stress recovery, led to the use of evidence-based design in many new hospitals.

This research is linked to the concept of **biophilia**. Not only do people have an aesthetic preference for certain forms of nature, but also contact with the natural world has real, measurable benefits. The idea that contact with nature is important to human physical, emotional, and intellectual well-being is known as biophilia.

The term biophilia, which literally means a love for nature, was coined in 1984 by Harvard biologist Edward O. Wilson, who proposed that humans have an innate and evolutionarily-based affinity for nature rooted in human biology and evolution (Wilson 2002b, 134). Biophilia evolved as an adaptive mechanism to protect people from hazards and to help them access such resources as food, water, and shelter. This translates in present conditions into the strong preference people exhibit for features that suggest those evolutionary roots. People are aesthetically drawn to environmental features that have proven instrumental in human survival, including clean flowing water, rich vegetation, bright flowering colors that frequently signify presence of food, promontories that offer prospect or the ability to see into the distance, and areas that offer refuge or a sense of enclosure and shelter. Humans are particularly attracted to parklike pastoral settings, which offer prospect, refuge, and suggestions of things to eat. Almost without exception they are strongly attracted to water, a necessity for survival. People are willing to pay a premium for homes and offices that have distant vistas, are located near water, or are surrounded by colorful, flowering plants. Biophilia research indicates this preference has ancient roots.

Biophilia means that, from a human perspective, healthy natural environments are more than just decorative; they are important to human well-being. **Biophilic design** is an approach to architecture which is evidence-based. **Evidence-based design** responds to growing evidence that the presence of natural daylight, fresh air, and connection to the natural world within the human environment affects our health, ability to learn, and productivity (Hamilton and Watkins 2009, 70). Humans are part of nature, and can be partners with nature. They can help make places healthy. It turns out that places can help make humans healthy, too.

Conclusion

Buildings and their sites play sizable roles in greenhouse gas emissions, fossil fuel use, and resource consumption; thus their design and operation have essential roles in addressing issues threatening planetary survival. Green buildings use the living world as their instruction manual. Constructed where possible of local, nontoxic materials, ideally they consume only as much energy and water as they can produce or capture, using local resources of sun, wind, and water available on site for lighting, heating, cooling, and water supply. Green buildings and their sites are citizens of their particular ecoregions and adapted to the places where they are. They support the environmental, economic, and social well-being of their occupants and communities, doing no harm and perhaps even regenerating the health of air, water, and biosphere.

Note

1 Directions of north and south related to sun and shade are given for the Northern Hemisphere; these directions are reversed for the Southern Hemisphere.

Further Reading

Calkins, Meg. *The Sustainable Sites Handbook: A Complete Guide to the Principles, Strategies, and Best Practices for Sustainable Landscapes*. New York: John Wiley, 2012.

Kellert, Stephen R., Judith H. Heerwagen, and Martin L. Mador, eds. *Biophilic Design: The Theory, Science, and Practice of Bringing Buildings to Life*. New York: John Wiley, 2008.

Kibert, Charles J. *Sustainable Construction: Green Building Design and Delivery*, 4th ed. New York: John Wiley, 2016.

Kwok, Alison G. and Walter T. Grondzik. *The Green Studio Handbook: Environmental Strategies for Schematic Design*. Oxford: Architectural Press, 2007.

Lechner, Norbert. *Heating, Cooling, Lighting: Sustainable Design Methods for Architects*. 3rd ed. New York: John Wiley, 2008.

McLennan, Jason F. *The Philosophy of Sustainable Design*. Bainbridge Island, WA: Ecotone Publishing Co., 2004.

Thompson, J. William and Kim Sorvig. *Sustainable Landscape Construction*. 2nd ed. Washington, DC: Island Press, 2008.

Chapter Review

1   What are three types of solar systems that can be used in buildings? Write an elevator speech that summarizes the types and how they differ.
2   Describe the fundamental elements used in passive solar design.
3   You notice a house in your neighborhood with a rectangular panel on top of its roof. How might you be able to tell whether it is used for generating electricity or heating water?
4   How does stack ventilation cool a building without using electricity?
5   What causes air to flow through a building that uses cross ventilation?
6   What kind of climate is appropriate for night ventilation?
7   Would a building up on stilts, with thin walls, be a good candidate for cooling with night ventilation? Why or why not?
8   What is the purpose of a roof ventilator?
9   A solar chimney is able to provide additional cooling when it is heated. How is this possible?
10   What is an absorption chiller? Under what circumstances would it be considered an energy efficient choice?
11   Name two benefits of daylighting, in contrast to electric lighting.
12   You work as a green building consultant for a school district. The school board is on a tight budget and wants to build a new school building with all-electric lighting. They say they will retrofit it for daylighting later on, when the budget improves. Is this a practical idea? Why or why not?
13   What is concrete? How is it different from cement?
14   What is fly ash, and how is it used as a building material?
15   What color roof uses less energy: black or white? Why?
16   What does albedo measure? What does high albedo indicate?
17   Describe the differences between an extensive green roof and an intensive green roof.
18   Does a green building always cost more than a similar size and type of conventional building? Does it make a difference how the costs are calculated?

Critical Thinking and Discussion

1   What are the benefits and tradeoffs of using geothermal heat pumps in the region where you live? Would it make a difference if you lived in another region where heating sources and air conditioning demand were different?
2   A building that uses passive solar heating can eliminate energy consumption that would have been required by a mechanical heating system. What are the tradeoffs? For example, do insulation and thermal mass increase the embodied energy in the building's materials? How might designers deal with requirements to reduce embodied energy?

3 Can a solar collector be used to heat water in freezing winter temperatures? If so, why?

4 Your organization is planning the construction of a new, single-story building. In a meeting, someone asks which is more sustainable, a wood building or a steel building. What would you say to them?

5 What factors in the surrounding site could contribute to an energy-efficient design in a building?

6 What is radiant cooling? Why is it considered a green building approach?

7 Could you use the same building design to provide passive heating and cooling in any climate? Why or why not?

8 Why don't we see more high-rise office buildings heated by passive solar heating?

9 Does it make any difference how wide the roof overhang is on the south side of a building? Would it be possible to design too wide an overhang? Why or why not?

10 If someone asked you whether their house could be heated with solar heat, what characteristics would you look for?

11 Is it possible to have too many windows in a passively solar-heated house? Why or why not?

12 On which side of a building will windows have a greater effect on the building's cooling load?

13 A letter to the editor in your local newspaper claims that cool roofs are not very effective because while they lower air conditioning costs in the summer, they result in higher heating bills in the winter. How would you respond?

14 Green roofs have many acknowledged benefits. Can you think of any disadvantages or tradeoffs?

15 Why is it important to include building occupants in the design process?

16 What are the benefits of charrettes? What are some disadvantages of charrettes?

11 Livable Cities

Demographers predict that world population will continue to grow in the next century, and all of that growth will take place in cities (OECD 2012, 20), which must grow either by expanding outward or by increasing in density. During that same period of time, much of our already-aging urban **infrastructure** will reach the end of its useful life and will need to be replaced. Cities will be impacted by a destabilized climate with drought, heat waves, altered growing conditions, increasingly severe storms, and sea levels at least several feet higher than today. At the same time, the passing of peak oil will mean an end to the era of cheap and available fossil fuels on which cities currently depend.

These converging trends point to an enormous opportunity to plan, design, build, and operate new or regenerated cities in ways that are different and better than before. Design and planning on an urban and regional scale have an even greater impact on sustainability than the design of individual buildings. The locations of roads, the types of transportation available, zoning decisions, and land-use patterns all impact how well an urban region can live in partnership with the quality of life of its citizens and the natural systems within which it sits. Getting these decisions right is critical, because once urban systems are in place they are extraordinarily difficult and costly to change (Condon 2010, 65).

A well-designed urban system offers amenities and a quality of life that people willingly choose because they are pleasant. A livable city provides mixed-use development with safe and healthy neighborhoods, places for social interaction, interconnected green space, food, clean air and water, power from renewable energy, multiple modes of easy-to-use transportation, economic opportunity, and social inclusion.

Sprawl

Modern urban conditions include a settlement pattern known as **sprawl**, characterized by low-density land use, single-use zoning, and automobile dependency. Sprawl has many negative side effects, including loss of agricultural land, habitat fragmentation or destruction, air pollution, greenhouse gas emissions, obesity, and social inequity. It began developing after World War II. Before that time, most communities consisted of compact neighborhoods where residents could get to work, school, and shopping either on foot or by public transportation. Since World War II, however, development has been dominated by automobiles.

Zoning regulations developed in an attempt to separate polluting industrial uses from places where people live. These rules separate land by uses, with residential use in one area, commercial uses in another, and industrial use in another. With land uses too far apart for walking and no effective public transportation system, the only practical way to travel between homes, work, school, shopping, and recreation is usually to drive in private cars.

Most sprawl is greenfield development: development on previously undeveloped land. These greenfield sites can include agricultural soil, forests, meadows, and prairie land. Density of greenfield development on suburban fringes averages 2 houses per acre (Farr 2008, 55). Many cities were originally established in regions with highly fertile soil such as river floodplains. Thus suburban expansion of cities tends to sprawl over agricultural land. Once farmland is converted to urban and industrial uses, its use is effectively lost and cannot be regained within the foreseeable future. One of the problems with greenfield development on prime farmland is that as population size continues to increase and as the passing of peak oil makes local food production a necessity, cities will need more, not less, farmland in order to feed their citizens.

The automobile, once hailed as the solution to a city's horse manure problem, is now a driving force in the problem of sprawl. New developments are almost always based on the assumption that people travel in automobiles every time they move from one place to another. Buildings are set back from roads, fronted by driveways or surrounding by parking. Half the land area in most suburbs and 80 percent of the land in commercial areas is taken up by paving for cars (Ferguson 1998, 16).

In order to move the large numbers of automobiles generated by sprawl, streets and roads linking disconnected land uses must be designed for traffic volume and speed. Distances between destinations are too great for walking and large, high-speed roads are not safe or comfortable for pedestrians or bicycles, forcing the use of cars to fulfill basic daily needs and cutting people off from the outdoors and each other. Cities construct wide arterial streets based on projections of future traffic demand. In turn the large, high-speed roads make new suburban development possible. As distances between land uses stretch farther apart and as other travel options narrow, greater speed is needed and vehicle ownership and use increases in a self-reinforcing cycle. New roads generate more traffic, and more traffic creates a demand for even more roads (Farr 2008, 56).

Transportation consumes 26 percent of the world's energy produced and is responsible for 23 percent of the world's energy-related greenhouse gas emissions (IPCC 2014c, 603). In order to stabilize global climate, we will need to cut current emissions by 50 percent (Levin 2013). That magnitude of reduction cannot be accomplished through vehicle technology alone. Nor can greenhouse gas emissions be reduced enough by designing energy-efficient buildings if buildings are separated by long distances and reachable only by automobiles. Fossil fuel consumption generated by buildings in suburban locations can easily be greater than any energy saved through building design. While building design is critical to climate stabilization, reaching greenhouse gas emissions targets will only be possible by also sharply reducing the number of vehicle miles traveled (VMT). That requires accommodating growth through compact, mixed-use urban development served by alternative modes of transportation.

Sprawl affects not only planetary health but social and individual health as well. Research surveys show significant links between the built environment and obesity. Physical inactivity is an independent risk factor for chronic diseases such as diabetes and heart disease. Walkable neighborhoods with nearby stores, community gardens, and parks encourage walking, biking, and other physical activity. At the same time they reduce social isolation and promote social cohesion.

Land-Use Planning

Planning is the process of deciding what to do and how to do it. Planning is a profession that deals with creating places and communities that are healthy, efficient, attractive, and equitable for present and future generations. It takes place at a variety of scales. The most common scales are urban planning, which deals with the planning of cities, and regional planning, which deals with the planning of larger regions. An important part of the work of planners is to facilitate active participation by public leaders and citizens. Planning is often done within one watershed, one metropolitan region, or one bioregion. These regions typically cross jurisdictional boundaries, making collaboration important.

As cities grow in population it is important to plan where growth will happen, using urban containment to encourage cities to grow inward and upward, rather than outward (IPCC 2014c, 972). One of the tools used by planners is the **urban growth boundary** (UGB), a line adopted by a government body that separates an urban area within which development may occur from surrounding open lands where development is restricted. The purpose is to promote compact development and thus protect farmland and other open-space land.

The State of Oregon in the western US is an example of an effective UGB program. In 1973 Oregon passed Senate Bill 100, a pioneering land-use law that created a framework for land-use planning statewide designed to preserve farmland, forest land, and water resources (Portland State University 2010). Farmers played an active role in the development and passage of this legislation. The law requires every city and county to prepare a comprehensive plan aligned with a set of 19 planning goals, which include citizen involvement, agricultural lands, natural resources, economic development, housing, transportation, and energy conservation. As part of its plan, each municipality is required to designate a UGB. The City of Portland's UGB has allowed it to curb sprawl and preserve surrounding farmland, while its comprehensive plan has allowed it to develop a thriving downtown and lively, compact mixed-use neighborhoods centered along transit corridors.

In regions where growth and development are imminent, one strategy for preserving farmland and open space is clustered development, also known as conservation development (Arendt 1996, 6). In this approach development is concentrated more densely onto less ecologically-important lands, leaving a larger proportion of land undeveloped. In a typical conservation development, 50 to 60 percent of the total area is set aside as open space, preserving habitat, allowing stormwater infiltration, and reducing the need for new sewer, water, and power connections. Infrastructure costs in conservation developments can be 10 to 25 percent lower than in comparable conventional developments (Kats 2010, 134). When practiced on greenfields, however, clustered development still consumes land and is less benign than urban infill.

Many regions encourage brownfield redevelopment in place of greenfield development. Brownfields are sites that have been contaminated by past industrial uses but are able to be regenerated to some extent through environmental cleanup. Pittsburgh, Pennsylvania, once known for its steel mills, is sometimes considered a model for successful brownfield redevelopment. Brownfields are often well-located within urban centers, near business districts or commercial corridors, where infrastructure already exists and where economic regeneration is possible. However, remediating and redeveloping brownfield sites is often more costly than new development on greenfield sites (IPCC 2014c, 975).

Box 11.1 The Oberlin Project

Oberlin, Ohio is a typical American rustbelt town. Over half its residents live below the poverty line. In earlier days, the town was a stop on the Underground Railroad. Today it is home to Oberlin College, whose environmental studies center was designed by a team of students and designers, led by Bill McDonough. The center produces more energy than it uses, uses geothermal wells and sunlight for heating and natural ventilation, treats its own wastewater, and grows food sustainably in gardens and fruit orchards. Professor David Orr believes they can do more; he thinks that colleges can be drivers for healthy communities. He has formed a partnership called the Oberlin Project (Orr 2011). Partners include the City of Oberlin, Oberlin College, the electric utility, and local businesses.

The heart of the project is the redevelopment of a 13-acre block to create a vibrant town center. A new green arts district is envisioned as a catalyst for economic revitalization with hotels, restaurants, and a conference center providing a lively downtown round the clock. One initiative has transformed a polluted brownfield site into a state-of-the-art mixed-use neighborhood.

The city and college have signed to be one of only 3 US cities in the Clinton Foundation Climate Positive Development Program, which means they have agreed to go beyond carbon neutral. Once dependent on coal, they are shifting to energy efficiency, renewable energy sources, and away from dependence on cars. The city believes demand for green energy will result in new jobs.

The project will preserve natural land by promoting agriculture and sustainable forestry in a 20,000-acre surrounding greenbelt while generating new economic opportunities. Forests and open space will supply fiber and wood for furniture shops. The area will grow 70 percent of the food it needs for its citizens, restaurants, and conference center (Alperovitz 2013, 57). The project has the support of advisors from the Department of Defense, who are calling on the US to focus on social policies, education, and sustainability as a national security strategy. They see the Oberlin Project as a model for addressing vulnerabilities in food, energy, social, and economic systems.

Finally, the project will equip students with the practical skills and vision to become leaders in the transition to a prosperous and sustainable future. An educational consortium of public schools, a community college, and Oberlin College will prepare people to live in a new world of unstable climate, declining fossil fuels, and depleted resources. People often implement sustainability as a series of one-off projects, unconnected to each other. The Oberlin Project recognizes that these separate parts are connected to each other and that stakeholders need to reach across siloes and walls that divide them. Team members call this full-spectrum sustainability. As David Orr says: "You are going to have lunch with a lot of people."

Urban Planning

Urban and regional planning presents difficult and complex problems and involves planning for a future whose outline is unknown. Particularly given new requirements for incorporating renewable energy, climate neutrality, and economic and social equity, integrated and interdisciplinary solutions are needed for this uncharted territory that are beyond the reach of any one specialist. Planning has always been a collaborative process, and collaboration has never been more essential than it is now.

Planning healthy, sustainable communities requires the integration of top-down professional skills from multiple disciplines with bottom-up, community-driven thinking and decision-making. Community participation is a bottom-up planning approach for exchanging information, finding creative solutions, and empowering citizens, including disenfranchised citizens, beginning early in the process. Real participation occurs when people who will be affected by planning are empowered to influence the actions that will be taken.[1] When innovative solutions actually come from members of a community, the solutions are far more likely to be implemented and to remain durable elements of community life. Real sustainability gains from an initiative depend a lot upon how people actually live in their homes and communities.

While brownfield and greenfield development are typically led by public agencies or developers, **eco-districts** come about through self-organized, collaborative efforts of municipalities, utilities, institutions, nonprofit organizations, developers, and neighborhood residents; they focus on regenerative urban development at the neighborhood scale, integrating building and infrastructure projects in existing neighborhoods. Eco-district members develop sustainability goals for economic opportunity, social equity, inclusion, and ecological health and co-develop district-scale projects, supported by investment and tracked by performance indicators. Examples include Vauban in Freiburg, Germany; Hammarby Sjöstad in Stockholm, Sweden; and the EcoDistricts initiative in Portland, Oregon (Girardet 2014, 151). EcoDistricts in Portland offers a planning protocol, certification, and resources.

Urban planning deals with the layout and function of towns and cities. Variables within the patterns of urban development are sometimes described as the "five Ds": density, diversity, design, destination accessibility, and distance to transit. Density refers to the number of people or dwelling units per acre. Diversity refers to land use, and whether areas are limited to a single use or are what is known as mixed use. Design covers a range of characteristics including streetscapes, building configurations, and vegetation. Destination is about transportation; it refers to the ease with which people can travel between home, work, school, shopping, and recreation. Distance from home to the nearest transit stop determines how many people will choose to use transit services.

Density

Density is a factor in reducing greenhouse gas emissions and in creating places with social and economic opportunity. Greater density can support public transportation, with less driving, more walkable neighborhoods, and more affordable infrastructure services; it also supports greater numbers of neighborhood stores and markets. The denser a city, the less its inhabitants drive and the more they walk and use bicycles and public transit; efficiencies are built in. The most dense US city, New York City, has per capita carbon dioxide emissions that are less than one-third the US average, while also providing walkability, ample public transportation, and low heating requirements within apartment buildings. A 2007 Urban Land Institute report calculated that if 60 percent of the new development in the US shifted to compact development, by 2030 carbon dioxide emissions would be reduced by over 93 million tons per year, or about 5 percent (Newman et al. 2009, 5).

The LEED standard for neighborhood development, LEED ND, requires a minimum of 7 dwelling units per acre. This is the minimum density needed to support public transportation and to provide retail services within walkable distances. At this density, stormwater runoff per dwelling drops sharply as well. A minimum of 15 to 20 dwelling units per acre are needed to support light rail or streetcar service (Farr 2008, 47). New greenfield development, or suburban sprawl, is an average of fewer than 2 dwelling units per acre.

Infill is one way to increase density in existing cities. Infill development is the process of building and developing on vacant or under-used parcels in a city where infrastructure is already in place. It can help provide enough density to support public transit and can improve the range of available services and activities in a compact, mixed-use area, helping to build more complete, well-functioning neighborhoods. Infill is a way of accommodating growth without expanding beyond a city's urban growth boundary.

Mixed-Use, Compact, and Walkable Neighborhoods

Sustainable urbanism is a term that encompasses mixed-use, compact, and walkable neighborhoods including a full range of housing types, with connections to nature, served by public transit corridors, and consisting of high-performance buildings and green infrastructure. The term, and the kind of development it represents, are related to the LEED ND standard. In such a neighborhood, inhabitants' needs can be met on foot, by bicycle, or using public transit, and meeting everyday needs on foot or by bicycle is pleasant and easy to do.

In mixed-use developments, housing is mixed with other land uses including schools, shops, businesses, restaurants, and entertainment. In such neighborhoods it is common to find buildings with commercial space on the ground floor, accessible to the street, with living spaces on the upper floors.

Mixed-use development has multiple benefits. The more varieties of activities are available within a neighborhood, the fewer numbers of automobile trips are required. Shops, inviting streets, and great public spaces help foster a sense of place, build a sense of community, and encourage casual social interactions among neighbors. Neighborhoods tend to have residents active at different times of day and days of the week; the result is more "eyes on the street," an important element in crime prevention.

Having a mix of housing types ensures that appropriate housing is available for people with diverse lifestyles and ensures that affordable housing is available for everyone. Diverse communities become more integrated rather than segregating people of differing economic means. In addition, providing housing suited to various phases of life allows people to age in place in their own communities and to build lifelong social connections.

Walkable neighborhoods allow most or all of one's daily needs to be met on foot. Schools, shops, work, recreation, and transit stops are all within distances short enough to walk, with streets and paths that are safe, comfortable, and attractive. People will walk only if it is easier than driving, but when places are well designed, most residents actually prefer to meet their needs on foot.

Being able to meet one's daily needs on foot provides independence for residents who are too young to drive and for older residents who can no longer drive, allowing them to age in place with dignity. With attention to universal accessibility, it provides independence to residents with mobility impairments and to parents pushing strollers. It provides greater economic independence for people with low income levels. It provides exercise-related health benefits and reduced air pollution as well.

How big is a walkable neighborhood? Urban planners say that the optimal size of a neighborhood is a quarter-mile from center to edge. Most people are willing to walk or use wheelchairs for a distance of about a quarter of a mile. Neighborhoods built before 1950 were compact and walkable, and tended to have a radius of a quarter-mile or a distance of half a mile across from edge to edge. If distances between uses are longer than that, residents who do not use bicycles may turn to their automobiles. For most people, a quarter-mile is a 5-minute walk, and for a neighborhood to feel walkable, daily needs should be supplied within this 5-minute walk. Experience shows an appropriate size for a walkable neighborhood to be 40 to 200 acres in extent (ibid., 42).

The layouts of walkable neighborhoods have networks of interconnected pedestrian-friendly streets. They have small block sizes and frequent intersections, with streets no more than 450 feet apart (ibid., 129) and designed for slow traffic speeds. The streets themselves, usually tree-lined, are public spaces and are designed for people. Buildings are set close to their property lines to help define the street spaces, with parking either along the curbs or hidden behind the buildings, rather than in parking lots in front. In the few cases where a building is set back from a sidewalk, it does so in order to create a public space such as a garden or plaza. Sidewalks are wide and include trees, planters, places to sit, and public art. Blank building walls can feel threatening and unsafe; on a walkable street building faces are human in scale, with display windows, attractive entryways, and a variety of access points to encourage frequent comings and goings and enliven the street.

Policymakers in cities promote walkable neighborhoods through ordinances and design guidelines. Design guidelines provide standards for characteristics such as height and form of building façades, architectural character, public spaces, and vegetation. They may be adopted independently or they may be included as part of a form-based code. A form-based code is an alternative to land-use zoning that specifies physical form rather than land use. It regulates the form and scale of buildings, streets, and public spaces.

Box 11.2 Freiburg's Vauban District

Vauban is a community of 5,000 households on a former military base in the city of Freiburg, Germany striving to integrate ecological, social, and economic resilience (Melia 2006). All new buildings must meet a low-energy standard, and about one in seven meets the German *Passivhaus* standard. Photovoltaic systems provide power to many of the buildings and a combined heat and power plant provides district heating. Biogas from sewage treatment is used for cooking (Newman et al. 2009, 75).

A school, markets, and businesses together with about 600 jobs are all within walking or bicycling distance. Walkable streets provide access to galleries, community gardens, and public open spaces. Parking spaces for cars are not permitted on private property; a community car park at the edge of the district allows neighborhoods to remain car-free.

Most building projects have been sold to co-housing groups and most buildings are four stories high. A planned density of over 50 dwelling units per acre supports public transit. When they are not walking or bicycling, citizens get around using buses, streetcar, light rail, and a car-sharing service.

A community group, Forum Vauban, worked collaboratively to plan the eco-district. Rather than having a plan imposed from outside, residents and professionals worked together, learning as they went. As a result, the ideas and innovations that emerged became their own and are durable (Scheurer and Newman 2008).

Smart Growth and New Urbanism

Smart growth is an approach to urban planning that is the antithesis of sprawl. It accommodates growth by locating development in city centers and older suburbs with existing infrastructure in ways that preserve open space and natural resources while supporting and revitalizing existing cities. Smart growth developments are compact, walkable, bikable, and transit-oriented, with a mix of uses, housing types, and affordability levels.

The term was first used in 1996 by former Maryland Governor Parris Glendenning, who worked for land-use legislation in that state. The Maryland Smart Growth Law became a prototype for legislation in other states. In the same year the EPA launched the Smart Growth Network in partnership with several governmental and nonprofit organizations.

Ten basic principles for smart growth were developed by the Smart Growth Network, based on information gathered from surveys of communities around the US. The principles are:

1 Mix land uses
2 Take advantage of compact building design
3 Create a range of housing opportunities and choices
4 Create walkable neighborhoods
5 Foster distinctive, attractive communities with a strong sense of place
6 Preserve open space, farmland, natural beauty, and critical environmental areas
7 Strengthen and direct development toward existing communities
8 Provide a variety of transportation choices
9 Make development decisions predictable, fair, and cost effective
10 Encourage community and stakeholder collaboration in development decisions.

These principles are in contrast to the characteristics of suburban sprawl. Sprawl features homogeneous land uses; low density; large-scale buildings and roads, with little detail for pedestrians; automobile-oriented streets, maximized for traffic volume and speed; greenfield development, with loss of farmland and open spaces; an unplanned development process; and an emphasis on the private developer and landholder. Studies of smart growth communities show that compared to residents of low-density sprawl, people who live in mixed-use communities with interconnected streets and twice the density drive about 30 percent fewer miles (Ewing et al. 2008, 6).

Thus smart growth is important for promoting resilient communities in the face of changing climate and declining oil supplies. People who live in compact, walkable, mixed-use developments have a variety of transportation and lifestyle options that residents of sprawl do not have, while these smart growth neighborhoods are better, more pleasant places to live.

New Urbanism is an urban design movement closely related to smart growth, focused on the elements of a neighborhood that make it attractive and successful, with a strong sense of community. Drawing on successful patterns from old European urbanism, its principles are similar to those of smart growth: compact, walkable neighborhoods; mixed use; transit-oriented development; highly connected street networks; human-scale buildings; and a range of housing types and affordability levels. New urbanism is promoted by the Congress for the New Urbanism, an organization of urban designers and planners.

Box 11.3 Mole Hill: A Garden in the City

Mole Hill, a 4-block neighborhood in the city of Vancouver, British Columbia, is the last remnant of Victorian and Edwardian houses that once made up Vancouver's West End, razed in the 1960s and 1970s to make way for modernist apartments. Originally built as boarding houses and later purchased by the city, these 100-year-old buildings were slated for demolition. In 1999, a grassroots partnership of affordable housing advocates and low-income residents calling itself the Mole Hill Community Housing Society (MHCHS) persuaded the city to preserve the area for social housing, which the MHCHS now leases from the city at no cost (Design Centre for Sustainability 2006, 110; Grdadolnik 2005).

Heritage buildings were carefully restored inside while the historic urban fabric was preserved outside. A geothermal heating and cooling system was installed and houses were upgraded for energy efficiency.

The city revised its parking policy, allowing parking spaces to be reduced from 100 to 28. The alley was narrowed and spaces once occupied by cars were converted to community gardens, fruit trees, and seating areas. A greenway passes through the site at mid-block, with a water feature that cleanses and retains stormwater. At the intersection of the alley and the greenway asphalt was replaced by brick pavers, marking a social center with benches, arbors, and shared workshops and laundries. Fruit trees, vines, and vegetables spill into the alley. Generous porches overlooking the gardens extend the living areas of small apartments.

The neighborhood now includes 170 units for low-income residents and a day center for people living with HIV/AIDS, together with 5 privately owned homes restored and sold at full market value. Renovation was funded by a loan from the city, which the MHCHS is repaying.

Green Infrastructure

Conventional infrastructure, sometimes informally referred to as "gray" systems, consists of technological support systems needed for the functioning of a community. "Green" systems consisting of vegetation and other living parts of the biosphere are needed for human well-being and the functioning of a community as well. When open spaces such as parks, green roofs, bioswales, and rain gardens are part of a stormwater system, some planners refer to this as green infrastructure. More broadly, the term "green infrastructure" can also mean any open space in which nature is used as an infrastructural system. In addition to providing residents a more immediate sense of living nature and the bioregion within which they live, green infrastructure can create safe, interconnected opportunities to walk or bicycle, reduce the urban heat island effect, cleanse stormwater and recharge groundwater, make urban air cleaner, provide movement corridors for wildlife, provide pathways for pollinators including bees and butterflies and, in some places, provide food.

Just as undeveloped open space is known as greenfields and abandoned industrial land is known as brownfields, aging suburban sprawl is sometimes known as grayfields. Locked into unsustainable transportation patterns and without the mix of services needed for daily life, these grayfields are candidates for neighborhood-based regeneration, what some planners refer to as greening the grayfields.

Some cities, recognizing the value of unbuilt space, actively look for ways to regenerate open-space networks. Opportunities for piecing together open-space networks and reweaving the green urban fabric can be found everywhere, in pockets large and small. Potential sites for parks include existing cemeteries, former landfills, and the possibility of shared spaces in schoolyards. Many cities install parks on the tops of underground parking structures; Chicago's Millennium Park is a well-known example. US cities are required by law to cover municipal water reservoirs and some, including Seattle, cover them with parks.

Streets are themselves public spaces and can become part of the green infrastructure. The Pearl District in Portland, Oregon, is a former warehouse and light industrial area that is now a walkable, mixed-use, mixed-income neighborhood served by streetcars and interwoven with a fabric of multiple parks and inter-block green space.

Some cities cover or even remove larger roadways and replace them with green infrastructure. In 1974 the city of Portland removed the urban freeway that separated people from its downtown river, replacing it with the 30-acre Waterfront Park. In 1976, the city of Seattle put a park over a freeway when it commissioned a 5.5-acre park above a busy interstate freeway in downtown Seattle known as Freeway Park, where visitors can lose themselves among trees, birds, and splashing water in a series of irregular plazas. In 1991, an elevated freeway slicing through downtown Boston was removed, relocated in a tunnel, and replaced by a series of parks and gardens known as the Rose Kennedy Greenway.

Abandoned railroad rights-of-way provide potential space for linear parks and greenways. New York City built the popular High Line Park on almost 1.5 miles of elevated rail structure in Manhattan, echoing the earlier Promenade Plantée built on almost 3 miles of elevated rail structure in Paris. The city of Washington, DC built the 11-mile Capital Crescent Trail on an abandoned B&O Railroad bed. The Rails-to-Trails Conservancy is a US nonprofit organization with the goal of "creating a nationwide network of trails from former rail lines and connecting corridors" that has preserved hundreds of pathways covering thousands of miles.

The reality behind urban open-space networks is that humans and nature are not separate. Rather than being something that is "out there" beyond the city, nature can be a central element of cities. The majority of the world's people live in cities, and this is where access and connections to green infrastructure are most needed.

Building Community

One of the benefits of smart growth neighborhoods is their role in building durable social communities. This social structure will be increasingly important for building resilient cities in the hotter, post-carbon years ahead.

Resilient communities provide walkable streets, common public spaces, ample places to sit, and opportunities for casual social interaction. The easier it is to walk and to interact with neighbors, the greater the number of spontaneous social contacts in a day and the greater the sense of community that can develop. A large body of evidence links social connectedness to physical and mental health. The ability to meet basic needs on foot and simultaneously to meet needs for social contact promote economic and social diversity, and are especially important for residents with disabilities, elders, and low-income residents.

Community-enhancing neighborhoods provide a variety of places for meeting and interacting. Planners talk about the importance of providing "third places," spaces that are neither home nor work, but that provide places to gather informally, develop trust, and form associations. Examples include community gardens, farmers' markets, public plazas, libraries, parks, cafés, and sidewalk seating.

Social ties and a sense of community have been shown to improve crime prevention. Evidence for this was first widely discussed following the publication of the classic urban planning book, *The Death and Life of Great American Cities* by Jane Jacobs (1961). Jacobs talked about the importance of community and the value of having many "eyes on the street." A specialization that deals with design strategies for discouraging crime and promoting safety is the field of crime prevention through environmental design (CPTED, pronounced "SEP-ted").

Urban-renewal housing projects of the 1960s provide counterexamples to CPTED. These large, modernist blocks that replaced city slums with public housing, known as "projects" in the US and "estates" in England, were expected to bring about social improvement. They were probably well-intended. However, they overlooked what we now know about how to build community. These massive, impersonal mega-parks lacked human scale, connection with nature, fine-grained personal space with opportunities for personalization, spaces and sub-spaces for a diversity of daily activity, or an adequate way to maintain "eyes on the street."

One such example was the award-winning Pruitt-Igoe housing development in St. Louis, Missouri, built in 1955. This public housing project consisted of 33 apartment towers, 11 stories each, housing a total of over 10,000 residents. Social conditions began to deteriorate shortly after its completion. Within 10 years it had become internationally famous for its extreme poverty, racism, and violence. It was finally declared a failure in the early 1970s and demolished (McLennan 2004, 168).

Brasilia, the capital of Brazil, is another example of massive spaces of inhuman scale, lacking connection to nature. Conceived in the late 1950s as a modernist utopia, whose city planner even refused to visit the site, the place contains award-winning concrete buildings set in unbroken paved areas (Schwartz 2008). Uses are segregated by zones and thoroughfares for cars dominate the spaces, with no people living above shops, no trees, places to sit, walkable streets or pedestrians. Generally regarded as a wrong turn in urban planning, Brasilia is now known for its crime, violence, and traffic jams.

Box 11.4 Curitiba, Brazil: Sustainability for All of Us

Curitiba, Brazil is a city of 1.6 million people. Relatively poor, it still fosters community well-being and a high quality of life (Edwards 2005, 131; ICLEI 2002, 2). Although it has more cars per capita than any city in Brazil, Curitiba's atmospheric pollution is the lowest in the country. This city that pioneered bus rapid transit (BRT) is known for its public transportation. At peak times buses arrive once a minute, less than a third of a mile from any spot in the city. In 1970 the city had less than 10 square feet of green space per person. Now there are 560 square feet per person, and nearly one-fifth of the city is parkland (ICLEI 2002, 3). Volunteers have planted 1.5 million trees, and builders get tax breaks if their projects include green space.

In response to the growing problem of the urban poor, the city bought and cleared a large lot renamed Novo Bairro, or New Neighborhood, which became home for 50,000 families. Each person gets a plot of land; two trees, one of them a fruit tree; and an hour's consultation with an architect. Landowners then build their own homes one room at a time as they acquire materials. Bus tickets are bought with a low-cost "social fare," and an attractive glass tube bus station connects Novo Bairro with the rest of the transit system.

People in low-income neighborhoods can exchange bags of trash for bus tickets and food. Children can exchange recyclables for school supplies, chocolate, toys, and tickets for shows. People who are homeless can get jobs at recycling separation plants. As a result of these and other programs, less garbage is dumped in natural areas and 70 percent of the city's trash is recycled (Edwards 2005, 131).

Two characteristics have made these successes possible: the first is an overarching planning strategy that integrates social, economic, and environmental programs and provides a framework. It is driven by a core value of respecting all the people who live there, both present and future generations. As a result, individual projects incrementally add to a sustainable whole.

The second is strong political leadership. Curitiba's former mayor, architect Jaime Lerner, first articulated the strategic vision. Lerner helped found the Urban Planning Institute of Curitiba (IPPUC). Core values in the city plan and the endurance of the IPPUC allowed the original vision to continue in spite of political dictatorship and economic crisis. Curitiba calls itself "the city of all of us," and it is that vision that shapes the city.

Transportation

Transportation is fundamental to any discussion of sustainability. It uses over a quarter of all energy consumed, is responsible for almost a quarter of all greenhouse gases emitted (IPCC 2014c, 603), and plays an integral role in determining development patterns and the livability of cities. Sustainable transportation planning works to find ways to move people and transport the goods they need without requiring each individual to use their own personal 2 tons of steel each time they do so. It offers people freedom to choose how they get around, providing multiple routes and multiple types of transportation, with alternatives that are faster, easier, and less expensive to users than single-occupant automobiles. Providing alternate modes of transportation does not mean that people cannot use private vehicles. It means that people will have affordable, efficient options from which to choose, and will not need to be dependent on private automobiles for every trip. Disincentives for automobile use must be combined with positive incentives that make alternate modes of transportation appealing.

Transportation demand management (TDM) is a set of tools and strategies for changing travel behavior to reduce the number of automobile vehicle trips and vehicle miles driven (Victoria Transport Policy Institute n.d.). TDM programs are common on college and university campuses and in some cities. Strategies include high-quality transit service with broad coverage, free or subsidized public transit, fees charged for parking, reduced parking supply, rebates to workers who do not use parking spaces, carpool and vanpool programs, safe bicycle routes, bicycle storage lockers and showers, guarantees of emergency rides home, compressed work weeks, telecommuting, carshare programs, bikeshare programs, and walkable, compact development.

Access to transportation affects people's economic and social opportunities, helping determine where people can work, shop, go to school, and recreate. Similar to the concept of **food deserts**, neighborhoods without access to healthy food, urban areas known as **transit deserts** have numerous transit-dependent residents but poor transit service (Litman 2015, 19). Transit-dependent people are typically unable to drive not by choice, but because they have disabilities or are too young, too old, or too poor. The presence of a transit desert is affected by how far a person must walk, the time it takes to access transit, and the relative safety and comfort of getting there.

Transit-dependent people are sometimes relocated to peripheral neighborhoods because of urban renewal, or they may be forced to move out of urban cores by rising housing costs; in other cases it is the jobs which move to suburbs accessible only to people with cars. Then, either low-income residents must spend a high percentage of their income on basic transportation, or they cannot can get there at all.[2] Smart growth, with its compact design, mix of uses and housing choices, safe and walkable neighborhoods, and multiple transportation options, promotes equity by improving access for people who cannot drive and making transportation more affordable for people with lower incomes.

Public Transit

Public transit choices include buses, bus rapid transit, and light rail. BRT combines some of the features of buses and subway systems including frequent service, large capacity, dedicated travel lanes, traffic signal priority, and quick passenger loading and unloading from accessible, platform-level doors. BRT was originally launched in the city of Curitiba, Brazil, known for its widely available public transit and sustainability initiatives. Curitiba planned the city's growth so that rather than expanding haphazardly, it would develop along designated transit corridors (IPCC 2014c, 975).

Light rail uses rail cars that travel on dedicated steel rails. It is called light rail because the rail and cars are lighter than the heavy track, cars, and locomotives used by railroads. It has a higher initial cost than BRT but much greater capacity and efficiency. Light rail systems are powered by electricity and are expected to play a significant role in supporting resilient cities in the coming years of changing climate and post-peak oil.

It is possible to combine light rail and highway roadbeds. Rail systems can be built more economically by using existing freeway rights-of-way, where slopes, curves, and bridges have been already engineered.

Compact development and public transit go together, particularly light-rail public transit. Transit in low-density sprawl cannot draw sufficient ridership. A minimum density of 7 dwelling units per acre is needed to support basic bus service, and a density of 15 to 20 dwelling units per acre is needed to support light rail (Newman et al. 2009, 96). Conversely, light rail is a factor that affects housing and employment patterns. Transit not only helps a city reduce greenhouse gas emissions and fossil fuel consumption, it also helps the city reconfigure its structure. Whatever transit methods are adopted, in order to ensure that people use them it is important that using them is easy, fast, and pleasant, with minimal wait times, and that curbside environments where passengers wait are clean, pleasant, and safe. The key is a network that knits together multiple modes of transport and multiple routes so that using public transport is at least as flexible and convenient as using a personal car (Mees 2010, 8).

Transit-Oriented Development

Transit-oriented development (TOD), in which neighborhood development is clustered around convenient transit stations and located along transit corridors, is a central element in smart growth. Walkable, compact, mixed-use neighborhoods allow people to meet most of their daily needs on foot. Convenient, nearby transit allows people to travel easily to other parts of a city for other activities. Experience has shown that TOD reduces total vehicle miles traveled by about 50 percent (Newman et al. 2009, 96). TODs affect real estate values. A study by the Urban Land Institute found that transit-oriented developments appreciate fastest in up markets and hold their value better in down markets (ibid., 119).

Complete Streets

Streets in automobile-dependent neighborhoods and cities were designed primarily for cars. Urban planners work to complete the streets, that is, to make them convenient and safe for all users, all travel modes, and all abilities. This involves a shift in thinking whereby transportation corridors are seen as public space for people, not just as movement corridors for cars. The Embarcadero in San Francisco is an example. Earlier in its history the elevated Embarcadero Freeway had separated the waterfront from downtown but was seen as essential to efficient traffic flow. However, when a 1989 earthquake damaged the freeway but no gridlock ensued, agencies and community leaders removed the freeway and redesigned the space as a tree-lined boulevard with accessible spaces for light rail, bicycles, and pedestrians.

Complete streets mean more walkable communities. For pedestrian safety, complete streets have no more than two travel lanes between curbs. Pedestrian safety is improved by shortening the crossing distance at intersections and using curb extensions. Separate lanes for parking and for bicycle travel may be marked by planters, vegetated planting strips and medians, and curb extensions, also known as bulb-outs. Space is provided for public life including street trees, seating, and outdoor cafés. Spaces are made accessible through wide, unobstructed sidewalks, curb ramps, and audible crossing signals. Space is provided for public transit with pleasant and comfortable transit stops, safe pedestrian routes to stops, curb extensions, and protected boarding islands. Larger complete streets are known in some cities as multiway boulevards.

Walkable and transit-oriented communities need not only complete streets, but complete street networks as well. Dead-end cul-de-sacs found in suburban sprawl eliminate connectivity and mean that cars must be used to get everywhere. By contrast, integrated networks of connected, walkable streets make it easy to move almost anywhere through a neighborhood. Walkable street networks need small block sizes, frequent intersections, and slow traffic speeds. Streets need to form connected webs, but they do not necessarily need to form rectangular grids. Streets need not look the same, and would be monotonous if they did. Differences in street hierarchy provide visual structure that helps pedestrians find their way easily, with primary connector streets serving as major pathways, smaller streets functioning as linkages, and alleyways providing intriguing shortcuts through blocks. The primary goal is to enable people to walk between activity centers using routes that are direct, comfortable, and attractive.

Cities and Climate Change

Cities will be impacted by changing climate in many ways. Drought, heat waves, changing precipitation patterns, reduced snowmelt, and changes in ecosystem structure will affect cities' abilities to provision themselves with food. Coastal cities will face increasing intensity of storm surges and rising sea levels which will inundate whole neighborhoods. Some inland cities will face increased flooding, perhaps together with water shortages. The need to transition away from planet-heating fossil fuels, coupled with the aftermath of peak oil, will necessitate fundamental changes in energy use and supply.

Many cities are developing climate action plans. These plans typically have parallel goals of mitigation and adaptation: to mitigate greenhouse gas emissions and move toward climate neutrality in order to help reduce the severity of climate change, and to prepare for responding to changes that are now inevitable. A number of cities are also simultaneously evaluating how to reduce their dependence on fossil fuels. Among the most comprehensive and detailed climate action plans developed to date have been the Chicago Climate Action Plan, the Seattle Climate Action Plan, and New York City's PlanNYC.

Many of the approaches taken by cities to develop compact, mixed-use neighborhoods, reduce vehicle miles traveled, promote high-performance buildings, increase the use of locally produced materials and products, increase renewable energy, restore functioning ecosystems, protect water resources, and provide food from urban agriculture are strategies that are relevant to adapting to climate change. These approaches help to reduce urban contributions to global warming while they also help increase urban adaptability, self-reliance, and resilience. Resilience is the capacity of a system to absorb disturbance and still retain its fundamental function and structure, whether that system is an ecosystem or a city.

Notes

1 Or as some disability rights advocates say, "Nothing about us without us" (Sanchez and Brenman 2008, 115).
2 When planners propose projects they believe will create jobs, landscape architect and sociologist Randy Hester measures their social equity broadly with three questions: Can I get it? Can I get there? Can I get in? (That is, am I qualified for jobs there? Is affordable transportation available? Are diversity and inclusion valued?) (Hester et al. 2015)

Further Reading

Beatley, Timothy. *Biophilic Cities: Integrating Nature into Urban Design and Planning*. Washington, DC: Island Press, 2010.
Farr, Douglas. *Sustainable Urbanism: Urban Design with Nature*. New York: John Wiley, 2008.
Newman, Peter, Timothy Beatley, and Heather Boyer. *Resilient Cities: Responding to Peak Oil and Climate Change*. Washington, DC: Island Press, 2009.
Toor, Will and Spenser W. Havlick. *Transportation & Sustainable Campus Communities*. Washington, DC: Island Press, 2004.

Chapter Review

1 How would you describe greenfield development?
2 How would you decide whether a particular vacant lot could be considered a brownfield?
3 Why would a city choose brownfield over greenfield development?
4 What could a city do to reduce its urban heat island effect?
5 Describe the causes of sprawl.
6 List some negative impacts of sprawl.
7 What kinds of federal or local laws and policies encourage sprawl?
8 If a city has a goal of preserving agricultural land, what are some policy approaches it could consider?
9 What examples of smart-growth characteristics, either fully developed or just beginning, can you observe in the city or region where you live?

10 What are some examples of green infrastructure a city might already have or might consider implementing?

11 How does public transit affect the health of the environment, economic well-being, and social equity, or the triple bottom line?

Critical Thinking and Discussion

1 If you were in a town meeting where someone said that making streets more pedestrian-friendly would lead to traffic congestion, how would you respond?

2 The city council in your town is developing plans for a new village on the site of a large restored brownfield. Some planners say streets in a hub-and-spokes pattern would be better; others say a general grid pattern would be better. What would you advise? What factors would you want to consider?

3 High-density cities preserve surrounding land and can reduce transportation demand in some cases, while low-density cities allow more space for plants to grow, and may even provide some habitat. List as many advantages and disadvantages as you can for each. Then list as many strategies as you can for creating green space and reducing the urban heat island effect within high-density urban areas.

4 Living along coastlines has many hazards, and they are increasing as the climate changes. Why do you think humans still choose to live there?

5 Why do you think the earliest cities developed along river valleys?

6 What types of animals are adapted or able to adapt to urban habitats?

7 In what ways do you think urbanization is beneficial to the human species? In what ways do you think it is not?

8 In what ways does urbanization affect the hydrosphere?

9 As a city works to become more sustainable and resilient, what roles do you think are appropriate for government and what roles are appropriate for community members and groups?

10 If a city were a kind of organism, what might indicate if the organism were healthy? What might indicate illness?

11 Why do so many people criticize suburban sprawl, yet still prefer living in suburbs themselves? What factors might explain this split?

12 Is there an ideal population size for a city? Does it vary by location?

13 What are some advantages and disadvantages of public transit systems?

14 Planners often use 25 years or 50 years as a planning horizon. Do you think this is an appropriate choice? Do you think it should be shorter or longer? Why?

15 Some cities refer to themselves as "sustainable cities." Is this name justified? What characteristics would make a city sustainable?

16 If you wanted to minimize your ecological footprint, would you live in a high-rise apartment in a big city or on a ranch next to a national forest? Why?

12 Food

Every living animal takes in food, metabolizes it to extract energy and nutrients, and discharges wastes. Perhaps nothing is more essential than food to the survival of every living organism, including us. Almost all of the food for humans comes either from **agriculture** or from harvesting animals from the oceans. Agriculture is the science of cultivating plants and animals as food crops. Currently agriculture occupies about 35 percent of the Earth's land surface (Wijkman and Rockström 2012, 52). By definition, it involves manipulating environments and ecosystems. The question is: how can we harvest seafood and practice agriculture in ways that are most sustainable for individual beings, ecosystems, and the biosphere as a whole?

For around 200,000 years, humans lived by gathering and hunting for their food.[1] Beginning around 10,000 years ago and continuing for several thousand years a change developed that was perhaps the most important transition in human history: the transition to agriculture. In exchange for greater effort, humans were able to extract larger quantities of food from smaller areas; they no longer had to travel to provide continuous sources of food, and permanent settlements became possible for the first time. In hunting and gathering societies, food sources were not seen as things to be owned, but as public goods available to all members of the group. With the transition to agriculture, surplus food could be produced and needed to be stored. The idea of ownership of food developed, and with it new ideas about social hierarchies along with leaders who had the power to control the distribution of supplies. Segments of societies became specialized, and crafts developed more rapidly. With more dependable supplies of food, populations grew larger. At the same time new health problems such as tooth decay came with changing diets (Ponting 2007, 237). This new way of life based on agriculture, cities, craft specialization, and political hierarchy is sometimes referred to as the Neolithic Revolution.

In the 1960s and 1970s, the so-called **green revolution** introduced the technology of industrial agriculture, with chemical fertilizers, pesticides, irrigation, and hybrid seeds. While the green revolution improved yields and ended the specter of mass famines, it came with environmental costs, and it did not end the problem of hunger. Over a billion people in the world are still hungry, and several million die of starvation each year (Wijkman and Rockström 2012, 49). Since the green revolution, food production in developing countries has increased, doubling or tripling in many places. However, because population has also nearly doubled, the amount of food produced per person has remained nearly unchanged in most parts of the world. At the same time, the green revolution has resulted in damage to soils, waters, and ecosystems, the final costs of which are not yet known.

Farming Methods

Organic Farms

Crops are grown using several methods at a range of scales. One method is known as **organic agriculture**. This is agriculture that does not use synthetic fertilizers or pesticides; instead, it relies on biological approaches. Organic farms return nutrients to the soil in the form of compost made of decayed plant matter. They use biological methods of controlling weeds and insect pests and techniques of crop rotation that prevent soil from becoming exhausted without the need for applying massive amounts of fertilizer. They may use manure recycled from the same farm. All food was grown organically before the advent of chemical fertilizers and pesticides in the twentieth century.

Small- and Mid-Level Farms

Small- and mid-size farms are owned by individual farmers or families, as opposed to corporations, and exemplify the traditional view of farmers. Farms at this scale may use either organic methods or chemical methods of fertilizing and pest control. Small farms rely on direct markets while very large farms owned by corporations have access to national distribution systems. Mid-size farms occupy an economic niche that is currently in flux. They tend to produce volumes too large for direct local markets but too small to compete against larger corporate farm systems.

Consumers increasingly want assurances that their food choices are healthy and safe. They want to know more about where their food comes from: who produced it, how it was grown, and perhaps even the name of the farmer. They want accountability. Farmers are increasingly selling not just products but also relationships.

Industrialized Farms

Industrialized agriculture, sometimes referred to as agribusiness, is farming on a large scale. Cultivation and harvesting are done with large, fossil fuel-driven machinery. Large quantities of irrigation water and synthetic fertilizers boost crop yield, while chemical pesticides reduce competition from weeds and damage from pests. As opposed to small- and midsize farms, which are typically operated by their owners, farms using industrial agriculture generally feature absentee owners, usually shareholders of corporations. Business objectives include reducing costs and development of national or international supply chains. Decisions made throughout often-distant supply chains are based on maximizing profit rather than on the long-term sustainability of the farm, the good of the surrounding community, or the health and diversity of natural resources that sustain the farm.

Large-scale producers who rely on long-distance shipping choose varieties for their ability to withstand harvesting equipment and 1 to 2 weeks of travel time rather than for flavor or nutritional value. Produce is grown with high-nitrogen fertilizer to make it reach marketable size more quickly, unfortunately before it reaches full nutritional value. Fruits that will be shipped long distances are picked before they are ripe so that they can be shipped without spoiling. Produce is often sprayed with pesticides designed to stay on the produce and to preserve it during its long trip. Once delivered, fruits are treated with ethylene gas to cause ripening, but the fruits never achieve natural ripeness and the flavor is never the same as fruits that ripen on the plant.

Industrialized agriculture uses a method of planting called **monoculture**, designed to boost efficiency, in which fields are planted with single types of crops. A kind of monoculture in a small-scale, non-agricultural application is the practice of growing turf, or lawns, using heavy irrigation, fertilizers, and herbicides to maintain a single and uniform species of grass. In agricultural fields, the same crop is planted in the same field year after year, in contrast to the traditional practice of crop rotation. Monoculture makes it possible to use large-scale machinery for cultivation and harvesting. It is a method that leads to soil depletion and a resulting dependence on fertilizer, and it makes plants more vulnerable to disease pathogens. About 25 percent of the world's cropland is currently planted in monocultures (Withgott and Brennan 2009, 145).

The **food sovereignty** movement is a global grassroots response to corporate control of food. Food sovereignty is "the right of peoples to healthy and culturally appropriate food produced through ecologically sound and sustainable methods, and their right to define their own food and agriculture systems" (Nyéléni 2007). Organizations fighting for food sovereignty work toward improving the resilience of local food systems and the health of ecological life-support systems; they focus on local food and local knowledge, promoting the right of farmers, fishers, and other food providers to have control over their land, seeds, and water, independent of control from transnational corporations (Akram-Lodhi and Kay 2008, 163).

Factory Farms

It is possible to approach the raising of animals as an industrial enterprise as well. Large-scale animal factories are known as **factory farms**. Industrial-scale yards housing animals at very high densities for feeding prior to slaughter are known as concentrated animal feeding operations (**CAFOs**) or **feedlots**. In the US, four companies produce 81 percent of cows, 73 percent of sheep, 57 percent of pigs, and 50 percent of chickens. Some 84 percent of pigs killed each year come from factory farms (Nierenberg 2005, 5).

Factory farms and feedlots come under criticism for a variety of reasons. Some critics raise environmental objections because these facilities produce large quantities of waste containing bacteria, chemicals, antibiotics, and hormones, with runoff that can pollute both surface water and groundwater. Some critics note the impacts on human health. Factory farm waste has been connected to outbreaks of disease in several states. Animals in feedlots suffer emotional stress from living conditions and physical stress from being forced to eat monotonous diets of corn or feed pellets, which their systems have not evolved to digest. To offset the stresses caused by their living conditions and unnatural diet they are preemptively fed antibiotics, which are then excreted and transferred up the food chain, leading to antibiotic-resistant bacteria.

Finally, some critics raise ethical objections to factory farms and feedlots. Animals in these facilities live miserable lives. The grotesque details are many and come in nightmarish variety, but the fundamental cause is the same: humans who work at these facilities must handle thousands of animals a day, and many do not see, or do not allow themselves to see, animals as living beings who think, feel emotions, and suffer pain. Two options are available to individuals concerned about the rights of animals. One option is to buy only meat from known local sources where it can be verified that animals are treated well and live moderately natural lives. The availability of such sources varies by region. The other option is not to eat animals, or at least to eat fewer of them, a choice sometimes known as "moving down the food chain."

Aquaculture

Aquaculture is industrial farming of fish or seafood in aquatic monoculture farming. While commercial fishing involves harvesting of wild fish or other animals, aquaculture involves growing and harvesting in tanks or similar controlled conditions. Aquaculture is a widespread industry in Asia, where farms raise animals including salmon, tilapia, and shrimp for export to the US, Europe, and Japan. Done responsibly, aquaculture has the potential to provide protein with minimal impact. However, in practice aquaculture also has the potential for environmental damage.

Farmed fish are packed densely in tanks or pens. Their close concentration makes them susceptible to disease, which requires treatment with antibiotics. Antibiotics and pesticides used in farming pollute the water, and heavy metals including copper and zinc accumulate on the bottoms of ponds and on the seafloor near salmon farms. Some fish are fed grain and soybean meal, which put demands on land and energy resources. Salmon are carnivores, so farmed salmon are fed wild ocean fish such as sardines and herring, placing stress on wild fish populations and reducing the food source for wild predators who depend on sardine and herring. Every pound of farmed salmon requires several pounds of wild fish as feed. Farmed fish are selectively bred for growth qualities and often genetically modified. When they escape from ponds and coastal pens into wild ecosystems, they grow larger and faster than native fish, whom they outcompete, while at the same time spreading disease and affecting the genetic pool by interbreeding.

Farming shrimp, too, results in ecological impacts. Coastal mangrove wetlands in southeast Asia provide critical habitat and protect coastlines from erosion and storm surges. Thirty-five percent of these tropical mangrove wetlands have vanished, primarily cleared to make room for shrimp farms (Primack 2008, 85). Shrimp can be grown in ponds, which reduces impact on mangroves, but this produces wastewater that contains pesticides and antibiotics. Both salmon farming and shrimp farming release antibiotics into waterways. From there they get into the food chain where they contribute to development of antibiotic-resistant strains of bacteria. Sludge containing pesticides and salts builds up on the bottoms of ponds, and after a few years contaminated pond sites must be abandoned.

Genetic Engineering

Perhaps no agricultural method provokes more disagreement than **genetically modified organisms** (GM, or GMOs). Some scholars believe that the risks are controllable and that GMO will play a role in providing food security (Sachs 2015, 350). Others believe that the uncertainty about risks remains too great to justify their use.

Selective breeding is an ancient method that involves influencing the genetic makeup of whole organisms by, for example, selecting wheat plants that produce the largest heads or dogs who have the best herding instincts to reproduce and create the next generation. By contrast, genetic engineering uses pieces of genetic material separate from organisms. Scientists add or remove segments of DNA, use splicing to recombine them in laboratories, and insert the pieces into genomes. Genes from entirely different species are routinely mixed together. A common example is "Bt crops," created by inserting genes from the bacterium *Bacillus thuringiensis* (Bt), which is toxic to insects, into the DNA of crop plants, particularly corn and cotton, to create a plant that produces its own pesticide.

Another common example of GMOs is a line of products called "Roundup-ready crops" engineered by Monsanto, the corporation that manufactures the herbicide glyphosate under the trade name Roundup. Roundup is the most commonly-used herbicide, widely used on crop fields. Roundup-ready soybeans, corn, cotton, and canola plants are not visibly affected by glyphosate, so farmers can spray Roundup at any time without killing their crops. Over two-thirds of US soybean, corn, cotton, and canola harvests now consist of genetically-modified plants. Critics observe that these plants promote increased use of herbicide, and that herbicide-resistant weeds are beginning to evolve.

A major criticism of genetic engineering is the potential for genetic pollution. Once GMOs breed with non-modified organisms, diverse stocks of genetic material may disappear from both crop species and wild species. Species and ecosystems could become increasingly uniform, without locally evolved and adapted variations that make species and ecosystems resilient. The loss of genetic diversity will mean plants and animals are less able to evolve in the face of new diseases and climate change. Critics of genetic modification believe that the precautionary principle should guide decision-making.

Other critics are concerned about threats to food sovereignty, with the potential for a few very large agribusiness corporations to dominate the world food supply. At issue is control over seeds themselves, with farmers being sued by corporations for saving their own seed (Toensmeier 2016, 124). They also point out that much of the research into the safety of genetic engineering is conducted, or at least funded, by large corporations who will profit if their GM crops are approved.

Irradiation

Many standard methods of processing food once it is harvested have been in use for decades or centuries, including drying, curing, canning, and freezing. A relatively new treatment method is called **irradiation**, done by exposing a food to a dose of radiation for the purpose of killing pathogenic bacteria and insects by disrupting their DNA. Irradiation is approved by the US Food and Drug Administration (FDA) for spinach, iceberg lettuce, fresh fruit, meat, and spices. Some vitamins and other nutrients are destroyed or reduced in the process of breaking molecular bonds, losses reported to be similar to losses caused by canning or pasteurization. In addition, flavor can be altered. The food does not become radioactive.

Human Health Issues

Human health can be impacted by materials that are added intentionally, such as food additives and sweeteners, and accidentally, such as pesticide contamination. Human health can also be impacted by too much food or food of the wrong kind, resulting in obesity and increased risk of disease; and by the reverse condition, food scarcity, resulting in malnutrition or starvation. Overnutrition is a food problem in affluent nations. Undernutrition is a food problem everywhere, including the US and Europe, but primarily in developing nations of the Southern Hemisphere.

Sweeteners

For early humans, a preference for sweetness may have conferred an evolutionary advantage by leading people to seek out ripe fruit, which is nutritious. Modern dependence on sugar taps into this powerful human preference for sweet taste. Researchers do not yet know whether sugar can lead to true physical addiction or whether it is simply a feature of preference. What is known, however, is that there is a link between increased sugar intake and increased blood levels of triglycerides and lowered levels of HDL, the so-called good cholesterol. And while eating sugar does not directly cause diabetes, a large body of research does show a strong association between amount of sugar eaten and risk of diabetes (Ballantyne 2009). Sugar adds calories to a person's diet, often displacing other, more nutritious foods.

High fructose corn syrup is a sweetener that first appeared on the market in 1967, became common in 1980, and is now ubiquitous in processed foods. In the US, federal farm policy and large subsidies keep corn prices low, making it the sweetener of choice for manufacturers. Recent research indicates that high fructose corn syrup may trigger more health problems than does sugar.

Food Additives

Chemicals are widely used in manufactured food as emulsifiers, to increase shelf life, to change color, and to provide flavors. According to the FDA, of the estimated 3,000 food additives used in the US, only about 2,000 have detailed toxicological data available (Knoblauch and Environmental Health News 2009). The FDA also has a category called "Generally Recognized As Safe" (GRAS) given to food additives that don't require approval because they have a proven track record based on either a history of use before 1958 or on published scientific evidence. Examples of GRAS substances include salt, sugar, spices and vitamins, as well as less recognized substances such as propyl gallate. Significant controversy continues over the potential risks of additives to food. Critics point to a history of additives formerly deemed safe and later banned after being shown to be carcinogens, including the root beer flavoring safrole, some food colorings, and the artificial sweetener cyclamate.

A laboratory discovery that two commonly used additives work as estrogen mimics has led researchers to suspect that other additives may be endocrine disruptors as well (ibid.). The two substances are 4-hexyl resorcinol, used to prevent shrimp, lobsters, and other shellfish from discoloring, and the GRAS additive propyl gallate, a preservative used to prevent fats and oils from spoiling and found in a range of foods including baked goods, shortening, dried meats, candy, pork sausage, mayonnaise, and dried milk. The FDA does not require food additives used in the US to undergo testing for estrogenic activity.

Pesticides

The EPA sets limits on how much of a particular pesticide residue can remain on food products, known as maximum residue limits (MRLs). The US Department of Agriculture maintains a MRL database, which can be accessed through the EPA website. In addition, several nonprofit organizations produce annual reports on residue pesticides found on foods, offering recommendations about which foods might be considered safest and which are best to avoid.

Obesity and Hunger

Problems of obesity and the related risks of heart disease, stroke, and diabetes in affluent nations arise from multiple factors. One cause is lack of activity, brought on by several cultural factors and exacerbated by the automobile culture and suburban sprawl. Another cause is food content, with two factors of particular concern: diets high in meat and diets high in sweeteners such as sugar and corn syrup.

People have **food security** when they have enough food and do not live in fear of hunger. The UN FAO says that "food security exists when all people, at all times, have physical and economic access to sufficient, safe and nutritious food to meet their dietary needs and food preferences for an active and healthy life" (FAO 2008, 1). The US Department of Agriculture (USDA) says that

> food security for a household means access by all members at all times to enough food for an active, healthy life. Food security includes at a minimum (1) the ready availability of nutritionally adequate and safe foods, and (2) an assured ability to acquire acceptable foods in socially acceptable ways (that is, without resorting to emergency food supplies, scavenging, stealing, or other coping strategies).
>
> (USDA ERS 2012)

Food security worldwide is threatened by a confluence of trends: rising population, rising water consumption, peak oil, collapse of fisheries, and declining stock of agricultural land (FAO 2011b, 2).

Hunger or food scarcity is a problem worldwide. The FAO reports that there are currently over one billion hungry people in the world (Conway 2012, 6). In absolute terms, the problem is one of distribution rather than quantity (Heinberg 2011, 218). The world produces enough grain to keep every person alive at a subsistence level and it produces enough grain plus vegetables, fruits, fish, and meat raised on grass rather than grain to provide a healthy diet to every person (Kimbrell 2002, 7; Meadows et al. 2004, 57). The shortages result from unequal distribution. People are not hungry because there is too little food to buy; they are hungry because they cannot afford to buy food. Much of the grain that could feed people instead goes into ethanol production and to feed animals to provide meat for affluent countries. In developing countries, food scarcity leads to political instability. The approach to food security as a basic human right is sometimes known as the food justice movement (Shiva 2005).

A set of goals, targets, and objectives known as the Millennium Development Goals was adopted by members of the UN in 2000; its successor, the Sustainable Development Goals, was adopted in 2015. Both established a framework for addressing the many dimensions of extreme poverty using a set of goals dealing with health, education, gender equity, and environmental sustainability. Goal number 1 is fundamental: "End extreme poverty, including hunger."

Planetary Health Issues

So far, humans as a whole do not take a sustainable approach to producing food. In the course of producing our food we put chemicals into the air, water, and soil faster than the capacity of natural systems to process them. Overfishing has led to the collapse of marine fisheries. We take more fish, water, forest, and topsoil than nature can replenish within time scales that are relevant for humans. Our food systems have overshot the planet's carrying capacity.

Soil

All terrestrial food comes from soil. Plants pull nutrients from soil, and other processes put them back. In intensive industrial agriculture, plants take nutrients from soil faster than they can be renewed. Soil becomes more and more depleted, so that the only way to continue growing on it is to add chemical fertilizer. This gives a boost to plant growth, which pulls even more nutrients from the soil. Although it is temporarily masked by the effects of fertilizer, the net result is depleted soil.

Habitat

Pesticide pollution of water and soil together with deforestation and habitat destruction are major threats to biodiversity. Industrial-scale agriculture smooths the surface of the land, shapes uniform fields to make planting and harvesting more efficient, and removes local pieces of habitat from fencerows, woodlands, and small creeks. Small- and mid-level farms are more likely to include habitat elements, which can be allowed to develop along fences and creeks without significantly impacting production quantities.

Box 12.1 Bees and Other Pollinators

Growing healthy food depends upon nutrients, water, soil, and pollinators. Globally, over 75 percent of all food plants and nearly 90 percent of all wild flowering plants rely on pollination by bees and other animals (Potts et al. 2016). Diversity and number of pollinators has a direct impact on crop yields and the resilience of the food supply.

Modern food crops rely primarily on a single species, the domesticated European honeybee. Yet there are more than 20,000 species of wild bees worldwide and over 4000 in North America, in addition to the numerous species of other insects, birds, and bats who contribute to pollination (Potts et al. 2016). Native bees are more efficient pollinators than domesticated bees but have smaller foraging ranges, so they accomplish more intensive pollination in small areas. As with other systems in the biosphere, diversity increases resilience. A diversity of wild bee species provides a greater chance of recovery from disease, extreme weather, and climate change. Conservation of native species plays an important role in food security.

In 2012 the UN established the Intergovernmental Platform on Biodiversity and Ecosystem Services (IPBES), a scientific body for the study of biodiversity and ecosystem services similar in structure to the IPCC. Under the auspices of UNEP, UNDP, FAO, and UNESCO, the IPBES consists of experts from governments, universities, and other organizations including indigenous communities who volunteer their time as peer reviewers to assess, evaluate, and synthesize existing research. Their first report, issued in 2016, was a global assessment of pollinators. The assessment was noteworthy for its inclusion of knowledge not only from scientific research but also from indigenous and local knowledge systems.

The IPBES assessment found that over 40 percent of invertebrate pollinators, especially bees and butterflies, are threatened with extinction, together with over 16 percent of vertebrate pollinators (Potts et al. 2016). Nicotine-based pesticides called neonicotinoids are implicated in declining bee populations, but they are only one of a set of interconnecting factors. Bees face multiple threats from loss of habitat, pesticides, disease and pests, and climate change. Climate change has led to changes and mismatches in the distribution of many species of bees and the plants that depend on them. In the US, the expansion of fields of corn for biofuels has converted land once

(continued)

(continued)

reserved for conservation, eliminating millions of acres of native plants. Industrial-scale farms often use genetically modified plants to allow broad use of herbicides, which kill all the plants except the genetically modified herbicide-resistant varieties. Bees need to forage for food much of the year, and they need a diverse diet, but mono-cultures eliminate the diversity of weeds and only offer flowers for a few weeks. Local bees live in the bee-equivalent of a food desert. If they are weakened by neurotoxins in pesticides they are more susceptible to pathogens; if they also must fly long distances to find food, or if the distances are too long and disoriented bees can't find their way home, their immune systems have more stressors than they can handle (Rosner 2013, 73). Agricultural beekeepers in the US follow the bloom time of crops, trucking millions of hives around the country in the back of tractor-trailers. In between crops, they supplement bees' diets with low-nutrition corn syrup or sugar water. During big pollination events, hives converge from around the country, making ideal conditions for the spread of disease.

Strategies for conserving wild bees involve providing a diversity of pollinator habitat patches and corridors in both agricultural and urban landscapes. These strategies nurture native bees and make domestic honeybees more efficient pollinators as well (ibid., 70). Sustainable agriculture supports bees by including diverse crops, crop rotation, and reduction or elimination of pesticides; ideal crop diversity would plan sections of farms that bloom at different times so that bees can always find food.

Hedgerows are bee-friendly farm elements, linear plant communities that support biodiversity and provide resources for pollinators. Used for thousands of years to mark property boundaries and keep livestock in, they became habitat refuges and movement corridors for wildlife and native plants as land became altered for agriculture. Although hedgerows are removed in large-scale industrial agriculture, they are increasingly seen in sustainable farming practices, where they have been shown to improve native bee populations (Morandin and Kremen 2013, 829).

In urban or suburban areas, linear bee-friendly corridors can be created, where they are sometimes known as pollinator pathways. These strips are planted with native plants to connect two or more pollinator-friendly patches, from large parks to tiny gardens, providing and linking foraging habitats for even the smallest bee.

Water

Agriculture puts a burden on the world's freshwater. About 70 percent of water use worldwide goes to the production of food (Sachs 2009, 36). Large-scale irrigation depletes underground aquifers such as the ancient Ogallala, while heavy use of irrigation water to grow crops on land that would not normally support them overtaxes some surface waters, such as the Colorado River in the US. In the scramble for decreasing water supplies, thousands of farmers find it more profitable to sell their irrigation rights to cities and to leave their land idle, taking their agricultural land out of production. Runoff from pesticide applications and from factory-farm sewage introduces pollution in the form of chemicals, antibiotics, and pathogens to lakes and rivers.

The Nitrogen Cycle

Widespread use of nitrogen fertilizers on many small and all industrial farms, much of it for biofuels and grain for meat production, contributes significantly to global warming and leads to coastal dead zones. Like many issues in sustainability, the difference between benefit and damage is a matter of degree. Billions of people today owe their lives to a discovery 100 years ago by Haber and Bosch, two German chemists who developed a way to transform inert nitrogen gas from the atmosphere into ammonia, which contains reactive nitrogen. The process requires fossil fuels. This development of synthetic nitrogen fertilizer was a pillar of the green revolution, allowing farmers to grow crops on previously infertile lands. Thanks to the dual discoveries of nitrogen fertilizer and fossil fuels, human population shot up from 1.5 billion to 7 billion in just one century.

Life depends on a group of bacteria, the nitrogen fixers, with the ability to break the strong triple bond holding together the two atoms in every nonreactive molecule of nitrogen, N_2, in the air. Another group of bacteria, the denitrifiers, convert reactive nitrogen back to N_2 gas. Until humans began exploiting the new technology for fixing nitrogen from air during the twentieth century, this cycle remained in delicate balance. Humans now create twice as much reactive nitrogen as all natural processes combined (Townsend and Howarth 2010, 66). Some nitrogen is released in the burning of fossil fuels, and some is released by fertilized fields and sewage runoff from farm animals.

On land, plants in ecosystems not equipped to deal with large nitrogen quantities lose out to new invasive species that are, with a net loss in biodiversity. In Europe, for example, grasslands have lost over a quarter of their plant species due to nitrogen deposition. The United Nations Environmental Programme (UNEP) ranks nitrogen pollution as one of the top three threats to biodiversity around the globe (ibid., 67).

Only a small percentage of synthetic fertilizer applied to crops is taken up by plants. In most of the US, about 10 percent of the fertilizer applied to fields goes into crops; 25 to 50 percent runs off in irrigation water immediately, and the rest ends up in the environment eventually (ibid., 69). Rivers carry fertilizer-laden runoff into the ocean, where excess nitrogen and phosphorus trigger explosive growth of algae, which consume oxygen as they decompose, killing virtually all aquatic life within the resulting dead zones.

In the atmosphere, reactive nitrogen in the form of nitrous oxide, N_2O, is a powerful greenhouse gas, with 300 times the global warming potential of carbon dioxide (IPCC 2014d, 87). Reactive nitrogen occurring as the other two forms of nitrogen oxides, NO and NO_2, leads to the development of ground-level ozone, also a significant greenhouse gas.

Peak Phosphorus

The nitrogen and phosphorus cycles make up one of nine major planetary boundaries identified by Wijkman and Rockström (2012, 45). Phosphorus is an essential building block for all cellular life and one of three essential components of commercial fertilizer. It is extracted from mined concentrations of phosphate rock.

Like fossil fuel, phosphate rock is a nonrenewable resource, cycling through the rock cycle over tens to hundreds of millions of years. Industrial agriculture dramatically altered the phosphorus cycle (Cordell and White 2011, 2029). Phosphorus in the form of phosphate is dug, transported all over the world in fertilizer, then transported again in food. Phosphorus removed from the soil in harvested plants must be replaced by the application of more fertilizer.

As with nitrogen, most of the phosphorus in synthetic fertilizer is not taken up by crops but runs off in irrigation water, resulting in eutrophication and dead zones in rivers and oceans. Of the phosphorus actually taken up by plants, some is discarded in the 30 to 40 percent of food that is wasted. More is flushed down toilets in urine and feces, drains through sewers, and contributes to eutrophication in rivers and lakes (Pearce 2011).

Policymakers and scholars are concerned about peak phosphorus (Cordell and White 2011, 2027). As with other nonrenewable resources, the higher quality, most easily accessible rock is mined first; as resources decline, the quality decreases and the environmental costs of extraction increase (ibid., 2039). The analytical framework developed by geologist M. King Hubbert to describe oil production also applies to other nonrenewable resources. As with the concept of peak oil, extraction of finite supplies of phosphorus results in peak phosphorus (Wijkman and Rockström 2012, 53).

About 95 percent of the world's phosphate reserves lie in 5 countries. Morocco, which controls 85 percent, is an occupied territory and the site of international human rights concerns (Elser and White 2010). China, the second largest source, has at times imposed stiff tariffs to block trade. The US has 12 phosphorus mines; the largest, in Florida, is owned by a company spun off from Cargill, an agribusiness corporation, and faces challenges from environmental groups over its negative impacts.

Like every element, phosphorus cannot be created or destroyed; it cycles throughout the lithosphere, hydrosphere, and biosphere.[2] In the absence of human activity, phosphorus is taken up by plants, then returns to the soil as dead plant matter decomposes, continually recycling through ecosystems. Thus the transition to a sustainable process involves circular life cycles rather than one-way use and discarding. Plants, crop residues, urine, and manure are all sources of phosphorus. This nutrient could be recycled through composting of crop residues and food waste and recycling of sewage, particularly urine (Pearce 2011).

Climate

Agriculture is responsible for 30 to 35 percent of the greenhouse gases emitted globally (Foley et al. 2011, 338), more than all transportation or all power plants (Sachs 2015, 339). Sources include tropical deforestation, soil degradation which releases carbon, methane emissions from livestock and flooded rice fields, and nitrous oxide emissions from fertilized soils. Other sources include the manufacture of fertilizers and pesticides and the combustion of fossil fuels for irrigation pumps, farm equipment, and the transport, packaging, and storage of food. Food systems are both major contributors to and at great risk from climate change (Schutter 2014, 8).

Fossil Fuels and Food Miles

Modern agriculture depends heavily on the use of fossil fuel to power tractors and harvesting equipment, run irrigation pumps, and manufacture pesticides and fertilizer. About 20 percent of energy used on US farms goes into producing synthetic fertilizer (Brown 2008, 34). While fossil fuels have increased the amount of food that can be produced, they have also increased the amount of energy needed to produce a given amount of food. As global oil production peaks and then declines in the years ahead, approaches to growing food will change. The years following peak oil, as well as peak water, may bring with them agricultural crises and increased food scarcity.

Consumption of food depends heavily on fossil fuels as well, as people in affluent societies have become accustomed to eating whatever food they want at any season of the year.

Food miles is a term that describes how far food travels from where it was grown to where it is eaten. Research conducted in 2001 by Iowa State University showed that at that time, food from a supermarket in the US traveled an average of 1,518 miles from farm to plate, a number often rounded down to 1,500 miles (Pirog and Benjamin 2003). Accurate data on food miles have been difficult to get since then, as the structure of the food distribution system has become less centralized and more complicated (Cockrall-King 2012, 52).

Not only how far food travels, but how it travels, influences its embedded energy and greenhouse gas emissions. Single-occupant automobiles and small trucks transporting small quantities of food to and from the grocery store are the least efficient; large trucks are somewhat better, trains better still, and oceangoing ships the most efficient simply in terms of energy consumed per unit of food (Bomford 2010, 125).

Biofuels

One of the greatest modern threats to food security may be the production of biofuels for cars (Brown 2009, 9). In the US, biofuel often means ethanol, a gasoline extender made from grain, usually corn. One-fourth of the US corn crop is now used to make ethanol, spurred by federal law requiring increases in ethanol production and use (Cimitile 2009).

The rush to the ethanol market has generated new demand for fertilizer, resulting in increased flows of excess nitrogen into the Mississippi River and the Gulf of Mexico, while some farmland has been diverted from soy and wheat to corn production, driving up the prices of grain and meat worldwide. Further, as the price of petroleum rises, the price of grain rises with it, so that grain and petroleum prices have become linked. According to the World Bank, 70 percent of food price increases from 2005 to 2010 were caused by diverting food crops to produce fuel for cars (Brown 2009, 49).

The EU emphasizes the use of biodiesel, rather than ethanol. In order to meet demand, the EU is increasingly turning to palm oil imported from southeast Asia (ibid.). Palm oil demand, in turn, is met by clearing rainforests to make room for oil palm plantations, removing the function of those rainforests as carbon sinks.

Ethanol is a gasoline extender, not a replacement. Driving cars with ethanol gasoline still emits pollutants and still releases greenhouse gases. Whether or not biofuels reduce carbon dioxide emissions depends on what land was used for before it was converted to biofuel production. Converting Midwestern grassland to corn production, for example, results in less carbon storage and increased carbon dioxide released into the air. One study done at Princeton University showed that diverting a soybean field to corn for biofuel resulted in an increase in soy prices, leading farmers in South America to clear more forestland in order to plant soy, thereby losing the carbon sequestration value of the forest. The study showed that this conversion actually doubled the amount of greenhouse gas emissions (Biello 2008). In addition, using biofuels can spur increased use of automobiles, as some drivers believe they are no longer contributing pollution or global warming potential.

Cellulosic ethanol, made from wood, grasses, and non-edible plant parts, is an alternative to corn ethanol. It emits fewer greenhouse gases and results in less deforestation than corn ethanol. Research and development are underway.

Impacts of the Modern Meat Diet

Meat is an agricultural product with a large and multidimensional Ecological Footprint. About 10 percent of the energy an organism gets from its food becomes tissue that organisms at the next trophic level can eat; that is, about 90 percent of the energy at one trophic level is lost to the next trophic level. Thus, the higher one goes up the food chain, the greater a food's Ecological Footprint. Every pound of beef, in fact, requires 20 pounds of grain to produce it (Withgott and Brennan 2009, 155). Numerous analyses have shown that the planet has the capacity to provide an adequate vegetarian diet for 10 billion people, more than the current world population (Cohen 2005, 51). For people who choose to live high on the food chain, however, the planet has the capacity to provide a meat diet for only a small fraction of that number.

The modern meat diet brings with it many stresses on planetary health. One is water consumption. The higher one goes up the food chain, the greater a food's water footprint or virtual water content. Thus, a pound of wheat has a virtual water content of 172 gallons, while a pound of beef has a virtual water content of 1,500 gallons (Kostigen 2010, xi).

A similar pattern applies to land and energy consumption. Grazing and growing animal feed account for 75 percent of all agricultural land (Foley et al. 2011, 338). As demand for meat continues to rise, with the rise in prices that accompanies rising demand, farmers in developing countries are motivated to enter the beef market; much of the large-scale destruction of tropical rainforests is done to make room for cattle. Each calorie of beef requires the input of 16 times more fossil fuel energy and emits 24 times more greenhouse gases than a calorie of vegetables and grains (Withgott and Brennan 2009, 155).

The FAO identifies livestock production as one of the major causes of climate change, land degradation, air and water pollution, and biodiversity loss (FAO 2006a). The FAO reports that livestock farming is a major contributor of methane and nitrous oxide, both with many times the global warming potential of carbon dioxide, with an estimated 18 percent of annual global greenhouse gas emissions attributed to meat and poultry production (ibid.). A 2009 report issued jointly by two World Bank analysts reexamined those data and concluded that livestock and their byproducts in fact account for 51 percent of global greenhouse gas emissions (Goodland and Anhang 2010). The supply chain that produces meat sends more greenhouse gases into the atmosphere than either transportation or industry (Fiala 2015).

Development on Agricultural Land

The conversion of agricultural land to nonfarm uses, primarily urban and suburban development, is another factor with potential to affect both food supply and ecosystem health. Formed from deposits transported by wind and water together with subsequent soil building by inhabitants of its ecosystems, agricultural topsoil develops at an average rate of about one inch of depth every 1,000 years (Wolfe 2001, 171) and is, for practical purposes, a nonrenewable resource.

Historically, it was common for cities to develop either in coastal zones or along floodplains of rivers, locations offering access to water which could be used for transportation and commerce. The rich soils of river floodplains are also prime areas of agricultural productivity. These situations place urban growth at odds with agricultural soil. Land planning to avoid consuming arable land will be critical to the ability of cities to feed their inhabitants in the future (OECD 2012, 20).

Food Waste

Much of the pressure on land, water, air, and climate comes not from food consumed but from food that is wasted. A study by the FAO estimates that about a third of all food produced is lost or wasted (Schutter 2014, 10); other studies suggest the figure is higher (Foley et al. 2011, 339). In developing countries, food loss is due to storage and transportation issues, while in developed countries, food is wasted in retail supply chains or thrown away by consumers. One of the goals of the 2015 UN Sustainable Development Goals (SDGs) is goal 12, "Ensure sustainable consumption and production patterns;" SDG Target 12.3 calls for the world to cut per capita food waste in half by 2030. A global accounting and reporting standard for quantifying food loss and waste, the Food Loss & Waste Protocol, was launched in 2016 for use by countries and organizations. The FLW Protocol was developed by a multi-stakeholder partnership led by WRI that includes FAO; UNEP; WBCSD; CGF, a manufacturers' and retailers' network; WRAP, a waste-prevention organization in the UK; and FUSIONS, a waste-prevention project funded by the EC.

Feeding Ourselves

Food sustains people and communities. Agriculture, the practice of growing food, touches all of us; every person on Earth has a connection to food. Involving learners in growing their own food fosters understanding of the larger, living world and their connection to it. For educators or sustainability professionals looking for ways to reach out to the general public, food can be a positive and engaging vehicle for building socially and economically healthy communities. Community gardens, urban farming, and edible landscapes are part of the transition to community resilience.

Food can be produced on a range of scales, from tiny containers on balconies, to small garden plots, to orchards in city parks, to farms of various sizes. It can be grown in an array of locations throughout a city including yards, parks, schools, utility easements, and street rights-of-way. It can even be grown on rooftops and inner-city vacant lots, where it can help people learn skills for escaping poverty while feeding themselves and others. Sustainable food production supports environmental well-being, economic stability, and social inclusiveness. There is room for all kinds of scales, with food from all kinds of places; resilience depends on diversity and redundancy.

In the years of declining oil supplies, changing climate, and economic contraction that probably lie ahead, the ability of a community to feed its inhabitants will be fundamental to its sustainability. Sustainable approaches to food incorporate familiar themes: they are place-based and local; they are diverse and resilient; they are made of networks of connections; they recycle nutrients; and there is room for everyone.

Local Food, in Season

Locally produced food is a basic component of food security and community resilience. Growing food close to where it will be eaten has many benefits. It sharply cuts greenhouse gas emissions associated with transporting the food. Local farms are small, compared to industrial operations, and typically operated by farmers with detailed knowledge of their land, a knowledge that allows them to produce food in ways that are more sustainable and tied to the ecological processes of a particular place. A new word has entered the modern lexicon: locavore. A locavore is someone who eats primarily locally produced food.

Before the invention of refrigeration and trucking, people had to grow food near where they lived and everyone was a locavore. Centuries ago gardens, farms, and grazing lands were interspersed with houses, commercial areas, and civic spaces. The Industrial Revolution and the subsequent green revolution have gradually separated humans from the sources of their food and food miles, the distance food travels, have grown.

Local food tastes better. Eating locally grown food allows customers to buy flavorful varieties of produce, picked when ripe, which would be too fragile to survive long distance shipping.

People who eat food grown locally eat produce when it is in season; the foods eaten change with the changing seasons. Consumers get to know the bioregions where they live as they become familiar with what foods are in season at which times of year. And since heated greenhouses use even more energy per unit to produce food out of season than field-grown food shipped from far away, eating food in season cuts energy consumption and emissions (Bomford 2010, 124).

Eating local food means greater food security. Food produced on large, far-flung farms is not likely to be reliably available in times of disaster, whether natural or human-made. A local and regional food network with food from a multitude of small- and mid-size farms makes a community less vulnerable to disruptions in food supply caused by natural disasters or political uncertainties.

Food Distribution

Even people who are able to grow their own food cannot grow every food item they need and will not have true food security unless they become part of a local food system with a network of producers and suppliers (Haeg 2010, 31).

Retail stores are sometimes an option; locally owned markets in some regions have been able to set themselves apart by stocking produce grown locally. However, the system of large supermarkets typically assumes access to automobiles and fossil fuel. In the years of energy descent that probably lie ahead, a more resilient food system will depend upon smaller shops and markets, more widely distributed, together with gardens and farmers' markets (O'Hara 2015, 52).

Farmers' markets are venues in public spaces where multiple farmers sell their produce directly. These markets allow customers to buy directly from the farmers who grew their food. Some farmers' markets are located in urban areas where they are accessible to inner-city residents.

Community-supported agriculture (CSA) is another option. Europeans call these services "box schemes" or "subscription farming." Customers buy memberships in a CSA offered by a farm. Farmers then deliver weekly allotments harvested immediately before delivery, bringing them either directly to the customer's door or to a drop-off location. Members pay less for organic produce than they would have paid by buying from a commercial market. However, the quantities and selections are generally fixed. In addition, CSAs are only a possibility for people who can afford to pay for food in advance, a luxury not available to everyone.

Food hubs are collaborative strategies that help make local food markets viable. A food hub is an organization that brings together local and regional food producers, processors, and distributors, actively managing the aggregation, distribution, and marketing of food products (Barham et al. 2012, 4). It gives small- and mid-size farmers access to wholesale and retail markets they might not be able to reach on their own and provides consumers stable, reliable access to local foods. A food hub can operate as a nonprofit organization, a cooperative, or a privately held corporation, or it can be publicly held by a municipality or other agency. Some are virtual food hubs, gathering and transmitting information without a physical facility.

Farming Methods

Sustainable agriculture methods emphasize creating healthy soil and strive to work in harmony with ecological processes. Various farming methods share these goals, including organic, biointensive, and permaculture farming. They can be practiced at a range of scales from large to small. Moving toward resilient food systems requires redundancy and diversity, with the coexistence of diverse farm sizes, landscape types, farming methods, and crop types (Bennett et al. 2014, 72), operating across multiple scales and each fulfilling different functions.

Organic farming is a general term for growing crops using environmentally healthy methods that "conserve soil and water and optimize the health and productivity of interdependent communities of plants, animals and people" (FAO 2011b, 150). Before the middle of the twentieth century and the advent of fertilizer and pesticides, all food was organically grown. The term often describes what it does not do: organic farming does not use synthetic fertilizers, synthetic pesticides, or genetically modified seeds. Other tools are used in place of chemical inputs. Soil fertility is increased by recycling nutrients with manure and compost and by crop rotation. Crop rotation changes the crops grown in a field each season, often by alternating nitrogen-fixing legumes, vegetables, and grains, and by alternating deep-rooted and shallow-rooted plants. Rotating crops prevents soil depletion, maintains soil fertility, breaks cycles of disease, and helps control insects and weeds. Pests are controlled with beneficial insects such as ladybugs and with companion planting, the interplanting of various plants that repel insects. Rather than monocultures, a diversity of crops is grown.

Box 12.2 Polyface Farm

Polyface Farm raises organic beef, sheep, chickens, pigs, rabbits, and turkeys on 550 acres of rolling hills in Virginia's Shenandoah Valley in the US, farmed by Joel Salatin and his family. Polyface is proof that sustainable farming can be profitable. The farm was featured in the best-selling book *The Omnivore's Dilemma* (Pollan 2006) and has received wide media coverage since then. The farm was featured in the 2009 documentary film *Food, Inc.* Salatin spends 100 days each year conducting lectures for colleges, universities, and environmental groups.

Demand for tours has grown so much that space on popular semi-monthly hay wagon tours must be reserved far in advance. Weekly guided group tours are offered for $500. Visitors can also take free self-guided tours; according to Polyface: "Anyone may come anytime Monday through Saturday to see anything anywhere" (Polyface Farms n.d.). The Salatins are eager to encourage organic farming by sharing what they know with everyone, including consumers and other farmers.

Polyface emphasizes healthy soil. Animals are treated humanely and respectfully. Salatin sells only to local customers, and refuses to ship food outside of his local **foodshed**. He encourages people who live more than a 4-hour drive away to find farms in their local communities.

The **biointensive** or French intensive method was developed in the nineteenth century in Paris, where it reliably supplied produce to city residents (Cockrall-King 2012, 82). The method uses a series of raised beds generally 12 inches deep and 3 to 6 feet on a side, with narrow paths between the beds. Soil is dug twice to a depth of two spade blades to create aerated, well-drained soil, and the double-dug soil is enriched with compost. Seeds are planted close together. The beds produce high yields in a small space, producing 4 times the quantity of traditionally managed plots. In a variation sometimes called "square foot gardening," a bed is divided into 1-foot squares with a single crop planted in each square. Using this method, a 4-foot by 4-foot bed can produce much of the food needed by an average family. Raised beds make it easier for people with mobility challenges to grow food.

Agroecology is an interdisciplinary approach that uses ecological principles to guide farm management. This discipline studies interconnections among ecosystems, plant and animal communities modified by humans, and human social and economic systems. Its goal is to manage agricultural crops as ecosystems that are environmentally safe, culturally sensitive, socially just, and economically viable. Agricultural systems are based on principles of nutrient cycling, biodiversity, and predator–prey relationships, combining methods from traditional knowledge, alternative approaches, and scientific research. Approaches can include the use of manure and compost, nitrogen fixers, mycorrhizae, seed saving, crop rotation, intercropping, agroforestry, habitat management, integrated pest management, dry farming, and minimum-till farming (Schutter 2014, 9).

In **no-till farming**, seeds are planted directly into a field that has not been tilled after harvesting the previous crop. One of the pioneers of this approach was plant pathologist and philosopher Masanobu Fukuoka, who advocated a minimalist approach to agroecology in his book *The One-Straw Revolution*. Based on a faith in the wholeness of the natural world and a recognition of the limits of human knowledge, Fukuoka's methods achieved yields as high as those from biointensive beds with his so-called "do-nothing" technique (Fukuoka 1978). No-till farming avoids the release of soil carbon that occurs with cultivation (Brown 2008, 159).

No-till farming is similar to **conservation tillage**, in which at least 30 percent of the crop residues left in place to provide nutrients to soil. Crop residue prevents soil erosion, retains soil moisture essential to the health of soil organisms, and provides food and cover for wildlife.

Conservation agriculture integrates multiple methods, building resilience by simultaneously combining no-till or minimal soil disturbance, permanent soil cover, and crop rotation (FAO 2011b, 149). This synergistic no-till approach improves rainwater infiltration, decreases erosion, increases biodiversity, and builds soil structure.

Agroforestry integrates trees or other woody plants into the agricultural system. Tree intercropping integrates trees with annual or perennial crops and may be in the form of alley cropping, hedgerows, and windbreaks. Silvopasture systems integrate trees with pasture understory for livestock. Homegardens and other multistrata systems in tropical regions can integrate annuals, perennials, and sometimes livestock with trees that provide crops (Toensmeier 2016, 40).

Permaculture is a design strategy based on observing patterns in nature. The term, introduced in 1978, is a combination of the words "permanent" and "agriculture." It is a way of living and growing crops in partnership with self-organizing, interconnected ecosystems using renewable energy and local resources. Permaculture emphasizes the use of perennial plants rather than annuals and avoids disturbing the soil by digging or plowing. Chickens and other animals have a variety of roles to play including nutrient cycling, pest control, and food production and are often part of permaculture farms. A system of design principles has been developed, which are taught through hands-on training courses.

Dry farming is an approach to growing crops without the use of irrigation. Grape growers sometimes choose dry farming because it results in plants with deeper roots and grapes with more concentrated flavor. Tomatoes were dry-farmed for many years in the Napa Valley of California before they were replaced by wine grapes, and dry-farmed tomatoes are again increasingly popular at farmers' markets because of their flavor (Kresge 2009, 9). Some farmers also use dry farming for fruit trees, nuts, melons, squash, and potatoes.

Certification

Certification is used to verify how food was grown. Thorough documentation and independent third-party verification are central components of certification.

The EU has legal standards under which foods can be certified as organically produced. Organic farming methods such as composting, crop rotation, and natural pest control must be used without synthetic inputs; GMO ingredients are prohibited. Organic meat, eggs, and dairy products must come from animals whose lives were as close as possible to their natural way of living. Farms and producers are inspected at least once a year. All foods certified as organic bear a green label with the EU organic logo featuring white stars tracing the outline of a leaf. A related European Action Plan promotes organic farming, animal welfare, research, and education.

In the US, farms can be certified as organic under the USDA's National Organic Certification Standards. Various state and local certifying agencies accredited by the USDA perform audits to verify that organic methods are used. Farms wanting to be certified organic must eliminate synthetic chemicals for 3 years, maintain a 50-foot buffer of land between production areas and possible contamination sources, use crop rotation, use cover crops incorporated into the soil, also known as green manure, maintain detailed records of every input and crop rotation, and be inspected annually.

In addition to the USDA label, organizations in several states have developed their own certification programs accredited by the USDA National Organic Program. California Certified Organic Farmers (CCOF), a trade association of farms, certifies about 80 percent of the organic farmland in California. Oregon Tilth is a similar organization providing education, advocacy, and certification services for farmers and food processors. Pennsylvania Certified Organic is another similar organization that provides education, advocacy, and certification services for farmers and food processors in 10 eastern states.

An agreement between the EU and the US allows products with organic certification under one system to be sold as certified organic under the other system. The US has a similar agreement with Canada. Food certified organic in Canada under Canada Organic Product Regulation (COPR) standards carries a label with the Canada Organic Biologique logo.

The Marine Stewardship Council (MSC) develops certification standards for wild-capture fisheries, with the goal of protecting both the health of the oceans and fishing-related livelihoods. The MSC **eco-label** indicates that the labeled seafood was captured from an MSC-certified sustainable fishery and was segregated from non-certified seafood.

For a fishery to be certified, fishing must be done at a level which ensures that the fish population can continue indefinitely and fishing operations must be environmentally responsible, so that the structure, function, and diversity of the ecosystem are maintained. A traceable chain of custody must be recorded along the entire supply chain as seafood products change hands from fisher to processor to supplier to final sale. Aquaculture Stewardship Council (ASC) certification is similar in structure; the ASC eco-label certifies responsibly farmed seafood.

Food Policy

Urban agriculture is often perceived as a grassroots, bottom-up effort. However, obstacles such as zoning regulations and the difficulty of freeing up public land parcels held by municipalities means that top-down intervention by local authorities is required as well. Among the tasks taken on by some city governments are to expand waste management systems to collect organic material for compost, to provide space for farmers' markets, to find space for food on public land including parks and rights-of-way, to enact ordinances allowing food to be grown in front yards or bees and chickens in backyards, to make community gardens legal in all zones, and to set aside funding for the acquisition of land for gardens.

In order to develop policy changes that support urban agriculture, the first step for a city is to conduct a citywide food assessment. Once existing conditions have been evaluated, the next step is to form a food policy council. A typical council includes members from city and regional government, nonprofit groups, citizens, and farmers. Councils recommend policy changes, such as including fruit and nut trees in lists of allowable street trees and designating city-owned land that can be used for community gardens and orchards, and develop strategies for increasing the amount of food grown on public and private land in the city.[3]

National governments, too, play important policy roles in shifting away from fossil fuels and greenhouse gas emissions. Examples of constructive changes include providing funding for agricultural habitat conservation programs; ending subsidies for fossil fuels, energy for irrigation pumps, dryland cotton production, and corn as biofuel; changing trade policies to favor small-scale, regional farming rather than industrial-scale production for export; restructuring taxes to tax environmentally destructive activities such as effluent discharges and carbon emissions, rather than taxing income; eliminating "use it or lose it" water-use laws; implementing tradable water rights; valuing ecosystem services through water rights, bonuses for habitat protection or reforestation, and other tax incentives for responsible water, soil and habitat conservation; providing tax incentives for agricultural cooperatives and food hubs; providing incentives for military and federal agencies to source some percentage of their food within a local or regional area.

Government leaders can shape public thinking. During World War II, the US government launched its Victory Garden campaign. By 1944, 40 percent of the nation's produce was being grown in backyard and community gardens (Nordahl 2009, 17). Eleanor Roosevelt dug up a large portion of the White House lawn to plant her own Victory Garden. In 2009, Michelle Obama again dug up part of the White House lawn to plant an organic garden as part of her initiative to promote healthy eating; local school classes participate in growing, harvesting, and eating, and food from the garden is used in White House dinners and donated to local homeless shelters.

Box 12.3 Cuba's Carbon-Neutral Food System

What if there were no more fossil fuels? What if there were no commercial fertilizers or pesticides? Could we grow our own food? Before the Industrial Revolution all food was grown without these things. Today, Cuba is proving that it can be done again.

During the Soviet era, Cuba practiced large-scale industrial agriculture like many other parts of the world. Then the Soviet Union collapsed. The robust Eastern bloc export market for agricultural products such as sugar disappeared, as did imports of food and equipment. The US strengthened an already-strict trade embargo, effectively cutting Cuba off from the rest of the world. Without food imports and without access to gasoline, tractor parts, or supplies for farming and daily life, Cubans had to figure out how to feed themselves. The alternative was starvation.

During the earlier era, many Cubans had taken advantage of free university education that was a Soviet priority. Their knowledge was put to work as the Cuban government focused on redesigning the food system as quickly as possible (Murphy and Morgan 2013, 333). Scientists experimented with organic farming methods including building healthy soil with compost and worms, crop rotation, companion planting, and biological pest control. Farmers learned to work their fields with teams of oxen and human labor.

The practice of growing food became decentralized and very local as the scale switched from big and industrial to thousands of small, local pockets. Patches of ground across every city became organic urban farms with farmers' markets and retail farm stands alongside. Ten years in, the capital city of Havana was growing 90 percent of its food this way (Cockrall-King 2012, 287).

Farms are cooperatively owned, although the land is still owned by the state. Farms are required to give a certain quantity of their produce to schools, hospitals, daycare facilities, and senior centers as part of the social contract. Beyond that quantity, all profits from farm stands go to the farmers or are reinvested. Farming pays well, relative to other professions in Cuba. The only job that pays better than farming is in the booming tourism business.

Life is still difficult. People work hard. Political dissent is not tolerated. Certain foods including oil, rice, and coffee, and certain products including soap and toothpaste, are still rationed, and the rations are never enough to meet basic needs.

But Cuba has shown that farming on a small, local scale is effective. And it has demonstrated that it is indeed possible to grow enough food and to eat well when fossil fuels are gone (McKibben 2005).

Finding Space for Food in the City

In the next century the world's population will continue to grow, from 7 billion to over 9 billion by 2050, to over 11 billion by 2100 (US Census Bureau 2015), with all that growth occurring in cities. With increasing numbers comes a growing need for food, at the same time that the passing of peak oil and the exigencies of climate change necessitate changes to our food distribution and long-distance transport systems. We will need to grow more food near where people live. Farming will continue to be needed in rural and peri-urban places, but there are many ways to integrate food production into city life, too. Food can grow wherever there is soil and sun: on rooftops, along sidewalks, in community gardens, at schools and other public institutions, in commercial urban farms, in parks and along city greenways. A farm is simply a piece of land used for growing food. As food production becomes integrated into city life, not every "farm" looks like a traditional farm.

Fast-Food Food Deserts

Food security is defined as having access to nutritionally adequate, safe, affordable, and culturally acceptable food on a daily basis. People in low-income urban neighborhoods are particularly at risk because they may not have access to healthy food; these impoverished areas are known as "food deserts." In a practice known as red-lining, grocery stores avoid locating in areas where profits are low and crime risk is high (Viljoen 2005, 58). Markets and convenience stores that do remain in inner cities tend to charge higher prices for the food they carry, so people on limited incomes often pay more for their food than more affluent shoppers in higher-income neighborhoods. Many inner-city residents do not own cars; their neighborhoods may be transit deserts as well as food deserts, so travel to suburban super-markets where they could get healthy food requires time-consuming and difficult bus trips. For people with disabilities, small children, or more than one job, getting nutritious food is a hardship. While hunger is a symptom of food insecurity, obesity is a symptom of food insecurity, as well. Inner city neighborhoods without grocery stores are still likely to have inexpensive fast-food restaurants and convenience stores selling high-fat snack food, often the only foods available in such areas.

Strategies for providing fresh and healthy food include community gardens and food grown in public spaces. Food can be grown wherever there is soil. In addition to farms on rural agricultural land, food production can be located in almost any space in a community or city. Plots can take any shape and be nearly any size. Finding space for food in urban settings is a way to provide multiple social and economic benefits.

Food at School

School grounds are popular places to grow food. Gardens are sensory, multidimensional places that support learning. While growing food, students learn about ecological cycles and the basics of where food comes from, how to grow it, and how to prepare and eat it. They develop an appreciation for the experience of fresh, whole food at an age when lifetime food preferences are being established.

Alice Waters, award-winning chef and owner of the Chez Panisse Restaurant, promotes edible educational gardens. Waters founded the Edible Schoolyard (ESY), a 1-acre garden and kitchen classroom at Martin Luther King, Jr. Middle School in Berkeley, California, which has inspired hundreds of similar programs around the country (Nordahl 2009, 130).

Farm to School is a US network of programs connecting schools with local farms. Fresh produce from these farms is used in school meals and educational activities. Each program is unique to its own community and region (Stone 2009, 41). In a typical program, students learn about planting gardens, composting, and what grows on local farms; they might also visit local farms and talk to farmers.

Food at Home

The concept of edible landscapes is a trend that encourages homeowners to replace monoculture front lawns with food, with a goal of creating gardens that are not only edible but also aesthetically appealing (Creasy 2010; Haeg et al. 2010). Edible landscape designers use food plants as primary design materials, just as they would use ornamental plants. Landscape structure can be provided by fruit and nut trees, grape vines can grow on arbors and trellises in place of wisteria, as can hardy varieties of kiwi and passion fruit vines, and raised beds can provide seating and easy access. Wild strawberry and thyme can provide low-maintenance ground covers while fennel and asparagus can provide lacy textures similar to ornamental grasses. Artichoke plants, rhubarb, and leafy greens such as chard, kale, and cabbage can provide dramatic forms, while other plants provide background.

Rooftops and Walls

Another option is rooftop gardens. Many city dwellers grow vegetables in pots on top of roofs. Some organizations convert whole roofs to urban farms. For full rooftop gardens, investigation by a structural engineer is required to be sure the roof can support additional load.

In Brooklyn, New York, the Eagle Street Rooftop Farm atop a 3-story warehouse includes chickens, bees, and drip-irrigated vegetables, and sells eggs, honey, and produce at a weekly farmer's market. A commercial-scale Gotham Greens greenhouse above a Whole Foods market in Brooklyn grows organic produce year round, sold in Whole Foods stores across New York City. Brooklyn Grange, another commercial organic farming business, operates a 1-acre intensive green-roof farm on its building in Queens, from which it sells its herbs, vegetables, and fruits to local restaurants and residents. The Rooftop Victory Garden above True Nature Foods in Chicago supplies produce sold in the food cooperative below. Rooftop gardens, apple trees, and apiaries at the Fairmont Hotels in Vancouver, British Columbia and Toronto, Ontario provide herbs, fruit, and honey to the hotels' restaurants.

Urban beekeeping on rooftops provides honey along with the essential pollination services provided by bees. Bees from Brooklyn's Eagle Street Rooftop Farm and Canada's Fairmont Hotels produce honey of different flavors at different times of year, depending upon what is in bloom within a 3-mile radius. The former mayor of Chicago ordered a colony of 200,000 bees for the roof of the Chicago City Hall; profits from honey sales are used to help support free public programs (Johnson 2010, 102). Bees in London produce more honey per capita than any other city. London is closely followed by Paris, where pesticides have been outlawed since 2000; Paris has become a refuge for bees while their populations continue to decline in the countryside (Cockrall-King 2012, 102).

Food gardens can grow vertically as well as horizontally. Fruit trees can be pruned and trained to grow flat against a wall or trellis, a practice known as *espalier* in Renaissance Europe and used as a way to conserve space in confined areas. Vines can be rooted in soil and trained to grow up flat screens or trellises. Another approach known as edible walls uses panels of metal slats welded to form a series of cells. The cells are filled with soil, planted with seeds, and hung from a structural wall as a vertical planter. Small holes in the slats allow roots to migrate between cells and drip irrigation provides moisture. A project known as the Urban Farming Food Chain, planted at 4 locations in the Skid Row area of downtown Los Angeles, uses this vertical planter approach; in one of the locations residents at an adjacent homeless shelter tend the crops, eating some of the produce and selling the rest (Belson 2009).

Urban Agriculture

Urban agriculture is the growing of plants or the raising of animals within and around cities and towns and can be practiced by commercial farmers, community gardeners, or backyard gardeners. Food can be grown in school programs and in therapeutic settings such as hospitals, drug treatment facilities, and long-term care facilities.

One successful example is Greensgrow Farm in Philadelphia, a commercial urban farm on the site of a former abandoned steel plant remediated by the EPA in the 1990s. In addition to supplying fresh produce to restaurants and CSA subscribers, Greensgrow runs a farm stand with honey from their apiary, plants and cut flowers from their year-round nursery, and local food products sourced from nearby. Working to build a local network, they have become a food hub offering an outlet for local jams, cheeses, breads, and pasture-raised meat, which they collect in trucks run on biodiesel made from waste grease from their restaurant clients (Rich 2012, 58).

Community Gardens

A garden is a way to bring not only food security but also social cohesion, community regeneration, new skills, and self-confidence to people living in a city. A community garden is any piece of land gardened by a group of people. The land may be owned by a city, a land trust, a community group, or a private owner. Some community gardens are large lots of land that have been divided into smaller private plots for each household's use. In Europe, such gardens are called allotments.

Some cities take an active role in promoting community gardens. The Comprehensive Plan for the City of Seattle, Washington, for example, mandates that at least one dedicated community garden be established for every 2,500 households and Seattle's P-Patch program, part of the city's Department of Neighborhoods, provides city-owned gardening space to households across the city.

Other community gardens are managed for and by local community groups. Sometimes groups do not own the land they use for growing food. Often perched on leftover bits of land or vacant lots, their existence can be precarious.

New York City is known for its thriving community gardens, planted by residents across the city and originally made possible by short-term leases with city agencies. In 1999, then-Mayor Rudolph Giuliani announced plans to sell 114 parcels of vacant city-owned land to help fund budget shortfalls. At the last minute entertainer Bette Midler, her nonprofit group New York Restoration Project, and the Trust for Public Land rallied and raised money to save these plots from destruction and they are now designated as public community gardens in perpetuity (Thompson 2000, 56). Renowned landscape architects from around the country have donated their design services for many of New York City's community gardens.

In the city of Detroit, Michigan, struggling with loss of jobs and a declining population, about 30 percent of land within the city is vacant (Nordahl 2009, 61). Community groups have been actively converting so many of these vacant lots into gardens that Detroit is often held up as an exemplar of successful community gardening.

The Peralta and Northside Community Gardens in Berkeley, California are perched over the opening of a Bay Area Rapid Transit (BART) tunnel, where the city leases the once debris-strewn lots from BART. Developed by landscape architect and Holocaust survivor Karl Linn, the gardens are intended not only to grow food but also to bring neighbors together and to foster a spirit of community. In addition to vegetable beds, the gardens include trellises and a circular commons formed by mosaic-covered benches. Linn says: "We're not only growing crops; we're growing community" (Thompson 2000, 53; Claessens 2000).

Food on Public Land

Planting community gardens on vacant city lots has value as a temporary measure, but urban land is high-value and gardens cannot compete with development investments in a real estate market. A more permanent solution is to take advantage of publicly owned bits of land. Public spaces for producing food can be woven throughout the urban fabric as part of fostering a self-sufficient local economy. The city itself is generally the largest single landowner, so the cooperation of municipal government is essential. Some people view access to safe, low-cost food as a service that could be provided to citizens in the same way as access to clean drinking water, protection from crime and natural disaster, and garbage collection. Many cities provide space for community gardens on public land.

One of the obvious locations of public land is city parks. For example, the Dr. George Washington Carver Edible Park in Ashville, North Carolina is a public orchard with 40 varieties of fruits and nuts planted on a former landfill which has become city park land. In Seattle, Washington, more than 30 city parks contain fruit trees, often remnants of former orchards, where volunteer orchard stewards harvest fruit and provide maintenance through a public-private collaboration with City Fruit, a nonprofit organization. The City of Seattle's 7-acre Beacon Food Forest provides a mix of fruit and nut trees, berries, and garden vegetables. Gleaning and foraging are free, and eat-all-you-need areas of the garden are open to everyone. Spaces for personal garden patches are also available. A **food forest** is a small-scale form of agroforestry in a multi-story combination of food-bearing trees, shrubs, perennials, and annuals. In the permaculture movement these edible forest gardens are known as food forests; in the tropics they are known as homegardens (Toensmeier 2016, 42).

Underutilized public spaces that could be used to grow food are everywhere. Patches of open ground can be found in schoolyards, around libraries and hospitals, in downtown plazas, in borders and planting islands within parking lots. Utility easements and transportation easements are additional strips of open ground that cannot be built on where food can be grown. In some cities, steep slopes and floodplain areas along rivers cannot be built on but are good places for food gardens.

Roadsides, planting strips along street rights-of-way, and landscape beds in medians constitute the most extensive network of public land in a city. All of these public spaces are woven through places where people live, work, shop, and play, so they offer opportunities to integrate food sources with community cohesion. Most US cities prohibit fruit-bearing trees in public rights-of-way, but some cities are changing policy to make public food possible in these places. For example, Drake Park in Des Moines, Iowa has an orchard with 33 fruit trees, with plans for grape arbors, streetside fruit and nut trees, and raised beds along streets adjoining the park.

A land trust is a mechanism often used in conservation for acquiring and holding land in order to protect it. The Trust for Public Land and The Nature Conservancy are two of the largest and best-known. Land trusts can also be used to support urban agriculture, buying land that is then deeded to community groups. One successful example is NeighborSpace, an intergovernmental partnership in Chicago, Illinois.

Foraging and Gleaning

Gleaning is the practice of gathering food from leftover crops in farmers' fields. Some farms advertise gleaning opportunities to nearby communities. In some areas near agricultural regions, local food banks have gleaning arrangements with farmers. Accepting handouts from food banks can feel humiliating to some people, while gleaning carries with it a feeling of self-sufficiency. However, taking the time and energy needed to work in a gleaning program is often difficult for people with limited incomes, who often have no childcare and may work more than one job, and gleaning takes place only during a brief interval at the end of a commercial harvest. The ability to forage provides a more durable source of food.

Foraging means simply looking for food. As more food is grown in public spaces, more opportunities for foraging appear. Foraging is common in the city of Berkeley, California, for example, where fruit and nut trees line many neighborhood streets. Because they are planted in strips between sidewalks and streets, the trees are growing in publicly owned rights-of-way and are public property. In many cities, fruits from plants that grow on private property but overhang a public space are also considered public property.

Foraging may be done by design. Village Homes, a residential development in Davis, California built in the 1970s and 1980s, was designed to include communal open space. In addition to offering individual plots in community gardens, fruit orchards, nut orchards, and vineyards are found throughout the community. All fruit and nuts are free except almonds, which are harvested as a cash crop.

The nonprofit organization Philadelphia Orchard Project, with support from the city, works to establish public orchards in schoolyards, community gardens, and other open spaces in low-income neighborhoods (McLain et al. 2014, 236). Residents in community organizations plant, care for, and harvest the fruit orchards, and the Philadelphia Orchard Project provides plants, technical assistance, and training in orchard care.

Nonprofit groups in some cities offer programs to match people with food. Fallen Fruit in Los Angeles, California began by creating maps of fruit trees growing on or hanging over public property in the city. The operation has expanded to include harvesting parties and communal jam-making. In addition to producing maps for neighborhoods to which they are invited in Los Angeles and surrounding areas, they now offer maps from several cities around the world.

Urban Edibles and the Portland Fruit Tree Project, both in Portland, Oregon, ask foragers and landowners to submit sites where fruit trees or other foods might be growing but not harvested. Urban Edibles offers maps and a database where residents can search by neighborhood or by type of plant. Portland Fruit offers a Fruit Tree Registry with maps showing locations of trees whose owners want to share their harvests. Harvesting parties arranged by Portland Fruit connect people who need help harvesting their trees with volunteers who will pick fruit; half the fruit goes to the pickers and half goes to local food banks. The Vancouver Fruit Tree Project offers a similar service in Vancouver, British Columbia.

Organizations in several cities offer programs matching landless gardeners with landowners willing to share space. Urban Garden Share is a service that matches homeowners with garden space to gardeners with experience in several regions of the US. Sharing Backyards in Greater Vancouver is a program from City Farmer, a nonprofit organization in British Columbia. A map of Vancouver shows locations of people looking for space to garden and those offering garden space to share. Landshare connects growers to people with land to share in the United Kingdom; Landshare Canada does the same across Canada.

Sustainability: Environment, Economy, and Equity

Food advocates and urban agriculture specialists emphasize the role that the growing of food plays in building strong, thriving communities with social equity and economic opportunity for everyone. One of the primary achievements of the community garden movement has been the economic and social opportunities that the growing of food can create in urban areas with low economic opportunity. These are examples of sustainability's triple bottom line in action.

Box 12.4 Food From the 'Hood and the Watts Garden Club

Food From the 'Hood (FFTH) is a student-managed nonprofit organization that arose in response to the 1992 Rodney King riots in South Central Los Angeles, California (CERT 2013). Students from Crenshaw High School, wanting to rebuild their community, transformed an abandoned lot behind the school into a 2-acre fruit and vegetable garden. They began by donating a quarter of what they grew to people in need and selling the rest for a profit. As the project grew the students, with help from local businesses, developed a line of salad dressings which they now market nationwide. Fifty percent of the profits are returned to the organization and 50 percent are awarded as scholarships to student managers. The students have generated thousands of dollars in scholarships while gaining life skills, work-based skills, and practical business experience.

The ideas that led to the Watts Garden Club in South Central Los Angeles, founded by master gardener Anna-Marie Carter known locally as The Seed Lady, also grew out of the 1992 riots (Carter 2003). The garden itself was finally launched in 2002 with the goal of transforming Watts, with its reputation as an impoverished, gang- and drug-infested area, to a place where children and families could help themselves and each other. When the Garden Club began, Carter told an interviewer: "The police say, 'I can't believe you got that kid over there planting flowers. Do you know about that kid?' I say, 'I know he's planting flowers'" (Hope Takes Root 2004). Now hundreds of children and adult volunteers grow food, build gardens for local housing projects, conduct training classes for other neighborhoods, deliver organic food to low-income neighborhood grandmothers who feed and care for grandchildren, operate an heirloom seed bank, sell organic foods and herbal products, and study marketing (Carter 2005, 364). Money raised by young gardeners is put into a fund; once they are 18 years old, participants can receive a cash grant to help them start their own business or go to school. Carter says: "They're learning life skills under the guise of growing a garden."

Healthy Soil: The Vital Foundation

The astronaut John Glenn was once asked what he thought would be the most essential piece of equipment to take when colonizing a planet. "Soil," he replied (Williams 2007, 33). Soil, the living skin of the planet, is far more than powdered rock. It is a complex ecosystem, a web of vast numbers of living beings, air, water, and mineral grains. Soil and its multitudes of inhabitants filter and cleanse stormwater, store rainwater, and minimize runoff. Water, oxygen, and carbon dioxide constantly move into and out of soil. Soil is an essential component of the global carbon and nitrogen cycles; the powerhouse for decomposition, storage, and release of nutrients; and a major storage compartment for carbon sequestration. Organic farmers express the fundamental importance of soil by saying, "grow soil, not plants." Soil makes plant growth possible and is the essential foundation of every food system.

Soil begins as solid rock, gradually broken apart by weathering. Cracks form and widen through cycles of expansion and contraction, freezing and thawing, impact of raindrops, sandblasting by wind, carbon dioxide in rainwater, acids produced by lichens, and tiny rootlets from mosses. Loosened particles are moved and deposited by flowing water, ice, and wind. Pioneer microbes, fungi, plants, and animals begin to colonize the particles. As they die and decompose, their remains add organic matter, which is consumed and recycled many times. Eventually humus forms, a dark, gelatinous material made of tiny bits of hard-to-digest organic matter including resins and lignins from plants and the remains of bacteria and fungi. Tiny animals burrow through soil, defecating and opening new spaces between particles as they go. Roots and tiny root hairs twine through soil, breaking down minerals and exuding sticky compounds that act like glue.

Organic matter is ingested, modified, and excreted multiple times as it cycles through the food web, and many particles that appear to be soil are actually fecal pellets from arthropods or earthworms. These fecal pellets are highly concentrated sources of nutrients, important to many bacteria and fungi. One creature's waste is another creature's food, and nothing is wasted.

Soil is a renewable resource that forms continuously. However, it forms very slowly. Rates of soil formation vary, but on average new soil forms at a rate of 4 thousandths of an inch per year. It takes from 200 to 1,000 years for 1 inch of topsoil to form (Wolfe 2001, 171).

Soil forms at an interface between realms, with atmosphere above it and lithosphere below it. The upper layers of soil, the plant and animal communities that grow from it, and the ecosystems within it constitute the thin layer of life that is the planet's skin, the biosphere. The layers of soil within the soil's profile form gradual layers along a gradient, expressing the transition from lithosphere to biosphere.

In most places, more life and diversity are found in the soil beneath our feet than above the surface. Just a teaspoon of topsoil contains from 100 million to 1 billion bacteria and around 10,000 different species of microbes (Soil and Water Conservation Society 2000, 18). The biomass of the bacteria in an acre of soil is equivalent to the mass of two average size cows (ibid.). A teaspoon of farm soil holds several thousand protozoa, 10 to 20 nematodes, and several yards of fungal threads, while a teaspoon of forest soil holds several hundred thousand protozoa, several hundred nematodes, and up to 40 miles of fungal threads. A square foot of farm soil contains up to 100 arthropods and 30 earthworms, while a square foot of forest soil contains up to 25,000 arthropods and 50 earthworms. More creatures live in a single handful of typical healthy soil than there are humans on the entire planet (Wolfe 2001, 1).

Soil ecosystems provide many kinds of niches for the creatures who live in them. Each type of organism finds niches where the amounts of air, moisture, and nutrients are just right for their way of life. Soil organisms live wherever organic matter exists. Populations are especially concentrated in the rich microhabitats around roots, known as the rhizosphere. These zones are dense with microscopic fungi, rich in sugars exuded by plant roots, teeming with bacteria who feed on the sugars and the decomposing root hairs, and filled with roaming protozoa and nematodes who graze on the bacteria.

The most essential organisms in the soil are the smallest ones, the bacteria. Without their recycling of organic materials, dead plant matter would pile up and smother the planet in layers of litter several miles deep. Without their unique ability to transform inert nitrogen into an accessible form, living plants would starve for lack of nitrogen. Without their ability to chemically transform other chemicals including carbon, iron, and sulfur, Earth's biogeochemical cycling of elements would come to a halt.

Fungi, along with bacteria, are also important decomposers, breaking down dead material and converting it back to nutrients. Microscopic filaments of fungi, called hyphae, bind tiny soil particles together into larger aggregates, improving both drainage and water-holding ability. Fungi and plant roots form essential symbiotic relationships known as mycorrhizae.

Earthworms are the soil's cultivators. In healthy soil, earthworms turn over the entire top 6 inches of soil every 10 to 20 years (Soil and Water Conservation Society 2000, 43).

As earthworms burrow in search of food and mates, they allow oxygen to enter the soil and create channels down which water can infiltrate and roots can grow. They tunnel to the surface and select freshly fallen plant litter, pull it back into their burrows to eat, then excrete nutrient-rich fecal matter known as castings. Worm castings become habitats for microbes and small arthropods, who further break down organic material.

Maintaining Healthy Soil

Soil on a site is an ecosystem. Thus taking care of the soil is essentially the practice of ecosystem conservation or ecosystem restoration, except that the system in question is underground. Keeping the ecosystem healthy means (1) not doing anything that would harm it, such as depriving it of water or poisoning its inhabitants with pesticides, and (2) doing things that maintain or improve its natural functions.

Compost is a universal maintenance and restoration tool that works on every site, in every situation. Compost is plant matter that has been converted to humus through the recycling work of organisms. Like humus on the forest floor or prairie, it is full of microbial and animal life. It absorbs water, provides minerals and other nutrients, and enriches soil ecosystems with the populations of creatures living within it. Compost improves soil structure and helps clay soils drain, loosening compacted soil particles so that air and water can move through. It helps sandy soils hold water, forming coherent clumps in loose soil particles and reducing risk of erosion.

On many commercial and institutional sites compost is applied in the form of compost tea, made by moving water through high-quality compost. Beneficial organisms are coaxed off the compost where they are living and into the water, which can then be applied to soil. Compost tea has a short shelf life, and must be used within two hours of its production.

Peat moss, dug from wetlands, and coir, from coconut palms, are sold as soil amendments. While they do improve soil structure, drainage, and water-holding ability, neither one contributes much in the way of nutrients or organisms. In addition, unlike locally produced compost, peat moss and coir must be shipped long distances and contain **embodied energy**. Embodied energy is the energy that is required to produce, transport, and dispose of a product.

Mulch is the other tool, in addition to compost, which can be used on every soil. Mulch is a layer of organic material spread over the surface of soil, typically in a layer 1 to 4 inches thick. The difference between a mulch and a soil amendment such as compost is that mulch is meant to remain on top of the soil, and soil amendments are worked into the soil. Often the same materials are used for both purposes. Mulch helps prevent loss of surface moisture and helps the root zone remain cool and moist. It suppresses weed growth and makes weeds that do sprout easier to pull out manually. A layer of organic material applied as mulch is frequently used to prevent soil erosion. As the mulch material decomposes it enriches the soil below with additional organic matter. Choices for mulch material include leaves, straw, and wood chips.

The two greatest threats to healthy soil are erosion and compaction. **Erosion** is a process in which soil is carried away by wind and water. The upper layer of topsoil, which is always the first to be eroded, is also where the majority of soil organisms and soil nutrients are found, so erosion leads to depleted soil quality as well as soil loss, sedimentation and pollution of streams, and increased flooding. Soil is a significant carbon sink, and soils can lose 75 to 80 percent of their carbon content when they are eroded (Ackerman-Leist 2013, 73).

Compaction is a process in which particles of soil are pushed together and the pore spaces between them are reduced in size or closed off. It can result from repeated foot traffic, vehicles, or the storage of heavy materials. Once soils are compacted, it may be impossible to restore their structure within a time span meaningful to humans. Compaction has a big effect on soil ecology. Bacteria, protozoa, and nematodes live in the nooks and crannies of soil pores. In compacted soils, those porous habitats are destroyed, leaving inadequate room for nutrient cycling to take place. As soil becomes more poorly drained, conditions become anaerobic, fatal to the majority of soil creatures who need oxygen to live.

Preventing soil compaction on a construction site often involves a written soil protection plan. Every construction project should also include a written tree protection plan, which specifies no vehicle traffic or parking, storage of building materials, stockpiling of soil, digging or trenching within an area known as the **critical root zone** (CRZ) or tree protection zone.

Soil is a large reservoir of carbon. It stores about twice as much carbon as does the atmosphere, and about 3 times as much as is contained in vegetation (Flannery 2010, 263). Work to stabilize global climate could be simplified to three primary approaches: stop using fossil fuels; cover as much of the Earth's surface as possible with plants; and protect ecosystems in healthy soil to allow them to sequester carbon in the form of decomposed plant material. As often happens with sustainability, the solutions are interconnected. Strategies that promote carbon sequestration in soils are the same strategies that protect soil from erosion, promote healthy plants, and nurture productive crops.

Soil Restoration

In some situations a site may have already been disturbed; soil erosion, compaction, or removal may have already occurred; and it may be too late for soil protection. In such cases it will be necessary to help the soil come back to health as a working ecosystem. In all but the most severe cases it is almost always better to restore and rebuild whatever soil remains on site rather than importing soil from somewhere else. A soil that has been damaged has in effect regressed to an earlier stage in the soil-formation life cycle. The goal of restoration is to re-establish conditions that allow the soil ecosystem to evolve once more.

The most effective method is to apply locally produced compost. If soil is too sandy, compost helps it hold water; if soil has too much clay content, compost helps water drain. Organic matter and bacteria are the two most critical elements to soil health, and compost, which is decomposed plant material, supplies both.

Conclusion

In spite of pressure from growing populations, we have enough land and resources to feed a healthy diet to every person on the planet (Meadows et al. 2004, 63). What we do not have is enough land and resources to absorb current levels of pollution or to allow all of us to live on meat-rich diets. Our food supplies face threats from changing climate, water shortages, soil loss, and diversion of land to produce grain for animal feed and biofuels. Likely solutions lie in stabilizing climate and population, protecting aquifers and soils, letting go of dependence on fossil fuels, eating lower down the food chain, and producing most of our food in our own communities using biosphere-friendly organic methods. Maintaining a sustainable food supply depends upon the basics: healthy soil, clean water, biodiversity, social equity, local technology, and community resilience.

Notes

1 The word "human" generally refers to the species *Homo sapiens*. Other species of hominids, mates who walked on two legs, were also hunter-gatherers. Some of these species lived severai million years ago.
2 Unlike nitrogen, phosphorus does not circulate in the atmosphere.
3 See, for example, the Providence Urban Agriculture Task Force in Providence, Rhode Island, and the Portland/Multnomah Food Policy Council in Portland, Oregon.

Further Reading

Ackerman-Leist, Philip. *Rebuilding the Foodshed: How to Create Local, Sustainable, and Secure Food Systems*. White River Junction, VT: Chelsea Green, 2013.

Haeg, Fritz, Will Allen, and Diana Balmori. *Edible Estates: Attack on the Front Lawn*. 2nd ed. New York: Metropolis Books, 2010.

Nordahl, Darrin. *Public Produce: The New Urban Agriculture*. Washington, DC: Island Press, 2009.

Pollan, Michael. *The Omnivore's Dilemma*. New York: Penguin Publishing, 2006.

Wolfe, David W. *Tales from the Underground: A Natural History of Subterranean Life*. New York: Basic Books, 2001.

Worldwatch Institute. *State of the World 2011: Innovations that Nourish the Planet*. Washington, DC: Worldwatch Institute, 2011.

Chapter Review

1 When did humans begin to change from hunting and gathering to agriculture, and what major social changes happened as a result?
2 What were the major elements of the green revolution? Why were they significant?
3 What are the differences between a large farm and an agribusiness?
4 What sustainability issues are associated with CAFOs?
5 How has the industrial fixation of nitrogen in the process of manufacturing fertilizer affected the nitrogen cycle?
6 How is genetic engineering similar to conventional plant breeding? How does it differ?
7 Describe some of the strategies used in organic farming. Then develop a definition of organic farming that is as succinct as possible.
8 What is food security?
9 Describe what is meant by a food desert. Why haven't supermarket chains fixed this problem?
10 Describe some of the benefits of eating locally grown food.
11 What is the difference between foraging and gleaning?
12 What are some of the benefits of school gardens?
13 How do community gardens relate to sustainability's triple bottom line?

Critical Thinking and Discussion

1 What benefits and what negative impacts were associated with the green revolution?
2 Discuss some advantages and disadvantages of fertilizer.
3 How do fossil fuels connect to food security?
4 Corn is the dominant field crop produced in the US. What are the benefits and problems associated with this crop?
5 Why does eating meat carry more adverse environmental impacts than eating grains, nuts, vegetables, and fruits?

6 How does high consumption of meat in some parts of the world contribute to scarcity of food in other parts of the world?

7 If you chose to eat primarily foods produced locally, but allowed yourself a few crops that must be imported long distances, which ones would you choose?

8 List some disadvantages of genetically modified organisms (GMOs). Are there advantages? What are they?

9 Locally grown foods have many benefits. What disadvantages, if any, can you foresee as communities become increasingly dependent upon local foods?

10 How does biofuel affect food security?

11 In what ways does food security relate to social equity?

12 For people who are meat-eaters, do you think it would be preferable to buy meat from a store, eat homegrown animals, or hunt wild animals?

13 What elements would you include in a program for food stewardship and food production in your local K-12 school district?

14 Think about the total time required to prepare a good meal at home versus the total time required to get a meal at a restaurant. Which one takes less time? What factors affect your answer?

15 Some people say that preparing a meal at home costs less than buying an equivalent meal in a restaurant. Others say the opposite is true, because a restaurant already has spices and auxiliary ingredients in stock, while a home chef may have to buy full packages of each. What factors determine whether a meal at home or a restaurant meal will have lower cost?

16 Compare local, conventionally grown food and organically grown food shipped from elsewhere. List the relative advantages and disadvantages of each.

17 Why does eating a vegetarian diet result in a smaller carbon footprint that a beef-based diet?

18 If everyone ate a vegetarian diet, how would that affect the number of humans that the planet could support?

19 List some of the personal, local, and global benefits and negative impacts that would result if everyone began eating only locally grown food.

13 Products

Matter on planet Earth is distributed within four major systems, or spheres: the atmosphere, biosphere, hydrosphere, and lithosphere. Modern manufacturing of products gets most of its materials from the lithosphere in the form of fossil fuels, stone, and metals, which are mixed and recombined, sometimes becoming toxic. The materials are used briefly and then spread out across the planet in small amounts where they cannot be retrieved.

Materials from the lithosphere are nonrenewable resources, which means there is no sustainable rate of consumption. In the US, 95 percent of the materials flowing through the industrial economy are nonrenewable; in China, the share is 88 percent (Worldwatch Institute 2013, 100). Consumption of these nonrenewable resources is accelerating exponentially as a result of the dual pressures of rising populations and growing affluence in China, India, and other developing countries. Their use is part of a complex picture in which products commonly seen as environmentally friendly have negative tradeoffs.[1] Platinum, a rare metal, is a vital component not only of catalytic converters that reduce pollutants from car exhausts but also of fuel cells. Solar cells can replace fossil-fuel power sources, and smartphones and computers can reduce the number of automobile miles driven by connecting people and businesses virtually instead of physically, but their manufacture requires rare metals including gallium and indium. Rare earth elements, 97 percent of which are produced in one country, China, are essential in climate-friendlier devices including neodymium used in wind turbines and dysprosium used in batteries for hybrid and electric cars (Worldwatch Institute 2013, 99). Not only are nonrenewable stores of these and other minerals being rapidly exhausted, but as ore deposits are depleted the amount of energy and water required to extract each unit of ore rises (Heinberg 2011, 144).

A concept called **Factor 4** was first introduced in the book *Factor Four: Doubling Wealth, Halving Resource Use* (von Weiszäcker 1997), which proposed that humans must rapidly reduce their consumption of resources to one-fourth of the current levels in order not to exceed the planet's carrying capacity. A parallel concept known as **Factor 10** subsequently proposed by Friedrich Schmidt-Bleek of the German Wuppertal Institute for Climate, Environment and Energy said that humans must reduce their consumption of resources to one-tenth the current levels within a few decades in order to be sustainable (Schmidt-Bleek 1998). Several committees within the EU are developing policies to implement Factor 10 (Kibert 2012, 52). Dematerializing the world's economies will require both governmental policy change and changes to industrial products and processes. Manufacturers have a fundamental role in reconfiguring human impact, as Paul Hawken noted years ago: "Business is the only mechanism on the planet today powerful enough to produce the changes necessary to reverse global environmental and social degradation" (Hawken 1992).

Toward a Circular Economy

Cradle to Cradle Design

The standard approach to product life cycle is sometimes referred to as cradle to grave, with materials and resources following a one-way trip from production to disposal. A different approach, an economy of "replenishing loops," was outlined in 1982 by Walter Stahel (Stahel 1982), a Swiss architect who first used the term "cradle to cradle." Twenty years later architect William McDonough and chemist Michael Braungart challenged the usual eco-efficiency approach to design thinking in their seminal book *Cradle to Cradle*. They pointed out that being less bad is still bad. Being less bad means that resources are still depleted and toxins still accumulate; they just do so gradually and quietly. They proposed an alternative approach based on nature's model in which waste equals food, with waste at one level becoming a nutrient at another level (McDonough and Braungart 2002).

Cradle to cradle design identifies two separate metabolisms, biological and technical, in which nutrients recycle continually. Biological nutrients are made of materials designed to return to the biosphere; they biodegrade and become food within biological cycles. The corn-based compostable fabric used in the Mirra chair is a biological nutrient. While it is possible to design packaging, shoes, clothing, and cleaning products as biological nutrients, some materials that appear to be biological nutrients may not be. For example, wool fabric treated with fire retardants could not be mixed into the biological cycle.

Technical nutrients are materials that will not biodegrade or become part of any ecosystem. They remain within closed-loop technical cycles, circulating within industry and not allowed to contaminate biological systems. Technical nutrients are durable substances for which the manufacturer is responsible. When a product has reached the end of its useful life it is returned to the manufacturer for disassembly and reuse. The plastic used in the Mirra chair is a technical nutrient. The fiber in Interface carpet tiles is a technical nutrient.

Toxic and hazardous substances, also known as X ingredients, are categorized as unmarketable; these are substances which should never be used. They include persistent organic pollutants, heavy metals, and PVC (ibid., 116, 174).

Manufacturers can apply for Cradle to Cradle (C2C) certification for products. In a certification audit, materials and manufacturing processes for a product are assessed in each of five categories: material health, material reutilization, renewable energy use, water stewardship, and social responsibility. A product can receive C2C basic certification or can be certified as C2C Silver, C2C Gold, or C2C Platinum. Similar to LEED certification, points are awarded with higher numbers of points required for successively higher categories. While the C2C certification process provides intensive technical support and expert advice to manufacturers, the certification audit itself has not yet achieved third-party status; C2C is a proprietary program from the private company of McDonough Braungart Design Chemistry (MBDC) (Atlee and Roberts 2007, 14).

Circular Economy

Cradle-to-cradle design is an example of an approach to the industrial economy known as the circular economy. The circular-economy concept is modeled on nature, where waste from one process becomes food for another, often summarized "waste equals food." Each part of the system is connected to other parts in closed loops and waste is designed out of the system entirely so that the system can function in the long term. The circular economy is envisioned to be not just "less bad" but restorative by relying on renewable energy, eliminating the use of toxic chemicals, and avoiding waste by design through the use of technical and biological nutrient cycles (Ellen MacArthur Foundation). Reports from the Ellen MacArthur Foundation (EMF), whose mission is the transition to a circular economy, have described why even practices such as recycling lead to downcycling and are not enough, establishing a framework that goes beyond simply recycling toward closed-loop, circular production systems.

In 2012 participants at the World Economic Forum in Davos, Switzerland, gathered to discuss, among other topics of global concern, how the circular economy could be scaled up; participants recognized that a large-scale collaboration, led by business, would be required in order to catalyze change at an economy-wide scale. Their work was summarized in the report "Towards the Circular Economy," prepared for the Forum by the EMF. The Circular Economy Framework from the EMF integrates Cradle-to-Cradle principles, principles from Stahel's Performance Economy, and principles from a parallel approach called Blue Economy (Brennan et al. 2015, 225).

Shifting policy thinking about nonrenewable resources, from throw-away material to irreplaceable resource, is a key piece of the circular economy framework. That means eliminating the linear, one-way flow of materials from use to disposal. Governmental subsidies of nonrenewable minerals and fuels encourage use and disposal. The European Commission plans to eliminate such subsidies by 2020 and to feed discarded substances back into technical nutrient cycles as raw materials (European Commission 2011; Worldwatch Institute 2013, 106). The EU's takeback laws promote reuse as well.

Industrial Ecology

The biosphere provides a model for the cycling of resources. Nature is a closed-loop system that circulates matter, where waste from one organism at one trophic level is food for another. In contrast, most industry is a collection of linear flows that Paul Hawken (1993, xiii) described as "take-make-waste," with resources flowing in one end and waste flowing out the other.

The science of **industrial ecology** studies material and energy flows through an industrial system, shifting them from a linear model to a closed-loop model. It identifies the industrial system as nested within the natural system rather than separate from it and strives for an industrial metabolism that interacts with the natural world in a sustainable way (Graedel and Allenby 2010, 41).

One industrial ecology strategy sets up closed-loop "food webs" among industries, where output from one industry is input for another and materials are reused. These networks of exchanges are sometimes referred to as industrial symbiosis or industrial metabolism. A complex of industrial facilities that applies these principles in an industrial ecosystem is referred to as an **eco-industrial park**.

The archetypal example of industrial symbiosis in an eco-industrial park is Kalundborg, Denmark, a town of 16,000 people with several companies within a 2-mile radius that use each other's by-products on a commercial basis. The 1,500 MW coal-fired Asnaes Power Station, Denmark's largest power station, produces heat, steam, fly ash, and sludge from scrubbers. Heat from the plant is sent to the town's district heating system and to a fish farm. Fly ash from the plant is sent to a cement factory. Steam from the plant is sent to a refinery and to Novo Nordisk, which produces industrial enzymes and pharmaceuticals. Sludge containing gypsum from the plant's scrubber is sent to the plasterboard plant Gyproc, which uses it to produce sheetrock. The Statoil Refinery, Denmark's largest oil refinery, produces waste cooling water that it sends to the power plant; it sends some of its flared gas to the power plant and some to the wallboard plant. Sludge from Novo Nordisk and from the fish farm is used as fertilizer on nearby farm fields (Hull 2007, 97–99).

Life Cycle Assessment

A core concept in industrial ecology is the life cycle of products. Life cycle assessment (LCA) is a method for measuring a product's impact on the environment throughout its entire life cycle, from "cradle to grave." The LCA methodology was first developed in the early 1990s by the Society for Environmental Chemistry and Toxicology (SETAC) (Fiksel 2009, 5). Guidelines and standards for LCA are described in ISO 14040, Life Cycle Assessment Principles and Framework, and ISO 14044, Life Cycle Assessment Requirements and Guidelines.

LCA quantifies energy flows, material flows, and environmental impacts of extraction, acquisition, production, use, and disposal, and typically involves a supply chain whose scope can be ever-expanding. Full LCA can be a complex, challenging, and time-consuming accounting process and is a separate field of expertise requiring specialized training. Many companies look for ways to conduct streamlined or abbreviated LCA, which, while not comprehensive, can still provide some understanding of relative impacts as a basis for making informed decisions (Fiksel 2009; Graedel and Allenby 2010, 189).

Process Design

Designing in environmentally responsible ways is sometimes referred to as design for **eco-efficiency**. Efficiency with the environment in mind means generating more value, that is, more product usefulness and more financial benefit, with less energy and resource consumption and less harmful environmental impact. The WBCSD in their 1992 manifesto *Changing Course* defined eco-efficiency as "the delivery of competitively priced goods and services that satisfy human needs and bring quality of life while progressively reducing the environmental impacts of goods and resource intensity throughout the entire life cycle" (Schmidheiny 1992).

Life-cycle thinking is a central feature of industrial ecology. Product and process designers consider the impacts of every step in the entire life of a product, from the processes of acquiring raw materials and producing components, through processes for manufacturing final products, to delivery, use, and disposal or recycling. This view involves evaluating not just the core manufacturing facility but the processes used by suppliers and customers as well. Processing choices can have long-term implications because once they are developed some manufacturing processes remain in place for decades, and designs for new products may depend on those processes as well. Depending upon the industry, the environmental impacts of some processes can be locked in for much longer time periods than is the case with individual product designs.

Many aspects of manufacturing processes are candidates for eco-efficiency. Each facility is unique, and improvements must be specific to the combination of products and processes in that particular place. A classic industrial ecology text, *Industrial Ecology and Global Change*, says that the goal of the process designer "(never achievable, always desirable) should be that every molecule entering a manufacturing process should leave the facility as part of a salable product" (Socolow et al. 1997, 36).

Product Alternatives

Buckminster Fuller once said,

> If you are in a shipwreck and all the lifeboats are gone, a piano top buoyant enough to keep you afloat that comes along makes a fortuitous life preserver. But this is not to say that the best way to design a life preserver is in the form of a piano top. I think that we are clinging to a great many piano tops in accepting yesterday's fortuitous contrivings.
>
> (Fuller 1969, 21)

Before designers begin working on product designs, systems thinkers may first want to consider defining product function. As Amory Lovins of the Rocky Mountain Institute observed: "If I want to hang a picture, I don't need a drill; I need a hole" (Friend 2009, 99). It may be more eco-efficient to design the function rather than the object. Perhaps the function can be achieved with a different product, or perhaps the function can be achieved in a different way.

One alternative is to provide a service instead of a product. Green engineers sometimes refer to this approach using the invented words "servicizing" or "servicization." Servicizing can be used for products with high initial costs, such as automobiles. For example, in some cities and universities a car-sharing service, also known as a car club, eliminates the need for each person to buy and maintain their own automobile. One such service company is Zipcar. Users purchase a membership, then reserve a car online, which they rent by the hour or by the day.

Providing a service instead of a product is common in consumer electronics. For example, instead of buying telephone answering machines, most customers now use electronic voicemail through their phone providers, and many companies use voicemail services instead of installing equipment on-site. Electronics manufacturers have replaced printed user documentation books with online documentation. Music services allow listeners to download and store music without needing to purchase physical CDs or similar media.

Some manufacturers offer rentals and leases for office equipment such as photocopiers and printers. The manufacturer owns the equipment, maintains it, and takes it back for recycling when the customer upgrades to a newer model. Renting a service instead of buying a product is an option for processes that use chemicals and solvents whereby chemical management companies store, handle, and recycle the chemicals, an approach used by some semiconductor fabrication facilities (Fiksel 2009, 133).

Leasing a service can apply to products such as carpet. Although carpet fibers are recyclable, typical carpeting is used for several years, then removed and sent to landfills, about 5 billion pounds of it a year. Ray Anderson, founder of Interface, the world's largest carpet manufacturer, realized that what customers wanted was not Interface's carpeting; what they wanted was comfortable and attractive floors to walk on. Interface began producing modular carpet tiles, which it leases rather than sells. The company provides monthly inspections and replaces carpet tiles as needed. Used carpet modules are returned to the factory where the materials are separated and recycled into new carpet fiber and other products (Friend 2009, 95; Anderson 2009).

Product Design

Design for the Environment

The practice of designing products and the processes for making those products in environmentally responsible ways is known as **Design for the Environment** (DFE, or DfE).

Its goals of protecting environmental systems from harm, protecting human health and safety, and the sustainability of natural resources apply over the full product and process life cycle. Its practice focuses on reducing the use of hazardous substances, minimizing consumption of energy and resources, reducing waste, and expanding the life cycle of products through recycling and reuse. DFE is also known as eco-design, life-cycle design, and design for eco-efficiency (Fiksel 2009, 5).

In the US, the EPA provides research and technical support in partnership with industry, academia, and environmental groups through its DFE program. Globally, the World Business Council for Sustainable Development (WBCSD) has been a driving force. The WBCSD is an association led by the CEOs of 200 major corporations working to develop tools and the best practices for businesses.

A company implementing DFE has a range of choices from which to select. It could change the process, making the same product but in a different way; it could change the product, for example, making the same product with different materials; or it could make a different product to achieve the same function.

A systems-level perspective might expand DFE thinking beyond simply finding ways to improve the product by asking the question: "Why do we need this product?" Consider the design of an automobile. To improve fuel efficiency and reduce emissions, designers might lower the weight, replacing steel body panels with high-strength aluminum or plastic composite materials. They might redesign batteries to last longer, so fewer batteries would be required over the lifetime of the vehicle. Perhaps components could be designed to be separated and disassembled easily so that parts could be recycled. Designers might rethink the idea of internal combustion engines and design a vehicle powered by fuel cells or electricity.

However, perhaps the real objective is not to design an automobile but to provide transportation, so systems thinkers might focus attention on developing better modes of public transportation. Planners might also focus attention on redesigning cities and towns so that public transportation is accessible and easy to use. Furthermore, they might also alter the need for transportation, for example by encouraging online college classes, by allowing employees to work from home, or by designing neighborhoods with homes and work near each other.

Implementing DFE in a company is a business decision with the potential for financial benefits that has organizational steps in common with implementations of other kinds of business programs. It must begin with commitment from top management and must involve stakeholders inside and outside the organization. After determining what kinds of metrics they will use, DFE teams assess the performance of existing processes and products, using collaborative methods to develop as many viable alternatives as they can, then evaluating and prioritizing the alternatives using a set of systematic criteria. After implementing the high-priority alternatives, they measure and assess the results and adapt as necessary, continuing to apply the lessons learned to other processes and products.[2]

It is important to use systematic methods for measurement and verification. A familiar business precept says "you can't manage what you can't measure" or "what gets measured, gets managed." Thus, improvements must be based on consistent, repeatable methodology and not just on anecdotal reports. It is important to communicate regularly with stakeholders, both inside and outside the company, and to recognize the accomplishments of individuals and teams who made positive contributions. DFE must be integrally designed into a system or set of processes; it is not something that can be stuck on at the end.

The goal of DFE is to design not just products but life cycles. Designers using DFE consider the impacts of products from sourcing and delivery of raw materials, through production and use, to eventual disposal. Design strategies include using or releasing less toxins, using less material, and designing for reuse of materials or components.

Design for Energy Efficiency

In addition to basic energy efficiency programs for lighting, heating, and cooling in manufacturing plants, product manufacturing can be designed to use less energy as well. Each raw material and component carries embodied energy. Formal life cycle analysis is used to calculate and evaluate embodied energy at each stage of the product life cycle. For example, life cycle assessments of laundry detergent by Seventh Generation and Proctor & Gamble revealed that the greatest energy consumption and greenhouse gas emissions occurred in the heating of water in users' homes, so the companies developed detergents that function in cold water (Makower 2009a, 119; Iannuzzi 2012, 7).

Extracting resources, transforming them, breaking chemical bonds and generating new chemical bonds, these all require energy and lots of it. Recycling and reuse of materials can save more than twice as much energy as can be saved by energy-efficiency measures in the production process (IEA 2015, 27). The second law of thermodynamics says that no conversion process is perfectly efficient; all processes produce residues and waste heat. The disciplines of DFE and industrial ecology look for ways to turn that waste into a resource. Combined heat and power (CHP) is one method for capturing and using process-heat energy.

Design for Detoxification: Healthier Materials

Products are full of hidden contaminants, and their total life cycles have many additional contaminants embedded. One of the steps in greening a product is to be sure the materials from which it is made are not harmful to life. Some choices are obvious, such as avoiding materials and components made with PVC, bisphenol A (BPA), formaldehyde, benzene, or lead.

This step of avoiding harmful materials can be surprisingly complex. Designers begin by specifying materials with as low an environmental impact as possible and this requires understanding their material chemistry and life cycles in detail—not only the toxicity of a material itself, but also where it came from and how it was produced. For example gold, used in many electronic circuit boards, may appear to be a benign ingredient; however, in addition to the fossil fuels burned in the mining of ore, substantial amounts of cyanide are also used in the process of extracting gold from the ore. As another example, cotton fiber is often considered a natural material, but unless it is grown in certified organic fields, cotton uses higher quantities of pesticides per acre than any other agricultural crop (Thorpe 2006, 36). The confusion about embedded toxins is compounded by the number of ingredients that may have originated in developing countries, where they may have been produced using chemicals which are banned in Europe and North America.

Rohner Textil, a Swiss company that makes textiles for commercial office furniture, wanted to develop a product to meet a growing demand for environmentally safe fabrics. Working with Cradle to Cradle consultants McDonough Braungart Design Chemistry, they first researched raw materials. Synthetic fibers can be made with petroleum products and can contain heavy metals; cotton is associated with heavy pesticide use. Instead, the company chose wool and ramie as materials. They next researched dyes, a challenge because most chemical dye manufacturing includes toxins and heavy metals. Of the 60 chemical companies contacted, the only company that agreed to submit data on the composition of its dyes was Ciba-Geigy. Although most of their dyes were deemed toxic as well, a small percentage did meet Rohner's environmental criteria. The end result of this research is a compostable, ecologically friendly upholstery fabric called Climatex (Phyper and MacLean 2009, 198).

Herman Miller is a manufacturer of office furniture with a rigorous DFE program. One of their products, the Mirra chair, needed a flexible seat back, usually achieved with chemical plasticizers. Herman Miller's designers developed an alternative honeycomb design, which gives the seat back flexibility without the need for synthetic polymers. The seat is upholstered with Kira, a fabric made from corn; at the end of the chair's life it is disassembled for recycling and reuse and the Kira fabric is composted. Two hundred chemicals are required for the manufacture of the Mirra chair; all 200 have been analyzed for environmental risk (Herman Miller 2007).

In 2008 Ford Motor Company began using a new kind of foam in the seats of its Mustang automobile in collaboration with seat manufacturer Lear Corporation, plastics manufacturer Bayer Corporation, and the United Soybean Board. While 60 percent of the foam is still petroleum-based, 40 percent of the foam is soybean-based. Ford reports that producing soy foam requires less energy and emits less carbon dioxide than petroleum-based foam (Epstein 2008, 259).

The largest sources of toxic substances occur in processes that involve physical or chemical transformations, as opposed to the assembly of components. **Green chemistry** is a technical specialty that focuses on chemical transformations with little or no toxicity. It integrates a combination of safer feedstocks or chemical ingredients, alternative solvents and catalysts, and alternative types of synthesis processes.

Box 13.1 The Twelve Principles of Green Chemistry

1   Prevention: it is better to prevent waste than to clean up or treat it after it is formed.
2   Atom economy: design synthetic methods to maximize incorporation of all materials used in the process into the final product.
3   Less hazardous chemical syntheses: design synthetic methods to use and generate substances that minimize toxicity to human health and the environment.
4   Designing safer chemicals: design chemical products to affect their desired function while minimizing their toxicity.
5   Safer solvents and auxiliaries: minimize the use of auxiliary substances (e.g., solvents and separation agents) wherever possible and make them innocuous when used.
6   Design for energy efficiency: minimize the energy requirements of chemical processes and conduct syntheses at ambient temperature and pressure if possible.
7   Use of renewable feedstocks: use renewable raw material or feedstock whenever practicable.
8   Reduce derivatives: minimize or avoid unnecessary derivatization, which requires additional reagents and can generate waste.
9   Catalysis: catalytic reagents are superior to stoichiometric reagents.
10 Design for degradation: design chemical products so they break down into innocuous products that do not persist in the environment.

11 Real-time analysis for pollution prevention: use real-time, in-process monitoring and control to avoid formation of hazardous substances.

12 Inherently safer chemistry for accident prevention: choose substances and the form of a substance used in a chemical process to minimize hazard and risk.

(Anastas 2010, 31; US EPA 2011)

Design for Dematerialization: Less Material

Design for dematerialization is the DFE strategy of reducing the amount of material required to make a product, which almost always results in lower energy requirements as well. These material and energy reductions are featured in Factor 4 and Factor 10 proposals. They can be achieved through straightforward design changes to minimize the material or packaging required. Virgin materials can be replaced with post-industrial or post-consumer wastes in some products.

One way to reduce material requirements is to reduce a part's physical dimensions. For example, in many injection-molded plastic parts thin ribs can be used in place of a thicker overall part to provide rigidity. Engineers working in the aluminum beverage-can industry perform calculations to determine minimum wall thicknesses needed to maintain structural integrity, minimizing the amount of aluminum required. Wall thicknesses in modern beverage cans vary from 0.005 inch at the neck of the can to 0.003 inch near the middle of the can, increasing to 0.012 inch at the base, where greater thickness is needed (Hosford and Duncan 1994, 48–53).

Product Longevity

One way to decrease the quantity of resources consumed is to design products for longer life by making items that are more durable, items that can be upgraded, or items that are easy to repair. The result is that fewer total resources are demanded per product use.

Some influences on product life are cultural. Before the industrial era, physical objects used in daily life were scarce, costly, or difficult to acquire, and were passed from one generation to another. Some kinds of objects such as farm equipment were shared by members of a community. In contrast, modern cultural expectations are that each individual or household will acquire its own set of objects and that many of the objects, such as cell phones or clothing, will be discarded and replaced frequently. Cultural norms may return to earlier patterns in the post-carbon years ahead.

Design for durability includes creating high-quality designs that people will want to keep. This means a search for designs that are timeless and less likely to pass out of style and implies the use of durable materials. Among the challenges for designers are the trade-offs between durability and recoverability; stronger fastening methods can make a product more durable, but can make materials more difficult to separate later for reuse or recycling. One solution is to develop simple, elegant designs made of single or limited numbers of materials.

On the other end of the lifespan spectrum, modern products such as food packaging and toothbrush heads are designed for short, temporary lives. For such products, designers aim for materials that are either fully recyclable or compostable.

Products can have longer lives when they are upgradeable. Upgrading means only some elements of a product are replaced rather than the entire product. A related idea is the use of reusable platforms. For example, an ink pen with a replaceable refill is an improvement over a disposable pen. A printer or copier in which the user adds toner is an improvement over disposable metal-and-plastic cartridges.

Products can also have longer lives when they are repairable. Components should be accessible, designed for easy replacement, and designed so that replaced or broken parts can be reused or recycled. Reparability overlaps with high-quality design. Designs must be comprehensible and self-explanatory to users (Norman 2002). A user who is frustrated by trying to service an object will be motivated to discard rather than repair it.

Modularity is a fundamental idea in the field of product design. A modular product is subdivided into components, or modules, which are interchangeable. An automobile is an example of modularity, with the manufacturer using the same frame and drive train components for multiple models. Customers can purchase vehicles with different engines or seat styles without needing changes to the body, frame, or suspension, and can later upgrade some of the modules without needing to replace the entire car. Originally, manufacturers pursued modularity because it was good for business: it streamlined production processes, reduced the amount of inventory they needed to keep on hand, reduced the number of components in each assembly, made products easy to upgrade without needing to scrap large numbers of obsolete parts, and provided economies of scale. Later, modularity became a tool for DFE as well (Vezzoli and Manzini 2008, 142).

Design for Reuse: Revalorization

DFE looks for opportunities to recover spent materials and components, reprocess them, and use them again. Revalorization, or getting new value from something, is a word sometimes used by product designers to describe this process of reuse.

Some companies reuse materials. Clothing manufacturer Patagonia reuses fiber from clothing in its Common Threads Initiative. This program explicitly asks people to get along with fewer clothes and to wear clothes until they are worn out. The company says this in turn means it needs to provide high-quality clothing that will last, and it offers free repairs to help clothing last as long as possible. For reuse, the company will help customers sell, trade, or donate clothes. Clothing that is too worn to be reused can be returned and reprocessed through Patagonia's recycling program. Customers return used garments to the company by mail or at retail stores, and Patagonia reprocesses the fiber into new clothing (Patagaonia 2013).

In heavy equipment, manufacturers refer to the reuse process as remanufacturing. Caterpillar, Inc. has emphasized this strategy and has 14 remanufacturing plants worldwide where it reclaims and reuses entire diesel engines, construction and mining equipment, and parts. Workers take products apart, clean the parts, fix or replace worn parts, and put them back together. Modularization makes the equipment upgradeable as well (Arndt 2005).

Some manufacturers accept used products in takeback programs. Most computer and cell phone companies and some television manufacturers have takeback programs. Used electronics that are still functional are refurbished for distribution to charitable organizations and those that are not are disassembled for recycling. EU regulations require automakers to take back any of their vehicles at no cost to consumers. Vehicles are disassembled, materials are recycled, and unrecyclable material is shredded. The law, the End-of-Life Vehicle Directive, mandates that at least 85 percent of a vehicle's weight must be recycled (European Commission 2013).

Box 13.2 Providing Shelter from the Elements by Reusing Scrap

In the Netherlands, an organization called the Sheltersuit Foundation uses tents left behind at music festivals, together with fabric seconds donated by TenCate Outdoor Fabrics, to make an insulated, wind- and water-resistant jacket and sleeping bag given free to homeless people. At night, the sleeping bag can be attached to the coat with a zipper to make a full-body sleeping bag. During the day, the sleeping bag can be unzipped and stored in an included waterproof duffle bag. Sheltersuits are made with the help of people who are homeless, long-term unemployed, and refugees from Syria and Afghanistan, many of whom are professional tailors. In exchange for their skills, the foundation offers assimilation courses, driving lessons, and help with accommodation for refugees.

In Detroit, Michigan, the Empowerment Plan makes the EMPWR, a water-resistant, self-heating coat that converts to a sleeping bag at night and a shoulder bag when not in use. The coat is made from scrap automotive insulation; wool army blankets; Tyvek, a thermal and moisture barrier used in building construction; and heavy-duty fabric, quilted nylon, and sherpa lining donated by workwear manufacturer Carhartt, who also donated industrial sewing machines and supplies. The coats are produced by homeless women from local shelters in exchange for room, board, minimum wages, and job-skill training (Hecht et al. 2014, 10).

Sheltersuits and the Empowerment Plan are examples of sustainability's triple bottom line in action: Scrap material is put to use instead of being sent to a landfill (environment); people in need gain employment (economy); and in the process they develop job skills, skills for living, and basic human dignity (social equity).

Design for Disassembly

To be able to reuse or recycle materials, product assemblies must be disassembled. Design for disassembly (DFD) is a major area of research and development within DFE. Designers strive to create logical structures with obvious access and disassembly points and products that can be disassembled using common tools and equipment (McDonough and Braungart 2002, 171). One design strategy is to reduce the number of different materials. When the EU mandated takeback programs for automobiles, in order to simplify recycling automakers drastically reduced the numbers of plastic types used, with material types identified by markings.

Fastening technology is important in DFD. Dissimilar materials that are glued or welded are difficult to separate; separable parts are preferable. Fasteners such as bolts and screws make it possible to disassemble products but add weight and complexity. Designers work to reduce the numbers of fasteners or to replace them with snap-on parts that can be removed without tools. When Hitachi adopted DFE in its washing machine division, their redesign for disassembly resulted in a machine that could be assembled and disassembled using just 6 screws. In addition to making recycling easier, their design reduced manufacturing time by 33 percent and reduced the number of separate parts needed in inventory (Esty and Winston 2009, 199).

The Mirra chair from Herman Miller was designed to be easily disassembled. At the end of its life cycle it can be returned to the factory, where the entire chair can be disassembled into a handful of parts in less than 15 minutes. Some 96 percent of the chair is recyclable and the fabric is compostable. Plastic in the molded plastic seat back can be recycled and remolded into backs 25 times. Material in the spine, made from Nylon, can be recycled into more spines or made into carpet fibers (ibid., 199).

Biomimicry

The word biomimicry was first introduced by science writer Janine Benyus in *Biomimicry: Innovation Inspired by Nature* (Benyus 1997, 118). She assembled the term from the Greek words *bios* (life) and *mimesis* (imitation). Biomimicry, recognizing that the biosphere has already conducted about 3.8 billion years of research and development, uses nature as a model for design. Benyus described a set of principles that guide nature's designs:

> Nature runs on sunlight. Nature uses only the energy it needs. Nature fits form to function. Nature recycles everything. Nature rewards cooperation. Nature banks on diversity. Nature demands local expertise. Nature curbs excess from within. Nature taps the power of limits.
>
> (ibid., 119)

These principles are recurring themes throughout the field of sustainability.

Biomimetic design can mimic physical form. One of the earliest technological examples was the hook-and-loop fastener design of Velcro, which imitated the barbs that allow seed pods to stick to passing animals. Automotive designers use biomimicry by studying the shapes of fish and the ways they move through water with minimal resistance. California research and design firm Pax Scientific uses biomimicry in its fluid-related equipment, such as propeller blades modeled on whale fins. Fog-collecting mesh screens are used in dry areas of some developing countries to capture potable water from condensation in the air. Designers of these screens developed the concept by watching the Namib Desert Beetle spread its wings every morning just as light fog rolls in, which collects on the beetle's back and rolls into its mouth, providing its only drink of the day.

Design can also mimic natural processes. Ceramic tiles require energy for extraction and transport of clay, then more energy for firing clay at temperatures of at least 2700°F; once produced, the ceramic does not readily break down and is typically sent to landfills at the end of its useful life. By contrast, naturally occurring ceramic in abalone shells is produced at ambient temperatures using materials from seawater, resulting in a ceramic that resists cracking and is twice as tough as human-made industrial ceramics. When the abalone shell is no longer needed by its inhabitant, it breaks down and provides materials for future shell-builders, with zero waste. Researchers are developing processes that attempt to mimic abalone shell-building. Rhinoceros horn contains no living cells, yet cracks in the horn are able to self-heal and could provide a model for self-healing materials if scientists can learn how the process works. Lubricant designers study synovial fluid in human joints and slime produced by snails and slugs; so far, they have not been able to develop lubricants as effective as those models (Benyus 2004).

Biomimicry reminds designers to define and focus on the design goal. For example, when designers are working on developing a better cleaning method, it is tempting to focus on finding the least toxic, most effective detergent. However, a biomimetic designer would ask how nature cleans surfaces. Structures such as leaves need to be clean in order to keep pores clear, yet nature does not use detergent. Researchers in Germany studied the leaves of lotus plants that grow in muddy swamps yet manage to stay clean, and discovered that leaf surfaces are covered in microscopic peaks and valleys. If the surfaces were smooth, water would be held in place by surface tension and unable to wash dirt particles away. The microscopic mountainous structure, however, keeps dirt particles on the tips of the peaks; when raindrops land, drops stay spherical, lifting the dirt particles off. Researchers looked at other leaves and found that most plant leaves use this same structure to keep clean. As a result, the German paint company Ispo has designed a paint that dries to form a surface like a lotus leaf so that rain can keep buildings clean (ibid.).

Researchers are investigating the photosynthesis process in leaves as a model for solar cells; leaves convert 93 percent of the sunlight that strikes them into energy-producing sugars, far more efficient and far more benign than current silicon photovoltaic cells (ibid.). Scientists focused on climate-change mitigation strategies are studying carbon-storing concrete modeled on coral reefs and bio-sequestration, the ways that ecosystems store carbon in soils (Green 2015).

An eco-industrial park such as Kalundborg is a form of biomimicry. Here, rather than mimicking natural forms or natural processes, engineers mimic natural ecosystems to develop industrial symbiosis. Mimicry of natural ecosystems is also the basis of the design philosophy known as cradle to cradle.

Shipping and Packaging

Packaging Design

Packaging design is a subspecialty within the engineering fields, with several professional societies, professional journals, and industry organizations devoted to more sustainable packaging.[3] One such group is the Sustainable Packaging Coalition, an industry group that is a project of the nonprofit sustainable design organization, GreenBlue.

Three packaging characteristics are relevant to DFE: type of material used, amount of material used, and whether the packaging is reusable. In packaging material, designers look for substances that avoid nonrenewable resources and toxic emissions. A few years ago polystyrene foam was commonly used for disposable packaging and packing peanuts. This foam is made from petroleum products and releases CFCs during manufacture and dioxins during incineration. Public opposition to this material, together with increased awareness of DFE issues among designers, has been somewhat effective in curtailing its use. However, many other types of plastic packaging are still widely used and its reduction is a key focus of sustainable packaging initiatives.

One of the issues with packaging is the practice of creating a package that is used once and immediately discarded. DFE designers work on developing alternatives to plastic packaging that can be made from renewable materials such as straw or corn and that can be composted after use. This technology is being used in compostable, corn-based fast-food and delicatessen containers. Challenges remain: while this packaging can be composted in a commercial composting process, it does not break down when buried in a landfill (Leonard 2010, 231).

Other designers look for ways to eliminate packaging altogether. The furniture manufacturer Herman Miller has eliminated 50 percent of its packaging materials by shipping its Mirra chairs in reusable blankets. The company states that all of its packaging is either reusable or recyclable (Herman Miller 2007).

The retailing chain Walmart introduced a packaging scorecard system in 2007, developed in cooperation with a packaging trade group and using feedback from suppliers. The company requires its suppliers to submit scorecards as part of their supplier evaluation.

Scorecards include criteria such as product-to-packaging ratio, recycled content, amount of renewable energy used in producing the packaging, and quantity of carbon dioxide emissions per ton of production.

Shipping containers and wooden pallets are often major sources of solid waste in supply chains. Earlier practice was to use wood pallets only once. Current practice is to return and reuse them, and a pallet recycling industry is active.

Transportation

Bulk quantities of materials are transported by ship and rail. Getting products from manufacturing plants to distribution centers and then to stores involves transport using trucks. Most trucks have diesel-burning engines and thus produce emissions including greenhouse gas. One way to reduce emissions is to reduce the number of miles driven.

When a truck unloads and then travels empty to another location, the trip is known as a deadhead trip. The National Private Truck Council estimates that 28 percent of trailers on the road are running empty. When a truck makes a delivery carrying a trailer that is less than full, the trip is known as less than a load (LTL). Deadhead trips and to a lesser degree LTLs waste fuel and produce unnecessary emissions. In 2009 a commercial group known as the Voluntary Interindustry Commerce Solutions Association (VICS) developed a program known as Empty Miles that works to match loads with empty trucks. Shipping managers enter their empty routes or the cargo they would like to ship onto a website where potential matches are arranged. Schneider National, a major US trucking company, reported that in the first year of the program it saved 5,554 gallons of diesel fuel and kept 61.65 tons of carbon dioxide from being emitted (VICS 2009).

Manufacturers can take other steps to reduce vehicle miles. Some companies arrange for modular components to be shipped directly from suppliers to final customers without intermediate handling. Some adjust their lead times to minimize the need for urgent, last-minute shipping of small quantities of parts. Product designers in some cases have redesigned their products so that they take up less volume or can be packed more tightly, resulting in less wasted space and fewer trips. When retail giant Walmart required its suppliers to reduce their packaging by 5 percent, General Mills changed the noodles in its Hamburger Helper from wavy to straight, making its boxes 20 percent smaller and taking 500 tractor-trailer rigs a year off the roads (Fishman 2011). In response to Walmart's requirement, detergent manufacturers Unilever, Church & Dwight, and Procter & Gamble removed water from their formulas; they now sell concentrated detergents in smaller bottles which require less plastic resin, less water, less cardboard, and fewer truck miles.

Some companies that own their own trucks convert their fleets to less-polluting models, but emissions come from more than driving. Many long-haul drivers idle their engines while stopped for the night in order to run air conditioning, heating, and appliances; the EPA estimates that truck idling releases 11 million tons of carbon dioxide per year (Erard 2007). Some states have laws that limit idling, some companies have policies limiting idling, and some truck stops provide plug-in power receptacles to which trucks can connect while parked in their lots. The first in the US was the Truck Stop Electrification (TSE) Project at one of the world's largest wholesale food distribution centers, located in the gritty Hunts Point neighborhood of South Bronx, New York, where high childhood asthma rates attributed to diesel exhaust had become a public health crisis. TSE was the result of a public–private partnership and the successful first project of a robust environmental justice organization, Sustainable South Bronx. Truckers save money on fuel and engine wear while neighborhood asthma rates and greenhouse gas emissions fall.

ISO 14000 Standards

ISO is the short name of the International Organization for Standardization, the developer and publisher of international standards established in 1947 and headquartered in Geneva, Switzerland.[4] ISO is a consensus-based network of national standards institutes from 163 countries, with standards developed by hundreds of ISO Technical Committees composed of volunteer stakeholders. Thousands of different standards cover almost every area of modern daily life. For example, an ISO standard for the size and shape of credit cards ensures that a card issued by any company will fit in any credit card slot.

ISO 14000 is a series of standards for environmental management. ISO defines the environment as the "surroundings in which an organization operates, including air, water, land, natural resources, flora, fauna, humans, and their interrelation." The standard says that the environment "extends from within an organization to the global system" (Sayre 1996, 14). An **environmental management system** (EMS) is an organization's formal system for developing, implementing, and maintaining its environmental policy, the framework by which it manages the quality of the environment over which it has influence.

The purpose of adopting the ISO 14000 standards is to be able to assure customers that the company consistently meets particular environmental goals. ISO management standards are organized around a familiar cycle known in quality management as Plan–Do–Check–Act. These steps refer to establishing objectives and processes, implementing, measurement and evaluation, and adaptation and improvement. The reiterative nature of this cycle reinforces the quality goal of continuous improvement.

The ISO 14000 standards lay out how to set up, document, implement, and maintain an EMS. Its structure is patterned on ISO 9000, a family of quality management standards widely used by companies, particularly large or international companies, since the early 1990s. In order to receive certification for either standard, a company must develop a set of procedures, document those procedures in writing, and be able to demonstrate that those procedures are actually followed at all times. A licensed third-party auditor is hired to perform a rigorous audit of the management system. The auditor verifies that the procedures are complete and comprehensive and that there is a non-falsifiable way of assuring they are followed.

Like ISO 9000, ISO 14000 does not prescribe any details for what the environmental management objectives should be or how to achieve them. It simply requires that there be a formal system and that it be followed. When asked to summarize what ISO 9000 or ISO 14000 are about, some managers describe them as: "Say what you do, then do what you say."

Box 13.3 The ISO 14000 Family of Standards for Environmental Management

ISO 14001: Environmental Management Systems Requirements

ISO 14004: Implementation Guidelines

ISO 14006: Eco-Design Guidelines

ISO 14010: Environmental Auditing

ISO 14020: Environmental Labels—General Principles

(continued)

(continued)

ISO 14021: Environmental Labels—Self-Declared Environmental Claims (Type II)

ISO 14024: Environmental Labels—Type I Environmental Labeling

ISO 14025: Environmental Labels—Type III Environmental Declarations

ISO 14031: Environmental Performance Evaluation

ISO 14040: Life Cycle Assessment

ISO 14050: Terms and Definitions

ISO 14060: Inclusion of Environmental Aspects in Product Standards

ISO 14062: Product Design and Development

ISO 14063: Environmental Communication

ISO 14064: Greenhouse Gas (GHG) Accounting and Verification

ISO 14065: Accreditation

ISO 14067: Carbon Footprint of Products

ISO 14069: Greenhouse Gas (GHG) Reporting

ISO 19011: Auditing 14000 and 9000

Certifications and Labels: Making Sense of Materials

The world of so-called green materials is complex and confusing. In addition to unverified claims by many manufacturers, certification standards have proliferated and not yet weeded themselves out. C2C certification is one of the more promising. One of the most comprehensive alternatives is the Sustainable Choice standard from Scientific Certification Systems (SCS), offering certifications for a wide range of products including furniture, carpet, building products, and food and including social factors in addition to environmental impacts. SCS was the developer and is now third-party certifier for Environmentally Preferable Products, a program widely used in making responsible purchasing decisions (Atlee and Roberts 2007, 13).

Green Seal, a large third-party certifier in the US, and EcoLogo, originally founded in 1988 by the Government of Canada but now used across North America and globally, are other certification and information services. Consumers Union also provides a website for consumers to help them sort through the complex web of labels and claims.

Sustainability Consortium

The Sustainability Consortium provides a set of science-based measurement and reporting systems that can be used by manufacturers, retailers, and consumers to allow them to compare and understand environmental, social, and economic impacts across the entire product supply chain. The Consortium is a global-scale collaboration of many of the world's largest corporations, academics, government agencies, and NGOs, jointly administered by universities in the US and The Netherlands, with an office in China.

The core goal of the Sustainability Consortium is an accessible life cycle assessment database covering 150 categories of consumer products across 9 sectors. Analyses of materials and products are conducted by sector working groups using detailed life cycle assessment methods and built on the framework of the Greenhouse Gas Protocol Standard.[5] Sensitive corporate data on emissions and labor practices have historically been difficult to uncover; the scope of the Consortium, the presence of the largest corporate players, and the structure of the measurement and reporting systems bring pressure to bear on suppliers to disclose closely held data and promote transparency.

Forest Stewardship Council

In 1993 a group of loggers, foresters, social activist groups, and environmental NGOs came together to form the Forest Stewardship Council (FSC), designed help prevent loss of the world's forests. Its strategy is to certify wood products that come from sustainably harvested forests.

Third-party auditors are accredited by FSC; the largest is the Rainforest Alliance. Auditors conduct assessments of forest operations and harvesting practices, which must meet criteria for issues such as use of chemicals, clearcutting, maintenance of old-growth forest ecosystem structure, and riparian management, while equitably meeting cultural and economic needs.

A product can change hands many times as it moves from forest to truck to mill to market. Therefore, wood must be tracked through the product chain, a process known as Chain of Custody certification. Once a wood product has been certified as sustainably harvested and its chain of custody has been certified, it is labeled with the FSC logo. Companies can be certified as well, and can then use the FSC logo on their products.

FSC is based on an understanding of the important role of social equity and economic survival in the health of the world's forests. Its mission is "to promote environmentally appropriate, socially beneficial and economically viable management of the world's forests" (Tollefson et al. 2008, 3). FSC has a participatory structure, governed by three bodies or chambers representing environmental, social, and economic interests. Each of those chambers has two sub-chambers representing the Northern and Southern Hemispheres. The social chamber includes representatives of indigenous groups, unions, and social welfare organizations. Although tropical deforestation is of particular concern, about 56 percent of the world's certified forest is located in North America (Hansen et al. 2006, 10).

In the 1990s an industry trade group, the American Forest & Paper Association, responded to the creation of the FSC by initiating their own certification system known as the Sustainable Forestry Initiative (SFI). Analyses of certification programs indicate that FSC has more prescriptive rules for practices such as ecosystem management, stream restoration, and social criteria, while SFI has criteria that deal with process, training, communication, and visual management (ibid., 4). FSC was designed and supported by environmental NGOs, while SFI is considered to be aligned with landowners and the forestry industry. SFI was originally an industry self-regulation program, but has added an optional third-party verification component.

A number of other forest-product certification programs have proliferated, with over 50 different systems worldwide. The largest is the Programme for the Endorsement of Forestry Certification (PEFC), which certifies forests in Europe, Asia, and North America (UNEP 2009, 58). A standard from the Canadian Standards Association (CSA), developed in 1996 at the request of Canadian forest industry companies, is similar to the SFI system.

Eco-Labels

The FSC logo is an example of an **eco-label**. An eco-label is any label on a product that tells consumers that the product provides environmental or social benefit. The best labels and the systems they represent are third-party verified, with meaningful standards for environmental protection or social justice developed through a process that is open, public, and transparent, with broad stakeholder involvement.

ISO 14020 recognizes 3 types of environmental labels. Type I labels indicate that products are independently verified by a third party based on specific criteria; these are referred to by ISO as eco-labels. Like a seal of approval, an eco-label is applied when the product meets a certifying standard. "USDA Organic" and "FSC" are examples of this type.

Type II labels are self-declarations about a product. They are claims that may or may not be verifiable. A Type II label makes claims using descriptive terms, such as "biodegradable."

Type III labels are also eco-labels that indicate independent third-party verification. In addition, award of a Type III label is based on a full life cycle assessment of the product.

Fair Trade Labels

The international Fairtrade Mark and the US Fair Trade Certified label are examples of Type I eco-labels. These third-party verified labels certify that an individual product meets international standards for fair prices, fair labor conditions, and environmental sustainability. The Fairtrade Mark is a circular blue, green and black logo from Fairtrade International (FLO) and is used worldwide. Products in the US are certified by Fair Trade USA and have a label bearing the words "Fair Trade Certified." US products can also use the international Fairtrade Mark.

Choice Editing

Most consumers make purchasing choices based on cost or performance rather than eco-labels, and if buyers must pay a premium for more sustainable products, those products will not be affordable for most people. Choice editing is an approach, practiced by retailers when deciding which products to offer and by governments when setting standards, which removes the most environmentally or socially damaging products from the market, pre-selecting the range of products available to consumers. For example, Walmart's requirement for more compact packaging from its suppliers was an example of choice editing, shifting the frame of choice for consumers without raising costs. Likewise, energy efficiency requirements for electrical equipment mean that consumers choose between more sustainable options. *Harry Potter* books are printed on FSC-certified paper, but people buy them not because of certification, but because the publisher Scholastic chose to produce all the books in the series on FSC-certified paper.

Conclusion

The consumption and economic-growth model of industrial society drives multiple risks to planetary health including climate change, pollution, and resource depletion. One course correction involves consuming less, finding ways to reduce demand for products. Another involves rethinking the ways we make products. These endeavors fall within the fields of

Industrial Ecology and Design for the Environment in which designers strive to improve process and product design and to find alternatives to products, often turning to nature's "instruction manual" for guidance. The move to produce more sustainable products is a turn away from once-through, linear cradle-to-grave systems and toward cyclical cradle-to-cradle systems. Standards and certification systems help producers and consumers evaluate processes and products for economic, social, and environmental performance.

Notes

1 This is an example of the fourth of Barry Commoner's "four laws of ecology," which says, "There is no such thing as a free lunch" (Commoner 1971).
2 This is the cycle business managers and ISO 14000 standards refer to as Plan–Do–Check–Act.
3 As many examples throughout this book illustrate, very few systems outside of the Earth system and biosphere could accurately be called sustainable. The word "sustainable" is often used loosely and, many would argue, incorrectly to mean simply "less bad." The word often appears in discussions of packaging, among others.
4 ISO is not an acronym. Translating "International Organization for Standardization" would have resulted in different acronyms in different languages. Instead, ISO founders selected a short name derived from the Greek word *isos*, meaning "equal."
5 The Greenhouse Gas Protocol Standard is the standardized method for measuring and reporting climate impact, developed through a partnership between the WRI and the WBCSD. It is discussed in Chapter 5, Climate.

Further Reading

Benyus, Janine. *Biomimicry: Innovation Inspired by Nature.* New York: Harper Collins, 2002.

Fiksel, Joseph. *Design for Environment.* 2nd ed. New York: McGraw-Hill, 2009.

Graedel, T. E., and B. R. Allenby. *Industrial Ecology and Sustainable Engineering.* Upper Saddle River, NJ: Prentice Hall, 2010.

Hawken, Paul, Amory Lovins, and L. Hunter Lovins. *Natural Capitalism: Creating the Next Industrial Revolution.* Boston, MA: Back Bay Books, 2008.

McDonough, William and Michael Braungart. *Cradle-to-Cradle.* New York: North Point Press, 2002.

Thorpe, Ann. *The Designer's Atlas of Sustainability.* Washington, DC: Island Press, 2006.

Chapter Review

1 What is Factor 4? What is Factor 10?
2 What is biomimicry?
3 List some examples of companies that provide services instead of products.
4 What stages are included in a product's life cycle?
5 Eco-efficiency means generating more value with less negative environmental impact. Why do some people think that eco-efficiency does not go far enough?
6 Summarize the basic concepts of cradle-to-cradle design.
7 What characteristics would you consider in evaluating the environmental impacts of a particular type of packaging?
8 Explain the concepts of certification and third-party certification.
9 If a coworker asked you what ISO 14000 was, what would you say?
10 Which ISO standard addresses life cycle assessment?
11 Briefly describe the 3 levels or types of eco-labels.

Critical Thinking and Discussion

1   Your neighbor says it is a physical law that matter is neither created nor destroyed, and therefore we will never run out of raw materials like metal ore. What would you say?

2   Critics allege that corporations sometimes buy patent rights to energy-efficient designs to prevent competition with their own products, then continue to manufacture their old model rather than introducing the new designs. If true, how might this practice be avoided?

3   If you were to write an environmental impact statement for a typical refrigerator, what would be included?

4   What does durability mean? Think of an everyday product. How long is that product's average lifetime? If this product were made to be durable, how long do you think its lifetime should last?

5   Can cradle-to-cradle design be used in buildings as well as manufactured products?

6   Why do you think that industrial ecosystems such as the one in the city of Kalundborg, Denmark have not been established in the US?

7   The EU mandates takeback programs for automobiles. Why do you think takeback programs are not required in the US? What kinds of changes might be needed in order to make such program requirements more attractive to business people or politicians?

8   Do product labels that claim qualities such as recycled or biodegradable affect your purchase decisions?

9   Do you think that every product claim about environmental benefits is greenwashing?

10   How can consumers determine whether claims on product labels are accurate?

11   A survey from Worldwatch Institute's 2010 *State of the World* reported that 83 percent of people in the US viewed a clothes dryer as a necessity, 50 percent viewed a cellphone as a necessity, and 33 percent viewed a high-speed Internet connection as a necessity. What do you think?

12   Some people have proposed imposing rules similar to takeback programs in which manufacturers are responsible for the cars they produce, whereby plastics manufacturers would be responsible for the plastic waste they generate. What do you think? Would such a program be feasible? How would it work? What problems do you think would need to be addressed?

14   Waste and Recycling

Waste is big business. Every day the average person living in the US throws away 4.6 pounds of solid waste (Center for Sustainable Systems Factsheets 2008, 1), and for every pound of household waste we discard, 40 to 70 additional pounds of industrial debris were generated during its production (Rogers 2005, 4).[1] But as one of Barry Commoner's "four laws of ecology" makes clear: "Everything must go somewhere. There is no 'waste' in nature and there is no 'away' to which things can be thrown" (Commoner 1971).

Every piece of material in a garbage can carries with it large quantities of embedded energy and invisible material resources that were part of its life history. Behind every object are the mining of resources or cutting of trees, the transport of ingredients and components by fossil fuel-burning vehicles, production in factories, more production for packaging, and transport again as the product is distributed. Most of the life cycle of a product remains invisible to us.

The idea of waste is a human construct. In other parts of the biosphere, matter moves in continuous cycles and waste from one organism is food for another, but in the industrial model of the world the movement is linear. We move materials into the waste stream when we can no longer find ways to use them. Waste is, as chemist Paul Connett says, "resources in the wrong place" (Leonard 2010a, 183). Specialists in an approach known as Zero Waste suggest we think of these materials not as waste but as "residual product" or as "potential resources" (Zero Waste Alliance n.d.). Consultant Gil Friend calls them "non-product output" (Friend 2009, 42).

The waste management hierarchy is a framework for minimizing waste streams. Pollution prevention and waste reduction are closely related and sometimes managed by the same work group within an organization. The Pollution Prevention (P2) hierarchy is a widely adopted framework for preventing or reducing pollution and waste (US EPA 2013a). Its steps, in descending order of priority, are prevention or reduction, reuse, recycling, treatment, and disposal. The highest priority is to prevent pollution at its source by reducing the amount generated. Following prevention, the next strategy is to reuse, then to recycle. Pollution that cannot be reduced or recycled is treated. As a last resort, pollution is disposed of as safely as possible.

The steps in the waste hierarchy familiar to most nonprofessionals are reduce, reuse, and recycle, sometimes referred to as the 3Rs. "Reduce" is a form of prevention: preventing waste from being generated in the first place, the most preferable strategy. Reuse comes next, as a way to minimize the generation of waste. Recycling what is left is the lowest priority. Additionally, waste managers treat and dispose of what cannot be recycled.

As an example, a person writing business memoranda would first "reduce" paper use by finding alternatives, such as sending memos electronically instead. If paper memos were required, the sender would then "reuse" by printing on both sides of each sheet. Finally, they would "recycle" by purchasing paper made with post-consumer waste and by recycling their own used paper.

A manufacturer designing a product could first "reduce" by designing for dematerialization or reduced material. They could then "reuse" by reprocessing waste material as a resource for additional products, by reusing pallets and packaging, by instituting a takeback program, or by leasing a service instead of selling a product. Where necessary, as a last resort they could then "recycle" to repurpose leftover waste material.

Waste Management

The practice of conventional waste management collects, transports, treats, and disposes of solid and liquid waste. Within the waste management industry, waste is divided into categories based upon its source, its chemical composition, and its industry sector. Knowing these categories helps the waste manager speculate on what might be in the waste and therefore make decisions about how it should be handled.

Municipal solid waste (MSW) is collected and treated by municipalities and is so-named because it is the responsibility of local governments. MSW includes waste from households, offices, institutions, and small businesses. Almost a third of the weight of MSW consists of discarded packaging materials (Imhoff 2005, 9).

Medical waste, also known as red-bag waste, is handled separately from MSW because it can be contaminated with pathogens. Electronic waste requires different methods of handling than MSW, so falls into its own category. Hazardous waste, most of which is generated by industrial activities, is another category, which is handled separately and either sealed in secure landfills or incinerated in special high-temperature hazardous waste incinerators.

Industrial waste, which results from materials and scrap left over from manufacturing processes, makes up perhaps 76 percent of the waste volume in the US (Leonard 2010a, 183). Construction and demolition (C&D) waste consists of scraps left over from construction and debris resulting from the demolition of structures. It can involve large volumes, and on job sites is placed in metal bins provided by hauling companies, called roll-off bins because they are carried directly on truck frames, then rolled off and onto the ground at a job site.

Waste Streams

A waste stream consists of the waste material produced in a region and the paths it follows from its sources to final disposal. Waste hauling companies are given contracts by municipalities to manage local waste streams.

In the language of waste managers, waste treatment means removing waste in some way so that it is no longer harmful (Maczulak 2010, 16). Physical treatment immobilizes waste so that theoretically it cannot pollute uncontaminated soil, air, or water; sealing waste within a capped landfill or encapsulating it within concrete are physical treatments. Chemical treatment uses chemical reactions to change the chemical makeup of substances; high-temperature combustion of hazardous wastes is a thermal method of breaking chemical bonds. Biological treatment uses bacteria, as in wastewater treatment plants, or plant life, as in phytoremediation processes, either to break down wastes or to immobilize them.

Waste is transported to centralized sites known as treatment, storage, and disposal facilities (TSDFs). TSDFs are transfer sites; they are not the final destination of waste. These sites perform some sorting, separating out hazardous waste and reusable or recyclable waste.

Transfer facilities allow trucks to spend less time driving and more time picking up loads. They also make more efficient use of trucks. Smaller trucks must maneuver through city streets as they pick up loads, while larger trucks from TSDFs bound for landfills or incinerators at outlying disposal sites can stay on main thoroughfares.

Some kinds of waste may also be taken to processing centers that accept specific material that has already been separated, such as metals, or that separate recyclable materials from loads before sending the balance to transfer stations. Some processing centers handle C&D waste and others handle organic waste. Some large transfer stations also have processing facilities, which may include places where individuals can deposit recyclable material.

Once sorted, waste that is not reused, recycled, or composted is consolidated into larger loads, which are then transported from TSDF transfer sites to one of two destinations: either to landfills or to incinerators. These loads are hauled by larger trucks, rail cars, or barges and may travel long distances to their final destinations. Waste from New York City, for example, is trucked to facilities in other states several hundred miles away (Hayes 2005, 481).

Landfills

Until the twentieth century waste was put into dumps. A dump could have been a hole in the ground filled with garbage or a heap of garbage piled on top of the ground. In either case, it was left uncovered and exposed to the elements.

In the twentieth century the technology of the sanitary landfill was developed. Modern landfills are called sanitary landfills because they use methods intended to keep surroundings clean by preventing leaks into soil and water. Landfills do not treat waste; they simply provide long-term storage.

A landfill begins with a large excavated hole. At the bottom is a layer of compacted soil several feet thick, then a layer of clay half an inch thick, topped by a waterproof membrane of high-density polyethylene (HDPE) plastic 1 to 2 inches thick and geonet, a plastic net-like drainage material. Above the membrane, a layer of sand and gravel several feet thick facilitates drainage. Perforated pipes within the gravel collect **leachate** and carry it to the lowest point of the pit, where a pump brings the leachate to the surface. The leachate goes to a sewage treatment plant or to an on-site treatment plant. As with wastewater treatment, leachate is treated mostly by bacteria. This biological method does not work when leachate is heavily contaminated with chemical pollutants (ibid., 488; Rogers 2005, 19).

After one area of a landfill has been filled it is covered with a cap consisting of bentonite clay and several feet of soil. Once landfills are closed and capped, they are covered with topsoil and repurposed. LaGuardia, Kennedy, and Newark airports are built on former landfills (Hayes 2005, 486). The 2,200-acre Fresh Kills landfill on Staten Island has been closed and capped, and will eventually become New York City's largest park. Many city parks are built above former landfills; some researchers worry that these sites emit VOCs and other pollutants in areas where children play.

Leachate is a liquid that forms when rainwater and liquid from food waste percolate through a landfill, dissolving pollutants along the way. Because it contains such a mix of chemicals, leachate is a complex pollution problem. When leaks form in landfill liners, leachate can contaminate surrounding soil and eventually percolate into groundwater. According to pollution specialists it is impossible to prevent all leaks; all landfills do eventually leak (Pepper et al. 2006, 271). Sensors are embedded within landfills for monitoring and series of monitoring wells are constructed around the outsides of landfills.

Leaking of pollutants is a present and future issue for landfills. Although their plastic liners are thick, the liners are eroded by some chemicals and can be punctured by items within the garbage, while their drainage pipes are sometimes crushed by the weight of garbage above them. Some items are banned from landfills, including batteries, switches containing mercury, fluorescent bulbs, insecticides, and aerosol cans, but these items are still occasionally dumped into household waste, where they form dangerous leachates. Most HDPE liners carry guarantees of 50 years or less. Landfill operators are not legally responsible for landfill contamination more than 30 years after a landfill is closed. Thus landfills can be thought of as temporary storage, and beyond 30 to 50 years, someone will still need to address these toxic legacies (ibid.).

Gas given off by landfills consists of about 50 percent carbon dioxide, 50 percent methane, and a little less than 1 percent other organic compounds (Maczulak 2010, 26). Anaerobic bacteria give off methane, a highly potent greenhouse gas, as they metabolize the paper, food, and other organic waste within a landfill. Landfills produce a third of the methane emitted in the US, and are the single largest methane source (Blockstein and Wiegman 2010, 19). Some landfills flare off or burn their methane to convert it to carbon dioxide, which is still a greenhouse gas but less dangerous than methane. Some capture methane and use it within gas turbines to generate power, a process known as **waste-to-energy** (WTE). Currently about half the methane produced by US landfills is emitted into the atmosphere and half is flared or burned to generate electricity (Center for Sustainable Systems Factsheets 2008, 1). One of the problems with burning landfill gas is that it picks up other VOCs from the waste in addition to methane, which can form dioxins when burned (Leonard 2010a, 209).

Incineration

In most regions the majority of municipal solid waste is sent to landfills, and the remaining amount is incinerated. An incinerator is a large furnace used for burning waste. Most medical wastes and hazardous wastes are incinerated. Incineration facilities may also be called plasma arc, pyrolysis, gasification, and WTE plants.

Waste-to-energy refers to the process of disposing of solid waste through incineration, then using the resulting heat to produce electricity (Connett 2013, 56). WTE power plants release more greenhouse gases than power generated using other fuels (Maczulak 2010, 27). Critics point out that by reducing consumption and reusing materials, every ton of trash not produced in the first place could save twice as much energy as could have been captured by incinerating a ton of trash, and a combination of recycling and composting materials will save 3 to 4 times more energy than would be generated by burning them (Connett 2013, 65).

When materials that contain chlorine, such as bleached paper, PVC, and clothing, are burned together with materials that contain carbon, such as paper, wood, and food, the high-temperature combustion breaks chemical bonds and forms new chemical bonds to produce dioxins (Rogers 2005, 5). Other new compounds form as well, many of which have not yet been tested for environmental and human health impacts. According to the United Nations Environmental Programme, 69 percent of the world's dioxin emissions are produced by MSW incinerators (ibid.). Waste incinerators also release particulates and acidic gases such as nitrous oxide (N_2O), a greenhouse gas with a global warming potential 265 times greater than carbon dioxide (IPCC 2014d, 87).

Incineration can be thought of as a method of reducing the volume of landfill waste. Burning MSW reduces its volume, but the waste does not completely disappear (Pepper et al.

2006, 140); about 25 percent of the waste by weight remains as ash, which must then be land-filled (Connett 2013, 67). Ash left from incineration contains heavy metals, dioxins, and other toxic pollutants, which become concentrated.

Incineration produces ash in two locations: Bottom ash collects at the bottom of the combustion chamber; lighter-weight and more-toxic fly ash forms in flue gases in the stack. When scrubbers and filters are added to stacks to remove pollutants such as dioxins from flue gases, the pollutants do not disappear but are transferred from the exhaust gas to the fly ash as it collects in the filter media (ibid.). The contaminated ash is sent to a landfill, where dioxin and other toxins can become mobile in leachate and enter soil and groundwater (Rogers 2005, 5; Leonard 2010a, 214).

Widespread public opposition to incinerators developed in the 1980s. Organized, well-informed community coalitions have prevented the construction of many new plants. In addition to having concerns about health risks, some organizations object on the basis of environmental justice since incinerators are usually built in low-income communities (Leonard 2010a, 214).

Recycling

Recycling is a disposal method that provides some improvement over landfilling and incineration. It extracts materials from the waste stream and processes them so that they can be reused in some way. Reprocessing materials and returning them to the supply chain in some form uses less energy and generates less additional waste than would be needed to produce the same materials from ore or virgin sources (Worrell and Reuter 2014, 5). However, recycling always requires energy inputs and machinery, losses occur at every stage, and materials can never be recycled 100 percent (ibid., 22). Household curbside recycling, which is quite popular, has been more successful than industrial recycling initiatives.

The Recycling Process

Materials collected for recycling are transported to a central material recovery facility, or MRF (pronounced "murf"), where they are sorted. In commingled, or single stream, recycling all the MSW material considered recyclable is mixed together. Material is dumped onto conveyor belts where preliminary manual sorting is done. Air blasts separate lightweight plastic containers, which are sorted by type either manually or using infrared spectroscopic scanners. Electromagnets remove ferrous metals such as food cans, and eddy current separators remove aluminum such as beverage cans. Other sorters separate corrugated cardboard, newsprint, and mixed paper.

Glass is readily recycled and can be remelted into products with the same characteristics as the original material (Worrell and Reuter 2014, 191). Glass is sorted by color into clear, green, amber, and blue. Crushed glass is called cullet. The manufacture of green glass can tolerate the most contamination by other colors; clear glass is more sensitive to contamination but can still tolerate up to 60 percent cullet content (ibid., 194). Because glass cullet melts at a lower temperature than sand, the raw material used to make glass, making containers from recycled glass requires less energy than new glass (Hayes 2005, 497). Washing and reusing of bottles uses even less energy.

Fifty-five percent of paper and cardboard is recycled, making up 31 percent of MSW (US EPA 2008). The fibers in paper break down and shorten each time they are reprocessed, so paper cannot be recycled indefinitely. It has been calculated that the paper produced in the US each year would be enough to build a wall from the east to the west coast 11 to 12 feet high (Maczulak 2010, 28). Millions of tons of paper are used each year for unwanted mail or junk mail. According to the Worldwatch Institute, junk mail consumes 100 million trees per year and as much energy as 3 million cars. In addition to recycling existing paper, one way for individuals to reduce paper use is to opt out of unwanted mail.[2]

Plastic consists of very long molecules, or polymers, typically made from petroleum. That is, it uses ancient carbon that was sequestered millions of years ago. Hundreds of varieties of polymers and additives are in use in industry, making them versatile to use but difficult to recycle. Containers and packaging make up most of the plastic found in MSW. The small percentage of plastic containers that are recycled are remade into products that are not themselves recyclable, including plastic lumber, textiles, and parking lot bumpers. Plastic packaging is not recycled, and no recycled plastic is used to make packaging or containers, although it would be possible if legislation required it (Plastics Task Force n.d.). Plastic containers are marked with resin identification codes, numerals from 1 to 9, indicating the general class of material used to make them.

The recycling logo was developed by the packaging industry. A few months after the first Earth Day the Container Corporation of America commissioned the recycling symbol, a triangle made of chasing arrows, leaving the design in the public domain so that other manufacturers could adopt it as well. In 1988 the Society of Plastics Industries (SPI) developed the idea of assigning a number to each of 9 grades of plastic and inserting those numbers inside the recycling logo. The symbol would identify what type of resin a plastic object contained. SPI then lobbied state legislatures to adopt this coding system in place of stricter laws such as bottle and can deposits or mandatory recycling laws. Over the next 8 years the SPI, together with the American Plastics Council (APC), successfully fought recycling legislation in 32 states. Meanwhile the triangular logo on every container implied that they were recyclable, and hinted that perhaps they were even made of recycled materials. This marketing inspiration deflected consumer awareness away from the need fundamentally to change the way design and production are conceived. Since that first Earth Day, plastic production has grown exponentially (Rogers 2005, 171).

Box 14.1 The Great Pacific Garbage Patch

In the middle of the Pacific Ocean lies a growing mass of trash currently believed to be about the twice the size of Texas. The garbage, mostly plastic, has come from many countries on both sides of the Pacific. Because plastic is lightweight and durable, it floats along for hundreds of miles until it becomes captured in a gyre, or circular ocean current, where it remains trapped. Plastic does not dissolve. Instead, constant wave energy breaks it apart into smaller and smaller pieces. Chemical sludge gets trapped in the gyre as well. Toxic chemicals such as PCBs and DDT cannot dissolve in water, but they are readily absorbed by plastic. The Pacific gyre has been found to contain several times more plastic than plankton; fish mistake the tiny plastic particles for plankton, eat them, and become part of a food chain in which the toxins bioaccumulate. The Pacific Garbage Patch is not visible by satellite because most of the plastic is broken into small bits suspended under the water's surface.

Larger pieces of plastic which have not yet broken apart are deadly to sea animals. Seabirds scoop up pieces of debris, mistaking them for fish or crustaceans; plastic pieces with jagged edges become trapped in the birds' digestive tracts, resulting in slow death. Albatross parents mistake pieces of plastic for squid, their main food, and feed the plastic pieces to their chicks whose stomachs fill with plastic and who then starve to death. Sea turtles and seals have been seen choking to death on chunks of plastic. Dolphins playing with plastic bags sometimes get the bags wrapped around their blowholes and suffocate. On Earth Day in 2010, a dead whale was found on the Washington coast with 50 gallons of plastic and textiles in its stomach. The UNEP estimates that plastic debris causes the death of 1 million seabirds and 100,000 marine mammals every year.

Similar massive garbage patches have been discovered in gyres in the Atlantic Ocean and the Indian Ocean. Researchers have found that the contents and their effects on wildlife are like those in the Pacific (Hill 2010, 326–27; Hoshaw 2009).

Visible sources of plastic include vast quantities of plastic floats, lines, and nets from the fishing and aquaculture industries (C. Moore 2014), along with discarded plastic toys, containers, and bags. Sources of microplastics include fibers from the washing of fleece clothing and plastic exfoliating microbeads from cosmetics, both of which enter the oceans from wastewater treatment facilities (Marine & Environmental Research Institute 2016), together with disintegrating bits of larger debris (Cole et al. 2011, 2588).

Prevention will involve fundamental changes to how we make and use products and to the economic growth model itself. The Ocean Conservancy, World Wildlife Fund, and industry partners are leading a large-scale plastic-reduction program as part of the Trash Free Seas Alliance. Strategies include eliminating illegal dumping, increasing waste collection rates, and increasing the economic value of waste to promote collection and recycling, particularly in low-income regions (Ocean Conservancy 2015, 8).

Meanwhile some organizations are striving to begin cleaning up the debris already in the oceans. Waste Free Oceans is a public-private partnership that includes the fisheries sector and the plastics industry, with support from the European Commission. The project uses fishing boats outfitted with special nets to collect plastic debris large enough to be trapped in the nets. Upcycle the Gyres is a similar initiative based in British Columbia. Both groups focus on education and prevention as well as remediation. Interface, the carpet manufacturer, is engaged in a similar initiative called Net-Works in partnership with the Zoological Society of London to retrieve discarded fishing nets from the oceans; recovered fibers are recycled into yarn for carpet tiles.

The Recycling Coordinator

One of the career paths in the field of sustainability is to work as a recycling coordinator for a company, institution, or public agency. The recycling coordinator is responsible for setting up and monitoring a recycling program and for providing education and training.

Careful recordkeeping is an important part of coordinating a recycling program. Setting up a program begins by evaluating existing conditions. Coordinators typically prepare an indicator report to serve as a benchmark against which future improvements can be measured. Measurements can include total solid waste quantity, current recycling rate, types and quantities of materials collected for recycling, details about current recycling infrastructure such as containers and their locations, and the status of education programs. Contracts are set up with local haulers and recyclers. The recycling coordinator files weight tickets and receipts and keeps an ongoing log recording information from these records, which are tracked over time and compared against the recycling program's stated goals.

Some coordinators calculate recycling rates by comparing the weight of material collected for recycling to the total weight of waste generated. However, some material may need to be rejected during processing, and for accuracy that amount should be subtracted from the weight so that only material actually marketed for recycling is counted.

Coordinators at sites such as schools and universities often do what is known as a waste audit or trash audit, a group exercise in which volunteers sort and weigh components of campus trash. The audit measures how much was discarded in each waste category and reveals how much of the material in garbage cans was uncaptured and could have been recycled instead. It is often eye-opening, and can provide a baseline for redesigning the school's waste management program. Some schools do a waste audit once a year and celebrate improvements they discover.[3]

Recycling depends upon the actions of many individuals. One thing the coordinator can do is to make it easy for people to recycle. An effective program provides attractive facilities such as bins for recycling, in as many convenient locations as possible. If a person must walk a long distance to get to a recycling bin, they may be tempted simply to throw an item in the trash instead. In addition, recycling bins should be set up in ways that minimize the risk of contamination, with clear, unambiguous, and easy-to-understand labeling so people immediately know what to do, and general trash containers should be placed adjacent to each recycling container so it is easy for people to put garbage in its appropriate spot. Trash containers must be emptied regularly. Recycling bins located in public areas must be kept securely covered.

One of the themes that recurs in the sustainability field is the need for communication and collaboration. The people who use a system should be acknowledged and their voices heard. In the case of recycling, custodial staff may be particularly impacted. Some recycling coordinators meet with custodial staff to ask them how recycling is working for them, whether their workload is impacted, whether they encounter any problems, and whether they have suggestions to make the recycling system work better.

Benefits and Costs of Recycling

Using recycled materials in manufacturing almost always uses less water and energy, releases less pollution, and emits less carbon dioxide than manufacturing with virgin materials.[4] In addition, perhaps one of the greatest benefits of recycling has been its effect on public awareness of environmental issues. Recycling is the first contact many people have with issues of planetary health and the connection between their own actions and the environment.

Unfortunately, recycling has intrinsic shortcomings. Materials collected in curbside recycling are only reprocessed if facilities are available and a market can be found for the materials. When virgin materials are the same price or lower, the recovered materials are discarded. Much of the material collected in curbside recycling bins can wind up being landfilled or incinerated, due either to lack of a market (Rogers 2005, 179) or lack of processing facilities.

Recycling is energy intensive, and it demands lengthy transport with additional energy consumption and greenhouse gas emissions. While there are energy savings, recycling still consumes more energy than either reusing a product or not producing it in the first place.

Most reprocessing involves a characteristic known as downcycling, in which the quality of the material decreases over time, rather than actual recycling. For example, the long fibers in paper break each time paper is recycled; shorter fibers do not hold together as well and result in lower-grade paper.

Sterilizing and refilling a plastic milk jug is an example of recycling; melting the plastic down to make other products is an example of downcycling. The long polymer chains of molecules in plastic shorten each time it is remelted, altering its strength and elasticity. Molders must mix in additives and high percentages of virgin material to achieve desired material properties. Plastics must be strictly grouped by resin type and are very sensitive to contamination, so even a small bit of nonrecyclable plastic in a recycling bin can render an entire batch of plastic unusable. Because of downcycling, most plastics are not reprocessed into the same kind of product as before. Plastic beverage bottles cannot be remade into more beverage bottles; they must be used in a lower grade, nonrecyclable product such as synthetic lumber, carpet backing, or fleece fabric, which must generally be discarded after use (McDonough and Braungart 2002, 177).

Recycling can increase the concentration of contaminants in a material or in the surrounding environment. Waste products that result from re-smelting aluminum contain dioxins and furans. Plastic from bottles contains heavy metals and plasticizers. Toxic chemicals must be used to remove ink from used paper; in Wisconsin, a paper-recycling facility is the second-largest polluter in the state (Rogers 2005, 178).

Recycling often encourages even greater consumption, an effect known as the rebound effect. Consumers seeing the recycling symbol on a plastic container may assume that consuming the product is without environmental cost, and may even feel that consuming and discarding are environmentally-responsible actions. Recycling may point us in the wrong direction and distract us from more effective and fundamental changes.

Composting: Recycling Organic Waste

Organic wastes include paper, yard trimmings, and food. In addition to consuming space in landfills, this organic matter is a major source of methane generation and liquid that becomes leachate. Throwing food waste into a landfill removes its carbon content from the biogeochemical carbon cycle and removes its other nutrients from the soil from which it was taken (Sims 2010, 420).

Composting, long a practice of organic gardeners, is increasingly part of many municipal waste management programs which provide composting of leaves and yard debris. Organic materials are mechanically shredded to increase the surface area on which aerobic bacteria can feed. The materials are then broken down and decomposed through the work of soil microorganisms and, in some processes, earthworms. Commercial composting includes mechanisms for irrigating, aerating, and turning composting material and operates at higher temperatures than home composters.

Some markets and food establishments offer compostable bioplastics made from plant material, often corn, as an alternative to regular disposable plastic dishes, packaging, and flatware. Unfortunately, while these products are technically compostable, they break down only under conditions available in large-scale commercial composting. In backyard composters, and even in small-scale commercial composters of the type found in campus food service programs, these plastics do not decompose. An additional problem occurs when bioplastics are mixed with other types of plastic in recycling bins. Unless they are removed, these materials clog recycling equipment and can contaminate entire batches of plastic resin (Leonard 2010a, 231). Plastics made from corn have some of the same problems as biofuels made from corn, including industrial-scale monoculture farming, deforestation, and pesticide use.

Recycling Electronic Waste

Electronic waste, or e-waste, is the name given to discarded electronics and electrical appliances including computers, cell phones, televisions, and refrigerators. Over 1 percent of solid waste in the US and 5 percent globally is e-waste (Maczulak 2010, 36). Banned from landfills, e-waste is handled differently from other waste and must be processed separately from MSW.

Electronic waste contains a mix of over 1,000 different types of embedded toxic materials (ibid., 40). Computer chips and circuit boards contain beryllium, cadmium, mercury, and lead. Computer monitors contain mercury and lead, while liquid crystal displays contain beryllium, lead, cadmium, and arsenic. Disc drives contain chromium. Batteries contain lead, cadmium, zinc, and mercury. Plastic cases, frames, hinges, cables, and hardware contain dioxins and PVC, and are treated with hexavalent chromium protectants and brominated flame retardants including PCBs. Ink in printers and fax machines contains various endocrine disruptors. All of these chemicals are released into the air when incinerated and leached into soil and water when placed in landfills.

Up to 80 percent of America's electronic waste is exported to developing countries, where environmental and worker protection laws and enforcement are less strict (ibid., 47). Low-wage workers without protective gear, including children, burn components, soak them in acid baths to separate small amounts of resalable materials, breath dioxin-filled smoke, and disassemble lead- and mercury-laden parts with their hands. Contaminated water is poured into lakes and rivers and contaminated solid waste is dumped in huge piles near villages, where toxins continue to leak into the soil and water supply (Sims 2010, 420).

Some electronics manufacturers have instituted voluntary takeback programs allowing consumers to return electronics to those manufacturers for recycling when buying new ones. In addition to promoting recycling, takeback programs motivate manufacturers to address e-waste problems during the design phase where decisions can have the greatest impact. Most US states have legislation mandating e-waste recycling.

Electronics recyclers can be certified through a third-party program known as e-Stewards. To be certified, recyclers are audited and must demonstrate adherence to strict environmental and social justice standards. E-Stewards is an environmental management system standard that uses ISO 14001 as its framework, with additional industry-specific performance requirements particular to electronics recycling and reuse (e-Stewards 2010).

The Basel Action Network (BAN), which developed e-Stewards, is a non-governmental watchdog organization that monitors an international treaty, the 1992 Basel Convention on the Control of Transboundary Movements of Hazardous Wastes and their Disposal, known as the Basel Convention, and its 1998 amendment, known as the Basel Ban. The Basel Convention was developed to reduce the movement of hazardous waste from industrialized countries to developing countries. The Basel Ban specifically bans hazardous waste exports from the countries of the Organization for Economic Cooperation and Development (OECD) to developing countries. The Basel Convention has been ratified by most OECD countries except the US (Basel Action Network 2011).

The Salvage Industry

The salvage industry is involved primarily with the recycling of metals including metal from automobiles. Modern steelmaking often takes place in minimills, using scrap steel rather than iron ore as its primary ingredient. After old cars are stripped of their nonmetallic components, the remainder of each car is flattened, then shredded in a hammer mill, and the resulting 1- to 2-inch bits of metal are melted into ingots and sent back to a steel mill. Steel is the most widely recycled material; the recycled content of structural steel is over 90 percent (AISC 2013).

Aluminum, copper, and other metals are part of the salvage industry as well but recycled at lower rates. Enough aluminum is discarded in the US each year to rebuild the entire fleet of aircraft (Maczulak 2010, 9). Virgin aluminum contains an extremely large amount of embodied energy; recycled aluminum can save 75 to 96 percent of that energy (GrassRoots Recycling Network 2001).

Over 200 million tires are produced and discarded in the US each year (Hayes 2005, 496). Salvaging of tires is a difficult challenge. Many states ban them from landfills but offer no other disposal or recycling options and as a result, many are dumped illegally. Piles of tires become breeding grounds for mosquitoes. When piles catch on fire, as they occasionally do, the fires release toxic smoke and are difficult to put out. Finding uses for tires is the subject of ongoing research. They have been used to fuel kilns in some cement plants, and companies have experimented with products made from recycled tires including material for shoes, sidewalks, and basketball courts.

Box 14.2 Urban Mining

As the richest sources of metal ores are mined out, the quality of raw ore declines and the cost of extracting it rises. While some engineers study ways to improve recycling rates, others are researching ways that previously discarded metals could be reclaimed. Landfills contain discarded metal of all types and in cities, large quantities of abandoned pipes, wires, pilings, streetcar rails, and other industrial detritus are buried under streets. Engineers have not yet been able to address the challenges of separating small bits of metal from the materials within which they are embedded, and the solutions are different for different applications. As with all waste issues, prevention through appropriate product design is the critical step.

Street sweepings and grassy roadsides contain platinum and palladium particles from automobile catalytic converters. Sludge from sewage treatment plants contains platinum from drugs used in hospitals and gold from electronics manufacturing. Scientists are investigating ways to partner with living organisms. Some strains of bacteria require particular elements for their metabolic functions; the theory is that they could be recruited to digest and concentrate precious metals and then be harvested. Plants known as hyper-accumulators could be grown in soils built of street sweepings, then harvested. Seaweeds could be used to extract metals from solvents. Urban planner Jane Jacobs once said, "cities are the mines of the future" (Jacobs 1969, 107). Her idea is still a long way from reality, but research continues.

(Van Nes and Cramer 2006, 1307–18;
Graedel 2011, 43–50; Ravilious 2013, 40–43)

Construction & Demolition Waste

Construction & demolition (C&D) waste is material left over from the building or taking down of structures. It includes pieces of wood, wallboard, steel reinforcing bar, chunks of concrete, shingles, pipes, wire, and metal hardware. In many areas C&D waste is 20 to 30 percent of the MSW waste stream (New York City Department of Design & Construction 2003, 9). Although it is a kind of MSW, because C&D is so large in volume it is often treated as a separate category. Hazardous construction waste must be handled and collected separately from C&D waste; it includes asbestos-containing materials, lead paint, lighting ballasts containing PCBs, fluorescent lamps, high-intensity discharge (HID) lamps, mercury-containing thermostats, and aerosol cans.

Contractors must pay to have waste hauled, so recycling saves them money. Nevertheless, in many areas only 10 to 20 percent of C&D is recycled (Napier 2012, 2). Some contractors separate and haul their own waste and recyclables, locating separate containers on the job site and sorting out recyclable materials as they are collected. Many recyclers of specific materials will arrange to pick up materials at the construction site.

Collecting recyclables in separate containers is known as source separation; it requires more space than collecting mixed waste in single containers but yields a higher recycling rate and a lower haulage fee. Recyclable materials include steel, asphalt shingles, concrete, rock, brick, lumber, carpet, architectural features, and sometimes excavated soil. Concrete and masonry can be recycled to produce aggregate. Wood scraps can be recycled for use as a mulch or fuel if they are not contaminated with preservative or lead-based paint. Structural and other steel is almost universally recycled.

On large construction projects, general contractors develop a waste management plan. A recycling coordinator is assigned to be responsible for developing details of the plan and to monitor its implementation and progress. The recycling coordinator includes all the prime contractors in developing the plan and provides training for each contractor and subcontractor. If space in staging areas is limited, the plan prioritizes materials, selecting key materials that are easiest to collect or most valuable, such as steel. Coordinators need to ensure that recyclable materials do not become contaminated by garbage or non-allowed materials, which cause processing facilities to reject the loads. Record-keeping is a significant part of coordination, and includes tracking weight tickets and receipts for the amount of material recycled, monitoring recycling progress, and comparing recycling rates to the goals established in the waste management plan (New York City Department of Design & Construction 2003, 22–26).

The greatest amount of waste is generated during the demolition phase of a project. An alternative is deconstruction, the process of selectively removing and salvaging building materials for reuse. Many contractors hire companies that specialize in deconstruction. Building materials and architectural elements are sold through specialized reclamation outlets or donated to nonprofit organizations such as Habitat for Humanity, which provides housing for low-income families. Some metropolitan areas maintain recycling databases and building materials exchanges to facilitate reuse of deconstructed materials.

Industrial Waste

Industrial waste is the leftover and discarded material produced as a byproduct of manufacturing, extraction, power generation, and other large-scale commercial enterprises. Although most consumers focus on MSW, it is industrial waste that makes up the majority of waste

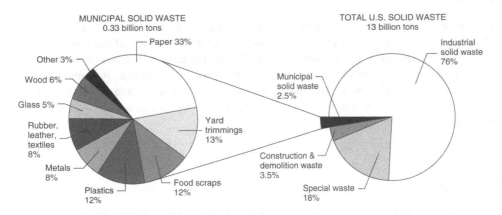

Figure 14.1 Municipal solid waste compared with total US solid waste. Note that MSW, the chart on the left, constitutes only a small percentage of the total volume, shown in the chart on the right.

Source: Adapted from Makower (2009c).

generated (Figure 14.1). Calculations indicate that industrial waste may be at least 90 percent of the total gross US waste (Leonard 2010a, 186). Other calculations show that the volume of industrial waste is somewhere between 40 times and 70 times that of MSW (Makower 2009b). Depending upon the industry and location, industrial waste may be included in sanitary landfills used for MSW or it may be sent to separate industrial waste landfills. The most effective way to deal with this massive quantity of refuse is through prevention, to change consumption patterns fundamentally.

Box 14.3 Keep America Beautiful

Industrial waste makes up around 90 percent of the total waste generated in the US. However, most of the responsibility for waste-related environmental impacts was deflected onto individuals in a marketing campaign of the 1960s and 1970s known as Keep America Beautiful (KAB). KAB is a nonprofit group developed by companies within the packaging industry who were concerned that government might make them responsible for solving the litter problem by regulating their industries (SourceWatch 2009). Originally founded in 1953 by the American Can Company, which invented the disposable can, and Owens-Illinois Glass Company, which invented disposable bottles, it was joined by Coca-Cola, the Dixie Cup Company, Phillip Morris, and several others. KAB worked to reframe waste as a problem that could be solved by individual behavior, rather than by stricter regulation. While actively lobbying against legislation that would require returnable containers, KAB simultaneously launched a marketing campaign focused on its newly developed concept: litter. KAB shifted the debate away from mass consumption, the rising volume of waste, and its

(continued)

(continued)

trail of resource depletion and pollution, "singling out the real villain: the notorious 'litterbug'" (Rogers 2005, 143). In 2009 KAB made a bid to buy out the financially struggling National Recycling Coalition (NRC), then the largest coalition of recycling advocates in the US. NRC members rejected the proposal, although it would have meant survival for the group, and the organization disbanded (Leonard 2010a, 196). Today KAB's members remain actively engaged in lobbying against environmental legislation such as bottle bills.

Zero Waste

In the waste hierarchy known as the 3Rs, the priorities for dealing with waste are to reduce, then reuse, and finally recycle as the last line of defense. Some sustainability specialists recommend adding a fourth, higher priority, "re-think," to the beginning of the hierarchy: re-think, reuse, reduce, recycle. They point out that we may be asking the wrong questions. Maybe the question should not be, "how can we recycle more?" Maybe the right question is, "how can we stop producing so much waste in the first place?"

The current industrial system is linear. In this "take–make–waste" model (Hawken 1993, xiii), raw material flows in, products are made and waste, a symptom of poor design, flows out. The more we make and the more time goes by, the more waste piles up, the more pollutants accumulate, and the more natural resources diminish.

Natural systems are not linear; they are closed-loop cycles. Waste from one system becomes food for another system, and everything gets reused. This is the fundamental concept behind cradle to cradle design and eco-industrial parks. It is also the organizing concept behind a shift in thinking known as Zero Waste.

Zero Waste looks at every material as a resource that can be used again. Instead of "take–make–waste" the system becomes "borrow–use–return" (Hawken et al. 2008). Waste is simply a resource in the wrong place. In a Zero Waste system, as in cradle-to-cradle design, every material is a nutrient, toxic substances are never produced or used, and "waste" does not build up as a legacy for future generations. Every material either returns to the biosphere through biological decomposition or recycles indefinitely as a technical nutrient.

Zero Waste begins with design. It means that products and packaging must be designed for durability, reuse, and recyclability, and the ways we live, including the ways we do business and the ways we lay out our cities, must be redesigned to minimize or eliminate the need for so many products.

Zero Waste uses the producer responsibility approach. Already seen in electronics and vehicle takeback laws, this approach involves a shift in responsibility. Responsibility no longer lies with consumer choices at the back end of a product's life, but with the manufacturer who designed and produced it. Although consumers can choose to buy or not buy a product, most of the choices made by designers and manufacturers lie beyond the reach of direct individual influence. Producers are held responsible to reduce consumption and to facilitate reuse and recovery. This shift in thinking explicitly takes into account the full life-cycle cost of each product, including extraction, production, transportation, and disposal.

To be widely implemented, Zero Waste requires changes in policies and laws. Extractive industries such as mining and timber currently receive tax subsidies that make resource extraction economical and that hide true life-cycle costs. Without subsidies, material prices would reflect their true costs and reused or recycled products would be able to compete in the marketplace on a level playing field (Eco-Cycle 2011).

Meanwhile, some cities with Zero Waste policies have changed their waste collection fee structures to provide incentives for reusing and recycling. Rather than a single monthly fee, users are charged based on the volume they discard, an approach sometimes known as pay-as-you-throw. Some regions have taken money that would have been spent on landfills or incinerators and instead have invested in infrastructure that supports reuse.

Some cities create resource recovery centers, sometimes known as discard malls, where multiple recycling and reuse businesses are grouped together in a single location (CalRecycle 2011). The Monterey Resource Recovery Park in California includes a sanitary landfill, recycling station, MRF, and resale facility. The San Leandro Resource Recovery Park in California includes a recycling center, building materials exchange, landscape products, and a tire recycling and crumb rubber facility. In Berkeley, California, an organization known as Urban Ore operates a resource recovery park with a building materials exchange, hardware exchange, arts and media exchange, salvage and recycling areas. Many cities in Japan, where re-use and recycling are emphasized, have attractive facilities where customers can shop for used clothing, toys, and household goods.

Zero Waste is more than simply reuse and recycling, although those are important. The so-called fourth R, "rethinking," is primary. Zero Waste involves rethinking the entire production and wasting system. This approach considers the entire life cycle of a product when analyzing its costs. It stresses prevention, recognizing that it is more efficient and healthier to prevent waste formation in the first place than to treat waste after it has formed. At its core, Zero Waste acknowledges that humans are part of the natural world. It aims for cradle-to-cradle, closed-loop cycling of non-toxic matter that will allow the biosphere in which we are embedded to continue intact into the future.

Notes

1 Rates are slightly lower in Europe, with per capita solid waste generation rates per day of 2.8 lb. in Sweden, 3.7 lb. in the UK, and 3.9 lb. in Germany (Center for Sustainable Systems Factsheets 2008, 1).
2 The Companion Website for this book lists websites for several organizations offering online instructions for opting out of unwanted mail.
3 Details about how to conduct a waste audit are available on the Companion Website.
4 According to the GrassRoots Recycling Network (2013), making paper with recycled pulp uses 58 percent less water and creates 74 percent less pollution than making paper from new wood; cans made with recycled aluminum require 96 percent less energy to manufacture than those made with new material, and plastic bottles made with recycled resin use 75 to 85 percent less energy to manufacture than those made with new plastic. According to the EPA, curbside recycling in the US prevents the emission of over 200 million tons of carbon dioxide per year, equivalent to removing 35 million automobiles from the road (Rogers 2005, 180).

Further Reading

Leonard, Annie. *The Story of Stuff*. New York: Free Press, 2010.
Maczulak, Anne. *Waste Treatment: Reducing Global Waste*. New York: Facts On File, 2010.
Rogers, Heather. *Gone Tomorrow: The Hidden Life of Garbage*. New York: The New Press, 2005.
Sheehan, Bill and Helen Spiegelman. "Climate Change, Peak Oil, and the End of Waste." In Richard Heinberg and Daniel Lerch, eds. *The Post Carbon Reader: Managing the 21st Century's Sustainability Crises*. Healdsburg, CA: Watershed Media, 2010, pp. 363–84.

Chapter Review

1   Describe the waste management hierarchy.
2   Why is domestic garbage referred to as MSW?
3   Describe the methods used for solid waste disposal.
4   What are the differences between a dump and a sanitary landfill?
5   What potential problems are associated with landfills?
6   What potential problems are associated with the incineration of waste?
7   What is the purpose of a transfer site?
8   Describe how recycling is different from reuse, and give an example of each.
9   What is downcycling? List some examples of downcycling.
10   What problems are caused by disposing of plastics in landfills, in incinerators, and through littering? Do you think one method is preferable?
11   Are there any negative impacts of using compostable plastics? If so, what are they?
12   What is Zero Waste?

Critical Thinking and Discussion

1   Some builders like to recycle discarded objects such as tires or bottles by embedding them in concrete or adobe walls. What advantages and disadvantages do you see in this type of recycling? Are these structures designed for disassembly?
2   Why are recycled-content paper napkins and facial tissues not recyclable?
3   Your neighbor says that he recycles when it is easy to do but that he is not willing to put any extra effort into recycling, because small personal efforts will not have much effect until structural, systemic changes in manufacturing and waste handling are put in place first. How would you respond?
4   A commentator suggests that if we could recycle every product we buy, we would not need any raw materials to make new products. What would you say?
5   Many communities have implemented facilities for composting yard debris, even though the market value of compost is low. Why?
6   What are some negative impacts of using the familiar triangular recycling symbol?
7   A letter to the editor in your local paper says that newspaper recycling is not a good use of resources. The writer argues that newsprint comes from tree farms, not old-growth forests; that the trucks that pick up old newspapers add greenhouse gas emissions; that newsprint can only be recycled a limited number of times anyway; and that removing ink from newsprint requires the use of toxic chemicals. The writer argues that it would be better to place old newspapers in the garbage and let them be buried in landfills. Write a letter to the editor in response.
8   Make a list of the types of waste you send to the landfill on a typical day at home, at work, and when traveling.
9   Some people have proposed imposing rules similar to automobile takeback programs whereby plastics manufacturers would be responsible for the plastic waste they generate. What do you think? Would such a program be feasible? How would it work? What problems do you think would need to be addressed?
10   If "there is no 'away' to which things can be thrown," why doesn't the world fill with waste from its myriad organisms?
11   In what ways does waste increase an organization's carbon footprint?

Part III
Becoming an Agent for Change

15 Working in an Organization

Sustainability professionals often guide sustainability planning in the organizations where they work. Such an organization might be a government agency, a school or college, a nongovernmental organization (NGO), or a private company which provides products or services, and it might be small or large. Each is unique, with its particular set of challenges and opportunities, problems and solutions. Sustainability is local and place-based, and strategies are tailored to each organization's particular situation. However, general principles and methods can be adapted and used in any type and size of organization.

Organizations decide to move toward sustainability for a variety of reasons; many involve either avoiding risk or gaining benefits. Part of the work of sustainability leaders is to help people in an organization determine which reasons make sense for them. In corporations, those new to sustainability may simply be aiming for regulatory compliance in order to avoid fines or legal liability, but as programs are put into place they may discover that many strategies also make business sense, for example, cutting costs by using less energy or by producing less waste. Some sustainability efforts are a response to customer demand over issues such as working conditions, waste, toxicity, or greenhouse gas emissions. Sustainability programs can lead to marketing advantages, distinguishing companies from their competitors and increasing their market share. Organizations of all types may be able to attract more qualified employees and to retain more of the high-quality employees they have.

Governance

The term "governance" refers to how an organization is run, whether at the scale of a company, a city, or a country. It is the process of steering an organization or society and includes what systems and processes are used, how groups are structured, how information is shared, how decisions are made, who is included, where they are included, and how and to whom authority is delegated (Doppelt 2003a, 17). When political scientists and geographers talk about governance they are referring to collective action by diverse communities of stakeholders working together in order to achieve common goals (Evans 2012, 22–26).

Governance is a key factor in successful sustainability programs. Initiatives such as recycling programs and energy efficiency are important, but these strategies alone will not make an organization more sustainable. Research shows that organizations that are successful at planning and implementing sustainability programs either already have in place cultures and governance systems that support these programs, or they make cultural and governance changes as part of overall sustainability strategies (Doppelt 2003a, 78).

In the 1990s management strategist Arie de Geus, formerly Corporate Planning Director at Royal Dutch Shell, conducted a study of Fortune 500 companies, most of whom had an average life expectancy of decades. A few companies had survived for centuries and he found that these long-lived companies all shared three characteristics: they were sensitive to the environment around them; they had a strong sense of cohesion and community; and they avoided centralized control while being tolerant of experimentation and change. Successful organizations, he said, were not just economic machines but were living beings (de Geus 1997). Several years later planning professor Bob Doppelt surveyed organizations that were making successful transitions toward sustainability to determine what characteristics they all had in common. His research revealed that of the range of potential factors, organizational culture and governance offered the greatest leverage (Doppelt 2003a, 78).

Two general approaches to governance can be recognized: the traditional hierarchical mode and a nonlinear model in which employees share information, participate in planning, and are empowered to take action. The traditional command-and-control model of governing is linear and is often seen in "take–make–waste" production systems (Hawken 2010, xiii). These linear systems appeared with the rapid commercial expansion of the Industrial Revolution and relied on mechanization and specialized semi-skilled laborers instead of master craftspeople. In the traditional take–make–waste system, each person or unit along a production line completes their specialized task, then passes the work onto the next station. Managers assume that workers need to understand only their particular job and do not need broad knowledge of the organization's work as a whole. In such systems only the people in positions of power at the top of the structure can see how all the pieces fit together.

An alternative governance model is necessary in what Hawken calls "borrow–use–return" systems, operating on cyclical models such as those found in cradle-to-cradle systems. When systems are such that materials must be reused in technical nutrient cycles or be returned to nature in biological nutrient cycles, members of the organization must understand the overall flows and must participate in making and implementing decisions. In fact, this kind of structure is analogous to living systems in the natural world. Such nonlinear models are made of self-organizing networks of communities, with flows of energy and information. As with living cells surrounded by membranes, these organizational systems are open to inputs from the outside world. As with living systems, such organizations are evolving, self-generating, adaptive systems that feature emergence of new forms and resilience in the face of change.

This may sound abstract. What it means in practice is that members participate in the life of the organization, developing a collective vision and strategies together. In such a structure, everyone affected by what the organization does has the ability to be engaged and information is shared widely, as are resources. Members are given the freedom and authority to make decisions and take action within the organization's agreed-upon framework. Innovation is supported and the organization is a learning organization that is able to evolve. In other words, it has the features of a resilient system (Evans 2012, 170–71).

Traditional, linear structures use approaches which feature what are known as silos. An organizational silo is analogous to a tall, narrow farm silo used to store just one type of grain. In an organization, a silo is an insulated, vertical unit with little outside exchange of information. The word "vertical," when applied to an organization, means that one of the most important characteristics is who has authority over whom. In this kind of structure, the people who actually do the work of the organization cannot see how the whole system functions, and so it is difficult to identify and understand the causes of systemic problems or to understand how to solve them (Barlett and Chase 2004, 11).

By contrast, an organization oriented around a circular borrow–use–return approach requires a more horizontal structure where employees and other stakeholders are seen as interdependent and the people who affect and are affected by sustainability issues are actively involved in finding solutions. This often means making use of the energy and collective intelligence of cross-functional teams. Organizations that do this successfully operate in ways that are similar to ecosystems, in which every niche fills an important role and every individual has a part to play.

This does not mean that a traditional hierarchical organization should not move toward sustainability, nor that such efforts are doomed. Organizations start where they are and take deliberate steps toward where they want to be. Developing a vision is essential for moving effectively in a positive direction.

Sustainability Professionals at Work

Sustainability professionals wear many hats and work in jobs requiring that they use both technical skills and so-called soft skills. They must work simultaneously as project managers, planners, report writers, analysts, educators, and inspirational change agents.

People work as sustainability professionals in a wide range of settings and scales and with a wide range of titles. Some jobs have broad responsibility, for example sustainability coordinator, sustainability director, or corporate social responsibility director. Some jobs are specialized, for example recycling coordinator, waste reduction analyst, pollution prevention specialist, energy analyst, or green building advisor. Practitioners can work for private businesses or corporations, cities, schools, colleges or universities, NGOs, nonprofit organizations, governments, the military, groups that work on generating national policies and laws, and international agencies. A professional may be hired for a particular project or they may be hired to do an evaluation and make recommendations. Often a person working in another kind of position is assigned a sustainability project as part of their other work, and as the organization begins to learn about the elements of sustainability their project grows into a job. Many sustainability practitioners have evolving job descriptions, and many create their own positions as they go along.

Each person works in this field with the goal of helping their particular organization become more sustainable. It is a multi-dimensional and constantly changing task. In general, the professional analyzes their system's current conditions, identifies what needs doing, lays out a prioritized plan often made up of many smaller projects, monitors to evaluate how much and what kind of progress is being made toward sustainability goals, and continuously adapts. Many sustainability programs begin with a specific, measurable project such as improving energy efficiency, reducing water consumption, increasing recycling rates, or tracking greenhouse gas emissions, then expand over time to become more inclusive and far-reaching.

In an organization with multiple departments and functions, the sustainability professional provides a unifying focus. The typical job includes writing reports, presenting data, publicizing goals and achievements, organizing events, working with committees, and having many conversations. It is collaborative work. Every sustainability job includes the responsibility to listen, to communicate, to educate others, and to include other people as true partners in the project of becoming more sustainable.

People who work in sustainability come to recognize the emergent properties of networks. Something happens when groups of people come together: the property of all living systems known as emergence, producing results that are greater than the sum of the parts, with novel qualities that are different from those in any of the individual parts. Part of the work of sustainability professionals includes promoting connections between people at all kinds of scales and fostering conditions where emergence can occur.

Whether expressed or unspoken, a larger purpose underlies every sustainability professional's work: the transformation of global civilization toward a regenerative system that promotes healthy ecosystems, consumes resources no faster than they can be replenished, releases toxins no faster than they can be absorbed, allows wastes from one cycle to become nutrients for another, fosters healthy, cohesive communities with opportunity for all, and continues into the long-term future. Sustainability professionals around the world are part of an effort not only to prevent large-scale catastrophe but also to bring into being a positive and regenerative vision. They work to change the world by changing the systems in which they work and live, often starting with small steps.

Corporate Social Responsibility

Corporate social responsibility (CSR) is a voluntary commitment by companies and other organizations to take responsibility and be held accountable for their environmental and social impacts. Such organizations go beyond legal requirements and fiduciary responsibilities to acknowledge a moral responsibility toward the environment and society of which they are a part, taking responsibility for their negative social and ecological impacts, striving to increase their positive impacts, and being accountable for both. This active willingness to accept responsibility for profit, people, and planet is integral to sustainable development (Moratis and Cochius 2011, 25).

ISO 26000: Guidance on Social Responsibility is an ISO standard which provides guidance to organizations. It defines terms, provides information on concepts and characteristics of social responsibility, and helps organizations to implement and promote socially responsible practices and to communicate information related to social responsibility (ISO 2010). It is not a management system standard and is not intended to be used for certification; it provides guidance for organizations and can be used in developing public policy.

Sustainability Initiatives

Working for sustainability in any organization follows steps that are similar to those for managing change in any business or institution. A sustainability professional maintains contact with a positive vision for the future while striving to understand the reality of where they are now.

Work begins by defining a goal. This is followed by inventory and analysis, as people work together to understand the current conditions and trends: what are the conditions, and how are they changing over time? Gathering this kind of detailed information is a fundamental part of doing sustainability work. Following the step of measurement, the next step is to identify where in the system to begin making a change. Leaders look for a leverage point, a place where a small change might lead to a bigger impact. Like much of sustainability work, this analysis is often done by people thinking and working together. Often cost–benefit analyses are conducted in order to understand the impacts or in order to make the business case for a sustainability initiative.

Implementing change is the most visible step in sustainability work and is where other people most often want to get involved. One approach to choosing a place to start is to pick what is known as "low-hanging fruit": projects that can be implemented with few obstacles to success, or projects with big impact and visible return on an investment in effort. Sustainability practitioners sometimes begin by launching a single targeted initiative, such as a "take back the tap" campaign to reduce the use of bottled water, or a recycling initiative, or a "lights out when you leave" campaign to reduce energy consumption and raise awareness. They might take steps to make impacts and improvements more visible, such as listing embedded energy or carbon footprints on a cafeteria menu, or installing dashboards, electronic screens that provide usage information in real time for attributes such as energy or water consumption. Sometimes there will be events to coordinate, such as an Earth Day celebration, a kickoff for a climate action plan, or a speaker series.

Some initiatives are large in scale. The professional might participate in planning green buildings, moving toward a low-carbon transportation system, launching a community garden network, setting up a community education center, restoring a local watershed, or regenerating economic vitality in a low-income neighborhood.

Whether initiatives are large or small in scale, sustainability professionals are aware that they are nested within other larger and smaller scales. They consider how changing one system might affect larger systems within which it is nested and smaller systems contained within it. They try, where possible, to work at multiple scales and across boundaries.

Sustainability practitioners need ways to know whether efforts to change are succeeding, so as with any kind of management, monitoring is an essential step. Monitoring maintains a connection between the original goal and the outcomes, providing feedback about whether efforts are headed in the right direction and showing where to make adjustments to keep an initiative on a positive trajectory. Vision, measurement, action, evaluation, and adaptation make up a cycle of continuous improvement.

Finance and Green Revolving Funds

Sustainability is essential, transformative work. It is collaborative and exciting work. However, it is almost always done within limited budgets, so an important question to ask is, "How are we going to pay for this?" One answer is that many efforts toward saving the planet also save money. For example, organizations must pay for garbage disposal. Instituting a recycling program reduces garbage collection fees by reducing the tonnage going to a landfill; at the same time, recycled material including paper and metal can be sold. A program for reusing materials such as equipment, office supplies, and furniture reduces purchasing costs. Instituting water and energy conservation programs or on-site renewable energy generation reduces the amount spent on monthly utility bills. Quantifying these savings, then reinvesting them to fund further initiatives, is part of the work of a sustainability professional.

Some institutions, cities, and corporations use a formal device called a green revolving fund, an internal fund that uses cost savings from sustainability projects to finance other projects. A loan provides the initial capital to support a project that mitigates greenhouse gas emissions or reduces resource use. The savings from that project are reinvested in the loan fund, where they can then be used to finance future projects. Typical projects that generate cost savings include energy efficiency, renewable energy, water conservation, waste reduction and recycling. A green revolving fund removes financial barriers, visibly makes the business case for sustainability, and provides a unified system for tracking financial aspects of sustainability projects as part of an integrated whole. It creates opportunities to engage the community, bringing diverse stakeholders together to make decisions about sustainability and investments, and clearly communicates an institution's commitment to sustainability goals.

Setting up a fund begins with research to understand thoroughly the accounting system, operations management, and sustainability project portfolio in the organization. Successful planning efforts typically involve staff with expertise in finance, operations, and sustainability, and often include participation by multiple stakeholders as well. A new fund needs seed capital to get started, which can come originally from an operating budget, an endowment fund, utility rebates, donations, or grants. Planners must decide whether to start small, allowing them to pilot a project before scaling up once the pilot demonstrates success; or whether to start at a larger scale, which allows greater flexibility in choosing projects. Planning includes developing criteria for evaluating and selecting projects to be funded.

Decisions need to be made about how the fund will be structured, how repayments will be made, by whom, and how often. The green revolving fund may be set up under a loan model, in which a project borrows money from the fund, or under an accounting model, in which both loans and repayments are handled by transferring funds between particular budgets. The system can be overseen by a single administrator; by staff from a relevant office such as finance, facilities, or sustainability; or by a management committee, which has the advantage of promoting broader stakeholder engagement and greater awareness (Indvik et al. 2013).

People

An important first step in any project is to get the right people involved. This entails two aspects: finding people who are motivated and engaged, and ensuring that an effective structure exists. Although some structures work better than others, leaders and sustainability champions can come from any level of the organization; change can be initiated from the bottom up or can be led from the top.

Transformation toward sustainability requires good governance and strong leadership. Eventually, involvement and support from senior management will be required; transforming the organizational culture and successful long-term maintenance of sustainability initiatives are nearly impossible without support from the power brokers in the organization (Doppelt 2003b, 5). Progress toward change typically occurs faster when initiatives are sponsored by or at least supported by senior leaders.

The sustainability change effort needs a sponsor or champion. The most effective original sponsors are typically people in leadership positions. They advocate for change, make the initiative visible and exciting, remove obstacles, minimize interference, and provide support. Once a sustainability initiative is launched, the original sponsor can be replaced by another, ongoing sustainability champion.

If governance is to be shared, sustainability efforts are led by some kind of steering committee. This group should be broadly representative, although members must be chosen with care and should include positions whose functions impact sustainability. For example, representatives might include a facilities manager and a purchasing manager; in a manufacturing facility they might also include a designer and in a university they might also include faculty and managers from food services and residence halls. At least one member should have decision-making authority. Similar to a steering device like a rudder or wheel that guides a vessel or vehicle in a direction, a steering committee guides an organization along a course of sustainability change. The steering committee looks at the big picture and helps establish a framework; it does not give orders, and it does not necessarily do all of the detailed work.

Teams are the heart of a sustainability change initiative. They can include many participants and they ensure that the sustainability vision and goals are embedded throughout the fabric of an organization in an authentic way. The more that goals and initiatives come from the people who are involved with planning, decision-making, and doing, the more the entire organization will embrace sustainability changes, rather than seeing them as edicts from above with little personal relevance (Willard 2009, 30).

Teams should include members from across the range of departments or job functions and from all levels of responsibility, as well as key stakeholders. Some are transition teams, launched primarily for planning and initiating change strategies. Some teams are known as task forces, organized to carry out specific short-term projects. Some groups are standing teams and are permanent elements of ongoing sustainability efforts, although individual members themselves may rotate on and off. In addition, it is important to get the buy-in of managers and supervisors to be sure that team members will be given time to participate in meetings and related activities.

Organizations that successfully implement sustainability ensure that everyone is included. People who are not members of specific teams still have roles in sustainability efforts, and each person is an expert in the area in which they work. For example, an organization implementing a new recycling program could host a breakfast for custodians and work crews to talk about how the system is working and what improvements could be made (Barlett and Chase 2004, 59). In 1995, Swedish hotel chain Scandic provided sustainability training for their entire staff using a framework called The Natural Step, and were surprised to learn that many of the best ideas came not from management but from housekeepers on the front line, who saw things no one else could see (Friend 2009, 167). Organizations with successful programs provide ways for employees to submit suggestions along with mechanisms for responding. Suggestion boxes became popular in the early 1940s, often featuring the slogan, "None of us is as smart as all of us." Modern suggestion "boxes" usually involve emails, websites, and meetings instead of pieces of paper.

While the fastest way to create change in an organization is through leadership from upper management in a top-down approach, momentum can also come from people in organizations without strong sustainability leadership in a bottom-up approach. Sometimes leaders at the top are insulated from the effects of poor social or environmental performance or are trapped in the inertia of business-as-usual, and it may be people in the lower or middle levels of an organization who generate interest first. Casual, informal gatherings can be a way to spark initial interest among volunteers. To be effective, however, a grassroots effort must be well organized. A productive approach is to gather data, prepare a high-quality presentation and slowly begin building a case, sharing ideas first with other like-minded employees and getting feedback, gradually expanding the circle of people who understand and support a more sustainable direction, and eventually making now-polished presentations to decision-makers. This is likely to be a long-term process, and sustainability champions must be prepared to be patient, persistent, and positive.

A theory known as Diffusion of Innovations was first introduced by sociologist Everett M. Rogers in 1962. Rogers described the categories of people who adopt a new idea as innovators, early adopters, early majority, late majority, and laggards. He showed that after enough people adopt an innovation it reaches critical mass, so that continued adoption of the innovation is self-sustaining. Rogers' calculations placed this number at about 16 percent of a population (Rogers 2003, 223). Since then, a number of management consultants and sustainability planners have affirmed that critical mass is reached when 15 to 20 percent of the members of an organization are involved in a change initiative such as sustainability; once that number is involved, cultural change across the entire organization is likely.

Many organizations create a job position with the title of sustainability coordinator or sustainability director to oversee and facilitate the change effort. Sustainability coordinators convene meetings of steering committees and task forces, prepare agendas, reserve meeting rooms, distribute meeting materials, send out notices, and chair or facilitate meetings. They function like internal consultants, helping steering committees and other groups develop visions and formulate strategies. They help develop implementation plans, indicator reports and other monitoring tools, job descriptions, and contracts for services such as recycling, energy services companies, and commissioning. Sustainability coordinators are communicators, writing articles for internal newsletters and external news media, developing websites, doing public speaking, conducting employee training, and writing annual sustainability reports. They are cheerleaders, conflict mediators, trainers, and resources for technical information. As effective leaders, they must willingly share ownership of projects and power and urge an organization on with energy, vision, and optimism. They may do this visibly, and they may also do it by supporting other leaders from behind the scenes.

A sustainability coordinator is sometimes like a trimtab on the rudder of a ship. A large ship moving through the water has great momentum in a particular direction, impossible to turn using just a rudder. A trimtab is a small flap on the edge of the main rudder; turning the trimtab allows the rudder to turn, which then allows the ship to turn. Airplane wings use trimtabs as well. Designer and visionary R. Buckminster Fuller (1895–1983) suggested the words "Call me Trimtab" as his epitaph; they are engraved on his tombstone.

The Planning Process

Planning is the essential foundation of sustainability work. Its importance cannot be overstated. Planning begins with a vision of where the team wants to be, then works backwards to milestones along the process. In contrast to forecasting or predicting the future, this approach to planning for a desired future is sometimes known as backcasting (Sachs 2015, 493). Careful planners construct a detailed map of how to get from the vision to reality, and they set up regular tracking systems with prioritized lists of tasks, people responsible, and timelines.

Vision

It is essential to create a clear vision of sustainability at the beginning of the planning process, a clear and compelling image of the future that defines what the organization is trying to achieve. Planning teams begin by imagining what the organization will look like 10, 20, or 50 years in the future when it is completely sustainable. How will it operate? What will its governance system be like? This is long-term, big-picture thinking.

A good vision statement describes ideal future conditions in terms that many different kinds of people can relate to. It is unambiguous and uses clear, simple language without technical jargon. A good vision statement describes a positive future state; assertions that describe what to avoid such as, "we will reduce our environmental damage" or "we will comply with all environmental regulations" are not vision statements. Vision statements should be generated without being concerned about cost or technological difficulty. This is the place to dream big.

Teams can use hypothetical stories to help them develop a vision. For example, they might think about a feature story about their organization in a magazine or television documentary 10, 20, or 50 years from now and imagine the details that might be presented in the story.

Box 15.1 Scenario Planning

Sustainability teams in some organizations use scenario planning, asking "what-if" questions to imagine possible futures. First used by military planners after World War II, then used by Royal Dutch Shell during the 1973 oil crisis, this approach is now used by the IPCC, the UN, the IEA in its *World Energy Outlook*, and many corporations, cities, and sustainability planners. Scenarios are plausible what-if stories. They are short, evidence-based fictional narratives about the future that enable an organization to make decisions that will be sound for all plausible futures (Hopkins and Zapata 2007; Schwartz 1996; van der Heijden 2005).

The process begins by brainstorming and identifying driving forces that could impact the future. Participants use group processes to cluster the driving forces, typically sorting driving forces into five categories: environmental, economic, social, political, and technological, then ranking them according to degree of impact and degree of uncertainty. If some forces are contrasting, they might become axes or ends of a spectrum.

Once the driving forces have been grouped, teams create four to six very different but plausible stories about the future. The more diverse the teams, the richer the scenarios will be. Participants try to describe each plausible future in as much detail as possible as if it had already come to pass, giving each one a vivid, memorable name. They flesh out these scenarios, thinking about how the world might get from the present to there and what events would need to occur to make a particular scenario plausible. They develop a set of indicators, small details to watch for that might indicate a particular future is possible.

After considering several varied stories of equally plausible futures, an organization can think about its vision—what it wants to become—and what it would take to achieve that vision under each of the possible futures. Teams can identify the future they most desire and the future with the greatest potential risk, working backward to identify ways to make their most cherished future more likely and their least preferred future less likely.

A good test for a vision statement once it has been drafted is a concise communication known as an "elevator speech." If someone asked you: "What is your organization's vision for sustainability?" as you were traveling in an elevator in a multistory building, would you be able to describe clearly what your organization is working toward, how it is different from past conditions, and why it is important by the time the elevator reached its destination floor? If you could, you probably have a vision.

Goals

A vision statement leads to actionable, measurable goals. When a goal is measurable, it is possible to know when it has been reached. It has, in effect, a finish line and people can know when the finish line has been crossed. Goals provide focal points for effort and help people take the next steps of developing strategies and tactics. Different people and departments will be interested in different aspects of the sustainability vision, and goals allow each to focus on their particular areas. Although some organizations are moving in a constructive direction, no organization on Earth is sustainable, and all of us are a long way from where we need to be. While we need some goals that are easily reachable, we also need to set some goals that require a stretch because that is what it will take to become sustainable. These stretch goals are sometimes referred to in planning circles as big, hairy, audacious goals (Friend 2009, 27; Hitchcock 2008, 46), or BHAGs (pronounced "Bee-hags").

Strategies

A vision describes what the future state should be and why; strategies describe how to reach it. Strategies are specific action plans generated by working backward from a vision. They include what steps will be taken and when. Sustainability planning in an organization involves developing two types of strategies: strategies for operations (such as product design, energy efficiency, transportation, or purchasing), and strategies for governance and process. If people are to think and behave differently, the way they are organized and empowered may need to be different as well.

Some sustainability plans develop strategies for two or three different time frames. Teams can use brainstorming and other group processes to generate ideas for short-term strategies, which are often easiest to conceive and appear achievable to the most people. Then groups can explore long-term strategies; these are where the vision of a fully sustainable organization can generate the most excitement. Finally, groups can develop transition strategies for an intermediate-term time frame.

Strategies include steps that will be taken. The use of the word "steps" is appropriate because the process is analogous to climbing a long hill one step at a time. The entire uphill distance is great but each step by itself is manageable. While some changes are dramatic and help sustain motivation, others are incremental. Many steps taken over time can add up to real progress. Regular reports help people recognize the progress that has been made through the accumulation of incremental steps.

Teams working to develop strategies need to understand the state of existing conditions by doing assessments. The vision shows where they want to be in the future, assessments show where they are in the present, and the differences are revealed as gaps that need to be closed. It is a little like shopping for a dinner party: the theme (vision) defines the overall experience, the menu (goals) defines the dinner that will be the end result, a list of ingredients (strategies) details what will be needed to produce the dinner, an inventory of the kitchen shelves (assessment) reveals what is already on hand, and comparing the two determines what still needs to be acquired.

At the scale of an organization, assessment can feel like a daunting task. One place to start is a process map, which maps the workflow in the organization using flowchart sketches, simple drawings, adhesive notes, or pieces of paper (Hitchcock 2008, 58; Sitarz 2008, 41–42). The mapping process itself can begin to clarify what might have seemed like a blurry picture. At each step, teams identify materials, energy, and people that are inputs and those that are outputs. With the overall whole thus broken into manageable discrete pieces, teams then evaluate components of the workflow methodically. They discuss which elements of each step match the goals they have established and which do not, what a sustainable version of each step would look like, and where in the process would be an appropriate place to begin working toward the vision and goals. As teams work together creating workflow diagrams, assessment details can be written on electronic boards or flip-charts, drawn directly on any diagrams that have been constructed, or recorded with image generators available in planning software. Seeing the flows in an organization diagrammed visually can help reveal opportunities for transforming linear processes into recirculating cycles. One of the challenges in instituting change is helping to make invisible impacts visible; sustainability assessments help to do that.[1] Naming the sustainability change initiative can make it seem significant, generate excitement, and help provide a sense of identity.

In an organization where a sustainability change initiative is well accepted, another useful activity is to conduct a walk-through assessment of the organization's facilities and work areas (Friend 2009, 49). As team members proceed they talk with people in each area, asking not only for explanations about how they do their work but also for suggestions about where improvements are possible. This may uncover ideas and innovations that others had not thought of, and is another way both to spread the word about sustainability work and to enable people to be involved.

Defining which indicators will be tracked and developing plans for reporting on them regularly is the next step following assessment. Teams in the Sustainable Seattle project, for example, created a collaborative vision, then developed targets organized around four goal areas in the natural, built, social, and personal environments. A set of 36 indicators were measured at the beginning of the project and are reevaluated at regular intervals in order to measure progress (Bell and Morse 2008, 164). Indicators are discussed later in this chapter.

Team members should think deliberately about timing of initiatives. If all the groundwork has been laid, management support and supporting systems are in place, and other members of the organization are generally in harmony with the vision of sustainability, then it may be appropriate to set big goals and make a dramatic launch. If so much time has been invested in preparation and assessment that people are beginning to lose interest or that what management consultants call "analysis paralysis" has set in, then it is time to move onto the next step and take action. If a company is facing pressure from shareholders, unhappy customers, or other imminent risk factors, a significant and visible change may be appropriate.

However, a gradual, quiet start may be preferable if management support, supporting systems, and employee goodwill are not yet in place. Building the case carefully and slowly is also important when the organization has a history of failed or forgotten initiatives, or when the majority of employees have a negative image of sustainability.

Tactics

The vision defines what an organization wants to achieve; goals and strategies lay out framework plans for reaching the vision. Tactics are the actions the organization takes in order to implement its strategies. Tactics are specific projects. Planning for and implementing tactics often gets greater numbers of people involved because this is the action step. Many people like to feel that something tangible is being accomplished.

Before selecting specific projects, teams should agree on criteria for selecting them (Hitchcock 2008, 59–61). There will probably be many more possible projects than there are time or resources to do immediately. At the least, projects must be prioritized. It is helpful to select several different projects so that everyone who chooses to has a place and a way to contribute.

One criterion is impact. Teams may want to select projects with the biggest or most lasting impact on social, economic, and environmental sustainability. An alternative criterion is immediacy. Teams may want to select projects which offer quick success. These quick wins, sometimes referred to as low-hanging fruit because they are easy to accomplish, help to generate enthusiasm and keep people engaged. A good approach is to choose some projects for quick results and some other projects that require greater time and effort and produce more significant, lasting impact. It may be helpful to begin with a prototype or pilot project, both to fine-tune elements of the sustainability plan and to demonstrate an immediate win. As a popular saying goes, you only get one chance to make a good first impression. After the pilot has been successful it may be able to be scaled up to encompass a larger scope.

Another set of criteria involves benefits and costs. Costs and benefits can be financial and are used in making the business case. They can also be intangible characteristics including employee engagement, image, market share, legal liability, and ethical principles.

Another criterion is feasibility. Organizations should evaluate their resources not only in terms of money but also in available time and in the particular skill sets and interests of their members. Organizations should also consider how many different projects they can simultaneously track and manage well. Visioning was the place to dream big; selecting tactics requires clear-headed realism.

Policies

Depending upon the type of organization, some teams may choose to develop written policies to guide sustainability, particularly in public agencies and educational institutions. In most cases policies help to provide guidance as an organization moves toward greater sustainability. Care should be taken that a policy does not simply become an excuse for doing the bare minimum. In addition, in some situations policies may constrain a process to incremental changes, limiting or preventing the kind of paradigm transformations that will be required if sustainability is to be achieved.

Making the Business Case for Sustainability

Initiating sustainability because "it is the right thing to do" is a nice idea, but typically it will not last. Regardless of the type of organization, whether a school, governmental agency, corporation, or nonprofit group, if an initiative does not also make business sense it is not likely to remain a priority. We need to build the business case.

A business case is an accurate assessment of the opportunities and risks connected with a proposed plan. It defines sustainability initiatives as investments that will improve the bottom line, and it calculates their return on investment (ROI). The business case should consider what people such as presidents and chief financial officers need to know and should then use the vocabulary and business language familiar to the audience to whom it is presented. Proposals for projects such as energy efficiency, waste reduction, or pollution reduction can highlight cost reductions, improved operational efficiency, increased market share, lower employee health costs, and improved employee productivity, with sustainability benefits mentioned as happy by-products of all the other benefits.

Risk analysis is a process that estimates what can go wrong, assesses the probabilities and potential consequences, and identifies how those consequences can be prevented or reduced. Risks include both financial and nonfinancial components. Some risks looming on the horizon are global in scale; the changing climate is an example. It has been shown that if all of us do not act to reduce the emission of greenhouse gases, all of us will face great costs (Stern 2006). Insurance carriers are particularly concerned about this risk. Issues of declining supplies of water or other natural resources, the disappearance of cheap fossil fuel, and the impacts of pollution present other large-scale risks. Some risks are more local and may include lawsuits and damage claims, regulatory fines, negative publicity, and lost customers.

Opportunities are often financial. For example, large potential savings from energy efficiency or waste reduction measures are usually relatively easy to demonstrate. One of the opportunities inherent in sustainability changes for businesses is competitive market advantage. Companies that are the first to transform their products and operations are seen in the market as innovators, and this image can remain with them in the form of market share and customer loyalty even after competitors have caught up (Hitchcock and Willard 2008, 20). Another opportunity is the benefit of being prepared in advance to meet new regulations. Preparing in a proactive, orderly way is almost always more cost-effective than having to respond reactively to a changing regulatory environment (Doppelt 2003a, 96, Willard 2002, 68).

A business case can demonstrate the potential for cost avoidance or cost savings. For example, in linear take–make–waste systems the so-called end-of-pipe solutions, such as scrubbers to remove pollutants from smokestacks or treatment plants to remove pollutants from waterways, are fixes that are applied after environmental impacts have occurred. Thus they are costs added to the original cost of doing business. In contrast, systemic shifts to circular borrow–use–return systems address the root causes and prevent damage from occurring in the first place; these kinds of changes often result in cost reductions (Doppelt 2003a, 57). When sustainable business consultant Gil Friend talks about the cost of waste he refers to waste as "non-product output," or NPO (2009, 42–45). Producing non-product requires resources that are paid for by the company but that cannot generate revenue. Thus eliminating waste or converting it to an input in a borrow–use–return cycle makes financial sense.

Teams that have trouble calculating cost savings or risk avoidance for their own organizations may be able to develop case studies of similar organizations which have implemented sustainability measures and use these in making the business case. In for-profit companies, it can be particularly helpful to research suppliers, major customers, and competitors to find which ones are already pursuing sustainability since the results can have an impact on a company's ability to remain competitive (Willard 2002, 12).

Implementation

Implementation is where the tactics that have been identified in the planning process become reality. Teams develop detailed implementation plans that list what is to be done, who will do it, timelines, responsibilities, funding, and feedback methods that lead to improvements and new opportunities.

If sustainability lacks management support, then implementation begins with small steps where teams select projects with relatively low risk and, if possible, high potential for pay-off. As projects continue, data on costs and benefits can be collected and the business case built gradually. Small successes add up and momentum can build over time.

If sustainability has support from top management and careful planning has resulted in an organized initiative, then symbolic actions and ceremonial events such as a kick-off event can be considered, perhaps with an employee luncheon, displays, and speakers including the organization's leaders. In some colleges, student groups conduct assessments and then present their results at the kick-off event. Some initiatives organize community-building activities such as nature walks, stream cleanup, or planting a community garden. If a logo has been developed for the sustainability program, the kick-off day is a good time to begin using it. Depending upon the type of event, teams may consider inviting local media. Subsequent events can include reports on improvements in sustainability performance, workshops and training sessions, awards or prizes, and other kinds of positive recognition. Celebrating together is important: it helps to strengthen community network bonds and it reinforces that sustainability is something that is valued by the group.

Communication is important. Everything the organization is doing to build a healthy, just, and sustainable society should be in front of everyone all the time. People need to understand why there is a need, what are the strategies, what are the benefits, what is the future vision, and where is the organization along the path toward that vision. They need to know not only what is being done but also how they can contribute. When people are well informed they are better able to make good decisions and to see new opportunities for improvement and innovation. Individuals feel optimistic when they believe that what they are doing is important and is actually making a difference.

People especially need to hear about the positive results of their efforts expressed in ways that are easily understood. For example, reporting that the amount of material recycled in two years would fill the local high school football stadium to the top bleachers is more meaningful to many people than simply expressing the same idea in tons of material diverted from the landfill.

Organizations that are leaders in sustainability change maintain a constant stream of communication to all the members of the organization and often to outside stakeholders as well. People receive floods of information from all directions every day, so sustainability information is more likely to get through if it is consistently presented and important part of the information landscape. Some sustainability practitioners develop a formal communication plan. Elements include internal communication which can take the form of regular newsletter articles, email updates, posters, discussion groups, sustainability agenda items in department meetings, speakers, brown bag lunches,[2] training sessions, and celebratory events. External communication can include sponsored events, news stories, providing public speakers to other venues, and websites that are regularly updated. Many organizations use websites both to report on progress and to provide links to additional resources where people can learn more.

Like annual reports from a corporation or agency, regular sustainability reports are part of a comprehensive communication plan. Assessments should be conducted regularly and reports on sustainability performance should be shared with employees and other stakeholders. These should be honest, transparent assessments of performance including both positives and negatives; reports will be ignored if they are seen as simply marketing efforts.

Sustainability involves new ways of looking at the world, and can seem abstract and hard to understand for people new to its ideas. Communication should use clear, nontechnical language that is easy to understand and to which everyone can relate in their own way. It should be simple and straightforward and must avoid the appearance of zealotry and preaching. Communications should be underpinned by the positive idea that we are all in this together, that we are all important, and that by working together and bringing our collective intelligence to bear we can solve problems. Communicators must be careful to avoid reinforcing erroneous notions that people who care about sustainability are somehow different from others. Every organization is a community; becoming more sustainable involves changing the culture of that community, and that requires a search for common ground.

The sustainability effort needs to be kept alive and growing through continuous improvement. Continuous improvement is a management concept that gained prominence through total quality management programs, later becoming one of the elements of environmental management systems laid out in ISO 14000. It involves steady progress, which can be either incremental or transformational; thinking about upstream processes rather than downstream damage control; the ongoing cycle of planning, implementing, assessing, and adapting; and wide participation. Continuous improvement will not come from top-down directives; it only happens when people at all levels work together.

Purchasing

Green purchasing is a systematic process in which buyers select goods and services based not only on price but on their full lifetime costs, with lower environmental and social impacts throughout their life cycles than would otherwise have been procured. Many organizations develop green purchasing policies to guide procurement. Green purchasing professionals and teams establish measurable, verifiable selection criteria; develop specifications for bidding and contract language; develop written green purchasing policy; collaborate with suppliers and communicate with end users.

Frameworks

As teams develop strategies and tactics, a framework can help to provide a common language and a common conceptual understanding. It can include standards and principles to help guide decision-making and it may suggest ways to conduct assessment and measurement. Commonly used frameworks include the triple bottom line, the Global Reporting Initiative (GRI), and The Natural Step. Some organizations develop their own hybrid sustainability framework.

The triple bottom line encompasses environmental, economic, and social dimensions of sustainability. As a reporting framework, the triple bottom line can be used to guide the measurement of sustainability performance in a business or region. Sustainable Seattle is an example of an initiative that uses a triple bottom line reporting framework.

The Global Reporting Initiative is probably the most widely used sustainability reporting framework worldwide. It provides detailed guidelines for measuring and reporting on environmental, economic, and social dimensions of an organization's activities. While it is a complex and comprehensive framework, particularly appropriate for large organizations and those with international audiences, its framework of sustainability indicators is useful in organizations of any size. The Sustainability Tracking, Assessment and Rating System (STARS) is a similar reporting framework used in institutions of higher education.

The Natural Step is a framework designed to help organizations measure and implement sustainable practices. This scientifically based framework was developed in 1989 by Dr. Karl-Henrik Robèrt, an oncologist from Sweden, as he began to think about the potential impact of environmental damage on the incidence of childhood cancers. Through a rigorous peer review process he and 50 ecologists, chemists, physicists, and medical doctors developed consensus about what is needed to sustain life and human civilization on Earth. From there, Dr. Robèrt developed a set of system conditions or principles and a planning method, which together are known as The Natural Step Framework (Edwards 2005, 59–62).

The four system conditions translate the laws of nature into understandable principles. Condition 1 relates to fossil fuels and minerals, Condition 2 relates to toxins, Condition 3 relates to resource extraction, and Condition 4 relates to equity and economics (Nattrass and Altomare 1999). Because these principles are based on incontrovertible science and derived through consensus, they offer a common ground for people with diverse values and backgrounds. The Natural Step assumes that each person is an expert in their particular niche and it trusts that people will be able to solve environmental, social, and economic problems themselves once they understand the basic principles.

The Natural Step uses graphics and metaphors to make the planning process practical and accessible. Its planning process is referred to as the ABCD approach, an acronym for the four steps. The first step is Awareness and Visioning. The second step is Baseline Mapping, in which the organization maps its major flows and impacts, then conducts a gap analysis to identify where the organization's activities violate the four sustainability principles. The third step is Creative Solutions, in which people use brainstorming to develop strategies. The Natural Step process uses backcasting, in which teams begin with the end in mind, envisioning a fully sustainable future and then working backward from that vision to develop strategies. The final step is to Decide on Priorities.

The Natural Step offers handbooks, webinars, and training programs to equip change agents with an understanding of sustainability principles and core skills for applying them. The framework is used by many cities, universities, design firms, and corporations (Nattrass and Altomare 2002).

Measurement and Reporting

Measurement is a fundamental element of sustainability work. An organization with a vision of sustainable products, sustainable services, or sustainable operation needs more than a vision; they need tools for understanding where they are, how far away or how close they are to their goals, and whether they are pointing in the right direction. They need measurement. Managers and planners often say, "what gets measured, gets managed." Measurement is the key to getting sustainability work done. Without measurement, plans and ideas remain disconnected abstractions; with measurement, they become physical reality.

It is common for sustainability professionals to measure progress toward sustainability goals by developing and using indicator reports or similar tools for measuring. Data that describe current conditions and trends are called **indicators**. Like an indicator needle on a gage, data in an indicator report point to conditions, telling us something about the state of the system being measured. These measurements are similar to taking an inventory; they help a company, institution, or community understand where they are, identify gaps, and decide what needs to be done. Indicators can include waste and recycling quantities, percentage of waste stream recycled, water quality, water use, energy consumption, local employment or local poverty rates, and greenhouse gas emissions.

An indicator is a marker that helps gage progress toward a goal. One indicator gives a snapshot; measuring an indicator more than once over time can reveal a pattern or trajectory. Sustainability work is about recognizing and changing trajectories. When sustainability indicators are tracked over time, they help to measure progress toward sustainability goals.

In addition to gathering data, people working on sustainability need to make sense of the data and to present them so that other people can make sense of them, too. An indicator report can take several forms. Some people report quantities in a simple table. Many professionals use spreadsheets to track large quantities of data, then write a summary report to explain and interpret the data. A spreadsheet provides the ability to sort, to track changes over time, and to generate graphs and charts easily.

Why measure?

Measurement provides multiple benefits. Sustainability indicators are used by organizations to provide a framework for deciding where to focus efforts; to motivate people toward process improvement; to demonstrate progress in environmental performance or social responsibility; and to communicate to customers, employees, shareholders, and other stakeholders. For companies using an environmental management system such as ISO 14001,[3] performance measurement is required as part of the standard. Sustainability indicators are used by scientists to clarify what is working, what is not working, and where additional effort is needed. They are used by decision-makers and people who develop policies to help set priorities and guide policy formulation. At the local and regional level, sustainability indicators are developed by community members in a participatory process; the process itself helps citizens and leaders identify key trends and come to a common understanding about issues and goals.

Types of indicators

Measurement can happen at any scale. A common method for measuring individual impact uses what is known as a Footprint, an approach originally used to measure a person's Ecological Footprint (Wackernagel and Rees 1995). Since then, other systems have developed for measuring other kinds of individual Footprint including the Water Footprint (Hoekstra et al., 2011) and the Carbon Footprint (Friend 2009, 58). Footprints can also be used to measure impacts at the scale of a company or other organization, a region, or a nation.

Indicators can be organized in various ways when deciding what to measure. One way is to organize by category. For example, a company or school might prepare an indicator report in each of several categories such as water use, energy use, waste and recycling rate, transportation, greenhouse gas emissions, pollution, economic development, and social impact. Reports organized by category tend to be easy for many people to understand.

Another approach is to organize measurement and reporting around a set of goals. Some communities work collaboratively to develop a set of sustainability goals, then organize their indicators to measure the extent to which each goal was addressed. At a national and global scale the United Nations established the Sustainable Development Goals, organized around a set of 17 goals subdivided into 169 quantifiable targets and indicators (UN 2012, 46).

Yet another way is to organize indicators around driving forces and responses, a method sometimes used by government agencies and other policymakers (Hart 2006, 10). Driving forces could include factors such as drought, rate of pesticide use, land conversion, or political instability. This was the method used by the United Nations Commission on Sustainable Development (CSD) in the past; more recently CSD reports are organized around themes, such as poverty or climate change (ibid.).

Businesses typically report measurements using performance indicators. A company with an environmental management system establishes goals, then uses indicators to measure their progress toward meeting those goals. Each measurable goal includes a benchmark or reference point. For example, a company goal might be to reduce volume of water used per year by 10 percent relative to the 2005 water consumption rate. Or a goal might be to reduce energy use compared to the regional average by 10 percent per year. Indicators can measure eco-efficiency, a concept introduced by the WBCSD. Eco-efficiency measures the ratio between product or service delivered and the amount of environmental impact such as resource consumption, waste generation, or pollutant emissions (Fiksel 2009, 102). For example, General Motors has measured the number of vehicles produced per kilowatt-hour used, per gallons of water used, and per ton of greenhouse gas emitted. As part of their performance assessment, most manufacturing companies use life cycle assessment, which measures impacts throughout the life of a product or service, including extraction or acquisition, manufacture, transport, use, and disposal.

Indicators can be a tool for community sustainability planning. For example, in 1990 business leaders, labor, educators, students, government representatives, and citizens of Seattle, Washington, came together to form a project known as Sustainable Seattle

(Bell and Morse 2003, 52). They worked together to agree upon goals, then selected regional sustainability indicators to measure progress toward those goals. Indicators are measured and reevaluated regularly. Their Regional Sustainability Indicators are organized around 4 environments: the natural, built, social, and personal environments, with 20 sustainability goals, measured with a set of 36 indicators.

Guidelines for Selecting Indicators

As with any planning or management task, the first step in preparing indicator reports is to clarify goals. Goals provide a framework, pointing toward indicators that can be used to measure progress toward those goals. Teams need to be clear about the purpose of collecting indicator data and need to clarify who makes up the intended audience. Time spent considering and developing a broad range of goals and being clear about ultimate goals before identifying indicators makes it more likely that the right things get measured (ibid., 49).

Providing diversity in the types of indicators helps to ensure a balanced picture and minimize distortion. Teams may want to consider a mix of lagging and leading indicators (Hitchcock and Willard 2008, 67). Lagging indicators measure past results, such as quantity of kilowatt-hours used in a month. Leading indicators help predict future trends; they are statistics that change before their results change, such as investment in energy conservation measures.

Teams must decide whether to measure absolute numbers, such as total tons of carbon dioxide equivalent (CO_2e) emitted, or whether to measure ratios, such as tons of carbon dioxide equivalent per item produced. Data expressed as a ratio are known as normalized data and often provide a clearer understanding of progress. However, normalized data sometimes appear to show progress when in fact the impact continues to worsen. For example, a computer manufacturer's indicator report may show that the amount of greenhouse gas emissions per unit produced is lower than the previous year, which is positive. However, if the manufacturer is producing more computers than in the previous year, the impact on Earth's climate is still increasing. The best solution is to track and report both absolute and normalized data (ibid., 74).

Teams sometimes get focused on what they want to measure rather than on their goals. There is a risk of tracking only indicators for which data are readily available and avoiding indicators for which data do not appear to exist. The advantage is that, if others are tracking similar indicators, it is possible to make comparisons and even to share knowledge. However, choosing indicators because they are easy to track can mean issues that should be analyzed, and that are perhaps the most significant issues, get overlooked. Thoughtfully developing sustainability goals first, and only selecting indicators once goals are established, helps to set priorities.

Sustainability indicators should be measurable; that usually means that they are quantitative rather than qualitative. Indicators should be relevant; that is, they should relate to the goals being assessed. They should be practical and easy to understand, including by people who are not experts. They should be based on data that are available and accessible, and data should be cost-effective to collect. Indicators should be reliable; they should dependably reflect conditions being measured, and their numbers should change as conditions change. Indicators need not be precise; given the complexity of sustainability issues precision is often not possible, and too much precision can imply reliability that is not realistic.

People can feel overwhelmed when dealing with numbers, so teams should limit the quantity of indicators. Twenty to 30 indicators are generally considered adequate for community sustainability indicators; for businesses, fewer indicators may be appropriate (Bell and Morse 2008, 177). One strategy for streamlining the amount of data people must deal with is to cycle through indicators over time. Teams can focus on 3 or 4 indicators in one year and a different 3 or 4 indicators the next year. Some indicators should be tracked on an ongoing basis; others may be project-specific and may only be needed to assess the effectiveness of a single project.

Another strategy for streamlining the management of data is for different people to track different indicators, with each person tracking the indicators that are most relevant to them. When tracking work is divided in this way, groups should come together periodically to discuss how indicators might be interacting and to reassess goals.

It can be tempting to create simplified indices by aggregating indicator measurements together. An **index** is a composite indicator that combines multiple sources of data into one number (Bell and Morse 2008, 24). For example, a multi-site corporation might decide to aggregate together measures of energy use, resource consumption, emissions, and social responsibility to produce a "sustainability index" for each of its facilities. However, if one facility's sustainability score improves, it can be difficult to understand the significance and meaning of this change. And if facilities in different regions have different sustainability scores, it can be difficult to understand what the drivers are in each facility's situation. Simplifying data into an index results in a loss of information; measurements are more meaningful when considered separately (Fiksel 2009, 102). Some organizations have accommodated both complexity and simplification by creating nested indicators and sub-indicators that can be rolled up into single indices or expanded to their detailed levels when needed (Hitchcock and Willard 2008, 67).

Sustainability is complex and multidimensional; practitioners and communities assess multiple indicators in an effort to form a more whole and accurate picture. Scholars acknowledge that direct, empirical indicators of sustainable development and sustainability per se do not exist (Costanza and Patten 1995, 58; IPCC 2014c, 12).

Monitoring and Using Indicator Reports

However indicator reports are organized, a system must be established that allows indicators to be monitored and evaluated at regular intervals. Once teams develop goals and define indicators to measure progress toward those goals, they then need feedback that tells them how well the related strategies are working, whether they are effective or whether more needs to be done. Help is available from environmental management system standards such as ISO 14001, which provide principles to guide measurement and monitoring (Fiksel 2009, 101).

Indicators are not ends in themselves; they are tools to foster learning and adaptation. Because they communicate the extent to which actions result in the achievement of performance goals, they can be used to guide policy change to make management decisions.

Indicators are communication tools as well as learning tools. When indicator data are communicated in written reports, names of categories should be unambiguous and descriptive. The language should be objective and descriptive, avoiding judgment, unnecessary adjectives, and words such as "should" or "ought." Data should be allowed to speak for themselves, without moralizing.

The easiest way to understand what large numbers of indicator data signify is to look at them graphically. There are many types of graphs, each one useful for revealing certain kinds of relationships and not so useful for others. Multiple sustainability indicators are sometimes illustrated together on a radar graph, also known as a star graph, spider graph, or amoeba graph (Bell and Morse 2003, 45). Laid out on a radial grid with multiple arms or axes with one sustainability characteristic displayed on each axis, the radar graph can help to illustrate strengths and gaps. Progress over time can be shown by representing past years with different line types.

Measurement and Reporting Systems

Ecological and Other Footprints

The Ecological Footprint, developed in the early 1990s by Mathis Wackernagel and William Rees, is a measure of the demand humans place on nature expressed as land area. It quantifies the amount of productive land and water area required to produce the resources we consume and to absorb the waste we generate. Calculating Footprints allows human demand to be compared to the biosphere's carrying capacity. Ecological Footprints are widely used and can be calculated at any scale, from an individual person to an entire nation. The global carrying capacity of the planet is estimated to be 4.45 acres per person; currently the global average Ecological Footprint is 6.67 acres per person (Ewing et al. 2010, 18), which indicates that humans have already overshot Earth's carrying capacity and are depleting natural capital rather than living off the interest. Meanwhile the average Ecological Footprint in the US is estimated to be 19.77 acres per person (ibid., 72).[4] Footprint calculators are available through the Global Footprint Network website and from several other organizations' websites.

Ecological Footprints are rigorous yet easily understandable tools for communicating impact, and they monitor the combined impact of a variety of indicators. However, they cannot measure some kinds of impacts, such as water use, pollution, ecosystem disturbance, or ecosystem resilience, or the economic and social dimensions of sustainability (ibid., 90). They document lagging indicators, or what happened in the past, but do not document leading indicators.

Water Footprint

Water Footprint is also known as virtual water content. A Water Footprint represents the volume of freshwater required per unit of product or per unit of time. Water Footprint is an indicator of water use related to consumption, and includes direct use, indirect use, and volume of water polluted. Water Footprint calculations include consumption of blue water: surface and ground water; green water: rainwater stored in soil; and gray water: the volume of freshwater required to assimilate pollution (Galli et al. 2012, 102).

Carbon Footprint

A Carbon Footprint when calculated as part of an Ecological Footprint expresses greenhouse gas emissions in terms of area of land needed for carbon dioxide sequestration (Ewing et al. 2010, 101). A number of carbon calculators are available online. Many of them calculate the amount of carbon in tons or carbon dioxide equivalent in tons, rather than the amount of land needed to sequester carbon dioxide emissions. Many sustainability practitioners use the term Carbon Footprint to mean the quantity of greenhouse gas emissions, rather than meaning Footprint expressed as area.[5]

Materials Footprints and Rucksacks

Manufacturing companies and other organizations often need to measure total material consumption and waste throughout the life cycle of a product. Some companies refer to these analyses as Materials Footprints, even though they do not actually measure land area.

A Carbon Footprint measures climate-warming greenhouse gas impacts, but it cannot quantify resource scarcity nor the consumption of raw materials. The **ecological rucksack** is an indicator concept used for describing the total material requirements of a product including the hidden material flows that become waste. It was developed in the 1990s at the Wuppertal Institute for Climate, Environment and Energy in Germany. An ecological rucksack is the total weight of material "carried" by a product when it arrives to the consumer, the total material that had to be displaced in order to extract, process, and use the material over the course of its lifetime (Kibert 2012, 48).

Life Cycle Assessment

Life cycle assessment (LCA) is a method for measuring a product's impact on the environment throughout its entire life cycle from cradle to grave. LCA quantifies energy flows, material flows, and environmental impacts of extraction, acquisition, production, use, and disposal.[6] By allowing planners to study an entire product system, rather than focusing on a single, local process, LCA helps to avoid shifting environmental impacts from one region to another (US EPA 2006, 3).

EMAS

EMAS, the EU's Eco-Management and Audit Scheme, is a sustainability management and reporting standard developed by the European Commission and used by organizations throughout Europe. Organizations seeking EMAS registration conduct an environmental review, develop an environmental policy, establish an environmental management system (EMS) with specific goals and targets, and submit to an audit by an accredited independent third party (European Commission 2016). Registered organizations commit to continuous improvement of their environmental performance and can display the EMAS logo. EMS requirements of ISO 14001 are a part of EMAS, so organizations registered with EMAS automatically comply with ISO 14001 requirements as well (ibid.)

Global Reporting Initiative

The most widely used comprehensive sustainability reporting standard is known as the Global Reporting Initiative (GRI). This international standard for sustainability reporting was the result of a consensus-based process by multiple stakeholders from business, labor, government, academia, and professional organizations in partnership with the OECD, UNEP, the Global Compact, and the Earth Charter Initiative. The GRI Reporting Framework sets out principles and performance indicators within its Sustainability Reporting Guidelines that organizations can use to measure and report their environmental, social, and economic performance. While the GRI is quite detailed, its list of indicators can provide a useful way of organizing measurements and adapting to changing conditions for any organization. Planners identify material aspects—subjects to be reported which are important to sustainability goals—that reflect the organization's economic, environmental, and social impacts. They assess boundaries, that is, whether the impact of each aspect lies within or outside the organization, and report on both. A GRI report includes a description of the organization and its management approach; discussions of each aspect, why it is important, the boundaries or where its impacts occur, and how it is managed; and indicator data for each aspect. Organizations can choose the Core option containing the essential elements of a sustainability report, or they can choose to conduct a full comprehensive report (Global Reporting Initiative 2013).

Another sustainability reporting framework is the Sustainability Tracking, Assessment & Rating System (STARS). STARS, an indicator report developed by the Association for the Advancement of Sustainability in Higher Education (AASHE), is used by institutions of higher education to track sustainability indicators.

Conclusion

Sustainability in an organization is a collaborative enterprise. The governance of an organization, its structure and operation, is an important factor in successful sustainability programs. Teams are the heart of sustainability change initiatives, and leaders and sustainability champions can come from any level of an organization; sustainability coordinators facilitate the change effort and help it continue into the future. A sustainability planning process begins with a vision statement that leads to measurable goals and then strategies, or specific action plans, and tactics, the actions an organization takes in order to implement its strategies. Organizations use assessments to describe the state of existing conditions, then track indicators over time in order to measure progress. They develop a business case for sustainability, an accurate assessment of the opportunities and risks connected with a proposed plan that defines sustainability initiatives as investments that will improve the bottom line. Teams can use a framework to help guide their work. Whatever framework is used, good communication is critical as teams work together to implement sustainability plans.

Notes

1 The use of words such as "vision" and "visible" is not meant to imply that planning processes are limited to people who are sighted. One of the benefits of working within organizations is their diversity, which includes people with a range of skills, specialties, and ways of understanding the world. Team members with visual impairment will see in different ways than members without visual impairment; diagramming in some format can be helpful to everyone.
2 A brown bag lunch is an informal, voluntary meeting held during an employee break such as a lunch break, typically lasting for an hour. In the past, many workers brought their lunches in brown paper bags, so the name "brown bag" symbolizes informal lunch events at which participants bring their own food. Brown bag lunches often feature speakers or discussions.
3 The ISO 14000 standards are discussed in Chapter 13, Products.
4 Ecological Footprint is typically calculated in global hectares, representing hectares of global average biological productivity. A hectare is a metric measure of area; Footprints in hectares have been converted to acres for purposes of this book.
5 Methods for conducting an inventory of greenhouse gas emissions for an individual, product, company, community, or region are discussed in Chapter 5, Climate.
6 LCA is introduced in Chapter 13, Products.

Further Reading

Bell, Simon and Stephen Morse. *Sustainability Indicators: Measuring the Immeasurable?* Sterling, VA: Earthscan, 2008.
Doppelt, Bob. *Leading Change toward Sustainability.* Sheffield: Greenleaf Publishing, 2003.

Friend, Gil. *The Truth about Green Business*. Upper Saddle River, NJ: FT Press, 2009.
Hitchcock, Darcy and Marsha Willard. *The Step-by-Step Guide to Sustainability Planning*. Sterling, VA: Earthscan, 2008.
——. *The Business Guide to Sustainability*. Sterling, VA: Earthscan, 2009.
Senge, Peter, Bryan Smith, Nina Kruschwitz, Joe Laur, and Sara Schley. *The Necessary Revolution: Working Together to Create a Sustainable World*. New York: Broadway Books, 2010.

Chapter Review

1   What is an elevator speech?
2   Discuss why shared governance might be more effective than command-and-control structures at implementing sustainability initiatives.
3   Who is responsible for developing ideas to improve sustainability performance?
4   What do people mean when they talk about organizational silos?
5   Describe the steps in an effective planning process.
6   List some of the business advantages of adopting a sustainability initiative.
7   List some of the business risks of not pursuing sustainability initiatives.
8   If you could pick only three methods to communicate sustainability information with others in your organization, what would they be?
9   Crafting a vision statement takes time. Why not save time and go directly to selecting strategies?
10   In what ways are organizations with borrow–use–return approaches analogous to living organisms?
11   What is the benefit of measuring an indicator more than once?
12   Give an example other than power consumption of a lagging indicator and a leading indicator.
13   What are the disadvantages of using a simplified index in place of multiple indicators? What are the advantages? How would you decide which method to use?
14   How does an ecological rucksack differ from an Ecological Footprint?
15   Write a job description for a sustainability coordinator in a small company.
16   Write a job description for a sustainability coordinator at a university.
17   If someone in a company where you work said that setting up a recycling program would cost too much money, what would you say?
18   What is emergence, and what does it have to do with working in the field of sustainability?

Critical Thinking and Discussion

1   What are some key differences between linear and nonlinear organizational structures?
2   Some businesses that adopt green business practices see real financial and market benefits. If that is the case, then why haven't more businesses moved in this direction?
3   You are hired as a sustainability coordinator for a business. They already have a recycling program. What would you suggest they undertake as the next companywide initiative? How would you decide?
4   A company where you work would like to implement a green purchasing policy. What are some potential barriers? What benefits might result from such a policy?
5   What guidelines would you suggest for a purchasing policy for paper and office supply purchases?
6   What guidelines would you suggest for a purchasing policy for the purchase of food products?

7 Do you think that implementing sustainability would be easier if an organization eliminated upper management? Why or why not?
8 Describe some dimensions of diversity in an organization. Why is diversity an advantage
   in sustainability initiatives?

1 Would you expect the Ecological Footprint of a person your age to have been smaller or
   larger if it had been calculated 20 years ago? 40 years ago? 100 years ago?
2 Do you think your Ecological Footprint as a working professional will be smaller or
   larger 10 years from now?
3 How might the Ecological Footprint of a person with a beef-based diet differ from that
   of a person with a vegetarian diet?
4 Briefly describe the different approaches to organizing indicators and measurement.
5 Why do graphs and other visual presentations of data often provide greater clarity than
   other ways of presenting information?
6 Evidence shows that people respond better to things that make them feel good than to
   things that are scary. Yet many people seem unconcerned and unaware of the gravity of
   issues such as global warming and mass extinctions. How can scientists communicate
   the seriousness of these issues without resorting to apocalyptic warnings? Or do you
   think apocalyptic warnings might be necessary?
7 As human animals we are wired to care most deeply about things that affect us and our
   immediate group and to care less about effects far away. What strategies can you suggest
   that could help people make a connection between their own behaviors, such as automobile and airplane trips, and things that happen far away, such as sea level rise in Asia?
8 Some people think numbers and reports are boring. How would you set up a sustainability effort in your organization so that you could track sustainability indicators without
   driving away potential volunteers?
9 You work for an organization that is planning to hire its first sustainability coordinator.
   One person on the hiring committee says that interpersonal skills are the most important
   attribute; another person counters that data analysis skills are the most important. What
   would you say?
10 You work for a university that plans to set up a training program for sustainability coordinators. List some courses you think it would be helpful for students to take.

16 Education

We live in a period of impending transition unprecedented in human history. Analyses by growing numbers of scientists and scholars are converging on a consensus: that some degree of the planetary destabilization humans have put into place is now irreversible, at least over the next century or more.

The educational system of the past 100 years worked well during the last half of the Industrial Revolution. Built upon a Cartesian, mechanical model of life and based upon the needs of an increasingly complex industrial system for division of labor and linear progress, it prepared learners to take their places in specialized niches of academia and the economy. Education has been based on abstract, theoretical knowledge and on reducing subjects to simple, relatively isolated parts. It was from this system that both the advantages and the problems of modern industrial development grew (Orr 1992, 2003; Rolston 1996).

As climate destabilization, fossil-fuel constraints, resource depletion, mass extinction, collapsing ecosystems, economic contraction, and social instability continue to rise in spite of the efforts of highly trained specialists, it seems clear that continuing with the same educational approaches can only lead to more of the same results. We have known and taught about these crises for decades, yet have been unable to avoid them or to bring forth large-scale strategies that could move us toward a sustainable future.

There is still hope that by a few centuries from now we will have been able to stabilize the carbon cycle, slow the rate of extinction, and allow the biosphere and the Earth system to begin the slow process of rebuilding. However, between now and then lies a long transition, and it appears now to be inevitable that conditions will get worse before these systems stabilize. Humans and all life on Earth will face changing circumstances, dislocations, and challenges that they have not encountered before. When the system begins to stabilize again, Earth will not be the same as it was before.

The ability of our species to survive and thrive will depend upon expanded and diverse knowledge and skills, with whole new approaches to thought and action. We will need both strategies for ensuring the survival of the living systems on which we depend and skills for living in a reconfigured reality. Meanwhile, we all will probably be reinventing society as we go along. The leaders who will help stabilize Earth's systems and who will help others face and adapt to the challenging circumstances ahead are students now, or will be students in the future. What they learn and how they learn it are critical.

We need citizens capable of systems thinking, able to understand how systems are nested and interconnected. We need citizens who see differences as opportunities, who recognize that diversity underlies all robust, resilient systems. As the era of fossil fuel comes to an end people will need skills of local adaptability and self-reliance, so we need institutions that recognize the value of local knowledge and the usefulness of traditional skills.

The old approach of memorizing facts is inadequate to address the crises bearing down upon us. We need frameworks that engage learners in forming their own questions, carefully evaluating quantitative and qualitative evidence, formulating their own responses, and in general able to think critically for themselves. We need inclusive systems that allow not only researchers and professionals but also every citizen to participate as equal partners in the process of learning, able to work collaboratively to solve complex problems.

The new project of education is to prepare learners to live in a changing world. Required are learner-centered pedagogy, systems thinking, values, and the ability to work collectively. In addition, three important concepts underpin much of education for sustainability: biophilia, bioregionalism, and learning by doing.

Biophilia

Biophilia, the genetically encoded emotional need of humans to affiliate with nature and with other living organisms, evolved as an adaptive mechanism to protect people from hazards and to help them access resources such as food, water, and shelter. In modern life, research shows that contact with the natural world has an impact on human health and well-being as well as on people's ability to think and to learn (Ulrich 1984, 420–21; Kellert 2005, 4; Li and Sullivan 2016, 149).

In the environments our early ancestors inhabited, people who learned to read the environment and responded to it long enough to survive to a reproductive age passed this trait on as an evolutionary advantage. This biophilic tendency to form positive connections with elements of nature is a weak genetic tendency that relies on learning and experience. Humans are predisposed to learn these associations readily when they are young, and to retain them, given the opportunity. Human children are innately curious and drawn to nature.

Children who spend time directly experiencing natural processes and materials are far more likely to grow into adults who care about the biosphere. They will have developed biophilia, love of life. However, these tendencies tend to atrophy if not fostered in childhood. The genes in a child's "genetic blueprint" are turned on and off based on their interactions with the world around them (Kellert et al. 2008, 208). Children need to spend time interacting with the natural world repeatedly and in a variety of ways in order to mature in a whole and healthy way. Thus biophilia has significant implications for the places in which children learn and the methods by which they learn.

Bioregionalism and Place-Based Learning

Sustainability is connected to place. Just as we are more likely to care for and protect another person when we know them intimately, the same is true of places; we are more likely to protect a place we have first come to love, and getting to know a place leads to loving it. In addition, communities with place-based knowledge can meet many of their own needs locally and are more self-reliant and resilient.

A **bioregion** is an area with similar climate, topography, plant and animal communities, and human culture, or as the Convention on Biological Diversity says, "a system of related, interconnected ecosystems" (Harding 2006, 228), often organized around a watershed.

Bioregionalism is an approach to living and learning that focuses on the particular bioregion where a person or group of people live. It represents local knowledge and local livelihoods that grow from a particular place, and often includes both formal learning and traditional knowledge and skills from local and indigenous communities, passed down from generation to generation.

Place-based learning is bioregional education, focused on the local bioregion and community of a student. Instead of reading discussions of places far away, learners go into the place where they live: touching it, studying it, getting to know it, and providing repair or restoration where appropriate.

Students who get to know a particular place learn skills of careful observation and the ability to think more accurately about cause and effect. With place-based learning students use hands-on, real-world activities to learn, to solve problems, and to discover that they are competent to solve problems.

Box 16.1 Where You At? A Bioregional Quiz

"Where You At? A Bioregional Quiz" first appeared in the *CoEvolutionary Quarterly* in 1981. The quiz tests place-based knowledge and is often used in design and environmental studies programs as a way to stimulate bioregional thinking. It asks:

1   Trace the water you drink from precipitation to tap.
2   How many days til the moon is full? (Slack of 2 days allowed.)
3   What soil series are you standing on?
4   What was the total rainfall in your area last year (July–June)? (Slack: 1 inch for every 20 inches.)
5   When was the last time a fire burned in your area?
6   What were the primary subsistence techniques of the culture that lived in your area before you?
7   Name 5 edible plants in your region and their season(s) of availability.
8   From what direction do winter storms generally come in your region?
9   Where does your garbage go?
10   How long is the growing season where you live?
11   On what day of the year are the shadows the shortest where you live?
12   When do the deer rut in your region, and when are the young born?
13   Name five grasses in your area. Are any of them native?
14   Name five resident and five migratory birds in your area.
15   What is the land use history of where you live?
16   What primary ecological event/process influenced the land form where you live? (Bonus special: what's the evidence?)
17   What species have become extinct in your area?
18   What are the major plant associations in your region?
19   From where you're reading this, point north.
20   What spring wildflower is consistently among the first to bloom where you live?

(Charles, Dodge, Milliman, and Stockley 1981,
1. Used by permission.)

Learning by Doing: Experiential Learning

Learning by doing is an essential part of education for sustainability. Making discoveries and putting lessons into practice in the real world helps people work out how to think about complex problems and to feel competent actually doing things. Learning by doing is known as **experiential learning**.

Alongside learning by doing is the very real necessity of planting hope. When learners are confronted only by the dangers of Earth's dire situation, the result can be feelings of despair and hopelessness, leading to the very opposite of the response that is needed. Students need facts, but then they need to know that they can make a difference. Beyond knowledge about sustainability, they need the ability to act on that knowledge (Orr 1992, 103; Stibbe 2009, 11). Once presented with a problem, the ability to focus on solutions enables them to feel empowered and to feel that these things are worth learning.

Learning by doing leads to competent citizens. When students are active they are more engaged, more areas of their brains are working, and they learn more. Students involved in real-world problems practice careful observation and develop skills that will help them analyze and address complex problems. These are skills that will be important in the uncertain years ahead.

Growing, preparing, and eating food is one example of experiential learning that can be accomplished by learners of all ages. Students with a schoolyard garden or orchard can learn about climate, ecosystems, the hydrologic cycle, and composting. Gardening allows them to be physically active and to incorporate all their senses. When they cook and eat the food, they can learn about nutrition and can incorporate learning about mathematics, recycling, history, geography, and other cultures.

Students learn about sustainability through both academics and work experience at Warren Wilson College in Asheville, North Carolina, a 'work college' where they are assigned to work crews essential to the operation of the college. All resident students work 10 to 20 hours per week running the power plant, farming, doing building maintenance including heating and cooling, or working in dining services. In return, each student earns money toward the cost of attendance. In additional **service learning** projects outside the campus they work on real solutions to community problems.

Service learning is a subset of experiential learning that combines direct learning with service to the community, as students apply what they have learned in the classroom to solving real-world problems. If students collect trash from a local stream, they are performing community volunteer work; if they collect trash from the stream, analyze water quality, determine the sources of pollution, examine the role of public policy, and share their findings with local residents, they are engaged in service learning. One of the most important outcomes of service learning is that students learn that they can make a difference. This confidence can help them go on to become motivated and active participants in reshaping the trajectory of the planet (Stone 2009, 112).

Box 16.2 The STRAW Project

In 1992 Laurette Rogers' fourth-grade class at Brookside School in northern California was watching a film about habitat loss and endangered species, when one student asked: "But what can we do?" Instead of giving them pat answers about donations and letter-writing, Rogers decided to find a local species in need of help. A state ecologist offered three choices and the students picked the California freshwater shrimp. First they studied the shrimp and its habitat. Students read scholarly scientific papers, with each student responsible for reporting to the group the main ideas from one or two pages of a paper. They analyzed data for the creeks where the shrimp live, and discovered a whole web of creatures and ecosystems all affected by habitat destruction. They visited local farmers and learned about agriculture, cattle, and the economic struggles that sometimes made restoration difficult for them. They formed a partnership with one farmer, working with professional restoration ecologists and planting willows on the banks of a creek running through his ranch. They made presentations to political groups and arranged for media coverage. Little by little the willows grew, shading and cooling the stream, stabilizing the streambanks, and providing branches for nesting birds who brought in seeds of other riparian trees. The students continued to monitor the site, and the next year another team continued the work at another site along the stream. They kept working, even after learning that it might take 50 to 100 years for their work to have significant impact on the shrimp's habitat, and talked about bringing their future grandchildren to see what they had done.

The students' Shrimp Club grew into an education program known as Students and Teachers Restoring a Watershed (STRAW). Today the STRAW Project is a network of schools, teachers, students, ranchers, community members, public agencies, and foundations across northern California offering training and restoration work in both rural and urban settings. The fundamental structure remains the same: students learn by doing and in the process see that the work they do makes a difference.

The Learning Environment

Natural Play Environments

The play environments that support healthy child development most effectively appear to be environments in nature. The theory that underpins natural play environment design is biophilia, and this theory is supported by a growing body of research from multiple disciplines. In addition to scholarly work, the concept of natural play environments was popularized by journalist Richard Louv in the influential book *Last Child in the Woods* (Louv 2008), which details the benefits of childhood interaction with nature and immersion in natural settings. Louv coined the term nature-deficit disorder which, as he explains, is not an actual medical condition but which does help to express the costs of a lack of connection with nature.

Louv argues that in addition to cognitive and emotional impacts, traditional schoolyards reward physical dominance and appear to foster bullying behavior, while natural play environments reward creativity and appear to foster collaborative interaction. In contrast to a traditional, single-purpose playground with limited options, a natural setting is flexible and open-ended, a place where imagination can flourish. These natural places for playing and learning go by names such as natural play environments, green schoolyards, or ecological schoolyards.

Children need opportunities for unstructured play in order to develop optimally. They need freedom to observe and experiment. They need opportunities to explore without having to pursue any particular goal. Children who are allowed to play creatively in open-ended settings do not depend on acquiring consumer goods for enjoyment, but instead learn to be resourceful and self-reliant (Worldwatch 2010, 62).

Embedded in biophilia is the genetic human need for exploration and discovery, both important elements in problem-solving. Thus the ideal play setting includes variety and mystery (Kellert et al. 2008, 13). It offers varied topography and alternative ways to move through, over, under, and around spaces, allowing children to build physical and spatial skills while getting to know a place in multiple ways. It offers a variety of microclimates to explore and learn about, with living things which change continually throughout the year.

The ideal setting includes natural materials and loose parts such as leaves, sticks, seedpods, and cones (Danks 2010, 24). Children need opportunities to experiment, to create things, and to change their environments. Not only do they learn a great deal from manipulating materials in their environments, but they also feel competent and empowered as a result.

Box 16.3 Risky Play and Adventure Playgrounds

Play, which includes some reasonable degree of risk, comes naturally to children, and we can assume that it never would have evolved, or would have been eliminated, unless it carried evolutionary benefits that outweighed its costs (Sandseter et al. 2011, 263). In infancy, children develop fears, such as heights or strangers, that protect them from situations they are not yet mature enough to handle (ibid., 257). Like most young mammals, they begin to use play not only to develop motor control but to learn what is dangerous and what isn't. They do this incrementally through confronting challenges and risks such as height or speed appropriate to their age, using activities in which they feel on the edge of being out of control before overcoming the fear and mastering the risk. They have a sensory need to experience what feels like danger: fire, heights, moving at a speed that feels too fast (Rosin 2014, 81); and they become better at judging risks through experience. Research shows six categories of risky play are consistently sought by children: great heights, high speed, dangerous tools, dangerous elements, rough-and-tumble, and disappear/get lost (Sandseter 2011, 3). The positive emotion from mastery is what drives children to engage in risky play (ibid.), developing skills that will be important later in life when watchful adults are no longer present (Sandseter et al. 2011, 259).

The concept of the adventure playground was introduced in Copenhagen in 1942 by Danish landscape architect Carl Theodor Sørensen, who had observed that children preferred to play everywhere but in the playgrounds that he built, happily building and demolishing structures on bombsites during the Second World War (A. Moore 2014). Sørensen provided an enclosed space originally known as a "junk playground," supplied with scrap materials and simple hand tools where children could work with earth, water, even fire, interact with farmyard animals, and build their own communities, overseen by skilled playworkers who provided materials and managed risk. At the end of World War II the model was imported to London by Marjory Allen, where the rubble of war was put to positive use as materials for adventure play (Moore and Cooper 2014, 165).

The central idea in modern adventure playgrounds is still a community space, supplied with scrap materials and nails that children can use and tools they can borrow, facilitated by trained playworkers who provide materials, lend tools, and administer risk management protocols. Children learn to collaborate, solve problems, and work together with people from diverse cultures as they build hideouts and manage their own affairs under the supervision of discretely watchful adults. Risk is the possibility of something unpleasant, such as injury, and can be more or less judged. Adventure playgrounds feature elements of risk: the ability to experience height and depth, movement and speed, building and using tools, and fire (Armitage 2011, 12). On a playground, a hazard is a source of danger that cannot be judged (Willoughby 2011, 8); while adventure playgrounds offer risk, they must be free from hazard and are operated under established risk-management protocols (Moore and Cooper 2014, 8).

Children need places that offer them choices in social interaction. Places for play and learning need a variety of sizes and types of accessible seating options for individuals and small groups, some of it movable. Some well-used learning environments include "council circles" made of logs, large rocks, or bales of hay.

Children sometimes need space and silence and should have the option of choosing solitude. Numerous surveys show that children want the opportunity to be part of a group at some times and to find solitude apart from a group at other times (Johnson 2000, 24). Particularly in the middle years, children need the ability to create personal nooks in places that offer both prospect and refuge (Kellert and Wilson 1993, 145). The middle years are a time when "the self is fragile and under construction" (Kellert 2005, 77), and secret refuges are important.

A refuge can be as simple as a spot under the leaves of a bush. Some schools plant living willow teepees, domes, or tunnels made from interwoven living willow whips. Children love the dappled light inside and the feeling of being in a secret place, while supervising adults can still see them safely from outside.

Environment as Curriculum

The environment in which children develop has a dual impact on learning: First, children learn directly from nature. Second, the learning environment, both landscapes and buildings, sends messages about what society genuinely values (Johnson 2000, 24). Students learn from everything their school does, including the food it serves; how it manages energy, water, and waste; how it makes decisions and who is included; and how it connects to its surrounding community (Heinberg and Lerch 2010, 414).

A building made of materials from far away, built in the same form as many buildings everywhere, tells students that knowing where you are is not important. A windowless building lit by light fixtures, heated by furnaces, and cooled by air conditioners tells students that energy is cheap and plentiful and can be squandered at little cost to the world.

In buildings that are made of local materials, powered by renewable energy, with systems for capturing and reusing water, students have increased opportunities to learn about energy flows and interconnectedness. But even so-called green building features may not teach if students do not know that the features are there or why they were done that way. Schools can take advantage of these potential opportunities by studying building features as part of class learning activities, by posting signs identifying and explaining the features, and by providing real-time feedback, such as a gage showing the amount of stored rainwater in a cistern or an electronic dashboard illustrating the current rate of energy use.

Some schools install sundials to help make visible how sun angles change with changing seasons. School buildings designed to use natural daylighting or passive solar heating also clearly illustrate the changing angles of the sun.

Ideally, the learning environment and the schoolyard are the same place. Every element in an educational environment should be connected to learning. Connecting all the parts of the curriculum to the landscape leads to a more supportive learning environment over time, and providing a more supportive learning environment leads to a better curriculum. Students at schools where schoolyards contain functioning ecosystems and healthy habitat learn that "the environment" is not just a place far away, in a tropical rainforest or on a mountain; it is the biosphere that surrounds and supports us all, including in our own neighborhoods.

A range of strategies help students learn about nature's rhythms and time scales. One of the most direct activities is planting, growing, and harvesting food in a garden. Other activities can involve wildlife, their habitats, and local native plants which change with changing seasons. Growing native plants that produce food for wildlife allows students to be part of the life cycles of wild birds and other animals. Students engaged in stream or ecosystem restoration projects can watch the changes over time as a system comes back to life.

Water in many forms offers a medium for learning. A genetic tendency in biophilia is to be drawn to water, and almost all humans are fascinated by it (Kellert et al. 2008, 23). Educators can find opportunities to use water, including measuring and monitoring rainfall, collecting and reusing rainwater, restoring wetlands or streams, creating and studying small ponds, and developing stormwater rain gardens and bioswales. Every school is in a watershed, and students can use water to learn to think about multiple scales. By studying rainfall, streams, and local geography, students learn not only about the water cycle but about their particular place within it.

Stages of Development: Humans as Lifelong Learners

While each person is unique and develops at their own rate, in general all humans pass through certain genetically driven stages of cognitive development (Moore and Cooper 2014, 19). Biophilia, bioregionalism, and experiential learning are elements of education for sustainability that apply at every stage of life.

Early Childhood

Early childhood, from birth through about age 7, is a crucial period when the brain develops in important ways. During this period, children investigate their world with all their senses. This is a time when neurological pathways are developing rapidly and when biophilic tendencies are most readily activated and reinforced. Sensory inputs and hands-on activities are the primary sources of learning. Natural settings with dirt, sticks, rocks, water, and plants offer a rich and constantly changing palette and have been shown to be the most effective environments for learning about the world.

For the youngest children still learning to walk, very small enclosed spaces made of natural materials allow interaction with smells, colors, and textures; ground surfaces should be clean, without loose materials, and can include undulating lawns, textured paving stones, and fragrant or colorful ground covers. For toddlers, physical exploration expands dramatically. Three-dimensional paths, stones, wood, and other surfaces offer opportunities to develop physical skills and to explore spatial relationships of up and down, in and out, around and through, over and under; water, stones, pieces of wood, and sand are highly attractive to toddlers, who love to fill, pour, stack, knock over, and interact with all kinds of objects.

From preschool through the elementary years, children are learning what things are. They learn how to tell apart things that are plants from things that are rocks or things that are animals (Kellert 2005, 76). They focus on naming or labeling things and on sorting them into categories. They experience cause and effect, an early form of scientific thinking. The brain is developing rapidly, and sensory stimulation in the natural world fosters "neurological development before the windows of opportunity close" (Moore and Cooper 2014, 21).

Early childhood, with its concrete, sensory approach to the world, is the best time to begin place-based education outdoors. Schools can move away from thinking of outdoor areas as playgrounds where children go for recess in between periods when they are learning. Instead, outdoor areas can be integral parts of the learning environment where students learn about the world first-hand. Research on childhood learning shows that children learn best when multiple senses are engaged, when the setting is part of daily life, and when they are actively involved and not just passively listening. Multisensory experiences, which are a feature of natural learning environments, promote healthy intellectual development as children integrate informal play with formal learning (Moore and Marcus 2008, 159).

Middle Childhood

From about age 8 to 12, children are learning how things work. They grow from simply identifying and classifying things to collecting empirical evidence and building an understanding of what it means. At this stage of learning, nature provides a laboratory with myriad opportunities for discovery. Children can develop the capacity for observation and interpretation in such settings. In nature children learn

> that snow falls at certain temperatures and rain at others; trees grow in soil and not in water or through asphalt; ducks and geese inhabit wet rather than dry or upland places; butterflies fly during the day and moths at night; [and] many trees, rather than one or a few, constitute a forest.
>
> (Kellert 2005, 76)

Children at this age can learn to follow the hydrologic cycle, to observe how things change with seasons, and to begin understanding that essential materials such as carbon go around and around in cycles. They can also begin to develop skills for living as thoughtful members of civil society, for example learning to work through conflict by generating and evaluating alternative solutions. The middle years as well are a time when children form strong bonds with other living creatures and learn to value and care for nature.

Children playing together outdoors learn to collaborate and to apply collective efforts to carrying out projects. They form self-directed groups, building cohesive communities and practicing the social skills that will help them be self-reliant and resilient in the face of challenges (Moore and Marcus 2008, 158). Their territory has expanded, and they need landscape qualities and enough space to be able to imagine they are lost, an experience helped by topography, vegetation, and tree cover (Moore and Cooper 2014, 23).

Adolescence

During the teen years young people are engaged in making the transition from childhood to becoming adult members of the world. Their understanding becomes more sophisticated and abstract. Their concept of scale is more finely developed, including an awareness of larger spatial and temporal scales, so that teens can grasp concepts such as the Earth system and ecosystem change over time. Feelings of moral obligation, including duties to the natural world, become more pronounced and keenly developed (Kellert 2005, 79).

Two primary concerns of adolescence are the building of social networks and the development of independence and self-reliance. Teens may temporarily become less focused on the sensory details of the natural world than they were as children and more focused on ideas and social connections.

Adolescence is a time for imagining possibilities. Students' range of understanding has expanded dramatically, life's hard lessons have not knocked back optimism and hope, and for most their attention is not yet distracted by the kinds of responsibilities that come with full adulthood. People in this age group are idealistic, full of passion and creativity, and want to contribute to society and the world (Giedd 2015, 37). This is a time when education for sustainability, reinforced by real-world projects and accomplishments, can really take hold.

Higher Education

Colleges and universities of the world have played a fundamental role in the problems now facing the planet. The people who are now leading us down an unsustainable path have come out of the best universities in the world. These institutions have armed us with knowledge suited for the conquest of nature, with the result that we are now misfits on our home planet (Orr 2009, 176; Rolston 1996).

Yet higher education holds opportunity. It generates most of the research being done and although research produced the current crisis, research also develops understanding and can lead us to solutions. Higher education nurtures future scientists, engineers, business leaders, and legislators, and it trains the teachers who will help guide the next generation. The combination of academic freedom, diversity of skills, substantial resources, and large numbers of people puts institutions of higher education in a position to forge new ways of thinking and to experiment with sustainable ways of living.

Colleges and universities are connected globally to other institutions and scholars, and they offer the potential to foster sustainable development in other parts of the world, for example as students and their professors help local people in developing regions to rebuild their water systems, set up resilient local food systems, build housing, train teachers, or educate young women. Institutions are also dependent upon and tied to their communities; they can be community partners, working with the local communities of which they are a part to assess, prepare, build local technical capacity, develop adaptation strategies, and foster community resilience in the face of changing climate and economic shifts. Campuses as living laboratories can model evidence-based strategies to address a range of technical concerns such as food, water, energy, and habitat, while working within community groups can foster a focus on economic inclusiveness, social cohesion, and governance.

Colleges and universities have tremendous leverage. Not only do they conduct research and turn out graduates who become leaders, they employ millions of faculty and staff, provision millions of students, and spend hundreds of billions of dollars each year. Each campus is like a small city. Together the magnitude of purchasing, investment, and construction decisions of these institutions has the potential to shape economic and ecological change while modeling sustainability.

One organization seeking to build on this potential is the Association for the Advancement of Sustainability in Higher Education (AASHE, pronounced "AY-shee"), an association of colleges and universities offering research, workshops, conferences, newsletters, and other resources. AASHE has developed a sustainability indicator report used by institutions of higher education, the Sustainability Tracking, Assessment and Rating System (STARS).

We are awash in data. The Internet has made vast amounts of information available at our fingertips, but the quality varies greatly. Learners need not so much an ability to remember facts but the ability to discern meaning from noise, to evaluate, to synthesize across multiple disciplines, and to apply that synthesis to real-world problem solving (Giedd 2015, 37). This has profound implications not just for what we teach but how we teach. Students need to engage in self-directed learning so that they can develop skills in practical research and critical thinking. At the same time they need practice at collaborating effectively in teams to solve complex problems.

Interdisciplinary thinking is the foundation of sustainability in higher education. In 1959 scientist and novelist C. P. Snow delivered a famous and still influential lecture on the division between the humanities and the sciences (Snow 2012). His premise was that the division between them was a major hindrance to solving global problems. As Snow noted, this division had its roots in the atomistic approach championed by the seventeenth-century philosopher Descartes, for whom the world consisted of simple mechanisms. The Cartesian view had no concept of a living, interconnected biosphere.

In the Cartesian model still prevalent in education, people learn facts and ideas in disciplinary silos. Academia tends to define work within disciplines as rigorous, while work across disciplines is traditionally considered non-rigorous. Sustainability, however, like the biosphere itself, is rooted in interconnected systems. It includes not only science and technology, but all the humanities. This is the concept of the triple bottom line, that a healthy environment, prosperous economies, and communities that are socially equitable are mutually interdependent.

The problems needing to be addressed are complex and interconnected; they cannot be understood through the lens of a single specialization and they cannot be solved when isolated into compartments. Sustainability leaders will need the ability to be flexible and innovative, to think and communicate with others outside narrow disciplines. Fundamentally, what we know about all systems is that they bring forth emergent properties that are always different from the sums of their component parts. Systems cannot be understood by focusing on their parts alone if we are to have any hope of understanding them at all. Higher education, which trains people in critical thinking, needs interdisciplinary vision so that learners are able to consider systems as the complex, interconnected wholes they are.

Adult Learners

While children often grasp systems thinking and interconnectedness readily, these ways of understanding the world are more difficult for many adults who are firmly attached to what they think they know (Stone and Barlow 2005, 253). Yet adults will need the ability to adapt to changing conditions in the years of transition that lie ahead. This will be a collective undertaking. More than any individual skill it is strong, diverse communities with a range of skills and experience that will build resilience. Approaches that promote lifelong learning and activities that build skills for living in a time of economic degrowth, fossil fuel scarcity, and changing climate will be especially valuable for helping adult learners survive and thrive into the future.

Conclusion

Kuan-Tzu, a collection of Chinese philosophical writings from the third century BCE, said: "If you are thinking a year ahead, sow seed. If you are thinking ten years ahead, plant a tree. If you are thinking a hundred years ahead, educate the people."

The Earth system and the human cultures contained within it are on the threshold of a transition unprecedented in all of human history. Education has a fundamental and essential role to play in giving us skills to navigate our way through an uncertain and unfamiliar future. The methods of education that were ubiquitous during the past century served us well but also contributed to the crisis we face. We will need to transform much about our current way of life, including how we educate ourselves and our children. Building on a foundation of the genetically encoded trait of biophilia, education for sustainability enables learners to discover the workings of the world through the places they inhabit (place-based learning) and helps them to build their own ability to reason and solve problems as they learn by doing (experiential learning). Education for sustainability is inclusive and interdisciplinary, equipping learners with observation skills, critical thinking skills, creativity, adaptability, skills for living well in place, and tools for building healthy and resilient communities.

Further Reading

Barlett, Peggy F. and Geoffrey W. Chase, eds. *Sustainability on Campus: Stories and Strategies for Change*. Cambridge, MA: MIT Press, 2004.

Danks, Sharon Gamson. *Asphalt to Ecosystems: Design Ideas for Schoolyard Transformation*. Oakland, CA: New Village Press, 2010.

Kellert, Stephen R. *Building for Life: Designing and Understanding the Human–Nature Connection*. Washington, DC: Island Press, 2005.

Orr, David W. *Ecological Literacy: Education and the Transition to a Postmodern World*. New York: State University of New York Press, 1992.

——. *Earth in Mind: On Education, Environment, and the Human Prospect*. Washington, DC: Island Press, 1994.

Sobel, David. *Place-Based Education: Connecting Classrooms and Communities*. Great Barrington, MA: The Orion Society, 2004.

Stone, Michael K. *Smart by Nature*. Berkeley, CA: University of California Press, 2009.

—— and Zenobia Barlow, eds. *Ecological Literacy: Educating Our Children for a Sustainable World*. San Francisco, CA: Sierra Club Books, 2005.

Worldwatch Institute. *State of the World 2010: Transforming Cultures from Consumerism to Sustainability*. New York: W. W. Norton, 2010.

Chapter Review

1   Describe some ways in which experiential learning differs from traditional classroom approaches.
2   What is a bioregion?
3   Make a list of ecological and cultural topics that students might learn about using place-based learning in your bioregion.
4   Why is childhood the optimal phase of life to develop biophilia?
5   What kinds of places and qualities enrich opportunities for learning?
6   Describe some of the differences between a natural play environment and a conventional playground.
7   What kinds of adult community education classes do you think would be useful for building skills for community resilience? List as many as you can.

Critical Thinking and Discussion

1   If a neighbor asked you, "what is biophilia?" what would you say? Write an elevator speech to explain the basic concepts of biophilia.

2   Describe the play environments that were the most significant to you when you were a child. Compare your descriptions with those of others. Are there any common themes?

3   When groups of people work together to plan and design school landscapes, who do you think should be included as stakeholders?

4   Do you think that only science teachers need to be involved in planning school landscapes? Why or why not?

5   Why do you think that only a small percentage of teachers or schools use experiential learning? What are some of the barriers?

6   If you were a school principal planning to convert your conventional playground to a natural play environment and a parent protested that natural play areas are unsafe, how would you respond?

7   Why do some people use the word "silo" when talking about academic disciplines?

17 Working as Agents for Change

People who choose to work in the service of a more sustainable world are change agents—a big, multidimensional job description. This work requires understanding environmental, economic, and social systems and their interconnectedness and the ability to think at multiple scales in the face of very big issues. Complex systems are unpredictable and connected, and so this work needs courage, including the courage to step outside of labels and disciplines and engage in big-picture thinking. Working for the transition to a sustainable world requires the ability to communicate clearly, listen, and collaborate; it demands humility, authentic appreciation for diverse ways of thinking and being in the world, and a recognition that we are all in this together. Global change in the Anthropocene is a collective problem which requires collective solutions (Rees 2014, 194).

Fostering Sustainable Behavior

Bringing about large-scale change may start small, but eventually it always involves moving beyond individual actions to acting collectively. The key is a positive vision: we need to know not so much what we are against as what it is we are for, the future we truly desire even while telling the truth about the current reality (Senge et al. 2010, 44, 52).

On perhaps even a subconscious level, people turn toward what feels good and away from what feels bad. While some activists work tirelessly fighting against something they believe is wrong, most people are not activists. The majority of people struggle with issues of everyday life and economic survival. Even if they believe that the planet is in crisis, changes that are difficult, that require ongoing effort or sacrifice, will not be lasting changes. Talk of a planetary crisis is not motivating to people facing their own personal crises (Jones 2009, 109).

People are willing to make changes if the changes are easy to do or if they look like solutions that lead to a better life. They may be small energy efficiency initiatives that lower a family's monthly energy bills, or initiatives that lead to green jobs in wind energy, or big projects that promote environmental justice and sustainable urban revitalization in places such as Curitiba, Brazil and the South Bronx neighborhood of New York City. Telling people that they "should" change causes a shield to go up. If we hope for people to change, we must give them something that is so compelling and so easy that they want to move toward it.

Social Marketing and Sustainable Behavior

Social marketing is the application of marketing principles to support social change for the well-being of individuals and communities. It can be used to promote such things as heart-healthy behavior, contraception, energy conservation, or environmental protection.

Various segments of the public have differing worldviews and respond in different ways to the same issues. A 2007 segmentation study by the nonprofit environmental law organization Earthjustice found that people in the US could be grouped into 10 distinct environmental worldviews, of whom about 12 percent could be considered 'environmentalists.' Other segments are typically motivated by other concerns (Earthjustice 2008, 5).

Recognizing that simply providing information is not enough to bring about behavior change and one size does not fit all, some social marketers segment their audience into groups based on attitudes or behaviors. They try to understand the attitudes and behaviors of the intended audience and the context within which they act, identify potential barriers to behavior change, then target their message to the preferences of their target audience. Such an approach overcomes an automatic tendency to stay within one's group and to reject ideas from outside group norms. However, while this may work well at the individual scale, there are questions about whether segmentation works at cross purposes to building social capital, an important attribute of resilient communities whose members can work collectively (Jones 2010, 121). And categorizing people into segments can lead to a self-reinforcing narrow focus and enhance differences. For example, focusing on how environmental behavior changes can save money in order to tailor messages to people who respond primarily to financial incentives strengthens the tendency to focus on financial factors and may obscure important ideas about long-term thinking (Crompton and Kasser, 2009).

Traditional marketing incorporates what are known as the "4 Ps": product, price, place, and promotion. In social marketing, the "product" is the benefits people reap by engaging in a particular behavior. The "price" is the cost of the behavior, which can include inconvenience or additional time; if the perceived costs outweigh the benefits, people will be unlikely to adopt a behavior. For people to change behavior, the benefits they receive must be greater than any costs they incur and the changes must feel easy. The "place" involves making the opportunities for change available in ways that reach the audience and fit its lifestyles. "Promotion" refers to communication and education (McKenzie-Mohr et al. 2011, 12).

We humans are networked, social animals, motivated by the behavior of others. When people observe behavior modeled by peers, that behavior can become a social norm to which people begin to conform, particularly when there is direct personal contact. An example occurred during the Dust Bowl of the 1930s. As farmers lost topsoil and the "black blizzards" swirled, the US Soil Erosion Service (or SES, which later became the Soil Conservation Service) put together educational materials explaining soil loss to farmers and giving them soil conservation strategies to help stop the loss of their soil. Surprisingly, these brochures failed to change farming practices. So the SES switched to an approach of working directly with a few farmers at a time, paying reluctant farmers a dollar an acre to implement new conservation practices. Once neighbors observed what was happening and talked with those farmers about the changes, the neighbors adopted the methods as well, and the practices then spread quickly (McKenzie-Mohr and Smith 1999, 73).

Several studies have shown that messages about what others are doing are more effective at shifting behavior than simple reporting. For example, a utility bill that rates one's energy use compared to neighbors in similar-size houses results in greater reduction in energy consumption than a bill which compares one's own use over time; a hotel-room sign stating that "x% of guests recycle towels" is more effective at shifting behavior toward conservation than a sign stating how much water recycling a towel could save (Ostrom 2010, 35).

The process in which an idea or behavior spreads through social contacts is known as social diffusion. The study of social diffusion is also known as the diffusion of innovation theory, introduced in a previous chapter. What this theory shows is that person-to-person contact is effective in spreading innovation and influencing sustainable behavior.

In addition to social contact, sustainable behavior is also influenced by information that is "vivid, concrete, and personal" (McKenzie-Mohr and Smith 1999, 84). This is the principle that drives interpretive and interactive museum exhibits. For example, instead of reporting that Californians generated 1,300 pounds of waste per person each year, psychology professor Shawn Burn described it as "enough to fill a two-lane highway, 10 feet deep from Oregon to the Mexican border" (ibid., 85). Instead of telling clients at a law firm how many cases of paper they consumed each year, sustainability consultants described how many times the height of their skyscraper that much paper represented, and how many stories high each individual attorney's stack of paper would be (Hitchcock and Willard 2008, 68). Some organizations use the EPA's Greenhouse Gas Equivalencies Calculator to convert miles driven or energy consumed into acres of trees or tanker trucks of gasoline. At a Third World Water Forum, instead of listing menu prices in dollars, the Water Footprint Network printed menus with prices shown in units of virtual water (Hoekstra and Chapagain 2008, 13). In New York City, menus at Otarian restaurants list the carbon footprints of each item on the menu, calculated using the standard Greenhouse Gas Protocol.

Lasting individual change is usually incremental. Any message too far outside familiar experience may be rejected and even cause hearers to be less supportive than before (Doppelt 2003a, 176). Although the scale of environmental damage is immense and what the planet needs are fundamental policy changes and a dramatic paradigm shift in global consumption and emissions, what most people are willing to do is incremental. When working with individuals, messages that allow them to take one small step at a time are more likely to be successful (McKenzie-Mohr and Smith 1999, 89).

To be effective, calls to action must strive for a balance between negative and positive messages (Doppelt 2003a, 176). On the one hand, it is true that people must be aware of the real threats of unsustainable behavior in order to be motivated and willing to take action. For example, in the 1960s books such as Rachel Carson's *Silent Spring* and Paul Ehrlich's *Population Bomb* conveyed the gravity of the planet's situation and resulted in some changes. On the other hand, once people become aware of threats, continued negative inputs will cause most people to tune out the messages and move on to other, more pleasant concerns (ibid., 92). It is more effective to focus on positive steps toward change. People must feel optimistic enough to avoid feelings of futility that settle into inaction. People must feel empowered to be part of solutions, and they need things to do that are positive and easy.

Making Sustainability Visible

A significant challenge in the work of change agents is to make the theories, issues, and potential solutions of sustainability visible (Worldwatch 2013, 27). People are continually inundated by information, accumulating a conglomeration of seemingly unconnected facts bewildering in their complexity (Makower 2009a, 61). We need context, we need to know what is important or unimportant, and we need to know what the facts mean. People working in the field of sustainability would do well to become familiar with methods of communicating graphically, whether we use graphics ourselves or hire graphics specialists to help us. The goal is to allow viewers to grab hold of the meaning with one look (White 2011, 9). A good way to communicate many words is with a picture, whether a photograph, an illustration, or a simple diagram. A good way to communicate many numbers is with a graph.

A good way to communicate processes is through a combination of interpretive signage, making processes visible, and letting the processes speak for themselves. For example, a building that collects rainwater or reuses graywater could make the collection and filtration systems visible rather than hidden in a mechanical room, could use an electronic dashboard to display quantities and flow rates, and could provide attractive interpretive signs to make sense of the system. Involving a designer to express the visible processes artfully further raises their stature, communicating the message, "this is something we value" (Haag 1998, 73; Johnson and Hill 2002, 179, 265; Hosey 2012, 5).

The Role of Language

The words we choose have impact. People who work in the sustainability arena recognize that language is not neutral and strive to consider the effects of the language they use. In the field of climate change, for example, scientists suggest that "global warming" is a misleading label. Not all of the planet is warming, and in addition many people think of warming as a pleasant thing. More accurate terms are "global climate change" or "climate destabilization."

In the waters around the islands of Indonesia, an area called the Coral Triangle produces what is thought to be the most diverse marine habitat on the planet. Damage from commercial overfishing threatens thousands of species with extinction. For several years Muhammad Korebima, a local conservationist, had talked with residents in nearby communities about establishing marine parks with no-take zones in order to protect the fisheries on which they depended. Local fishers saw these parks as threats to their livelihood and remained adamantly opposed. When a global recession hit, Korebima got an idea. He stopped talking about no-take zones and started talking about parks with "fish banks." He helped villagers think about how if fishing were banned in some areas, which he called "banks," fishers could reap the interest on these savings in the form of new fish born inside the banks but caught outside them. Communities became interested, and in 2009 The Nature Conservancy helped them implement several "fish saving banks," or marine reserves (Sanjayan 2010, 8).

Sustainability consultant John Elkington coined the term "triple bottom line" in 1994 after a long period of "trying to come up with a term that would capture the full business agenda." While businesses had been looking at environmental and financial efficiency, according to Elkington many were steering away from the social agenda. He wanted to develop a term which was couched in familiar business language that business people could connect to, and eventually hit upon triple bottom line, together with a related phrase, "people, planet, and profit." As Elkington described it, the term was "almost a Trojan horse," but "once they started to use the language and commit to it to some degree, we could then define it in ways that could stretch their imaginations a little" (Finfrock 2008, 10; Elkington 2012, 55).

Although the concept of sustainability is understood as positive by some people, for others "sustainability" is a controversial issue and the word itself is a barrier. So we can talk about outcomes that are positive for everyone without using provocative language. Instead of labeling sustainability projects, practitioners sometimes use descriptive terms such as healthy, zero waste, energy efficiency, or livability. While words such as "sustainability" and "social justice" are disturbing to some people, everyone can support the idea of healthy communities with living-wage jobs. We share similar goals, qualities most of us can agree are desirable: strong, thriving, secure communities, with economic opportunity for everyone and participation by as many people as possible in the governance of society; the biosphere is our life support system and so in order have those other conditions we want, we have to keep the life support system in good shape (Cortese 2012, x).

Cognitive linguistics professor George Lakoff advises environmental organizations on how to present issues to the public. He talks about a phenomenon called framing, the way that language shapes how we think. For example, when we talk about "protecting the environment," listeners form an (inaccurate) image of the environment as a category separate from themselves and with humans as the powerful protectors (Butler 2004, 54; Makower 2009a, 55). Reframing issues of pollution, renewable energy, clean air and water in terms of health and security can help us see connections between "the environment" and other aspects of survival.

Ecolinguistics is a subdiscipline of linguistics that attempts to understand the role of language in the current ecological crisis. Ecolinguistics says that humans perceive reality through filters, with language one of the most important (Mühlhäusler 2003, 12).

One of the topics ecolinguists study is how our use of words frames selected characteristics as positive, reinforcing various "-isms" such as growthism, bias in favor of economic growth; classism, bias in favor of one social or economic class; sexism, bias in favor of one gender; and **anthropocentrism**, bias in favor of one species, *Homo sapiens*.[1] Just as sexist language degrades women and makes them invisible, speciesism does the same to animals and other organisms by failing to acknowledge them as beings who live and feel. Various groups choose language to reflect their particular views of reality. For example, wildlife biologists may use euphemisms such as "culled" or "population control" rather than using direct words such as "killed," while wildlife and animal rights advocates may refer to a wolf or seal hunt as "slaughter" and the animals killed as "victims" (ibid., 50).

Some words in modern usage are examples of what is known to linguists as semantic vagueness, words whose meanings are unclear and indefinite. One example is the word "sustainable," which although it has a specific meaning, is frequently overused or misused in combinations such as sustainable pollution, sustainable development, and sustainable consumption. In some cases its misuse is an example of a phenomenon known as "**ecobabble**," highlighted by ecolinguists and defined in modern dictionaries as "using the technical language of ecology to make the user seem ecologically aware."

"Green" is another commonly used word with semantic vagueness. An even more overused example of semantic vagueness is the word "natural" (ibid., 68). Examples of its use include products with labels such as "natural plastic" or "all natural ingredients." If "natural" means something existing or growing without the influence of deliberate human action, then by this definition there can be no such thing as "natural potato chips" or "natural shampoo." A fourth example, the word "environment," is misused almost as much.

Greenwashing

The use of deliberately misleading terms in order to portray an environmentally responsible image is a practice known as **greenwashing**. The term, coined by Greenpeace, combines the word "whitewashing," an attempt to hide unpleasant facts, with the word "green," associated with an environmental context (Makower 2009a, 175). For example, the term "photodegradable" is applied to some plastic products, which means they break down in sunlight. However, when these materials are dumped into landfills and covered, their ability to break down under exposure to sun has little effect. A similar phenomenon occurs when the term "biodegradable" is applied to plastics or other materials, since when these materials are buried in landfills, aerobic bacteria cannot break them down.

The consulting firm TerraChoice issues an annual greenwashing report. Their publications identify "Seven Sins of Greenwashing:" the hidden tradeoff, such as citing recycled content without mentioning greenhouse gas emissions; lack of proof, a claim with no supporting evidence available; vagueness, such as use of the term "all natural;" irrelevance, such as claiming a product is CFC-free when all CFCs have been outlawed since the 1970s; the lesser of two evils, such as promoting organic tobacco; falsehoods; and false labels, such as implying a third-party endorsement where none exists (ibid., 177; Iannuzzi 2012, 169).

Images are powerful tools in greenwashing as well. Examples from automobile manufacturers and oil companies are particularly common, where visual language built on decades of cognitive research is used in advertising to influence readers. For example, a gas-guzzling sport-utility vehicle (SUV) may be photographed in a verdant forest. A car advertisement from a few years ago showed leaves apparently sprouting from automobile tailpipes and another from an oil company showed oil refinery smokestacks producing clouds of flowers (Hogben 2009).

Efforts Big and Small

A question commonly asked is: at what scale should we work (Maniates 2002)? The brief answer is that there are multiple scales and we need them all.

Taking action at a person level is one scale, allowing individuals to illustrate without preaching what kinds of changes are appropriate and possible. Individual actions by many people have the potential to send signals to the market and, given critical mass, to influence political process. Personal actions build resilience: adjusting our eating habits to begin to match food that grows locally, perhaps learning to grow some of our own food, making our households as energy efficient as possible, learning how to buy less and reuse more, learning skills for making and repairing, and making connections with other people in our local communities build skills that will be needed in the years of transition ahead (Heinberg and Lerch 2010, 437–43). However, typical sustainability campaigns which emphasize small, simple lifestyle solutions, though attractive and plausible, are ineffective at tackling the real problems (Rees 2010; Maniates 2013, 260).

If we are to restructure the global economy, individuals must become informed and active politically as well, each picking an issue that is meaningful to them to which to contribute effort: organizing, joining a group, or contacting elected representatives (Brown 2011, 201). We cannot wait for someone else to fix the problems; there is no one else (Gilding 2011, 263). Political action is not monolithic (Alperovitz 2013, 66); some paths may be blocked, but others may be open enough to allow some kind of incremental progress.

Individual actions are a good place to start, but are capable of only small impact in the face of underlying systems of extraction, production, and disposal, which are global in scale (Makower 2009a, 203; Worldwatch 2013, 252). Because the planetary crisis is so pressing and the issues reach across state and national boundaries, mobilizing all the parts of global social networks is essential, including communities, profit and nonprofit organizations, educational institutions, governance, and policy (Evans 2012, 77; Sachs 2015, 496). Hoping to address the crisis through individual actions alone obscures the enormous force of power and privilege (Maniates 2002, 55). Systemic problems require systemic solutions.

To have significant impact requires people working together. Broad change is built around a compelling vision and it always involves collective effort. In the Indian Independence Movement led by Mahatma Gandhi in the early twentieth century, the US Civil Rights Movement of the 1960s, the environmental movement of the 1970s, and the movement opposing apartheid in South Africa, which ended in the 1990s, people did express their views through what they bought and what they boycotted. But these individual acts alone were not enough. No organizers argued that individuals caused the wrongs or that changing daily behaviors could stop the wrongs. Rather, people in these movements shared a vision of how life could be different and they joined en masse to protest, to lobby, to take legal action, and to call for broad change (Worldwatch 2013, 248). Likewise, it will take many people working together to build resilient communities, larger transformative movements, and political change for sustainability.

Resilient communities and resilient democratic societies require broad participation by significant numbers of people. That means inclusion and an openness to participation by people who may have different needs or may see the world differently than we do. It means an openness to and welcoming of a diversity of possible pathways, many of which may be hidden (Leach 2013, 235).

Policy and legislation are critical if we are to have any hope of dealing with the systemic global problems facing us. Only governments have the power to levy taxes and enforce laws, and the challenges facing us in the long emergency ahead (Kunstler 2005) are primarily political rather than technological (Orr 2009, 160). It can be argued that a bottom-up approach that is a feature of local governance is not powerful enough to address global problems such as resource depletion and climate change, since the work of local communities involves experimenting and learning together, always tuned to the needs of their particular places, lacking the impact of rolling out a single large-scale response (Evans 2012, 185).

However, the robustness of networks holds potential. Networks—a feature of ecosystems, brains, the Internet, power distribution grids, social and political systems—are flexible, operate across scales, and are resilient in the face of instability (ibid., 211–13; Barabási and Bonabeau 2003, 52; Buchanan 2002, 20). Coping with the complexity of climate destabilization and the crossing of planetary boundaries will require substantial change at all scales: of individuals, families, organizations, communities, and governments. An expectation that effective policies will appear at a global level is unreasonable; a more plausible and realistic strategy is to encourage simultaneous actions explicitly at multiple scales (Ostrom 2010, 27). Network governance as part of the global democracy (Gilding 2011, 263) is community resilience writ large; it takes an integrated approach to policymaking, including people and groups at multiple scales, across disciplines and across jurisdictional boundaries (Worldwatch 2013, 131, 241).

Box 17.1   Collective Learning: The Deeper Roots of Working in Groups

The impact of *Homo sapiens* on our planet is so great that many scientists use the term "Anthropocene" to describe the current geological epoch. What is it that makes our species so extraordinarily adaptable and thus such a powerful global force? It turns out not to be our use of tools or our brain size. Many other animals use tools, and some appear to be at least as intelligent as we are. Other animals, too, communicate with their own languages, so it is not simply that we use language that makes us different. What makes us so good at adapting to any environment is that our species has developed a unique ability to exchange large amounts of learned information precisely, using symbolic language. It is this adaptation, an emergent property known as collective learning, which has enabled us to consume resources and modify our environment at such an unprecedented rate (Christian 2011, 146).

Organisms adapt to changing environments in various ways. Natural selection is one method of adaptation used by all organisms in which genetic variations are recorded and reproduced by DNA. But because it involves passing on and accumulating genetic changes one generation at a time, the method is slow, requiring thousands or millions of years. Individual learning is another way organisms with brains adapt. It is fast, but most learning dies with the individual and cannot be transmitted to others. While parents do pass on certain skills, most of what each individual animal learns has to be learned from scratch. Humans have stumbled upon a third, unique way of adapting to the environment which combines the cumulative ability of genetic change with the speed of individual learning (ibid., 171).

What is different about humans is that they are networked. Humans adapt by sharing ideas. Human symbolic language can describe with great precision something which has been learned, and through social networks each piece of information can be stored within an entire community, then passed on and built upon across long distances and times. Other people can add to this stored collective knowledge, and over time it grows. Through this vast network, each human has access to great quantities of accumulated information from the brains of other humans. As a species, we appear to be wired to work collectively, powered by the unique cooperative structure of human communication. When we work cooperatively we tap the natural potential of this collective, networked brainpower (Tomasello 2009, 46-47). Cooperative social interaction is a defining characteristic of our species. Collective learning, taken to a planetary scale, offers a way to implement planet-wide foresight as a species (Worldwatch 2013, 221).

Working Together

Working together is where the messy work of trying to find sustainable solutions takes shape. Effective groups are microcosms of healthy ecosystems, in which diversity and multiple connections promote resilience and can lead to the emergence of novel properties. The participation of different people with diverse perspectives may result in conflict and dissent, but when committed stakeholders acknowledge this conflict explicitly and work through it with debate, dialog, and negotiation, the result can be information richness, resilience in the face of crises, and the emergence of new perspectives that may point in sustainable directions (Leach 2013, 237). An African proverb says, "If you want to walk fast, walk alone. If you want to walk far, walk together."[2]

Working in Groups

One of the roles of sustainability professionals is to coordinate and facilitate meetings. In some situations, particularly those with complex or controversial issues to address, the group may use a facilitator in addition to the leader, a neutral third party trained in effective group facilitation methods, whose task is to guide the group process. While the leader deals with the content of the meeting, the facilitator deals with the process. A facilitator is particularly helpful at times of transformation and change and can help a group use conflict constructively to maximize its collective wisdom and to produce positive outcomes with everyone's participation.

The two basic methods of making group decisions are voting and consensus. The word consensus means "agreement" and comes from the Latin word *consentire*, "to feel or perceive together." Reaching consensus usually involves a lot of listening and exchanging of ideas. Consensus is reached after all participants have had the opportunity to voice their opinions, each person's concerns are heard and understood, and the group working together has developed a solution that everyone agrees is the best solution given all the factors. Consensus does not mean that people are in 100 percent agreement; it means that the members of the group have generated a decision together that all of them can live with.

Box 17.2 Consensus in the Applegate Watershed

The Applegate Watershed in southern Oregon covers an area of about 500,000 acres, with an economy supported by the timber industry, ranching, and farming. For years the watershed had been a source of conflict between environmentalists and the timber industry, with the two sides polarized over how forests should be managed. Over time, a number of factors set people at odds including clearcutting of old growth forests, the listing of the northern spotted owl as a threatened species, lawsuits, stalled timber sales, increased fire hazard, depleted fisheries, and subsequent unemployment. The economy was shifting from farming, fishing, and logging to trade and service jobs, environmental advocates were active, and an influx of new urbanites and retirees added to the mix. Political gridlock reigned.

In 1992 two people, an environmental activist and a long-time logger, began talking to each other about the possibility of collaborating. For the next several months they talked with their neighbors and the more they talked, the more they heard about common goals. Motivated by these conversations, they invited community stakeholders to a meeting, and at that meeting a group of residents, environmental advocates, and timber industry representatives formed an alliance called the Applegate Partnership.

As this grassroots coalition began to meet, participants frequently asked a key question: "Who else needs to be at the table?" As a result of persistent outreach, they were joined by farmers, ranchers, loggers, miners, environmental groups, and representatives from the US Forest Service and the US Bureau of Land Management. The various interest groups distrusted each other but each of them, for their own reasons, was impacted by land use decisions. As they began to talk they discovered that they shared similar goals: to maintain the health of the watershed and to stabilize the local economy.

In the midst of this contentious climate, the former adversaries established some principles for working together. They struggled to overcome stereotypes about "the other."[3] They began repeating a slogan, "No 'they'" (Senos 2008, 223). In other words, they agreed to accept diverse viewpoints and they agreed to put effort into finding common ground.

With the help of skilled facilitators who volunteered their time, the first thing the participants did was to craft a vision statement. The vision they agreed to said:

> The Applegate Partnership is a community-based project involving industry, conservation groups, natural resource agencies, and residents cooperating to encourage and facilitate the use of natural resource principles that promote ecosystem health and diversity. Through community involvement and education, this partnership supports management of all land within the watershed in a manner that sustains natural resources and that will, in turn, contribute to economic and community well-being.

(Sturtevant and Lange 2001, 81–95)

The partnership sponsored numerous workshops, field trips, and open forums. It created a newspaper, the *Applegator*, distributed free to all residents and landowners in the watershed. Articles from diverse viewpoints, including such topics as streams, fish, fire danger, the timber industry, history, local businesses, and neighborhoods, along with a map of the entire watershed depicting some aspect of the area, helped people to develop a sense of community identity. The articles helped residents to feel that they were all in this together.

This inclusive, collaborative partnership promoted forest health and watershed health, and these were explicitly linked to overall community health. Before launching ecological assessments, the group initiated community assessments by professionals which included evaluations of employment, economics, recreation, and residents' likes and dislikes about their community. Citizens conducted monitoring and ecosystem research. Three hundred landowners and volunteers implemented streamside restoration projects, installed fish-protection screens on irrigation ditches, and planted 250,000 trees (Senos 2008, 219). They helped develop forest management policies, advised agencies on regulations for gravel extraction, and formed an active and effective watershed council.

Still active today, the unlikely success of this collaborative, grassroots process has drawn national attention from politicians and planners. Environmentalists, industry representatives, farmers, ranchers, and federal agencies sat at the same table as equals and looked at a common problem. With the help of facilitators, they were able to place the issues and problems at the center of their work and then work together to find science-based, community-based solutions.

Social Equity

At the dawn of the Anthropocene epoch, when humans have become such a powerful force that they have major, planet-scale impact on climate and on every living system, it is clear that a sustainable world will only be possible if all people can live secure, healthy lives within the carrying capacity of supporting ecosystems, a state known as sustainable development. Work toward sustainable development involves three goals: environmental sustainability, economic opportunity, and social inclusion.

Social inequity is a fundamental barrier to sustainability. One marker of social inequity is income inequality. The degree of income inequality can be quantified by a number known as the Gini coefficient, measured on a scale of 0 to 1. Among the countries with the lowest Gini coefficient and income inequality are the Scandinavian countries; the highest inequality is found in the US, followed by the UK (Sachs 2015, 268). Historical research directly links high levels of economic stratification to overconsumption and depletion of resources as well as to social collapse (Motesharrei et al. 2014, 90).

True sustainable development in a country is marked not by industrialization and income level, but by the degree of freedom of its citizens (Heinberg 2011, 218). The freedom to do and to be what one wants requires fair and reliable governance with the ability to participate in decision-making, transparency, educational opportunities, and an absence of discrimination.

Environmental justice, that is, the fair distribution of environmental benefits and burdens, is a dimension of social equity. It is the concept that access to a clean, healthy environment is a fundamental human right. Uneven access, often due to market forces and government policy and driven by social stratification or racial inequity, results in a range of social burdens including health problems, food insecurity, poverty, and poor education. Social issues are sustainability issues. Environmental justice works to ensure equal distribution of access to clean air, clean water, healthy food, parks and open space, walkable streets, low-cost and accessible transportation, economic and social opportunities, and full participation in the decisions about one's community.

Box 17.3 Sustainable South Bronx

In the final decades of the twentieth century, South Bronx in New York City had become poor, was primarily non-white, and bore a heavy environmental burden for the rest of the city. With one of the lowest ratios in the city of parks to people, it was home to contaminated land, burned-out buildings, waste facilities, power plants, and massive truck yards, along with pollution, high asthma rates, obesity, unemployment, poverty, and crime.

Then in 1998 Majora Carter and a few neighbors organized and got a small seed grant to clean up a polluted waterfront along the Bronx River, with the tiny Hunts Point Riverside Park giving residents their first access to the river in over 60 years. Carter subsequently formed an environmental justice organization known as Sustainable South Bronx. They applied for larger grants to create the South Bronx Greenway, a system of connected parks and greenways with street networks, public transportation, bike paths, waterfront access, improved air quality, retail, and mixed-use affordable housing, all developed in collaboration with community residents.

Their organization wanted to link environmental change with social and economic change, so they started one of the first green jobs training programs in the country. They wanted to ensure that work on infrastructure projects on their waterfront was done by people in the community. So residents, many of whom had faced significant obstacles to employment, got training in wetland restoration and habitat creation. Now known as BEST Academy, or Bronx Environmental Stewardship Training, the job-training program trains people in well-paying skill areas (which can't be outsourced) such as ecological restoration, hazardous waste cleanup, green roof installation and maintenance, urban forestry, and landscaping. To promote economic development, Sustainable South Bronx started a green roofing company, and they played a key role in creating a green-roof tax abatement program in New York City.

Hundreds of diesel trucks each day once idled for 8 to 12 hours a day at Hunts Point, one of the world's largest wholesale food distribution centers, leading to high childhood asthma rates and other health issues, an example of environmental injustice. Sustainable South Bronx, in partnership with the New York Power Authority, the Hunts Point Cooperative Market, and the Clean Air Communities Foundation, instituted the anti-idling Truck Stop Electrification (TSE) Project to cut diesel exhaust, lower asthma rates, and reduce greenhouse gas emissions. Some residents saw that large numbers of shipping pallets came through their community and went to a landfill, so they began a green manufacturing firm making high-quality furniture from the discarded pallets.

In 2012, a design competition and a New York City grant led to the construction of Via Verde, a LEED-certified, mixed-use affordable housing development. Proximity to schools, jobs, and mass transit now make access to the activities of daily life affordable. The ground floor houses a community health center. Energy efficiency, solar power, and rainwater harvesting cut utility costs for residents. Narrow building footprints wrap around a central courtyard, allowing cross ventilation and natural light. Multiple stepped roofs are topped with community gardens where residents grow fresh food, and one roof includes fruit trees. A garden amphitheater is used for community events. The highest floor has spectacular views; it is not the usual private penthouse but common space for community use.

Equity for future people, known as intergenerational equity, is a significant focus of sustainability and at the core of sustainable development (IPCC 2014c, 14). Much of the planetary damage being done, including climate change, pollution, resource depletion, and extinction, has costs that will be borne primarily not by those who impose the damages but by future generations of people not yet born. In addition, the benefits to future generations from actions taken today are often evaluated using an approach known as 'discounting the future,' in which benefits today have greater value than benefits in the future (ibid., 30).

Those who will suffer the greatest harm are people who are least responsible for causing the harm. These future generations have no representation and cannot speak as decisions are being made in the present. Decisions of people alive in the present affect the number, identity, and existence of future people and other species: how many will exist, who will exist, and whether any will exist at all (Moore and Nelson 2013, 227; Meyer 2015, 2).

Building Community

As the world makes its transition out of the industrial era perhaps our most important asset will be healthy communities of people able to work together to provision themselves and create thriving local economies (Heinberg 2011, 269; Orr 2013, 289). The more we work now to build inclusive social infrastructure, the more robust our communities will be during times of disruption and transition that probably lie ahead. That does not mean it will be easy; collaboration is hard work, and it is messy (Senge et al. 2010, 49). It requires innovation and a willingness to try untested approaches with the understanding that some of our experiments will fail. It means a willingness to form partnerships among people and groups who do not usually cooperate. Something happens when groups of people come together, with results that are larger than the sum of the parts: emergence, a property of all living systems. None of us has the knowledge or resources to address sustainability issues alone. Facing them and coming out the other side successfully will require all of us as part of networks in various forms.

Within communities of all scales, diversity is an essential asset. Sustainability has many goals, the issues are many and varied, and each of us has our own sets of skills and understandings. Sustainability is not a single pathway (Worldwatch 2013, 234). The more we are open to alternative voices, the stronger our social fabric and the richer our choice of potential futures. As we begin to work together, we should constantly be asking, whose voices are not yet included? Who else should be at the table? Learning to be open to other perspectives and learning to work through conflict are easier to talk about than to accomplish. They, too, are skills developed through hard work.

One of the fundamental themes running through strategies for living sustainably is the importance of modeling our choices on how living systems work: looking at the world and reading it as our "instruction manual." One thing we notice about living systems that are resilient is that they all feature diversity. Resilient systems endure not because they remain stable in the face of change, but because they are able to shift to new states that allow them to retain their core functions (Evans 2012, 170). A system with diverse components has a range of ways it can respond to disturbance and more ways to absorb shock (Walker and Salt 2006, 121). It is more likely to generate novel responses to changing conditions, and some of this innovation leads to solutions with good fit to new conditions (Worldwatch 2013, 357). Keeping in mind our instruction manual we can value diversity and embrace change, remembering that change is inevitable and that the ability to adapt to changing circumstances is a feature of all resilient systems (Heinberg and Lerch 2010, 448).

Building community involves real participation with people actively engaged, creating options, and making decisions about them; it is the practice of genuine democracy[4] (Alperovitz 2009, 141). Self-reliance, including skills of self-governance at a local level, will become increasingly important as climate destabilizes, ecosystems are rearranged, and economies falter (Orr 2013, 289; Assadourian 2013, 300). Governance is not learned simply by being told about it but by practicing, beginning at a limited scale. We practice, build understanding, and gain experience with small, decentralized democracy by doing it in towns and workplaces (Alperovitz 2013, 141-42). As political economist Gar Alperovitz points out, "If we are to counter the dangers both of corporate domination and of traditional forms of socialist states, decentralization is essential, both of economic institutions and of political structure" (ibid., 144). Strategies for stabilizing local economies and building community include small independent firms, cooperatives, worker owned companies, neighborhood corporations, municipal utilities, and new approaches to banking and investing.

In a worker-owned cooperative, workers have a direct role in decision-making. Wealth is owned by the members, rather than shareholders, who can choose to invest in capital and do long-term planning since they are not driven solely by short-term profit. Cooperatives foster economic opportunity and build social capital, and may be early elements of necessary systemic transformation of a brittle economic structure dominated by corporate power (Alperovitz 2013, 47).

Green Worker Cooperatives in the South Bronx of New York City, with a mission of building a healthy local economy rooted in democracy and environmental justice, serves as an incubator with training programs for worker-owned green businesses, such as ReBuilders Source, a worker-owned cooperative that reuses salvaged building materials.

Mondragon Corporation is a federation of over 100 independent cooperatives, based in the Basque region of Spain with facilities on five continents. Workers in each cooperative own a share of their company and participate in all major decisions. The salary of an executive cannot be more than 6.5 times that of the lowest paid employees.

Evergreen Cooperative Laundry in Cleveland, Ohio, is a large-scale network of over 100 cooperatively owned businesses with a structure drawn on the Mondragon model. Worker-owned cooperatives within the group include the eponymous laundry service for the healthcare industry, a solar-panel installation and weatherization company, and a large food-production greenhouse.

The planetary crisis in which we find ourselves cannot be addressed without confronting the issue of how wealth is owned and controlled. Corporations not only have legal status as 'people,' they are required by law to make decisions that financially benefit their stockholders (Alperovitz 2013, 39). This restriction is at odds with goals of environmental protection, economic equity, and social justice. This led a group of private equity experts to invent a new legal form, the benefit corporation or B Corp, which permits the use of business profits for social and environmental benefit. B Corps are certified through the nonprofit organization B Lab and are now allowed by law in many countries. A small but growing number of banks operate as cooperatives, B Corps, or both.

Transition

The twenty-first century will be a time of transition. Humans have gone through several major transitions in their history: the discovery of fire, the development of language, the development of agriculture and settlements, and the Industrial Revolution. We live at the threshold of another major turning at the beginning of the Anthropocene epoch, as humanity moves away from an industrial age built upon fossil fuel and economic growth and toward what could turn out to be a steady-state economy within a regenerative, sustainable society (Heinberg and Lerch 2010, 284). A great deal of the effort of sustainability practitioners is aimed toward equipping humanity for this transition.

The Tellus Institute and its Great Transition Institute refer to this as the Great Transition (Raskin et al. 2002, 11). Deep ecologist Joanna Macy and economist David Korten refer to this transition as "The Great Turning" (Seed et al. 2007; Worldwatch 2013, 232). Post Carbon Institute Senior Fellow Richard Heinberg refers to it as humanity's "fifth great turning" (Heinberg and Lerch 2010, 284).

Transition Towns, founded by permaculturist Rob Hopkins, is a global network of hundreds of communities each working to build local resilience in response to peak oil, economic instability, and climate destabilization. Many develop local food and resource systems, handle their own waste, generate renewable energy, and craft energy descent plans; some offer re-skilling workshops or develop local currencies. All are built on networks of relationships and centered around hope and action, or as Hopkins calls it, "engaged optimism" (Hopkins 2011, 24). A central idea is that the ending of the fossil fuel era can be an opportunity rather than a threat, that life after oil can be more abundant and fulfilling than before. As Heinberg says: "If it's not fun you're not doing it right" (Heinberg and Lerch 2010, 446).

Planning for Turbulence

Working together, growing food, building resilient communities, planning our energy descent, and pressing for better approaches to governing could help ease humanity's transition. Nevertheless, great momentum is already built into the system, and we are in for a bumpy ride no matter what we do (Orr 2009, xi; Senge et al. 2010, 32; Gilding 2011, 48; Heinberg 2011, 280; Maniates 2013, 259).

We have entered a period of unknown duration in which we can expect turbulence. Economic degrowth, extinctions, disappearing resources, and the nasty side effects of climate destabilization will be painful. We can expect conflicts and social disruption alongside the more pleasant aspects of transition. We would do well to work at training ourselves to handle these with resilience and equanimity while we work at keeping a positive vision of the future always in mind (Maniates 2013, 268).

What Now?

A number of groups have worked to envision what life on the other side of the transition might be like (Raskin et al. 2002; Edwards 2005; Corcoran 2007; Orr 2009; Heinberg and Lerch 2010). It seems clear that nearly every aspect of our modern way of living will be transformed to some degree (Senge et al. 2010, 32), from where and how we grow our food to how we transport ourselves and our goods to how those goods are made. We can expect a resurgence in high-quality, durable, hand-crafted goods, locally made, maintained, and reused for generations. The mission of education will expand, teaching learners about local ecology and giving them experience with skills for self-reliance. Civics will become important as people re-learn skills for participating in democratic governance. Humans will take a more active role in the health of the biosphere. The job market will shift as some jobs become obsolete while new green-economy jobs appear. Although we may still occasionally drive personal vehicles, most people will take advantage of interconnected public transit networks. Energy will come increasingly from renewable sources, transmitted over distributed, intelligent microgrids. Communities will become more decentralized and more resilient, with greater control over many aspects of their daily lives. Buildings, landscapes, food, and social structures will look different in each place as placelessness becomes a relic of an earlier time. Human connections across the globe using information technology will continue to build collective learning even as local clusters become more self-reliant and resilient, a robust exemplar of classic scale-free networks at a planetary scale.

A question often posed to sustainability practitioners is whether we should be optimistic or pessimistic, whether we should feel hope or despair. This may be an unhelpful dichotomy, for both positions ask us to predict a future that is in fact unknown, and both give us reasons not to act.

What we know based on reliable evidence is that, at the least, Earth's climate will be changing and its oceans will be rising for centuries to come; the era of a petroleum-powered, ever-expanding economy will necessarily come to an end; and a significant portion of species alive today will no longer be with us. To feel sorrow and even despair in the face of this reality is reasonable, a stage of grieving as we move from denial to a more productive stage.

Blind optimism, the belief that all will be well because nature is in charge and its cycles always find a way, is moral complacency (Worldwatch 2013, 228), a weakness of character that is not so productive. Unthinking optimism leads to inaction. We should remember that if nature makes adjustments, its new state may well not include us.

There is a third path: action, compelled by our own ethical values and a belief that the rights of future generations, of other species, and of the Earth system itself are worth struggling for (Ehrlich and Ehrlich 2013). A Latin proverb says, *Si ventus non est, remiga*: "If there is no wind, row." The way to move away from both debilitating despair and paralyzing optimism is to choose to act from a position of active, engaged hope based upon a positive vision. At the beginning of the Civil Rights era, when Dr. Martin Luther King looked around he saw evidence of racism everywhere. Its presence was indisputable. It was ugly, and it was deeply embedded. And yet, in the face of this grim reality, his speech was not "I have a nightmare." His speech was a call to action: "I have a dream" (Gilding 2011, 112).

Find a place to stand. Choose what you love. Start from there, do what you can, and connect with others. Foresters have a saying: "The very best time to plant a tree is decades ago. The second best time is today" (Worldwatch Institute 2013, 83).

Notes

1 Anthropocentrism is a human-centered view of reality that sees humans as the most important species and views nature in terms of its usefulness to humans.

2 Africa is an enormous continent of many cultures. Although this proverb is quoted often, its origin is never located more specifically than "Africa," and its provenance is uncertain.

3   "The Other" is a term used in philosophy, sociology, and literature to describe people outside one's own group. It implies alienation and a sense that those outside the group, who are different in some way, have less worth than those inside the group. Various writers have noted that perceiving fellow creatures as "The Other" is the basis of discrimination, inequity, and warfare.

4   The word "democracy," which means essentially rule by the people, literally people-power, is made from two Greek roots: *dēmos*, the people, and *-kratia*, power or rule.

Further Reading

Alperovitz, Gar. *What Then Must We Do?* White River Junction, VT: Chelsea Green, 2009.

Gilding, Paul. *The Great Disruption.* New York: Bloomsbury Press, 2011.

Heinberg, Richard and Daniel Lerch, eds. *The Post Carbon Reader: Managing the 21st Century's Sustainability Crises.* Healdsburg, CA: Watershed Media, 2010.

Hopkins, Rob. *The Transition Companion: Making Your Community More Resilient in Uncertain Times.* White River, VT: Chelsea Green, 2011.

Worldwatch Institute. *State of the World 2013: Is Sustainability Still Possible?* Washington, DC: Island Press, 2013.

Chapter Review

1   How does a facilitator differ from the person who leads a meeting?

2   Why do so many meeting leaders use flipcharts or their electronic equivalents?

3   Describe the difference between majority vote and consensus.

4   What is a stakeholder?

5   Briefly describe the history behind development of the term "triple bottom line."

6   List some commonly used words with semantic vagueness.

7   Name 5 to 10 examples of practices that you think illustrate greenwashing.

8   What is meant by the term "change agent"?

Critical Thinking and Discussion

1   Why does "collective learning" appear to give the human species an adaptive advantage? Why is it important to sustainability?

2   What do you think might happen if a meeting were held without an agenda?

3   Do you think that social marketing manipulates people?

4   What can you do as an individual citizen to enable your voice to be heard by government officials and policymakers?

5   Evidence shows that people respond better to things that make them feel good than to things that are scary. Yet many people seem unconcerned and unaware of the gravity of issues such as global warming and mass extinctions. How can scientists communicate the seriousness of these issues without resorting to apocalyptic warnings? Or do you think apocalyptic warnings might be necessary?

6   Some environmentalists believe that collaborative groups with consensus approaches can give disproportionate advantage to industry representatives and other people with power. What do you think? Do you think ordinary citizens and less-privileged people can influence decisions on an equal footing with power brokers in consensus groups? What factors do you think are required for consensus to be effective?

7   In a group whose members have a common background and common values, conflict is often minimal and consensus relatively easy to reach. Participating in a diverse group

such as a watershed council, however, can be more challenging. What kinds of outcomes can a diverse partnership achieve that cannot be accomplished by a more homogeneous group?

8 When trying to make decisions about difficult issues, such as oil drilling in fragile wilderness areas or protecting critical endangered species habitat on privately owned property, do you think that compromise or consensus are possible?

9 The label on one pesticide product claims that it "kills all insects but is safe for the environment." What do you think about this statement?

10 As human animals we are wired to care most deeply about things that affect us and our immediate group and to care less about effects far away. What strategies can you suggest that could help people make a connection between their own behaviors, such as automobile and airplane trips, and things that happen far away, such as sea-level rise in Asia?

Bibliography

AAAS Climate Science Panel. *What We Know: The Reality, Risks and Response to Climate Change*. Washington, DC: American Association for the Advancement of Science (AAAS), 2014.

Ackerman-Leist, Philip. *Rebuilding the Foodshed: How to Create Local, Sustainable, and Secure Food Systems*. White River Junction, VT: Chelsea Green, 2013.

Adams, Lowell W. *Urban Wildlife Habitats: A Landscape Perspective*. Minneapolis, MN: University of Minnesota Press, 1994.

AGI (American Geological Institute). *Environmental Science: Understanding Our Changing Earth*. Clifton Park, NY: Delmar, 2011.

Agyeman, J. *Sustainable Communities and the Challenge of Environmental Justice*. New York: New York University Press, 2005.

—— and Alison Hope Alkon, eds. *Cultivating Food Justice: Race, Class, and Sustainability*. Cambridge, MA: MIT Press, 2011.

Aiken, William. "Ethical Issues in Agriculture." In Tom Regan, ed. *Earthbound: Introductory Essays in Environmental Ethics*. Philadelphia, PA: Temple University Press, 1984, 247–288.

AISC (American Institute of Steel Construction). "Designing for Sustainability." 2013. www.aisc. org/sustainability.

Akram-Lodhi, A. Haroon and Christóbal Kay, eds. *Peasants and Globalization: Political Economy, Rural Transformation and the Agrarian Question*. London: Routledge, 2008.

Alcott, Blake. "Jevons' Paradox." *Ecological Economics*, 54 (2005): 9–21.

Alexander, Martin. *Biodegradation and Bioremediation*, 2nd ed. San Diego: Academic Press, 1999.

Allen, Will, Diana Balmori, and Fritz Haeg. *Edible Estates: Attack on the Front Lawn*. 2nd ed. New York: Metropolis Books, 2010.

Allenby, B. *Industrial Ecology: Policy Framework and Implementation*. Englewood Cliffs, NJ: Prentice Hall, 1999.

Alonso, Elisa et al., "Evaluating Rare Earth Element Availability: A Case with Revolutionary Demand from Clean Technologies." *Environmental Science and Technology*, 46, 6 (2012): 406–414.

Alperovitz, Gar. *What Then Must We Do?* White River Junction, VT: Chelsea Green, 2013.

Altieri, Miguel A. and Fernando R. Funes-Monzote. "The Paradox of Cuban Agriculture." *Monthly Review*, January 2012.

Anastas, Paul. "Introduction to Green Chemistry." In John W. Hill, Terry W. McCreary, and Doris K. Kolb, *Chemistry for Changing Times*. 12th ed. Upper Saddle River, NJ: Prentice Hall, 2010, 31.

—— and J. B. Zimmerman. "The Twelve Principles of Green Engineering as a Foundation for Sustainability." Chapter 2 in Martin A. Abraham, ed. *Sustainability Science and Engineering: Defining Principles*. Amsterdam: Elsevier B. V., 2006, 11–32.

Andel, Jelte van and James Aronson, eds. *Restoration Ecology: The New Frontier*, 2nd ed. Chichester: Wiley-Blackwell, 2012.

Anderson, Ray C. *Mid-Course Correction: Toward a Sustainable Enterprise: The Interface Model*. Atlanta, GA: Peregrinzilla Press, 1999.

——. *Confessions of a Radical Industrialist*. New York: St. Martin's Press, 2009.

Ansell, C. and C. Gash. "Collaborative Governance in Theory and Practice." *Journal of Public Administration Research and Theory*, 18 (2008): 543–571.

Anthropocene Working Group, Subcommission on Quaternary Stratigraphy, International Commission on Stratigraphy. Updated February 23, 2016. http://quaternary.stratigraphy.org/workinggroups/anthropocene/ (Accessed June 16, 2016).

Apfelbaum, Steven I. and Alan W. Haney. *Restoring Ecological Health to Your Land.* Washington, DC: Island Press, 2010.

Aral Sea Foundation. N.d. http://www.aralsea.org/.

Architecture 2030. 2013. http://architecture2030.org/.

Arendt, Randall. *Conservation Design for Subdivisions: A Practical Guide to Creating Open Space Networks.* Washington, DC: Island Press, 1996.

Armitage, Marc. "Risky Play Is Not a Category—It's What Children Do." *Childlinks* issue 3 (2011): 12–16.

Arndt, D. S., M. O. Baringer, and M. R. Johnson, eds. "State of the Climate in 2009." *Bulletin of the American Meteorological Society*, 91 (2010): S1–S224.

Arndt, Michael. "Caterpillar Remanufacturing." *Bloomberg Businessweek*, December 5, 2005.

Arnstein, S. "The Ladder of Citizen Participation." *Journal of the Institute of American Planners*, 35 (1969): 16–24.

Arrhenius, Svante. "On the Influence of Carbonic Acid in the Air upon the Temperature of the Ground." *The London, Edinburgh, and Dublin Philosophical Magazine and Journal of Science*, April 1896.

Ash, Caroline, Barbara R. Jasny, Leslie Roberts, Richard Stone, and Andrew M. Sudden. "Reimagining Cities." *Science* special issue, 319, 5864 (February 8, 2008): 739.

Assadourian, Erik. "The Living Earth Ethical Principles: Spreading Community." *World Watch Magazine*, September/October 2009: 38–39.

——. "The Path to Degrowth in Overdeveloped Countries." In Worldwatch Institute. *State of the World 2012.* Washington, DC: Island Press, 2012, 22–37.

——. "Re-engineering Cultures to Create a Sustainable Civilization." In Worldwatch Institute, *State of the World 2013: Is Sustainability Still Possible?* Washington, DC: Island Press, 2013, 113-125.

AtKisson, Alan. *The ISIS Agreement: How Sustainability Can Improve Organizational Performance and Transform the World.* London: Earthscan, 2008.

Atlee, Jennifer and Tristan Roberts, "Cradle to Cradle Certification: A Peek inside MBDC's Black Box." *Environmental Building News*, February 1, 2007.

Atsom, Yuval et al. "Winning the $30 Trillion Decathlon: Going for Gold in Emerging Markets." *McKinsey Quarterly*, August 2012: 4.

Attaran, A. "An Immeasurable Crisis? A Criticism of the Millennium Development Goals and Why They Cannot Be Measured." *PLoS Medicine* (2005). www.ncbi.nlm.nih.gov/pmc/articles/PMC1201695/.

Attari, Shahzeen Z., Michael L. DeKay, Cliff I. Davidson, and Wändi Bruine de Bruin. "Public Perceptions of Energy Consumption and Savings." *Proceedings of the National Academy of Sciences* 107, 37 (2010): 16054–16059. www.pnas.org/content/107/37/16054.abstract.

Ayres, Robert U. and Leslie W. Ayers, eds. *A Handbook of Industrial Ecology.* Cheltenham: Edward Elgar, 2002.

—— and Edward H. Ayres. *Crossing the Energy Divide.* Philadelphia, PA: Wharton School Publishing, 2010.

Bäckstrand, K. "Civic Science for Sustainability: Reframing the Role of Experts, Policy-Makers and Citizens in Environmental Governance." *Global Environmental Politics*, 3, 4 (2003): 24–41.

Ballantyne, Coco. "Not All Sugars Are Created Equal." Health & Medicine, *ScientificAmerican.com.* April 20, 2009. www.scientificamerican.com/blog/post. cfm?id=not-all-sugars-are-created-equal-2009-04-20.

Balmori, Diana and Gaboury Benoit. *Land and Natural Development (LAND) Code: Guidelines for Sustainable Land Development.* New York: John Wiley & Sons, 2007.

Banerjee, S. "CSR: The Good, the Bad and the Ugly." *Critical Sociology*, 34 (2008): 51–79.

Banks, Suzy and Richard Heinichen. *Rainwater Collection for the Mechanically Challenged.* Dripping Springs, TX: Tank Town Publishing, 2004.

Barabási, Albert-László and Eric Bonabeau. "Scale-Free Networks." *Scientific American*, May 2003: 50–59.

Barlett, Peggy F., ed. *Urban Place: Reconnecting with the Natural World*. Cambridge, MA: MIT Press, 2005.

—— and Geoffrey W. Chase, eds. *Sustainability on Campus: Stories and Strategies for Change*. Cambridge, MA: MIT Press, 2004.

Barlow, Connie. *Green Space, Green Time: The Way of Science*. New York: Copernicus, 1997.

Barnofsky, Anthony D. et al. "Approaching a State Shift in Earth's Biosphere." *Nature*, June 7, 2012: 52–58.

Barham, James, Debra Tropp, Kathleen Enterline, Jeff Farbman, John Fisk, and Stacia Kiraly. *Regional Food Hub Resource Guide*. Washington, DC: US Dept. of Agriculture, Agricultural Marketing Service. April 2012. http://dx.doi.org/10.9752/MS046.04-2012.

Barnosky, Anthony D. et al. "Approaching a State Shift in Earth's Biosphere." *Nature* 486 (June 2012): 52–58.

Bartlett, L. J., et al. "Robustness Despite Uncertainty: Regional Climate Data Reveal the Dominant Role of Humans in Explaining Global Extinctions of Late Quaternary Megafauna." *Ecography* 38 (2015): 1–10. doi: 10.1111/ecog.01566.

Basel Action Network. "About the Basel Ban." 2011. www.ban.org/about-the-basel-ban/.

BASMAA (Bay Area Stormwater Management Agencies Association). *Start at the Source: Design Guidance Manual for Stormwater Quality Protection*. New York: Forbes, 1999.

Batterman, Sarah A. et al. "Key Role of Symbiotic Dinitrogen Fixation in Tropical Forest Secondary Succession." *Nature* vol 502 no 7470 (October 10, 2013): 224–227. doi:10.1038/nature12525.

Beatley, Timothy. *Biophilic Cities: Integrating Nature into Urban Planning and Design*. Washington, DC: Island Press, 2010.

Beattie, Andrew and Paul R. Ehrlich. *Wild Solutions: How Biodiversity Is Money in the Bank.* 2nd ed. New Haven, CT: Yale University Press, 2004.

Bell, Simon and Stephen Morse. *Measuring Sustainability: Learning from Doing*. Sterling, VA: Earthscan, 2003.

——. *Sustainability Indicators: Measuring the Immeasurable?* Sterling, VA: Earthscan, 2008.

Bellwood, Peter. *First Farmers: The Origins of Agricultural Societies*. Oxford: Blackwell, 2005.

Belson, Ken. "The Rooftop Garden Climbs Down a Wall." *New York Times*, November 19, 2009.

Benedict, Mark A. and Edward T. McMahon. *Green Infrastructure: Linking Landscapes and Communities*. Washington, DC: Island Press, 2006.

Bennett, E. M., et al. "Toward a More Resilient Agriculture." *Solutions*, vol. 5 no. 5 (September–October 2014): 65–75.

Bennett, M., P. James, and L. Klinkers. *Sustainable Measures: Evaluation and Reporting of Environmental and Social Performance*. Sheffield: Greenleaf, 1999.

Benson, M. "Regional Initiatives: Scaling the Climate Response and Responding to Conceptions of Scale." *Annals of the Association of American Geographers*, 100 (2010): 1025–1035.

Benyus, Janine M. *Biomimicry: Innovation Inspired by Nature*. New York: HarperCollins, 1997.

——. *Biomimicry Discussion Guide*. N.p.: Bioneers, 2004.

Berkes, F. "Rethinking Community Based Conservation." *Conservation Biology*, 18 (2004): 621–630.

——, J. Colding, and C. Folke, eds. *Navigating Social-Ecological Systems*. Cambridge: Cambridge University Press, 2003.

Biello, David. "Biofuels Are Bad for Feeding People and Combating Climate Change." *Scientific American*, February 2008.

——. "Green Buildings May Be Cheapest Way to Slow Global Warming." *Scientific American*, March 2008.

Bierman, F. and P. Pattberg. "Global Environmental Governance: Taking Stock, Moving Forward." *Annual Review of Environment and Resources*, 33 (2008): 277–294.

——, —— and F. Zelli. *Global Climate Governance Beyond 2012*. Cambridge: Cambridge University Press, 2010.

Biomimicry Institute. "Ventilated Nests Remove Heat and Gas: Mound-Building Termites." N.d. www.asknature.org/strategy/8a16bdffd27387cd2a3a995525ea08b3.

Birkeland, Janis. *Design for Sustainability: A Sourcebook of Integrated Eco-logical Solutions*. London: Earthscan Publications, 2000.

Black, Maggie and Jannet King. *The Atlas of Water: Mapping the World's Most Critical Resource*. 2nd ed. Berkeley, CA: University of California Press, 2009.

Blanc, Patrick. *The Vertical Garden: From Nature to the City*. rev. ed. New York: W. W. Norton, 2012.

Blaustein, Richard. "Predicting Tipping Points." *World Policy Journal* vol 32 no 1 (Spring 2015): 32–41. doi:10.1177/0740277515578622.

Blockstein, David E. and Leo Wiegman. *The Climate Solutions Consensus: What We Know and What to Do About It*. Washington, DC: Island Press, 2010.

Bollier, David. *Green Governance: Ecological Survival, Human Rights, and the Commons*. Cambridge: Cambridge University Press, 2014.

Bomford, Michael. "Getting Fossil Fuels off the Plate." Chapter 9 in Richard Heinberg and Daniel Lerch, eds. *The Post Carbon Reader: Managing the 21st Century's Sustainability Crises*. Healdsburg, CA: Watershed Media, 2010.

Boswell, Michael R., Adrienne I. Greve, and Tammy L. Seale. *Local Climate Action Planning*. Washington, DC: Island Press, 2012.

Boucher, Doug, Pipa Elias, Katherine Lininger, Calen May-Tobin, Sarah Roquemore, and Earl Saxon. *The Root of the Problem: What's Driving Tropical Deforestation Today?* Cambridge, MA: Union of Concerned Scientists, 2011.

Bourne, Joel K. "California's Pipe Dream." *National Geographic*, 217, 4 (April 2010): 132–153.

Braasch, Gary. *Earth under Fire: How Global Warming Is Changing the World*. Berkeley, CA: University of California Press, 2009.

Bradshaw, Vaughn. *The Building Environment: Active and Passive Control Systems*. 3rd ed. New York: John Wiley, 2006.

Brennan, Andrew and Lo, Yeuk-Sze, "Environmental Ethics." In Edward N. Zalta, ed., *The Stanford Encyclopedia of Philosophy*, 2015. http://plato.stanford.edu/entries/ethics-environmental/.

Brennan, Geraldine, Mike Tennant, and Fenna Blomsma. "Business and Production Solutions: Closing Loops and the Circular Economy." Chapter 10 in Kopnina, Helen and Eleanor Shoreman-Ouimet, eds. *Sustainability: Key Issues*. London: Routledge, 2015.

Briscoe, John and R. P. S. Malik. *India's Water Economy: Bracing for a Turbulent Future*. New Delhi: Oxford University Press, 2006.

Broad, William. "Tracing Oil Reserves to Their Tiny Origins." *New York Times*, August 2, 2010.

Brown, G. Z. and Mark DeKay. *Sun, Wind & Light*. 2nd ed. New York: John Wiley, 2000.

Brown, J. and M. Purcell. "There's Nothing Inherent about Scale: Political Ecology, the Local Trap, and the Politics of Development in the Brazilian Amazon." *Geoforum*, 36 (2005): 607–624.

Brown, Lester R. *Building a Sustainable Society*. New York: Norton, 1981.

———. *Plan B 3.0: Mobilizing to Save Civilization*. New York: W. W. Norton & Company, 2008.

———. *Plan B 4.0: Mobilizing to Save Civilization*. New York: W. W. Norton & Company, 2009.

———. *World on the Edge: How to Prevent Environmental and Economic Collapse*. New York: W. W. Norton, 2011.

———. *The Great Transition: Shifting from Fossil Fuels to Solar and Wind Energy*. New York: W. W. Norton, 2015.

Brown, Robert D. *Design with Microclimate: The Secret to Comfortable Outdoor Space*. Washington, DC: Island Press, 2010.

Bruges, James. *The Biochar Debate: Charcoal's Potential to Reverse Climate Change and Build Soil Fertility*. White River Junction, VT: Chelsea Green, 2010.

Buchanan, Mark. *Nexus: Small Worlds and the Groundbreaking Science of Networks*. New York: W. W. Norton & Company, 2002.

Bulkeley, H. and S. Moser. "Responding to Climate Change: Governance and Social Action beyond Kyoto." *Global Environmental Politics*, 7 (2007): 1–10.

—— and P. Newell. *Governing Climate Change*. London: Routledge, 2010.

——, V. Castán Broto, M. Hodson, and S. Marvin, eds. *Cities and Low Carbon Transitions*. London: Routledge, 2010.

Bullard, Robert D. "Anatomy of Environmental Racism," in R. Hofrichter, ed. *Toxic Struggles: The Theory and Practice of Environmental Justice*. Gabriola Island, BC: New Society Publishers, 1993, 25–35.

Burke, Edmund III and Kenneth Pomeranz, eds. *The Environment and World History*. Berkeley, CA: University of California Press, 2009.

Butler, Katy. "Winning Words." *Sierra*, 89, 4 (July/August 2004): 54.

Butler, Tom, Daniel Lerch, and George Wuerthner, eds. *The Energy Reader: Overdevelopment and the Delusion of Endless Growth*. Healdsburg, CA: Watershed Media, 2012.

Butti, Ken and John Perlin. *A Golden Thread: 2,500 Years of Solar Architecture and Technology*. New York: Van Nostrand Reinhold, 1980.

Cahill, Thomas H. *Low Impact Development and Sustainable Stormwater Management*. New York: John Wiley, 2012.

Calkins, Meg. *Materials for Sustainable Sites: A Complete Guide to the Evaluation, Selection, and Use of Sustainable Construction Materials*. New York: John Wiley, 2009.

——. *The Sustainable Sites Handbook: A Complete Guide to the Principles, Strategies, and Best Practices for Sustainable Landscapes*. New York: John Wiley, 2012.

Callicott, J. Baird. *In Defense of the Land Ethic: Essays in Environmental Philosophy*. Albany, NY: State University of New York Press, 1989.

CalRecycle. "Resource Recovery Parks." 2011. www.calrecycle.ca.gov/LGCentral/Library/Innovations/recoverypark/.

Cambridge Systematics, Inc. *Moving Cooler: An Analysis of Transportation Strategies for Reducing Greenhouse Gas Emissions*. Washington, DC: Urban Land Institute, 2009.

Campbell, Craig S. and Michael Ogden. *Constructed Wetlands in the Sustainable Landscape*. New York: John Wiley, 1999.

Campbell, Robert Wellman, ed. 2001. "Aral Sea, Central Asia: 1964, 1973, 1987, 1999." Earthshots: Satellite Images of Environmental Change. USGS. February 14, 1997. Revised August 14, 2000 and August 14, 2001. http://earthshots.usgs.gov.

Capra, Fritjof. *The Web of Life*. New York: Anchor Books, 1996.

——. *The Hidden Connections: Integrating the Biological, Cognitive, and Social Dimensions of Life into a Science of Sustainability*. New York: Doubleday, 2002.

Caradonna, Jeremy L. *Sustainability: A History*. New York: Oxford University Press, 2014.

Carson, Rachel. *Silent Spring*. New York: Houghton Mifflin, 1994.

Carter, Anna Marie. "Seeds of Justice, Seeds of Hope." *YES! Magazine*, March 31, 2003.

——. "Seeds of Justice, Seeds of Hope." In Jack Canfield et al. *Chicken Soup for the Soul: Stories for a Better World*. Deerfield Beach, FL: Health Communications, 2005, 364–368.

Casselman, Anne. "Strange but True: The Largest Organism on Earth Is a Fungus." *Scientific American*, October 2007.

Cassio, Jim and Alice Rush. *Green Careers: Choosing Work for a Sustainable Future*. Gabriola Island, BC: New Society Publishers, 2009.

Center for Sustainable Systems Factsheets. *Municipal Solid Waste*. Ann Arbor, MI: University of Michigan, 2008. http://css.snre.umich.edu/facts/.

CERT (Corporation for Educational Radio and Television). "Food From the 'Hood." 2013. www.certnyc.org/ffth.html.

Chandy, L. and G. Gertz, *Poverty in Numbers: The Changing State of Global Poverty from 2005 to 2015*. Washington, DC: The Brookings Institution, 2011.

Chapin, F. Stuart III et al. "Ecosystem Stewardship: Sustainability Strategies for a Rapidly Changing Planet." *Trends in Ecology and Evolution*, November 24, 2009, 241–249.

Charles, Leonard, Jim Dodge, Lynn Milliman, and Victoria Stockley. "Where You At? A Bioregional Quiz." *CoEvolution Quarterly*, 32 (Winter 1981): 1.

Chertow, M. "The IPAT Equation and Its Variants: Changing Views of Technology and Environmental Impacts." *Journal of Industrial Ecology*, 4 (2001): 13–29.

Christian, David. *Maps of Time: An Introduction to Big History*. 2nd ed. Berkeley, CA: University of California Press, 2011.

——. "Big History for the Era of Climate Change." *Solutions*, March 2012.

Cimitile, Matthew. "Corn Ethanol Will Not Cut Greenhouse Gas Emissions." *Scientific American*, April 2009.

Claessens, Marilyn. "An Ecological Neighborhood." *The Berkeley Daily Planet*, June 17, 2000.

Clark, William C. "Sustainability Science: A Room of Its Own." *Proceedings of the National Academy of Sciences*, 104, 6 (February 6, 2007): 1737–1738.

Cleveland, C., ed. *Encyclopedia of Earth*. Washington, DC: Environmental Information Coalition, National Council for Science and the Environment, 2007.

Cleveland, Cutler J. "Net Energy from Extraction of Oil and Gas in the United States," *Energy*, April 2005.

Cockrall-King, Jennifer. *Food and the City: Urban Agriculture and the New Food Revolution*. Amherst, NY: Prometheus Books, 2012.

Cohen, Joel E. "Human Population Grows Up." *Scientific American*, September 2005: 48–55.

Colborn, Theo, Dianne Dumanoski, and John Peter Meyers. *Our Stolen Future: Are We Threatening Our Fertility, Intelligence and Survival? A Scientific Detective Story*. New York: Dutton, 1996.

Cole, David N. and Laurie Yung, eds. *Beyond Naturalness: Rethinking Park and Wilderness Stewardship in an Era of Rapid Change*. Washington, DC: Island Press, 2010.

Cole, Matthew, Pennie Lindeque, Claudia Halsband, and Tamara S. Galloway. "Microplastics as Contaminants in the Marine Environment: A Review." *Marine Pollution Bulletin* vol 62 no 12 (December 2011): 2588–2597.

Commoner, Barry. "The Four Laws of Ecology." In *The Closing Circle: Nature, Man, and Technology*. New York: Knopf, 1971.

Comprehensive Assessment of Water Management in Agriculture (CA). *Water for Food, Water for Life: A Comprehensive Assessment of Water Management in Agriculture*. London: Earthscan and Colombo, Sri Lanka: International Water Management Institute, 2007.

Condon, Patrick M. *Design Charrettes for Sustainable Communities*. Washington, DC: Island Press, 2007.

——. *Seven Rules for Sustainable Communities: Design Strategies for the Post-Carbon World*. Washington, DC: Island Press, 2010.

Connett, Paul. *The Zero Waste Solution*. White River Junction, VT: Chelsea Green, 2013.

Conservation International. N.d. Biodiversity Hotspots. www.biodiversityhotspots.org.

"Constructed Wetlands for Wastewater." *Environmental Building News*. BackPage Primer. August 1, 2009.

Container Recycling Institute. "Keep America Beautiful: A History," Culver City, CA, n.d.

Conway, Gordon. *One Billion Hungry: Can We Feed the World?* Ithaca, NY: Cornell University Press, 2012.

Cook, E. A. *Landscape Planning and Ecological Networks*. Amsterdam: Elsevier, 1994.

Cooperative Extension Washington State University. *Hybrid Poplars in the Pacific Northwest*. Symposium Proceedings. Pullman, WA: Washington State University, 1999.

Corcoran, Peter Blaze, ed. *The Earth Charter in Action: Toward a Sustainable World*. Amsterdam: KIT Publishers, 2007.

Cordell, Dana and Stuart White. "Peak Phosphorus: Clarifying the Key Issues of a Vigorous Debate about Long-Term Phosphorus Security." *Sustainability* 3 (2011): 2027–2049. doi:10.3390/su3102027.

Cortese, Anthony. "Foreword." In Holley Henderson. *Becoming a Green Professional: A Guide to Careers in Sustainable Architecture, Development and More*. New York: John Wiley, 2012, xi–xiii.

Costanza, Robert and Bernard C. Patten. "Defining and Predicting Sustainability." *Ecological Economics* vol 15 no 3 (1995): 193–196.

—— and Ida Kubiszewski, eds. *Creating a Sustainable and Desirable Future.* Singapore: World Scientific, 2014.

——, John H. Cumberland, Herman Daly, Robert Goodland, and Richard B. Norgaard. *An Introduction to Ecological Economics.* 2nd ed. Boca Raton, FL: CRC Press, 2014.

—— et al. "The Value of the World's Ecosystem Services and Natural Capital." *Nature,* 387 (1997): 253–260.

——. "Principles for Sustainable Governance of the Oceans." *Science,* July 10, 1998, 198–199.

——. "Sustainability or Collapse: What Can We Learn from Integrating the History of Humans and the Rest of Nature?" *Ambio* vol 36 no 7 (November 2007): 522–527. doi: 10.1579/0044-7447(2007)36[522:SOCWCW]2.0.CO;2.

Coulter, Liese, Josep G. Canadell, and Shobhakar Dhakal, eds. *Carbon Reductions and Offsets.* Earth System Science Partnership Report No. 5. Global Carbon Project Report No. 6. Canberra: Global Carbon Project, 2008.

Council on Environmental Quality. *Interim Framework for Effective Coastal and Marine Spatial Planning.* Washington, DC: White House, 2009.

Cox, J. Robert. *Environmental Communication and the Public Sphere.* 3rd ed. London: SAGE Publications, 2012.

Crabtree, G. and J. Misewich. *Integrating Renewable Electricity on the Grid, American Physical Society.* American Physical Society, Washington, DC, 2010. www.aps.org/policy/reports/popa-reports/upload/integratingelec.pdf.

Cradle to Cradle Products Innovation Institute. N.d. www.c2ccertified.org/.

Creasy, Rosalind. *The Complete Book of Edible Landscaping.* 2nd ed. San Francisco, CA: Sierra Club Books, 2010.

Creighton, Sarah Hammond. *Greening the Ivory Tower: Improving the Environmental Track Record of Universities, Colleges, and Other Institutions.* Cambridge, MA: MIT Press, 1998.

Crist, Eileen and H. Bruce Rinker, eds. *Gaia in Turmoil.* Cambridge, MA: MIT Press, 2010.

Crompton, T. and T. Kasser. *Meeting Environmental Challenges: The Role of Human Identity.* Surrey: WWF UK, 2009.

Crutzen, Paul J. "Geology of Mankind." *Nature,* 415 (January 2002): 23.

——. "Albedo Enhancement by Stratospheric Sulfur Injections: A Contribution to Resolve a Policy Dilemma?" *Climatic Change,* August 2006: 212, 217.

—— and W. Steffen. "How Long Have We Been in the Anthropocene Era?" *Climate Change,* 61, 3 (2003): 251–257.

Cryan, Paul. "Bat Fatalities at Wind Turbines: Investigating the Causes and Consequences." Fort Collins, CO: USGS Fort Collins Science Center, October 21, 2015. https://www.fort.usgs.gov/science-feature/96.

—— et al. "Behavior of Bats at Wind Turbines." *PNAS* vol 111 no 42 (October 21, 2014): 15126–15131. doi: 10.1073/pnas.1406672111.

Csutora, Maria. "One More Awareness Gap? The Behaviour-Impact Gap Problem." *Journal of Consumption Policy,* March 2012: 149.

Cullon, Donna L., Mark B. Yunker, Carl Alleyne, Neil J. Dangerfield, Sandra O'Neill, Michael J. Whiticar, and Peter S. Ross. "Persistent Organic Pollutants in Chinook Salmon (*Oncorhynchus Tshawytscha*): Implications for Resident Killer Whales of British Columbia and Adjacent Waters." *Environmental Toxicology and Chemistry* vol 28 no 1 (January 2009): 148–161.

Cunningham, William P. and Mary Ann Cunningham. *Environmental Science: A Global Concern.* 11th ed. New York: McGraw-Hill, 2010.

Czech, B. *Shoveling Fuel for a Runaway Train: Errant Economists, Shameful Spenders, and a Plan to Stop Them All.* Berkeley, CA: University of California Press, 2000.

Daily, Gretchen, ed. *Nature's Services: Societal Dependence on Natural Ecosystems.* Washington, DC: Island Press, 1997.

—— et al. "Ecosystem Services: Benefits Supplied to Human Societies by Natural Ecosystems." *Issues in Ecology* 2 (Spring 1997): 1–18. Washington, DC: Ecological Society of America, 1997. www.wvhighlands.org/VoicePast/VoiceJun99/EcoServices.JS.June99Voice.txt.htm.

Daly, Herman E. *Steady State Economics.* Washington, DC: Island Press, 1990.
——. "Economics in a Full World." *Scientific American,* 293, 3 (September 2005): 100–107.
—— and Joshua Farley. *Ecological Economics: Principles and Applications.* Washington, DC: Island Press, 2003.
Daly, Lew and Stephen Posner. *Beyond GDP: New Measures for a New Economy.* New York: Demos, 2012.
Daniel, Terry C. et al. "Contributions of Cultural Services to the Ecosystem Services Agenda." *Proceedings of the National Academy of Sciences,* 109, 23 (June 5, 2012): 8812–8819.
Danks, Sharon Gamson. *Asphalt to Ecosystems: Design Ideas for Schoolyard Transformation.* Oakland, CA: New Village Press, 2010.
DARA International. *Climate Vulnerability Monitor: A Guide to the Cold Calculus of a Hot Planet.* 2nd ed. Washington, DC: 2012.
Davidson, E. A. and I. A. Janssens. "Temperature Sensitivity of Soil Carbon Decomposition and Feedbacks to Climate Change." *Nature,* 440 (2006): 165–173.
Davies, Paul and John Gribbin. *The Matter Myth: Dramatic Discoveries that Challenge Our Understanding of Physical Reality.* New York: Simon & Schuster, 2007.
Davis, Mark. "Researching Invasive Species 50 Years after Elton: A Cautionary Tale." In David M. Richardson, ed. *Fifty Years of Invasion Ecology.* Oxford, UK: Blackwell, 2011. 269–274.
____ et al. "Don't Judge Species on Their Origins." *Nature* 474 (June 9, 2011): 153–154.
Deneven, W. "The Pristine Myth: The Landscape of the Americas in 1492." *Annals of the Association of American Geographers,* 82 (1992): 369–85.
Denison, William C. "Life in Tall Trees." *Scientific American,* 228, 6 (June 1973): 74–80.
DePalma, Anthony. "City's Catskill Water Gets 10-Year Approval." *New York Times,* April 13, 2007.
Desai, Pooran. *One Planet Communities: A Real-Life Guide to Sustainable Living.* Chichester: John Wiley Ltd., 2010.
Design Centre for Sustainability. *Greater Vancouver Green Guide: Seeding Sustainability.* Vancouver: Design Centre for Sustainability, University of British Columbia, 2006.
Dessler, A. E. and E. A. Parson. *The Science and Politics of Global Climate Change: A Guide to the Debate.* Cambridge: Cambridge University Press, 2006.
Devall, Bill and George Sessions. *Deep Ecology: Living as if Nature Mattered.* Layton, UT: Gibbs Smith, 1985.
Diamond, Jared. *Collapse: How Societies Choose to Fail or Succeed.* New York: Penguin, 2004.
Dierderen, Andre. *Global Resource Depletion: Managed Austerity and the Elements of Hope.* Delft: Eburon Academic Publishers, 2010.
Dietz, Rob and Dan O'Neill. *Enough Is Enough: Building a Sustainable Economy in a World of Finite Resources.* San Francisco: Berrett-Koehler, 2013.
Dillard, Jesse, Veronica Dujon, and Mary C. King, eds. *Understanding the Social Dimension of Sustainability.* London: Routledge, 2009.
Dodds, Felix and Jamie Bartram, eds. *The Water, Food, Energy and Climate Nexus: Challenges and an Agenda for Action.* New York: Routledge, 2016.
Donlan, C. Josh. "Restoring America's Big, Wild Animals." *Scientific American,* June 2007: 70–77.
Donlan, Josh et al., "Re-wilding North America." *Nature* 436 (Aug. 18, 2005): 913–914.
Doppelt, Bob. *Leading Change toward Sustainability.* Sheffield: Greenleaf Publishing, 2003a.
——. "Overcoming the Seven Sustainability Blunders." *The Systems Thinker,* 14, 5 (2003b): 2–7.
——. *The Power of Sustainable Thinking.* London: Earthscan, 2008.
Dornelas, Maria et al. "Assemblage Time Series Reveal Biodiversity Change but Not Systematic Loss." *Science* vol 344 no 6181 (April 18, 2014): 296–299. doi: 10.1126/science.1248484.
Dramstad, Wenech E., James D. Olson, and Richard T. T. Forman. *Landscape Ecology Principles in Landscape Architecture and Land-Use Planning.* Washington, DC: Island Press, 1996.
Drew, Jeannine. *Mastering Meetings: Discovering the Hidden Potential of Effective Business Meetings.* New York: McGraw-Hill, 1994.

Du, Xiaoyue and Thomas E. Graedel. "Global In-Use Stocks of the Rare Earth Elements: A First Estimate." *Environmental Science & Technology*, 45, 9 (May 2011): 4096–4101.

Dunnett, Nigel and Clayden, Andy. *Rain Gardens: Managing Water Sustainably in the Garden and Designed Landscape*. Portland, OR: Timber Press, 2007.

Duram, Leslie A. *Good Growing: How Organic Farming Works*. Lincoln, NB: University of Nebraska Press, 2005.

Dyer, Betsy Dexter. *A Field Guide to Bacteria*. Ithaca, NY: Comstock, 2003.

Earth911. N.d. http://earth911.com/recycling/glass/facts-about-glass-recycling/.

Earthjustice. *Re: Green – The Ecological Roadmap*. San Francisco: Earthjustice, 2008.

Easterlin, Richard. "Does Economic Growth Improve the Human Lot? Some Empirical Evidence." In Paul A. David and Melvin W. Reder, eds. *Nations and Households in Economic Growth: Essays in Honor of Moses Abramowitz*. New York: Academic Press, 1974, 89–125.

Eccleston, Charles H. *Environmental Impact Assessment: A Guide to Best Professional Practices*. Boca Raton, FL: CRC Press, 2011.

Eco-Cycle program (Boulder, CO). "Zero Waste." 2011. www.ecocycle.org/zerowaste.

EcoDistricts. http://ecodistricts.org/ (Accessed December 15, 2015).

Edenhofer, Ottmar et al., eds. *Renewable Energy Sources and Climate Change Mitigation: Special Report of the Intergovernmental Panel on Climate Change*. New York: Cambridge University Press, 2012.

Edwards, Andrés R. *The Sustainability Revolution: Portrait of a Paradigm Shift*. Gabriola Island, BC: New Society Publishers, 2005.

——. *Thriving Beyond Sustainability: Pathways to a Resilient Society*. Gabriola Island: New Society Publishers, 2010.

Ehlers, Eckart and Thomas Karfft, eds. *Earth System Science in the Anthropocene: Emerging Issues and Problems*. New York: Springer, 2006.

Ehrenfeld, John R. "Can Industrial Ecology Be the 'Science of Sustainability'?" *Journal of Industrial Ecology*, 8, 102 (2004): 1–3.

——. *Sustainability by Design*. New Haven, CT: Yale University Press, 2008.

—— and Gertler, N. "Industrial Ecology in Practice: The Evolution of Interdependence at Kalundborg." *Journal of Industrial Ecology*, 1, 1 (1997): 67–79.

Ehrlich, Paul R. *The Population Bomb*. New York: Ballantine, 1971.

—— and Anne Ehrlich. *Extinction: The Causes and Consequences of the Disappearance of Species*. New York: Random House, 1981.

—— and Anne H. Ehrlich. "Can a Collapse of Global Civilization Be Avoided?" *Proceedings of the Royal Society B: Biological Sciences*, March 7, 2013, 280 (1754): 2012–2845.

—— and John P. Holdren. "Impact of Population Growth." *Science*, 171 (1971): 1212–1217.

——, Peter M. Kareiva, and Gretchen C. Daily. "Securing Natural Capital and Expanding Equity to Rescale Civilization." *Nature*, 486 (June 2012): 68–73.

Elkington, John. *Cannibals with Forks: The Triple Bottom Line of 21st Century Business*. Gabriola Island, BC: New Society, 1998.

——. *The Zeronauts: Breaking the Sustainability Barrier*. New York: Routledge, 2012.

Ellen Macarthur Foundation. www.ellenmacarthurfoundation.org. (Accessed January 30, 2016).

Elser, James and Stuart White. "Peak Phosphorus." *Foreign Policy,* April 2010.

Elton, Charles. *The Ecology of Invasions by Animals and Plants*. 1958; repr., Chicago: University of Chicago Press, 2000.

Empire State Building, "Sustainability & Energy Efficiency." June 24, 2013. www.esbnyc.com/sustainability_energy_efficiency.asp.

Engelman, Robert. "Beyond Sustainababble," in Worldwatch Institute. *State of the World 2013: Is Sustainability Still Possible?* Washington, DC: Island Press, 2013, 4–16.

Epstein, Marc J. *Making Sustainability Work: Best Practices in Managing and Measuring Corporate Social, Environmental and Economic Impacts*. San Francisco: Berrett-Koehler Publishers, 2008.

Epstein, P. R. et al. "Full Cost Accounting for the Life Cycle of Coal." *Annals of the New York Academy of Sciences*, 1219 (2011): 73–98.

Erard, Michael. "Call of the Truck Stop: Gentlemen, Stop Your Engines." *New York Times*, March 7, 2007.

Erickson, W. P., G. Johnson, D. Strickland, and D. Young. *Avian Collisions with Wind Turbines: A Summary of Existing Studies and Comparisons to Other Sources of Avian Collision Mortality in the United States*. Portland, OR: American Wind Energy Association Conference, 2002.

e-Stewards, "e-Stewards Certification." 2010. http://e-stewards.org/certification-overview/.

Esty, Daniel C. and Andrew S. Winston. *Green to Gold*. New York: John Wiley, 2009.

European Commission, *Roadmap to a Resource Efficient Europe*. Brussels: European Commission, 2011.

——. "End of Life Vehicles." European Commission, 2013. http://ec.europa.eu/environment/waste/elv_index.htm.

——. EMAS. European Commission, 2016. http://ec.europa.eu/environment/emas/.

Evans, J. P. *Environmental Governance*. London: Routledge, 2012.

Ewing B., D. Moore, S. Goldfinger, A. Oursler, A. Reed, and M. Wackernagel. *The Ecological Footprint Atlas 2010*. Oakland, CA: Global Footprint Network, 2010.

Ewing, Reid, Keith Bartholomew, Steve Winkelman, Jerry Walters, and Don Chen. *Growing Cooler: The Evidence on Urban Development and Climate Change*. Washington, DC: Urban Land Institute, 2008.

Faga, Barbara. *Designing Public Consensus: The Civic Theater of Community Participation for Architects, Landscape Architects, Planners, and Urban Designers*. New York: John Wiley, 2006.

FAO (Food and Agriculture Organization of the United Nations). "Livestock Impacts on the Environment." *Spotlight*. November 2006a. www.fao.org/ag/magazine/0612sp1.htm.

——. *Livestock's Long Shadow: Environmental Issues and Options*. Rome: FAO, 2006b.

——. *An Introduction to the Basic Concepts of Food Security*. EC–FAO Food Security Programme, 2008. www.fsnnetwork.org/resource-library/nutrition/introduction-basic-concepts-food-security.

——. *Global Food Losses and Food Waste: Extent, Causes and Prevention*. Rome: FAO, 2011a.

——. *The State Of the World's Land and Water Resources For Food and Agriculture: Managing Systems at Risk*. London: FAO and Earthscan, 2011b.

——. *Coping with Water Scarcity: An Action Framework for Agriculture and Food Security*. FAO of the UN, 2013.

Farr, Douglas. *Sustainable Urbanism: Urban Design with Nature*. New York: John Wiley, 2008.

Fatal Light Awareness Program. N.d. www.flap.org/.

Fearn, Eva, ed. *State of the Wild 2010–2011: A Global Portrait*. Washington, DC: Island Press, 2010.

Ferguson, Bruce K. *Introduction to Stormwater: Concept, Purpose, Design*. New York: John Wiley & Sons, 1998.

Few, Steven. *Information Dashboard Design*. O'Reilly Media, 2006.

Fiala, Nathan. "The Alarming Environmental Costs of Beef." *Scientific American* vol 24, no 2s (June 2015).

Fiksel, Joseph. *Design for Environment*. 2nd ed. New York: McGraw-Hill, 2009.

Finfrock, Jesse. "Q&A: John Elkington." *Mother Jones*, November/December 2008, 10.

Fishman, Charles. *Has Wal-Mart Found Its Soul? A New Introduction to The Wal-Mart Effect*. New York: Penguin, 2011.

——. *The Big Thirst: The Secret Life and Turbulent Future of Water*. New York: Free Press, 2012.

Flannery, Tim. *The Eternal Frontier: An Ecological History of North America and Its Peoples*. New York: Grove Press, 2001.

——. *The Weather Makers: How Man Is Changing the Climate and What It Means for Life on Earth*. New York: Grove Press, 2006.

——. *Now or Never: Why We Must Act Now to End Climate Change and Create a Sustainable Future*. New York: Atlantic Monthly Press, 2009.

——. *Here on Earth: A Natural History of the Planet*. New York: Atlantic Monthly Press, 2010.

Fleming, J. "The Climate Engineers: Playing God to Save the Planet." *Wilson Quarterly*, spring 2007: 46.

Folke, Carl et al. "Resilience Thinking: Integrating Resilience, Adaptability and Transformability." *Ecology and Society*, 15, 4 (2010): 1–9. www.ecologyandsociety.org/vol15/iss4/art20/.

———. "Reconnecting to the Biosphere." *Ambio*, 40, 7 (2011): 719–738.

Foley, Jonathan. "Boundaries for a Healthy Planet." *Scientific American* April 2010, 54–57.

—— et al. "Solutions for a Cultivated Planet." *Nature* 478 (October 20, 2011): 337–342.

Folke, Carl. "Respecting Planetary Boundaries and Reconnecting to the Biosphere," in Worldwatch Institute. *State of the World 2013: Is Sustainability Still Possible?* Washington, DC: Island Press, 2013, 19–27.

Fong, Mei. *One Child: The Story of China's Most Radical Experiment.* New York: Houghton Mifflin Harcourt, 2016.

Forde, C. Daryll. *Habitat, Economy and Society: A Geographical Introduction to Ethnography.* London: Routledge, 2010. Reprint edition of 1949 7th ed.; originally published in 1934.

Foreman, Dave. *Rewilding North America: A Vision for Conservation in the 21st Century.* Washington, DC: Island Press, 2004.

Fosket, Jennifer and Laura Mamo. *Living Green: Communities that Sustain.* Island, BC: New Society Publishers, 2009.

France, Robert L. *Wetland Design: Principles and Practices for Landscape Architects and Land-Use Planners.* New York: W. W. Norton, 2002.

——, ed. *Handbook of Regenerative Landscape Design.* Boca Raton, FL: CRC Press, 2008.

Fraser, Caroline. *Rewilding the World: Dispatches from the Conservation Revolution.* New York: Picador, 2009.

Friend, Gil. *The Truth about Green Business.* Upper Saddle River, NJ: FT Press, 2009.

Frosch, Robert A. "Industrial Ecology: A Philosophical Introduction." *Proceedings of the National Academy of Sciences, USA,* 89 (February 1992): 800–803.

—— and Nicholas E. Gallopoulos. "Strategies for Manufacturing." *Scientific American,* 261, 3 (1989): 144–155.

Frumkin, Howard. *Environmental Health: From Global to Local.* 2nd ed. New York: Jossey-Bass, 2010.

Fukuoka, Masanobu. *The One-Straw Revolution.* New York: Rodale, 1978.

Fuller, R. Buckminster. *Operating Manual for Spaceship Earth.* Carbondale, IL: Southern Illinois University Press, 1969.

Fund for Peace. Failed States Index. 2013. http://ffp.statesindex.org/.

Funes, Fernando, Luis Garcia, Martin Bourque, Nilda Perez, and Peter Rosset. *Sustainable Agriculture and Resistance: Transforming Food Production in Cuba.* Oakland, CA: Food First Books, 2002.

Galaz, Victor et al. "Institutional and Political Leadership Dimensions of Cascading Ecological Crises." *Public Administration,* June 2011: 360–380.

Galileo Galilei. *Il Saggiatore*, Opere VI. 1623. Quoted in Lynn Margulis and Dorion Sagan. *Microcosmos: Four Billion Years of Microbial Evolution.* Berkeley, CA: University of California Press, 1997.

Galli, Alessandro, Thomas Wiedmann, Ertug Ercin, Doris Knoblauch, Brad Ewing, and Stefan Giljum. "Integrating Ecological, Carbon and Water Footprint into a 'Footprint Family' of Indicators: Definition and Role in Tracking Human Pressure on the Planet." *Ecological Indicators* 16 (2012): 100–112.

Gaskill, Melissa. "Rise in Roadkill Requires New Solutions." *Scientific American,* May 16, 2013.

Gauthier S., P. Bernier, T. Kuuluvainen, A. Z. Shvidenko, D. G. Shchepaschenko. "Boreal Forest Health and Global Change." *Science,* vol 349 no 6250 (August 21, 2015): 819–822.

Geels, F., A. Monaghan, M. Eames, and F. Steward. *The Feasibility of Systems Thinking in Sustainable Consumption and Production Policy: A Report to the Department for Environment, Food and Rural Affairs.* London: DEFRA, 2008.

GE Global Research. *How Loud Is a Wind Turbine?* www.gereports.com/how-loud-is-a-wind-turbine/. GE Reports, November 18, 2010.

German Advisory Council on Global Change (WBGU). *Solving the Climate Dilemma: The Budget Approach.* Berlin: German Advisory Council on Global Change, 2009.

Geus, Arie de. *The Living Company.* Boston: Harvard Business School Press, 1997.

Giancoli, Douglas C. *Physics: Principles with Applications.* 6th ed. Upper Saddle River, NJ: Prentice Hall, 2005.

Giedd, Jay N. "The Amazing Teen Brain." *Scientific American* June 2015, 33–37.

Gilding, Paul. *The Great Disruption.* New York: Bloomsbury Press, 2011.

Gillis, Justin. "Climate Accord Is a Healing Step, if Not a Cure." *New York Times*, December 12, 2015, A1.

Girardet, Herbert. *Cities People Planet: Urban Development and Climate Change.* 2nd ed. New York: John Wiley, 2008.

——. *Creating Regenerative Cities.* London: Routledge, 2014.

Giudice, Fabio, Guido La Rosa, and Antonino Risitano. *Product Design for the Environment: A Life Cycle Approach.* Boca Raton, FL: Taylor & Francis, 2006.

Gleick, Peter. *The World's Water, The Biennial Report on Freshwater Resources: 2004–2005.* Washington, DC: Island Press, 2004.

——. *Bottled and Sold: The Story Behind Our Obsession with Bottled Water.* Washington, DC: Island Press, 2011.

——. *The World's Water 2011–2012: The Biennial Report on Freshwater Resources.* Washington, DC: Island Press, 2012.

Glikson, Andrew Y. and Colin Groves. *Climate, Fire and Human Evolution: The Deep Time Dimensions of the Anthropocene.* New York: Springer, 2016.

Global Reporting Initiative. *G4 Sustainability Reporting Guidelines.* Amsterdam: Global Reporting Initiative, 2013.

Glock, Clarinha. "Rio+20 Doubts over Impact of Sustainable Development Dialogues." *Inter Press Service*, June 19, 2012.

Goldsmith, Edward. *Blueprint for Survival.* New York: Signet, 1974.

Goldstein, D. B. *Invisible Energy: Strategies to Rescue the Economy and Save the Planet.* Pt. Richmond, CA: Bay Tree Publishing, 2010.

Goleman, Daniel. *Ecological Intelligence: How Knowing the Hidden Impacts of What We Buy Can Change Everything.* New York: Broadway Books, 2009.

Goodall, Chris. *How to Live a Low-Carbon Life: The Individual's Guide to Tackling Climate Change.* 2nd ed. London: Routledge, 2010.

Goodland, Robert and Jeff Anhang. "Livestock Emissions: Still Grossly Underestimated?" *World Watch Magazine*, 23, 4 (July/August 2010): 11–19.

Goodstein, Eban S. *Economics and the Environment.* New York: John Wiley, 2010.

Gordon, Larry. "'All You Can Carry' College Cafeterias Go Trayless." *Los Angeles Times*, September 14, 2009.

Graedel, T. E. "The Evolution of Industrial Ecology." *Environmental Science and Technology*, 34 (2000): 28A–31A.

——. "The Prospects for Urban Mining." *The Bridge* 41, 1 (Spring 2011): 43–50.

—— and Allenby, B. R. *Industrial Ecology.* 2nd ed. Upper Saddle River, NJ: Prentice Hall, 2003.

—— and ——. *Industrial Ecology and Sustainable Engineering.* Boston: Prentice Hall, 2010.

—— and Jennifer A. Howard-Grenville. *Greening the Industrial Facility: Perspectives, Approaches, and Tools.* New York: Springer, 2005.

Grafton, R. Quentin, Libby Robin, and Robert J. Wasson, eds. *Understanding the Environment: Bridging the Disciplinary Divides.* Sydney: University of New South Wales Press, 2004.

Grant, M. and J. Mitton. "Case Study: The Glorious, Golden, and Gigantic Quaking Aspen." *Nature Education Knowledge*, 1, 8 (2010): 40.

GrassRoots Recycling Network. "Aluminum Can Waste: Bigger Impact than Plastic Bottle Waste." 2001. http://archive.grrn.org/beverage/shareholders/articles/can_waste.html.

——. 2013. www.grrn.org/.

Grdadolnik, Helena. "Garden City." *Canadian Architect*, November, 11, 2005. www.canadi anarchitect.com/news/garden-city/1000199577/.

Green, Deborah. *Water Conservation for Small- and Medium-Sized Utilities.* Denver: American Water Works Association, 2010.

Green, Jared. "Interview with Janine Benyus on How to Design Like Nature." *The Dirt,* ASLA, November 4, 2015.

Gribbin, John and Mary Gribbin. *James Lovelock: In Search of Gaia.* Princeton, NJ: Princeton University Press, 2009.

GRID-Arendal. *Kick the Habit: A UN Guide to Climate Neutrality.* Nairobi: UNEP, 2008.

———. *Environment & Poverty Times* September 6. Nairobi: UNEP, 2009.

Grim, John A. *Indigenous Traditions and Ecology: The Interbeing of Cosmology and Community.* Cambridge, MA: Harvard University Press, 2001.

Grossman, David. "Breaking the Bottled Water Habit." *USA Today*, September 22, 2008. Guevara-Stone, Laurie. "La Revolucion Energetica: Cuba's Energy Revolution." *Renewable Energy World Magazine*, April 2009, 2.

Guillette, Elizabeth A. et al. "An Anthropological Approach to the Evaluation of Preschool Children Exposed to Pesticides in Mexico." *Environmental Health Perspectives*, 106, 6, (June 1998): 347–353.

Gunderson L. H. and C. S. Holling, eds. *Panarchy: Understanding Transformations in Human and Natural Systems.* Washington, DC: Island Press, 2002.

———, Craig R. Allen, and C. S. Holling, eds. *Foundations of Ecological Resilience.* Washington, DC: Island Press, 2010.

Haag, Richard. "Eco-Revelatory Design: The Challenge of the Exhibit." *Landscape Journal*, 17, special issue (1998): 72–79.

Haeg, Fritz, Will Allen, and Diana Balmori. *Edible Estates: Attack on the Front Lawn.* 2nd ed. Metropolis Books, 2010.

Hagens, Nathan Jon. "Energy, Credit, and the End of Growth." In Worldwatch Institute. *State of the World 2015: Confronting Hidden Threats to Sustainability.* Washington, DC: Island Press, 2015.

Hambrey, Michael and Jürg Alean. *Glaciers.* 2nd ed. Cambridge: Cambridge University Press, 2004.

Hamilton, D. Kirk and David H. Watkins. *Evidence-Based Design for Multiple Building Types.* New York: John Wiley, 2009.

Hansen, E., R. Fletcher, B. Cashore, and C. McDermott. "Forest Certification in North America." EC 1518-E, February 2006.

Hansen, James. *Storms of My Grandchildren.* New York: Bloomsbury, 2010.

Hardin, Garrett. "The Tragedy of the Commons." *Science*, 162, 3859 (December 13, 1968): 1243–1248.

Harding, Stephan. *Animate Earth: Science, Intuition and Gaia.* White River Junction, VT: Chelsea Green Publishing, 2006.

Harnik, Peter. *Urban Green: Innovative Parks for Resurgent Cities,* 2nd ed. Washington, DC: Island Press, 2010.

Harris, Mark. *Grave Matters: A Journey through the Modern Funeral Industry.* New York: Scribner, 2007.

Hart, Maureen. *Guide to Sustainable Community Indicators.* 2nd ed. West Hartford, CT: Sustainable Measures, 2006.

Harte, John. *Consider a Spherical Cow: A Course in Environmental Problem Solving.* Sausalito, CA: University Science Books, 1988.

Hawken, Paul. "The Ecology of Commerce." *Inc. Magazine*, July 1992.

———. *The Ecology of Commerce.* New York: HarperCollins, 1993.

———. *Ecology of Commerce, Revised Edition: A Declaration of Sustainability.* New York: Harper Collins, 2010.

———. *Blessed Unrest.* New York: Penguin, 2007.

———, Amory B. Lovins, and L. Hunter Lovins. *Natural Capitalism: Creating the Next Industrial Revolution.* Boston, MA: Back Bay Books, 2008.

Hayes, Brian. *Infrastructure: A Field Guide to the Industrial Landscape.* New York: W.W. Norton, 2005.

Hazen, Robert M. *The Joy of Science.* Chantilly, VA: Great Courses, 2001.

———. *The Story of Earth: The First 4.5 Billion Years, from Stardust to Living Planet.* New York: Viking, 2012.

Hecht, Alan D., Joseph Fiksel, and Marina Moses. "Working toward a Sustainable Future." *Sustainability: Science, Practice, & Policy* vol 10 no 2 (2014): 65–75.

Heckenberger, Michael et al. "Amazonia 1492: Pristine Forest or Cultural Parkland?" *Science* vol 301 no 5640 (September 19, 2003): 1710–1714.

Heinberg, Richard. *The End of Growth: Adapting to our New Economic Reality.* Gabriola Island, BC: New Society Publishers, 2011.

——— and Daniel Lerch, eds. *The Post Carbon Reader: Managing the 21st Century's Sustainability Crises.* Berkeley, CA: University of California Press, 2010.

Heintz, Jim. "Aral Sea Almost Dried Up: UN Chief Calls It 'Shocking Disaster.'" *Huffington Post*, June 4, 2010.

Helvarg, David. *Blue Frontier: Dispatches from America's Ocean Wilderness.* San Francisco, CA: Sierra Club Books, 2006.

Henson, Robert. *The Rough Guide to Weather.* New York: Penguin Putnam, 2002.

———. *The Rough Guide to Climate Change.* 3rd ed. New York: Rough Guides Ltd, 2011.

Herman Miller. *Herman Miller Environmental Advocacy.* Zeeland, MI: Herman Miller, 2007.

Hester, Randolph T. *Design for Ecological Democracy.* Cambridge, MA: MIT Press, 2010.

———, Kurt Culbertson, Cali Pfaff, and Lara Lasky. *Measuring Environmental Justice.* Chicago, IL: American Society of Landscape Architects Annual Meeting, 2015.

Hey, Donald L. and Nancy S. Philippi. "Flood Reduction through Wetland Restoration: The Upper Mississippi River Basin as a Case History." *Restoration Ecology*, March 1995: 4–17.

Hill, Marquita K. *Understanding Environmental Pollution.* 3rd ed. Cambridge: Cambridge University Press, 2010.

Hillel, Daniel. *Out of the Earth: Civilization and the Life of the Soil.* Berkeley, CA: University of California Press, 1992.

Hitchcock, Darcy and Marsha Willard. *The Step-by-Step Guide to Sustainability Planning.* Sterling, VA: Earthscan, 2008.

———. *The Business Guide to Sustainability.* New York: Earthscan, 2009.

Hodgson, Kimberly, Marcia Caton Campbell, and Martin Bailkey. *Urban Agriculture: Growing Healthy, Sustainable Places.* Washington, DC: American Planning Association Planning Advisory Service, 2011.

Hobbs, Richard J. "Environmental Management and Restoration in a Changing Climate." Chapter 3 in Jelte van Andel and James Aronson, eds. *Restoration Ecology: The New Frontier*, 2nd ed. Chichester, UK: Wiley-Blackwell, 2012, 23–29.

———, Eric Higgs, and James Harris. "Novel Ecosystems: Implications for Conservation and Restoration." *Trends in Ecology and Evolution* 24, no 11 (November 2009): 599–605.

Hoekstra, Arjen Y. *The Water Footprint of Modern Consumer Society.* Routledge, 2013.

——— and Ashok K. Chapagain. *Globalization of Water: Sharing the Planet's Freshwater Resources.* Oxford: Blackwell Publishing, 2008.

———, ———, Maite M. Aldaya, and Mesfin M. Mekonnen. *The Water Footprint Assessment Manual: Setting the Global Standard.* London: Earthscan, 2011.

Hoff, Holger. *Understanding the Nexus.* Background Paper for the Bonn 2011 Conference: The Water, Energy and Food Security Nexus. Stockholm: Stockholm Environment Institute, 2011.

Hogben, Susan. "It's (Not) Easy Being Green: Unpacking Visual Rhetoric and Environmental Claims in Car, Energy and Utility Advertisements in the UK." *Language & Ecology*, 3, 1 (2009): 1–16.

Holdren, John P., Gretchen C. Daily, and Paul R. Ehrlich. 1995. "The Meaning of Sustainability: Biogeophysical Aspects." In M. Munasinghe and W. Shearer, eds. *Defining and Measuring Sustain-ability: The Biogeophysical Foundations.* Washington, DC: World Bank, 3–17.

Hölldobler, Bert and Edward O. Wilson. *The Superorganism: The Beatuy, Elegance, and Strangeness of Insect Societies.* New York: W. W. Norton, 2009.

Holling, C. S. "Understanding the Complexity of Economic, Social and Ecological Systems." *Ecosystems*, 4 (August 2001): 390–405.

———. "From Complex Regions to Complex Worlds." *Ecology and Society*, 9 (2004): 11.

Hönisch, Bärbel et al. "The Geological Record of Ocean Acidification." *Science*, March 2, 2012: 1058–1063.

"Hope Takes Root." *Garden Ideas & Outdoor Living Magazine*, Fall 2004.

Hopkins, Lewis D. and Marisa A. Zapata, eds. *Engaging the Future: Forecasts, Scenarios, Plans, and Projects*. Cambridge, MA: Lincoln Institute of Land Policy, 2007.

Hopkins, Rob. *The Transition Handbook: From Oil Dependency to Local Resilience*. White River, VT: Chelsea Green, 2008.

——. *The Transition Companion: Making Your Community More Resilient in Uncertain Times*. White River, VT: Chelsea Green, 2011.

——. *The Power of Just Doing Stuff: How Local Action Can Change the World*. Dartington: Green Books, 2013.

Hosein, Neesha. "Apollo Astronaut Shares Story of NASA's Earthrise." Houston, TX: Johnson Space Center, March 29, 2012. www.nasa.gov/centers/johnson/home/earthrise.html.

Hosey, Lance. *The Shape of Green: Aesthetics, Ecology, and Design*. Washington, DC: Island Press, 2012.

Hosford, William F. and John L. Duncan. "The Aluminum Beverage Can." *Scientific American*, September 1994: 48–53.

Hoshaw, Lindsey. "Afloat in the Ocean: Expanding Islands of Trash." *New York Times*, November 10, 2009.

Hoskins, Tansy. "Cotton Production Linked to Images of the Dried Up Aral Sea Basin." *Guardian Sustainable Business*, October 1, 2014.

Hough, Michael. *Cities and Natural Process*. London: Routledge, 1994.

Houghton, John. *Global Warming: The Complete Briefing*. 4th ed. Cambridge: Cambridge University Press, 2009.

Hughes, J. David. *Drill, Baby, Drill: Can Unconventional Fuels Usher in a New Era of Energy Abundance?*, 2nd ed. Santa Rosa, CA: Post Carbon Institute, 2013.

Hull, Ruth N., Constantin-Horia Barbu, and Nadezhda Goncharova. *Strategies to Enhance Environmental Security in Transition Countries*. New York: Springer, 2007.

Humblet, Emmanuelle M., Rebecca Owens, Leo Pierre Roy, David McIntyre, Peggy Meehan, and Leith Sharp. *Roadmap to a Green Campus*. Washington, DC: USGC, 2010.

Hutchison, David and David W. Orr. *A Natural History of Place in Education*. New York: Teachers College Press, 2004.

Iannuzzi, Al. *Greener Products: The Making and Marketing of Sustainable Brands*. Boca Raton, FL: CRC Press, 2012.

ICLEI (International Council for Local Environmental Initiatives). *Case Study 77: Curitiba: Orienting Urban Planning to Sustainability*. Toronto: ICLEI, 2002.

IEA. *Energy for All: Financing Access for the Poor*. Paris: IEA, 2011.

——. *Key World Energy Statistics 2012*. Paris: IEA, 2012.

——. *World Energy Outlook 2015*. Paris: IEA, 2015.

Imhoff, Daniel. *Paper or Plastic: Searching for Solutions to an Overpackaged World*. San Francisco, CA: Sierra Club Books, 2005.

Indvik, Joe, Rob Foley, and Mark Orlowski. *Green Revolving Funds: An Introductory Guide to Implementation & Management*. Sustainable Endowments Institute and Association for the Advancement of Sustainability in Higher Education, 2013.

IPCC (Intergovernmental Panel on Climate Change). *Climate Change 2007: The Physical Science Basis. Contribution of Working Group I to the Fourth Assessment Report of the Intergovernmental Panel on Climate Change* (S. Solomon, D. Qin, M. Manning, Z. Chen, M. Marquis, K. B. Averyt, M. Tignor and H. L. Miller, eds.). Cambridge: Cambridge University Press, 2007a.

——. *Climate Change 2007: Synthesis Report. Contribution of Working Groups I, II and III to the Fourth Assessment Report of the Intergovernmental Panel on Climate Change* (Core Writing Team, R. W. Pachauri and A. Reisinger, eds.). Geneva: IPCC, 2007b.

——. *Special Report on Emissions Scenarios (SRES): Summary for Policymakers. A Special Report of Working Group III of the Intergovernmental Panel on Climate Change* (Nebojša Nakićenović et al., eds.). Geneva: IPCC, 2007c.

——. *Climate Change 2007: Mitigation. Contribution of Working Group III to the Fourth Assessment Report of the Intergovernmental Panel on Climate Change* (B. Metz, O.R. Davidson, P.R. Bosch, R. Dave, L.A. Meyer, eds.). Cambridge: Cambridge University Press, 2007d.

——. *Climate Change 2013: The Physical Science Basis. Contribution of Working Group I to the Fifth Assessment Report of the Intergovernmental Panel on Climate Change.* (Stocker, T.F., D. Qin, G.-K. Plattner, M. Tignor, S.K. Allen, J. Boschung, A. Nauels, Y. Xia, V. Bex and P.M. Midgley, eds.). Cambridge: Cambridge University Press, 2013.

——. *Climate Change 2014: Impacts, Adaptation, and Vulnerability. Part A: Global and Sectoral Aspects. Contribution of Working Group II to the Fifth Assessment Report of the Intergovernmental Panel on Climate Change.* (Field, C.B., V.R. Barros, D.J. Dokken, K.J. Mach, M.D. Mastrandrea, T.E. Bilir, M. Chatterjee, K.L. Ebi, Y.O. Estrada, R.C. Genova, B. Girma, E.S. Kissel, A.N. Levy, S. MacCracken, P.R. Mastrandrea, and L.L. White, eds.). Cambridge: Cambridge University Press, 2014a.

——. *Climate Change 2014: Impacts, Adaptation, and Vulnerability. Part B: Regional Aspects. Contribution of Working Group II to the Fifth Assessment Report of the Intergovernmental Panel on Climate Change.* (Barros, V.R., C.B. Field, D.J. Dokken, M.D. Mastrandrea, K.J. Mach, T.E. Bilir, M. Chatterjee, K.L. Ebi, Y.O. Estrada, R.C. Genova, B. Girma, E.S. Kissel, A.N. Levy, S. MacCracken, P.R. Mastrandrea, and L.L. White, eds.). Cambridge: Cambridge University Press, 2014b.

——. *Climate Change 2014: Mitigation of Climate Change. Contribution of Working Group III to the Fifth Assessment Report of the Intergovernmental Panel on Climate Change.* (Edenhofer, O., R. Pichs-Madruga, Y. Sokona, E. Farahani, S. Kadner, K. Seyboth, A. Adler, I. Baum, S. Brunner, P. Eickemeier, B. Kriemann, J. Savolainen, S. Schlömer, C. von Stechow, T. Zwickel and J.C. Minx, eds.). Cambridge: Cambridge University Press, 2014c.

——. *Climate Change 2014: Synthesis Report. Contribution of Working Groups I, II and III to the Fifth Assessment Report of the Intergovernmental Panel on Climate Change.* (Core Writing Team, R.K. Pachauri and L.A. Meyer, eds.). Geneva, Switzerland: IPCC, 2014d.

ISO. *Guidance on Social Responsibility.* Geneva: ISO, 2010.

IUCN (International Union for Conservation of Nature). "From Death Zone to Lifeline: Iron Curtain Becomes Green Belt." Press release, IUCN, September 10, 2004.

——. *Species Extinction: The Facts.* Gland: IUCN, 2007.

Jackson, Stephen T. "Vegetation, Environment, and Time: The Origination and Termination of Ecosystems." *Journal of Vegetation Science* 17 (2006): 549–557.

Jackson, Tim. *Prosperity without Growth: Economics for a Finite Planet.* London: Earthscan, 2009.

Jackson, Wes. *New Roots for Agriculture.* Lincoln, NB: University of Nebraska Press, 1980.

Jacobs, Jane. *The Death and Life of Great American Cities.* New York: Random House, 1961.

——. *The Economy of Cities.* New York: Random House, 1969.

Jacobson, Mark Z. and Mark A. Delucchi. "A Path to Sustainable Energy by 2030." *Scientific American,* 301 (November 2009), 58–65.

Jedliĉka, Wendy. *Packaging Sustainability: Tools, Systems, and Strategies for Innovative Package Design.* New York: John Wiley, 2008.

Jenkins, Willis. *Berkshire Encyclopedia of Sustainability, Volume 1: The Spirit of Sustainability.* Great Barrington, MA: Berkshire Publishing Group, 2010.

Jerneck, Anne et al. "Structuring Sustainability Science." *Sustainability Science,* 6 (2011): 69–82.

Jevons, W. S. *The Coal Question: An Inquiry Concerning the Progress of the Nation, and the Probable Exhaustion of Our Coal-Mines.* 2nd ed. London: Macmillan and Co., 1866.

Johnson, Bart R. and Kristina Hill, eds. *Ecology and Design: Frameworks for Learning.* Washington, DC: Island Press, 2002.

Johnson, Julie M. *Design for Learning: Values, Qualities and Processes of Enriching School Landscapes.* Landscape Architecture Technical Information Series. Washington, DC: American Society of Landscape Architects, 2000.

Johnson, Lorraine. *City Farmer: Adventures in Urban Food Growing.* Vancouver: Greystone, 2010.

Johnston, David and Scott Gibson. *Green from the Ground Up: A Builder's Guide*. Newtown, CT: Taunton Press, 2008.

Jones, N. "Environmental Activation of Citizens in the Context of Policy Agenda Formation and the Influence of Social Capital." *The Social Science Journal* 47 (2010): 121–136.

Jones, Van. *The Green Collar Economy*. New York: HarperOne, 2009.

Kalundborg Centre for Industrial Symbiosis. www.symbiosis.dk/en.

Kaner, Sam. *Facilitator's Guide to Participatory Decision-Making*. 2nd ed. New York: John Wiley, 2007.

Kareiva, Peter, Heather Tallis, Taylor H. Ricketts, Gretchen C. Daily, and Stephen Polasky, eds. *Natural Capital: Theory and Practice of Mapping Ecosystem Services*. New York: Oxford University Press, 2011.

Kates, Robert W. "What Kind of a Science Is Sustainability Science?" *Proceedings of the National Academy of Sciences*, 108, 49 (December 6, 2011): 19449–19450.

Kates, R. et al. "Sustainability Science." *Science*, 292 (2001): 641–642.

Kats, Greg. *Greening Our Built World: Costs, Benefits, and Strategies*. Washington, DC: Island Press, 2010.

Kay, J. "On Complexity Theory, Exergy, and Industrial Ecology." In C. J. Kibert, J. Sendzimir, and G. B. Guy, eds. *Construction Ecology: Nature as the Basis for Green Buildings*. London: Spon, 2002, 72–106.

Keeler, Marian and Bill Burke. *Fundamentals of Integrated Design for Sustainable Building*. New York: John Wiley, 2009.

Keen, Mike F. and Krista Bailey. "The Natural Step for Colleges and Universities." *Sustainability: The Journal of Record*, 5, 3 (June 2012): 147–151.

Keller, Edward A. and Daniel B. Botkin. *Essential Environmental Science*. New York: John Wiley, 2008.

Kellert, Stephen R. *Building for Life: Designing and Understanding the Human–Nature Connection*. Washington, DC: Island Press, 2005.

—— and Edward O. Wilson, eds. *The Biophilia Hypothesis*. Washington, DC: Island Press, 1993.

——, Judith H. Heerwagen, and Martin L. Mador, eds. *Biophilic Design: The Theory, Science, and Practice of Bringing Buildings to Life*. New York: John Wiley, 2008.

Kemp, R., S. Parto, and R. Gibson. "Governance for Sustainable Development: Moving from Theory to Practice." *International Journal of Sustainable Development*, 8 (2005): 12–30.

Keniry, Julian. *Ecodemia: Campus Environmental Stewardship at the Turn of the 21st Century*. Washington, DC: National Wildlife Federation, 1995.

Kennedy, Christopher, John Cuddihy, and Joshua Engel-Yan. "The Changing Metabolism of Cities." *Journal of Industrial Ecology*, 11, 2 (April 2007): 43–59.

Kennedy, Donald, ed. *Science Magazine's State of the Planet 2006–2007*. Washington, DC: Island Press, 2006.

Kibert, Charles J. *Sustainable Construction: Green Building Design and Delivery*, 3rd ed. New York: John Wiley, 2012.

Kim, Ke Chung. "Preserving Biodiversity in Korea's Demilitarized Zone." *Science* 278 (October 10, 1997): 242.

Kimbrell, Andrew, ed. *The Fatal Harvest Reader: The Tragedy of Industrial Agriculture*. Washington, DC: Island Press, 2002.

King, Carey W. and Charles A. S. Hall. "Relating Financial and Energy Return on Investment." *Sustainability*, 3, 10 (2011): 1810–1832.

Kinkade-Levario, Heather. *Forgotten Rain: Rediscovering Rainwater Harvesting*. Phoenix, AZ: Granite Canyon, 2004.

——. *Design for Water*. Gabriola Island, BC: New Society Publishers, 2007.

Kinter-Meyer, Michael, Kevin Schneider, and Robert Pratt, "Impacts Assessment of Plug-In Hybrid Vehicles on Electric Utilities and Regional U.S. Power Grids, Part 1: Technical Analysis." Pacific Northwest National Laboratory, US DOE, DE-AC05-76RL01830.

Kintisch, E. *Hack the Planet*. Hoboken, NJ: John Wiley, 2010.

Klein, Naomi. "Capitalism vs. the Climate." *The Nation*, November 21, 2011.

Klingle, Matthew. *Emerald City: An Environmental History of Seattle*. New Haven, CT: Yale University Press, 2007.

Knoblauch, Jessica A. and Environmental Health News. "Some Food Additives Mimic Human Hormones." Health & Medicine, *ScientificAmerican.com*, March 27, 2009.

Kolbert, Elizabeth. *Field Notes from a Catastrophe: Man, Nature, and Climate Change*. New York: Bloomsbury, 2006.

——. *The Sixth Extinction: An Unnatural History*. New York: Picador, 2014.

Komiyama, Hiroshi, Kazuhiko Takeuchi, Hideaki Shiroyama, and Takashi Mino, eds. *Sustainability Science: A Multidisciplinary Approach*. Tokyo: UN University Press, 2011.

Kopnina, Helen and Eleanor Shoreman-Ouimet, eds. *Sustainability: Key Issues*. London: Routledge, 2015.

Korten, David C. *When Corporations Rule the World*. 2nd ed. San Francisco, CA: Berrett-Koehler, 2001.

Kostigen, Thomas M. *The Green Blue Book*. New York: Rodale Press, 2010.

Kresge, Lisa. *California Water Stewards: Innovative On-Farm Water Management Practices*. Davis, CA: California Institute for Rural Studies, 2009.

Kubiszewski, Ida et al. "Beyond GDP: Measuring and Achieving Global Genuine Progress." *Ecological Economics* 93 (2013): 57–68.

Kump, Lee R. "The Last Great Global Warming." *Scientific American*, July 2011: 56–61.

——, James F. Kasting, and Robert G. Crane. *The Earth System*. 3rd ed. Upper Saddle River, NJ: Prentice Hall, 2010.

Kunstler, James. *The Long Emergency: Surviving the Converging Catastrophes of the 21st Century*. London: Atlantic Books, 2005.

Kwok, Alison G. and Walter T. Grondzik. *The Green Studio Handbook: Environmental Strategies for Schematic Design*. Oxford: Architectural Press, 2007.

LaChapelle, Dolores. "Ritual Is Essential: Art and Ceremony in Sustainable Culture." *In Context*, Spring 1984. Reprinted in Alan R. Drengson and Yuichi Inoue, eds. *The Deep Ecology Movement: An Introductory Anthology*. Berkeley, CA: North Atlantic Books, 1995, 219–22.

Lakoff, George. "Winning Words." *Sierra Magazine*, July/August 2004.

Landsberg, Dennis R. and Mychele R. Lord. *Energy Efficiency Guide for Existing Commercial Buildings: The Business Case for Building Owners and Managers*. Atlanta: ASHRAE, 2009.

Lang, Kerryn. *The First Year of the G-20 Commitment on Fossil-Fuel Subsidies: A Commentary on Lessons Learned and the Path Forward*. Geneva: Global Studies Initiative, International Institute for Sustainable Development, 2011.

Lasat, Mitch M. *The Use of Plants for the Removal of Toxic Metals from Contaminated Soil*. Washington, DC: US Environmental Protection Agency, 2000.

Lazarus, Richard J. *The Making of Environmental Law*. Chicago, IL: University of Chicago Press, 2004.

Leach, Melissa. "Pathways to Sustainability: Building Political Strategies," in Worldwatch Institute. *State of the World 2013: Is Sustainability Still Possible?* Washington, DC: Island Press, 2013, 234–243.

——et al. "Transforming Innovation for Sustainability." *Ecology and Society*, 17, 2 (2012): 1–6. www.ecologyandsociety.org/vol17/iss2/art11/.

Lechner, Norbert. *Heating, Cooling, Lighting: Sustainable Design Methods for Architects*. 3rd ed. New York: John Wiley, 2008.

LEED Visual GA, V3. The Modulus, 2009.

Lehmann, Johannes. "A Handful of Carbon." *Nature*, 447 (May 10, 2007): 143–144.

——and Stephen Joseph, eds. *Biochar Environmental Management: Science and Technology*. London: Routledge, 2009.

Lennertz, Bill and Aarin Lutzenhiser. *The Charrette Handbook: The Essential Guide for Accelerated, Collaborative Community Planning*. Chicago: American Planning Association, 2006.

Lenton, Timothy M. et al. "Tipping Elements in the Earth's Climate System." *Proceedings of the National Academy of Sciences*, 105 (2008): 1786–1793.

Leonard, Annie. *The Story of Stuff.* New York: Free Press, 2010a.

____. "The Story of Bottled Water." Story of Stuff website, 2010b. www.storyofbottledwater.org.

Leopold, Aldo. *A Sand County Almanac and Sketches Here and There.* New York: Oxford University Press, 1987.

Leopold, Luna B. *A View of the River.* Cambridge, MA: Harvard University Press, 2006.

Lerch, Daniel. *Post Carbon Cities: Planning for Energy and Climate Uncertainty.* Sebastopol, CA: Post Carbon Press, 2008.

Levin, Kelly. "Developed Nations Must Cut Emissions in Half by 2020, Says New Study." *WRI Insights*, World Resources Institute, March 6, 2013. http://insights.wri.org/news/2013/03/developed-nations-must-reduce-emissions-half-2020-says-new-study.

Levy, Sharon. "The Giving Trees." *OnEarth*, Spring 2008.

Li, Dongying and William C. Sullivan. "Impact of Views to School Landscapes on Recovery from Stress and Mental Fatigue." *Landscape and Urban Planning* 148 (2016): 149–158.

Lidula, N. S. A. and A. D. Rajapakse. "Microgrids Research: A Review of Experimental Microgrids and Test Systems." *Renewable and Sustainable Energy Reviews*, 15, 1 (2011): 186–202.

Light, Andrew and Holmes Rolston III, ed. *Environmental Ethics: An Anthology.* Oxford: Blackwell Publishers, 2003.

Lingl, Paul, Deborah Carlson, and the David Suzuki Foundation. *Doing Business in a New Climate: A Guide to Measuring, Reducing and Offsetting Greenhouse Gas Emissions.* London: Earthscan, 2010.

Litman, Todd. *Evaluating Transportation Equity: Guidance for Incorporating Distributional Impacts in Transportation Planning.* Victoria, BC: Victoria Transport Policy Institute, 2015.

Lohan, Tara, ed. *Water Consciousness.* San Francisco: AlterNet Books, 2008.

Louv, Richard. *Last Child in the Woods: Saving Our Children from Nature-Deficit Disorder.* Chapel Hill, NC: Algonquin, 2008.

——. *The Nature Principle: Reconnecting with Life in a Virtual Age.* Chapel Hill, NC: Algonquin, 2012.

Lovelock, James. *Gaia: A New Look at Life on Earth.* Oxford: Oxford University Press, 2000.

——. *The Revenge of Gaia.* New York: Basic Books, 2006.

——. *The Vanishing Face of Gaia: A Final Warning.* New York: Basic Books, 2008.

Lovins, Amory B. *Reinventing Fire.* White River Junction, VT: Chelsea Green Publishing, 2011.

——. "Farewell to Fossil Fuels: Answering the Energy Challenge." *Foreign Affairs*, 91, 2 (2012): 134–146.

Lustgarten, Abrahm, David Sleight, Amanda Zamora and Lauren Kirchner. "Killing the Colorado: What You Need to Know About the Water Crisis in the West. Causes of — and potential solutions to — the Water Crisis on the Colorado River." *ProPublica*, May 27, 2015. https://projects.propublica.org/killing-the-colorado/story/what-you-need-to-know.

Lyle, John Tillman. *Regenerative Design for Sustainable Development.* New York: John Wiley & Sons, 1994.

Lyson, Thomas A., G. W. Stevenson, and Rick Welsh, eds. *Food and the Mid-Level Farm.* Cambridge, MA: MIT Press, 2008.

MacArthur, Robert H. and Edward O. Wilson. *The Theory of Island Biogeography.* Princeton, NJ: Princeton University Press, 1967.

Macaulay, David R. and Jason F. McLennan. *The Ecological Engineer. Volume One: KEEN Engineering.* Kansas City, MO: Ecotone, 2006.

McCutcheon, Steven C. and Jerald L. Schnoor, eds. *Phytoremediation: Transformation and Control of Contaminants.* New York: Wiley-Interscience, 2003.

McDonough, William and Michael Braungart. *Cradle to Cradle.* New York: North Point Press, 2002.

MacFarquhar, Neil. "Experts Worry about Feeding the World as Its Population Grows." *New York Times*, October 22, 2009.

MacKay, David JC. *Sustainable Energy—Without the Hot Air*. Cambridge: UIT Cambridge Ltd., 2009.
Mackenbach, Johan P. "René Dubos and Jared Diamond Dream of Dutch Polders." *European Journal of Public Health*, 16, 6 (2006): 575.
McKenzie-Mohr, Doug and William Smith. *Fostering Sustainable Behavior*. Gabriola Island, BC: New Society Publishers, 1999.
——, Nancy R. Lee, P. Wesley Schultz, and Philip A. Kotler. *Social Marketing to Protect the Environment: What Works*. Los Angeles: Sage Publications, 2011.
McKibben, Bill. "The Cuba Diet: What Will You Be Eating When the Revolution Comes?" *Harper's Magazine*, April 2005.
——. *Deep Economy: The Wealth of Communities and the Durable Future*. New York: Henry Holt and Company, 2007.
——. "Breaking the Growth Habit." *Scientific American*, April 2010: 63–65.
——. "Global Warming's Terrify New Math." *Rolling Stone*, August 2, 2012.
McKinsey & Company. *Unlocking Energy Efficiency in the US Economy*. 2009.
Mackova, Martina, David N. Dowling, and Tomas Macek, eds. *Phytoremediation and Rhizoremediation: Theoretical Background*. Dordrecht: Springer, 2006.
McLain, Rebecca J., Patrick T. Hurley, Marla R. Emery and Melissa R. Poe. "Gathering 'Wild' Food in the City: Rethinking the Role of Foraging in Urban Ecosystem Planning and Management." *Local Environment: The International Journal of Justice and Sustainability*, vol 19 no 2 (December 2014): 220–240. doi: 10.1080/13549839.2013.841659.
McLennan, Jason F. *The Philosophy of Sustainable Design*. Bainbridge Island, WA: Ecotone Publishing Co., 2004.
McPhee, John. "Atchafalaya." In *The Control of Nature*. New York: Farrar, Straus and Giroux, 1989, 3–93.
McShane, Katie. "Environmental Ethics: An Overview." *Philosophy Compass* 4/3 (2009): 407–420.
Macy, Joanna, L. "A Wild Love for the World." Interview by Krista Tippett, *On Being*, American Public Media, November 1, 2012.
Maczulak, Anne. *Waste Treatment: Reducing Global Waste*. New York: Facts on File, 2010.
Magoc, Chris J. *Environmental Issues in American History: A Reference Guide with Primary Documents*. Westport, CT: Greenwood Press, 2006.
Makower, Joel. *Strategies for the Green Economy*. New York: McGraw-Hill, 2009a.
——. "Calculating the Gross National Trash." GreenBiz.com, March 20, 2009b. www.greenbiz.com/blog/2009/03/20/calculating-gross-national-trash.
——. "Industrial Strength Solution: You Recycle. Why Doesn't Industry?" *Mother Jones*, May/June 2009c.
Malthus, T. R. *An Essay on the Principle of Population*. 1798. Reprint, New York: Oxford University Press, 2008.
Maniates, Michael, "Individualization: Plant a Tree, Buy a Bike, Save the World?" in Thomas Princen, Michael Maniates, and Ken Conca, eds. *Confronting Consumption*. Cambridge, MA: MIT Press, 2002.
——. "Editing Out Unsustainable Behavior." In Worldwatch Institute, *State of the World 2010*. New York: W. W. Norton, 2010, 3–20.
——. "Teaching for Turbulence." In Worldwatch Institute. *State of the World 2013: Is Sustainability Still Possible?* Washington, DC: Island Press, 2013, 255–268.
Mann, Charles C. *1491: New Revelations of the Americas before Columbus*, 2nd ed. New York: Vintage Books, 2011.
Mann, Michael E. and Lee R. Kump. *Dire Predictions: Understanding Global Warming—The Illustrated Guide to the Findings of the IPCC*. New York: DK Publishing, 2008.
Mapes, Lynda V. "Elwha: Roaring Back to Life." *Seattle Times,* February 13, 2016.
Margulis, Lynn and Dorion Sagan. *Microcosmos: Four Billion Years of Microbial Evolution*. Berkeley, CA: University of California Press, 1997.
——. *What Is Life?* Berkeley, CA: University of California Press, 2000.

Marine & Environmental Research Institute (MERI). *Plastics and Microplastics.* Blue Hill, ME: MERI, 2016. http://www.meriresearch.org/focus/plastics-and-microplastics.

Marris, Emma. *Rambunctious Garden: Saving Nature in a Post-Wild World.* New York: Bloomsbury, 2011.

Marshall, Michael. "Fungal Threads Are the Internet of the Plant World." *New Scientist* vol 208, no 2786 (November 13, 2010): 14.

Martin, Paul S. *Twilight of the Mammoths: Ice Age Extinctions and the Rewilding of America.* Berkeley, CA: University of California Press, 2005.

Mathews, John A. and Hao Tan. "Progress toward a Circular Economy in China: The Drivers (and Inhibitors) of Eco-industrial Initiative." *Journal of Industrial Ecology*, June 2011: 435–457.

Meadowcroft, J. "What about the Politics? Sustainable Development, Transition Management, and Long Term Energy Transitions." *Policy Science*, 42 (2009): 323–340.

Meadows, Donella. *Indicators and Information Systems for Sustainable Development.* Four Corners, VT: The Sustainability Institute, 1998.

——. *Thinking in Systems: A Primer.* White River, VT: Chelsea Green, 2008.

——, Jorgen Randers, and Dennis Meadows. *Limits to Growth: The 30-Year Update.* White River Junction, Vermont: Chelsea Green, 2004.

——, ——, ——, and William W. Behrens. *The Limits to Growth: A Report for the Club of Rome's Project on the Predicament of Mankind.* New York: Universe Books, 1972.

Mees, Paul. *Transport for Suburbia: Beyond the Automobile Age.* London: Earthscan, 2010.

Meffe, Gary K. *Principles of Conservation Biology.* Sunderland, MA: Sinauer Associates, 1997.

Meisel, Ari. *LEED Materials: A Resource Guide to Green Building.* New York: Princeton Architectural Press, 2010.

Melia, Steve. *On the Road to Sustainability: Transport and Carfree Living in Freiburg.* Bristol: UWE Faculty of the Built Environment, 2006.

Mendler, Sandra, William Odell, and Mary Ann Lazarus. *The HOK Guidebook to Sustainable Design.* 2nd ed. New York: John Wiley, 2006.

Merchant, Carolyn. *American Environmental History: An Introduction.* New York: Columbia University Press, 2007.

Metz, B., O. Davidson, H. de Coninck, M. Loos, and L. Meyer, eds. *Special Report on Carbon Dioxide Capture and Storage.* Cambridge: Cambridge University Press, 2005.

Meyer, Lukas, "Intergenerational Justice." *The Stanford Encyclopedia of Philosophy* (Fall 2015 Edition), Edward N. Zalta (ed.), 2015. http://plato.stanford.edu/archives/fall2015/entries/justice-intergenerational/.

M'Gonigle, Michael and Justine Starke. *Planet U: Sustaining the World, Reinventing the University.* Gabriola Island, BC: New Society Publishers, 2006.

Millennium Ecosystem Assessment. *Ecosystems and Human Well-Being: Synthesis.* Washington, DC: Island Press, 2005.

Miller, G. Tyler, Jr., and Scott E. Spoolman. *Living in the Environment: Concepts, Connections, and Solutions.* 16th ed. Belmont, CA: Brooks/Cole, 2009.

Miller, Kivi Leroux. *The Nonprofit Marketing Guide: High-Impact, Low-Cost Ways to Build Support for Your Good Cause.* San Francisco, CA: Jossey-Bass, 2010.

Millstone, Erik and Tim Lang. *The Atlas of Food: Who Eats What, Where, and Why.* Berkeley, CA: University of California Press, 2008.

Mitsch, William J. and James G. Gosselink. *Wetlands.* 4th ed. New York: John Wiley, 2007.

Moe, Richard. Acceptance address for Vincent Scully Prize, National Building Museum, Washington, DC, December 13, 2007.

Monbiot, George. "How Wolves Change Rivers." *The Guardian* March 3, 2014.

Montgomery, David. *Dirt: The Erosion of Civilizations.* Berkeley, CA: University of California Press, 2007.

Moore, Anna. "Is This the Perfect Playground, Full of Junk?" *The Guardian,* May 10, 2014.

Moore, Charles J. "Choking the Oceans With Plastic." *New York Times,* August 26, 2014.

Moore, Kathleen Dean and Michael P. Nelson, eds. *Moral Ground: Ethical Action for a Planet in Peril.* San Antonio, TX: Trinity University Press, 2010.

____. "Moving toward a Global Moral Consensus on Environmental Action." In Worldwatch Institute, *State of the World 2013: Is Sustainability Still Possible?* Washington, DC: Island Press, 2013, 225–233.

Moore, Robin C. and Clare Cooper Marcus. "Healthy Planet, Healthy Children: Designing Nature into the Daily Spaces of Childhood." In Stephen R. Kellert, Judith H. Heerwagen, and Martin L. Mador, eds. *Biophilic Design: The Theory, Science, and Practice of Bringing Buildings to Life.* New York: John Wiley, 2008, 153–203.

Moore, Robin C. and Allen Cooper. *Nature Play & Learning Places: Creating and Managing Places Where Children Engage with Nature.* Raleigh, NC: Natural Learning Initiative and Reston, VA: National Wildlife Federation, 2014.

Morandin, L.A. and Kremen, C. "Hedgerow Restoration Promotes Pollinator Populations and Exports Native Bees to Adjacent Fields." *Ecological Applications,* vol 23 no 4 (2013): 829–839.

Moratis, Lars and Timo Cochius. *ISO 26000: The Business Guide to the New Standard on Social Responsibility.* Sheffield, UK: Greenleaf, 2011.

Motesharrei, Safa, Jorge Rivas, and Eugenia Kalnay. "Human and Nature Dynamics (HANDY): Modeling Inequality and Use of Resources in the Collapse or Sustainability of Societies." *Ecological Economics* 101 (2014): 90–102.

Mougeot, Luc J. A. *Growing Better Cities: Urban Agriculture for Sustainable Development.* Ottawa: International Development Research Centre, 2006.

Mozingo, L. A. "The Aesthetics of Ecological Design: Seeing Science as Culture." *Landscape Journal,* 16, 1 (1997): 46–59.

Mühlhäusler, Peter. *Language of Environment, Environment of Language: A Course in Ecolinguistics.* London: Battlebridge Publications, 2003.

Müller, Daniel B., Tao Wang, and Benjamin Duval. "Patterns of Iron Use in Societal Evolution." *Environmental Science & Technology,* 45, 1 (January 2011): 182–188.

Muller, Richard A. *Physics and Technology for Future Presidents.* Princeton, NJ: Princeton University Press, 2010.

Mumovic, Dejan and Mat Santamouris, eds. *A Handbook of Sustainable Building Design & Engineering.* London: Earthscan, 2009.

Murphy, Pat and Faith Morgan. "Cuba: Lessons from a Forced Decline." In Worldwatch Institute, *State of the World 2013: Is Sustainability Still Possible?* Washington, DC: Island Press, 2013, 332–342.

Musser, George. "The Climax of Humanity." *Scientific American,* September 2005: 44–47.

Myers, Nancy J. and Carolyn Raffensperger, eds. *Precautionary Tools for Reshaping Environmental Policy.* Cambridge, MA: MIT Press, 2006.

Myers, Norman, Russell A. Mittermeier, Cristina G. Mittermeier, Gustavo A. B. da Fonseca, and Jennifer Kent. "Biodiversity Hotspots for Conservation Priorities." *Nature,* 403 (February 2000): 853–858.

Nair, P. K. Ramachandran et al., "Carbon Sequestration in Agroforestry Systems," *Advances in Agronomy* 108 (2010): 237–307.

Napier, Tom. "Construction Waste Management." *Whole Building Design Guide.* 2012. www.wbdg. org/resources/cwmgmt.php.

NASA Earth Observatory. "World of Change: The Shrinking Aral Sea." August 25, 2000. http://earth observatory.nasa.gov/Features/WorldOfChange/aral_sea.php.

——. "The Aral Sea Loses Its Eastern Lobe." September 26, 2014. http://earthobservatory.nasa.gov/ IOTD/view.php?id=84437.

Nash, Roderick Frazier. *The Rights of Nature.* Madison: University of Wisconsin Press, 1988.

Nassauer, Joan I. "Messy Ecosystems, Orderly Frames." *Landscape Journal,* 14 (1995): 161–170.

Nattrass, Brian and Mary Altomare. *The Natural Step for Business: Wealth, Ecology & the Evolutionary Corporation.* Gabriola Island, BC: New Society Publishers, 1999.

——. *Dancing with the Tiger: Learning Sustainability Step by Natural Step.* Gabriola Island, BC: New Society Publishers, 2002.

Natural Resources Conservation Service (NRDC). *Stream Corridor Restoration: Principles, Processes, and Practices*. Washington, DC: Natural Resources Conservation Service, 1998.

Nestle, Marion. *Food Politics: How the Food Industry Influences Nutrition and Health, 2nd ed.* Berkeley, CA: University of California Press, 2007.

Newman, Peter, Timothy Beatley, and Heather Boyer. *Resilient Cities: Responding to Peak Oil and Climate Change*. Washington, DC: Island Press, 2009.

New York City Department of Design & Construction. *Construction & Demolition Waste Manual.* 2003. Nicol, Fergus, Michael Humphreys, and Susan Roaf. *Adaptive Thermal Comfort: Principles and Practice.* New York: Routledge, 2012.

Nierenberg, Danielle. *Happier Meals: Rethinking the Global Meat Industry.* Worldwatch Paper 121. Washington, DC: Worldwatch Institute, 2005.

Nobis, C. "The Impact of Car-Free Housing Districts on Mobility Behaviour—Case Study." In E. Beriatos, C.A. Brebbia, H. Coccossis and A. Kungolos, eds. *International Conference on Sustainable Planning and Development.* Southampton: Wessex Institute of Technology Press, 2003, 701–720.

Nordahl, Darrin. *Public Produce: The New Urban Agriculture.* Washington, DC: Island Press, 2009.

Nordhaus, Ted, Michael Shellenberger, and Linus Glomqvist. *The Planetary Boundaries Hypothesis: A Review of the Evidence.* Oakland, CA: Breakthrough, 2012.

Norman, Donald A. *The Design of Everyday Things.* New York: Basic Books, 2002.

Norman, Jonathan, Heather L. McLean, and Christopher A. Kennedy. "Comparing High and Low Residential Density: Life-Cycle Analysis of Energy Use and Greenhouse Gas Emissions." *Journal of Urban Planning and Development*, March 2006, 10–21.

Novotny, Vladimir and Paul Brown, eds. *Cities of the Future.* London: IWA Publishing, 2007.

——, Jack Ahern, and Paul Brown. *Water Centric Sustainable Communities: Planning, Retrofitting, and Building the Next Urban Environment.* New York: John Wiley, 2010.

Nyári, J., E. Bailleul, S. Gow and M. Arbinolo. *The Effects of Wind Turbines on Bat Mortality and Available Solutions: An Executive Review.* Helsinki, Finland: EKOenergy, May 2015.

Nyéléni Forum for Food Sovereignty. Mali, 2007. http://www.nyeleni.org/.

Ocean Conservancy. *Stemming the Tide: Land-Based Strategies for a Plastic-Free Ocean.* McKinsey Center for Business and Environment, 2015.

OECD (Organisation for Economic Co-operation and Development). *OECD Environmental Outlook to 2050: The Consequences of Inaction.* Paris: OECD Publishing, 2012.

Ogden, Joan. "High Hopes for Hydrogen." *Scientific American*, September 2006: 94–101.

O'Hara, Sabine. "Food Security: The Urban Food Hubs Solution." *Solutions* vol 6 no 1 (January–February 2015): 42–53.

Olajire, A. "CO_2 Capture and Separation Technologies for End-of-Pipe Applications: A Review." *Energy*, 35 (2010): 2610–2628.

Olson, Eric G. *Better Green Business: Handbook for Environmentally Responsible and Profitable Business Practices.* Upper Saddle River, NJ: Prentice Hall, 2009.

Olsson, P. et al. "Shooting the Rapids: Navigating Transitions to Adaptive Governance of Social-Ecological Systems." *Ecology and Society*, 11, 1 (2006): art. 18.

Orr, David W. *Ecological Literacy: Education and the Transition to a Postmodern World.* New York: State University of New York Press, 1992.

——. "Walking North on a Southbound Train." *Conservation Biology*, 17 (2003): 348–351.

——. *Earth in Mind: On Education, Environment, and the Human Prospect.* Washington, DC: Island Press, 2004.

——. *Down to the Wire: Confronting Climate Collapse.* New York: Oxford University Press, 2009.

——. "Resilience, Security, and Education." Plenary presentation, annual conference of Association for the Advancement of Sustainability in Higher Education, October 10, 2011.

——. "Governance in the Long Emergency," in Worldwatch Institute. *State of the World 2013: Is Sustainability Still Possible?* Washington, DC: Island Press, 2013, 279–291.

Ostrom, Elinor. *Governing the Commons: The Evolution of Institutions for Collective Action.* Cambridge: Cambridge University Press, 1990.

——. "A Multi-Scale Approach to Coping with Climate Change and Other Collective Action Problems." *Solutions* vol 1 no 2 (February 2010): 27–36.

——. *The Future of the Commons: Beyond Market Failure and Government Regulation.* London: Institute of Economic Affairs, 2012.

Owen, Nick A., Oliver R. Inderwildi, and David A. King. "The Status of Conventional World Oil Reserves—Hype or Cause for Concern?" *Energy Policy*, 38, 8 (2010): 4743–4749.

Owens, S. and L. Driffil. "How to Change Attitudes and Behaviours in the Context of Energy." *Energy Policy*, 36 (2008): 4412–4418.

Pacala, S. and R. Socolow. "Stabilization Wedges: Solving the Climate Problem for the Next 50 Years with Current Technologies." *Science*, 305, 5686 (August 13, 2004): 968–972.

Pahl, Greg. *Power from the People: How to Organize, Finance, and Launch Local Energy Projects.* White River Junction, VT: Chelsea Green Publishing, 2012.

Palaniappan, M. and Gleick, P. H. "Peak Water." In P. Gleick, H. Cooley, M. J. Cohen, M. Morikawa, J. Morrison, and M. Palaniappan, eds. *The World's Water 2008–2009.* The Biennial Report on Freshwater Resources Washington, DC: Island Press, 2009, 1–16.

Palazzo, Danilo and Frederick R. Steiner. *Urban Ecological Design: A Process for Regenerative Places.* Washington, DC: Island Press, 2012.

Parish, Billy and Dev Aujla. *Making Good.* New York: Rodale, 2012.

Patagonia. 2013. Patagonia Common Threads Partnership. www.patagonia.com/us/common-threads/.

Pauly, Daniel. "Major Trends in Small-Scale Marine Fisheries, with Emphasis on Developing Countries, and Some Implications for the Social Sciences." *Maritime Studies*, 4, 2 (2006): 7–22.

Pearce, David. *Blueprint 3: Measuring Sustainable Development.* London: Earthscan, 1993.

Pearce, Fred. *When the Rivers Run Dry.* Boston: Beacon Press, 2006.

____. "Phosphate: A Critical Resource Misused and Now Running Low." *Yale Environment 360*, July 7, 2011. http://e360.yale.edu/feature/phosphate_a_critical_resource_misused_and_now_running_out/2423/.

____. *The Landgrabbers: The New Fight Over Who Owns the Planet.* London: Eden Project, 2012.

____. "A Successful Push to Restore Europe's Long-Abused Rivers." *Yale Environment 360*, December 10, 2013.

____. *The New Wild: Why Invasive Species Will Be Nature's Salvation.* Boston, MA: Beacon Press, 2015.

Pepper, Ian L., Charles P. Gerba, and Mark L. Brusseau, eds. *Environmental and Pollution Science.* 2nd ed. Boston, MA: Academic Press, 2006.

Perlman, Dan L. and Jeffrey C. Milder. *Practical Ecology for Planners, Developers, and Citizens.* Washington, DC: Island Press, 2004.

Petts, J., ed. *Handbook of Environmental Impact Assessment. Volume 1, Environmental Impact Assessment: Process, Methods and Potential.* Oxford: Blackwell, 1999.

Pharos Project. 2012. www.pharosproject.net/.

Phillips, Anne. *Holistic Education: Learning from Schumacher College.* Dartington: Green Books, 2008.

Phyper, John-David and Paul MacLean. *Good to Green: Managing Business Risks and Opportunities in the Age of Environmental Awareness.* New York: John Wiley, 2009.

Pickett, S. T. A., M. L. Cadenassso, and J. M. Grove. "Resilient Cities: Meaning, Models, and Metaphor for Integrating the Ecological, Socio-Economic, and Planning Realms." *Landscape and Urban Planning*, 69, 4 (2004): 369–384.

Pickett, S. T. A. and P. S. White. *The Ecology of Natural Disturbance and Patch Dynamics.* London: Academic Press, 1985.

Pimm, S.L. and C. Jenkins. "Sustaining the Variety of Life." *Scientific American*, 293, 3 (September 2005): 66–73.

Piore, Adam. "The Ultimate Sustainability Index." *Scientific American*, December 2012, 40–41.

Pirog, Rich and Andrew Benjamin. *Checking the Food Odometer: Comparing Food Miles for Local Versus Conventional Produce Sales to Iowa Institutions.* Leopold Center for Sustainable Agriculture. Ames, IA: Iowa State University, July 2003.

Plant, Judith, Christopher Plant, Van Andruss, and Eleanor Wright. *Home! A Bioregional Reader*. Philadelphia: New Catalyst Books, 2008.

Plastics Task Force, Ecology Center, Berkeley. N.d. http://ecologycenter.org/plastics/.

Pollan, Michael. *The Omnivore's Dilemma*. New York: Penguin Publishing, 2006.

Polyface Farms. N.d. www.polyfacefarms.com/.

Ponting, Clive. *A New Green History of the World: The Environment and the Collapse of Great Civilizations*. New York: Penguin, 2007.

Poole, Robert. *Earthrise: How Man First Saw the Earth*. New Haven: Yale University Press, 2010.

Portland State University. "Land Use Planning." *The Oregon Encyclopedia*, 2010. www.oregonency clopedia.org/entry/view/land_use_planning/.

Postel, Sandra and Brian Richter. *Rivers for Life: Managing Water for People and Nature*. Washington, DC: Island Press, 2003.

Potsdam Institute for Climate Impact Research and Climate Analytics. *Turn Down the Heat: Why a 4°C Warmer World Must Be Avoided*. Washington, DC: World Bank, 2012.

Potts, Simon G. et al. *Thematic Assessment of Pollinators, Pollination and Food Production*. [n.p.]: Intergovernmental Science-Policy Platform on Biodiversity and Ecosystem Services (IPBES), 2016.

Preservation Green Lab. *The Greenest Building: Quantifying the Environmental Value of Building Reuse*. National Trust for Historic Preservation, 2011.

Prigogine, Ilya and Isabelle Stengers. *Order Out of Chaos*. New York: Bantam, 1984.

Primack, Richard B. *A Primer of Conservation Biology*. 4th ed. Sunderland, MA: Sinauer Associates, 2008.

Pulliam, H. R. and N. M. Haddad. "Human Population Growth and the Carrying Capacity Concept." *Bulletin of the Ecological Society of America*, 75 (1994): 141–157.

Ramus, C. and I. Montiel. "When Are Corporate Environmental Policies a Form of Greenwashing?" *Business and Society*, 44, 4 (2005): 377–414.

Randers, Jorgen. *2052: A Global Forecast for the Next Forty Years*. White River Junction, VT: Chelsea Green, 2012.

Randolph, John and Gilbert M. Masters. *Energy for Sustainability: Technology, Planning, Policy*. Washington, DC: Island Press, 2008.

Rappaport, Ann and Sarah Creighton. *Degrees that Matter: Climate Change and the University*. Cambridge, MA: MIT Press, 2007.

Raskin, Paul, Tariq Banuri, Gilberto Gallopin, Pablo Gutman, and Al Hammond. *Great Transition: The Promise and Lure of the Times Ahead*. Boston: Stockholm Environment Institute, 2002.

Ravilious, Kate. "Mid-Town Miners: The Hunt for Urban Treasure." *New Scientist*, 2919 (June 5, 2013): 40–43.

Ray, Justina C., Kent H. Redford, Robert S. Steneck, and Joel Berger, eds. *Large Carnivores and the Conservation of Biodiversity*. Washington, DC: Island Press, 2005.

Reck, Barbara K. and T. E. Graedel. "Challenges in Metal Recycling." *Science*, August 10, 2012.

Redman, Charles L. *Human Impact on Ancient Environments*. Tucson, AZ: University of Arizona Press, 2001.

Redman, Charles L. "Should Sustainability and Resilience Be Combined or Remain Distinct Pursuits?" *Ecology and Society* [online] vol. 19 no. 2 (2014): 37. http://www.ecologyandsociety.org/vol19/iss2/art37/.

Reed, Christina. "Hot Trails." *Scientific American*, 295 (September 2006): 28.

Rees, William E. "What's Blocking Sustainability? Human Nature, Cognition and Denial." *Sustainability: Science, Practice and Policy*, vol 6, no. 2 (2010).

____. "The Way Forward: Survival 2100." in Robert Costanza and Ida Kubiszewski, eds. *Creating a Sustainable and Desirable Future*. Singapore: World Scientific, 2014.

Register, Richard. *EcoCities: Rebuilding Cities in Balance with Nature*. Gabriola Island, BC: New Society Publishers, 2006.

Renne, John L. and Billy Fields, eds. *Transport Beyond Oil: Policy Choices for a Multimodal Future*. Washington, DC: Island Press, 2013.

Rice, J. "Climate, Carbon and Territory: Greenhouse Gas Mitigation in Seattle, Washington." *Annals of the Association of American Geographers*, 100, 4 (2010): 929–937.

Rich, Sarah C. *Urban Farms*. New York: Abrams, 2012.

Richey, Alexandra S. et al. "Quantifying Renewable Groundwater Stress with GRACE." *Water Resources Research* 51 (July 2015): 5217–5238. doi:10.1002/2015WR017349.

Riley, Ann L. *Restoring Streams in Cities*. Washington, DC: Island Press, 1998.

"Rio+20: After Dialogues, Citizens to Make Recommendations on Rio+20 Issues." UN News Centre, June 20, 2012.

Roaf, Sue, David Crichton, and Fergus Nicol. *Adapting Buildings and Cities for Climate Change*. Oxford: Architectural Press, 2005.

Robbins, Jim. "The Rapid and Startling Decline of World's Vast Boreal Forests." *Yale Environment 360*, October 12, 2015.

Robèrt, Karl H. *The Natural Step Story: Seeding a Quiet Revolution*. Gabriola Island, BC: New Society, 2002.

—— et al. *Strategic Leadership towards Sustainability*. Karlskrona: Blekinge Institute of Technology, 2004.

Roberts, K. et al. "Life Cycle Assessment of Biochar Systems: Estimating the Energetic, Economic, and Climate Change Potential." *Environmental Science & Technology*, 44, 2 (2010): 827–833.

Rochman, Chelsea M. et al. "Classify Plastic Waste as Hazardous." *Nature*, 494 (February 14, 2013): 169–171.

Rockström, Johan et al. "A Safe Operating Space for Humanity." *Nature*, 461, 7263 (2009a): 472–475.

——. "Planetary Boundaries: Exploring the Safe Operating Space for Humanity." *Ecology and Society*, 14, 2 (2009b): 1–3. www.ecologyandsociety.org/vol14/iss2/art32/.

Rogers, Elizabeth Barlow. *Landscape Design: A Cultural and Architectural History*. New York: Harry N. Abrams, 2001.

Rogers, Everett M. *Diffusion of Innovations*. 5th ed. New York: Free Press, 2003.

Rogers, Heather. *Gone Tomorrow: The Hidden Life of Garbage*. New York: The New Press, 2005.

Rolston, Holmes, III. *Environmental Ethics: Duties to and Values in the Natural World*. Philadelphia, PA: Temple University Press, 1989.

____. "Earth Ethics: A Challenge to Liberal Education." In J. Baird Callicott and Fernando R. da Rocha, eds. *Earth Summit Ethics: Toward a Reconstructive Postmodern Philosophy of Environmental Education*. Albany, NY: State University of New York, 1996, 161–192.

____. *A New Environmental Ethics: The Next Millennium for Life on Earth*. New York: Routledge, 2012.

Rosenzweig, Michael L. *Win–Win Ecology*. New York: Oxford University Press, 2003.

Rosenthal, Elisabeth. "Paying More for Flights Eases Guilt, Not Emissions." *New York Times*, November 17, 2009, A1.

Rosin, Hanna. "The Overprotected Kid." *The Atlantic*, April 2014, 73–83.

Rosner, Hillary. "Return of the Natives." *Scientific American* September 2013, 70–75.

Roth, Charles E. "Education for Life in the Sky." *The Environmentalist*, 1, 4 (Winter 1981): 293–297.

Royal Society. *Geoengineering the Climate: Science, Governance and Uncertainty*. London: Royal Society, 2009.

Rubin, Jeff. *Why Your World Is about to Get a Whole Lot Smaller*. Toronto: Vintage Canada Editions, 2010.

Ruppental, R. J. *Fresh Food from Small Spaces: The Square-Inch Gardener's Guide to Year-Round Growing, Fermenting, and Sprouting*. White River Junction, VT: Chelsea Green, 2008.

Russell, David L. *Remediation Manual for Contaminated Sites*. Boca Raton, FL: CRC, 2012.

Rydin, Y. "Indicators as a Governmentality Technology? The Lessons of Community-Based Sustainability Indicator Projects." *Environment and Planning D*, 25, 4 (2007): 610–624.

Sachs, Jeffrey. "Transgressing Planetary Boundaries." *Scientific American*, 301 (December 2009): 36.

Sachs, Jeffrey D. *The Age of Sustainable Development*. New York: Columbia University Press, 2015.

San Diego County Water Authority (SDCWA). "Seawater Desalination." SDCWA 2015. http://www.sdcwa.org/seawater-desalination.

Sanchez, Thomas W. and Marc Brenman. *The Right to Transportation: Moving to Equity.* Chicago: APA Planners Press, 2008.

Sandford, Robert William. *Restoring the Flow: Confronting the World's Water Woes.* Surrey: Rocky Mountain Books, 2009.

Sandom, Christopher, Søren Faurby, Brody Sandel, and Jens-Christian Svenning. "Global Late Quaternary Megafauna Extinctions Linked to Humans, Not Climate Change." *Proceedings of the Royal Society* B 281 (2014): 20133524.

Sandseter, Ellen Beate Hansen. "Children's Risky Play in Early Childhood Education and Care." *Childlinks* issue 3 (2011): 2–6.

Sandseter, Ellen Beate Hansen and Leif Edward Ottesen Kennair. "Children's Risky Play from an Evolutionary Perspective: The Anti-Phobic Effects of Thrilling Experiences." *Evolutionary Psychology* vol 9 no 2 (2011): 257–284.

Sanjayan, M. A. "Seaworthy Semantics." *Nature Conservancy*, summer 2010: 8.

Sanoff, Henry. *Community Participation Methods in Design and Planning.* New York: John Wiley, 2000.

Sayan, Charles and Daniel Blumstein. *The Failure of Environmental Education (And How We Can Fix It).* Berkeley, CA: University of California Press, 2011.

Sayre, Don. *Inside ISO 14000: The Competitive Advantage of Environmental Management.* Delray Beach, FL: St. Lucie Press, 1996.

Schaefer, Valentin, Hillary Rudd, and Jamie Vala. *Urban Biodiversity: Exploring Natural Habitat and Its Value in Cities.* Concord: Captus Press, 2004.

Schendler, Auden. *Getting Green Done: Hard Truths from the Front Lines of the Sustainability Revolution.* Philadelphia, PA: Public Affairs, 2009.

Scheurer, Jan and Peter Newman, "Vauban: Integration of the Green and Brown Agendas," UN Global Review of Human Settlements, 2008.

Schiller, Ben. "Trash to Cash: Mining Landfills for Energy and Profit." *Fast Company*, September 7, 2011.

Schmidheiny, Stephan. *Changing Course: A Global Business Perspective on Development and the Environment.* Cambridge, MA: MIT Press, 1992.

Schmidt, Gavin and Joshua Wolfe. *Climate Change: Picturing the Science.* New York: W. W. Norton, 2009.

Schmidt, H. et al. "Solar Irradiance Reduction to Counteract Radiative Forcing from a Quadrupling of CO_2: Climate Responses Simulated by Four Earth System Models." *Earth System Dynamics*, 3 (2012): 63–78.

Schmidt-Bleek, Friedrich. *Das MIPS Konzept—Faktor 10.* Munich: Droemer Knaur, 1998.

Schumacher, E. F. *Small Is Beautiful: Economics as if People Mattered.* New York: Harper & Row, 1973.

Schutter, Olivier De. *The Transformative Potential of the Right to Food.* UN General Assembly, Human Rights Council. January 2014.

Schwarz, Benjamin. "A Vision in Concrete." *The Atlantic*, July/August 2008.

Schwartz, Peter. *The Art of the Long View: Planning for the Future in an Uncertain World.* New York: Currency Doubleday, 1996.

SDCWA (San Diego County Water Authority). "Seawater Desalination." SDCWA 2015. http://www.sdcwa.org/seawater-desalination

Seed, John, Joanna Macy, Pat Fleming, and Arne Naess. *Thinking Like a Mountain: Towards a Council of All Beings.* Philadelphia: New Catalyst Books, 2007.

Senge, Peter, Bryan Smith, Nina Kruschwitz, Joe Laur, and Sara Schley. *The Necessary Revolution: Working Together to Create a Sustainable World.* New York: Broadway Books, 2010.

Senos, René. "Rebuilding Salmon Relations: Participatory Ecological Restoration as Community Healing." In Robert L. France. *Handbook of Regenerative Landscape Design.* Boca Raton, FL: CRC Press, 2008, 205–235.

Sheldon, Christopher and Mark Yoxon, *Installing Environmental Management Systems: A Step-byStep Guide.* London: Earthscan, 2002.

Shiva, Vandana. *Earth Democracy: Justice, Sustainability and Peace*. Cambridge, MA: South End Press, 2005.

Sibbet, David. *Visual Meetings: How Graphics, Sticky Notes and Idea Mapping Can Transform Group Productivity*. New York: John Wiley, 2010.

Sims, Mike. "Waste." In Willis Jenkins, ed. *Berkshire Encyclopedia of Sustainability: The Spirit of Sustainability*. Great Barrington, MA: Berkshire Publishing Group, 2010, 418–421.

Sinclair, Minor and Martha Thompson. *Cuba, Going Against the Grain: Agricultural Crisis and Transformation*. Boston, MA: Oxfam America, 2001.

Sitarz, Daniel. *Agenda 21: The Earth Summit Strategy to Save Our Planet*. New York: Nova, 1994.

——. *Greening Your Business: The Hands-On Guide to Creating a Successful and Sustainable Business*. Carbondale, IL: Earthpress, 2008.

Slavin, Matthew I., ed. *Sustainability in America's Cities: Creating the Green Metropolis*. Washington, DC: Island Press, 2011.

Smil, Vaclav. *The Earth's Biosphere: Evolution, Dynamics, and Change*. Cambridge, MA: MIT Press, 2002.

——. *Energy at the Crossroads*. Cambridge, MA: MIT Press, 2003.

——. *Energy: A Beginner's Guide*. Oxford: Oneworld, 2006.

——. *Crossing the Energy Divide*. Philadelphia, PA: Wharton School Publishing, 2009.

——. *Energy Myths and Realities: Bringing Science to the Energy Policy Debate*. Washington, DC: AEI Press, 2010.

Smith, Adam. *An Inquiry into the Nature and Causes of the Wealth of Nations*. 1776. Reprint, Chicago, IL: University of Chicago Press, 1976.

Smith, Gregory A. and Dilafruz R. Williams, eds. *Ecological Education in Action: On Weaving Education, Culture, and the Environment*. Albany, NY: State University of New York Press, 1999.

Smith, Peter F. *Architecture in a Climate of Change*. 2nd ed. Oxford: Architectural Press, 2005.

——. *Building for a Changing Climate: The Challenge for Construction, Planning and Energy*. London: Earthscan, 2009.

Smith-Sebasto, Nicholas. *Annual Editions: Sustainability 12/13*. New York: McGraw-Hill, 2011.

Smolin, Lee. *The Life of the Cosmos*. New York: Oxford University Press, 1997.

Snow, C. P. *The Two Cultures and the Scientific Revolution*. New York: Cambridge University Press, 2012 (reissued).

Sobel, David. *Place-Based Education: Connecting Classrooms and Communities*. Great Barrington, MA: Orion Society, 2004.

Socolow, Robert H. and Stephen W. Pacala. "A Plan to Keep Carbon in Check." *Scientific American*, September 2006: 50–57.

——, C. Andres, F. Berkhout, and V. Thomas, eds. *Industrial Ecology and Global Change*. Cambridge: Cambridge University Press, 1997.

Soil and Water Conservation Society. *Soil Biology Primer*. Revised ed. Ankeny, IA: Soil and Water Conservation Society, 2000.

Solnit, Rebecca. *A Paradise Built in Hell: The Extraordinary Communities that Arise in Disaster*. New York: Viking Press, 2008.

Soulé, Michael and Reed Noss. "Rewilding and Biodiversity: Complementary Goals for Continental Conservation." *Wild Earth* 8 (Fall 1998): 19–28.

SourceWatch. "Keep America Beautiful." 2009. www.sourcewatch.org/index.php?title=Keep_America_Beautiful.

Speth, James Gustave. *Red Sky at Morning*. New Haven, CT: Yale University Press, 2004.

——. *The Bridge at the Edge of the World*. New Haven, CT: Yale University Press, 2008.

——. *America the Possible: Manifesto for a New Economy*. New Haven, CT: Yale University Press, 2012.

Stahel, Walter R. The Product-Life Factor. Houston, TX: Mitchell Prize Competition on Sustainable Societies, 1982.

Stanley, Steven M. *Earth System History*. 2nd ed. New York: W. H. Freeman, 2004.

Steffen, Alex, ed. *World Changing: A User's Guide for the 21st Century, Revised ed.* New York: Abrams, 2006.

——. *World Changing: A User's Guide for the 21st Century, Revised ed.* New York: Abrams, 2011.

Steffen, Will. "Connecting the Solution to the Problem." *Solutions,* vol. 5 no. 4 (July–August 2014): 1.

—— et al. "The Anthropocene: From Global Change to Planetary Stewardship." *Ambio,* 40 (2011): 739–761.

——, Paul J. Crutzen, and John R. McNeill. "The Anthropocene: Are Humans Now Overwhelming the Great Forces of Nature?" *Ambio,* 36, 8 (December 2007): 614–621.

——, Wendy Broadgate, Lisa Deutsch, Owen Gaffney, and Cornelia Ludwig. "The Trajectory of the Anthropocene: The Great Acceleration." *Anthropocene Review.* January 16, 2015.

Steinfeld, Henning, Pierre Gerber, Tom Wassenaar, Vincent Castel, Maricio Rosales, and Cees de Haan. *Livestock's Long Shadow: Environmental Issues and Options.* Rome: FAO of the UN, 2006.

Steingraber, Sandra. *Living Downstream.* 2nd ed. Philadelphia: Da Capo, 2010.

Stephens, J. C. and D. W. Keith. "Assessing Geochemical Carbon Management." *Climatic Change,* 90 (2008): 217–242.

Stern, Nicholas. *The Economics of Climate Change: The Stern Review.* Cambridge: Cambridge University Press, 2006.

——. *The Global Deal: Climate Change and the Creation of a New Era of Progress and Prosperity.* New York: PublicAffairs, 2009.

Stibbe, Arran, ed. *The Handbook of Sustainability Literacy: Skills for a Changing World.* Dartington: Green Books, 2009.

Stiglitz, Joseph, Amartya Sen, and Jean-Paul Fitoussi. *Report of the Commission on the Measurement of Economic Performance and Social Progress,* 2009. www.stiglitz-sen-fitoussi.fr/documents/ rapport_anglais.pdf.

Stockholm Convention on Persistent Organic Pollutants. *Global Status of DDT and Its Alternatives for Use in Vector Control to Prevent Disease.* Geneva: UNEP Stockholm Convention, 2008.

Stone, Christopher D. "Should Trees Have Standing? Toward Legal Rights for Natural Objects." *Southern California Law Review,* 1972.

Stone, Michael K. *Smart by Nature.* Berkeley, CA: University of California Press, 2009.

—— and Zenobia Barlow, eds. *Ecological Literacy: Educating Our Children for a Sustainable World.* San Francisco, CA: Sierra Club Books, 2005.

Stoyke, Godo. *The Carbon Charter: Blueprint for a Carbon-Free Future.* Gabriola Island, BC: New Society Publishers, 2009.

Sturtevant, Victoria E. and Jon I. Lange. "The Applegate Partnership Case Study: Group Dynamics and Community Context. Seattle: US Forest Service." Pacific Northwest Research Station, Oregon, USA. Summarized in Jonathan Kusel and Elisa Adler, *Forest Communities, Community Forests: A Collection of Case Studies of Community Forestry.* Taylorsville, CA: Forest Community Research, 2001, 81–95.

Suh, Sangwon, ed. *Handbook of Input–Output Economics in Industrial Ecology.* New York: Springer, 2009.

Sullivan, Chip. *Garden and Climate.* New York: McGraw-Hill, 2002.

Sullivan, Robert and Mark Meyer. *Guide to Evaluating Visual Impact Assessments for Renewable Energy Projects.* Denver, CO: National Park Service, 2014.

Susskind, Lawrence, Sarah McKearnan, and Jennifer Thomas-Larmer, eds. *Consensus-Building Handbook: A Comprehensive Guide to Reaching Agreement.* Thousand Oaks, CA: Sage Publications, 1999.

Sustainable Scale Project. *Limits to Growth.* 2003. http://www.sustainablescale.org/ ConceptualFramework/UnderstandingScale/MeasuringScale/LimitstoGrowth.aspx.

Sustainable Seattle. www.sustainableseattle.org/.

Sustainable Sites Initiative. *Guidelines and Performance Benchmarks 2009.* Austin, TX: Sustainable Sites Initiative, 2009.

Sutton, Mark A. et al. "Too Much of a Good Thing." *Nature,* April 10, 2011: 159–161.

Svanström, Magdalena, Francisco J. Lozano-García, and Debra Rowe. "Learning Outcomes for Sustainable Development in Higher Education." *International Journal of Sustainability in Higher Education*, 9, 3 (2008): 339–351.

Taylor, M. "Community Participation in the Real World: Opportunities and Pitfalls in New Governance Spaces." *Urban Studies*, 44 (2007): 297–317.

TEEB (The Economics of Ecosystems and Biodiversity). *The Economics of Ecosystems and Biodiversity: Mainstreaming the Economics of Nature: A synthesis of the approach, conclusions and recommendations of TEEB*. 2010.

Tennesen, Michael. "Bioacoustics: Calls of the Wild." *Scientific American*, October 2008: 24.

Thayer, Robert L. *LifePlace: Bioregional Thought and Practice*. Berkeley, CA: University of California Press, 2003.

Theis, Tom and Jonathan Tomkin, eds. *Sustainability: A Comprehensive Foundation*. Houston, TX: Connexions, Rice University, 2012.

The Nature Conservancy. "Where We Work." N.d. www.nature.org/success/art13910.html.

Thiele, Leslie Paul. *Sustainability*. Cambridge: Polity, 2013.

Thompson, J. William. "Lots in Common." *Landscape Architecture Magazine*, August 2000, 2–59.

—— and Kim Sorvig. *Sustainable Landscape Construction*. 2nd ed. Washington, DC: Island Press, 2008.

Thoreau, Henry David. *The Journal, 1837–1861*. New York: New York Review Books, 2009. Quoted in Roderick Frazier Nash. *The Rights of Nature*. Madison, MI: University of Wisconsin Press, 1988.

Thorpe, Ann. *The Designer's Atlas of Sustainability*. Washington, DC: Island Press, 2006.

——. *Teaching Guide for The Designer's Atlas of Sustainability*. Version 3, June 2008. www.designers-atlas.net/teaching-resources.

Toensmeier, Eric. *The Carbon Farming Solution*. White River Junction, VT: Chelsea Green, 2016.

Tollefson, Chris, Fred Gale, and David Haley. *Certification, Governance, and the Forest Stewardship Council*. Vancouver: UBC Press, 2008.

Tomasello, Michael. *Why We Cooperate*. Cambridge, MA: MIT Press, 2009.

Toor, Will and Spenser W. Havlick. *Transportation & Sustainable Campus Communities*. Washington, DC: Island Press, 2004.

Townsend, Alan R. and Robert W. Howarth. "Fixing the Global Nitrogen Problem." *Scientific American*, 302 (February 2010): 64–71.

Trefil, James and Robert Hazen. *The Sciences: An Integrated Approach*. 6th ed. New York: John Wiley, 2010.

Ulrich, Roger. "View through a Window May Influence Recovery from Surgery." *Science*, New Series, 224, 4647 (April 27, 1984): 420–421.

UN (United Nations). Millennium Development Goals. 2000. www.un.org/millenniumgoals/.

——. *Report of the World Summit on Sustainable Development, Johannesburg*, A/CONF.199/20. New York: UN, 2002.

——. *Water in a Changing World: United Nations World Water Development Report, 3rd ed*. Paris: UNESCO, 2009.

——. *The Future We Want*. New York: UN, 2012.

——. *Millennium Development Goals Report*. New York: UN, 2015.

UNCOP (United Nations Conference of the Parties). *Framework Convention on Climate Change*, FCCC/CP/2015/L.9 (December 12, 2015). Paris: UN, 2015.

UNDESA (United Nations Department of Economic and Social Affairs). *The Millennium Development Goals Report 2013*. New York: UN, 2013.

UNEP (United Nations Environment Programme). *Communicating Sustainability: How to Produce Effective Public Campaigns*. Nairobi: UNEP, 2005.

——. *Green Jobs: Towards Decent Work in a Sustainable, Low-carbon World*. Nairobi, UNEP: 2008.

——. *Vital Forest Graphics*. Nairobi: UNEP, 2009.

——. *Recycling Rates of Metals: A Status Report*. Paris, UNEP: 2011.

——. *The Emissions Gap Report 2012*. Nairobi: UNEP, 2012.

UN Habitat. *State of the World's Cities 2012/2013*. London: Earthscan, 2006.

UNICEF and World Health Organization. *Progress on Drinking Water and Sanitation: 2012 Update*. New York: UN, 2012.

University of Arkansas Community Design Center. *Low Impact Development: A Design Manual for*

UN Population Division. *World Population Prospects: The 2010 Revision, Volume I: Comprehensive Tables*. New York: UN, 2011.

UN Sustainable Development. *Earth Summit Agenda 21: The United Nations Programme of Action from Rio*. New York: UN Department of Public Information, 1992.

UN University-International Human Dimensions Programme and UNEP. *Inclusive Wealth Report 2012: Measuring Progress toward Sustainability*. Cambridge: Cambridge University Press, 2012.

Urban Area s. Fayetteville, AZ: University of Arkansas Press, 2011.

US Census Bureau. "World Population: Total Midyear Population for the World: 1950–2050." http://www.census.gov/population/international/data/worldpop/table_population.php (Accessed October 17, 2015).

USDA ERS (Economic Research Service). "Definitions of Food Security." 2012. www.ers.usda.gov/topics/food-nutrition-assistance/food-security-in-the-us/definitions-of-food-security.aspx.

US DOE (Department of Energy). *Microhydropower Systems*. N.d. http://energy.gov/energysaver/microhydropower-systems

US DOE Buildings Energy Data Book. N.d. http://buildingsdatabook.eren.doe.gov/ChapterIntro6.aspx.

US DOE and EPA. *Combined Heat and Power: A Clean Energy Solution*. Washington, DC: US Department of Energy and EPA, August 2012.

US DOI (Department of the Interior). *Best Management Practices for Reducing Visual Impacts of Renewable Energy Facilities on BLM-Administered Lands*. Cheyenne, WY: Bureau of Land Management, 2013.

US EPA (Environmental Protection Agency). *Life Cycle Assessment: Principles and Practice*. Cincinnati, OH: National Risk Management Research Laboratory, 2006.

——. *A Wedge Analysis of the Transportation Sector*. Washington, DC: Transportation and Climate Division, 2007.

——. "Twelve Principles of Green Chemistry." *EPA Science Matters Newsletter*, June 2011.

——. *Green Building*. N.d. www.epa.gov/greenbuilding/pubs/about.htm.

——. *Nitrogen Dioxide: Health*. N.d. www.epa.gov/oaqps001/nitrogenoxides/health.html.

——. *Pollution Prevention (P2)*. 2013a. www.epa.gov/p2/.

——. "Reduce Your Outdoor Water Use." EPA Fact Sheet, May 2013b.

US Geological Survey. *USGS Water Science School*. 2013. http://ga.water.usgs.gov/edu/drinkseawater.html.

——. "Metal Stocks in Use in the United States." Fact Sheet 2050–3090. Reston, VA: July 2005.

US Government Accounting Office. *Wind Power Impacts on Wildlife and Government Responsibilities for Regulating Development and Protecting Wildlife*. GAO-050906, September 2005.

Vale, Thomas, ed. *Fire, Native Peoples, and the Natural Landscape*. Washington, DC: Island Press, 2002.

Van der Heijden, Kees. *Scenarios: The Art of Strategic Conversation*. 2nd ed. New York: John Wiley, 2005.

Van der Ryn, Sim and Stuart Cowan. *Ecological Design, 10th Anniversary Edition*. Washington, DC: Island Press, 2007.

Van Nes, Nicole and Jacqueline Cramer. "Product Lifetime Optimization: A Challenging Strategy towards More Sustainable Consumption Patterns." *Journal of Cleaner Production*, 14, 15–16 (2006): 1307–1318.

Venhuas, Heather. *Designing the Sustainable Site*. New York: John Wiley, 2012.

Vesilind, P. Aarne, Susan M. Morgan, and Lauren G. Heine. *Introduction to Environmental Engineering*. Stamford, CT: Cengage Learning, 2004.

Vezzoli, Carlo and Ezio Manzini. *Design for Environmental Sustainability*. Milan: Springer, 2008.

Vickers, Amy. *Handbook of Water Use and Conservation*. Amherst, MA: WaterPlow Press, 2001.

Victoria Transport Policy Institute. "Online TDM Encyclopedia." N.d. www.vtpi.org/tdm/.

Viljoen, André, ed. *CPULs: Continuous Productive Urban Landscapes*. Oxford: Architectural Press, 2005.

Vincent, Shirley. *Interdisciplinary Environmental Education on the Nation's Campuses: Elements of Field Identify and Curriculum Design*. Washington, DC: National Council of Science and Environment, 2010.

Vleuten, E. van der and R. Raven. "Lock-in and Change: Distributed Generation in Denmark in a Long-Term Perspective." *Energy Policy*, 34, 18 (2006): 3739–3748.

Vogt, K. A. et al., eds. *Forests and Society: Sustainability and Life Cycles of Forests in Human Landscapes*. Cambridge, MA: CAB International, 2007.

Vogt, William. *Road to Survival*. New York: William Sloane Associates, 1948.

Volk, Tyler. *CO2 Rising: The World's Greatest Environmental Challenge*. Cambridge, MA: MIT Press, 2010.

Voluntary Interindustry Commerce Solutions (VICS) Association. "Macy's and Schneider National Filling Empty Miles for Sustainability and Savings." October 2009. www.vics.org.

Vries, Bert J. M. de. *Sustainability Science*. New York: Cambridge University Press, 2013.

Wackernagel, Mathis and William Rees. *Our Ecological Footprint: Reducing Human Impact on the Earth*. Gabriola Island, BC: New Society Publishers, 1995.

Waddell, Steve. *Global Action Networks*. New York: Palgrave-Macmillan, 2011.

Walker, Andy. *Solar Water Heating. Whole Building Design Guide*. Washington, DC: National Institute of Building Sciences, 2010. www.wbdg.org/resources/swheating.php.

Walker, Brian and David Salt. *Resilience Thinking: Sustaining Ecosystems and People in a Changing World*. Washington, DC: Island Press, 2006.

——. *Resilience Practice*. Washington, DC: Island Press, 2012.

Walker, B., C. S. Holling, S. R. Carpenter, and A. Kinzig. "Resilience, Adaptability and Transformability in Social-Ecological Systems." *Ecology and Society*, 9, 2 (2004): 5.

Walker, Brian et al. "Resilience Management in Social Ecological Systems: A Working Hypothesis for a Participatory Approach." *Conservation Ecology*, 6, 1 (2002): 14.

——. "Looming Global-Scale Failures and Missing Institutions." *Science*, September 11, 2009: 1345–1346.

Wang, Heming et al. "Resource Use in Growing China: Past Trends, Influence Factors, and Future Demand." *Journal of Industrial Ecology*, August 2012: 481–492.

Wang, T. "Forging the Anthropogenic Iron Cycle." Doctoral dissertation, Yale University, 2009.

Ward, Barbara and René Dubos. *Only One Earth: The Care and Maintenance of a Small Planet*. Toronto: Report on the Human Environment, 1972.

Warde, Paul. "The Invention of Sustainability." *Modern Intellectual History*, 8 (2011): 153–170.

Wargo, John. *Green Intelligence: Creating Environments that Protect Human Health*. New Haven, CT: Yale University Press, 2010.

WCED (World Commission on Environment and Development). *Our Common Future*. Oxford: Oxford University Press, 1987.

Webber, Michael E. "Catch-22: Water vs. Energy." *Scientific American* Special Issue: Earth 3.0. vol 18 no 4 (2008): 34–41.

——. "Energy, Water and Food Problems Must Be Solved Together." *Scientific American* 312 (January 2015): 62–67.

Weber, C. L. *An Examination of Energy Intensity and Energy Efficiency*. Pittsburgh: Carnegie Mellon University, 2008.

—— and H. S. Matthews. "Embodied Environmental Emissions in US International Trade, 1997– 2004." *Environmental Science & Technology*, 41, 14 (2007): 4875–4881.

Weiszäcker, Ernst von, Amory Lovins, and L. Hunter Lovins. *Factor Four: Doubling Wealth, Halving Resource Use*. London: Earthscan, 1997.

Wells, Malcolm. *Infra Structures*. Brewster, MA: Malcolm Wells, 1994.

——. *Recovering America: A More Gentle Way to Build*. Brewster, MA: Malcolm Wells, 1999.

Wendt, Allyson. "The Living Building Challenge: Can It Really Change the World?" *Environmental Building News*, June 1, 2009.

Wengenmayr, Roland and Thomas Buhrke, eds. *Renewable Energy: Sustainable Energy Concepts for the Future*. Weinheim: Wiley-VCH, 2008.

Wessels, Tom. *The Myth of Progress: Toward a Sustainable Future*. Burlington, VT: University of Vermont Press, 2006.

Westley, Frances et al. "Tipping Towards Sustainability: Emerging Pathways of Transformation." *Ambio*, 40, 7 (2011): 762–780.

Wheeler, Stephen M. *Planning for Sustainability: Creating Livable, Equitable and Ecological Communities*. 2nd ed. New York: Routledge, 2013.

White, Alexander W. *The Elements of Graphic Design: Space, Unity, Page Architecture, and Type*. 2nd ed. New York: Allworth Press, 2011.

White, I. and J. Howe. "Planning and the European Union Water Framework Directive." *Journal of Environmental Planning and Management*, 46 (2003): 62–131.

Whitson, Alan and Yudelson, Jerry. *365 Important Questions to Ask about Green Buildings*. Portland, OR: Corporate Realty, Design & Management Institute, Inc., 2003.

Wijkman, Anders and Johan Rockström. *Bankrupting Nature: Denying Our Planetary Boundaries*. London: Routledge, 2012.

Wilcove, David S. *No Way Home: The Decline of the World's Great Animal Migrations*. Washington, DC: Island Press, 2010.

Wilcove, David S., David Rothstein, Jason Dubow, Ali Phillips, and Elizabeth Losos. "Quantifying Threats to Imperiled Species in the United States." *BioScience*, vol 48 no 8 (August 1998): 607–615. University of California Press.

Wildlands Network. http://www.wildlandsnetwork.org (Accessed November 21, 2015).

Willard, Bob. *The Sustainability Advantage: Seven Business Case Benefits of a Triple Bottom Line*. Gabriola Island, BC: New Society Publishers, 2002.

——. *The Sustainability Champion's Guidebook: How to Transform Your Company*. Gabriola Island, BC: New Society Publishers, 2009.

Willers, Bill. *Learning to Listen to the Land*. Washington, DC: Island Press, 1991.

Williams, Daniel E. *Sustainable Design: Ecology, Architecture, and Planning*. New York: John Wiley, 2007.

Williams, Dilafruz and Jonathan Brown. *Learning Gardens and Sustainability Education*. New York: Routledge, 2011.

Willoughby, Marie. "The Value of Providing for Risky Play in Early Childhood Settings." *Childlinks* issue 3 (2011): 7–9.

Wilmoth, John. *Global Population Projections by the United Nations*. Joint Statistical Meetings, session 151. Population Division, DESA, UN, August 10, 2015.

Wilson, Edward O. "Bottleneck." *Scientific American*, February 2002a: 84–91.

——. *The Future of Life*. London: Abacus, 2002b.

——. *The Diversity of Life*. Boston: Belknap Press of Harvard University Press, 2010.

Wise, Steven M. *Rattling the Cage: Toward Legal Rights for Animals*. Perseus Books, 2000.

Withgott, Jay and Scott Brennan. *Essential Environment: The Science behind the Stories*. 3rd ed. San Francisco, CA: Pearson Benjamin Cummings, 2009.

Wolfe, David W. *Tales from the Underground: A Natural History of Subterranean Life*. New York: Basic Books, 2001.

Wolfson, Richard. *Earth's Changing Climate*. Chantilly, VA: The Teaching Company, 2007.

——. *Energy, Environment, and Climate*. New York: W. W. Norton, 2008.

World Bank. *Kazakhstan—First Phase of the Syr Darya Control and Northern Aral Sea Project*. Washington, DC: World Bank, 2011. http://documents.worldbank.org/curated/en/2011/06/15404043/kazakhstan-first-phase-syr-darya-control-northern-aral-sea-project.

——. *Moving Beyond GDP*. Washington, DC: WAVES Partnership, 2012.

Worldwatch Institute. *State of the World 2002*. New York: W. W. Norton, 2002.

——. *State of the World 2003*. New York: W. W. Norton, 2003.

——. *State of the World 2004: Special Focus: The Consumer Society*. New York: W. W. Norton, 2004.

——. *State of the World 2005: Redefining Global Security.* New York: W. W. Norton, 2005.

——. *State of the World 2006.* New York: W. W. Norton, 2006.

——. *State of the World 2007: Our Urban Future.* New York: W. W. Norton, 2007.

——. *State of the World 2008: Innovations for a Sustainable Economy.* New York: W. W. Norton, 2008.

——. *State of the World 2009: Into a Warming World.* New York: W. W. Norton, 2009.

——. *State of the World 2010: Transforming Cultures from Consumerism to Sustainability.* New York: W. W. Norton, 2010.

——. *State of the World 2011: Innovations that Nourish the Planet.* Washington, DC: Worldwatch Institute, 2011.

——. *State of the World 2012: Moving Toward Sustainable Prosperity.* Washington, DC: Island Press, 2012.

——. *State of the World 2013: Is Sustainability Still Possible?* Washington, DC: Island Press, 2013.

——. *State of the World 2015: Confronting Hidden Threats to Sustainability.* Washington, DC: Island Press, 2015.

——. *State of the World 2016: Can a City Be Sustainable?* Washington, DC: Island Press, 2016.

Worrell, Ernst and Markus Reuter, eds. *Handbook of Recycling: State-of-the-Art for Practitioners, Analysts and Scientists.* Waltham, MA: Elsevier, 2014.

Wright, Richard T. and Dorothy F. Boorse. *Environmental Science: Toward a Sustainable Future.* 11th ed. Boston, MA: Benjamin Cummings, 2011.

World Wildlife Fund (WWF) et al. *Living Planet Report 2012.* Gland: WWF, 2012.

Yudelson, Jerry. *Green Building A to Z: Understanding the Language of Green Building.* Gabriola Island, BC: New Society Publishers, 2007.

Zalasiewicz, Jan et al. "Are We Now Living in the Anthropocene?" *Geological Society of America,* 18, 2 (February 2009): 4–8.

——, Mark Williams, Will Steffen, and Paul Crutzen. "The New World of the Anthropocene." *Environmental Science & Technology,* 44, 7 (2010): 2228–2231.

Zimov, Sergei. "Mammoth Steppes and Future Climate." *Science in Russia,* 2007 (n.d.), 105–112.

Zero Waste Alliance. N.d. www.zerowaste.org/.

Index